THE **OFFICIAL**
ILLUSTRATED HISTORY OF
Arsenal
1886–2002

THE **OFFICIAL**
ILLUSTRATED HISTORY OF
Arsenal
1886–2002

Phil Soar Martin Tyler

TED SMART

Records by John Burt and Daniel Feinstein with assistance from Jonathan Culverhouse and Kevin Connolly

Additional text: Adam Ward, Peter Arnold, Ivan Ponting and Kevin Connolly.

This edition published in 2002 by Hamlyn, a division of Octopus Publishing Group Ltd, 2–4 Heron Quays, London E14 4JP

This edition produced for The Book People Ltd., Hall Wood Avenue, Haydock St Helens WA11 9UL

First published in 1986
Revised and updated 1994, 1995, 1996, 1997, 1998, 1999, 2000, 2001, 2002

ISBN 0 600 60815 8

A CIP catalogue record for this book is available from the British Library

Printed and bound in Italy

10 9 8 7 6 5 4 3 2 1

PHOTOGRAPHIC ACKNOWLEDGMENTS

Picture Research: Daffydd Bynon

In source order

ALLSPORT 79 Top Left, 79 Top Centre, 79 Centre Left, 154 Main Picture, 155 Centre Right, 158 Top Left, 160 Top Left, 190 Main Picture, 191 Bottom Right, 196 Top Centre, 196 Top Right, 200 Top Right, 201 Top Left, 201 Bottom Centre, 202 Bottom, 204 Top, 205 Centre Left, 207 Top, 208 Bottom.
ALLSPORT HISTORICAL COLLECTION 72 Bottom Left, /Hulton Getty 10 Main Picture, 11 Main Picture, 19 Main Picture, 49 Bottom Right, 54 Top Left, 56 Bottom Left, 57 Main Picture, 58 Main Picture, 59 Main Picture, 67 Bottom Right, 70–71 Main Picture, 73 Top Left, 73 Bottom Right, 75 Bottom Right, 76 Top Right, 76 Bottom Centre, 77 Main Picture, 89 Main Picture, 102 Main Picture, /MSI 122 Centre Right
Alpha 170 Top Left, 171 Top
ARSENAL FOOTBALL CLUB 16 Main Picture, 20 Main Picture, 24 Main Picture, 25 Bottom Right, 27 left, 27 right, 30 Main Picture, 31 Bottom Right, 32 Top Left, 33 Top Centre, 33 Bottom Right, 35 Main Picture, 38 Bottom, 41 Top Right, 53 Main Picture, 66 Top Left, 67 Top Centre, 86 Main Picture, 87 Bottom Left, 90 Main Picture, 94 Main Picture, 95 Main Picture, 100 Main Picture, 111 Main Picture, 85 Top Right, 125 Top Right/Stuart McFarlane 3, 209 Bottom, 221, 220, 222, 223, 224, 225, 226, 227 Right, 227 Left, 229, 230
COLORSPORT 8 Main Picture, 13 Main Picture, 14 Main Picture, 28 Main Picture, 29 Top Right, 37 Top Right, 39 Top Right, 42 Main Picture, 44 Main Picture, 48 Main Picture, 55 Top Right, 68 Main Picture, 74 Main Picture, 78 Top Centre, 78 Top Right, 84 Main Picture, 85 Main Picture, 96 Main Picture, 97 Top, 101 Main Picture, 108 Main Picture, 109 Bottom Left, 113 Top Left, 114–115 Main Picture, 115 Bottom Left, 116 Main Picture, 117 Top Right, 117 Bottom Right, 118 Top Left, 119 Main Picture, 122 Top Right, 123 Top Left, 123 Bottom Left, 132 Main Picture, 133 Main Picture, 134 Main Picture, 135 Main Picture, 136 Top Left, 137 Bottom Right, 138-139 Main Picture, 140-141 Main Picture, 141 Bottom Centre, 142 Main Picture, 144 Top Right, 146 Bottom Right, 147 Main Picture, 148 Top Right, 151 Main Picture, 153 Top Right, 156 Top Left, 157 Top Right, 158 Bottom Centre, 159 Top Left, 160 Bottom, 161 Top Right, 162 Main Picture, 163 Main Picture, 164 Bottom Centre, 165 Top Right, 166 Top Right, 167 Bottom Left, 168 Top Left, 168 Bottom Right, 169 Top Right, 170 Centre Right, 171 Top Right, 171 Centre Left, 193 Top Right, 194 Top Right, 195 Main Picture, 198 Bottom Left, 199 Top Left, 202 Top Centre, 203 Top Left, 203 Bottom Centre, 127 Bottom Centre Right, 129 Bottom Left, 187 Main Picture, 202 Top, 203 Top, 203 Bottom, 204 Bottom, 205, Top Right, 206, 207 Centre Right, 207 Bottom, 208 Top, 209 Top, 209 Centre, 211—221.
HULTON GETTY PICTURE COLLECTION 36 Top Left, 47 Main Picture, /hulton 83 Top Right
MIRROR SYNDICATION INTERNATIONAL 36 Top Right, 36 Bottom Right, 112 centre left 1
NEWS INTERNATIONAL SYNDICATION 69 Main Picture

INTRODUCTION AND ACKNOWLEDGEMENTS

It was the 92nd minute of the very last match of the 1988-89 season, probably the most significant and dramatic in English football history. For only the third time in the 101-year existence of the Football League the two leading teams were playing for the Championship on the final day of the season. Uniquely, there were no other games this day. It really was the last game of the season. Arsenal were winning 1–0 at Anfield, in any other circumstances an outstanding result. But here, at that moment, it meant that Liverpool were going to win the League and the Double by a single goal. Both clubs had the same number of points but Liverpool had a goal difference advantage of just one. It would be Liverpool's second Double in four seasons, an astonishing achievement in a season which will always be remembered primarily for the Hillsborough disaster.

It was all over bar the presentation of the trophy to Ronnie Whelan. A late injury to Kevin Richardson had taken the match into injury time. There were just seconds for the Kop to wait before they acclaimed their double-Double winning team as, perhaps, the greatest English club side ever.

And then Alan Smith, as he had been doing all night, cleverly picked up a pass from Lee Dixon and moved it deftly on to Michael Thomas, some yards out from goal on the right side of the pitch. Thomas moved forward, went past Steve Nicol by taking a rebound off the defender's body and sped into the penalty area. Bruce Grobbelaar, hero of so many similar situations, a keeper who had saved from the same Thomas just 10 yards out a few minutes before, came out and spread himself. Nicol and Ray Houghton flung themselves at the Arsenal man. But Thomas deftly flicked the ball to his right, over Grobbelaar's body and into the corner of the goal. 2–0. Seconds left. Pandemonium. Arsenal were Champions by virtue solely of scoring more goals. On points and goal difference Arsenal and Liverpool had identical records. If goal average rather than difference had still been the arbiter, Liverpool would have been Champions and so winners of the Double. No Championship has ever had a closer finish. None has gone to the last 30 seconds. None has deprived a team of the Double in such an impossible-to-script manner.

History takes many years in the making and as long in the writing. It is probably too early to place Michael Thomas's goal securely in its rightful context. But it is already arguable that it will become the most famous goal ever scored in league football – comparable with Geoff Hurst's second in the 1966 World Cup final or Blackpool's fourth in the 1953 FA Cup final.

It was a game and a finale which no fantasist would have dreamed of writing. It was surely enough that these two teams had come together to decide the Championship in the very last game of the season, a season forever to be remembered for Hillsborough. For the season to end that way, with just seconds remaining, and at that venue, was to live and rewrite every boy's childhood fantasies.

It was inevitable that there should be reminders of another goal in another game against Liverpool. The comparisons were close: a yellow and blue shirted young star scoring in the dying minutes of the last match of the season; red shirted Liverpool were the opponents and the Double was at stake. But Charlie George lay down after his goal in 1971, while Michael Thomas turned a flying somersault of, in all probability, utter astonishment. And Arsenal were to win their Double of 1971, while Liverpool were to lose theirs of 1989. To have played each other twice for the Double; that alone is worth its place in the history books, particularly this book which was originally devised to celebrate Arsenal's centenary year in 1986.

One hundred years is a long time. How long can perhaps the best be judged when we realise that 1886, the moment of Arsenal's birth, was also the year that the world's first motor car was built. And, even then, the 15 young men who founded Royal Arsenal were probably well into their thirties before they actually saw a motor vehicle and certainly grandfathers before they would have seen an aeroplane.

Much can happen in a century. Too much to record fully here. To give our story meaning we must seek out landmarks, find moments when it is possible to explain much in a short space of time, perhaps even in a single game. That is why we begin our story not with 1886, or even the magical Doubles of 1971, 1998 and 2002, but with the FA Cup final of 1930. The story is more precise even than that. It homes in on the two captains that day, Tom Parker and Tom Wilson, walking onto the field together. In that one innocent gesture they told so much; in a way they revealed the underlying story of inter-war football. And that is the heart of Arsenal's story; a tale essentially of the 1920s and 1930s.

By some chronological freak, Arsenal's world changed at the turn of the 1930s. The glories that followed can probably be traced to a dramatic few minutes against a team of Second Division nobodies at Elland Road, the first of the games which are the real cornerstones in the Highbury story. Forty-one years later, on another ground in Yorkshire, those few minutes were to be eerily re-run. If we must pick landmarks, if that is how this history should be told, then these few minutes from these two matches shine like beacons from the dusk of history. It is these two games, rather than the 1971 FA Cup final or the last game of the 1989 League Championship, which will be the centre-points of our story.

Both were semi-finals. Both games had seen Arsenal, at half-time, 2–0 down and virtually out. Both finished 2–2. The first game eventually led to the 1930 final, the game which defined an era. It was Arsenal's first ever trophy and from it they went on to the glories of the next ten years. Without that conclusion, it is entirely possible the Arsenal of today would be no more significant than a middle-of-the-road club.

The second game was dramatic for its dénouement, a last minute Peter Storey penalty which was perhaps the second most important goal in the club's long history. It was to lead to the 1971 FA Cup final and the Double, a feat Herbert Chapman's team of the 1930s could never achieve. We say this was the second most important goal for one simple reason. Peter Storey's penalty was not so much the moment the Double was won, but was certainly the moment it could have been lost. The first Double is a central, vital and highly emotional part of the Arsenal story. But it is ultimately not as important as 1930. With or without the Double of 1971, Highbury would still be Highbury. The ground, the club and the worldwide reputation were built by Herbert Chapman, Tom Whittaker and the teams of the 1930s. The 1971 Double was the icing on an already substantial cake.

This book is about those men and those landmarks, and about more moments and matches and the players that created them. In particular it is about Herbert Chapman, the greatest manager the game has ever seen.

A first-class football club is a complex organism. It is of course about players, directors, grounds and games, but it is also about the far greater numbers who watch each week. A soccer team is often a deeply significant part of a man's three score years and ten. Having been born under the star of a football club, it is almost impossible to stray elsewhere in the mind, no matter where he may go physically. That one team will always slightly increase the pulse rate at 5 pm on a Saturday evening. The heights of exultation that a Cup final or, in Arsenal's case, the Double, can bring to tens of thousands should not be doubted or devalued. For many it will be one of the two or three most emotional and moving moments they will ever experience in their lives.

All football clubs have their peculiarities; Arsenal's most interesting is one of location and historical accident. Football in England has long been about provincialism. Arsenal are not (at least since their move from Woolwich) a provincial club. Chapman's efforts, coupled with the lack of any alternative, allowed them to become the capital's club, at a time which corresponded with London imposing its economic as well as political dominance over the rest of a depressed and uncertain nation. It was this historical good fortune which was ultimately to determine the character of Arsenal. A team supported by rich and poor, but somehow, then and now, the rich relation. Herbert Chapman chose his time and his location well.

Since their foundation in 1886 Arsenal have played around 6,000 first-class games. We cannot talk about them all, but we can at least record them. Throughout the book you will find a complete match-by-match, week-by-week record (up to August 2002) of every first-class game the club has played. We have chosen 1970, the year the club's modern history began with that sensational start to their record-breaking unbroken spell in the First Division, as the year from which we cover not only all the games and their results, but also all the team line-ups and goalscorers. The statistical sections of the book has been a massive undertaking for all concerned and we should like to thank John Burt, who provided the original material, and checked and corrected it; Daniel Feinstein, who prepared the players' records which give every first-class appearance since the club was founded; Kevin Connolly for his updates; Roger Walker for his work on the original typography and layout; and Jonathan Culverhouse for his expertise.

Numerous people assisted us in our research and talked to us of their own experiences and recollections, including many Arsenal players, past and present, who kindly took time to help. There are simply too many to thank here. Instead we would like to mention just a handful – Bertie Mee, Don Howe, Don Roper, Billy Wright, Ken Friar, David Miles, and especially Bob Wilson who made his own archives available to the authors. At Hamlyn, we would like to mention our art director Chris Pow, editors Sarah Bennison and Peter Arnold, picture researcher Jean Wright, Diana Godwin-Austen, supporters Charles Fowkes and Terence Cross.

But above all others we would like to record our debt to Tony Bagley. It was he who originally commissioned the book, argued about its contents and enthused over its preparation. A great lover of the game, he sadly died before the book's completion.

Phil Soar and Martin Tyler

CHAPTER 1
HERBERT CHAPMAN

The beginning of everything can really be traced to 2.45 pm on Saturday 26 April 1930. The place was London's vast Empire Stadium. Two men stood together in the Wembley tunnel, tense with just 15 minutes to go before the start of only the eighth FA Cup final to be played there.
Soon they were to emerge into the sunlight together, the first captains ever to lead out their teams side-by-side for a major football match. One of those men was Tom Wilson, captain and centre-half of Huddersfield Town, the dominant team of the age. In the 12 years since the First World War, Huddersfield had won a unique hat-trick of League Championships and reached four FA Cup finals. But, though no one could have believed it that day, the parade had already passed Huddersfield by. For the remainder of the 20th century they would not win a major honour.

The second man, Tom Parker, captained Arsenal, a north London club of no great distinction which, in nearly 50 years, had won absolutely nothing. And yet in the decade that remained between that April day in 1930 and the start of another world war, Arsenal, originally Royal Arsenal, later Woolwich Arsenal and briefly The Arsenal, would win five Championships, match Huddersfield's League hat-trick and reach two more FA Cup finals. By 1939 they would have become the richest, best supported and most successful club side in the world, a bright shining star that has yet to be dimmed in the football firmament.

For that fleeting moment in 1930 the pendulum stood still. Midway between the two world wars the centre of gravity of English football gently moved south. And, as if to mark such a uniquely symbolic game, the teams not only took the field together but crowded into the same dressing room at the end to congratulate the winners and even shared the same celebration dinner that night at the Café Royal.

There had to be more to it than that, of course, much more, certainly another reason for such a peculiarly portentous day. The reason was to be found in the slightly portly, commanding figure of the 52-year-old Arsenal manager, Herbert Chapman. It was he who had earlier led Huddersfield to their hat-trick in the mid-1920s, left that team before the end of it and moved to small, struggling, trophyless Arsenal. When he arrived at Highbury in May 1925 he had said it would take five years to build a winning team. Here he was at Wembley, literally five years to the week later, presumably intending to make good his boast.

In retrospect, with the useful hindsight of more than 70 years, it is easy to see what happened and why. But it was not so clear then. Huddersfield were clearly the better team; Arsenal were in the bottom half of the First Division and had

survived several close shaves on their way to the final. If the Gunners had lost that day it is not unreasonable to argue that the whole history of Arsenal FC might have been very different. There may never have been the 1930s; we may never have had reason to speak of the marble halls of Highbury; Arsenal may have remained, at best, as they had since their 1927 FA Cup final defeat, a middle-of-the-road First Division club. The 1930 FA Cup final might have been remembered primarily for the dramatic appearance of the *Graf Zeppelin*, another peculiarly poignant moment in this symbolic final midway between the two wars. The hopes and fears of years gone by, and of years to come, rested heavily on the shoulders of Tom Parker and Herbert Chapman that day.

It is the measure of this one game, of its remarkable portents, of the future that it promised for one of the two clubs and the past chapter that it closed for the other, that virtually the whole history of inter-war football can be told in its 90 minutes.

And, by the same token, the history of Arsenal FC, which remains in essence a tale of the 1930s, can be related in the day's dominant figure – Herbert Chapman. That is why we must start our story of Arsenal Football Club on this one day, with the life of that one man, and with one single, all-encompassing football match.

Birth of the legend

Saturday 26 April 1930 had begun fine and warm; temperatures were in the sixties, perfect for the 55th FA Cup final. The morning papers had said King George V would not be well enough to attend, but he surprised everyone by arriving to a rousing reception for his first outdoor appearance since an illness 18 months before. The leading story in *The Times* that day had been the arrival home from India of the Prince of Wales, his plane touching down in front of the cameras in Windsor Great Park. But even *The Times* took a more than passing interest in the day's football, pointing out to its readers that: 'The broadcast from Wembley Stadium this afternoon will begin at 2.30 pm with community singing conducted by Mr T. P. Radcliff and accompanied by the band of the Welsh Guards. At 2.45 pm Mr George F. Allison will open the commentary on the Cup final match between The Arsenal and Huddersfield Town, and this is expected to last until about 4.45 pm. The position of the ball in the field of play and the score will be called at intervals by Mr Allison's assistant in the stand.'

George Allison was, as it happened, also an Arsenal director and the club's second biggest shareholder. It was only the fifth time that a game had been broadcast live and the effects of this exciting new medium, wireless, were far from being fully felt. For one thing, the Football League still organised a full programme on Cup final day. The crowds who stayed away to listen to the radio missed some good matches – Wolves drew 4–4 with Bradford Park Avenue, Fred Cheesmuir of Gillingham scored all six goals in his side's 6–0 defeat of Merthyr Town and Lincoln City beat New Brighton 5–3. Sheffield Wednesday stayed five points clear at the top of the First Division with a 1–0 defeat of Grimsby. Arsenal were little concerned about League results. With just two matches left of the season they were in 12th place and the Wembley crowd of 92,488 was understandably only interested in what was about to happen there and then. Only one London club had won the FA Cup in the 20th century (Tottenham Hotspur) and the capital had still never applauded a League Championship winner.

The 1930 FA Cup final

As a match, it was one of the better finals. The Arsenal team was Charlie Preedy in goal, Tom Parker and Eddie Hapgood at full-back, Alf Baker, Bill Seddon and Bob John the half-backs, and Joe Hulme, David Jack, Jack Lambert, Alex James and Cliff Bastin the forwards. Nine of the 11 had been brought to Highbury by Chapman himself and, with the substitution of Moss for Preedy, Roberts for Seddon and Charlie Jones for Baker the team was probably close to the greatest one of an era that lived long in the memories of those fans who witnessed it.

Above: Photo-calls and player pools are nothing new; the Arsenal team made a 'talkie' to be shown in news theatres on 16 April 1930 – ten days before the final. Chapman (wearing a suit) stands between Joe Hulme and Charlie Preedy, with Tom Parker peering over his shoulder.

Huddersfield were, at the time at least, a rather more distinguished 11. Former England captain Roy Goodall was at full-back, the magnificent centre-half Tom Wilson (a famous Huddersfield surname) remained as stopper, and the right-wing pair of Alex Jackson and Bob Kelly was the best in the country. 'Flying Scotsman' Jackson, scorer of a hat-trick in Scotland's famous 5–1 defeat of England at Wembley two years earlier, had also scored nine of Huddersfield's 11 goals on the way to the final. Eddie Hapgood was given the job of shadowing him wherever he went, Bob John taking the role of subduing Kelly. The defensive plan worked superbly, though it was in no sense a one-sided game.

Memories, however, are not made of defensive tactics but of goals, and never more so than in Cup finals. The first remains one of Wembley's most famous. In the team coach on the way from the club's hotel in Harrow, Alex James had spoken to winger Cliff Bastin: 'If we get a free-kick in their half early on, I'll slip it out to you on the wing. You give it me back and I'll have a crack at goal.' Most of the players thought James was joking – since joining the Gunners from Preston he had ceased to be anything other than a very occasional goalscorer. But in the 17th minute just such a free-kick occurred; James was fouled 40 yards from goal, sprang to his feet and looked at referee Tom Crew, who nodded to the Scotsman to take the kick

1886–1939

without any ado. Out went the ball to the left-wing, off hared Bastin, drawing Goodall out toward him. At just the right moment Bastin slipped the ball back inside for James, following through, to hit it into the corner of the net. The Huddersfield players protested briefly, but the referee had been quite correct in allowing the instant restart. It was, said *The Times*: 'The skill and bold tactics of James that turned the scale in favour of his side ... to his remarkable control of the ball, he added the craft that both sees and makes openings.'

Some minutes later, in yet another incident redolent with symbolism, the *Graf Zeppelin*, Germany's giant airship and pride of a nation slowly rebuilding its self-confidence, suddenly loomed over the stadium like a massive cloud. Flying at 2,000 feet, well below the legal limit, it dipped its nose in salute to the King and flew on. The players barely noticed; those who did were apparently annoyed at the break in their concentration.

Arsenal win the Cup

Huddersfield attacked for the rest of the game, greatly helped by Arsenal's erratic goalkeeper, Charlie Preedy, who was deputising for the injured Dan Lewis. In the programme pennotes he had explained how he liked coming out to meet the

Below: The 1930 final will be remembered for a remarkable number of reasons, not least the fact that the captains came out side by side for the very first time before a major game. Celebrating Herbert Chapman's association with the two finalists were captains Tom Parker of Arsenal (left) and Tom Wilson of Huddersfield. It was the Yorkshire club's fourth Cup final since the First World War, a period during which they had also won a hat-trick of Championships under Chapman's management.

ball at the earliest opportunity. Unfortunately he appeared not to have explained this to his defence, used to playing in front of a more conservative keeper. Said *The Times* on Monday: '... at times Preedy took risks which hardly deserved to succeed as they did. Three times he let the ball slip from his hands as he was trying to clear.'

The Arsenal goal led something of a charmed life, often unguarded after a Preedy dash had failed to connect with the ball, and the Gunners' centre-forward Jack Lambert spent much of the second half virtually alone on the centre line as his colleagues defended frantically. With just seven minutes left, a sudden long clearance from James found Lambert in the centre circle. Somehow he slipped between Goodall and Spence and the centre forward hared nearly half the length of the pitch toward the Huddersfield goalkeeper, Turner, who seemed suddenly dazed by this disastrous turn of events. Lambert shot from the edge of the area past the badly placed keeper, the ball hit the back of the net and Lambert turned, arms outstretched, expecting to greet his onrushing colleagues. But there was no one there; the rest of the side were still in their own half. So Lambert set off alone, applauding himself as he went, to provide one of football's more enduring memories at the end of one of football's most famous matches. It is probably no exaggeration to say that this game, which ended 2–0, along with the FA Cup final and semi-final in the Double year of 1971 and the 1989 title decider at Anfield is the most memorable in the history of Arsenal Football Club. It was not only the moment when the greatness began, it was also the moment when everything could so easily have slipped away.

The 1930 FA Cup final was the forerunner of two more in the decade that followed – 1932 and 1936 – and of five League Championships – 1931, 1933, 1934, 1935 and 1938. By the time Hitler's war began, Arsenal were without doubt the greatest, the most famous, the most widely supported football club in the world. Since then, only Liverpool and Manchester United have had a comparable dominance and, even then, without quite the same emotional commitment, for and against. One cannot begin to compare, for instance, Liverpool's two defeats by Brighton in the 1983 and 1984 FA Cups with the sensation caused by Walsall when they knocked the Gunners out of the same competition 50 years before. Since the 1930s the glories have inevitably been fewer, the trophies more widely spaced, but the reputation and image that Herbert Chapman built remain essentially as he left them. And so dominant is Chapman in Arsenal's history that, although it was nearly half a century before the club won a major prize, it is surprising to recall that it is also more than 65 years since Chapman died so tragically in 1934.

The history, status and wealth of the club are so bound up with this one man that it is surely necessary to go back and discover what we can about him, to find what it was that he brought

The Herbert Chapman story

Herbert Chapman was born eight years before Arsenal, on 19 January 1878 in Kiveton Park, a small mining village on the borders of South (then West) Yorkshire and Nottinghamshire. His father was an illiterate miner who had five other sons and one daughter. Herbert was an exceptionally bright child in an age when working class children had virtually no opportunities, so much so that he eventually reached Sheffield Technical College to complete a course in Mining Engineering. He was to use his academic qualifications, and hold down various jobs in industry, for nearly all of his life. Indeed, it was not until Huddersfield Town first became League Champions, when Chapman was already 46, that he finally turned his back on an engineering career.

He was a moderate footballer, a roly-poly inside forward or wing half, but nothing like as good as his brother Harry, who was a forward with the Sheffield Wednesday Championship winning sides of 1903 and 1904. Herbert remained an amateur through most of his playing career, which took him through a remarkable range of clubs and locations. In the ten years between 1897, when he was 19, and 1907, when he became player-manager of Northampton, he played for Stalybridge Rovers, Rochdale, Grimsby, Swindon, Sheppey United, Worksop, Northampton, Sheffield United and Notts County before heading to north London and Spurs.

In most of these towns he also took an engineering job, which was wise as his playing career could only be described as unmemorable. But ten clubs in as many years also had its advantages. He got to know people in the game throughout the country, he saw numerous styles of management (most of them poor) and he began to develop his own theories about how best to run a football club and win football matches. His longest spell in a single place was two years at White Hart Lane and, though he was usually in the reserves, the potential for a major club in north London (Arsenal were still south of the river) cannot have escaped his attention.

When he took over at Northampton in 1907 they had just finished bottom of the Southern League. In 1908–09 Northampton were Champions. Chapman finished playing the same year and in 1910 Northampton were fourth, in 1911 second and in 1912 third. By that time Chapman had returned to his native Yorkshire as manager of Second Division Leeds City. His first job was to canvass for votes at the League's AGM, where City were facing re-election. The club improved dramatically, just missing out on promotion in 1914 and then, in the different

Below: Herbert Chapman (indicated) had joined Spurs as an inside forward in 1905 and finished as their top scorer in the 1905-06 season with 11 goals in 28 games. It was his most successful season in a playing career which spanned ten clubs. Years later, his willingness to join downtrodden Arsenal was partially prompted by a desire to see Spurs' great rivals become a success, for he had generally been poorly treated by Spurs' fans. By a peculiar quirk of fate, his very first game in charge of the Gunners was against Spurs at Highbury – and the visitors won 0-1.

atmosphere of wartime football, being good enough to win the unofficial League Championship of 1918. Chapman had taken over the management of a munitions factory in 1916, a move which was probably and paradoxically to save his future career for, in 1919, Leeds were summoned before a League commission to answer allegations of making illegal payments between 1916 and 1918. This had always been, in theory, a major offence in the eyes of the League but was a much more sensitive issue in wartime. The club refused to release their books and were simply thrown out of the League. The club's officials, including their ex-manager, were suspended and Chapman remained in various industrial jobs for the next two years, suffering at least one spell of unemployment.

Chapman probably knew about the payments involved (he had been fined by the League once before, though on something of a technicality, in 1912) but as he was not at the club during the critical period the judgement seemed a little harsh. It was, understandably, to have a lasting effect on him and its echoes were to affect Arsenal in a truly dramatic way a decade later. That part of the story must, however, wait its turn.

Success at Huddersfield

When Leeds City were ejected from the League in 1919, Second Division neighbours Huddersfield Town sensibly decided to move up the road to Elland Road in their place

1886-1939

('From Leeds Road to Leeds City' went the headlines). Town were based in a rugby league stronghold, had little support to speak of and were literally facing collapse. But in a classic instance of 'out of adversity coming strength', meetings of supporters rejected the decision to move towns (though the League had already approved it), raised cash and reinvigorated the board. Coincidentally there was a miraculous transformation on the field. Within a year Town were promoted to the First Division and were playing in the first post-war Cup final. Late in 1920 the Huddersfield secretary-manager, Ambrose Langley (an old playing colleague of Chapman's brother Harry) approached the then unemployed Chapman with an offer of a job as his assistant. Langley had been one of the main advocates of the move to Leeds and he was obviously aware that his own days must be numbered. Chapman had now been out of football for more than four years and as a consequence, the League felt able to cancel his suspension without further question, but it shows just how far his star had fallen that his new appointment at Huddersfield did not receive a single mention in even the local press.

Within a month Langley handed over the reins to Chapman (this must have been agreed in advance), within three years Huddersfield were League Champions and within five they had completed the first League hat-trick in history.

Back to London

By that time, however, Chapman had again left Yorkshire and returned to north London. Though Arsenal advertised their manager's job in *The Athletic News* on 11 May 1925, Chapman had already been approached. Arsenal chairman Henry Norris offered him £2,000 a year to take the job, easily the highest salary in the game, and Chapman took little persuading. His days at Tottenham had shown him the potential of London, and when he had visited Highbury before the war he had been particularly struck by the adjacent underground station, only 12 minutes from Piccadilly. In a period of mounting unemployment he was also conscious of the better opportunities his two teenage sons would have in the capital.

The visionary

So what sort of man was Herbert Chapman? The image that has been best preserved is that of a strict authoritarian, the man who once refused to allow Joe Hulme to spend a weekend at home in Lancashire (though Arsenal were playing at Bolton) because Hulme's two goals on the Saturday were not enough, the man who insisted none of the staff at Highbury left at 6.00 pm before asking whether there was anything more he wanted them to do. But if he was an authoritarian, it was in a far more

Above: David Jack joined Arsenal in the 1928–29 season, and played in Arsenal's 1930 FA Cup win. Jack was no stranger to success at Wembley having scored the first goal ever at the stadium, for Bolton against West Ham in the 1923 final. He scored again in the 1926 final, and secured winners' medals in both games, before picking up a third medal with Arsenal. In 206 games for the Gunners he scored 123 goals.

authoritarian age. Jobs were scarce, jobs at football clubs were good ones, particularly at Highbury. A player earned £8 per week, four times as much as the average working man. To be the most successful club in Britain, you had to have the best players and staff. There was no gainsaying that, and it applied across the board. Early on he called the 50 club stewards into his office and told them he was ending the various free perks they received. He wanted everything above board and out in the open. Though his teams were tough, he never advocated unfair play. There are two celebrated incidents demonstrating this when Chapman immediately transferred players who had been guilty of very bad tackles – Islip from Huddersfield and Black from Arsenal.

He was a committed man. He wanted to build the greatest of all football teams. Bernard Joy said of him: 'There are two kinds of visionary; those that dream of a whole new world, and those who dream of just one thing. Chapman's vision was of the greatest football team in the world. His genius was in actually creating something close to that.'

His players, in their reminiscences, spoke of him with affection rather than fear; some go even further. Cliff Bastin wrote in 1950: 'There was an aura of greatness about him. He possessed a cheery self-confidence. His power of inspiration and gift of foresight were his greatest attributes. I think his qualities were worthy of an even better reward. He should have been Prime Minister, and might have been but for the lack of opportunities entailed by his position in the social scale.' An extreme view perhaps (and inaccurate as Ramsay MacDonald had been PM at the time), but Chapman believed that his players were worth the very best, hence the tremendous facilities at Highbury, in particular, the medical and physiotherapy side, years before its time, run by Tom Whittaker. He also insisted on his players having part of their earnings saved by the club. 'He was not a bully,' said Bastin, '... he gave few words of praise and fewer of blame.' The signing of Bastin himself also shows other essential elements in Chapman's success as a manager – his absolute commitment to the job and his willingness to back his judgement and take chances.

Chapman signs Bastin

Chapman had first seen Bastin playing for Exeter at Watford when he and George Allison had gone to size up a member of the home side named Barnett. Bastin, playing for the Devon club in a Third Division South game, was then only 16 years old but his amazing ball control and composure struck Chapman instantly and Barnett was completely forgotten. In the inter-war period youngsters developed much more slowly and it was very rare to see a teenager even in the Third Division. But Bastin was a natural (when he eventually arrived at Highbury the commissionnaire wouldn't let him in, thinking he was a boy seeking autographs). Chapman set off immediately the following morning for Devon. Bastin, always a phlegmatic man, was unimpressed by Chapman's overtures, even though he had played just a handful of matches for his local club, Exeter City. He was more concerned with a tennis match he was due to play that afternoon. But Chapman persisted and persisted. 'I had visions of a lifetime spent sitting there listening to him,' said Bastin a quarter of a century later. Bastin, of course, eventually gave in, signed and became one of the all-time great names in British football, uniquely winning every honour in the game before his 21st birthday.

It was a good example of Chapman personally overseeing Arsenal as a close, family club. He had a very happy home life of his own. His wife was a teacher from the same Yorkshire village, and they had four children. His commitment to his family can be judged by the answer he gave immediately when asked

1886-1939

what the proudest moment of such a successful life had been: 'When my son Ken qualified as a solicitor.' Oddly neither of his sons was to play soccer, but both were accomplished at rugby. Indeed, Ken, the elder, was to become President of the Rugby Football Union. Perhaps the proximity to such tremendous success was a disincentive rather than an encouragement.

Tactics for success

When Chapman joined Arsenal in 1925 he had been playing and managing in the senior game for nearly 30 years, apart from his four-year break. While it would be wrong to say that his conception of the ideal tactical approach was fully formed, it is certainly the case that, over this period, his successes had been based on certain constant themes.

Chapman was, above all else, a believer in great players. He brought Clem Stephenson to Huddersfield as soon as he became manager, and later won the signature of Alex Jackson. At Arsenal he immediately insisted on having Charlie Buchan, and later David Jack and Alex James – among the greatest, if not the greatest, players of their generation. He believed that a great player could fit into any tactical system, and was to prove it, even with the complex Alex James. The fact that a player, like Stephenson or Buchan, might even be past his best was not in itself important.

It is arguable that Chapman was actually not a great tactician – when the offside law was changed from three defenders to two in 1925 Chapman was rather slow to spot the changes required to deal with the extra freedom it gave to attackers. The introduction of a centre-back and midfield link was suggested by Charlie Buchan, who could see the problem from the field, and it took Arsenal some time to settle down to the new system. Where Chapman was obviously magnificent was in fitting the man to the system required; to pursue the example, he found and then developed Herbie Roberts into the definitive stopper centre-back.

If there is another simple key to understanding Chapman's view of the game it is perhaps in the phrase: 'A team can attack for too long.' He is first quoted as saying that while at Northampton in November 1907, after his side had attacked for most of a Cup match but Norwich had stolen a 1–0 victory. Chapman soon instructed his wing halves not to press forward behind the attack quite so readily, and directed the whole team to drop back sometimes, to bring the opposition forward and create the opportunity for a counterattack.

Chapman was to say the same 25 years later: 'You can attack too long, though I do not suggest that the Arsenal go on the defensive even for tactical purposes. I think it may be said that some of their best scoring chances have come when they have been driven back and then have broken away to strike

Opposite: Alex James and Cliff Bastin (right) both joined Arsenal in the 1929–30 season and went on to become two of the great players of Herbert Chapman's side. James both initiated and scored Arsenal's first goal in their 1930 FA Cup win, after linking up cleverly with Bastin. Between them, they made a total of 651 appearances for Arsenal, scoring 203 goals.

suddenly and swiftly.' That almost sums up a general view of Arsenal in the 1930s, the 'lucky' Arsenal of myth and legend. As with most myths, there is certainly something in it. The speed of Bastin and Hulme, the strength of Lambert and later Drake, the cunning of James, were all essential pieces of a clear plan. But in 1930–31 Arsenal scored 127 First Division goals – three per game. They can't all have come from breakaways.

Defence and attack

Chapman has been misinterpreted as saying that a team goes on the pitch with one point and, if it doesn't concede a goal, keeps that point. He did indeed say almost exactly that, but not as an advocate. In fact he was criticising the fact that so many teams, particularly in the early 1920s when goalscoring was at an all-time low, were basically defensive, offside orientated tactical units. He once even advocated 11 up and 11 down as a means of forcing teams to look for goals. There is no doubt, nonetheless, that Chapman was one of the first to put to really good effect the very obvious truth that the best side is the one which scores most goals, not the one which attacks longest or shows most endeavour. This was a surprisingly difficult point for many fans to appreciate in the 1930s, and beyond.

Chapman was never reluctant to admit the necessity of strong defence above all else. As he wrote in 1933: 'I confess I am out to win, and so are my players. It is laid down by law that the team who scores the most goals wins. To accomplish this, you must be sure that the defence is sound. All this, I know, is elementary but it is also the rock bottom of football.' Arsenal's system was designed on a pivotal principle, wrote Chapman: 'First, as to the attack, we have ceased to use our wing forwards in the old style, in which they hugged the touchline. Not only is it the aim of Hulme and Bastin to come inside when the Arsenal attack, but also the aim of the wing halves. This gives us seven men going up on goal. Now, as to defence, the team swing the other way, but the same principle applies so we have eight defenders when the goal is challenged. The defence pivots toward the position of attack, the opposite back coming in to support the centre. It is, of course, essential that the two insides should come back and it is on this account that you get what is called the W formation. The two wing halves are therefore the key men, either in defence or attack, and no defence can be sound unless it has the support of two inside forwards.'

All of this is relatively familiar today, going under terms such as 'closing down space' or 'getting behind the ball'. In the 1930s it was genuinely still a mystery. Programmes were always printed with a 5–3–2 formation (five forwards and two full-backs) and crowds continued to believe that this is how teams like Arsenal played right through to the 1950s – despite the clear weekly evidence to the contrary in front of their eyes.

The right mix

Because Arsenal so completely dominated English football in the decade after the 1930 Cup final, it is perhaps worth examining exactly what it was about the manager, the club and their tactics that brought such astonishing success.

First of all, it is nonsense to suggest that Chapman arrived at Highbury with a plan in mind and then went out to find the players to fit it. If anything, the reverse was the case. Between his arrival in 1925 and his first game in charge, three months later, the offside law was changed and a whole new era had

begun. Chapman had achieved considerable success in refining and exploiting the old system and it would be unrealistic to have expected him, or any other manager, to understand all the implications of the law change overnight. His Leeds and Huddersfield teams had been tight, defensive units, and his roving centre-half at Leeds Road, Tom Wilson, was a key, if now obsolescent figure. When Charlie Buchan forced the third-back tactic on the team (the phrase 'policeman' came in later) the other changes required were reasonably obvious – the full-backs moving out to mark the wingers and one of the inside

1886-1939

forwards dropping back to become the midfield link. Arsenal may have adapted to these changes better than most other clubs but there was nothing secret or particularly subtle about them and, by the end of Chapman's first season (1925–26), most of his opponents were using the same formation. The tactical reason for Chapman's successes definitely lay elsewhere.

While it is undeniably true that the use of Alex James as the link-man was the *key* to Arsenal's success, its *essence* was further forward. The added dimension in Arsenal's game was actually the use of the wingers Cliff Bastin and Joe Hulme, and the club's relative decline toward the end of the 1930s was due more to the fact that these two could not be replaced than for any other reason.

Chapman did not plan it that way. By the late 1920s it had simply become apparent to him that, in the astonishingly fast Hulme and the cool, clever Bastin, he had two players of very unusual quality. The basic difference in Arsenal's game from that point on was that they generally played only three real front men. There was always a strong centre-forward (Jack Lambert being the most celebrated). Behind him David Jack was a goalscorer of quality but not a true front-runner. The wingers did not play in the manner of their equivalents at other First Division clubs. Their role was not, in other words, to hug the touchline, beat the full-back, get to the goalline and cross for the centre-forward to head home. They were both capable of doing this, but Chapman saw it as essentially wasteful. A normal winger spent too much time waiting. He must be used more extensively and far more effectively.

The result was that both Hulme and Bastin would cut in far more often than they would go outside, that Alex James' most famous pass would become the ball inside the full-back, and that both wingers became goalscorers of importance (in the great era between 1929 and 1935 Bastin scored 116 League goals and Hulme 75; an average between them of almost exactly a goal a game – meaning that Arsenal expected one or other of their wingers to score every week). As long as no other club played this way, it was always likely to work. The opposing full-backs had 40 games a year dealing with conventional wingers going outside; twice a season they met Arsenal and had to deal with a totally different threat. But, and here is the rub, Chapman could only do it because he had Hulme and Bastin and, eventually, Alex James to feed them. His competitors couldn't match his success simply because they didn't have the players.

New formations

Chapman did not create all of this overnight. Parts of his post-1925 system – the stopper centre-half, the midfield link – were quite straightforward and the manager's strength here was in finding the perfect men for the job. The more subtle development involving the wingers was probably largely chance but, having seen the potential, Chapman worked at the conclusions and maximised them. He didn't just win an odd League Championship, he completely dominated the game. What happened, bluntly, was that he moved one player back through each department of the team. The stopper centre-half actually meant a line of three at the back rather than two. The need to replace the centre-half in midfield meant one of the inside forwards had to fall back to create three in midfield and four up front. This is where most teams left it – at 3–3–4. As they continued to use conventional wingers they had to have at least two goalscoring forwards – otherwise there was no one for the wingers to serve. Chapman went further by dropping another man some way back as well, creating a system far closer to 3–4–3 than 3–3–4.

The benefit (as was also to be seen in the 1970s when 4–4–2 became the norm) was that the extra man in midfield helped Arsenal gain much more possession of the ball. In purely technical terms, it was a defensive alteration. It moved a man backward. But Arsenal could make it work and scored a lot of goals because they had the genius of James, Hulme and the phenomenal goalscoring of Bastin. Any other club trying the same thing was almost certain to fail because they lacked such talent. Hence, in general, they didn't try.

Chapman knew it was a scheme perfectly geared for scoring goals on the break. It was arguably the ultimate fulfilment of his old belief that 'you can attack for too long'. It was, in many ways, an away team's approach (in the six great seasons between 1929–30 and 1934–35 Arsenal won 187 points at home and 147 points away) but, at the same time, it in no way blunted the greatness of the other parts of the team when they wanted to attack and faced opponents who were their inferior. Their goalscoring record was second to none in the 1930s. Nevertheless, one can see the seeds of the tactics of the 1960s (using wingers in such unconventional ways found remarkable echoes in Alf Ramsey's seminal Ipswich side of 1962) and one can understand how the cries of 'Lucky Arsenal' arose from the unsophisticated terraces of the era. Chapman's instinct for fitting the right man to parts of a plan while being able to develop other parts of that plan to the particular skills of the men available was, of course, the mark of footballing genius.

First professional manager

Another important part of Chapman's philosophy was that the whole club should play to the same system – in other words the first, reserve, third and junior team all tried to play, within their capabilities, to the same pattern. The reasoning was obvious – if a reserve came into the first team he would be familiar

Opposite: Eddie Hapgood, Cliff Bastin and Alf Kirchen (right) march down the street as purposefully as the Arsenal side to which they belonged marched on to become the most famous club in the world. Hapgood was a fantastic servant to the club, playing 434 games over 11 seasons at left-back, while Bastin's 17-season service made him a club legend. Kirchen joined from Norwich in 1935 after Herbert Chapman's death, but was still able to secure winners medals in two League Championships and one FA Cup during his four seasons with the Gunners.

with the behaviour of the players around him. This was obviously most important in defence, but was not insignificant in attack. The club's classic moves, the ball from James inside the full-back, or the cutting in of the wingers and the playing of the ground ball sideways, would not have come naturally to any player had they not also played that way in the reserves.

To ensure the tactical messages came across, Chapman turned part of his desk into a plan of the field, with models to represent the players. When players came to see him, it was easy to discuss moves, ideas and developments in a practical way. Chapman introduced weekly team-talks for the whole side; everyone was invited to contribute, and it was from these meetings that many of the best ideas emerged.

One needs to put all this in perspective if one is to understand its significance. This was an era when directors chose the team, whether or not they knew a thing about the game. There was no such animal as a team manager – technically he was secretary-manager, deputed basically to run the club. Attempts to integrate tactics, combine the best team (as opposed to the 11 players the directors might have thought were best in 11 individual positions) and develop a pattern of consistency were largely outside the control of the average secretary-manager, or were easily frustrated if he tried. Chapman, having seen throughout his playing career how not to run a whole range of clubs, was probably the first real professional in a world of semi-amateurs. These were the days when success was a Cup semi-final here and there, finishing fifth or sixth in the League now and again, and bringing in large enough crowds to balance the books. If further proof is needed, and with the possible exceptions of Wolves' Frank Buckley and Charlton's Jimmy Seed, who now can name any other manager of the inter-war era?

Chapman the innovator

What was really remarkable about Chapman was his influence on, or attempts to influence, the game outside the playing area as well. Many of his proposals were firmly opposed by the FA, to whom he must have seemed a constant irritation. He introduced numbering on the Arsenal shirts on 25 August 1928, when the Gunners visited Hillsborough. This was the first time a team had ever been numbered and the FA told him to desist. He had a minor revenge by having the reserves continue to wear the same shirts. He introduced a 45-minute clock and was told to stop that (it was simply turned into the 60-minute clock that for so long stood on Highbury's southern terracing), he wanted to start floodlit matches (midweek games then kicked off at 3.00 pm, when very few people could attend, causing the obvious loss of revenue) but was not allowed to, and Arsenal proposed the ten-yard penalty semi-circle ten years before it

was finally adopted. Other ideas he put forward have still to come to fruition – goal judges (which he felt very strongly about), two referees rather than one, and far more clubs promoted and relegated (although the number was increased from two to three in the 1973–74 season).

England 'manager'

He was a keen advocate of a single England manager, rather than a selection committee. In 1932 he wrote: 'The idea may be startling, but I would like the England selectors to bring together 20 of the most promising young players for a week under a selector, coach and trainer. The idea would be to practise definite schemes and ... at the end have them hold a conference at which views might frankly be exchanged. I would keep these players together during the season ... if this proposal were carried out, I think the result would be astonishing. I may say that I have no hope of this international building policy being adopted.' Note that not even Chapman dared suggest that a single manager actually pick the players. It was, of course, 30 years before these ideas began to be put into practice, and we are still some way from the ultimate conclusion but, surprisingly, the FA did give Chapman a chance to carry out some of his ideas during an England tour in 1933. He travelled with the England party to Italy and Switzerland and, despite the objections of some of the selectors, was allowed to act as team manager, giving pre-match talks and trying to decide tactics in advance. With several Arsenal players in the team, this was obviously reasonably practical and the tour was undoubtedly a success – England drawing 1–1 with future World Champions Italy in Rome and beating a strong Switzerland side 4–0.

Though the idea was not repeated, there is no reason to suppose it might not have been eventually, largely because Stanley Rous, secretary of the FA from 1934 and later, of course, President of Arsenal, was very much in favour of giving the responsibility for coaching and selecting the side to a single manager. Chapman's death might have ended a good idea prematurely: with no obvious candidate really qualified to take his place the possibility died with him. It is arguable that, had Chapman lived longer, and applied all his persistence to the project, the principle might have been accepted and the whole history of post-war English international football could therefore have been very different.

Tube station renamed

The exploits of Arsenal as a team are covered elsewhere in this history, but to end a celebration of Herbert Chapman, the man who made the team and the club we know today, we should

1886-1939

Above: Herbert Chapman at a football lesson for schoolboys in 1933. Chapman's approach to the game was as distinctive off the pitch as on it, proposing a host of innovations, ranging from floodlit matches to a single manager to select the England team.

perhaps mention the most symbolic and yet most visible of all the man's achievements. When he took Leeds City to Highbury for the first time (on 6 December 1913) he had been particularly struck by the fact that the club had an underground station virtually in the ground. It was minutes from Piccadilly on the quickest and most direct of all the tube lines. The station, on what was then the Great Northern, Piccadilly and Brompton Railway, was actually opened in December 1906, when Chapman was still playing for Spurs. There was only one problem, the station was called Gillespie Road. This was obviously a major advertising opportunity missed; what if all of the millions of people who travelled by the Piccadilly Line or looked at maps of the underground could see the name Arsenal right in front of their eyes? There was not much Chapman could do about it when he first arrived at Highbury, but by 1932 the influence of the club had grown so much, through its success on the field and the support it was drawing, that he could invite the London Electric Railway (as it was by then called) to discuss the matter.

Changing the name was not as simple as it sounds. In those days the destination was printed on each ticket, not to mention on all of the maps, in all of the timetables, and in all of the carriages. The LER was also no doubt wary of numerous other clubs requesting similar things (Chelsea are close to Fulham Broadway, then called Walham Green, though Fulham FC are not, and neither West Ham or Queen's Park Rangers are actually anywhere near those stations). On the other hand, Arsenal drew so many supporters, Chapman argued, that actually promoting the name might bring more passengers for the LER. Initially the railway proposed a compromise name of Highbury Hill, but Chapman was not satisfied with this. Eventually, his persistence paid off, and on 5 November 1932, the name Arsenal became a fixture on maps throughout London. It remains the single greatest tribute to the skill, persuasion and perseverance of the man, and Arsenal celebrated the honour with a 7–1 win at Molineux on the same day.

By the time Arsenal's half century came around Chapman was gone, having died from pneumonia at the age of 55. His bust, created by the famous sculptor Jacob Epstein, was later placed in the magnificent entrance hall of the East Stand, from where he has been able to watch over the club he raised to greatness. There are few clubs who can say with any certainty that they have already had their greatest manager and most influential era. It may not even be true of Arsenal, but it seems unlikely that there will ever be another manager who will do as much for the Gunners as Herbert Chapman.

CLOSE TO ARSENAL
—OPEN EVERY EVENIN

CHAPTER **2**

ROYAL ARSENAL

All in all, 1886 was a memorable year for football. Blackburn Rovers completed a hat-trick of FA Cup wins, winning a replay against West Bromwich Albion 2–0 on Derby Racecourse in the first final played outside London. It was the first year of professionalism and, though the Scots banned their clubs and players from any involvement with English professional teams, there did not seem to be any obvious ill-effects south of the border. But when James Forrest, a professional with Blackburn Rovers, played at half-back for England in Glasgow the Scots objected and the England selectors made Forrest wear a different shirt to distinguish him from the England amateurs. The Football Association was already 23 years old, the FA Cup 15, but the game was still very different from the one we know today. Apart from the centre line, there were no pitch markings; there was no need to provide a crossbar; there were no nets or penalties; a goalkeeper could handle the ball anywhere on the pitch, and the referee had no power to award a free-kick or even a goal unless the players appealed to him. There was not even any requirement that all members of a team wear the same coloured shirts.

In the wider world, 1886 was not particularly momentous. Prime Minister William Gladstone introduced his first Irish Home Rule Bill, saw it defeated in the Commons and was replaced by Lord Salisbury, after whom the new capital of Rhodesia was to be named. Great Britain extended her African empire even further by annexing Zanzibar, and the Severn railway tunnel, then the longest in the world, was opened. Frances Hodgson Burnett wrote *Little Lord Fauntleroy*, Robert Louis Stevenson published *Dr Jekyll and Mr Hyde* and, on the sporting front, the foundation of the Lawn Tennis Association remains the most significant fact that the history books record.

Left: The first badge adopted by Royal Arsenal FC, probably around 1888. It was essentially the Borough of Woolwich's coat of arms. The vertical columns are not chimneys but cannons. Until the end of the 19th century Woolwich was a separate town and not part of London. It was mentioned in the 'Domesday Book' in 1086 and the first known reference to the famous ferry (for centuries the lowest public crossing point of the Thames) was as early as 1308, when the rights to operate it were sold for £10. The military connections began with the Royal Dockyard (thriving by Henry VIII's time), and then developed with the Arsenal, the Royal Military Academy, the Royal Artillery Regiment and the various military hospitals which still dot the local landscape. At the time of the club's foundation there were no fewer than 28 military units based in the area. It is easy nowadays to forget that the club is called Arsenal because it was an offshoot of the single most important military town in England at the end of the last century.

Opposite: Above: Arsenal returned to the Manor Ground in 1893. Very few pictures exist of matches there because, unless you lived very locally, it took so long to get to the ground, either by rail to Plumstead station or by tram.

But, tucked away in a backwater on the borders of rural Kent and the southern sprawl of the largest city in the world, other events were taking place of which the newspapers and public at large were, understandably, totally ignorant.

Founding fathers

It was a small group of Scotsmen that was really behind what happened at the Woolwich Arsenal toward the end of 1886, first among them one David Danskin from Kirkcaldy in Fife. What he actually did was to found a works football team. At that time Kent was firmly rugby and cricket country, both alien games to a Scot like Danskin. The only local clubs which can claim a prior place in football history are Blackheath and Blackheath School, both attenders at the historic first meeting of the Football Association in 1863. Both defected to play rugby and Blackheath are, oddly, the only founder members of the FA still in existence. The local cricketers were no more sympathetic to Danskin – earlier in 1886 one Joseph Smith had tried to persuade the cricket club at the Woolwich Arsenal to allow part of their pitch to be used for football, but they would not hear of it. None of this was perhaps too surprising. The Arsenal, one of the government's main munitions factories, was rather out of place in both Kent and the Home Counties, as were many of the men who came to work there.

The real spur came with the arrival in Woolwich of two Nottingham Forest players, Fred Beardsley and Morris Bates. Forest were already one of the leading sides in the country, having been the first northern club to reach the semi-finals of the FA Cup, which they did in 1879, 1880 and 1885. On that last occasion they had forced the great Queen's Park to two matches with Fred Beardsley as their goalkeeper. Nottingham also had an ordnance factory next door to the old Forest ground at Trent Bridge, and no doubt this was where Beardsley and Bates had worked before they moved to similar jobs in Woolwich. Their arrival pushed Danskin and three friends, Elijah Watkins, John Humble, and Richard Pearce, into action. They asked around to see who might be interested and 15 men were prepared to pay sixpence (2½p) each to start up a club. Danskin added three shillings (15p) out of his own pocket (a tenth of the weekly wages of a man at the Arsenal at that time) and the club bought a football with the money. Apparently they had threepence (1½p) change.

It is interesting to relate that Fred Beardsley had worked for a previous spell at Woolwich Arsenal, back in 1884, and had helped form another team then. Beardsley told his grandson, R. A. Beardsley-Colmer, many years later that this club had been called Woolwich Union and had played on 'Piggy' Walton's field in Plumstead. Beardsley was always a football fanatic – he changed jobs in 1887, going to work for Siemens unofficial historian by virtue of eventually being associated with Arsenal longer than anyone else. Humble and Danskin naturally related their own experiences, the story of their earliest involvement with organised football in the Arsenal as they knew it. If another of the players, Beardsley for instance, had happened to become honorary secretary, then he might have handed down a slightly different story for us to ponder today.

Humble beginnings

It is important to try and put ourselves in the position of those 15 founding fathers over a century ago. As far as they were concerned, the team was a means of providing themselves with a little fun, exercise and, no doubt, a convivial social circle. They gave no thought to the future, of what their team might become. This was entirely sensible, for how could men who had yet to see a motor car and who would be grandfathers before they saw an aeroplane, possibly envisage an FA Cup final watched by 30 million people?

There were, to be sure, thousands of similar groups of young men dotted around the country whose identical efforts would never reach a history such as this. Naturally, only a tiny number of these sides were to rise, by fortune and genuine endeavour, to the national prominence of the next century.

The closest date we have for the initial subscriptions to Danskin's new club is October 1886, but it is unlikely that the founding of the Arsenal can accurately be attributed to any single day. Apart from the seven names mentioned earlier, others who paid at that point were named Price, Whitehead, Porteous, Gellatly, Ratcliffe and Brown (the other two must remain unrecorded by history). Danskin, Humble, Beardsley and Brown all lived to see Arsenal's first honour, the FA Cup victory in 1930. David Danskin himself was fortunate enough to witness all the successes of the decade that followed, writing to manager George Allison from his hospital bed after listening to the 1936 Cup final on the radio, an arrangement surely not even vaguely imagined by his colleagues exactly half a century before when he put the whole thing in motion.

Engineering, but they quickly dismissed him because he took too much time off to play the game. Although it is possible that many of the same men who played for Woolwich Union also joined the new club, it would not be accurate to say that the one was the forerunner of the other, particularly as Danskin and John Humble were apparently not involved.

The likelihood is that there was more than one football team comprised of men from the Arsenal at that time. The better players probably turned out for several of them and the team that eventually became Royal Arsenal was no doubt a composite of some or all of these teams. The reason we today regard Danskin's Dial Square as the forerunner is that John Humble (and, to a lesser extent, Danskin himself) became the club's

Above: Dial Square a century after the formation of the team; for the first few weeks of its existence it had no name and was later referred to by Danskin as Dial Square simply because many of the 15 founders worked there.

First success

The first game of the new club was actually arranged against a team called Eastern Wanderers on 11 December 1886. There were one or two problems, such as the lack of a name, a pitch and any kit. For the time being the side, if it called itself anything at all, had simply used the name of one of the workshops within the Arsenal where many of the players were employed – Dial Square. The actual Dial Square had been erected as long ago as 1717, and acquired its name when a sundial was built over its entrance in 1764. The building was actually situated

1886-1893

between Woolwich and Plumstead which in part explains why, despite their name, Woolwich Arsenal never played a single match in Woolwich itself.

Sadly, the historic first game did not take place anywhere near the Arsenal or Woolwich. The players crossed the Thames by the famous ferry to a piece of open ground someone had found on the Isle of Dogs. Elijah Watkins, whom Danskin had asked to be the first secretary, described it as follows: 'It eclipsed any pitch I ever heard of or saw; I could not venture to say what shape it was, but it was bounded by backyards for two thirds of the area and the other portion was ... I was going to say a ditch, but an open sewer would be more appropriate. We had to pay handsomely to have ... the mud cleaned out of our dressing room afterward!'

There was some dispute about the result, as there were no crossbars, hardly any pitch markings and the ball apparently spent a fair amount of its time in either the back gardens or the sewer. Nonetheless, Dial Square decided they had won 6–0.

A name, a kit and a pitch

The players met in the Royal Oak, next to Woolwich Arsenal station, on Christmas Day 1886 full of enthusiasm. They immediately set about solving their three major problems; a shortage of name, kit and somewhere to play. The name was easy – Dial Square was clearly far too unprepossessing and nothing less than Royal Arsenal would satisfy their ambitions. The name probably came from simply combining that of the pub they were sitting in with their place of work, though that was also referred to on occasions as the Royal Arsenal. It was to remain Royal until 1891, when Woolwich Arsenal was formally adopted though, strangely, the Football League insisted on calling the club Royal Arsenal until 1896.

The kit was almost as easy. Red was adopted because Beardsley and Bates already had shirts of that colour (first-class goalkeepers, like Beardsley, wore the same shirts as their colleagues until 1909), and in future players were supposed to provide their own shorts (several continued to wear knickerbockers) and real boots, as opposed to working boots with bars nailed across them. As the regal Royal Arsenal could not actually afford any of this kit, Fred Beardsley wrote to Nottingham Forest asking if they could help. Forest, who were the first team in the country to adopt uniform red when they began wearing caps of that colour in 1865, generously sent a complete set of red shirts and a ball and Arsenal have worn red and white, like Forest, ever since in consequence. The white sleeves, to add just a little extra distinction, were added before a Highbury match against Liverpool on 4 March 1933.

Forest's ball was also useful for the club didn't have one of those either, having lost the original somewhere along the line,

now all they lacked was somewhere to kick it. The only option was to use any convenient public land nearby and the obvious choice was Plumstead Common. This is not the flat, pleasant recreation area that the name conjures up, though it was also where Woolwich Union had played. Not only is it uneven and hilly, it was then also stony and rutted owing to it being used by the Royal Horse Artillery as a manoeuvring ground. While part of the old Common still exists, housing has been built on much of it in the intervening years and it is no longer possible to determine exactly where Royal Arsenal raised their goalposts. One thing we do know, however, is that the said goalposts were kept nearby in Fred Beardsley's back garden during the week. Many current League clubs started the same way. Spurs played on the Tottenham Marshes for five years before they were able to fence off an enclosure, being forced to do so by a combination of unruly spectators throwing mud at the players, their inability to take money and finding, on more than one occasion, that their carefully marked pitch had simply been usurped by another pair of teams.

The Reds (as they were then nicknamed) invited nearby Erith to Plumstead Common for a match on 8 January 1887, the first under the name Royal Arsenal, and their first formal 'fixture'. The first team ever to play under the name Arsenal was: Beardsley in goal, Danskin and Porteous at full-back, Gregory, Price and Wells at half-back, and Smith, Moy, Whitehead, Crighton and Bee as forwards. Another eight fixtures had been completed by the end of the season. The strength of Beardsley and Bates (who became known as the 'iron-headed man' because he regularly used his forehead, rare in an era of solid, heavy balls) was at the core of the team's early success, helped by the skills and occasional experience of several of the Scots, and they lost only two of their ten matches that season.

Below: The only known match report on the first ever meeting between Spurs and Arsenal, on 19 November 1887. The game was played on the Tottenham Marshes and Spurs won 2–1.

Rapid rise

Progress from here onward was more than steady. Despite their humble origins, Arsenal actually had one of the fastest rises of all the early League clubs (Chelsea and Bradford City later went straight into the Football League without having kicked a ball, but that's another story). Within seven years of their foundation, Woolwich Arsenal were members of the Football League, a tribute to their entrepreneurial foresight rather, it must be said, than to their playing record.

The first few seasons, nonetheless, had their fair share of local success. As early as 1889 the club reached the semi-final of the London Senior Cup, where they were beaten 0–2 by Clapton. The following season they won the Kent Senior Cup, the Kent Junior Cup and, more significantly, the London Charity Cup. The latter was concluded with a 3–1 win over Old Westminsters (the old boys of Westminster School) at the Manor Field in front of 10,000 people. The team was Beardsley, McBean and Connolly (both full-backs were from Kirkcaldy, Danskin's home town), Howatt, Bates (the captain) and Julian, Offer, Christmas, Robertson, Barbour and Fry. The Old Westminsters had their revenge in the London Senior Cup final, winning 1–0 in what was then the premier competition for

Below: The Arsenal line-up in the summer of 1890. The trophies are the Kent Senior Cup, the Kent Junior Cup, the London Charity Cup (probably the Shield in fact) and a cup won in a six-a-side competition at the Agricultural Hall, Islington. The picture seems to have been taken at their new ground, the Invicta, to which they moved that summer. Founder David Danskin is second left on the bottom row.

clubs in the capital. These four competitions were no easy option, although it must be remembered that the London Football Association at this time was fiercely amateur in nature and that Arsenal had the advantage of being a works team. Good players who they wanted to join them were found jobs at the Woolwich Arsenal by a sympathetic management and, on occasion, the club even bought out the contracts of footballing soldiers who they discovered stationed at the nearby barracks or enlisted with the Horse Artillery.

The next season, 1890–91, the Gunners won the London Senior Cup for the first time, beating Casuals 3–2 in the quarter-finals, Clapton 3–2 at the Oval in the semis (having been 2–0 down 25 minutes from the end) and St Bartholomew's Hospital 6–0 in the final, also at the Oval. This was the first really important success for the club and, as the *Kentish Independent* reported: 'Excitement is a mild description for the scenes in Woolwich and Plumstead on the return of the football champions on Saturday night. A host of admirers met them at the Dockyard Station and drove them in open carriages, shouting and singing. There were celebrations everywhere all evening and, we fear, a good deal of drinking was mixed with the rejoicing and exultation.'

1886-1893

It was when they came up against the professionals, or even the leading amateur sides, that Royal Arsenal were made aware of their status. The club first entered the FA Cup, by far and away the most prestigious competition throughout the country, as early as 1889–90. Their first three ties were relatively easy, against Lyndhurst (an 11–0 victory in their first ever FA Cup match), Thorpe (who could not afford to come to London from Norwich for a replay after a 2–2 draw) and Crusaders. But Swifts beat them easily 5–1 in the next round and Derby County won 2–1 at the new Invicta ground in the first tie of the next season. Two Arsenal players, Peter Connolly and Bobby Buist, played so well in that game that John Goodall, the Derby captain and acting secretary-manager, offered them contracts. In the end they did not go, but the event set the alarm bells ringing in the Arsenal committee and was to begin the train of events which took Royal Arsenal into the Football League and also led to the foundation of the Southern League.

On the move again

By this stage the club had settled at a formal address, the Invicta Ground (Invicta is the motto of the county of Kent). After playing on the Common in 1886–87, for the 1887–88 season they had occupied the Sportsman Ground in Plumstead, an old pig farm situated on the edge of Plumstead Marshes, but because of its site this pitch had a predictable tendency to become waterlogged. On the morning of their first home game against prime local rivals Millwall (to be precise on 11 February 1888), the committee arrived at the Sportsman Ground to find that it was under water.

Looking up Manor Road toward Plumstead Station, they noticed that the field next door, which was used as pastureland, appeared dry. Jack Humble rushed round to the owner, a Mr Cavey, and asked permission to use it. He agreed, Woolwich Arsenal drew 3–3, and for the next two years (1888–90) they played on the Manor Field, which they rather grandly called the Manor Ground. After the Cup successes of 1889 and 1890, they decided to move just across Plumstead High Street, to a new ground which already had a stand, terraces and dressing rooms – the Invicta. At the Manor Field, they had to rope off the pitch and bring in wagons (borrowed from the nearby barracks) if they expected a big crowd, which would mean around 500 to 1000. The players usually changed at the Green Man in Plumstead High Street or at the Railway Tavern beside the station (neither exists today), and often had to help with collecting the money.

All this seemed behind them at the Invicta, particularly when, on Easter Monday 1891, they attracted 12,000 fans to see a game against Scottish Champions Hearts. But when the landlord put a massive increase on the rent (from £200 to £350

per annum) hoping to exploit the club's election to the Football League in 1893, they could not pay and had to move again. The Invicta's owner was one George Weaver, of the Weaver Mineral Water Company, who built two rows of houses on the site, named Mineral and Hector Streets, after Arsenal left. The old Manor Ground was repurchased and club and supporters worked through the summer of 1893 to get it ready for the Second Division. The club stayed there, opposite Plumstead Station, for 20 years until a final move far further afield than anyone could have envisaged in these early days.

The move toward League status

Back in 1891, committee member and occasional goalkeeper John Humble was shaken by the ease with which his better players could be lured away by a Football League club if they were playing well. As Royal Arsenal were nominally amateur (although their players were undoubtedly paid 'expenses') there was nothing to stop any of them accepting offers from professional clubs. The next step was bold, for everyone knew the obsessive hatred the London FA had of that evil northern virus, professionalism, and few had yet dared challenge it. This

Below: Arsenal used various sites around Plumstead and in 1888–90 and 1893–1913 were based at The Manor Ground. Nothing is left to indicate that crowds of 25,000 once watched football here: it is now occupied by Manor Way, a roundabout and Plumstead bus garage.

was to be a problem for another decade and a half, eventually ending in virtually a complete break when the London, Surrey and Middlesex FAs formed the Amateur Football Association as an entirely separate body from the official FA in 1907.

Jack (as he was usually known) Humble deserves something of a diversion for, apart from being the most important influence on the club's history after Herbert Chapman and his chairman Henry Norris, he seems to typify the men who worked at the Arsenal and who founded the football club. He was born in a village called East Hartburn in County Durham in 1862. His father and mother died within three months of each other in 1880 and Jack and his elder bother decided to leave the relatively depressed north-east. Not being able to afford the train fare, they walked from Durham to London and had both found jobs as engine fitters at the Arsenal by the time of the 1881 census. Theirs was a hard but common story of the times. The Arsenal drew large numbers of poor men from the Midlands, the north and Scotland, of whom Danskin, Beardsley and Humble were unusual probably only in their devotion to, and skill at, football. Humble was to remain connected with the club for four decades, for much of that time the last link with the real working men who had founded the club.

At the 1891 AGM, held in the Windsor Castle Music Hall, Humble proposed taking the chance of going professional to ensure they kept their best players and this was carried by a large majority. Jack Humble declared at this meeting that: 'The club (has been) carried on by working men and it is my ambition to see it carried on by them.' This was in objection to an additional proposal that a limited liability company should be formed simultaneously. Although this proposal was to be adopted two years later, in 1893, it seems to have been regarded as a retrograde step, against the sporting ethos of the club and (rightly as it proved) endangering the control of the working men who had founded it. Humble, nonetheless, remained a director until a scandal in 1927 forced him, though wholly innocent, to resign.

Exile from the London FA

The London FA were apoplectic about professionals in any form, and immediately banned Arsenal, their previous Cup winners, from all competitions under their auspices and expelled them into the bargain. The only modern-day equivalent was, until recently, the reaction of the Rugby Union to anyone who had played rugby league or written a book about his playing career. But for Woolwich Arsenal (the AGM had also changed the name – presumably because calling a professional club Royal might have invoked even more fury from above) the arguments were not as arcane as they are today; the problems were very practical and very real.

They were effectively banned from playing in all competitions except the FA Cup or in friendlies against professional clubs from the north or Midlands. The FA Cup was therefore financially critical, but their first round tie in January 1892 took them to Small Heath (later renamed Birmingham) and they went down ignominiously 5–1. The following year was even worse – a first round proper 6–0 defeat by Sunderland.

There seemed only one solution – to form a southern version of the Football League, providing real competitive fixtures, and thus staunching the ebb of support that the club was experiencing. In February 1892, just after their Cup ejection by Sunderland, Woolwich Arsenal called a meeting of possible southern members and, initially at least, there was real enthusiasm. Twelve sides were elected: Chatham, Chiswick Park, Crouch End, Ilford, Luton, Marlow, Millwall, Old St Mark's, Reading, Swindon, West Herts (forerunners of Watford) and Arsenal. If the inclusion of Old St Mark's and Crouch End suggests that the meeting was not particularly prescient, then this is further confirmed by the fact that Spurs came bottom of the poll, un-elected with just one vote (presumably their own). Nine years later Tottenham were to become the first southern professional club to win a major honour, the FA Cup. The meeting was held on 24 February 1892 in Anderton's Hotel, Fleet Street. There was an obvious symbolic significance in the location, for it was in the very same hotel that the Football League itself had been formed four years before.

Election to the Football League

The London FA predictably exploded again, threatening to ban the other 11 clubs as well as Arsenal. Surprisingly, the other clubs all backed down, although the idea was successfully revived a year later by Millwall. Arsenal, with no one local to play against, were now getting desperate. There seemed only one gamble they could make, and that a tremendous long shot at best. This was to apply for membership of the Football League, although the Woolwich club had never previously played in any league competition.

At the end of the 1892–93 season the Second Division was extended from 12 to 15 clubs. This created three vacancies, and two more surprisingly yawned when Bootle resigned and Accrington (a different club from the later, ill-fated, Stanley) refused to play in the Second Division after being relegated from the First. Newcastle United and Rotherham Town were given places without a vote, and Liverpool, Arsenal and Middlesbrough Ironopolis were elected at a later meeting. There were actually only seven recorded new candidates for membership, the others being Doncaster Rovers and Loughborough Town.

The simultaneous addition of Liverpool, Newcastle and Arsenal, who were to win an astonishing 26 of the next 80

1886-1893

Championships of the organisation they joined together, must surely be the most distinguished of all the League's annual elections. It was also clearly Arsenal's good fortune to have applied at a time when there were so many vacancies. In a typical year they would have stood no chance, and even in a year with two new vacancies (the most at any normal time) they could have had little hope of success. On such random chances do great stories depend.

As there were no League clubs south of Birmingham and Burton, it was a considerable step for the League to take. Most journeys would be overnight, costs would be high, Woolwich Arsenal had no record of massive crowd support and they were hardly attractive visitors. On the playing front, the FA Cup was usually the acid test for new applicants, and here Arsenal could only be said to have failed dismally. They had never progressed beyond the first round proper and, oddly, were never to achieve even that small distinction in the remainder of the nineteenth century. Nonetheless, someone on the League Management Committee had the foresight to recognise the benefits. Firstly, if the League was ever to become a national institution, it must have members in London, the capital and the country's dominant city. Secondly, travel was becoming less onerous. Cities like Manchester and Liverpool were now only four-and-a-half hours from London by the fastest trains (even if Plumstead was nearly another hour on the other side). And thirdly, and perhaps the telling point in the end, to admit Arsenal would be to reward the club's brave stand on professionalism and to encourage others to do the same.

All in all, the summer of 1893 was a critical moment for the

Above: In April 1948 the Gunners invited the only three living members of their first professional team of 1891 to a game versus Chelsea. The three are (left to right) Bill Julian, Gavin Crawford and John McBean. Julian had gone to work at the Arsenal in 1889 and became the first professional captain two years later. Gavin Crawford was a Scot who became the first professional imported by the club in 1891.

Above, right: The Manor Ground was Arsenal's main home south of the river until 1913. They moved there on 11 February 1888. The game above was against Liverpool on 2 September 1905 (Arsenal won 3–1).

future of football. The Scottish FA finally accepted professionalism at their AGM in the same month as Arsenal's admittance to the League, and 16 southern clubs were also persuaded to form the Southern League, though only half were professional at the time. In creating a general acceptance of professionalism, all three decisions were major stepping-stones on the road to legitimacy for the League and the FA and, a mere seven years old, Arsenal were playing a major part.

Raising funds

It was Arsenal's first significant contribution to the history of British football. For the club and its board, however, one rather more immediate consequence of the club's arrival in the League, and the raising of the rent at the Invicta ground, was the decision to try to buy a ground of their own. The only way to raise enough money was to form a limited liability company, and this, despite those earlier objections, happened in the summer of 1893.

The new company had a nominal capital of 4,000 £1 shares. In all 860 people subscribed for 1,552 shares (the rest were left unissued) and most of the shareholders were actually manual workers at the Arsenal who lived locally. There were only three holdings of 20 shares or more, the highest being 50 by a coffee house proprietor. The first board of directors contained a surgeon, a builder and six engineers from the Arsenal. At that moment in time, without a ground, large crowds, or obvious playing resources, the problems were actually only just beginning.

CHAPTER 3

WOOLWICH ARSENAL

The 20 years between Woolwich Arsenal joining the Football League in 1893 and their departure for Highbury in 1913 could not exactly be described as a period of unqualified success. Indeed, apart from the six-year spell following Harry Bradshaw's arrival as manager in 1901, it could better be termed one of financial struggle and footballing mediocrity. The Gunners were never a bad Second Division side. They chuntered along in mid-table until Bradshaw's arrival resulted in a fourth, third and second in successive seasons, the last gaining them promotion to the top division for the first time, in 1904. They stayed there nine years, but never finished better than sixth and even that performance was not as outstanding as it sounds for they won 14, lost 14 and drew 10.

The FA Cup is perhaps a better guide to their real status, for Arsenal went beyond the second round (the equivalent of today's fourth) only twice between 1893 and the First World War. Admittedly, these years, 1906 and 1907, were the highlight of the whole era, for Arsenal reached the semi-final in both seasons, but that proved the last gasp of the team Bradshaw built. He had already left, being lured away to Fulham in 1904.

Problems of geography

So, 1904 to 1907 apart, the era was really the story of a struggle against geography. Despite seeming to be relatively close to the middle of London, Woolwich is actually something of a backwater. No one passes through; it is difficult to reach from the eastern side, and the river effectively cut Arsenal's geographical circle of support by half. It was also a good 20- to 30-minute tram ride further out than the nearest major club (at the time Millwall Athletic).

George Allison used to be a junior sports reporter with Hulton's before the First World War and was given Woolwich Arsenal as his regular team to report on. He told more than a few amusing stories about trying to get there: 'From Fleet Street to Plumstead was heavy going. Other sports writers were more than happy when I offered to undertake all the reporting of Arsenal's home games. The payment I received softened the monotony of the long and tedious journey. One could travel on the South Eastern and Chatham Railway from London Bridge, Cannon Street or Charing Cross. The trains

Above: The first team squad at the start of the 1895–96 season; top: Boyle, Powell, Storer, Caldwell, Hollis; centre: Davis, Jenkyns, Ward; bottom: Mills, Hare, Buchanan, O'Brian, Mortimer. It was an average season, the side finishing seventh in the Second Division. John Boyle's season was particularly interesting – he played six times at half-back and four times in goal. The club tried six men between the posts during the season in an attempt to replace the departed Storer.

Opposite: Harry Storer, the first choice keeper in 1894 and 1895. When he was chosen to represent the Football League against the Scottish League on 13 April 1895, he became the first Arsenal player to win representative honours. Storer is wearing the red and light-blue striped shirt that the club briefly tried in 1895. As the idea was not pursued, one can only assume that just the single set of kit was ever purchased. Goalkeepers wore the same shirts as the rest of their team until 1909.

stopped at every station. There were the same halts on the return journey, with the added difficulty that no one knew where the trains were going.'

No longer the big guns

When Woolwich Arsenal joined the Football League in 1893, they were London's only professional club. Some 15 years later, there were five in the Football League alone (Chelsea, Fulham, Spurs and Clapton Orient were the others), and a range of Southern League sides like Millwall Athletic and Crystal Palace. Arsenal's unique position was eroded quickly.

Additionally, there was the Boer War between 1899 and 1902, an enormous blow to a club whose dependence on the military, in its earlier days, cannot be overestimated. This took both players and support out of the area, particularly as the Arsenal itself introduced a Saturday afternoon shift. The tradition throughout the country at that time was for men to knock off at Saturday lunch time, have a drink and go to the game. The war was to prove almost as much a disaster for Arsenal as it was for the British troops in South Africa.

By the turn of the century the Reds had so far managed to hold their own in the Second Division. The long distances were something of a help to them, for they rarely lost at home (only 13 defeats in the first five seasons). On the other side of the coin, they never won more than three games on the road in a single season until 1897–98.

There were occasional highlights – the very first game of their League career was on Saturday 2 September 1893 against

Arsenal's Caesar capped

The next few seasons were similarly unspectacular, though the club soon gained its first representative honours. Goalkeeper Harry Storer was chosen between the posts for the Football League against the Scottish League in April 1895 and the gloriously named Caesar Llewellyn Jenkyns became the first current full international when he represented Wales against Scotland on 21 March 1896. Typically, both men were too good for the club and had been transferred within a year. Also too good were, surprisingly, Loughborough Town, who beat the Gunners 8–0 away in a Second Division game on 12 December 1896.

The Loughborough defeat came during a peculiar spell which has never been surpassed before or since by the club. Between October 17 and Christmas Day 1896, their League results went as follows: a 3–5 defeat at Walsall, a 6–1 win over Gainsborough Trinity, a 4–7 defeat by Notts County, a 2–5 defeat by Small Heath, a 4–2 win over Grimsby, a 3–2 victory over Lincoln, the 0–8 defeat at Loughborough, a 4–2 win over Blackpool and a 6–2 Christmas Day romp past Lincoln. In nine games they had scored 32 goals and conceded 34.

The result at Loughborough remains Arsenal's record defeat, but the compliment was quickly returned on 12 March 1900 when Loughborough came to the Manor Ground and were themselves beaten 12–0. This is still Arsenal's record victory and is one of only 18 occasions when a side has scored a dozen goals in a Football League fixture.

Sadly, these talking points only serve to brighten an essentially dour period. A disastrous FA Cup defeat by non-League Millwall (2–4 away) on 16 January 1896 proved one turning point for the committee. They decided to appoint a secretary-manager, one T. B. Mitchell from Blackburn, who was quickly succeeded by George Elcoat from Stockton. When Harry Bradshaw took over at the turn of the 20th century the club were going nowhere very fast. He soon brought in the two most notable players of the period, an Australian left-back, Jimmy Jackson, who became club captain, and a new goalkeeper from Sheppey United, Jimmy Ashcroft. When Ashcroft played in all three internationals in 1905–06, he became the first Arsenal player to be capped for England. Results and support improved slowly. By February 1903, over 25,000 were prepared to turn out to see Cup holders Sheffield United win a first round FA Cup tie 3–1 in Plumstead. The receipts were a healthy £1,000, the first time the club had reached the four-figure mark.

Gunners promoted

The following season, 1903–04, led to promotion to the First Division. This was almost entirely the result of an excellent home record, with an astonishing goal ratio of 67 to 5. Not a

another newly elected club, Newcastle. It ended 2–2, Shaw and Elliott being the scorers. Arsenal's first League win did not come until 11 September, at home to Walsall Town Swifts, when John Heath scored a hat-trick in a 4–0 home victory. Newcastle scored six against the Gunners at the end of the month, and Burton Swifts did the same in November, but Arsenal returned the compliment twice during the season – against opponents Middlesbrough Ironopolis (away from home) and Northwich Victoria, both long since gone from the Football League. All in all, ninth place out of 15 in their first season, with 28 points from 28 games, was acceptable, though Liverpool took all the attention by winning the division undefeated.

1893-1915

match was lost at home (all were won but the last two) and there were 8–0 wins over Burton United and Leicester Fosse. The away record was not so impressive, with just six wins, but the overall goal tally of 91–22 remained impressive. Proud Preston won the division a point ahead of Arsenal, with Manchester United another point behind in third. The team which gained promotion was Jimmy Ashcroft (who played in every game), Archie Cross (a local lad from Dartford), captain Jimmy Jackson, John Dick, Percy Sands (a schoolteacher who taught in Woolwich), Roddy McEachrane (a neat Inverness-born schemer who played left-half), Tommy Briercliffe (signed from Blackburn), 'Tim' Coleman, Bill Gooing (the centre for-ward, who was another ever-present player), Tommy Shanks (the leading scorer with 25 League goals) and Bill Linward (signed from West Ham). Of the 20 players to appear in the promotion season, only two had been with the club before Bradshaw's arrival as manager.

Woolwich Arsenal's success quickly brought problems in its wake. Bradshaw was lured away to Fulham for a large salary before the next season had even begun and his Woolwich successor, Phil Kelso, was to follow him to Craven Cottage five years later. Fulham have a strange affinity for Arsenal when choosing their managers – no fewer than nine of the first 14 managers at Craven Cottage either played for or managed the Gunners.

Kelso was a Scotsman, previously manager of Hibernian, and he reinforced the side, as many have done before and since, with his countrymen. Initially gates were good (aver-aging over 10,000) and the club made a particular point of encouraging season-ticket holders, one result being that for a time they had more than any other club in the country.

Cup form improves

Those supporters were well rewarded in 1906 when the club managed to get past the second round for the first time in their 20-year history and reach the semi-finals of the FA Cup. Nor was it an easy run: West Ham were beaten away after a home draw, then Watford 3–0, Sunderland (already having been League Champions four times) 5–0, which was a sensational result at the time, and then Manchester United 3–2 away in the quarter-final.

The semi-final was at Stoke, against the all-conquering might of Newcastle. Between 1905 and 1911 the Magpies were to reach five FA Cup finals and Arsenal did not really stand in their way. Newcastle won 2–0 with goals from the great Colin Veitch and Jimmy Howie, although they then lost the final 1–0 to Everton. Arsenal had fielded one of their best ever forward lines and, early on, centre-forward Bert Freeman hit the bar before Newcastle had scored. Arsenal could not hold onto

Above: A corner of the Manor Ground in 1904. In the background are some of the workshops of Royal Arsenal East, which was situated in the middle of Plumstead.

Below: The Liverpool keeper trying to parry an Arsenal shot on goal during a League match at the Manor Ground on 6 October 1906. Arsenal went on to win 2–1.

Freeman for more than a couple of years, and eventually had to sell him to Everton. He was to lead the Football League's goalscorers three times between 1908 and 1913 and finally won an FA Cup winners' medal when he scored the only goal of the game for Burnley against Liverpool in 1914. The two wingers were also internationals – Bill Garbutt on the right (capped for England later when he was with Blackburn) and the unpre-dictable Scot Bobby Templeton on the left. Templeton had won caps when with Aston Villa and Newcastle.

Considering that they had never before gone beyond the second round, it was a great surprise to see Arsenal pop up in the semi-final again the following year. This time their progress was easier, past Grimsby, Bristol City (at the time lying second in the First Division), Bristol Rovers and

Above: The 1907 Arsenal Cup squad, who got as far as the semi-final for the second successive year. They lost 3–1 to Wednesday.

Barnsley. They met mighty Wednesday at St Andrew's in the semi-final and Arsenal went one up after only ten minutes when Garbutt headed in a Satterthwaite cross.

Then came tragedy; keeper Ashcroft was injured in a collison with centre-forward David Wilson when coming outside his area to collect a loose ball (at this time keepers could handle anywhere in their own half) and Wilson scored from the free-kick which referee Jack Howcroft had controversially awarded Wednesday. The incident turned the game and Wednesday scored twice more (making it 3–1) to reach Crystal Palace for the final, which they won by beating Everton 2–1.

Nonetheless, it had been a very successful season for the Reds, perhaps a sign of things to come. They were seventh in the First Division, the reserves had won the London League and the South Eastern League, inside right John 'Tim' Coleman had played for England and full-back Jimmy Sharp for Scotland. As it happened, it was actually the top of the roller-coaster, not part of a careful ascent. The club's support and finances were not strong enough to survive a decline in results, and, once things started to go wrong, they accelerated virtually out of control.

Financial problems mount

The problems were initially much more acute off the field than on it, where the side finished 15th, 6th and 18th between 1907–08 and 1909–10. Phil Kelso resigned, initially to run a hotel in Scotland, but almost immediately joined Fulham instead, replacing Harry Bradshaw. The new Arsenal manager, George Morrell, found himself having to sell to survive. Within 12

months virtually all of the important names had gone – Coleman, Freeman, Sharp, Ashcroft and Garbutt. After leaving Woolwich Arsenal for Blackburn, Bill Garbutt moved further and further afield. In 1914 he went to Genoa as coach, where his team won the Italian League the following year. By 1927 he was in Rome, and two years later he went on to Naples. In the 1935–36 season he coached the Spanish champions Athletic Bilbao but the Spanish Civil War drove him back to Italy. During the Second World War he was hidden there by friends and in 1946 emerged from hiding to take up his old post again at Genoa.

Morrell's first full season in charge began on 2 September 1908. The first programme of the season was not shy about discussing the fact that the best players had all gone: 'Here we go again,' began the editor 'and the followers of Arsenal look forward to the advent of another season with a great number of the players on whom we rely practically unknown quantities. The 'Reds' will look somewhat strange without such faces as Ashcroft, Sharp, Coleman, Freeman, Kyle and Garbutt but we believe capable men have been engaged to replace them and we look forward to a successful season.'

The hope was misplaced for it was to be nearly two decades before the 'Reds' had another genuinely successful year. Even the greatest of all the pre-war Gunners, Andy Ducat, eventually had to be transferred to Villa. Right-half Ducat appeared for England in all three internationals in 1909–10, when he was only 23. He had scored a hat-trick in his first ever game for Arsenal, on Christmas Day 1905, versus the mighty Newcastle United. It was particularly sad that his best playing days were lost to the First World War. For their part Woolwich Arsenal never recovered from those sudden sales of their best players in 1908, particularly missing keeper Ashcroft. The crowds melted away, as did the results, and by 1910 the club was effectively bankrupt and up for sale.

Gunners to go west?

For the next decade the Arsenal story is really to be told off the field rather than on it. The main reason for this was one Henry Norris, the Chairman of Fulham. As we have seen, the links between the two clubs were already close, if not necessarily friendly, and in 1910 Norris was able to use the Woolwich club's problems to effect a takeover of Arsenal as well.

Fulham had experienced a remarkably rapid rise since Henry Norris became chairman. In 1902 and 1903 they won the Second Division of the Southern League, were then elected to the First and, under Bradshaw, won that Division in 1906 and 1907, upon which they applied to join the Football League and were immediately accepted. This was the first concrete evidence of Henry Norris' remarkable powers of political

1893-1915

persuasion where the Football League was concerned. At the 1907 election Fulham easily received the highest number of votes (28) and replaced Burton United.

Henry Norris was a self-made man, his fortune based on property development in south-west London. He was Mayor of Fulham for seven years, was knighted in 1917 and represented Fulham East in Parliament from 1918 to 1922. A dictatorial man, he ran his football clubs like his businesses. A thin autocrat with a walrus moustache, he welcomed neither criticism nor advice; nonetheless, he was influential and persuasive. Over the years he developed close friendships with members of the League Management Committee, particularly the president, John McKenna.

Leslie Knighton, Arsenal manager to Norris' Chairman between 1919 and 1925, has left us perhaps the best descriptions of Norris. Knighton said in his autobiography: 'I soon found out that everyone was afraid of Sir Henry. And no wonder! I have never met his equal for logic, invective and ruthlessness against all who opposed him. When I disagreed with him at board meetings and had to stand up for what I knew was best for the club, he used to flay me with words until I was reduced to fuming, helpless silence. Then, as I sat not knowing what to say, and trying to bottle up what I was tempted to say, he would whip round and shout: "Well Knighton, we pay you a great deal of money to advise us and all you do is sit there as if you were dumb".' But afterwards, says Knighton: 'Sir Henry would ask my advice, smile, wheedle and I was falling over myself to help him again. He did it with everyone. Those board meetings took years off my life.'

Like many influential Londoners with lower-class roots in the Edwardian era, Norris was sensitive to the fact that London appeared to be unable to compete with the provinces in what had become the national winter sport. For whatever personal reasons, he became determined to create a side capable of competing with the best from the north and Birmingham. His attention first turned to his local club, Fulham, but by 1908 he had obviously become convinced that they would never have a strong enough base for the success he sought.

Although Fulham had not been unsuccessful on the field, they, like Arsenal, were quite poorly supported. By 1910 the Cottagers had an accumulated overdraft of over £3,000 – an enormous sum in those days – while the Woolwich club were to all intents and purposes completely bankrupt.

Although this was the year in which Norris took over Arsenal, he remained a Fulham director until the war. His co-director at Woolwich, William Hall, was also Fulham chairman until the same date and the two men obviously controlled both clubs. It was partially because of this possible conflict of interests that the League later insisted no one could have a controlling interest in two League members.

Above: Advertising in match programmes is nothing new: the official programme for the match on 4 December 1906 carried details about forthcoming concerts at the Royal Artillery Theatre and Opera House, Woolwich.

Right: Half-back Alec Graham joined Arsenal for their disastrous final season before the move to Highbury, scoring 20 goals in his 179 matches for the 'Reds'.

Norris takes charge

Norris had no doubt been putting out feelers for some time, but it was not until the summer of 1910, with the Gunners having escaped relegation by only a couple of points, that he was able to take control. His initial plan was very simple – he wanted to amalgamate Woolwich Arsenal with Fulham, move them to Craven Cottage and have a First Division team play there. When the League said no, he proposed an even more financially attractive solution – Arsenal and Fulham could play at Craven Cottage on alternative Saturdays. The other London clubs objected and that was turned down as well. The League also pointed out the obvious disadvantages of having one man controlling two clubs and Norris was in the position, having failed to achieve either of his objectives, of being informally forced to choose one club or the other.

In the end he came down in favour of the Woolwich club, no doubt because they were still in the First Division. Sadly, this was not to be the case for much longer. After a couple more years of mid-table insignificance, 1912–13 was a disaster. Arsenal finished bottom with only 18 points, 26 goals scored and three wins. The points, goals and wins were all the lowest ever recorded in the First Division and remained records, though equalled, until the end of the two point-system.

Arsenal in dire straits

By the end of the 1912–13 season, the club was reported as having only £19 in the bank. The size of the disaster had been clear from the first few matches and Henry Norris and William Hall had been looking for some rapid solution to their plight throughout the year.

ALEC. GRAHAM.

Their conclusion was as dramatic as it was simple. If the club was to have any chance of becoming the power in the land that Norris desired, then it would simply have to move.

There were four necessary guidelines for a new location for the club. It should be within greater London so as not to lose the backbone of the support which the club had relied upon over the years; it should be in a heavily populated area, preferably not bounded by the river or any other restriction to access; thirdly, it should not be too close to another major club; and, most important of all, it should be very easy to reach by public transport such as the underground or railway. In 1913 the last point was a prerequisite for any side that hoped to attract really big crowds. Among the open spaces that Hall and Norris negotiated for were ones in Battersea and Harringay, but they found nothing that met all of their requirements. Nor were they to, in the end, accepting that they would probably have to be in the north or west and therefore inevitably close to either Spurs or Chelsea.

A new home at Highbury

When and how Highbury came into the reckoning is unknown. The land in question was the site of St John's College of Divinity, but relatively little of it was built upon. Most was taken up by the two football pitches, two cricket pitches and tennis courts used by the students. The keys to the site, for Hall and Norris, were its availability and its proximity to Gillespie Road underground station. Negotiations were not exactly easy and went on for several months, Norris bringing all his considerable influence to bear on the Ecclesiastical Commissioners. In the end, Arsenal paid a massive £20,000 for a 21-year lease and agreed not to stage matches on Good Friday and Christmas Day (this restriction was eventually lifted in 1925 when the club paid another £64,000 to buy the whole site outright). The college itself remained at the southern end of the ground until it burned down at the end of the Second World War.

The actual deed of transfer was signed by the Archbishop of Canterbury, but if Norris thought that this implied heavenly blessing for his plans then he was quickly to discover others disagreed. The objections to Arsenal moving to Highbury came from three main sources. The most predictable was from the other clubs, particularly Tottenham and Clapton Orient, then playing at Homerton. Both were within four miles of Highbury but Arsenal would be closer to the centre and, with that vital underground station, much easier to reach. Spurs had only joined the League five years before and had just spent enormous sums (around £50,000) on improving their ground.

Local residents joined in the outcry – it was one thing having a college of divinity on the doorstep, quite another to see it suddenly turn into a football ground. It is impossible to imagine such a transfer being approved today, but at that time there was very little in the way of planning permission required.

Tottenham, Orient, the local residents and even Chelsea appealed to the League Management Committee and a special meeting was called in March 1913. It went on until two in the morning, a not too friendly and highly argumentative debate. To cut a long story short, Arsenal won the day. This was less because the Management Committee agreed with their plans than because: '... of the opinion that under the rules and practice of the League (we) have no right to interfere.'

Many clubs had moved in the past but no one had ever objected before and the transfers had usually been local and to everyone's benefit. Arsenal's case was, by any standards, different. It is only ten miles as the crow flies from Woolwich to Highbury, but in terms of travelling times within greater London that is very different from Blackburn Rovers or Sunderland moving a mile up the road. Never before had there been a clear incursion into a competitor's catchment area.

Farewell to Woolwich

The last first-class game at the Manor Ground took place on Saturday 26 April 1913 against Middlesbrough and Woolwich Arsenal said goodbye to their name, their home and southeast London with a 1–1 draw, a rather better result than most of that season for they had won only two games in all first-class competitions at the Manor Ground in the previous 12 months.

Woolwich was dropped from the name and, though the club apparently never officially called itself The Arsenal, that was to be the name by which it was publicly known until Chapman insisted on the single word some 12 years later. Oddly, the official *Football League Fiftieth Anniversary History* said: 'Thus the new Arsenal club was reborn and, on 3rd April of the following year (1914) it was given permission to drop the Woolwich from the name and was henceforth known as "The Arsenal".'

Now the spending really began. In four months the new pitch was levelled (the north end had to be raised 11 feet and the south end lowered five feet), a new grandstand partly built and turnstiles and terracing installed. It cost Norris another £80,000. Including bank guarantees and loans, by the time the first match was played at Highbury on 6 September 1913 he had found an astonishing £125,000 to put into the club. Cash was so short that the builder of the stand agreed to take a percentage of the weekly gate in order to pay for its construction.

All Norris had to show for this investment at that time, of course, was a Second Division football team. The first game was against Leicester Fosse and the Reds did well enough, winning 2–1. Scottish international inside left Andy Devine scored the first goal, but it is centre-forward George Jobey whose contribution that day has gone down in the history

1893-1915

Above: the 1912–13 squad at the start of the season. It was a disastrous time for Woolwich Arsenal as they were relegated to the Second Division of the Football League.

books. He sprained an ankle during the game and was helped off by trainer George Hardy. As there were no dressing rooms or running water, Hardy decided to take Jobey to the player's lodgings nearby. To do so, and not wanting the player to walk, he borrowed a cart from the local milkman David Lewis, who lived in Gillespie Road.

All in all, the team did quite well in that Second Division season – finishing third and failing to go up only on goal average behind Bradford Park Avenue. The critical game was the last home match of the season, on 18 April against Clapton Orient, who were sixth in the division. In a bitter hangover from the controversy over Arsenal's move a year before, Orient fought like tigers to draw 2–2. The following week, though Arsenal won 2–0 at Glossop (the Hill-Wood family club), Bradford beat Blackpool 4–1 and were up.

The war to end all wars

But a far greater shock was about to face Norris. He desperately needed First Division football and seemed to have a team that might achieve it but, within a year of that first game at Highbury, Europe was at war. The result was disaster. Players, particularly the many with Woolwich Arsenal connections, went back to munitions work, others joined the forces, the crowds declined and the League, though it was contested in 1914–15, was something of an irrelevance.

The most notable players of the era were right-back Joe Shaw, who was to stay with the club during and beyond the inter-war period as assistant manager, and his full-back partner Bob Benson. Benson was one of the many players who went back into munitions work and therefore lost his match fitness. Having gone to watch the club play at Reading in February 1916, Benson volunteered to take Joe Shaw's place as Shaw himself could not get away from his own job. Benson was clearly unfit, had to leave the field and, having gone to the dressing room, died a few minutes later in the arms of George Hardy. In a fitting tribute he was buried in an Arsenal shirt.

Benson's was a personal tragedy and there were many more in that 'war to end wars'. For the club, having taken such a gamble only a year before, the war was a source of total despair. At the end of the 1914–15 season manager George Morrell was unceremoniously sacked to save money and, financially, things just got worse. By 1918 the club was £60,000 overdrawn and Norris was, not surprisingly, again desperate.

On Saturday 24 April 1915 Arsenal had played their last game of the season against Forest at Highbury. The programme detailed Morrell's departure and the club's plight. It was, nonetheless, their best display of the year, a 7–0 win with Harry King scoring four goals, Jock Rutherford one, and the tragic Bob Benson, less than a year before his death, playing up front and getting two. What no one knew at the time was that it was to be Arsenal's last game in the Second Division.

The actor, writer and Arsenal fanatic Tom Watt sums up the passion of the North London derby: 'Arsenal-Spurs games tend to be fired by a bitterness all their own. There's little hint of a local occasion to be proud of. The match – and the rivalry between the fans – is unremittingly competitive. Victory is the only satisfactory outcome.'

The roots lay in the distant past. When the Gunners moved from Plumstead to Highbury in 1913, they invaded Spurs' territory. In 1919, after much lobbying by Arsenal chairman Sir Henry Norris, the Gunners were elected to the enlarged first division ... at Tottenham's expense.

As former Spurs Chairman Irving Scholar said: 'It always means so much to beat Arsenal. If Spurs win, you can hold your head high. If you lose, you dread meeting the next Arsenal fan.'Even when Arsenal were at their peak in the 1930s, Spurs occasionally managed to pull out something extra for the derby. In 1934, for instance, Tottenham beat the Gunners 3–1 at Highbury.

Arsenal took revenge the following year. They were on their way to a third consecutive title. Spurs were relegated. At Highbury, Ted Drake grabbed a hat-trick as the Gunners won 5-1. At White Hart Lane, Arsenal blew Tottenham's offside tactics apart. Drake netted twice. So did ex-Norwich winger Alf Kirchen, on his Arsenal debut. Reserve inside forward Peter Dougall and Cliff Bastin, from the spot, made it 6-0. That's still the biggest win in a north London derby.

Hostilities resumed four years after the war, in the 1949 FA Cup third round. Ian McPherson, Don Roper and Doug Lishman scored as Arsenal crushed second division Spurs 3–0.

The early 50s were one of those rare periods when both clubs enjoyed success. Arsenal won the FA Cup in 1950 and clinched their seventh championship three years later. In 1951, promoted Tottenham won their first title.

As the decade wore on, both had to rebuild. Spurs did it better than Arsenal. Bill Nicholson's return, as manager, in 1958, galvanised Tottenham. The early 60s were no time to be an Arsenal fan. In 1961, Spurs became the first 20th-century

Above left: Charlie Buchan shakes Spurs' Arthur Grimsdell's hand on 29 August 1925. This was Chapman's first game as manager.

Above: By the late 1960s the balance of power had shifted towards Arsenal, although this meeting in 1969 ended in a 3–2 defeat.

Opposite: Wenger's Arsenal are too powerful for the Lillywhites. Nwankwo Kanu scores in a 3–1 victory at White Hart Lane in May 1999.

Below: During the early 1980s the derbies were thrilling games as both sides wrestled results off one another.

team to do the 'double.' They won the FA Cup again the following year, then became the first English team to lift a
European trophy.

Yet the Gunners offered spirited resistance. Two of the
most famous derbies of that era finished 4–4. The first was at
Tottenham in October 1962. Spurs led 3–0 after 26 minutes.
David Court, deputising for the injured Joe Baker, pulled one
back The 18-year-old striker scored again. Cliff Jones made it
4–2 to Tottenham at the interval. In the second half, George
Eastham dominated midfield, created a third goal for Johnny
MacLeod – then sliced open Spurs defence for Geoff Strong to
hit the equaliser.

A year (and nine days) later, it finished 4–4 at Highbury.
Tottenham galloped into a two-goal lead. Eastham replied from
the spot. Dave Mackay cracked Tottenham's third. Eastham
scored again. Bobby Smith restored Spurs two-goal margin.
Arsenal staged an amazing late recovery. Joe Baker struck
with five minutes left. In injury time, Strong rose to head home
MacLeod's corner.

By 1967, the tide was starting to turn. On the morning of
September 16, the best man at George Graham's wedding was
Spurs midfielder Terry Venables. That afternoon Graham slid
in Arsenal's third goal as they overwhelmed the FA Cup
holders 4–0. The Gunners confirmed the shift of power in the
League Cup semi-final the following season. John Radford
scored the only goal at Highbury. In a bruising return, Jimmy
Greaves put Spurs ahead – but Radford levelled three minutes
from time. The Arsenal fans celebrated long and loud in
Tottenham High Road. They celebrated even more in 1971,
when Ray Kennedy's last-gasp header at White Hart Lane
clinched the Championship and the first leg of the 'Double'.

In 1978 Liam Brady gave Gunners fans an early Christmas
present when he orchestrated the 5-0 destruction of Spurs on
their home ground. Alan Sunderland scored a hat trick. Not
until April 1983 – when they annihilated the Gunners 5–0 –
could Tottenham wipe out the memory of that defeat.

Enter Graham as Arsenal manager in 1986. Cue three
thrilling matches in the 1987 League Cup semi-final. Spurs won
the first leg, 1–0 at Highbury. Clive Allen netted again at White
Hart Lane. At half time, the stadium announcer read out
Tottenham's Wembley ticket arrangements. Arsenal were
inspired. Viv Anderson and Niall Quinn scored to force extra
time and a replay. Spurs won the choice for venue. Allen struck
again. Charlie Nicholas had to go off injured. With eight minutes left, Arsenal looked finished. Then Ian Allinson, sub for
Nicholas, tucked away a close-range effort and ensured a furious finale. With time running out, Allinson's shot rebounded
into the path of David Rocastle, who ran on to stroke Arsenal's
winner past Ray Clemence. The Gunners came from behind
again, to beat Liverpool at Wembley.

In 1991, Arsenal and Spurs met in the FA Cup semi-final: at
Wembley. It was Gazza's match. Terry Venables gambled on
the semi-fit England midfielder. He lashed a magnificent free-
kick goal past David Seaman to give Spurs an early lead; then
started the move for Gary Lineker to stab Tottenham's second.
Alan Smith headed in Lee Dixon's cross to revive Arsenal
hopes. The Gunners dominated much of the second half. But
Lineker's breakaway goal killed the contest. Two years later,
they met at Wembley again. This time, Tony Adams' goal
decided. With ten minutes left, the Gunners skipper stole in
unmarked at the far post to bury Paul Merson's free kick with a
stooping header.

In 1995, Graham left Arsenal. In 1998, he returned to north
London – as manager of Tottenham. His joy when Spurs held
out for a goalless draw at Highbury last November was obvious. But on May 5, 1999, Dennis Bergkamp and Kanu took
Tottenham apart. Bergkamp created gilt-edged chances, converted by Manu Petit and Nicolas Anelka. Then – after Darren
Anderton's free-kick had given Spurs a lifeline – sub Kanu
wrapped up the points with a wonderful goal: a delicate flick
over Luke Young, followed by a crashing volley past Ian
Walker. 3–1 to Arsenal. Surely, after victory at White Hart Lane,
the destiny of the title was in the Gunners' hands? David
O'Leary's Leeds destroyed Arsenal's dream six days later.

On November 17 2001, Sol Campbell played his first
derby in Arsenal colours and enjoyed a consummately professional match in defence. It seemed as though Arsenal
were destined for victory until Poyet equalized in the third
minute of injury time. But on 6 April, the Gunners gained
revenge with a 2–1 victory with Ljungberg and Lauren scoring – Arsenal were back on top of the Premiership table and
on their way to a third Double.

CHAPTER 4
THE ARSENAL

When the long, terrible conflict known then as the 'War to End All Wars' reached its exhausted conclusion in the November of 1918, first-class football had effectively ceased to exist. Three quarters of a million young British men had been killed, and of those no small number had been professional footballers.

Amid all this, The Arsenal's problems were clearly relatively small ones, but to the club's owner and bankroller, Sir Henry Norris, they were real enough. When the war began the club had been fielding a side which should have quickly fought its way back into the First Division and hence helped with the £60,000 standing debt and Norris' immense investment of £125,000. But those players who had survived the traumas of the war were all five years older and there was absolutely no telling how any club would perform in the season that was to begin in September 1919.

Political games begin

It was at this point that Henry Norris set out on the single most outrageous enterprise ever to be conceived in the history of English football. There is still no convincing explanation of how Norris achieved his object and it is almost inconceivable that any other individual, before or since, could have carried it off at all. Norris' aim, very simply, was to talk The Arsenal back into the First Division.

In 1914–15 the team had finished fifth in the Second Division. Above Arsenal were Derby, Preston, Barnsley and Wolves. In 1919 it was decided to extend the First Division from 20 to 22 clubs. Extensions of the divisions had happened on several occasions since the League was founded in 1888 and the almost invariable procedure when extending the First Division was to re-elect automatically the bottom clubs from the previous season and promote the top clubs from the Second Division. Given the unfortunate intervention of the war, there seemed every reason to suppose that this is exactly what would happen.

By chance, two other London clubs, Chelsea and Spurs, had finished 19th and 20th in the First Division in 1915. Showing remarkable stealth and political judgement, Norris used the eight intervening months between the end of the war and the AGM of the Football League in mid-1919 to canvass the other major clubs and various influential friends in the game. He had received his knighthood in 1917 and became a Tory MP in 1918, and one must assume that many were flattered by the attentions of this successful luminary in a game which then had few figures of note outside its own confines.

Norris seemed to have little material to work on with which to prove his case. But there was just one small chink of hope.

Above: Joe Shaw's playing career with Arsenal began in 1907 and went on until 1923. Apart from a short spell at Chelsea, his distinguished career as part of the management team was to continue until the mid-1950s.

Opposite: Before and after; the top picture shows the ground as it was at the time of Leslie Knighton's departure and Herbert Chapman's arrival in 1925. The lower picture was taken just after the Second World War and shows the new East and West Stands.

At the end of the 1914–15 season it had become obvious that the League would have to be abandoned completely for the duration of the war. There had been some allegations of match fixing by one or two players (who had apparently bet on the results) and, in one instance, this accusation was proven after a number of lengthy court cases. That particular game was Manchester United versus Liverpool, and United had won it 2–0 to finish 18th, just one point ahead of Chelsea. Although United would have dropped below Chelsea if Liverpool had beaten them, they would still have finished ahead of bottom-placed Spurs, but the whole business did serve to create an understandable uneasiness that something about the 1914–15 season was not quite as it should have been. It should be said immediately for the record that there was never the slightest suggestion that either Tottenham or Chelsea were ever involved in any wrongdoing.

Norris makes claim for promotion

What Norris said to the other chairmen has never been revealed, but his desperation for First Division status and the size of the investment at risk clearly persuaded enough of them that he had a worthwhile case. Leslie Knighton described his Chairman's technique at the time thus: 'His influence was enormous. (He would) speak to an important person there, suggesting a favour, remind a certain financier who was interested that he had once done him a good turn and been promised something in return.'

When the AGM was convened, Norris' strategy became clear. It must have been agreed with League President 'Honest' John McKenna, a close friend of Norris and the owner of Liverpool, in advance. Firstly, Chelsea were detached from Spurs and their position taken separately. There was no vote, and the fact that Chelsea would have finished third from bottom in 1915 rather than only one place above Spurs had Liverpool beaten United in the fixed match undoubtedly influenced the meeting. McKenna proposed they they be re-elected on the nod and this was accepted. Then Derby and Preston, first and second in the Second Division in 1914–15, were elected to the First Division without debate.

Then came the bombshell. McKenna, who might have been more reticent given that he was the force behind Liverpool FC, made a brief speech recommending that Arsenal be given the remaining First Division place because of their service to the League and their longevity, particularly pointing out that Arsenal had been in the League 15 years longer than Spurs.

The arguments used were, of course, complete and utter nonsense. The League is not (and never has been) run on the basis of the most experienced clubs being given the higher places, and, in any event, Wolves, who finished fourth, had been members of the League four years longer than Arsenal. Spurs chairman Charlie Roberts found it (not surprisingly) very difficult to counter the illogicalities of this Alice in Wonderland meeting in which he had suddenly, unexpectedly and inexplicably become entrapped. The vote was taken; Arsenal got 18, Spurs got 8, Barnsley (who finished third) 5, Wolves 4, Forest (who finished 19th and had no claim to a place whatsoever) got 3, Birmingham 2 and Hull 1. Hence Arsenal were elected and Sir Henry Norris had his First Division club again.

A mysterious decision

To this day it is impossible to explain what went on at that AGM. The most plausible explanation is actually the most irrational; the individual representatives assumed that, if McKenna was prepared to support so unlikely a cause, then he must have some very good, if well-hidden, reason for doing so.

If there was such a reason, it has remained very well hidden indeed, though it would clearly have been assumed to be something to do with the results at the end of the 1914–15 season. For the sake of completeness, it should be mentioned that for many years there were rumours of the involvement of significant sums of money.

Paradoxically, it was a conclusion that probably favoured Spurs more than Arsenal. Only six years after failing to prevent the upstart's arrival on their patch, the Tottenham board went back to White Hart Lane pondering the injustice of it all. Their response was on the field. In 1919–20 they scored 102 goals and broke all the records for points (70) and wins (32). Straight back in the First Division, they finished sixth, and won the FA Cup at Stamford Bridge. Until Chapman was bedded in at Highbury, Spurs were clearly north London's leading club. There was, not surprisingly, a heavy residue of bitterness between the clubs, thankfully unparalleled before or since in the English game.

In September 1922 the bitterness led to a particularly vicious match, two sendings off, censures, suspensions and an FA Commission of Inquiry.

Bitter north London rivals

As late as 1928, Arsenal were accused of throwing games at the end of the season to ensure Spurs went down. The games concerned in that 1927–28 season were both at home – a 0–2 defeat by Portsmouth (who themselves finished 20th) on 28 March and, more relevantly, a 0–1 defeat by Manchester United (who finished 18th) on 28 April, the last week of the season. Both of those clubs finished one point above Spurs, who had finished their programme earlier, and if Arsenal had managed even a draw with either Portsmouth or United then Spurs would have stayed up.

On the other hand, the table in 1927–28 was astonishingly tight. Seven points covered Derby, who finished fourth, and Middlesbrough, who finished bottom. Arsenal, in 19th place, were only three points ahead of Spurs themselves and would therefore, one must assume, have endangered their own position by such unlikely behaviour. The Gunners only very rarely got the better of Spurs in the inter-war period anyway; between Chapman's arrival in 1925 and October 1934 Spurs did not once lose at Highbury.

The Arsenal did not exactly enjoy a successful spell for the few seasons after 1919, but at least they stayed where they were. It was a happy coincidence that the centenary was also the point that Arsenal equalled the record for the longest unbroken spell of First Division membership. Sunderland stayed there from 1890 to 1958, a run of 68 years. Arsenal's 68th year arrived in the second half of the season 1986–87.

1918-1925

Mission impossible

Norris had appointed Leslie Knighton as manager in June 1919. Knighton, who had previously had quite successful spells with Huddersfield and Manchester City, was, however, rarely allowed to manage. Among Norris' other edicts, Knighton was not allowed to sign players smaller than 5ft 8in, was not allowed to spend more than £1,000 on anyone (Norris was either not prepared to spend any more money or, more likely, was running short of it), was expected to sign and create a team of purely local players and, to compound all these problems, had to save money by abandoning the scouting system. The task tended to verge on the impossible and the playing record reflects this.

The best position between 1919 and Chapman's arrival six years later was ninth in 1921, the only time the club won more games than they lost. In the Cup The Arsenal got beyond the second round just once, in 1922, when they lost to Preston in the quarter finals after a replay. Knighton's last FA Cup game as manager (and probably one of the reasons behind his dismissal soon afterward) actually provides one of the funniest stories in football history.

A. BAKER

Right: The 'utility' player and England international Alf Baker joined Arsenal in the 1919–20 season, and remained with the club for 12 seasons, scoring 26 goals in 351 games.

Knighton's 'pluck pills'

The Arsenal were drawn against West Ham in the first round in January 1925 and Knighton told how he was surprised to be approached by a Harley Street doctor who was also an Arsenal fan: 'I trust you agree that we have a poor chance of survival against West Ham, Mr Knighton,' said the doctor. 'What the boys require is something in the nature of a courage pill. They do no harm, but tone up the nerves to produce the maximum effort.' Knighton investigated the doctor, who was genuine, and his remedy, which did not appear poisonous or illegal, and decided to go ahead. The team were, naturally enough, reluctant. Knighton tried to reassure them by promising to take one of the pills himself. At 2 pm on the Saturday of the match they all took their pills. At 2.50 pm the referee came into the dressing room and told them he'd called the game off because of fog. 'Getting the boys back to Highbury that afternoon was like trying to drive a flock of lively lions,' said Knighton. 'The pills not only left us raring to go but also developed the most red-hot, soul-destroying thirst I've ever known.'

On the following Monday Arsenal went to Upton Park again and went through the same routine. Down went the pills ... and down came the fog. The game was called off again. The after-effects were the same.

On the Thursday the game finally began, the Arsenal team and their manager having taken their pills for a third time. By half time the Gunners were running around like maniacs. 'They were giants suddenly supercharged. They tore away with the ball and put in shots like leather thunderbolts. They monopolised the play – and yet they couldn't score ... For West Ham there was no defence against the pluck pills. The ball crashed and bounced against the West Ham goal. The Arsenal players ran like Olympic sprinters, jumped like rockets to reach the high ones and crashed in shots from all angles and distances. It is no disparagement to West Ham to say that they had the most incredible luck that half.' The game ended as a goalless draw. But Knighton's troubles were only just beginning. 'I forgot my frightful thirst,' he recounts, 'croaking out congratulations and sympathy to the team. But you should have heard them! Running about had made their thirst and bitter throats a thousand times worse. That night those pills created a riot.'

An hour before the replay at Highbury Knighton took out his box of pills. The team refused point-blank to go through it all again. They drew 2–2. The fifth attempt was at Stamford Bridge. There were no pills and no goals for Arsenal. With the last kick of the game, George Kay scored from a Jimmy Ruffell corner and West Ham won 1–0. The doctor never told Knighton what was in the pills, nor ever offered them again.

Talented but underachieving

Knighton's team had its strengths, despite the poor playing record. Joe Shaw was still at full-back, Scot Billy Blyth was used everywhere and Tom Whittaker was a very reliable, intelligent, wing half- or full-back until a knee injury in Woolongong,

Above: The view from the
terraces of the North Bank to
the Main Stand on a dull grey
day during the 1927–28 season.

Australia, while on tour with the FA party, ended his playing
career and directed him to becoming the most famous
trainer/physiotherapist soccer has known. Knighton also made
one or two clever signings. Alf Baker, later an England international at right-half, signed for Arsenal after Knighton met him
at the pithead in Ilkeston (near Nottingham) to forestall other
clubs waiting at Baker's home. Baker was to play in all 11
positions for the club during his career.

Another international who was whisked away for nothing
from under the noses of others was Bob John. He came from
Caerphilly, where Knighton painted a glowing picture of the
glories of the capital (which John was, indeed, later to enjoy
with the club) compared with Cardiff, to whom John was
pledged. He was in the Welsh national side within six months.
Also from south Wales (though he was born in Bristol) came
Jimmy Brain, who was to lead the attack for several seasons.
Both Knighton and Peter McWilliam, manager of Spurs, reput-
edly had to disguise themselves when they visited south Wales

because of the anger expressed when the two London clubs
had stolen away Jimmy Seed, Cecil Poynton and Bob John,
and Spurs were at a crucial disadvantage because all their
negotiations for Brain had to be carried out in secret.

Because of Norris' transfer edicts (he tried in both 1922 and
1924 to get the League to impose a limit on fees of £1,650 –
rarely for a League AGM, they chose to ignore Norris' wishes),
Knighton also had to indulge in some rather unusual transfers.
Dr Jimmy Paterson was an amateur winger with Queen's Park
in Glasgow, when his sister happened to marry the Arsenal
club doctor, J. L. Scott. Paterson joined Scott's practice
(based in Clapton) and also started to play for the club.

Midget Moffat signs

A more celebrated transfer was that of the famous 'Midget'
Moffat of Workington. Again, this is a story worth telling
largely in Leslie Knighton's words.

1918-1925

Knighton had been told about Midget Moffat, the 5 ft tall Workington winger, by an old Huddersfield colleague, who had also warned him that other sides were beginning to take an interest. But chairman Norris had recently imposed one of his absolute edicts – no small men, all new signings had to be at least 5 ft 8 in tall and weigh in at a minimum of 11 stones. Nonetheless, Knighton trusted his source enough to go to Workington by an overnight train and watch the player.

The manager was as mesmerised as the opposing full-back: '... a tiny footballer spinning rings around two perfectly competent full-backs, a midget with a kick like a horse,' Knighton said later. He immediately offered the player a job but Moffat strangely failed to turn up at Highbury the following day. Knighton arrived at the ground the subsequent morning to find the groundsman waiting for him. 'I've got a little tiny chap waiting for you. Says he's come to play for Arsenal. He's asleep in the dressing room.' And, said Knighton: 'There was Moffat, fast asleep on some kit in a corner, his shock of hair sticking out like a squirrel's tail.' Moffat had arrived at Euston and gone straight to Woolwich, thinking the club still played there (they had moved 12 years earlier). When he arrived it was dark. A road sweeper explained things, and offered Moffat a lift on his cart all the way to Highbury.

Knighton took Moffat straight off on a continental tour to Scandinavia, where the winger was apparently a great success. Norris, who had been on a summer holiday in Nice, returned at the start of the new season to find a midget in his midst. 'Norris smiled and said nothing,' wrote Knighton, 'but, as always, he got his way. Moffat had to go, to Luton and thence on to Everton.'

Norris grows impatient

Sadly, Midget Moffat rather sums up Knighton's career at Highbury – clever, thoughtful, but unfortunately bound hand and foot by Norris' peculiar restraints. Whether Knighton would have been a more successful manager for Arsenal in different circumstances is difficult to assess; it certainly seems possible, for he went on to achieve a fair deal with Chelsea and Birmingham.

For his part, it appears that Norris could not work out what was going wrong. As far as we can tell, it doesn't seem to have occurred to him that his restriction on transfers could be affecting the team's potential. He saw the game with an outsider's eye – each of the players seemed good enough, why wouldn't they knit together properly, why did they keep losing by the odd goal? There were other pressures on Norris. As we have seen, Spurs had recovered well from the shenanigans of 1919 and were established as the leading, and best supported, club in the area.

And Henry Norris wasn't getting any younger. If he was ever to do it, to realise the dreams of the past two decades for his club, it would have to be soon. He was no longer an MP, no longer the Mayor of Fulham. Highbury had become his career and, in his own eyes perhaps, the remaining symbol to crown a very successful life.

Knighton sacked

Knighton was dismissed toward the end of the 1924–25 season. In his autobiography, the manager gives his own explanation of the event. Early on in his Highbury days, he had decided to get married. As his future wife lived in Manchester, and a house was available there, Knighton decided to move back north. Norris, according to Knighton, persuaded him to stay by offering his own apartment for Knighton's use (which Knighton accepted) and a benefit game in 1925–26, specifically the Arsenal versus Spurs match that season. This game could be expected to bring in perhaps £3,000 to £4,000 for Knighton, as a benefit then meant that the player or manager simply kept the takings of a regular season fixture.

As it happened, the Arsenal-Spurs match proved to be the first of the 1925–26 season. Knighton believed that Norris fired him simply to avoid paying over the gate receipts of this game. Knighton actually wrote: 'I believe Norris sacked me to get round offering me the big benefit he promised ... when I tackled him about it, he made it clear I had nothing but a verbal promise, but he offered me £500 "without prejudice".' It is worth mentioning that Norris remembered Knighton in his will nine years later, by which time Knighton appears to have forgiven him.

It is certainly an interesting story, but matters are rarely so simple and it does not ring entirely true. A more likely explanation surely lies in the fact that The Arsenal had been knocked out of the Cup by West Ham in the first round, and had finished 20th in the League.

Norris probably approached Chapman in April 1925. The chairman managed one final dig at everything he had railed against with a superfluous advertisement in the *Athletic News* on 11 May 1925. It read: 'Arsenal Football Club is open to receive applications for the position of TEAM MANAGER. He must be experienced and possess the highest qualifications for the post, both as to ability and personal character. Gentlemen whose sole ability to build up a good side depends on the payment of heavy and exhorbitant (sic) transfer fees need not apply.'

It was a final, forceful restatement of at least one of his beliefs before they were allowed to rest in peace. From this point on, Arsenal and Sir Henry Norris were in the hands of the first football professional.

5

LEGENDARY ARSENAL

Herbert Chapman's first few months at Highbury were not exactly uneventful. In the close season the old offside law was changed. Previously to remain onside required three defenders between the foremost attacker and the goal, and now this was reduced to two. This was in response to the deadening effect of the offside game, refined during the early 1920s by teams such as Newcastle and Notts County. The immediate effect was a flood of goals and a change in tactics which allowed far more goalscoring in the English game until around the late 1960s. To take one good example of the effect of the change, Huddersfield's first two Championships (1923–24 and 1924–25) under Chapman had been achieved with 60 and 69 goals scored. Chapman's two Championships with Arsenal saw the Gunners score 127 in 1930–31 and 118 in 1932–33. Chapman does not appear to have developed any immediate tactical variations in the light of the new law. His first season started relatively poorly – the very first game was a 1–0 home defeat by Tottenham though this was followed by 1–0 away wins at Manchester United and Leicester. However, on 3 October 1925 came a truly critical match, a resounding 7–0 defeat at Newcastle. This defeat so upset Arsenal new man Charlie Buchan that he demanded a tactical change by dropping the centre-half (previously the free-ranging link between defence and attack) back between the full-backs. The centre-half could thus cut out forwards coming through the middle who hoped to exploit having to be behind only one defender rather than two. Apparently Newcastle, with Charlie Spencer at centre-half, played this very system during their 7–0 win and Buchan, who had suggested the idea at every Arsenal team meeting since the opening day of the season, clearly thought himself vindicated.

Buchan prompts tactical switch

Charlie Buchan was a player Chapman would always listen to, a good example of Chapman's determination to bring the very best players, irrespective of age or price, to his clubs. He had used Clem Stephenson at Huddersfield in the same way in 1920 and Chapman also took the great Alex Jackson to Leeds Road. At Highbury he paid a record fee for David Jack and captured Alex James, the outstanding schemer of the inter-war period.

Opposite: Once Herbert Chapman had taken over the club and money was available from the new owners, more of it could be spent on bringing in new blood. Both Charlie Buchan and Jimmy Brain were brought in for the 1925–26 season.

A significant signing

Charlie Buchan was Chapman's first purchase at Highbury, and one that was to reverberate round the club for many years. Buchan had actually been born in Plumstead, had watched Arsenal as a boy, studied at Woolwich Polytechnic, and had played four games for Arsenal Reserves. He walked out on the club in 1909 when the notoriously mean George Morrell turned down an expense claim for 11 shillings (55p). He joined Northfleet, then Leyton, and was transferred to Sunderland (after turning down Norris and Fulham) for a massive £1,200 when aged only 18. He played in their Championship side of 1913 and in the Cup final that year, became captain of England and, after his retirement, became a very well known journalist and broadcaster. He was nearly 34 years old when he came to Highbury, and had, a couple of months before, already been the subject of an approach by Leslie Knighton, who had clearly decided to go out with a bang by (unbeknown to Norris) offering £7,000 for Buchan's signature. Buchan's main concern was his sports shop in Sunderland, from which he took a great deal of income. The maximum wage at the time was only £8 per week and the need for sweeteners and compensations was not uncommon in persuading very good players to move.

Chapman was presumably a much more persuasive negotiator than Knighton, for Sunderland were eventually prepared to consider and accept a much lower fee. The signing has, of course, gone down as one of the most celebrated in football history and is worth recounting. Buchan was serving in his shop in May 1925 when in walked Chapman. 'I've come to sign you for Arsenal,' he told Buchan immediately, and the player assumed he was joking. On being told that Chapman had spoken to the club, Buchan telephoned Sunderland manager Bob Kyle, finding it difficult to believe that the club would release him so easily. It was to be another ten weeks before he finally put pen to paper and in the meantime the deal had been thrashed out. It was actually Norris, and not Chapman, who had insisted on handling the financial negotiations. Sunderland had asked for £4,000, but Norris was not prepared to pay that for a 33-year-old player. Kyle argued that Buchan might now be 33 but that he would still score 20 goals in his first season with Arsenal. Norris asked Kyle to put his money where his mouth was – £2,000 down and £100 for every goal scored. Kyle agreed and Buchan scored 19 League goals and two in the Cup. So Kyle got his £4,000 and £100 interest on top. For Arsenal the deal turned out to be a publicity godsend, a ready-made headline every time Buchan scored. The crowd responded as well: 'There goes another £100,' they would chant whenever Buchan got near goal.

Financial irregularities

Norris must already have given Chapman *carte blanche* on transfer fees, for within a few weeks the manager had also bought the Scottish international keeper Bill Harper from Hibs for £5,000. The Buchan transfer dragged on for those ten weeks because of the player's insistence that he must somehow be compensated for the likely loss of revenue from his shop if he moved.

Chapman, no doubt remembering only too clearly what had happened when Leeds City were suspended in 1919 and how difficult it had been for him to find work afterward, would not get involved in any illegal payments but, according to Norris, pleaded for the chairman to meet Buchan's demands. The chairman later claimed that Chapman left the room when this delicate point was reached. The payments involved came to light as part of a much wider League commission two years later, which found Norris and William Hall guilty of various financial irregularities. Though the hearing was supposedly secret, the *Daily Mail* published the details and Norris sued the FA for libel in suggesting he had acted dishonestly. Norris had a reputation for being quick to take legal action, which he usually won, but in February 1929, the case having gone as high as the Lord Chief Justice, the FA were vindicated and were able to exclude Norris from any further involvement in football.

The significant findings of the commission were that between 1921 and 1924 Norris' chauffeur had been paid by the club, and that in 1926 the club had paid for his motor car. During the case, Norris and Chapman clashed, the chairman saying that the manager and club had known about various payments and Chapman (perhaps again with his mind on 1919) denying it. Norris called Chapman a liar and particularly mentioned that £125 for the team bus was the sum he had given to Buchan, under the counter, to come to Highbury. It should be said that Buchan, in his autobiography, disputed this – though only in general terms: 'Let me say here that I made nothing out of my transfer ... In fact, I lost rather a lot of money through changing quarters like that.' One is, nonetheless, struck by Buchan's careful choice of words, which seem chosen to cloud rather than clarify.

When asked why he had done it, Norris replied very simply and obviously: 'Because (otherwise) we would not have got the players.' It all sounds desperately petty now, but at the time there were many scores to be settled and, in the fashion of a true Greek tragedy, the opportunity was not regretted by some. It was a genuine tragedy for Norris; since 1910, in addition to the money he had found for the club via various business ventures and from his own companies, he had sunk over £15,000 directly from his own pocket and no one could seriously claim that he was alone or unique in his supposed mis-

demeanours. Most of the leading clubs were doing the same thing one way or another.

During the case Norris declared that: 'I only made one mistake in my career, and that was sacking Knighton.' Leslie Knighton took this as a signal compliment, but in its context one is tempted to believe that it was more a none-too-subtle jab at Herbert Chapman than praise for Knighton. Nonetheless as a final epitaph to the man who, almost as much as Herbert Chapman, built the modern Arsenal, we should return to the manager he had fired, Leslie Knighton:

'Despite everything,' said Knighton in his autobiography, 'I still say he was the best Chairman I ever had (Knighton managed eight clubs). He did miles more for football and for footballers than the public will ever know. If he had not been (such) a rebel against petty authority he would have risen to the greatest position in the game.

A financial genius, football was his hobby and delight, even though only a bagatelle compared with some of his business dealings. The game was immensely the poorer for his passing out of it, and it was a tragedy indeed that such a man should have gone under a cloud.' In a sense the greater regret was that the dreams were about to come true – the year after his exclusion saw the first major trophy arrive at Highbury. Norris lived to see the FA Cup and League won before dying, an outcast from the game, just six months after Chapman on 30 July 1934.

Hill-Wood takes control

The new Chairman was Sir Samuel Hill-Wood, whose family had run Glossop North End before the war as a sort of works team, and with some success. Glossop, in Derbyshire, remains by far the smallest town ever to have hosted a First Division club. Hill-Wood had his own place in the sporting record books already. Playing for Derbyshire versus the MCC at Lord's in May 1900, he had scored ten runs off a single ball, the highest ever recorded before or since from a single hit. He was content to leave the running of the club to Herbert Chapman, who was no doubt greatly shaken by the court case but mightily relieved at its outcome.

But back to October 1925 and to the team meeting after that appalling 7–0 thrashing by Newcastle; it was here Buchan persuaded Chapman that centre-half Jack Butler had to drop back. The meeting was in the Royal Station Hotel in Newcastle and Buchan had started the debate by refusing to catch the train back to London. 'Oh no,' said Chapman. 'You're playing at West Ham on Monday. I know what you want so let's discuss it.' Buchan outlined his ideas to the team. He didn't actually want a centre-half 'policing' the centre-forward, rather a man given a geographical 'beat' on the edge of the area. The

1925-1934

rest of the defence would wheel around him to provide support. Buchan then pitched hard to be given the now necessary roving inside forward job needed to replace the centre-half's attacking role (he described it as being like the fly half in rugby) but Chapman refused, wanting Buchan to continue as a goalscorer up front. There was no other obvious candidate for the job, so Chapman apparently put it to Buchan: 'It's your plan Charlie, do you have any suggestions?' Buchan suggested occasional inside forward Scotsman Andy Neil, who, though not fast could kill the ball instantly and distribute it quickly and accurately with either foot. After some argument the plan was accepted and Neil took on the role for the following day's match at West Ham. The plan worked perfectly, Arsenal won 4–0 and, for a year at least, they barely looked back. Jimmy Ramsey and then Billy Blyth later took over the link-man's job from Neil.

The WM formation

It would not be true to say that the new system was in any sense invented by Buchan and Chapman. As we have seen, Newcastle were already experimenting, as were Queen's Park and several other sides, including Spurs. What Chapman did do, of course, was to refine it and find the players to fit the positions as perfectly as was ever likely to be possible.

He quickly moved his full-backs out to mark the wingers (that job had regularly been done by the half-backs), dropped a second inside forward back half-way between the midfield line and the forwards, and decided that three very fast-moving and adaptable forwards were probably the best attacking answer to the new defensive formations and the revised offside law. This was not developed overnight, but over a period of years, ending with the 3–4–3 or WM formation of the great Arsenal teams. The key was never the scheme itself, but the players whom Chapman fitted into it.

Chapman had retained relatively few of the men he inherited from Knighton. Alf Baker continued at right-half, Bob John for a time at left-back and then at wing half. Bernard Joy said of John that: '... next to Joe Mercer, he is the finest wing half Arsenal have had and I have played alongside giants like Jack Crayston, Wilf Copping and Archie Macaulay. There was nobody like him for plucking the ball out of the air with his foot, whatever its height or pace, and bringing it to the ground. He did his job quietly, efficiently and unobtrusively, and there lay his strength.' Charlie Buchan was equally unstinting in his praise of John, whom he regarded as the core of the Arsenal side: 'He deserves a place in any list of famous players ... yet one rarely hears him mentioned nowadays (this was in 1955). You could depend on Bob in every game but this dapper player was not showy. He just got on

Above: A handshake begins one of the most symbolic games ever played at Highbury. The date was 29 August 1925, the captains Charlie Buchan of Arsenal and Arthur Grimsdell of Spurs. It was Chapman's first game as Arsenal manager, Buchan's first as an Arsenal player and the first day of the revolutionary offside law.

with the job.' Bob John eventually played 421 First Division matches (a club record until surpassed by George Armstrong) over 16 seasons, won three Cup medals, three Championship medals and 16 caps. If there was a cornerstone of the great teams, it was surely Bob John.

Chapman moved Jimmy Brain, who had recently been playing as an inside forward, to centre-forward and Brain immediately established a new club scoring record with 33 goals in 1925-26. By February 1926 another of the critical influences had arrived – right-winger Joe Hulme. Reputed to be the fastest winger in British football, Hulme had previously played for York and Blackburn and eventually won nine England caps, a lot for a winger at the time.

He was right remains elusive despite the speculations about the gathering legal storm clouds over Norris and his manager. The next four years in the League were almost a definition of mediocre – 11th, 10th, 9th and 14th. Perhaps it was because the team was always in a state of flux as Chapman added to it, or tried to incorporate the skills of a Jack or a James. Certainly it was to continue to be a period of team-building.

The next significant purchase was Tom Parker, Southampton's right-back. He was relatively slow but very good positionally, and Chapman particularly wanted him as a steadying, intelligent captain. He played 155 consecutive League games and was easy to pick out (there were no numbers in the League until 1939) because of his bald head. Chapman always had a penchant for miners, not surprisingly given his own mining background, and there were over a dozen on the staff during his regime. One of the most popular was the ungainly but highly effective Jack Lambert, acquired as an inside forward for £2,000 from Doncaster Rovers. Chapman was always trying to find the perfect centre-forward and constantly seemed to be buying, or trying to buy, Lambert's replacement. But he always returned to the big fellow and the quest for the ideal was not actually satisfied until after the manager's death, with the arrival of Ted Drake. Lambert stayed with the club after his playing career had finished, going down to Margate to manage Arsenal's nursery club in that town. Tragically the big centre-forward was to be killed in a road accident at the start of the Second World War.

For the other side of the field from Hulme, Chapman bought Welsh international Charlie Jones from Nottingham Forest. Jones was a very intelligent, worrying type of player, but an odd choice in the long term for outside left as he lacked speed. Chapman later moved him to right-half, where he became a permanent fixture in the great team of the early 1930s. Jack Butler, on the other hand, failed to adapt to his new stopper centre-half role, all too often venturing upfield and being caught out of position. In December 1926 Chapman somehow found a tall 21-year-old redhead playing for Oswestry on the Welsh borders and bought him for just £200. Herbie Roberts became such a feature of Arsenal's success that he has remained identified forever as the basic mould for the stopper, policeman, centre-half. Rarely moving upfield, he performed his role consistently and effectively season after season.

False dawn for Chapman's Gunners

All in all, 1925–26 proved to be a successful first season for Chapman. The results were not spectacular, but kept going the right way and Arsenal finished with 52 points, which took them to second place in the League. They never really challenged Huddersfield, who took their third consecutive Championship and the first ever hat-trick. Arsenal's 52 points was the most they had ever achieved in the First Division (eight more than in 1920–21) and the greatest number ever achieved by a London club. Second place was also the highest ever reached by a club from the capital, equalling Spurs' performance of 1922.

But if anyone at Highbury thought that here was the brave new world, then they were wrong. Chapman said it would take five years to win a trophy and he was right, though quite why

Above: Joe Hulme was another Chapman acquisition for Arsenal. An outside right, he scored 124 goals in 372 games for the Gunners.

Policeman Roberts called in

Roberts was never a particularly skilful player, but he became an essential part of the tactical formation. As Cliff Bastin said: 'As an all-round player he may have had his failings, but he fitted in perfectly with the Arsenal scheme of things. Seldom was it that he wasted a ball ... Alex James picked up ball after ball

1925-1934

Left: At Stamford Bridge on 26 March 1927, Arsenal finally won an FA Cup semi-final. Their opponents were Southampton and the goals in a 2–1 success were scored by Joe Hulme and Charlie Buchan.

winning goal being a remarkable one. A Joe Hulme centre was headed straight into the net from around 25 yards by centre-half Jack Butler, who was yet to be replaced by Roberts. Arsenal were in the semis for the first time in 20 years and were lucky enough not to have to leave London as they were drawn against Southampton, then in the middle of the Second Division, and the game was played at Stamford Bridge. The Gunners were even luckier to win on a blustery, wet day. Southampton pressed for much of the match but could only score once, late on, through their centre-forward Rawlings. By that time Hulme and Buchan had made the game safe.

FA Cup surrendered to Welshmen

The final is remembered for three things. One is the very first Cup final radio commentary, the second is Cardiff City taking the Cup out of England for the only time. The third is the tragic goal, the only one of the match, that, in truth, lost it for Arsenal rather than won it for Cardiff. Keeper Dan Lewis, a Welshman himself, had only come into the side for the third round tie at Sheffield. He replaced Bill Harper, who immediately set off for the States in search of fame and fortune (and returned to the club slightly disillusioned four years later). Lewis was also to find fame in the final, but not the kind he would have sought.

It had not been a very good game, played on a greasy pitch with much commitment but little skill. Arsenal had been the better side, winning all of the game's eight corners. With just 16 minutes left, Cardiff skipper Fred Keenor took a throw and

from him in midfield.' Roberts rarely scored a goal, though he won the 1932 FA Cup quarter final at Huddersfield with a totally unexpected header from a corner right at the start of the match. He is also remembered for scoring two identical own goals in the same game for Derby at Highbury. His case is an interesting one for, by everyone's admission, not only was he not a skilful player, he was a relatively poor kicker of the ball.

Whittaker said that: 'Roberts' genius came from his intelligence and, even more important, that he did what he was told.' His orders were to stay in the centre of the defence, to intercept all the balls down the middle and either head them clear or pass them short to a team-mate. 'Because he carried out his orders,' said Whittaker, 'his inability to kick a ball hard or far was camouflaged.'

While 1926–27 was not a notable year in the League, it did end on a high note. After 40 years, Arsenal made their first appearance in an FA Cup final. It was, incidentally, Chapman who at this time insisted on changing the common name from The Arsenal to plain Arsenal, arguing that it would mean the club always came first in any alphabetical list – a point which remained valid only until 1932, when Aldershot joined the Third Division South.

In 40 years the club had only gone beyond the second round/fourth round stage (i.e., last 32) on four occasions, frankly a dreadful record for a first-class club. The run to the final was a tough one. Sheffield United were beaten 3–2 at Bramall Lane, then Port Vale 1–0 in a replay. Liverpool were beaten 2–0 at Highbury in the fifth round with both goals coming from headers at free-kicks. Wolves also came to Highbury for the quarter final. Arsenal won the game 2–1, the

Below: The Arsenal first team pictured behind Highbury's southern terracing two days before the 1927 FA Cup final. Left to right: Billy Blyth, Bob John, Horace Cope, Andy Kennedy, Tom Parker, Dan Lewis, Bill Seddon, Jack Butler, Alf Baker, Joe Hulme, Jimmy Brain, Syd Hoar and Charlie Buchan.

found his Scots centre-forward Hugh Ferguson around 25 yards out. Ferguson advanced and tried a half-hearted, weak ground shot which should have given Lewis no trouble. The keeper did indeed stop the ball but, turning away slightly to avoid the oncoming Ferguson, it slid out of his grasp and under his left arm. Even now the situation was not lost but, in an attempt to gather the ball up again, Lewis turned and simply knocked it with his elbow so that it trickled gently over the line. The film of the incident is appalling to behold – the whole thing happens in slow motion, as if the projector was running at half speed.

Even then the game was not over: Arsenal were offered the best chance of the match. Sid Hoar put in a long, high centre. Cardiff keeper Tom Farquharson misjudged the flight, it bounced once and passed over his head. Brain and Buchan both rushed into nod the ball into the empty net. But as Buchan then describes it: '... at the last moment Jimmy left it to me; I unfortunately left it to him.' The ball bounced harmlessly away past a post and, with it, Arsenal's remaining hopes.

After the presentations, Lewis threw his losers' medal to the turf, from where it was retrieved by fellow Welshman Bob John. 'Never mind, you'll have another chance,' said John, but he was wrong and Lewis was to be injured just before the 1930 final. The Arsenal team in 1927 was Lewis, Parker, Andy Kennedy, Baker, Butler, John, Hulme, Buchan, Brain, Billy Blyth and Sid Hoar. Grease on Lewis' new jersey was partly blamed for the disaster, and when Arsenal reached the 1930 final Tom Whittaker told Charlie Preedy to wear an old, unwashed jersey rather than a new one. The ritual was observed in all the subsequent finals through the Chapman, Allison and Whittaker eras.

Chapman continues to build

Chapman was not discouraged. He had lost important matches before. The team-building continued. The left full-back position was something of a weakness, the current incumbents being Horace Cope and Andy Kennedy. To fill the slot, Chapman showed another of his strengths, that of finding rare talents in unlikely places. He had shown this with Roberts and was to show it again with Bastin. Eddie (actually Edris Albert) Hapgood was particularly special because he had played only 12 games for non-League Kettering and in no way looked the part. A 19-year-old milkman who had not been signed at the crucial moment by his home town club, Bristol Rovers, he weighed only 9 stones 6 pounds. Although he was, and remained, a physical fitness fanatic, he was relatively weak and was often literally knocked out when heading the wet, heavy, leather ball of the period. Arsenal invested heavily in their £750 signing, Tom Whittaker forcing the ex-vegetarian to eat steaks

Above: Joe Hulme cuts in to score from the right wing past Sheffield United full-back Green on 3 September 1927. Note that the letters have been removed from the stand. Arsenal won the game 6–1. Hulme was the fastest winger in the game in the 1920s and it was the use Chapman made of his two outstanding wingers (Bastin was the other) which was really the key to Arsenal's unstoppable style in the 1930s.

and build up both his strength and weight. A few years later, after an accident in which Hapgood had been burned quite badly, Tom Whittaker built a special leather harness for his body so that he could play without the burns rubbing the whole time, proof of Hapgood's remarkable physical courage and unswerving commitment to the game and to the club.

It was sad that Hapgood eventually became estranged from the game. His relations with Allison were never as good as with Chapman, and between him and Whittaker strains gradually developed as they appeared rivals for future senior roles at the club. This was a great pity, as Hapgood had written in 1944 (before Whittaker took over from Allison as manager) that: 'Tom Whittaker has, perhaps of all the people who helped me at Highbury, been my closest friend.' Hapgood was later manager at Blackburn, Watford and Bath but, after losing the Bath job in 1956, he asked Arsenal for a retrospective benefit and was very upset when the club was unable to agree.

1925-1934

Gunners target Jack and James

Whatever else he now had, by 1927 Chapman clearly felt he lacked the great names and, with the exception of perhaps Buchan and Hulme, the great players. His two great transfer coups were still to come – David Jack and Alex James. The David Jack story has been told so often that it has become part of soccer folklore, but no doubt it bears repetition.

By 1928 David Jack was one of the great names known in English football. A cultured, stylish inside forward (he used to arrive at the ground in spats), he was one of those always rare animals, an automatic choice for England. He had scored the first ever goal at Wembley, in the 1923 Cup final, and won winners' medals with Bolton in that year and again in 1926. Bolton were one of the handful of top teams at the time, but in the close season of 1928 they informed other clubs that they would consider offers for any player, excepting only David Jack. Chapman and George Allison went to Bolton to see their board, initially meeting a blank refusal. Eventually, however, the question was asked: 'How much would we have to offer for you to change your minds?' Bolton, probably to get Chapman and Allison to go away, said £13,000 – almost double the existing record transfer fee.

Allison and Chapman returned to the Midland Hotel in Manchester for dinner, eventually invited the Bolton chairman and secretary to join them and haggled until the small hours. In the end an offer of £11,500 plus the accrued benefit to be paid to Jack was accepted (players then received a benefit after five years, but if they left a club after, say, three years, they could be given a sum to represent three-fifths of what they might have expected to receive). David Jack was roused from his bed and belatedly asked his opinion. After talking to his father (then the

Plymouth manager) he was amenable and agreed to come to London the following day to sign for Arsenal.

That day was coincidentally the first time Bob Wall had ever been involved in the transfer of a player. He had just been taken on at the club as secretary/assistant to Herbert Chapman. Wall takes up the story as he and Chapman headed off for the Euston Hotel to meet the Bolton party off the Manchester train: 'We arrived at the hotel half-an-hour early. Chapman immediately went into the lounge bar. He called the waiter, placed two pound notes in his hand and said: "George, this is Mr Wall, my assistant. He will drink whisky and dry ginger. I will drink gin and tonic. We shall be joined by guests. They will drink whatever they like. See that our guests are given double of everything but Mr Wall's whisky and dry ginger will contain no whisky and my gin and tonic will contain no gin".' According to Bob Wall, their guests were in a very cheerful mood by the time the deal was finalised and were not inclined to question anything further.

Charlie Buchan had by now retired, his last game being the famous 3–3 draw at Everton on 5 May 1928 when Dixie Dean got a hat-trick and broke the League scoring record with 60 goals in a single season. Without Buchan, Chapman lacked a commander on the field. There was actually no obvious candidate whom Chapman could pay the earth for. David Jack was Buchan's counterpart in goalscoring ability, but not as a leader. As Bernard Joy rightly pointed out, the way the Arsenal system had developed, the key man had become the foraging inside forward, the centre of the W, the man who picks up clearances from the defenders and sends the forwards away. Clem Stephenson had done a similar job for Chapman at Huddersfield, but there were very few players in the game with either the technical or strategic skills, never mind both.

One player who did have the vision was Alex James, the creator behind the Scots Wembley Wizards of 1928, infamous 5–1 humiliators of England. He had gone from Raith to Preston, where he was less a schemer than an attacking inside forward. In four years there (admittedly in the Second Division) he had scored 60 goals. In June 1929 Preston, surprisingly, put him up for sale and Chapman beat most of the big clubs – including Villa, Liverpool and Manchester City – for his signature.

Bargain fee sparks inquiry

George Allison said of James: 'No one like him ever kicked a ball. He had a most uncanny and wonderful control, but because this was allied to a split-second thinking apparatus, he simply left the opposition looking on his departing figure with amazement.' The small size of the transfer fee (£8,750) was such a surprise that the Football League held an inquiry before Arsenal were allowed to register James. With so many

Below: The classic Arsenal golfing party of the great years – Tom Parker, David Jack, Herbert Chapman and Alex James. The picture was taken at Hatch End on 14 November 1929. It was not a good period for the club – they were to win only three of their next 16 League games but had still, by season's end, won a first major trophy and laid the foundations for the decade that was to follow.

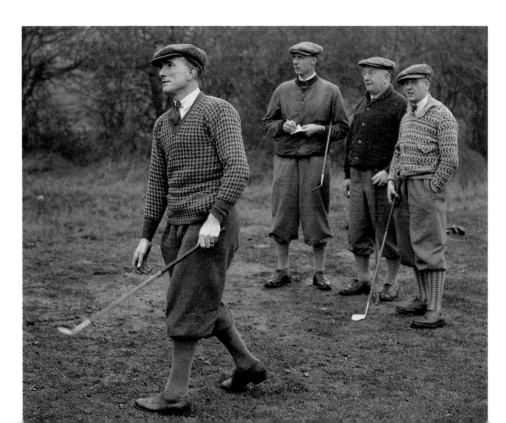

clubs interested it had naturally been assumed that the transfer fee would break the David Jack record, and the Lancashire clubs, possibly with the recent Norris case in mind, were muttering about financial inducements. The inquiry showed that Arsenal were completely clean – all they had done was to help find James a job in Selfridges, the famous London store. But even the inquiry had more to it than met the eye. Chapman knew that he would face rumours about the impending transfer (he had already secretly obtained James' signature) and it was actually the manager himself who quietly asked the League to set up the inquiry into the deal. He then publicly insisted he would not sign James (something of a deceit) until *after* such an investigation had taken place.

It could not be said that James was the perfect club man. It took a season for him to settle in to his new role, after which he virtually gave up scoring goals. Chapman always treated him slightly differently from the other players (he was allowed to stay in bed until noon on matchdays, for instance). Alex was the key, that was the message; and it is certainly true that the side did not win anything before James arrived but started winning everything soon afterward.

Herbert Chapman's patience was, nonetheless, sorely tested. In the summer of 1931 James refused to re-sign, presumably looking for some sort of extra inducements. In August the club sent him on holiday, then Chapman called him back saying the club had decided to despatch him on a cruise instead. He hurried back to London Docks, only to find that Chapman had booked him into a berth on a banana and general cargo boat. John Peters, the assistant secretary, somehow persuaded James to go on board and he was finally released in Bordeaux. He always claimed to have quite enjoyed it. James eventually signed his new contract the week before the season began. When the team, who were training, heard the news they raided the Arsenal band room and serenaded James into the ground by murdering 'See the Conquering Hero Comes.' More serious was James' failure to turn up at the celebration banquet after the Championship success of 1933. He had refused to go to Belfast to play Cliftonville in the last week of the season and was dropped. As club captain he should have received the trophy from League President John McKenna. James' place was left empty and Charlie Jones accepted the award as vice-captain.

Arsenal were the team of the era, and James was the heart of the team, the definition of football success. Without him the style, the system and the successes would probably never have been achieved. Whether James would have done as much in another era is an interesting point. Some of the greats would arguably not have achieved as much at a different time – Stanley Matthews in the 1970s, for instance – but James was probably a player for any age and every era.

The James-Hulme-Bastin triangle

All of this is probably rather peripheral to the essential truth about Alex James – that at the critical time he was the hub of the whole team. He foraged so far back that he was no longer an inside forward, and Bastin therefore had no one inside him for most of the time. For many teams this would have caused problems, but for Arsenal it was an encouragement to develop different moves. The classic was the James-Hulme-Bastin triangle. James, often facing his own goal, would hit a long pass up the right wing. Hulme would race past the defence, and hit his centre way over to the left for Bastin either to shoot or dribble in on goal. Up the middle would steam Lambert, looking for any crumbs that might fall from the table.

In 1932–33 Bastin and Hulme scored 53 goals between them, perfect evidence that Arsenal did play the game very differently from their contemporaries, who tended to continue to rely on the wingers *making* goals for the centre-forward, rather than scoring themselves. By playing the wingers this way, Chapman was able to have one more man in midfield, and thus control the supply of the ball, primarily through James. But it was only possible because both wingers were exceptional footballers – Hulme because of his speed and Bastin because of his tactical brain and coolness. Bastin's calm was legendary. Tom Whittaker said of him in 1950: 'Coupled with his sincerity and his loyalty to all his bosses, he had a trait few of us are blessed with – that is, he had an ice-cold temperament.'

Bastin was the last of the major signings, coming a couple of weeks after James. Bastin is very amusing on his first meeting with the Scotsman. James was already a star, while Bastin was hoping just to play for the reserves. James came up and introduced himself to Bastin in an accent which, Bastin says: 'I have never heard rivalled, before or since. I must confess,' Bastin goes on, 'that my chief reaction, apart from feeling rather more at home than I had a few moments earlier, was of trying to understand just what Alex was saying. Alex and I may have developed a well-nigh perfect understanding on the field, but off it I always found him a trifle incomprehensible.' Bastin knew him well of course, and had enormous admiration for the man, particularly for his self-confidence. 'Nobody had greater faith in the qualities of Alex James than Alex James himself – not even Herbert Chapman, and that is saying something. Alex needed all his self-confidence during his first few months at Highbury, for he was very slow to settle down.'

As part of the settling down process, James established his own trademark – the baggy shorts. They were apparently not his idea at all. Cartoonist Tom Webster drew him playing for Preston in the *Daily Mail* one Monday with rather long shorts, possibly to emphasise James' small stature. James liked the idea, and insisted on going out to buy a pair to fit the cartoon. They kept his knees warm, he would tell admirers.

1925-1934

celebrated 1930s. For it was the turn of the year, the passing of the 'gay twenties', that was the turning point for Arsenal. In the League they achieved no more than respectability (finishing 14th), but in the Cup they truly achieved glory.

Glory years commence

The second week of the new decade saw the third round of the FA Cup. Arsenal drew Chelsea at Highbury, never an easy game. Chapman made a courageous decision, possibly the most difficult in his career, and dropped James. If the team wasn't scoring with the class of forward they had, then it had to be the provider who was at fault. David Halliday was also dropped, in came John, Thompson and Lambert. Arsenal won 2–0 in a rainstorm. Two weeks later Chapman simply ordered James to bed. The Scotsman had always suffered from a form of rheumatism in the ankles, which made it difficult for him to play golf, and Chapman felt James needed a complete rest. In the fourth round Birmingham (who reached the final the following year) came to Highbury and went away with a 2–2 draw. Leslie Knighton was now their manager and Chapman knew the replay would be a tough one. If Arsenal lost it, then the whole season would have gone.

Bernard Joy, who was with the team in the 1930s and whose opinion has always been highly respected, argued in 1952 that Chapman's decision after the first Birmingham game that Saturday night, 25 January 1930, was the turning point in the modern history of the club.

Chapman had to win the replay at St Andrew's the following Wednesday. On the Sunday morning he went round to Alex James' home, got him out of bed and took him off to Highbury for training. Chapman gambled that James would react to the crisis, to the obvious placing of responsibility on his shoulders. It worked, not spectacularly, but it worked. Alf Baker scored from the penalty spot, the only goal of a hard game. The fifth and six rounds were no easier – a 2–0 win away at Ayresome Park and a convincing 3–0 win at West Ham, banishing memories of the pep-pill farce of five years before.

Gunners evade McCracken's trap

The semi-final looked easy – Hull City at Elland Road. Hull were at the bottom of the Second Division and were relegated to the Third a month later. It was also their first semi-final. Quite what they were doing there was anyone's guess, but most knowing observers put it down to the wily management of Bill McCracken, the full-back who had perfected the offside game ten years before. All the interest was in the other semi-final between the two Yorkshire giants, Huddersfield and League Champions Wednesday. This was indeed to be a

No sign of improvement

By 1930 James was beginning to fit, but there must have been frustration in the boardroom as well as on the terraces. In five years under Chapman, Arsenal had spent a fortune but the world remembered them only for an excruciating goal in the 1927 Cup final and a chairman banned from the game.

It is interesting to speculate what would have happened if Chapman had died exactly four years earlier, in January 1930. Certainly his own reputation would have been dramatically lessened, his days at Huddersfield perhaps questioned as a peculiar fluke or the work of Clem Stephenson.

But would the team have gone on to greatness in the 1930s? Who can say, but in the last month of the 1920s no one would have predicted anything very much for the club, Chapman or not. The season had begun so badly that relegation looked the only sort of news Arsenal were likely to make. The forward line had cost £34,000, by a mile the most expensive in football history, and yet it couldn't score goals. But perhaps there was something magic in that new decade, in the rather-less-than

Above: The fourth round FA Cup tie against Birmingham at Highbury on 25 January 1930. The match ended 2–2 with Jack and Bastin scoring goals. The next morning Chapman went to see Alex James – who had earlier been dropped and sent to bed for a complete rest – to tell him that Arsenal could not succeed without him, in the hope that James would respond to the responsibility. Many people felt that this was the turning point that led to all of Arsenal's success of the following decade.

much so that, in the second half, the Hull centre-half Arthur Childs became the first (and for another 50 years the only) man to be sent off in a semi-final. He was despatched for taking a kick at Jack Lambert. That was the end for Hull. Soon afterward Joey Williams (taking the place of the injured Hulme) hared off down the right wing, pulled the ball back from the goalline and David Jack connected with a right-foot volley to score the game's only goal. Arsenal were at Wembley for the second time in four years, Huddersfield were there for the fourth time in a decade.

Success breeds confidence

The defeat of Hull seemed to lift a great weight from the Arsenal attack. Two weeks before the Cup final the Gunners ran up their biggest First Division win to date, 8–1 over Sheffield United. And five days before the final they set yet another record when, having been 3–1 down at half-time, they eventually drew 6–6 at Leicester. It remains the highest scoring draw in any English first-class game, having only been equalled by Charlton v Middlesbrough in 1960. Oddly, Lambert's deputy, David Halliday, had an excellent game at Leicester, scoring four times. But the centre-forward spot was firmly Jack Lambert's by now, a decision that was to be fully justified five days later at Wembley.

A record-breaking season

The final against Huddersfield (*see* Chapter One) was formally the start of the great decade, but it was the following year that has always been known as the great season. 1930–31 saw the establishment of the record points total for a Championship side (66 – later to be surpassed by Leeds United under the now defunct two-point system), and the remarkable total of 127 goals scored would have then been, and remained for all time, a First Division record had Aston Villa not, incredibly, scored 128 the same year. In London, Birmingham and elsewhere it was a wonderful season for spectators.

The season was a massive success for the Gunners from start to finish. The first two games were away, at Blackpool and Bolton. They were both won 4–1. Arsenal were not defeated until their tenth game, at the Baseball Ground against one of the best sides of the 1930s, Derby County. Despite Arsenal's tremendous performance through the whole season, strangely they were never clear of challengers and were not sure of the trophy until two weeks before the end of the contest, when Liverpool went down 3–1. Villa were, of course, the biggest threat, countering a 5–2 defeat by the Gunners at Highbury with a 5–1 win at Villa Park and the friendly rivalry between the clubs was marked by Villa's attendance at the season's end

famous match; with Huddersfield leading 2–1 a Wednesday shot entered the net just as the whistle blew for full time. The referee disallowed the goal but many of the crowd went home not knowing whether there would be a replay or not.

Back at the supposedly less interesting semi-final at Elland Road, shocks were in store. After 15 minutes keeper Dan Lewis cleared a ball from the edge of his area. It was a poor kick, travelling only 30 yards or so, and it went straight to the Hull inside left Howieson. He lobbed it straight back on the volley and it flew over Lewis' head into the net from a full 45 yards out. After 30 minutes Eddie Hapgood sliced a Duncan shot into his own net and Arsenal were 2–0 down at half-time. In the second half, the goals just wouldn't come. And it was not until 20 minutes from the end that whichever gods control football ended their little joke. Those last few minutes are among the most important in the club's history, and they bear a remarkable similarity to the last minutes of the 1971 semi-final against Stoke at Hillsborough, when the Gunners also came back from a 2-0 deficit. In both 1930 and 1971, the semi-final result was vital to the history of the club, just as vital as the finals themselves.

Firstly Alf Baker got Joe Hulme away on the wing, he crossed and David Jack finally defeated McCracken's offside trap and converted the centre. Just 12 minutes later Cliff Bastin picked up a ball from Alex James, took on the defenders in a solo run and hit the ball into the top right-hand corner. Arsenal were unlucky not to get a third, but the teams met again for a midweek replay at Villa Park. Hull seemed bitter about being robbed so late in the first game and the tackling was fierce. So

Above: Arguably the most important goal in the history of Arsenal Football Club. The only goal of the game, it was scored by David Jack in the second half of the semi-final replay against Hull at Villa Park on Wednesday 26 March 1930.

1925-1934

celebration banquet. Villa were also the first opponents in the Cup, and went 2–0 up at Highbury before Lambert and Jack forced a draw. Arsenal played well to win the replay 3–1 but surprisingly went out 2–1 at Stamford Bridge. Though a disappointment, it did not upset the team. Four days later they beat Grimsby 9-1 at Highbury, their biggest ever First Division win and, a week later, won 7–2 at Leicester, to make it 13 goals in consecutive appearances at Filbert Street.

The team of the thirties

The Gunners lost only four games in all, and, coincidentally, their home and, away records were identical – 14 wins, 5 draws and 2 defeats. The team for the final game of the season is probably the one that is best remembered as the great team of the whole era – Ted Harper in goal, Tom Parker and Eddie Hapgood at full-back, Herbie Roberts at centre-half, Charlie Jones and Bob John at half-back, Joe Hulme and Cliff Bastin on the wings, Alex James, as the provider, and David Jack and Jack Lambert up front.

Harper had just returned from his four-year sojourn in the United States, and was re-signed. He replaced Dutchman Gerry Keyser, a wholesale fruiterer who was an amateur with both Arsenal and Charlton.

With Jack Lambert now established as Chapman's first choice forward the manager let David Halliday go to Manchester City in November. The first of the two meetings between Arsenal and Villa at Villa Park in the 1930–31 season was the celebrated occasion when the Midlanders' magnificent England international centre-forward Pongo Waring cheerfully taunted Chapman with his obsession for buying centre-forwards: 'I bet you'd like to get me Herbert, wouldn't you?' said Waring. And Chapman would have, for Waring was the best in the country until Drake came along, but he was also one of the few players Chapman could never manage to get his hands on. Underrated Jack Lambert actually set up an Arsenal record in 1930–31 with his 38 League goals, although this was soon to be beaten by Drake.

Male sent back

Those 11 names for the last game of 1930–31 would certainly have to be supplemented by one or two others to complete the real first-class roll of honour for the era. The three obvious omissions are George Male, Wilf Copping and Frank Moss. Male became Hapgood's full-back partner late in 1932 before Tom Parker went to Norwich as manager. Male actually played in the 1932 Cup final in his normal position, left-half, but with Parker ready to retire Chapman needed a replacement and selected Male, who already had a reputation for all-round skill,

Right: George Male was Arsenal's right-back during the 1930s. Male, whom Chapman had converted from a left-half role, made 316 first-class appearances in an 18-year playing career before joining the coaching staff. He never scored a goal for the senior side, but was capped 19 times for England.

strength and steadiness. Male told how Chapman called him into his office and astonished him by explaining how Male was about to become a right-back. Chapman was so convincing about Male's skills that, said Male: 'I wasn't only convinced I was a right-back, I knew I was the best right-back in the country!' And so it proved, Male eventually taking over the England captaincy from Hapgood. He played his first game at right-back on 15 October 1932 and within months he had been chosen for an international trial.

Bernard Joy argued that the success of the Male-Hapgood combination was a matter of contrasts: 'Hapgood was enthusiastic, volatile and poised, the born captain. Male was determined, rugged and fast in recovery; as a person quiet, retiring and modest, the ideal first mate.' Not only did both of them captain England, they also played together for their country 14 times.

Wilf Copping was already an international when he came from Leeds in 1934, he and Jack Crayston (from Bradford) effectively replacing Charlie Jones and Bob John. Copping is probably best remembered for his remarkable display in the 'Battle of Highbury' against Italy on 14 November 1934 when Arsenal provided seven of the England team and the World Cup holders were beaten, in a bitter game, 3–2.

Frank Moss was actually only the reserve keeper at Second Division Oldham when Chapman signed him. Apparently Chapman pretended to be pursuing the first-team keeper Jack Hacking and, when Oldham wouldn't release him, switched his interest to the reserve as an apparent afterthought (this particular story has been told about several of Chapman's signings). He was another agile keeper, totally fearless and a natural for the England jersey. His career was sadly cut short because of a recurrent shoulder injury. His last effective game for the club was at Everton on 16 March 1935, when he was injured, dislocating his troubled shoulder early on and playing the rest of the match on the wing. He was always a very good forward and scored an excellent goal, cutting in past his defender and shooting into the corner for a peculiarly unfitting end to a goalkeeper's career. He did try to come back for a few games the following season, but the shoulder and collarbone were continually causing problems and he was forced to give up the game completely.

Whittaker keeps Gunners primed

The team that brought the League Championship to the south of England for the very first time in 1931 was hardly anonymous, but it was unusual in that its back-up was far more sophisticated than at any other club of the period. The cornerstone was Tom Whittaker, who eventually became manager after George Allison in 1947. It is almost impossible to do full justice to Whittaker either as coach, physiotherapist or inspiration. The stories about him are legion, almost invariably extremely complimentary. Bernard Joy said that: 'Chapman's success would have been impossible without Whittaker,' but Allison reaches the essential Whittaker more succinctly. Allison was once asked: 'Is it true, what Tom Whittaker says?' 'Of course it is,' was Allison's reply. 'What did Tom say?'

Below: Frank Moss kept a clean sheet against Manchester City in the 1932 semi-final at Villa Park on 12 March 1932. Cliff Bastin scored the only goal of the game. Moss was the club's most celebrated keeper in the 1930s, but his career was effectively ended by a double dislocation of the collar bone at Everton on 16 March 1935.

Cliff Bastin was as effusive: 'I can never thank him enough for the care and expert treatment he lavished on me whilst I was at Highbury. Perhaps "expert" is a badly chosen word, for Tom was something more than an expert. There was about him a touch of genius.' Bastin explained how men who would have remained on the injured list for three or four weeks at another club would be fit at Highbury within three or four days. Bastin, on one occasion, scalded his foot in a boiling hot bath and couldn't stand on it. The foot was agony, but Whittaker built a special soft cast inside Bastin's boot so that the winger felt no pain. His only sensation when he ran, as he explained, was the water inside the blister running up and down his foot. Whittaker also would regularly snap Bastin's cartilage back into place on the field, doing this on at least a dozen occasions, and when Bastin eventually had to have an operation, Whittaker attended and assisted.

'The greatest trainer in the game'

Tom Whittaker was born in Aldershot in 1898. His father was a sergeant major and Tom also had a military career, studying as a marine engineer and joining the Royal Artillery as, very appropriately, an ordnance engineer. It was while he was playing for the Army that Arsenal spotted him and brought him to Highbury, where he played as a wing half and later full-back until his injury in Australia in 1925. His arrival at Highbury, on 11 November 1919, has a touch of the times about it – Leslie Knighton, newly installed as manager, met him off the tube!

The surgeon who told Whittaker he would never play again in 1925, Sir Robert Jones, was so impressed by the player that he arranged a year's course in anatomy, massage and electrical treatment of injuries, particularly associated with muscles. Whittaker returned to Highbury after that injury unsure about his future. Arsenal had apparently been intending to let him go in 1925, but he was retained so that he could go on the FA tour (players without clubs were not allowed to represent the FA). For six months Whittaker was unable to train and helped in the treatment room. Officially, he was just a player under treatment. One day in February 1926, Chapman called Whittaker up to the top of the stand. For a few moments there was silence, says Whittaker, then Chapman turned and, with his arm stretched out toward the pitch and emphasising every word, said: 'I am going to make this the greatest club ground in the world, and I am going to make you the greatest trainer in the game. What do you say to that?'

Whittaker later built the most modern treatment room in football, and possibly in the country, at Highbury. It was full of sunlamps, heating and electrical apparatus and attracted all sorts of sportsmen who had no association with Highbury. Whittaker was, for instance, also the official trainer for Britain's

1925-1934

obviously the man Chapman wanted and he remained as trainer, apart from a spell during the Second World War, for 20 years. He finally took over as manager from Allison in 1947.

Double disappointment

Before the 1931–32 season began the talk was of the chances of the Double, a feat not performed since Aston Villa in 1896–97 and not to be performed again for another three decades. After a month the talk was what happened to the League Champions? Arsenal lost their opener at home to West Bromwich and didn't take both points until their fifth match. They never made up the gap and, although it was a good season, eventually finishing second was something of an anticlimax. Everton were Champions, two points ahead. Bernard Joy says the team was overconfident, pushing forward too eagerly, leaving too many holes for the counterattack. It was a lesson that was learned for subsequent seasons.

The Cup should have provided compensation for the League disappointment, but failed to do so after the most controversial goal in British domestic football.

The run to the 1932 final was straightforward but hard work, and there were to be no replays. Lancashire Combination side Darwen provided an 11–1 walkover in the third round, then Plymouth, with Ted Harper in goal, were removed 4–2. After a 2–0 away win against gradually improving Portsmouth (they reached the final in 1929 and 1934) the quarter final brought Arsenal back to old adversaries Huddersfield at Leeds Road. After only two minutes Hulme won a corner; the winger held the ball until Herbie Roberts came up on a rare (but obviously pre-planned) foray, placed it right on Roberts' forehead and Arsenal had scored the only goal of the game.

The semi-final at St Andrew's also saw just one goal, this time at the end of the game rather than the beginning. The opponents were Manchester City, who were to reach the next two finals as compensation. The 1932 semi-final was already in time added on, with City frantically attacking. But they left their defence undermanned and as a final clearance came out from the Arsenal penalty area Bastin picked it up and hopefully knocked it toward the right-hand corner. The defender let the ball go, thinking it would go over the line, but Lambert suddenly appeared, hooked it back and there was Bastin to touch it home with the last kick of the match.

James a final doubt

The final was to be against Newcastle. The preparations were dominated by whether or not Alex James would be fit as he had damaged knee ligaments in a match against West Ham a couple of weeks earlier.

highly successful Davis Cup tennis team in the 1930s, as well as the regular England soccer team trainer.

He worked seven days a week and his ability to get players back quickly was a crucial element in the club's consistent pattern of success between 1930 and 1936. The other great contribution Whittaker made to Chapman's personal success was relieving the manager of day-to-day control of the players. This was vitally important for it allowed Chapman time to watch new players, negotiate transfers and consider other essential matters for the club.

Whittaker actually became first-team trainer in February 1927. George Hardy, who had held the job since before the First World War, shouted a tactical switch to the players from the bench during a Cup match against Port Vale on 2 February 1927. Chapman said he wouldn't tolerate the trainer influencing tactics and relegated Hardy to the reserves, giving the 29-year-old Whittaker the job. Straight after that Port Vale game Chapman marched into the dressing room and, in front of everyone, told Whittaker to take over the first team immediately. Whittaker, who lodged with Hardy, was shocked, but he and Hardy remained friends. Chapman's action was only an excuse. Hardy was of the old school, whereas Whittaker was

Above: Planning department. Bob John, Herbert Chapman and Alex James discuss the aspects of the forthcoming FA Cup final against Newcastle in 1932.

Three days before the Cup final Chapman announced his team – James and Hulme were not fit enough so in came George Male and Pat Beasley. The news was a surprise, and L. V. Manning, sports editor of the *Daily Sketch*, got James and Hulme to jog around the Highbury pitch and published a picture captioned: 'The two fittest men in football.' Chapman was furious, and ordered the pair down to Brighton, where the team were staying. Tom Whittaker gave them both a tough try-out the following morning on the Brighton ground, in front of 40 or so photographers. Both came through and were reinstated in the team for Saturday's final. Then, as everyone was making their way back to the dressing room, another photographer, whose car had broken down, came rushing into the ground to plead with Whittaker for a final shot. Whittaker agreed, tackled James once more and, suddenly, James fell to the ground clutching his knee. He was carried to the dressing-room where, says Whittaker: '... almost crying with pain and disappointment, he would not let the doctor touch him and shouted at me to get everyone out of the room. Even Chapman had to go.'

George Male, signed from the London amateur side Clapton earlier that season, had been in, out, and back in a Cup final side within the space of an hour. Male played left-half, and it was on that side that the critical moment was to occur.

Ref's mistake costs Gunners the Cup

It was almost half-time (with Arsenal 1–0 up after Bob John had headed the ball home when United had made a hash of a clearance) when Newcastle centre-half Davison overhit a long pass up the right wing for inside forward Jimmy Richardson to chase. The ball appeared to cross the goalline and the Arsenal defenders relaxed, but Richardson carried on and hooked the ball into the centre. Eddie Hapgood could probably have intercepted it, but didn't bother. Centre-forward Jack Allen did bother, flicking it neatly into the net. Referee Bill Harper gave a goal, the Arsenal players were incredulous but did not argue. L. V. Manning said in the *Sunday Graphic* the next day: 'One cannot praise too highly the restraint of the Arsenal players

1925-1934

when the first Newcastle goal was scored. Every man must have known what was so clear to the onlookers – that the ball had crossed the line – but there was not the slightest attempt at a demonstration or protest.' Tom Parker got their minds back on the game but the timing was perfect for Newcastle, who came out for the second half a different team and Allen scored again for United to win 2–1. Arsenal had thus finished runners-up in both major competitions, only the second time this had ever happened.

Though it has always been claimed that the ball was over the line, in fairness it must be said that no convincing photograph exists and the angle of the most reproduced photograph is not necessarily a good one. Newcastle were the first team to win the final at Wembley after being behind in the match, and the first to come from behind in any final since they did the same thing themselves in 1910.

Arsenal dominate the League

The disappointment of 1932 was only short-lived. For many years afterward regret was expressed that, despite their dominance of the decade, the Arsenal of the 1930s never performed the Double. 1931–32 was to be the nearest they came for they did not seem to be able to concentrate on the FA Cup when they were leading the League. And for the next three seasons Arsenal were to do exactly that, equalling Huddersfield's hat-trick with an impeccable period of dominance covering 1932–33, 1933–34 and 1934–35.

Above: The 1932 semi-final success took the Gunners to Wembley for the infamous 'over-the-line' final against Newcastle. Although Arsenal went 1–0 ahead through Bob John, the over-the-line goal by Jack Allen changed the pattern of the game and his second goal settled it.

Opposite: An unusually shy Alex James poses for the camera before a reserve team game at Highbury on 13 April 1932. His fitness was being tested before the Cup final, then ten days away. A week later one final tackle by Tom Whittaker, in a practice game to please a photographer who had arrived late, caused James' knee to break down again and he left the field in tears, unable to play at Wembley.

Most clubs which have such a successful spell do so with a very settled side. Indeed, it is almost a truism of the game that a great side lasts for no more than three good seasons. The Arsenal of the first half of the 1930s were almost exactly the opposite. By 1935 no more than three of the regulars of 1932 were still in the team – Hapgood, Roberts and Bastin. Most of the missing had simply succumbed to age, though Frank Moss was an exception. Much more significantly, Herbert Chapman was dead and had been replaced by George Allison. Yet the period was one of remarkably consistent results, with only 24 League games lost and a points average of 58. By Championship standards, none of the three seasons was particularly outstanding, certainly not to be compared with the record breaking efforts of 1930–31, and their number of defeats (9, 8 and 7 in the three seasons) was no better than average for a Championship side. On the other hand, the pattern of consistency during a period when the team was being rebuilt was most certainly outstanding. If this sounds like grudging praise, it is only so in the context of the heady two years which followed the 1930 Cup win.

Many of the individual replacements proved to be the match of their predecessors. George Male was already a Highbury stalwart when he replaced Parker in 1932, Eddie Coleman and an ageing Jimmy Dunne appeared in Lambert's shirt, although neither of them truly became a fixture, and the great David Jack played only 14 games in 1933–34 and then went to Southend as manager. He was replaced by Ray Bowden, who arrived from Plymouth in March 1933. Cliff Bastin was still a youngster, although he suffered from periods of injury and his deafness was beginning to be a worry, but Joe Hulme proved very difficult to duplicate.

Allison seeks replacements

The Arsenal wingers had performed very different jobs compared with men in the number 7 and 11 shirts at other clubs and it was not easy to slot new men into Arsenal's unique system. They had not only to be very fast in the conventional sense, but also significant goalscorers as well. Only Alex James was allowed the liberty of not appearing on the scoresheet. As has been said before, it was the role of Hulme and Bastin, more than any other aspect of their style, which marked the Arsenal of the early 1930s apart from their competitors. That meant the club's wingers could, and would, often also double up as inside forwards. Pat Beasley, who arrived from Stourbridge, would play in either Bastin or Hulme's place if they were injured, or act as Bastin's inside forward. He would have played in the 1932 Cup final if Hulme had not recovered from that injury but, ironically, he and Hulme then played on opposite wings for Huddersfield in the 1938 Cup final. Ralph Birkett, who later won an England cap while with Middlesbrough, was bought from Torquay specifically to take over from Hulme, but was never an adequate replacement, and by 1935 Alf Kirchen from Norwich was on the right wing.

The midfield men were more easily replaced, Jack Crayston from Bradford and Wilf Copping from Leeds coming in for

Above: The Prince of Wales meets the teams at the inauguration of the new West Stand. The opening of the two new stands (the West on 10 December 1932 and the East on 24 October 1936) was football's equivalent of the unveiling of the Taj Mahal. There was nothing like them anywhere in the country.

Charlie Jones and Bob John with remarkably little disruption in the summer of 1934. When Alex James was unavailable the remarkable Peter Dougall would take his place. By all accounts he was an even cleverer player, but could never consistently harness his fabulous ball skills to the team effort, but then it was perhaps unfair to expect anyone to replace the hub of the wheel. In goal Alex Wilson replaced Moss in a quiet, competent way. He had come from Morton in May 1933. When Moss was injured at Goodison in March 1935, however, Wilson was also hurt and George Allison had no other first-class keeper. That day also happened to be the transfer deadline, so he asked Everton if Arsenal could sign their reserve keeper George Bradshaw there and then. Bradshaw was a little bemused by this sudden turn of events, but eventually agreed and came to Highbury for a number of years.

A trio of titles

The first year of the hat-trick, 1932–33, did not start well. Charlie Jones was injured and, in their first home match, Arsenal lost to West Brom for the second consecutive year. But this season was to be different, with 32 of the next 36 points finding their way back to Highbury. Yet again, though, Villa managed to score five goals in Birmingham and the 5–3 defeat was Arsenal's only setback in that 18-game run. The final match in the sequence was the Christmas Eve 9–2 thrashing of Sheffield United at Highbury. Jack Lambert scored five, his best ever for the club, in what was virtually his valedictory performance. That particular game is often recalled as the height of Arsenal's powers in the whole inter-war period, though, oddly, two days later they went down 1-2 at home to Leeds.

Villa and Wednesday continued to press until April when, though Arsenal were ahead, both their challengers had games in hand. By chance both came to Highbury in April, where Arsenal finished things off in fine style. Villa went down 5–0 and ended four points behind, Wednesday lost 4–2 and were eventually three points further back. The month saw five wins in a row and the last, 3–1 versus Chelsea at Stamford Bridge, confirmed the Gunners' second title in three years. The forwards had been magnificent all season, and the total of 118 goals was the club's second highest ever and included one 9, two 8s and one 7. Cliff Bastin's 33 goals still remain a Football League record for a winger.

The next season, 1933–34, was a strangely subdued one compared with those before and after. It was marred, of course, by Herbert Chapman's death, but, though it saw one more point won (59 rather than 58) the goalscoring record was completely different. Only 75 were scored compared with 118 the season before and 115 the season after. One major reason was Alex James' injury against Birmingham in the first match

1925-1934

of the season. He was out for half of the campaign, as was Joe Hulme. However, Arsenal quickly went to the head of the table, putting together a spell of 27 points out of a possible 32. Derby and Huddersfield both took the lead briefly, but they had to play the Gunners in consecutive matches in Easter week. Arsenal beat Derby 4–2 at the Baseball Ground and followed up with a 3–1 defeat of Huddersfield at Highbury. In the end only Huddersfield kept up the challenge, eventually finishing three points in arrears.

It was actually one of those strangely quiet seasons when not a lot seems to happen and no team can really impose its authority. Both Villa and Wednesday had lost their sparkle, finishing mid-table, and Arsenal, despite the loss of Chapman, were able to hold their ground by virtue of their established patterns of play and their consistency. Even so, they had to survive a number of poor results – home defeats by Everton and Spurs within the space of four days, a 4–1 crushing at Leicester and a 3–0 defeat at Sunderland – and were perhaps lucky that their crisis season coincided with a corporate lethargy among their competitors.

New boy Drake is the hero

The third year of the hat-trick saw a genuine new star in the making. He was Ted Drake, George Allison's first signing (from Southampton) in March 1934. Drake was to score a record 42 goals with the Gunners in this, his first season. That total included four matches in which he scored four goals and three in which he notched mere hat-tricks. The newcomer almost carried the team. There were numerous major injuries – Dunne, Copping and Bastin all had cartilage operations and even the two trainers, Tom Whittaker and Billy Milne, both had to be hospitalised during the season. Most of the reserves had fair spells in the first team, but still went on to win the Football Combination for the seventh time in nine seasons. Had Chapman lived, he would have seen it as the perfect validation of his insistence that the reserves play to the same patterns and tactics as their seniors.

The 1934–35 season had started well with an 8–1 crushing of Liverpool and the first four home games produced 21 Arsenal goals. Away from home, matters did not give rise for similar congratulations, with only a single victory prior to the New Year. But none of their regular challengers could put together anything like a convincing set of results and Arsenal headed the table until March when Sunderland, inspired by the young Raich Carter, went a point ahead. Arsenal had games in hand, however, and though Sunderland held them to a goalless draw at Highbury, Arsenal made Sunderland's task almost impossible with a 2–0 win at Everton on 16 March 1935. This was the game in which Frank Moss scored Arsenal's second, magnifi-

cent goal as a highly inappropriate finale to his mainstream goalkeeping career. Sunderland ended the season four points behind Arsenal.

Cup success proves elusive

Chapman was always surprised, and perhaps a little distressed, that Huddersfield could not get to a Cup final during their hat-trick years. The Yorkshiremen were there in 1920 and 1922, and again in 1928 and 1930, but in the middle years, 1924 to 1926, when they should by rights have made it, they were nowhere to be seen. Arsenal had a peculiarly similar record. They reached the final in 1930, 1932 and 1936, but missed out in 1933, 1934 and 1935. Oddly, they never even reached a semi-final during those seasons.

We have skirted around what happened on 14 January 1933. It is not usual in the history of a great club, when there is so

Right: The shield which hangs outside the boardroom at Highbury commemorating the hat-trick of Championships between 1932 and 1935. Huddersfield and Liverpool have almost identical trophies. The bust is of Denis Hill-Wood.

much to tell, to dwell for very long on a game that was lost, particularly in the third round of the Cup, but this one is an exception. Exactly 50 years later, when Walsall came to Highbury, still as a Third Division side, and surprisingly won again (this time in the Milk Cup) no one tried to make any serious comparison between the two matches. There was no way they could. Walsall's 2–0 defeat of Arsenal in 1933 remains, very simply, the greatest act of giant-killing in English club history. This is vaguely peculiar. There have been giant-killers whose performances have seemed far more praiseworthy since, there have been non-League clubs knocking out top flight sides, but whenever a giant-killer arises, the comparison is automatically made, above all other games, with Walsall 2 Arsenal 0.

We need to stand back a little to judge the real significance of this result. Arsenal, it should be remembered, had just gone through a run obtaining 32 points from 18 matches. Three weeks before meeting Walsall, they had crushed Sheffield United 9–2. They were well clear at the head of the First Division and were, in a sense, at their very peak, for they had no obvious rivals. In the three previous seasons Arsenal had won the Cup, then the League, then been runners-up in both. The Double in 1932–33 seemed a very strong possibility.

A popular result

The game must also be put in a social and economic context. This was the height of the depression. Three million were out of work, a far higher percentage of the work force then than 50 years later, and benefits were far less generous where they existed at all. As in the 1980s, there was real resentment in the provinces against London, Westminster, 'them' as opposed to 'us'. Walsall may not have corresponded with Lancashire or Tyneside in the 1980s, but it was a moderate-sized provincial town with problems enough of its own. Arsenal, in its way, was a very visible representative of London, a symbol of the richness of life there compared with the provinces. The fact that this was unfair, that most of the players were from the north and many had been miners, was not the point. What mattered were the symbols, what people wanted to believe was true.

It is also realistic to point out that Arsenal were not a popular club outside London, compared with, say, the Spurs side of the early 1960s. This was a difficult attitude to analyse, for it was a feeling abroad without any rational base, rather than a justifiable dislike. In part it was due to the 'Bank of England' reputation, Chapman's and later Allison's apparent desire to buy success at almost any price, though many clubs had gone the same route and failed dismally. In part it was also the tactical style; the holding back, occupying midfield space, the numerous goals which came from quick breaks from James to

Bastin and Hulme, rather than the constant attacking pressure which was the traditional approach of the day. Spectators, having come to expect fast dribbling wingers crossing from the goal line for thundering centre-forwards in the Dixie Dean or Pongo Waring mould, found Arsenal's style odd and, therefore, somehow 'lucky'.

Fans had yet to realise the simplest of all football truths, that the winning team is, by definition, the one which scores most goals. Perhaps 85 minutes of unrewarded but naive pressure may seem more valuable than a single breakaway goal, but that isn't what the laws of the game say. Actually, such perceptions as they related to Arsenal were not only extremely unfair but, very simply, wrong – Arsenal scored 127 League goals in 1931, 118 in 1933 and 115 in 1935, overall considerably more than any of their competitors, and, to repeat the obvious, they couldn't all have come from lucky breakaways. What is true is that, like all teams, Arsenal tended to play differently away from Highbury than at home. Equally, other sides would attack them more on their own grounds, forcing Arsenal toward the use of their 'smash and grab' style. It is very difficult for fans born after the Second World War to imagine how little exposure pre-war crowds had to the big clubs. North London fans could watch Arsenal every other week but a Liverpudlian or a Mancunian was only able to see this dominating force once or twice a year – thus his views about the sort of team they were, and the way they played, could only be based on very limited evidence. He had no opportunity of seeing Arsenal 20 or 25 times a year on television and thus building a more balanced view. Arsenal at Villa, Hillsborough or Roker would always face a hard game, would always forced to defend, and would probably rely on Hulme and Bastin for a winning goal. It was the fact that they succeeded so often which bred the resentment.

In any event, the key to the Walsall result, the way it was greeted and the reason it has remained the giant-killing feat *par excellence*, lies as much in the times as in the football. Walsall were the small, underprivileged, provincial David overthrowing the rich, lucky London-based Goliath and the Midland side's success was fêted far and wide, often by people who probably had not the slightest idea where Walsall was.

A surprising selection

Chapman has been accused of underestimating Walsall, but there is little evidence to support this contention. Walsall had been watched, and, though their last four matches comprised three draws and a 5–0 defeat, Chapman was under no illusions as to the kind of game he was facing. His real problem had been influenza, earlier claiming Bob John, Jack Lambert and Tim Coleman. Eddie Hapgood and Joe Hulme had been

1925-1934

injured and Chapman therefore had to decide whether to play recently unavailable men or some of his well-prepared reserves. He chose the reserves – it would be a hard match but here would be a good opportunity for the second-teamers to push their claims for a first-team place. In many respects, they were less likely than the internationals to be upset by rough Third Division tackling. So in came Scot Tommy Black at left-back, Norman Sidey at left-half, Billy Warnes at outside right and Charlie Walsh at centre-forward. The last two had both been recruited from local amateur clubs. Too much has been made of the side's inexperience – it still contained Moss, Male, Roberts, Jack, James and Bastin. Tom Whittaker later dismissed the suggestion that the first-teamers were unavailable, though, afterward, Chapman seems to have encouraged this belief. Everyone travelled to Walsall says Whittaker, in the team's own railway coach the day before. During the journey Chapman announced the team to, in Whittaker's own words: '... murmurs of amazement.'

The newspapers, always loving a David v Goliath story, gave the game the usual build-up and their angles were predictable enough. Said one: 'Arsenal, the Rich, the Confident, the League leaders, the £30,000 aristocrats, against the little Third Division team that cost £69 all-in. Arsenal train on ozone, brine-baths, champagne, gold and electrical massage in an atmosphere of prima donna preciousness. They own £87 worth of football boots. Walsall men eat fish and chips and drink beer, and the entire running expenses of the club this season have been £75.'

The players didn't quite see it like that. One or two of the reserves were particularly edgy. Just before leaving the dressing room Chapman came over to Charlie Walsh: 'I'm expecting a lot of you today, son, we're relying on you to show us your best.' Walsh, who had been nagging Chapman for a first-team chance for months, replied: 'OK Mr Chapman, I'm ready to play the game of my life.' Chapman answered: 'Good lad, you'll do,' and then, just as he was turning away, paused: 'Oh, and by the way, you'd better put your stockings on or the crowd will laugh at you.' Poor Walsh was so nervous he had put on his boots before his socks.

Walsh's apprehensions were more justified than his teammates would have guessed. Walsall employed classic cup-tie tactics. Their enthusiasm was overwhelming, their tackling, especially on James, could only be described as grim. Arsenal failed to settle throughout the match, but should still have won it. Walsh, now complete with socks, made a complete hash of the easiest chance of the first half when he missed a simple Bastin centre and the ball came off his shoulder. In the second half the centre-forward's intervention was even more disastrous when he took the ball off David Jack's toe just as Jack seemed certain to score.

Above: The cover of the programme for the greatest giant-killing feat in English club history. Arsenal came to Walsall on top of the First Division, having reached two of the three previous finals. The guns and reproduction of James confronting the teddy bear are a delight for a Third Division programme of 1933.

Walsall take their chance

As Arsenal failed to score, Walsall became more confident, the inches of mud which covered the pitch being much more to their liking. After 60 minutes Gilbert Alsop, the home side's centre-forward, headed home a Lee corner-kick to put Walsall a goal up. Even 50 years later Alsop, still marking out the pitches at the age of 73, remembered: 'We had a corner and their full-back (Black) was marking me. He didn't get up. The ball was just a big plum pudding that day and I headed it off my forehead straight into the corner of the net.' Alsop also remembered the foul which, five minutes later, sealed the game for Walsall. He could still point to a scar on his knee which, he claimed, was caused by Tommy Black's violent tackle after 65 minutes. It was in the penalty area and, as a result, Billy Sheppard scored from the spot.

The Arsenal players had been getting more and more irritated by Walsall's tactics. 'They could not have complained if five of their men had been sent off in the first quarter of an hour,' said Bastin, 'We had ten free-kicks in the first ten minutes.' Black had become particularly irate, the more so after failing to prevent Alsop's goal, and Arsenal paid the penalty.

The Gunners could do nothing to retrieve the two-goal deficit in the last 25 minutes and the packed 11,000 crowd

Left: Herbert Chapman, who guided Arsenal through the rocky years of the late 1920s to greatness in the early 1930s until his untimely and tragic death.

chaired the Walsall players off at the end. For the Arsenal team, retribution was swift. Chapman was apoplectic. He refused to let Black return to Highbury and had transferred him to Plymouth within a week. Whether this was because of Chapman's anger at Black's tackle on Alsop, or because of his all-round performance in the match, was never absolutely clear, though Chapman certainly said the former. Walsh, whose display was almost as wretched as Black's, was sold to Brentford by the end of January, having, despite his ambitions, played just that one first-team match for Arsenal. Warnes went to Norwich at the end of the season. Only Sidey remained in the reserves, a competent back-up for Roberts.

For Walsall the game was something of an inspiration. Though they were knocked out by eventual finalists Manchester City in the next round, they managed to finish the season third in the Third Division North. For Arsenal it was a hiccup, though one that was to echo down the years as, in all probability, the most famous Cup tie the club have ever contested. Exactly 50 years later the fact that it was Walsall, rather than any other Third Division club, who knocked the Gunners out of the Milk Cup at Highbury must have made some small contribution to Terry Neill's departure from the manager's office.

Chapman's death rocks Highbury

Walsall was the last FA Cup defeat Herbert Chapman ever suffered. By the time Villa defeated the Gunners in the quarter final of 1934 Chapman was dead. It was so sudden, so unexpected, that it was almost prosaic. There is somehow very little that can be said about it. On Saturday 30 December 1933 Arsenal had drawn 0–0 at Birmingham. They were a comfortable four points clear at the top of the League. It was to be a typical, perhaps slightly busy, week for Chapman. On the Monday, New Year's Day, he went to see Bury play Notts County, who had someone in whom he was interested. He then crossed the Pennines to watch Sheffield Wednesday play Birmingham on the Tuesday. Wednesday were the visitors at Highbury on the following Saturday and were Chapman's greatest fear as rivals for the title. By the Wednesday he had clearly developed a heavy cold but ignored the advice of Dr Guy Pepper, the club doctor, and went down to Guildford to see the third team play. 'I don't get a chance to see the lads very often,' he commented. On returning home to Hendon he was much worse and went to bed. By the Friday, some 36 hours later, he seemed rather better but the pneumonia, as it presumably was, suddenly worsened and he died at 3 am on the Saturday morning.

The news came as a complete shock. The players arrived at Highbury a few hours later to discover suddenly that the Boss, who was perfectly healthy when they had last seen him in Birmingham, was dead. Bastin told of the terrible blow the players felt: 'As I approached the ground, the newspaper-sellers were shouting out the news of Chapman's death. It seemed just too bad to be true. In the dressing room, nobody had anything to say, yet each of us knew what (the others) were thinking. Herbert Chapman had been loved by us all.' George Male was walking past a tube station when he saw the newspaper board: 'Herbert Chapman Dead.' ... 'That was the first I knew about it. I couldn't believe it.' Arsenal and Wednesday stood to attention before the game. 'I suppose Arsenal gave quite a good display that day, considering that to the players the game was just an unimportant incident,' said Bastin. 'Even the crowd was practically silent throughout the 90 minutes of a game which seemed to go on for 90 years.' Arsenal and

1925-1934

Wednesday drew 1–1, but the team collapsed afterward and lost three consecutive games, including two home matches against Spurs and Everton.

Herbert Chapman was buried at Hendon, where he had attended church regularly, four days later. The pallbearers were among the greatest names in the game's history – David Jack, Eddie Hapgood, Joe Hulme, Jack Lambert, Cliff Bastin and Alex James. The crowds were huge and the Reverend A. Hunt Cooke, a close friend of Chapman's at St Mary's, recalled that the scenes were a little shocking: 'There were people climbing all over the graves with cameras. Mr Chapman would not have approved.'

Below: 10 January, 1934; the saddest day of the glorious 1930s. The cortege carrying Herbert Chapman's body moves slowly through the streets of Hendon, where he was buried in the churchyard of what was then still a quiet village.

Bob Wall, then Chapman's secretary, said that, for several years after Chapman's death, he regularly heard his measured footsteps in the Highbury corridors late in the evening, going along the upper landing, through the boardroom and cocktail bar, into the Press Room and on into the stand. He, and other members of the staff, often looked down the corridors to see if there was anyone there – but no one ever was. If there are such things as ghosts, then if Herbert Chapman's still watches over Highbury it would be perfect. In every sense, he has continued to live on in the club and the ground that he raised, just as he promised Tom Whittaker he would, to the very heights of football.

It all happened the best part of a lifetime ago, but as long as men gather together to kick a football, the players who earned Arsenal their first wave of glory will never be forgotten.

Foremost among them was Alex James, the chief entertainer and midfield string-puller of Herbert Chapman's wonderful side. Beloved of cartoonists for his baggy shorts, flapping sleeves and sleek centre hair-parting, the little Scot was the outstanding creative inside forward of his generation.

He was blessed with supreme technique, his distribution was both uncannily accurate and ruthlessly penetrating, and he played the game with a natural swagger which made him a magnet to crowds.

Born at Mossend, Lanarkshire, in 1901, James served Raith and Preston before joining the Gunners for £8,750 in June 1929. He netted in the Wembley triumph over Huddersfield in his first campaign, then went on to collect four title medals and a second FA Cup gong.

Alex made 259 League and Cup appearances and scored 27 goals for Arsenal before retiring in 1937, but was capped only eight times by his country due to a surfeit of Scottish riches at that time. Later he coached youngsters at Highbury.

A man who benefited hugely from James' guile was the dashing Devonian, Cliff 'Boy' Bastin, signed from Exeter in 1929. A strong, hard-running left-winger with an explosive shot, he was the leading scorer in Arsenal's history until Ian Wright took his record, and a fair proportion of his strikes emanated from Alex's cunning despatches inside the full-back. A magnificent athlete, Bastin created plenty of goals for colleagues, too, and played 21 times for England. He retired in 1947, having netted 176 times in 392 appearances.

On the opposite wing, Joe Hulme was a veritable grey-

hound and and a reliable finisher, too, contributing 124 goals in his 372 outings between 1925–26 and 1937–38. A Midlander who served York and Blackburn before becoming one of Chapman's first Highbury signings, Joe specialised in pin-point crosses and played nine times for England. He was transferred to Huddersfield in 1938 and bossed Spurs for four years after the war.

Another immense talent was the tall, elegant inside forward David Jack, for whom Chapman shattered the British transfer record when he paid Bolton £10,890 in 1928. A born predator and bountifully endowed with ball skills, Jack was a thorough-bred and he justified the great man's faith to the tune of 123 goals in 206 games. During the course of his nine-cap interna-tional career, he became the first Gunner to captain England, then left the club in 1934 to manage Southend.

Arsenal were served by two outstanding centre-forwards during the 1930s, first Jack Lambert and then Ted Drake. The former's contribution tends to be rather overshadowed by the latter's, but there should be no doubt about the mettle of Lambert, a one-time miner in his native Yorkshire, who played for Rotherham, Leeds and Doncaster before enlisting as a Gunner in 1926. True, he was not over-endowed with delicacy on the ball, but he was a courageous bustler who hit the target 109 times in 159 matches, a formidable strike rate. He was sold to Fulham in 1933, later returning to Arsenal as a coach.

As for Drake, he remains one of the most illustrious figures in Highbury history. Ted was a rampaging marauder who con-tributed an avalanche of goals – 136 in 182 appearances – to the Gunners' cause between 1934 and 1939 after costing £6,500 from his hometown club, Southampton, in 1934. On acquiring the ebullient, charismatic marksman, manager George Allison described him as 'the best centre-forward in the world'; a trifle

Right: Arsenal versus the World Champions Italy on 14 November 1934. No fewer than seven Gunners were chosen to play on their own ground against the recently crowned Jules Rimet Trophy winners. It fully reflected the balance of power in the mid 1930s. The line up, left to right, of the seven: George Allison (club manager), Wilf Copping, Ray Bowden, George Male, Frank Moss, Ted Drake, Eddie Hapgood, Cliff Bastin and Tom Whittaker (trainer for both club and country). England won 3–2.

Right: Alex James was a fiery inside forward who recorded 259 games for the Gunners during their most successful period from 1929 to 1937.

steep, perhaps, though soon the broad-shouldered newcomer was demonstrating that the description might not be entirely fanciful. After the war Ted, who scored six times in five matches for England, became a successful manager, leading Chelsea to their only title in 1955.

Another attacker of note was Cornishman Ray Bowden (1932–33 to 1937–38 (136 games, 47 goals), who was capped six times.

Of course, while the forwards captured most of the head-lines, Arsenal possessed a fabulous defence, too (some things never change). There were three exceptional full-backs in Tom Parker (1925–26 to 1932–33, 292 games), George Male (1930–31 to 1947–48, 314 games) and Eddie Hapgood (1927–28 to 1938–39, 434 games). The Male-Hapgood partnership was as effective as any the game has seen and it is a testimony to their stature that both men captained Arsenal and England.

Big Herbie Roberts (1926–27 to 1937–38, 333 games) was famed as one of the first 'stopper centre-halves while there was inspirational input from three wing-halves, the Welshman Bob John (1922–23 to 1936–37, 467 games), Wilf 'Iron Man' Copping (1934–35 to 1938–39, 185 games) and 'Gentleman' Jack Crayston (1934–35 to 1938–39, 184 games), a cultured footballer and a future Gunners boss.

Goalkeeping honours were shared by Frank Moss (1931–32 to 1935–36, 159 games) and Alex Wilson (1933–34 to 1938–39, 89 games).

NOTE: figures for appearances and goals refer to Football League and FA Cup games only.

STARS OF THE 30s

CHAPTER 6
ALLISON'S ARSENAL

Chapman's death was so unexpected that there was no obvious successor. The players probably favoured Joe Shaw, who was popular and fully versed in Arsenal's ways. Shaw, apparently, was not particularly keen on the glare of publicity that was now an essential part of the job as manager at Highbury and stayed behind the scenes. Whether George Allison, the director in charge, actually formally offered him the job is unclear. The choice of a successor was an almost impossible one for the board – to follow Chapman was the hardest task in football. As it turned out, the problems were not as intractable as the board probably imagined. The club was run on a day-to-day basis by Joe Shaw, Tom Whittaker and John Peters, all of them highly competent, and the fact that between Chapman's death and the outbreak of war Arsenal won three Championships and the FA Cup (more trophies, interestingly, than when he was alive) is largely due to them. It was also true that the club had established a style and approach to the game that could survive even the passing of a Herbert Chapman.

Allison fills the breach

The solution that the board came up with, while unlikely, proved in the end to be rather clever. George Allison, who had been involved with the club since its Woolwich days and who became a director in the early 1920s, moved from the boardroom to the manager's office. For some months after Chapman's death, Allison had been acting as Managing Director/Secretary. He did not actually become manager until the end of the 1933–34 season. It was a clever move because it avoided any great disruption, it allowed Shaw and Whittaker to continue to manage the team, the training and the tactics, and it saved the club from facing any new broom that an outsider would probably want to bring, even to so successful a club as the Gunners.

Technically Joe Shaw had become team manager, John Peters secretary and Tom Whittaker trainer. The 'official' job of secretary-manager was not advertised, but there were hundreds of applications anyway, to which Allison had to reply. One from Wales claimed the ability to run 14 miles in an hour, a mile in 3½ minutes and '... to have developed a private system of team control on the field by verbal orders that will break any defence or attack that does not use my methods ...' As Allison said, presumably tongue in cheek, being the only one who saw the applications gave him ample opportunity to put examples like that to one side, lest they endanger his prospects.

Left: George Allison talking to journalists at Highbury before the 1936 FA Cup final.

Below: The most famous of all Arsenal pictures: Alex James leaves a trail of Manchester City defenders behind him during a game at Highbury on 13 October 1934. The view is towards the old North Bank, then graced by the famous clock. The FA had recently told the club to change it from a 45-minute timer to a proper clock. It was eventually moved to the southern end when the North Bank stand was built. Arsenal won this particular game against City 3–0 and ended the season as Champions for the third consecutive time (picture by courtesy of *The Sunday Times*).

Allison was actually three years older than the Arsenal, having been born in Darlington in 1883. He had built a reasonable reputation for himself as a journalist, and had for a time been the manager's assistant at Middlesbrough, but his name came to national attention when he was chosen to be Britain's first ever radio sports commentator. The very first major event to be broadcast live was to be the 1927 Cup final, played on 23 April between Arsenal and Cardiff City. Oddly, no one seemed to think it unreasonable that the commentator for the Cup final should also be a director of one of the teams playing.

A hard act to follow

Bernard Joy, who played for Allison, described him as: '... tactful, friendly and good-hearted. But he fell short in his handling of footballers and lacked the professional's deep knowledge of the game. (Allison) wisely left dressing-room discipline in Tom Whittaker's hands and it was Whittaker and Joe Shaw who took the brunt of the strained relations which occasionally developed between management and players. The two of them were loyalty itself to Allison – they had to be or the club would have fallen apart.' Cliff Bastin, who also played for the next five years under Allison, clearly agreed with Joy, but there is a slight edge to comments in his autobiography. Having pointed out that Joe Shaw was unhappy with the glare of publicity, Bastin comments: 'The man who did take over the position was one to whom the limelight was far from unwelcome ... he was not, however, a successor shaped in the Chapman mould. Indeed, relations between him and Mr Chapman had not always been of the happiest ... He (Allison) had the name of Arsenal splashed across the front pages of the press, but he lacked Herbert Chapman's gift of getting the best out of his players.'

These were commonly held views when Allison took over, and were to be heard often enough through the rest of the decade. But others were prepared to look at the results and accept what was plain to see; few men, if any, could have taken over from Chapman, and there were still plenty of trophies on the boardroom sideboard. Frank Carruthers, one of the leading journalists of the period, wrote in 1937: 'The continuance of Arsenal's power is a wonderful tribute to Mr George Allison, who has borne his office through a period of extreme difficulty which would have taxed the ingenuity of a Herbert Chapman to surmount.' And to sum up his views about George Allison's success he said, simply: 'Well, we have all been wrong.'

For the season-and-a-half after Chapman's death things went as well as they could have done for anyone. No other man has come into a manager's seat and won the Championship in each of his first two seasons. But while Arsenal clearly remained the team to beat through the rest of the 1930s they were no longer the best. In the last four seasons prior to the outbreak of war in 1939 their record was a creditable sixth, third, first and fifth, though the Championship of 1938 was won with a mere 52 points, the lowest ever in a 42-match season. The Cup was again highly creditable, but arguably not outstanding compared with the impossibly high standards set by Chapman between 1930 and 1934. There were, nonetheless, three quarter finals and the 1936 final victory over Sheffield United.

When Allison's third season in charge began in August 1935 success had become a habit. It was seven seasons since Arsenal had not won or threatened to win one or both trophies. In 1930 there was the FA Cup, in 1931 the League, in 1932 the runners-up slot in both, in 1933, 1934 and 1935 the Championship. Could they do it again? After seven matches and only two wins it didn't look likely.

All great teams come to the end of their eras. Some settle slowly, as Arsenal did, some rapidly, as Manchester City did after their Championship of 1937. For Arsenal, as we have seen, nearly all the major players had already gone. Alex James and Herbie Roberts were nearing retirement, Frank Moss' shoulder injury recurred in a Cup tie against Blackburn and his career was finally over, reserve centre-forward Ronnie Westcott, of whom great things were expected, injured a knee in only his second League match and never played again.

Allison later wrote that, just before the manager's death, Chapman had told him: 'The team's played out Mr Allison, we must rebuild.' At the time the club was top of the First Division and half-way through the hat-trick. In many ways the quote rings untrue. Perhaps it was just Chapman's way of loosening up a director for yet more major expenditures, or perhaps it was a throw-away line after a single poor game. Nonetheless, the team was rebuilt, and not so much because of Allison's desire to buy new players as the ageing of the first-team squad.

Drake hits Villa for seven

Allison's first signing was Ted Drake, the reluctant gas inspector from Southampton, in March 1934. And the highlight of the 1935–36 season was to be one game involving the same Ted Drake. The date was 14 December 1935 and the match was one of the standard classics of the decade – Aston Villa versus Arsenal at Villa Park. About 70,000 were packed inside the ground to see another instalment in a rivalry which had provided a series of highly memorable encounters since 1930. They were not to be disappointed though, for once, neither Arsenal nor Villa were heading the League. The Gunners were

Right: Alex James, dressed in unlikely garb, watches the Barnsley keeper, Ellis, during the FA Cup quarter final tie at Highbury on February 29, 1936. Arsenal won 4–1 with goals from Bastin, Bowden and Beasley (2).

already eight points behind Sunderland while Villa, having conceded 52 goals in 18 games were bottom. Founder members of the League in 1888, Villa had never been relegated and, in an attempt to stave off that ignominy, had recently spent so heavily that Chapman's and Allison's earlier behaviour looked like that of paupers by comparison. Villa fielded six internationals, Arsenal were without James and Hulme. Centre-forward Ted Drake had been in the reserves and was carrying a knee injury, which was heavily strapped for the first time.

For the first quarter hour Villa were better, but at half time were 3–0 down and Drake had a hat-trick. All the goals were classic Arsenal – a long ball from Pat Beasley for Drake to run on to, a long pass from Bastin which Drake picked up and ran with to the edge of the area before scoring, and a rebound from a Pat Beasley shot from the wing. At the end of an hour Drake had a double hat-trick and Arsenal were 6–0 up. This time the goals came from a mistake by Villa centre-half Tommy Griffiths, who assumed a ball was going over the goalline only to see it rebound off the post for Drake, another pass from Bastin to Drake and an instant return from a bad clearance.

Drake was controlling the ball perfectly, beating defenders at will and shooting so accurately that the Villa keeper, Merton, had no chance. It was the exhibition of a complete centre-forward. By this stage the entire Villa half-back line was marking Drake, but it made little difference for his seventh shot actually hit the bar and bounced down to be cleared. It was one of only two goal attempts of the whole afternoon which missed its mark (the other was saved). Villa did score once, but Drake had the last word in the final minute with yet another goal from a Bastin cross-field pass; seven goals away from home with just nine shots.

One reason it was the highlight of the season for Drake was that he was injured for much of it. As the 1936 Cup final approached, in which Arsenal were to play Sheffield United, Allison needed to test Drake's fitness after a cartilage operation. The game before the final was against Villa at Highbury. Ted Drake scored the winning goal and it was the final nail in Villa's relegation coffin.

Drake's seven goals in Birmingham were a League record, equalling Jimmy Ross Junior's alleged total for Preston against Stoke set way back in 1888 (and since found to be incorrect). By one of those peculiar statistical coincidences, however, Drake's was to remain the record for just 12 days, when Bunny Bell of Tranmere scored nine against Oldham in the Third Division North, though Drake's record remains for the First Division. Drake's goals made little difference to the title race – Sunderland beat the Gunners 5–4 in an exciting game at Roker and went on to win the Championship easily. Arsenal finished sixth, their worst position since 1930.

Bastin strikes decisive goal

The Cup was to be a different story that season. Bristol Rovers were defeated 5–1 at Eastville, then Liverpool 2–0 at Anfield. 'Recorder' in the Arsenal programme was particularly effusive about that display: 'It will go down in Arsenal history as one of the most glorious performances. The form of our team ... was superb and would probably have accounted for any team in the land.' The next game was again away (their seventh consecutive away draw) at Newcastle, who had beaten them in the 1932 final. Moss, Roberts and Drake were all out injured, and the Gunners did well to draw 3–3. The replay at Highbury was easier, a 3–0 win including two penalties by Cliff Bastin. The sixth round finally saw a home draw and a 4–1 defeat of Barnsley. The semi-final was at Huddersfield against highly unfashionable Grimsby (but who were then a First Division club) and some concerns were voiced that this might be another hard struggle like the semi-final against Hull of six years before. It was certainly a hard game, Bastin's goal being the only one of the match and taking Arsenal to Wembley for the fourth time in ten years. Cliff Bastin had a useful habit of scoring the critical goal in semi-finals and in this case, he struck from a Bowden through-ball in a move which had been rehearsed repeatedly on the training ground.

Gunners back at Wembley

With no chance of winning the Championship, Allison had been resting his injured players (such as Roberts and Drake) between Cup ties. This did not please the League, who fined Arsenal £250 in a show of displeasure which became almost an annual ritual directed at some club or other between the wars. When the final came round Drake, Roberts, James and Hapgood were all unwell. Drake was barely recovered from a cartilage operation and had only played his comeback game one week before. Allison decided he had to risk the centre-forward and reshuffled his attack – putting Ray Bowden at inside forward and moving Bastin back to the left-wing (he had been playing inside). The upshot was that Pat Beasley, who had been in Bastin's spot for much of the season, was dropped before the final, just as he had been hours before the 1932 game. The FA again refused to mint an extra medal for him. The team that therefore took the field was Wilson, Male, Hapgood, Crayston, Roberts, Copping, Hulme, Bowden, Drake, James and Bastin.

Their opponents were Second Division Sheffield United, who had beaten Burnley, Preston, Leeds, Spurs and finally Fulham to get to Wembley. For most of the game United were on top, almost going ahead in the first minute when Alex Wilson dropped the ball in the six-yard box, and later unluckily

hitting the bar with a Jock Dodds header after half-an-hour. There were no goals until the 74th minute, when Bastin picked up a clearance and passed the ball through the middle to Ted Drake. Drake side-stepped past United captain Tom Johnson and hit the ball hard, left-footed, past keeper Smith. United attacked for the rest of the match and suffered further wretched luck when Dodds hit the woodwork a second time. Drake, who had been uncomfortable for the whole game, said afterward that when he got the ball from Bastin he knew it was now or never. After he had scored James and Bastin were first to reach him, but he was on his hands and knees in the grass, unable to get up because of the pain in his injured knee. Drake stayed on the field for the rest of the game, but took no further part. It was the only goal of the game and Alex James took the trophy. Hapgood had not realised he wouldn't be captain until he read the morning papers, a communication slip by Allison which appears to have rankled with Hapgood afterward.

The captain and the manager never had a particularly close relationship, Hapgood being another who has described Allison as lucky to take over when he did and not possessing the football knowledge of Chapman. Later Hapgood was particularly hurt that Allison was prepared to let him go to Luton at the start of the 1943–44 season, when the player wanted a final year with the Gunners. But the full-back tells a good story about Allison in his autobiography, admitting that the manager was also very amused by it. Shortly after taking over, Allison was running a team-talk preparing for the following day's match: 'The danger man for Wednesday is Charlie Napier,' he told Jack Crayston, 'and you have the job of marking him and not letting him have the ball.' Crayston tried to interrupt but Allison stopped him: 'Wait a moment, let me finish and then give me your views.' When Allison had finished he asked what Crayston wanted to say. 'Napier does play well for Wednesday, Mr Allison,' the half-back commented, 'but we're playing Blackpool tomorrow.'

Still good but no longer great

Having been largely outplayed by a Second Division side in the 1936 final, Arsenal were forced to face the realities of their new position. They were no longer *the* outstanding side. Others, having watched what Chapman had achieved, had begun to copy many of his methods. Arsenal's tactical game was no longer a surprise, particularly when Bastin, Hulme and James became older, slower and less effective. The strain of a decade with every game played like a Cup tie was taking its toll.

And yet there was still no single club ready to take over the mantle – Sunderland were always in at the kill, Preston often looked good, Huddersfield kept popping up, Wolves and Derby threatened to win everything and eventually won nothing. So,

Below: The 1936 FA Cup final against Sheffield United was not to prove the most glittering moment in the club's history, but the demand for tickets never faltered. The Monday after the semi-final the Highbury staff faced this postbag of requests for Cup final tickets.

1934-1939

Above: The only goal of the 1936 FA Cup final: Drake picked up a pass from Bastin, side-stepped the Sheffield captain Tom Johnson and hit the ball hard, left-footed past keeper Smith.

at the end of the day, Arsenal still maintained a better overall record than any other club – it is just that we are tempted to judge them by the standards not of the Chapman era as a whole, but solely against the 1930–34 period.

The realities of Arsenal's slightly diminished status were clear in the first few games of 1936–37. The Gunners won only two of their initial nine matches and, by the end of October, were 17th. In a now familiar story, though, the side fought back until, by mid-March, they were on top and seemed to be on the way to a seventh trophy in eight years. But, in true fairy story tradition, Manchester City came with an astonishing run of 36 points out of 40 from the New Year onward. The crucial game was at Maine Road on 10 April 1937, when the Gunners went down 2–0 and left City clear to take the title.

Below: 1936–37 was an anticlimax as Arsenal came third in the League and were knocked out of the Cup in the quarter finals, but Ted Drake carried on his heroic efforts, here in a 4–1 win against Sunderland at Highbury.

fle onto the field for the first time that there was one who might lay claim to genius. Some held that James' slovenly appearance was natural, others said it was a pose. But it was in sharp contrast to one of the tidiest minds in football. James hated waste, particularly wasted effort. To him it was the surest mark of inadequate technique. "Let the ball do the work" was his motto.' After he had begun to heed Chapman's advice to: '... cut out the circus tricks until we're winning 3–0,' James was at the centre of everything. That was why he was always treated differently from the rest. Chapman would not have put up with his antics, his disappearances in the night and lying in bed until noon from any other player. When he finished playing he took up a job with one of the pools companies. He later became a Sunday paper reporter and eventually returned to Highbury as a coach. He was to die in 1953, aged 51, one of several of the great names of the 1930s to die tragically young.

James proved almost impossible to replace, though Allison tried. He bought Bobby Davidson from St Johnstone, but he was not to be the playmaker Arsenal needed. Nor, in the end, was Cliff Bastin, who featured for most of the 1936–37 season where he had started out, at inside forward. Allison searched further afield, buying Leslie Jones from Coventry (already a Welsh international) and George Drury from Sheffield United to fill the gap, but they didn't work either. In the end, he made the move which was, to a large extent, to become the albatross around the neck of his reputation – the purchase of Bryn Jones from Wolves.

Bob John retired on the same day as Alex James, Herbie Roberts never came back from his injury and a bloodclot complication and Joe Hulme was out for virtually a year-and-a-half after injuring his back when he ran into a concrete wall at one end of the Huddersfield pitch. Oddly, it was back there to Leeds Road that Hulme eventually went in January 1938, and within three months he was playing outside right in the famous FA Cup final against Preston. Hulme was the first man to play in

Alex James retires

For Arsenal, the season's most significant event was probably Alex James' retirement. His last League game was against Bolton on 1 May 1937 and was hardly the send-off he might have wished. Bernard Joy, now in the team in place of the injured Herbie Roberts, called the goalless draw 'dismal'.

It is impossible to underestimate James' contribution to the successful Arsenal side of the 1930s. He was simply the key man. Before he arrived, as has often been repeated, they had won nothing, despite the big signings. In the six years after his arrival they won four Championships and reached three FA Cup finals. 'You might have suspected,' said Don Davies in an obituary in the *Manchester Guardian*, 'when you saw him shuffive Wembley FA Cup finals, a club record later to be equalled by Pat Rice. The 1938 Cup final was actually Joe Hulme's last ever first-class match, a wonderful way to end any career.

Herbie Roberts had a less happy sequel to his Arsenal career, which ended after that bad injury on 30 October 1937 versus Middlesbrough. He became part of the backroom staff, moving down to train the nursery club at Margate. After only a brief time there, shortly after the outbreak of the war, he died of erysipelas, a rare bacterial infection of the skin which penicillin can cure relatively easily today. He was a great loss to Arsenal and to football and was the second (after Jack Lambert) of the great team to die soon after moving to Margate.

Margate: Arsenal's nursery by the sea

The nursery club idea had been another of Chapman's brain waves. It was much better to have your youngsters competing in a real league than against other juniors, he reasoned. His first move was to try to take over Clapton (later Leyton) Orient, then a Third Division South club, who were threatened with expulsion by the FA in 1931 unless they paid off their debts. Chapman effectively took over the club late that year and all of the players were registered with Arsenal. It was a nice, if short-

Left: Cliff Bastin was one of the few members of the rapidly ageing Cup-winning squad of 1936 to return as a player after the war. During his 396 games for Arsenal he scored an amazing 178 goals, a record that remained unbroken until Ian Wright finally managed it in September 1997.

lived, irony as, 20 years before, Orient had been one of the main objectors to the move to Highbury. Needless to say, the League objected strongly and ordered Chapman to desist (they had clearly had enough of Arsenal bosses running two clubs 20 years earlier). The upshot was that Jimmy Seed, Orient manager since April 1931, found himself just a few weeks from the start of the 1932–33 season with no team, no directors and no registered players.

It was not Chapman, but Allison, who later turned to the Southern League, which was not concerned about the two clubs idea, and Arsenal acquired Margate instead. Seed was to have his own revenge on Arsenal – between 1934 and 1936 he took Charlton from the Third Division to the First and in 1936–37 he squeezed into second place between Manchester City and the Gunners.

Fifth championship in eight years

So, having finished third in 1936–37 and been knocked out of the Cup in the quarter finals at the Hawthorns, it did appear that Arsenal were in decline. All the more surprising, then, was their Championship in 1937–38, their fifth in eight years. Their record was almost identical to that of 1936–37, with exactly the same number of points, 52. They lost as many as 11 games (their highest number of defeats in any season in the 1930s to date, with the sole exception of 1935–36 when they lost 12) and scored only 77 goals, their lowest total since 1929–30 apart from the 75 in 1933–34, that peculiarly quiet season containing Chapman's death.

The side was in no sense settled and the season was tough and inconsistent. At the end the Gunners were to just squeeze past Wolves and Brentford, who were performing the surprise Charlton role one season later. George Hunt had been bought from Spurs to partner Drake up front and did so well that it was a surprise when Allison transferred him to Bolton at the end of the season. Joy had replaced Roberts, and Bastin and Male were now the only survivors from the great days, making another Championship both surprising and impressive.

By February, Arsenal and Wolves were favourites for both major competitions and found themselves drawn together in the Cup one week after meeting in the League. Wolves won the League game 3–1 to go ahead of Arsenal in the table, though both were then several points behind Brentford. In the Cup the roles were reversed, Arsenal winning a very tough game 2–1 with goals from Drake and Kirchen in what Bernard Joy called the most exciting tie he ever played in. It must have exhausted them, for they went out 1–0 to eventual winners Preston in the next round at Highbury.

Brentford, despite having been seven points ahead of Arsenal at one stage, were like many clubs who rise through

1934-1939

the divisions quickly. The elements of unfamiliarity and surprise carry them so far for so long, but the lack of strength in depth tells in the end. Brentford walked the tightrope for a long time, but when they fell they fell heavily. In eight games Brentford took only two points and were out of contention.

At Highbury new names were making their mark – Mel Griffiths at outside right, Eddie Carr, a successful centre-forward when Drake was injured, as he so often was. A long run of success put Arsenal three points clear of Wolves, at Easter, but then came disaster. Over the holiday period the Gunners could only draw 0–0 at Birmingham and then lost both games against Brentford. The matches against their London rivals, who were back in form now that their chance had virtually gone, were particularly inept, notable for Ted Drake's injury at Griffin Park, where he was knocked out and then came back on the field despite having blood pouring down his face from a head wound. That was the Drake of Arsenal inter-war legend. He ended this game half-conscious and hung over Tom Whittaker's shoulder (see picture on p.176).

Final-day decider

The Easter debacle put Wolves back on top and the contest went to the last match. Preston had made a late run from behind and were being tipped for the Double. Arsenal were perhaps fortunate to go to Deepdale a week before the Cup final (in which Preston defeated Huddersfield) and, with the Preston players no doubt tense and afraid of injury, the Gunners won 3–1. On the very last day Wolves were away to Sunderland. If Wolves won, they were Champions no matter what the opposition did, but if they drew, and Arsenal beat Bolton at Highbury, then Arsenal would be Champions again. The Bolton game was easy for a committed Arsenal, who won 5–0. But, though Sunderland had nothing to play for, they threw themselves into their game with Wolves with a vengeance. Such was their determination that, despite having a defender sent off, they still won 1–0. The game at Roker had kicked off 15 minutes before that at Highbury, and when the result came through on the scoreboards and the crowd started cheering Bernard Joy called to Eddie Hapgood: 'They've lost Eddie.' Hapgood, typically, was so embroiled in the game, though Arsenal were already 4–0 up, that he simply didn't understand what Joy was talking about.

Money talk

The final season before the Second World War proved to be notable for little but the purchase of Bryn Jones. This was really the point at which Allison was accused of taking over Chapman's 'money bags' reputation with a vengeance.

Interestingly such criticisms were a source of unusual irritation to Allison, who usually took disagreements and press comment in his stride. He was very quick to point out that, between 1925 and 1934, Chapman spent £101,000 in fees and received £40,000 for those he sold – a balance of around £7,000 per annum. Between Allison taking over and the war, Arsenal spent £81,000 and received £51,000, a net expenditure of £30,000. This was certainly more than manageable when, during the six seasons 1933–39, the total profit amounted to £136,000, a massive sum for any football club or moderate sized company of the period. In 1934–35 the club became the first ever to have gate receipts of over £100,000, and made a profit of £35,000. Of the other clubs only Portsmouth, with £14,961, even got into double figures. The financial reserves were then £60,000 and even programme sales brought in nearly £2,500.

The grandest of stands

Financially more debatable, as it happened, was the building of the stands. The West Stand cost £45,000 and was opened by the Prince of Wales (later the Duke of Windsor) on 10 December 1932. It had actually been first used on 12 November for a game against Chelsea (Arsenal won 1–0) and was, by a large margin, the grandest and most expensive structure on any League ground at the time. It incorporated three flats, an electric lift, and 4,100 seats, and the lower level, which was originally all standing, could theoretically hold another 20,000. Work had actually begun on redeveloping the ground in 1931, when the club started building up the banking on all four sides. Local inhabitants were encouraged to bring in their rubbish to help the process and, as Simon Inglis mentions in his

Below: Television comes to Highbury; the first match shown live anywhere in the world was played at Highbury on Thursday 16 September 1937. Excerpts were shown on the BBC from a practice game between the first team and reserves.

invaluable *The Football Grounds of England and Wales*, one coal merchant backed up too close to a hole in the North Bank and saw his horse and cart disappear into the cavity. The animal was so badly injured that it had to be destroyed and it was buried where it fell, in the middle of the North Bank terracing.

The North Bank roof was originally built in 1935 (the clock then being moved to the South Bank) but was destroyed by bombs in the war. A new East, or Main, Stand was not planned to be built until 1941, but the original stand was deteriorating so fast, and the finances appeared to be so favourable, that the decision was made to rebuild it in 1935.

As the club had already borrowed quite heavily to erect the other stands, by early 1937 Arsenal had debts of £200,000 and needed average crowds of 40,000 simply to pay the running expenses and finance the debt. The Main Stand, though planned to be identical to the West Stand, finally cost far more (£130,000 to be precise) and when the war came in 1939 the club found themselves in a similar position to that of Henry Norris in 1914. The war years clearly left the problem unsolved but, with the enormous boom in attendances between 1945 and 1952, and some intelligent management, the problem happily, and perhaps a little fortuitously, solved itself. One reason why the East Stand cost more than the West was that it had an expensive public frontage – the West is built entirely behind a row of houses and is effectively invisible from that side.

Gunners break transfer record

When George Allison finally decided he had to buy Bryn Jones in August 1938, the record fee was still the £11,500 he and Chapman had paid out for David Jack ten years before. Eventually Wolves forced Allison up to £14,000, and Jones was left to carry the very distracting tag of 'most expensive player'. Many players before and since have found this difficult, not least Bryn's own nephew Cliff Jones when he joined Spurs for £35,000 two decades later. Bryn started well enough though, scoring in his first game, against Portsmouth, and getting two more in the next three matches. But he never really settled that season, not enjoying the limelight and feeling the crowd and club's expectations weighing very heavily on his light shoulders.

It was the sort of pressure he could never escape from at Highbury – when he and Allison agreed that a run in the relative calm of the reserves might improve his form, 33,000 turned up to see his second-team debut. As they had nearly all come to see Jones, this was even worse than being in the first team and the experiment was never repeated. Allison was understandably unrepentant about his purchase, pointing out that: '... he was not a prolific goalscorer (though he had scored 52 goals in 163 games for Wolves) just like Alex James, because

Above: The tense end to the 1937–38 season included more heroic efforts from Drake. During the Brentford match on 18 April he suffered two broken bones in his wrist, needed nine stitches in his head and was finally carried off unconscious.

Below: Denis Compton, like most of the Arsenal players, joined the forces, becoming (appropriately) a gunner in the army.

his chief asset was the holding together of the line and the making of openings for the more vigorous of his team-mates.'

Allison said that Jones often asked to be saved from the ever-present, ever-insistent limelight, and believed that, given time to settle down, he would have made the grade: 'My faith never failed and I have never for a moment considered him a bad buy.' Allison's point seems a fair one. It took Alex James a season to settle down and there was no reason to expect Jones, just as important a buy, to adapt any faster. He played exceptionally well on the team's close-season tour of 1939 but never really had another chance except in the very different atmosphere of wartime football. Like many great players, notably Stan Cullis of Wolves, his best years were inevitably lost to the war.

Interestingly, other members of the club did not share Allison's optimism. Cliff Bastin, in his autobiography, said: 'I thought at the time this was a bad transfer, and subsequent events did nothing to alter my views ... I had played against Bryn in club and international matches and had ample opportunity to size him up. To my mind, he was essentially an attacking player, who was successful at Wolverhampton largely because the rest of the team was playing well.'

Bastin argued that James had a first-class footballing brain and that Jones, while being a first-class footballer, did not. James, whom Bastin, of course, called one of the most self-confident people he had ever met, was able to weather the bad patch of the transition, while Jones, quiet, modest and self-effacing, was not. Bastin was the wing partner of them both, of

1934-1939

course, so his judgement is possibly the most reliable available. Sadly, his conclusion is rather dismissive: 'It was his (Jones) natural instinct to play as far upfield as I. Arsenal's attempt to curb that instinct failed ... (He) would have been much happier if he had never left Wolverhampton.'

Teenage keeper dies

Apart from Jones, the goalkeepers were also in the news in the last season before the war. George Marks, hailing from the non-footballing town of Salisbury, became the first-team keeper and was England's first choice for much of the war, losing his place only after a bad head injury sustained against Wales toward the end of hostilities. Much more serious was the tragedy that befell the reserve keeper David Ford. Aged only 18, he had played well in a Combination game for the second team against Portsmouth at Highbury. On the way home, he collapsed in the tube station, was rushed to hospital and found to have a duodenal ulcer. He never recovered and died the following Saturday.

More were to die in the hostilities that followed – of the 42 players on the staff in 1938–39, nine were dead by the end of the war. Nearly all the players joined the forces (Whittaker had served in the First World War and Bastin's deafness disqualified him so the two of them manned the Air Raid post on top of the main stand). The ground was bombed several times – Eddie Hapgood recalled one occasion when the incendiaries

missed the stands but managed to set fire to both sets of goalposts. Soon afterward a barrage balloon arrived and was moored on the practice pitch. This did not prevent a 1,000-pound bomb hitting the same pitch, nor various other aerial objects destroying the North Stand and some of the terracing.

The Arsenal Stadium Mystery

Arsenal were to conclude their inter-war glories with a flourish in 1939. Though they had never been in the hunt for the League title (Everton won it easily) the Gunners did win five of their last six games to finish, as in 1914–15, fifth. By this time Hitler had already invaded Czechoslovakia and the normality of football already seemed a little unreal. Although three games were played at the start of the aborted 1939–40 season, it was fitting that the last official pre-Second World War match should have been as peculiar, in its own way, as the last game in 1914–15. That was at Highbury on 6 May 1939, against bogey team Brentford, and was used to film the playing sequences for a thriller called *The Arsenal Stadium Mystery* by one Leonard Gribble. Brentford wore white shirts and black shorts instead of their usual change strip (to provide contrast for the black and white cameras) and played the part of the mythical Trojans. Several Arsenal players, as well as George Allison, enlivened the plot. Whether the script called for a 2–0 home win is not clear, but that's the way the game ended. It was Arsenal's last official first-class match for over six years.

Below: Ted Drake in action again, against bogey team Brentford at Griffin Park on 8 September 1938.

As befits a club of such colossal stature and tradition, Arsenal have been blessed with the services of numerous international stars down the decades.

Most notably there was the all-conquering 1930s side, festooned by England alumni plus, among others, Scotland's Alex James and Bob John of Wales; then came the 1971 Double-winners, packed with men who represented their countries; and now there is Arsene Wenger's sumptuously talented multi-national combination, of which every regular member has graced the world stage.

But also there has been a steady flow of gifted Gunners who were capped frequently in between those golden eras. For instance, there was goalkeeper Jack Kelsey and wing half Dave Bowen, who were at the heart of Wales' greatest team, which reached the quarter finals of the World Cup in 1958 before losing 1-0 to the eventual winners, Brazil.

With every respect to the massive achievements of Pat Jennings, Bob Wilson and David Seaman, there is no shortage of shrewd judges who would name Kelsey as the most outstanding net-minder in Highbury history. Unfortunately for genial Jack, his mid-century prime coincided with a relatively humdrum period for the north Londoners and his only club honour was a League Championship medal in 1952–53.

A former steelworker, he was formidably strong and possessed of shovel-like, appararently prehensile hands with which he specialised in claiming shots and crosses with confident aplomb. It was just as well because, week after week, he was called upon to perform near-miracles between the posts, his brilliance hugely instrumental in maintaining Arsenal's mid-table status in the old First Division.

In addition to earning 41 full caps between 1954 and 1962, he represented Great Britain against the Rest of Europe in 1955 before his career was ended by a back injury sustained against

Above left: Jack Kelsey won 41 Welsh caps between 1954 and 1962. He was the first the forefather of the great Arsenal keepers: Jennings, Wilson and Seaman.

Above: The playmaking talents of Liam Brady made him a regular in the Republic of Ireland side for 16 years.

Above right: His immaculate reading of the game earned David O'Leary 68 Republic of Ireland caps between 1976 and 1993.

Above far right: Arsenal's Republic of Ireland connection of the 70s and 80s was started by Dubliner Frank Stapleton.

Right: Kenny Sansom held the left-back position for England 86 times the majority of which were during the early 1980s.

Brazil. Thereafter he extended his Highbury service to 40 years, running the club lottery and shop before retiring as Commercial Manager in 1989. Jack died in 1992.

Dave Bowen, capped 19 times between 1954 and 1959, skippered Wales throughout their 1958 World Cup campaign and his input was inspirational. His tackling was ferocious and his passing perceptive, but it was for his immense strength of will and uplifting motivational powers that he was renowned. Indeed, colleagues maintained that this storming, passionate leader made more noise on the pitch than any dozen fans, and he was at his peak in the Brazil quarter final, when he locked horns with a 17-year-old genius. True, Pele scored the only goal of the game, but Bowen, who died in 1995, covered himself in glory for his valiant display.

In that same Wales side was a versatile performer named Mel Charles, not then a Gunner but destined to move to Highbury from Swansea Town in April 1959. The brother of the more famous John, he turned out at centre-half against the Brazilians, but later showed his most effective Arsenal form as between 1974 and 1990, though he departed Highbury in 1980, going on to serve Juventus, Sampdoria, Internazionale, Ascoli and West Ham United before retiring. Later he coached and managed before re-enlisting with Arsenal as head of youth development in 1996.

O'Leary was an exceptional footballing centre-half, a polished thoroughbred whose reading of the game and distribution were invariably immaculate. Despite his willowy frame, David was no physical pushover, as he proved by enduring for a decade and a half at the heart of the Gunners' rearguard. He was capped 68 times between 1976 and 1993, then finished his career with Leeds before stepping up at Elland Road to become arguably the Premiership's most promising young boss.

Stapleton was a centre-forward of compelling all-round quality who made his mark initially as a deputy for John Radford, then excelled as the foil for free-scoring Malcolm Macdonald. Frank scored his share of goals but also he was a magnificent leader of the line, adept at first-time lay-offs with head, foot and all points between and most Gooners were desperately disappointed when he departed to Old Trafford in 1981. At the time he was widely deemed the equal of any centre-forward in Europe, and his 70 caps accumulated between 1976 and 1990 are an accurate reflection of his status.

Arsenal's most capped player, though, remains left-back Kenny Sansom, who made 77 of his 86 England appearances while a Gunner, between 1980 and 1988.

Other international luminaries to have served Arsenal include Joe Mercer, Tommy Lawton, George Eastham, Alan Ball, Paul Mariner and Tony Woodcock of England; Charlie Nicholas of Scotland; Wally Barnes, Ray Daniel and Peter Nicholas of Wales; Pat Jennings and Terry Neill of Northern Ireland; Joe Haverty and Niall Quinn of the Republic; and Sweden's Anders Limpar.

a centre-forward. When his international career ended in 1962, Mel had been capped 31 times.

Moving forward to the 1970s, the Gunners boasted another outstanding triumvirate of players who had arrived from another country, the Republic of Ireland's Liam Brady, David O'Leary and Frank Stapleton.

Schemer Brady would be many fans' choice as the club's finest footballer of all time, a midfield general of sublime vision and skill whose left foot was an instrument of almost celestial precision and who could drift past opponents as though they were not there. Liam represented the Irish on 72 occasions

INTERNATIONALS

SEASON 1886-1887
FRIENDLIES

Date	Opponent			Score
11 Dec	Eastern W	A	W	6-0
8 Jan	Erith	H	W	6-1
15 Jan	Alexandria U	H	W	11-0
22 Jan	Eastern W	H	W	1-0
29 Jan	Erith	A	W	3-2
5 Feb	Millwall Rov	A	L	0-4
12 Feb	Alexandria U	A	W	6-0
25 Feb	2nd Rifle Brigade	H	D	0-0
12 Mar	Millwall Rov	H	W	3-0
26 Mar	2nd Rifle Brigade	A	L	0-1

	P	W	L	D	F:A
Arsenal	10	7	2	1	36:8

SEASON 1887-1888
FRIENDLIES

Date	Opponent			Score
30 Sep	Alexandria U	H	W	5-1
15 Oct	Clapton Pilgrims		D	2-2
22 Oct	St Lukes		W	4-0
5 Nov	Grange Institute		W	4-0
12 Nov	Iona Deptford		D	1-1
19 Nov	Tottenham H	A	L	1-2
26 Nov	Millwall Rov	A	L	0-3
2 Dec	Grange Park	H		
10 Dec	Brixton Rangers	H	L	1-2
16 Dec	Shrewsbury Park		W	4-0
31 Dec	Forest Gate Alliance	A	L	1-4
14 Jan	Iona Deptford	A	W	3-2
28 Jan	Champion Hill		W	6-0
3 Feb	Tottenham H	H	W	6-0
11 Feb	Millwall Rov	H	D	3-3
17 Feb	Erith		W	2-1
24 Feb	Forest Gate Alliance	H	D	1-1
2 Mar	Grange Institute		W	2-1
9 Mar	Brixton Ran		W	9-3
16 Mar	Ascham		W	5-0
30 Mar	Millwall Rov	H	W	3-0
6 Apr	Alexandria U	A	W	3-1

London Senior Cup

Date	Opponent			Score
8 Oct	Grove House	H	W	3-1
29 Oct	Barnes		L	0-4

Junior Matches

Date	Opponent			Score
10 Nov	Woolwich Pupils & Teachers	H	W	1-0
26 Nov	Erith	A	L	0-1
24 Feb	Thistle		L	1-2

	P	W	L	D	F:A
Arsenal	24	14	6	4	66:33

SEASON 1888-1889
FRIENDLIES

Date	Opponent			Score
15 Sep	London Scottish		D	3-3
22 Sep	Tottenham H		L	0-1
29 Sep	Old St Pauls		W	7-3
6 Oct	Grove House		W	2-0
13 Oct	London Scottish		W	4-0
20 Oct	2nd Rifle Brigade		L	1-3
27 Oct	Brixton Ran		L	1-3
10 Nov	Millwall Rov			
17 Nov	St Lukes		D	1-1
1 Dec	Phoenix		D	0-0
22 Dec	St Brides			
5 Jan	Vulcan		D	1-1
12 Jan	Unity		D	0-0
26 Jan	St Lukes			
2 Feb	Ilford		L	1-2
16 Feb	Millwall Rov			
23 Feb	Ilford		L	0-1
2 Mar	London Caledonians		L	1-2
9 Mar	Tottenham H		W	1-0
16 Mar	South Eastern Ran		L	1-2
23 Mar	Royal Artillery		W	9-0
30 Mar	2nd Rifle Brigade		W	6-1
1 Apr	2nd Rifle Brigade		W	6-1
6 Apr	Old St Pauls		W	3-0
13 Apr	Millwall Rov		W	3-0
19 Oct	Boston T		L	1-4
20 Apr	Spartan Rov		W	1-0
23 Apr	Scots Guards		W	7-2
27 Apr	London Caledonians		L	0-1

London Association Cup

Date	Opponent			Score
3 Nov	Phoenix		W	3-0
24 Nov	Dulwich		W	4-2
8 Dec	Old St Pauls		W	3-1
19 Jan	Clapton (Semi-Final)		L	0-2

Kent County Challenge Cup

Date	Opponent			Score
10 Nov	Horton Kirby		W	6-2
29 Dec	Iona		W	5-1
9 Feb	Gravesend		D	3-3*

*Arsenal disqualified for refusing
to play extra time.

	P	W	L	D	F:A
Arsenal	32	16	10	6	83:40

SEASON 1889-1890
FRIENDLIES

Date	Opponent			Score
7 Sep	London Caledonians	H	D	2-2
14 Sep	Casuals	H	W	6-0
21 Sep	Tottenham H	H	W	10-1
28 Sep	Unity	A	W	2-1
19 Oct	St Old Marks College	A	W	2-1
30 Nov	Marlow	A	L	0-2
21 Dec	Ilford	A	W	2-0
25 Dec	Preston Hornets	H	W	5-0
26 Dec	Chatham	A	D	2-2
27 Dec	Reading T	H	W	5-1
4 Jan	Windsor Phoenix	H	W	3-1
18 Jan	Old Harrovians	H	W	2-1
25 Jan	Foxes	H	W	7-2
8 Feb	Chiswick Park	H	D	1-1
1 Mar	Birmingham St George	H	L	1-4
15 Mar	Ilford	A	W	4-1
28 Mar	Clapton	A	L	0-2
31 Mar	W. H. Loraine XI	H	W	2-1
7 Apr	1st Lincs. Regt.	H	W	2-1
12 Apr	Marlow	H	W	1-0
19 Apr	Chatham	H	W	1-0
26 Apr	Clapton	H	W	6-1
3 May	London Cal/Clapton Comb	H	W	3-2
10 May	Millwall Athletic	A	D	3-3

FA Cup

Date	Opponent			Score
5 Oct	Lyndhurst (Q1)	H	W	11-0
26 Oct	Thorpe (Q2)	A	D	2-2*
16 Nov	Crusaders (Q3)	H	W	5-2
7 Dec	Swifts (Q4)	H	L	1-5

*Thorpe withdrew

London Cup

Date	Opponent			Score
2 Nov	Unity	H	W	4-1
23 Nov	Foxes	H	W	4-1
14 Dec	St Martins Ath	H	W	6-0
11 Jan	London Caledonians	H	W	3-1
8 Mar	Old Westminster (Final)		L	0-1

London Charity Cup

Date	Opponent			Score
1 Feb	Marlow	H	W	4-1
22 Feb	2nd Batt Scots Guards	H	W	3-0
5 Apr	Old Westminster (Final)	H	W	3-1

Kent Senior Cup

Date	Opponent			Score
12 Oct	5th Northern Fusilliers	H	W	6-1
9 Nov	West Kent	H	W	10-1
14 Dec	Gravesend	H	W	7-0
15 Feb	Chatham	H	W	5-0
22 Mar	Thanet W (Final)		W	3-0

Six-a-Side Competition

Run by National Physical Recreation
Society at Agricultural Hall

Date	Opponent			Score
31 May	London Caledonians		W	15-7

	P	W	L	D	F:A
Arsenal	41	31	5	5	158:49

SEASON 1890-1891
FRIENDLIES

Date	Opponent			Score
6 Sep	93rd Highlanders	H	D	1-1
13 Sep	Casuals	H	W	5-4
20 Sep	Ilford	H	W	6-0
27 Sep	London Caledonians	H	W	3-0
4 Oct	Chiswick Park	A	W	4-0
11 Oct	93rd Highlanders	A	W	4-0
18 Oct	Old St Marks	A	W	4-0
25 Oct	St Bartholomews Hospital	H	W	1-0
1 Nov	South Shore (Blackpool)	H	D	2-2
8 Nov	Ilford	A	W	1-2
15 Nov	Clapton	A	L	1-2
22 Nov	Gainsborough Trinity	H	W	2-1
1 Dec	Cambridge Univ	H	W	5-1
6 Dec	Casuals	H	D	0-0
24 Jan	Millwall Athletic	A	W	1-0
26 Jan	Everton		L	0-5
7 Feb	St Bartholomews Hospital	H	W	5-4
14 Mar	Old Harrovians	H	W	5-1
21 Mar	Sheffield U	H	D	1-1
27 Mar	Highland Light Infantry	H	W	3-1
28 Mar	Old Harrovians	H	W	5-0
30 Mar	Heart of Midlothians	H	L	1-5
31 Mar	Nottingham F	H	L	0-5
18 Apr	Clapton	H	W	3-1
25 Apr	Sunderland	H	L	1-3
30 Apr	London Caledonians	H	D	1-1
2 May	1st Highland Light Infantry	H	W	5-1
3 Jan	London Caledonians (abandoned)			

FA Cup

Date	Opponent			Score
17 Jan	Derby Co (1)	H	L	1-2

London Cup

Date	Opponent			Score
13 Dec	Old Westminster	A	W	4-1
31 Jan	Old Westminster	A	L	4-5
21 Feb	Casuals	H	W	3-2
28 Feb	Clapton	A	W	3-2
7 Mar	St Barts Hosp (Final)	H	W	6-0

London Charity Cup

Date	Opponent			Score
14 Feb	Crusaders	H	W	1-0
4 Apr	Old Carthusians	A	D	1-1
8 Apr	Old Carthusians	A	D	2-2
11 Apr	Old Carthusians	A	L	1-2

	P	W	L	D	F:A
Arsenal	37	22	6	7	98:58

SEASON 1891-1892
FRIENDLIES

Date	Opponent			Score
5 Sep	Sheffield U	H	L	0-2
12 Sep	Casuals	H	W	2-1
19 Sep	Gainsborough Trinity	H	L	1-4
26 Sep	W B A	H	D	1-1
3 Oct	St George Birmingham	H	L	1-5
8 Oct	Royal Engineers	H	W	8-0
10 Oct	Crusaders	H	W	4-1
17 Oct	Bootle	A	D	2-2
19 Oct	Sheffield Wed	H	L	1-8
24 Oct	Long Eaton Rangers	H	W	3-1
29 Oct	Royal Artillery	H	W	10-0
31 Oct	Clapton	A	W	7-0
5 Nov	Notts Co	A	L	3-4
7 Nov	London Caledonians	A	W	4-3
12 Nov	Erith	H	W	7-0
14 Nov	Cambridge University	H	W	5-1
19 Nov	Woolwich League	H	W	6-1
21 Nov	St Bartholomews Hospital	H	W	9-0
23 Nov	2nd Scots Guards	H	W	6-0
28 Nov	Canadians	H	D	1-1
30 Nov	Sheffield W	A	L	1-5
3 Dec	Canadians	H	W	4-0
5 Dec	Lincoln C	H	W	3-1
10 Dec	2nd Royal West Kent Reg	H	L	1-2
12 Dec	Chiswick Park	H	W	5-1
19 Dec	Preston N E	H	L	0-3
25 Dec	Sheffield U	A	D	3-3
26 Dec	1st Lincolnshire Reg	H	W	6-0
2 Jan	Cowlairs (Glasgow)	H	L	1-2
7 Jan	City Ramblers	H	W	3-0
9 Jan	Crusaders	H	W	4-1
21 Jan	Windsor Phoenix	H	W	3-1
23 Jan	Grimsby T	A	D	3-3
30 Jan	Burton W	H	W	3-1
4 Feb	Sheffield U	H	L	1-4
13 Feb	Chatham	H	W	3-2
20 Feb	Burton Swifts	H	W	3-1
25 Feb	Windsor Phoenix	A	W	5-0
27 Feb	Derby Co	H	L	3-4
3 Mar	Borough Road College	H	W	5-1
5 Mar	Wolverhampton W	H	L	1-4
10 Mar	Casuals	H	W	3-1
12 Mar	Marlow	A	W	5-2
14 Mar	3rd Lanark Rovers	H	L	0-1
19 Mar	Highland Light Infantry	H	W	3-2
22 Mar	Preston N E	H	D	3-3
26 Mar	Everton	H	D	2-2
31 Mar	Notts Co	H	L	2-4
2 Apr	Chatham	H	W	5-3
9 Apr	South Shore Blackpool	H	D	1-1
15 Apr	Small Heath	H	W	2-1
16 Apr	Crewe Alexandra	H	W	2-1
18 Apr	Bootle	H	D	1-1
23 Apr	Corinthians	H	W	4-1
26 Apr	Bolton W	H	W	3-2
30 Apr	Glasgow Ran	H	L	2-3

FA Cup

Date	Opponent			Score
16 Jan	Small Heath (1)		L	1-5

	P	W	L	D	F:A
Arsenal	58	33	17	8	183:107

SEASON 1892-1893
FRIENDLIES

Date	Opponent			Score
2 Sep	Highland Light Infantry		W	9-0
7 Sep	Gainsborough T		W	4-2
8 Sep	Scots Guards		W	5-1
10 Sep	Casuals		W	4-0
12 Sep	Sheffield U	A	L	0-1
16 Sep	Darlington		W	3-2
24 Sep	Crusaders		W	4-0
1 Oct	Marlow		W	3-0
6 Oct	3rd West Kent Rangers		W	3-0
8 Oct	Clapton		W	4-1
20 Oct	Sheffield U	H	W	1-0
22 Oct	Staffordshire Reg	H	L	0-4
27 Oct	Oxford University	A	L	0-4
5 Nov	Lincoln C	H	W	4-0
7 Oct	Fleetwood Rangers		L	1-2
12 Nov	Cambridge University		D	6-6
14 Nov	Sunderland	H	L	0-4
23 Nov	Ipswich T		W	5-0
26 Nov	Clapton		W	5-0
3 Dec	W B A	H	W	3-1
12 Dec	Mr Armitage XI		W	4-1
17 Dec	Nottingham F	H	L	2-3
23 Dec	Leith Athletic	H	W	1-0
25 Dec	Burslem P V		L	1-3
26 Dec	Stockton		W	1-0
27 Dec	Blackpool	H	D	1-1
2 Jan	Glasgow Thistle		L	1-2
7 Jan	Middlesbrough		L	0-2
11 Jan	Sussex Martelos		W	2-0
12 Jan	Brighton		W	2-0
14 Jan	Wolverhampton W	H	L	1-3
25 Jan	Oxford University	A	L	0-1
28 Jan	Chatham		L	1-3
31 Jan	1st Batt Sherwood Foresters		W	3-0
3 Feb	Casuals		W	4-1
6 Feb	Royal Lancaster Regiment		W	2-0
9 Feb	Cambridge University		L	2-4
11 Feb	Small Heath	H	W	3-1
13 Feb	Millwall		W	5-0
25 Feb	Notts Greenhalgh		W	4-0
27 Feb	Notts Co		L	1-3
3 Mar	Middlesbrough		L	0-2
11 Mar	Dumbarton		W	3-1
13 Mar	Aston Villa	H	L	0-1
18 Mar	Middlesbrough		W	4-2
25 Mar	Millwall		W	1-0
31 Mar	Middlesbrough		W	4-1
1 Apr	Accrington St	H	W	3-1
3 Apr	Grimsby T	H	L	3-5
8 Apr	Casuals		W	2-0
15 Apr	Crusaders		W	3-0
22 Apr	Derby Co	H	D	0-0
24 Apr	London Welsh		W	11-0
26 Apr	Sevenoaks		W	11-0
29 Apr	Stoke	H	L	0-1

FA Cup

Date	Opponent			Score
15 Oct	Highland Light Infantry (Q1)	H	W	3-0
29 Oct	City Ramblers (Q2)	H	W	10-1
19 Nov	Millwall (Q3)	H	W	3-2
10 Dec	Clapton (Q4)	H	W	5-0
21 Jan	Sunderland (1)	A	L	0-1

	P	W	L	D	F:A
Arsenal	62	41	18	3	172:76

SEASON 1893-1894
FOOTBALL LEAGUE (DIVISION 2)

Date	Opponent			Score
2 Sep	Newcastle U	H	D	2-2
9 Sep	Notts Co	A	L	2-3
11 Sep	Walsall	H	W	4-0
25 Sep	Grimsby T	H	W	3-1
30 Sep	Newcastle U	A	L	0-6
21 Oct	Small Heath	A	L	1-4
28 Oct	Liverpool	H	L	0-5
11 Nov	Aldwick		W	3-1
13 Nov	Rotherham	H	W	3-0
18 Nov	Burton Swifts	A	L	2-6
9 Dec	Northwich Victoria	A	D	2-2
25 Dec	Burslem	H	W	4-1
26 Dec	Grimsby T	H	W	1-0
30 Dec	Ardwick	A	W	1-0
1 Jan	Liverpool	A	L	0-5
6 Jan	Burslem	A	L	1-2
3 Feb	Lincoln C	A	L	0-3
6 Feb	Rotherham	A	D	1-1
10 Feb	Crewe Alexandra	H	W	3-2
12 Feb	Walsall	A	W	1-0
17 Feb	Lincoln C	H	W	4-0
24 Feb	Middlesbrough Ironopolis	A	W	6-3
3 Mar	Crewe Alexandra	A	D	0-0
10 Mar	Middlesbrough Ironopolis	H	W	0-0
23 Mar	Northwich Victoria	A	W	1-0
24 Mar	Notts Co	H	L	1-2
31 Mar	Small Heath	H	L	1-4
14 Apr	Burton Swifts	H	L	0-5

FA Cup

Date	Opponent			Score
14 Oct	Ashford University (Q1)	H	W	12-0
4 Nov	Clapton (Q2)	H	W	6-2
25 Nov	Millwall (Q3)	H	W	2-0
16 Dec	2nd Scots Guards (Q4)	A	W	2-1
27 Jan	Sheffield W (1)	H	L	1-2

Friendlies

4 Sep	Doncaster Rov		W	4-1
16 Sep	Charlton		W	5-0
23 Sep	Middlesbrough	H	W	3-1
7 Oct	Casuals		W	5-1
9 Oct	Sunderland	H	L	1-4
12 Oct	London Caledonians		W	10-3
23 Oct	Mr Roston Bourkes XI		W	4-3
30 Oct	Wolverhampton W		W	2-0
30 Nov	London Caledonians		D	1-1
2 Dec	W B A		D	1-1
11 Dec	Preston N E		D	1-1
23 Dec	Crusaders		W	7-0
13 Jan	Accrington Stanley		W	1-3
15 Jan	Aston Villa	H	L	1-3
20 Jan	Chatham		W	4-0
29 Jan	Blackpool		W	5-2
1 Mar	London Caledonians		W	1-0
5 Mar	Luton T	A	W	2-0
12 Mar	Sheffield U	A	W	2-0
17 Mar	Millwall		D	2-2
26 Mar	St Mirren		L	1-3
2 Apr	Nottingham F	H	L	1-3
7 Apr	Millwall		W	4-1
9 Apr	Sheffield U	H	L	0-1
11 Apr	New Brompton		W	4-1
12 Apr	Westerham District XI		W	3-1
16 Apr	Luton T		D	3-3
21 Apr	Burnley		W	2-0
25 Apr	Corinthians	A	L	3-4
28 Apr	Stoke	H	D	3-3

Position in Football League Table

	P	W	L	D	F:A	Pts	
Liverpool	28	22	0	6	77:18	50	1st
Arsenal	28	12	12	4	52:55	28	9th

SEASON 1894-1895
FOOTBALL LEAGUE (DIVISION 2)

Date	Opponent			Score
1 Sep	Lincoln C	A	L	2-5
10 Sep	Grimsby T	H	L	1-3
15 Sep	Burton Swifts	A	L	0-3
22 Sep	Bury	H	W	4-2
29 Sep	Manchester C	H	W	4-2
6 Oct	Lincoln C	H	W	5-2
13 Oct	Newton Heath	A	D	3-3
20 Oct	Rotherham	A	W	2-2
27 Oct	Notts Co	H	W	2-1
3 Nov	Notts Co	A	L	1-4
10 Nov	Walsall	A	L	1-4
24 Nov	Newcastle U	A	W	4-2
8 Dec	Darwen	H	W	4-0
15 Dec	Manchester C	A	L	1-4
25 Dec	Burslem Port Vale	A	L	2-4
26 Dec	Grimsby T	A	L	2-4
1 Jan	Darwen	A	L	1-3
7 Jan	Leicester Fosse	A	L	1-3
12 Jan	Newcastle U	H	W	3-2
19 Jan	Burslem P V	H	W	1-0
26 Jan	Burton Wanderers	H	D	1-1
9 Feb	Rotherham	H	D	1-1
23 Feb	Burton Swifts	H	W	3-0
2 Mar	Bury	A	L	0-3
9 Mar	Leicester Fosse	H	D	3-3
23 Mar	Crewe Alexandra	H	W	7-0
30 Mar	Newton Heath	H	W	3-0
6 Apr	Crewe Alexandra	H	W	7-0
12 Apr	Walsall	H	W	6-1
20 Apr	Burton W	A	L	1-2

FA Cup

Date	Opponent			Score
2 Feb	Bolton W (1)	A	L	0-1

Friendlies

Date	Opponent			Score
3 Sep	Nottingham F	H	W	3-2
8 Sep	Fleetwood Rovers		W	4-0
17 Sep	W B A		L	0-1
24 Sep	Renton		W	6-1
4 Oct	Casuals		W	8-0
15 Oct	Sunderland	H	W	2-1
29 Oct	Luton T		W	5-0
12 Nov	R. Bourkes XI		W	6-2
17 Nov	Casuals		W	4-1
21 Nov	Marlow		W	4-2
1 Dec	Stoke C	H	W	3-1
3 Dec	St Bernards	H	L	1-2
24 Dec	New Brompton		L	0-5
29 Dec	Dresden University		W	6-1
5 Jan	Sheppey University		W	6-1
11 Feb	Luton T		W	2-1
16 Feb	Chatham		W	6-0
25 Feb	Liverpool		W	4-0
6 Mar	Eastbourne		W	5-1
13 Mar	Bromley & District		W	7-0
16 Mar	Gainsborough Trinity	H	W	2-0
20 Mar	Home Park Plymouth		W	2-1
21 Mar	Weymouth		W	5-0
25 Mar	Millwall	H	D	1-1
1 Apr	Blackburn Rov	H	D	2-2
8 Apr	Millwall	A	D	0-0
13 Apr	Dumbarton		W	5-1
15 Apr	Small Heath	H	L	3-4
25 Apr	Royal Ordnance		L	0-1
27 Apr	Millwall	A	W	3-1
30 Apr	Grimsby T		L	0-2

Position in Football League Table

	P	W	L	D	F:A	Pts	
Bury	30	23	5	2	78:33	48	1st
Arsenal	30	14	10	6	75:58	34	8th

SEASON 1895-1896
FOOTBALL LEAGUE (DIVISION 2)

Date	Opponent			Score
2 Sep	Grimsby T	H	W	3-1
7 Sep	Manchester C	H	L	0-1
14 Sep	Lincoln C	A	D	1-1
21 Sep	Lincoln C	H	W	4-0
28 Sep	Manchester C	A	L	0-1
5 Oct	Rotherham	H	W	5-0
12 Oct	Burton W	H	W	3-0
19 Oct	Burton Swifts	H	W	5-0
26 Oct	Rotherham	A	L	0-3
2 Oct	Notts Co	A	W	4-3
9 Nov	Newton Heath	H	W	2-1
16 Nov	Liverpool	H	L	0-2
30 Nov	Newton Heath	A	L	1-5
7 Dec	Leicester Fosse	H	D	1-1
14 Dec	Burton W	H	W	3-0
21 Dec	Burton Swifts	A	L	2-3
23 Dec	Crewe Alexandra	A	W	1-0
25 Dec	Burslem Port Vale	H	W	6-0
4 Jan	Loughborough	H	W	6-0
11 Jan	Liverpool	A	L	0-3
18 Jan	Newcastle U	A	L	0-1
25 Jan	Leicester Fosse	A	L	0-1
15 Feb	Burslem Port Vale	A	W	1-0
29 Feb	Loughborough	A	L	1-2
7 Mar	Notts Co	H	W	3-0
14 Mar	Darwen	A	D	1-1
21 Mar	Crewe Alexandra	H	W	7-0
4 Mar	Grimsby T	A	D	1-1
7 Mar	Newcastle U	H	L	1-3
18 Apr	Darwen	H	L	1-3

FA Cup

Date	Opponent			Score
2 Feb	Burnley (1)	A	L	1-6

Friendlies

9 Sep	Millwall	A	W	3-1
23 Sep	Sheffield W	H	W	2-1
14 Oct	Everton	H	L	0-2
4 Nov	Royal Ordnance		W	3-1
21 Nov	Casuals		W	3-0
23 Nov	Barnsley St Peters		W	4-1
9 Dec	Sunderland	H	L	1-2
26 Dec	Cliftonville	H	W	10-1
28 Dec	Darlington		W	6-2
1 Jan	Hastings		W	12-0
20 Jan	Cambridge University	A	W	3-0
10 Feb	Royal Ordnance		W	3-0
22 Feb	Stirlingshire		W	5-0
24 Feb	Newton Heath		W	6-1
2 Mar	Casuals		L	1-3
16 Mar	Tottenham H		L	1-3
23 Mar	Sheffield U	H	W	3-1
26 Mar	Tottenham H	H	W	3-1
28 Mar	Millwall	H	L	1-3
2 Apr	Stockton		W	2-0
3 Apr	Dundee		W	3-1
7 Apr	Gravesend		W	4-0
11 Apr	Millwall	H	D	2-2
13 Apr	Everton	A	W	3-1
20 Apr	Whittaker XI		W	3-1
25 Apr	Luton T	H	W	5-2
27 Apr	Luton T	A	L	0-2
29 Apr	Chatham		W	1-0
30 Apr	Tottenham H		L	2-3

Position in Football League Table

	P	W	L	D	F:A	Pts	
Liverpool	30	22	6	2	108:32	46	1st
Arsenal	30	14	12	4	59:42	32	7th

SEASON 1896-1897
FOOTBALL LEAGUE (DIVISION 2)

Date	Opponent			Score
5 Sep	Manchester C	A	D	1-1
12 Sep	Walsall	H	D	1-1
14 Sep	Burton Wanderers	A	W	3-0
19 Sep	Loughborough	H	W	2-0
26 Sep	Notts Co	H	L	2-3
12 Oct	Burton Wanderers	H	W	3-0
17 Oct	Walsall	A	L	3-5
24 Oct	Gainsborough	H	W	6-1
7 Nov	Notts Co	A	L	4-7
14 Nov	Small Heath	A	W	4-2
28 Nov	Grimsby T	H	W	4-2
5 Dec	Lincoln C	A	W	3-2
12 Dec	Loughborough	A	L	0-8
19 Dec	Blackpool	H	W	4-2
25 Dec	Lincoln C	H	W	4-0
26 Dec	Gainsborough	A	L	1-4
1 Jan	Darwen	A	D	1-1
4 Jan	Blackpool	A	D	1-1
23 Jan	Newcastle U	A	L	0-2
13 Feb	Leicester Fosse	A	L	3-6
20 Feb	Burton Swifts	H	W	3-0
13 Mar	Burton Swifts	A	W	2-1
22 Mar	Newton Heath	A	D	1-1
29 Mar	Small Heath	H	L	0-2
3 Apr	Newton Heath	H	L	0-2
8 Apr	Grimsby T	A	L	1-3
16 Apr	Newcastle U	H	W	5-1
17 Apr	Leicester Fosse	H	W	1-0
19 Apr	Darwen	H	W	1-0
28 Apr	Manchester C	H	L	1-2

Abbreviations:

Appearances (goals)
refer to League games only

Figures shown as '2' etc.
refer to goals scored by
individual players

* own-goal

FA Cup
12 Dec Leyton (Q) — H W 5-2
2 Jan Chatham (Q) — H W 4-0
16 Jan Millwall (Q) — A L 2-4

United League
7 Sep Rushden — W 3-2
3 Oct Luton T — D 2-2
5 Oct Rushden — L 3-5
19 Oct Wellingborough — W 2-1
2 Nov Kettering — D 1-1
9 Nov Tottenham H — W 2-1
23 Nov Kettering — W 1-0
30 Nov Wellingbrough — W 1-4
9 Jan Loughborough — W 5-3
25 Jan Tottenham H — D 2-2
27 Feb Millwall — W 3-1
20 Mar Luton T — L 2-5
7 Apr Loughborough — L 0-4
24 Apr Millwall — L 1-3

Friendlies
1 Sep Rossendale — W 4-0
10 Sep Millwall — W 2-1
10 Oct Millwall — L 1-5
26 Oct Luton — L 1-3
31 Oct Clyde — W 3-0
21 Nov Millwall — D 2-2
7 Dec Aston Villa — L 1-3
30 Jan Ilkeston — W 7-0
8 Feb Luton — W 5-1
15 Feb Celtic — L 4-5
1 Mar Reading — W 6-2
6 Mar Casuals — L 3-5
10 Mar Reading — W 2-1
15 Mar St Mary's, Southampton — L 1-3
27 Mar Nottingham F — L 1-2
20 Apr Norfolk — L 3-4
28 Apr Sheffield U — D 1-1

Position in Football League Table

	P	W	L	D	F:A	Pts	
Notts Co	30	19	7	4	92:43	42	1st
Arsenal	30	13	13	4	68:70	30	10th

Position in United League Table

	P	W	L	D	F:A	Pts	
Millwall	14	11	2	1	43:22	23	1st
Arsenal	14	6	5	3	28:34	15	3rd

SEASON 1897-1898
FOOTBALL LEAGUE (DIVISION 2)

1 Sep Grimsby T — H W 4-1
4 Sep Newcastle U — A L 1-4
6 Sep Burnley — A L 0-5
11 Sep Lincoln C — H D 2-2
18 Sep Gainsborough — H W 4-0
25 Sep Manchester C — A L 1-4
2 Oct Luton T — A W 3-0
9 Oct Luton T — H W 3-0
16 Oct Newcastle U — H D 0-0
23 Oct Leicester Fosse — H L 0-3
6 Nov Walsall — A L 1-2
13 Nov Walsall — H W 4-0
27 Nov Blackpool — H W 3-0
4 Dec Leicester Fosse — A L 1-2
18 Dec Loughborough — A W 3-2
27 Dec Lincoln C — A W 3-2
1 Jan Blackpool — A D 3-3
8 Jan Newton Heath — H W 5-1
15 Jan Burton Swifts — A W 2-1
5 Feb Manchester C — H D 2-2
12 Feb Grimsby T — A W 4-1
26 Feb Newton Heath — A L 1-5
5 Mar Small Heath — H W 4-2
12 Mar Darwen — H W 4-1
19 Mar Loughborough — H W 4-0
26 Mar Gainsbrough — A L 0-1
2 Apr Burnley — H D 1-1
9 Apr Darwen — A L 1-3
11 Apr Burton Swifts — H W 3-0
23 Apr Small Heath — A L 1-2

FA Cup
30 Oct St Albans (Q) — H W 9-0
20 Nov Sheppey United (Q) — H W 3-0
11 Dec New Brompton (Q) — H W 4-2
29 Jan Burnley (Q) — A L 1-3

United League
22 Sep Loughborough — A W 3-1
4 Oct Kettering — H W 4-0
11 Oct Wellingborough — A W 3-2
13 Dec Rushden — H W 3-0
20 Dec Southampton — H D 1-1
25 Dec Tottenham H — H L 2-3
10 Jan Wellingborough — H W 3-1
22 Jan Millwall — A D 2-2
19 Feb Millwall — H D 2-2
21 Feb Luton T — H D 2-2
28 Mar Rushden — A W 3-2
1 Apr Loughborough — H W 4-1
4 Apr Kettering — A W 2-0
8 Apr Tottenham H — A D 0-0
13 Apr Southampton — A L 0-1
16 Apr Luton T — A L 1-2

Friendlies
15 Sep Gravesend — A W 3-1
1 Nov Reading — H W 3-1
8 Nov Blackburn Rov — H W 3-0
15 Nov Bristol C — A L 2-4
9 Feb Maidstone — A W 3-1
21 Mar Bristol C — H W 3-1
26 Apr Thames Iron Works — A D 2-2
27 Mar Tottenham H — H W 5-0
30 Apr Millwall — A L 0-2

Position in Football League Table

	P	W	L	D	F:A	Pts	
Burnley	30	20	2	8	80:24	48	1st
Arsenal	30	16	9	5	69:49	37	5th

Position in United League Table

	P	W	L	D	F:A	Pts	
Luton	16	13	1	2	49:11	28	1st
Arsenal	16	8	3	5	35:24	21	3rd

SEASON 1898-1899
FOOTBALL LEAGUE (DIVISION 2)

3 Sep Luton T — A W 1-0
5 Sep Burslem PV — H L 0-3
10 Sep Leicester Fosse — H W 4-0
17 Sep Darwen — H W 4-1
24 Sep Gainsborough — H W 5-1
1 Oct Manchester C — A L 1-3
15 Oct Walsall — A L 1-4
22 Oct Burton Swifts — H W 2-1
5 Nov Small Heath — H W 2-0
12 Nov Loughborough — A W 1-0
26 Nov Grimsby T — A L 0-1
3 Dec Newton Heath — H W 5-1
10 Dec New Brighton — A L 1-3
17 Dec Lincoln C — A L 1-2
24 Dec Barnsley — A L 1-2
31 Dec Luton T — H W 6-2
7 Jan Leicester Fosse — A L 1-2
14 Jan Darwen — H W 6-0
21 Jan Gainsborough — A W 1-0
4 Feb Glossop — A D 0-2
11 Feb Walsall — H D 0-0
13 Feb Glossop — H W 3-0
18 Feb Burton Swifts — A W 2-1
25 Feb Burslem PV — H W 1-0
4 Mar Small Heath — A L 1-4
13 Mar Loughborough — H W 3-1
18 Mar Blackpool — H W 6-0
22 Mar Blackpool — A D 1-1
25 Mar Grimsby T — H D 1-1
1 Apr Newton Heath — A D 2-2
3 Apr Manchester C — H L 0-1
8 Apr New Brighton — H W 4-0
15 Apr Lincoln C — A L 0-2
22 Apr Barnsley — H W 3-0

FA Cup
28 Jan Derby Co (1) — H L 0-6

Chatham Charity Cup
18 Jan Chatham — A D 1-1
20 Feb Chatham — H D 3-3
6 Mar Chatham — A L 1-2

United League
14 Sep Reading — A D 1-1
3 Oct Reading — H W 2-0
8 Oct Millwall — A D 1-1
10 Oct Luton T — H W 3-2
17 Oct Rushden — H W 2-0
24 Oct Kettering — A L 1-2
29 Oct Southampton — A L 1-5
31 Oct Brighton & HA — H W 5-2
9 Nov Bristol C — A W 2-1
14 Nov Wellingborough — A L 0-3
19 Nov Southampton — H W 2-1
21 Nov Rushden — A W 6-0
12 Dec Bristol C — H L 1-3
26 Dec Millwall — H L 1-3
27 Dec Luton T — A D 1-1
4 Jan Brighton & HA — H W 4-1
6 Feb Kettering — H W 4-2
11 Mar Tottenham H — H W 2-1
31 Mar Wellingborough — H W 3-0
29 Apr Tottenham H — A L 2-1

Friendlies
1 Sep Gravesend — H L 0-1
19 Sep Thames Iron Works — H W 4-0
25 Oct Gravesend — W 1-0
23 Nov Corinthians — A L 1-4
28 Nov Chatham — A L 1-3
8 Dec Thames Iron Works — A W 2-1
25 Jan Sevenoaks — A W 7-1
30 Jan Millwall — H L 2-4
15 Feb Gravesend — A W 2-3
23 Feb Clapton — A W 3-0
9 Mar Casuals — A W 4-0
23 Mar Past XI v Present XI — Present won 3-1
4 Apr Millwall — A D 0-0
24 Apr Notts Co — H W 2-1
26 Apr Woolwich Locals — W 3-0

Position in Football League Table

	P	W	L	D	F:A	Pts	
Manchester C	34	23	5	6	92:35	52	1st
Arsenal	34	18	11	5	72:41	41	7th

Position in United League Table

	P	W	L	D	F:A	Pts	
Millwall	20	14	3	3	42:19	31	1st
Arsenal	20	10	6	4	40:30	24	4th

SEASON 1899-1900
FOOTBALL LEAGUE (DIVISION 2)

2 Sep Leicester Fosse — H L 1-2
9 Sep Luton T — A W 2-1
16 Sep Burslem PV — H W 1-0
23 Sep Walsall — A L 0-2
30 Sep Middlesbrough — H W 3-0
7 Oct Chesterfield — A L 1-3
14 Oct Gainsborough — H W 2-1
21 Oct Bolton W — A L 0-1
4 Nov Newton Heath — A L 0-2
11 Nov Sheffield Wed — H L 1-2
25 Nov Small Heath — H W 2-0
2 Dec New Brighton — H D 1-1
16 Dec Burton Swifts — H D 1-1
23 Dec Lincoln C — A L 0-5
30 Dec Leicester Fosse — A D 0-0
6 Jan Luton T — H W 3-1
13 Jan Burslem PV — A D 1-1
20 Jan Walsall — H W 3-1
3 Feb Middlesbrough — A L 0-1
10 Feb Chesterfield — H W 2-0
17 Feb Gainsborough — A D 1-1
24 Feb Bolton W — H L 0-1
3 Mar Loughborough — A W 3-2
10 Mar Newton Heath — H W 2-1
12 Mar Loughborough — H W 12-0
17 Mar Sheffield Wed — A L 1-3
24 Mar Lincoln C — H W 2-1
31 Mar Small Heath — A I 1-1
7 Apr New Brighton — H W 5-0
14 Apr Grimsby T — A L 0-1
16 Apr Grimsby T — H W 2-0
21 Apr Burton Swifts — A L 0-1
23 Apr Barnsley — A L 2-3
28 Apr Barnsley — H W 5-1

FA Cup
28 Oct New Brompton (Q) — H D 1-1
1 Nov New Brompton (QR) — A D 0-0
6 Nov New Brompton (QR) — A D 2-2
8 Nov New Brompton (QR) — A D 1-1
14 Nov New Brompton (QR) — A L 0-1

Southern District Combination
11 Sep Millwall — L 0-2
27 Sep Reading — W 3-0
11 Oct Southampton — L 0-3
23 Oct Portsmouth — L 0-1
30 Oct Bristol C — W 3-0
10 Jan Bristol C — W 3-1
29 Jan Chatham — W 4-0
7 Feb Portsmouth — L 1-3
26 Feb Chatham — W 2-1
5 Mar Southampton — W 2-1
19 Mar Q P R — W 5-1
26 Mar Reading — L 0-1
2 Apr Millwall — L 0-1
9 Apr Q P R — L 0-1
17 Apr Tottenham H — L 2-4
24 Apr Tottenham H — W 2-1*
*unfinished

Friendlies
4 Sep Stoke — W 5-3
2 Oct Aston Villa — W 1-0
29 Nov Eastbourne — W 2-1
9 Dec Southampton — D 1-1
23 Dec Swindon T — W 2-1
27 Jan Bedminster — W 3-0
19 Feb Derby Co — L 0-1
13 Apr Burnley — W 2-0

Position in Football League Table

	P	W	L	D	F:A	Pts	
Sheffield Wed	34	25	5	4	84:22	54	1st
Arsenal	34	16	14	4	61:43	36	8th

Position in Southern District Combination League

	P	W	L	D	F:A	Pts	
Millwall	16	12	2	2	30:10	26	1st
Arsenal	15	7	7	1	61:21	15	4th

(Exclusive of match unfinished 24 April, against Tottenham H, Arsenal leading 2-1)

SEASON 1900-1901
FOOTBALL LEAGUE (DIVISION 2)

1 Sep Gainsborough — H W 2-1
8 Sep Walsall — H D 1-1
15 Sep Burton Swifts — A L 0-1
22 Sep Barnsley — H L 1-2
29 Sep Chesterfield — A D 1-1
6 Oct Blackpool — A D 1-1
13 Oct Stockport Co — H W 2-0
20 Oct Small Heath — A L 1-2
27 Oct Grimsby — H D 1-1
3 Nov Leicester — H W 2-1
10 Nov Newton Heath — H W 2-1
17 Nov Glossop — A W 1-0
24 Nov Middlesbrough — H W 1-0
1 Dec Burnley — A L 0-3
8 Dec Burslem PV — H W 3-0
15 Dec Leicester — A L 0-1
22 Dec New Brighton — H W 2-1
24 Dec Walsall — A L 0-1
29 Dec Gainsborough — A L 0-1
12 Jan Burton Swifts — H W 3-1
19 Jan Barnsley — A L 0-3
26 Jan Lincoln C — A D 3-3
16 Feb Stockport Co — A L 1-3
19 Feb Chesterfield — A W 1-0
2 Mar Grimsby T — A L 0-1
9 Mar Lincoln C — H D 0-0
16 Mar Newton Heath — A D 0-0
23 Mar Glossop — H W 2-0
30 Mar Middlesbrough — A D 1-1
6 Apr Burnley — H W 3-1
8 Apr Blackpool — H W 3-1
13 Apr Burslem PV — A L 0-1
22 Apr Small Heath — H W 1-0
27 Apr New Brighton — A L 0-1

FA Cup
5 Jan Darwen (Q) — A W 2-0
9 Feb Blackburn Rov (1) — H W 2-0
23 Feb W B A (2) — H L 0-1

Friendlies
1 Oct Aston Villa — H W 3-0
21 Nov Southampton — L 1-4
25 Dec West Ham U — A L 0-1
26 Dec Newcastle U — H D 1-1
1 Jan Newcastle U — L 1-5
4 Mar Southern League XI — H W 3-0
1 Apr Millwall — D 1-1
1 Apr Nottingham F — W 1-0
5 Apr Notts Co — H W 3-0
20 Apr West Ham U — D 0-0

Position in Football League Table

	P	W	L	D	F:A	Pts	
Grimsby T	34	20	5	9	60:33	49	1st
Arsenal	34	15	13	6	39:35	36	7th

SEASON 1901-1902
FOOTBALL LEAGUE (DIVISION 2)

2 Sep Barnsley — H W 2-1
4 Sep Leicester — H W 2-0
14 Sep Preston NE — A L 0-2
21 Sep Burnley — H W 4-0
28 Sep Burslem PV — A L 0-1
5 Oct Chesterfield — H W 3-2
12 Oct Gainsborough — A D 2-2
19 Oct Middlesbrough — H L 0-3
26 Oct Bristol C — A W 3-0
9 Nov Stockport Co — A D 0-0
16 Nov Newton Heath — H W 2-0
23 Nov Glossop — A W 1-0
30 Nov Doncaster Rov — H W 1-0
7 Dec Lincoln C — A D 0-0
21 Dec Burton Un — H L 0-1
25 Dec Blackpool — H D 0-0
26 Dec Burslem PV — H W 3-1
28 Dec Barnsley — A L 0-2
4 Jan Leicester — A L 1-2
11 Jan Preston NE — H D 0-0
18 Jan Burnley — A D 0-0
1 Feb Chesterfield — A W 3-1
8 Feb Gainsborough — H W 5-0
15 Feb Middlesbrough — A L 0-1
22 Feb Bristol C — H W 2-0
1 Mar Blackpool — A W 3-1
8 Mar Stockport Co — A W 1-0
15 Mar Newton Heath — A W 1-0
22 Mar Glossop — H W 1-0
29 Mar Doncaster Rov — A L 0-1
31 Mar W B A — H W 2-1
5 Apr Lincoln C — H W 2-0
12 Apr W B A — A L 1-3
19 Apr Burton Un — A L 0-1

FA Cup
14 Dec Luton T (Q) — H D 1-1
18 Dec Luton T (QR) — A W 2-0
25 Jan Newcastle U (1) — H L 0-2

Southern Charity Cup
7 Apr Portsmouth — A W 2-1
23 Apr Tottenham H (Semi Final) — H D 0-0
29 Apr Tottenham H (Semi Final) — A L 1-2

London League
16 Sep Tottenham H — L 0-2
30 Sep Millwall — D 1-1
21 Oct West Ham U — L 0-1
4 Nov Tottenham H — L 0-5
3 Feb Q P R — D 2-2
17 Feb Q P R — W 3-0
24 Feb Millwall — L 1-2
28 Mar West Ham U — W 2-0

Friendlies
2 Nov Reading — H W 1-0
18 Nov Southampton — H L 0-1
1 Apr Blackburn Rov — H W 2-0
25 Apr Plymouth Arg — A W 4-1
26 Apr W B A — H L 0-1

Position in Football League Table

	P	W	L	D	F:A	Pts	
W B A	34	25	4	5	82:29	55	1st
Arsenal	34	18	10	6	50:26	42	4th

Position in London League Table

	P	W	L	D	F:A	Pts	
West Ham U	8	5	2	1	19:9	11	1st
Arsenal	8	2	4	2	9:13	6	5th

SEASON 1902-1903
FOOTBALL LEAGUE (DIVISION 2)

6 Sep Preston NE — A D 2-2
13 Sep Burslem PV — H W 2-0
20 Sep Barnsley — A D 1-1
27 Sep Gainsborough — H W 6-1
4 Oct Bristol C — A L 0-1
11 Oct Glossop NE — A W 2-1
18 Oct Glossop — H W 2-0
25 Oct Manchester U — H L 0-1
1 Nov Manchester C — H W 1-0
8 Nov Blackpool — H W 2-1
15 Nov Burnley — A W 3-0
22 Nov Doncaster Rov — A W 1-0
29 Nov Lincoln C — H W 2-1
6 Dec Small Heath — A L 1-4
20 Dec Manchester C — A L 1-4
25 Dec Burton Un — A L 1-2
27 Dec Burnley — H W 5-1
1 Jan Stockport Co — H W 2-0
3 Jan Preston NE — A L 0-3 (?)
10 Jan Burslem PV — H W 3-1
17 Jan Barnsley — H W 4-0
24 Jan Gainsborough — A W 1-0
31 Jan Burton Un — H W 1-0
14 Feb Glossop NE — H D 0-0
28 Feb Stockport Co — A D 3-1
7 Mar Blackpool — A L 0-1
9 Mar Manchester U — A L 0-3
14 Mar Chesterfield — H D 2-2
21 Mar Doncaster Rov — H W 2-1
28 Mar Lincoln C — A D 2-2
4 Apr Small Heath — H W 6-1
10 Apr Chesterfield — H W 3-0
11 Apr Leicester — A L 0-3
13 Apr Leicester — H D 0-0

FA Cup
13 Dec Brentford — A D 1-1
17 Dec Brentford (QR) — H W 5-0
7 Feb Sheffield U — H L 1-3

Southern Charity Cup
9 Feb Millwall — H L 2-3

London League
1 Sep West Ham U — A W 3-1
15 Sep Q P R — H W 3-1
27 Oct Q P R — A W 3-0
10 Nov Brentford — H W 3-0
17 Nov Tottenham H — A L 0-1
1 Dec Tottenham H — A L 0-1
26 Dec Millwall — H W 3-0
21 Mar West Ham U — H L 0-1
23 Mar Brentford — A W 1-0
18 Apr Millwall — H L 0-2

Friendlies
8 Sep New Brompton — A W 3-2
18 Mar Brighton & HA — A W 1-1
14 Mar Northampton T — A D 1-1
20 Apr Bristol C — A W 2-1
25 Apr Chesterfield — H W 1-0

Position in Football League Table

	P	W	L	D	F:A	Pts	
Manchester C	34	25	5	4	95:29	54	1st
Arsenal	34	20	6	8	66:30	48	3rd

Position in London League Table

	P	W	L	D	F:A	Pts	
Tottenham H	10	7	2	1	19:4	15	1st
Arsenal	10	6	4	0	14:10	12	3rd

SEASON 1903-1904
FOOTBALL LEAGUE (DIVISION 2)

5 Sep Blackpool — H W 3-0
12 Sep Gainsborough — A W 2-0
19 Sep Burton Un — H W 8-0
26 Sep Bristol C — A W 4-0
3 Oct Manchester U — H W 4-0
10 Oct Glossop — A W 3-1
24 Oct Burslem PV — A W 3-2
26 Oct Leicester — H W 8-0
31 Oct Barnsley — A L 1-2
7 Nov Lincoln C — H W 4-0
21 Nov Chesterfield — H W 6-0
28 Nov Bolton W — H L 1-2
19 Dec Grimsby T — H W 5-1
25 Dec Bradford C — H W 4-1
26 Dec Leicester — A D 0-0
1 Jan Stockport Co — A D 2-2
2 Jan Blackpool — A D 2-2
9 Jan Gainsborough — H W 6-0
16 Jan Burton Un — A L 1-3
30 Jan Manchester U — A L 0-1
27 Feb Barnsley — H W 3-0
29 Feb Burnley — A W 2-0
5 Mar Lincoln C — A W 2-0
12 Mar Stockport Co — H W 5-2
14 Mar Bristol C — A W 2-0
19 Mar Chesterfield — A L 0-1
26 Mar Bolton W — H W 4-0
1 Apr Preston NE — A D 0-0
2 Apr Burnley — H W 2-1
4 Apr Glossop — A W 2-1
9 Apr Preston NE — H W 2-1
16 Apr Grimsby T — A W 2-2
19 Apr Bradford C — A W 3-0
25 Apr Burslem PV — H D 0-0

FA Cup
12 Dec Bristol Rov (Q) — A D 1-1
15 Dec Bristol Rov (QR) — H D 1-1
21 Dec Bristol Rov (QR) — A* W 1-0
6 Feb Fulham (1) — H W 1-0
20 Feb Manchester C (2) — H L 0-2
*at Tottenham

Southern Charity Cup
12 Oct West Ham U — W 1-0
18 Jan Reading (Semi-Final) — W 3-1
28 Apr Millwall (Final) — L 1-2

London League
1 Sep Tottenham H — W 1-0
7 Sep Fulham — W 2-0
14 Sep West Ham U — W 4-1
14 Nov Tottenham H — D 1-1
23 Nov Brentford — D 1-1
7 Dec Millwall — L 1-3
11 Jan Q P R — W 6-2
8 Feb Brentford — W 3-2
22 Feb West Ham U — W 4-2
7 Mar Millwall — L 0-3
21 Mar Q P R — L 1-3
30 Apr Fulham — L 0-1

Friendlies
17 Oct Luton — D 2-2
30 Nov Army — W 4-0

Position in Football League Table

	P	W	L	D	F:A	Pts	
Preston NE	34	20	4	10	62:24	50	1st
Arsenal	34	21	6	7	91:22	49	2nd

Position in London League Table

	P	W	L	D	F:A	Pts	
Millwall	12	11	0	1	38:8	23	1st
Arsenal	12	6	4	2	24:19	14	3rd

SEASON 1904-1905
FOOTBALL LEAGUE (DIVISION 1)

3 Sep Newcastle U — A L 0-3
10 Sep Preston NE — H D 0-0
17 Sep Middlesbrough — A L 0-1

24 Sep Wolverhampton W H W 2-0
1 Oct Bury A D 1-1
8 Oct Aston Villa H W 1-0
15 Oct Blackburn Rov A D 1-1
22 Oct Nottingham F H L 0-3
29 Oct Sheffield Wed A W 3-0
5 Nov Sunderland H D 0-0
12 Nov Stoke H W 2-1
19 Nov Derby Co A D 0-0
3 Dec Small Heath A L 1-1
10 Dec Manchester C H W 1-0
17 Dec Notts Co A W 5-1
24 Dec Sheffield U H W 1-0
26 Dec Aston Villa A L 1-3
27 Dec Nottingham F A W 3-0
28 Dec Sheffield U A L 0-4
31 Dec Newcastle U H L 0-2
7 Jan Preston NE A L 0-3
14 Jan Middlesbrough H D 1-1
21 Jan Wolverhampton W A L 1-4
28 Jan Bury H W 2-1
11 Feb Blackburn Rov H W 2-0
25 Feb Sheffield Wed H W 3-0
4 Mar Sunderland A D 1-1
11 Mar Stoke A L 0-2
18 Mar Derby Co H D 0-0
1 Apr Small Heath H D 1-1
5 Apr Everton A L 0-1
8 Apr Manchester C A L 0-1
15 Apr Notts Co H L 1-2
22 Apr Everton H W 2-1

FA Cup
4 Feb Bristol C (1) H D 0-0
8 Feb Bristol C (1R) A L 0-1

Southern Charity Cup
10 Oct Tottenham H H L 1-3

Friendlies
1 Sep Bristol C H W 3-2
12 Sep West Ham U A D 1-1
31 Oct Cambridge Univ H W 2-0
22 Nov Cambridge Univ A W 4-3
5 Dec French International Team H W 26-1
18 Feb Corinthians A L 1-2
27 Feb Queens Park (Glasgow) H W 6-1
25 Mar Burnley A W 2-0
12 Apr Southend U A W 2-0
21 Apr New Brompton H W 3-0
24 Apr Dundee H W 3-0
26 Apr Ipswich T A W 3-1
27 Apr Norwich C A L 1-2
29 Apr Sheffield U A L 2-3

Position in Football League Table

	P	W	L	D	F:A	Pts	
Newcastle U	34	23	9	2	72:33	48	1st
Arsenal	34	12	13	9	36:40	33	10th

SEASON 1905-1906
FOOTBALL LEAGUE (DIVISION 1)

2 Sep Liverpool H W 3-1
9 Sep Sheffield U A L 1-3
16 Sep Notts Co H D 1-1
18 Sep Preston NE H D 2-2
23 Sep Stoke A L 1-2
30 Sep Bolton W H D 0-0
7 Oct Wolverhampton W A W 2-0
14 Oct Blackburn Rov A L 0-2
21 Oct Sunderland H W 2-0
28 Oct Birmingham A L 1-2
4 Nov Everton H L 1-2
11 Nov Derby Co A L 1-5
18 Nov Sheffield Wed H L 0-3
25 Nov Nottingham F A L 1-3
2 Dec Manchester C H W 2-0
9 Dec Bury A L 0-3
16 Dec Middlesbrough H D 2-2
23 Dec Preston NE A D 2-2
25 Dec Newcastle U H W 4-3
27 Dec Aston Villa A L 0-3
30 Dec Liverpool A L 1-6
1 Jan Bolton W A L 1-6
6 Jan Sheffield U H W 5-1
20 Jan Notts Co A L 0-1
27 Jan Stoke H L 1-2
10 Feb Wolverhampton W H W 2-1
17 Feb Blackburn Rov H W 3-2
3 Mar Birmingham H W 5-0
17 Mar Derby Co A W 1-0
21 Mar Everton A W 1-0
24 Mar Sheffield Wed A L 2-4
2 Apr Nottingham F H W 3-1
7 Apr Manchester C H W 2-1
13 Apr Aston Villa H W 2-1
14 Apr Bury H W 4-0
16 Apr Newcastle U A D 1-1
21 Apr Middlesbrough A L 0-2
25 Apr Sunderland A D 2-2

FA Cup
13 Jan West Ham U (1) H D 1-1
18 Jan West Ham U (1R) A W 3-2
3 Feb Watford (2) H W 3-0
24 Feb Sunderland (3) H W 5-0
10 Mar Manchester U (4) A W 3-2
31 Mar Newcastle U (Semi-final)* L 0-2
*at Stoke

Southern Charity Cup
9 Oct West Ham U H W 3-2
9 Apr Tottenham H A D 0-0
28 Apr Tottenham H H W 5-0
30 Apr Reading (Final) A W 1-0

Friendlies
21 Sep Faversham Rangers A W 9-0
18 Oct Corinthians A L 1-2
30 Oct Oxford Univ H W 3-1
26 Dec Corinthians H D 1-1
15 Jan Cambridge Univ H W 4-2
22 Jan Oxford Univ A W 2-0
18 Apr West Hartlepool A W 4-0

Position in Football League Table

	P	W	L	D	F:A	Pts	
Liverpool	38	23	10	5	79:46	51	1st
Arsenal	38	15	16	7	62:64	37	12th

SEASON 1906-1907
FOOTBALL LEAGUE (DIVISION 1)

1 Sep Manchester C A W 4-1
3 Sep Bury A L 1-4
8 Sep Middlesbrough H W 2-0
15 Sep Preston NE A W 3-0
22 Sep Newcastle U H W 2-0
29 Sep Aston Villa A D 2-2
6 Oct Liverpool H W 2-1
13 Oct Bristol C A W 3-1
20 Oct Notts Co H W 1-0
27 Oct Sheffield U A L 2-4
3 Nov Bolton W H D 2-2
10 Nov Manchester U A L 0-1
17 Nov Stoke H W 2-1
24 Nov Blackburn Rov A W 3-2
1 Dec Sunderland H L 0-1
8 Dec Birmingham A L 1-5
15 Dec Everton H W 3-1
22 Dec Derby Co A D 0-0
26 Dec Bury H W 3-1
29 Dec Manchester C H W 4-1
1 Jan Sheffield Wed A D 1-1
3 Jan Middlesbrough H L 3-5
19 Jan Preston NE H W 1-0
26 Jan Newcastle U A L 0-1
9 Feb Liverpool A L 0-4
16 Feb Bristol City H L 1-2
2 Mar Sheffield U H L 0-1
9 Mar Manchester U A W 4-0
23 Mar Bolton W A L 0-3
28 Mar Sheffield Wed H W 1-0
30 Mar Blackburn Rov H W 2-0
1 Apr Aston Villa H W 3-1
6 Apr Sunderland A W 3-2
10 Apr Everton A L 1-2
13 Apr Birmingham H W 2-1
15 Apr Stoke A L 0-2
17 Apr Notts Co A L 1-4
27 Apr Derby H W 2-1

FA Cup
12 Jan Grimsby T (1) A D 1-1
16 Jan Grimsby T (1R) H W 3-0
2 Feb Bristol C (2) H W 2-1
23 Feb Bristol Rov (3) H W 1-0
9 Mar Barnsley (4) H W 2-1
23 Mar Sheffield Wed (Semi-final)* L 1-3
*at Birmingham

Southern Charity Cup
10 Dec Millwall H L 1-2

Friendlies
12 Sep Reading A W 1-0
19 Sep West Norwood A W 1-0
5 Nov Oxford Univ H W 7-1
19 Nov Clapton Orient A W 3-1
3 Dec Cambridge Univ A W 3-1
25 Dec Celtic H L 0-2
14 Jan Cambridge Univ H W 6-3

On Tour
5 May Racing Club, Brussels W 2-1
7 May The Hague W 6-3
9 May BFC Pressen, Berlin W 9-1
12 May SP Sportorina, Prague W 7-5
16 May Klub Slavia, Prague W 4-2
18 May Combined Vienna Team W 4-2
19 May Magyaren Buda Pesth W 9-0
20 May Buda Pesth D 2-2

Position in Football League Table

	P	W	L	D	F:A	Pts	
Newcastle U	38	22	9	7	74:46	51	1st
Arsenal	38	20	14	4	66:59	44	7th

SEASON 1907-1908
FOOTBALL LEAGUE (DIVISION 1)

2 Sep Notts Co H D 1-1
7 Sep Bristol C H L 0-4
9 Sep Bury A L 2-3
14 Sep Notts Co A L 0-2
21 Sep Manchester C H W 2-1
28 Sep Preston NE A L 0-3
5 Oct Bury H D 0-0
12 Oct Aston Villa A W 1-0
19 Oct Liverpool H W 2-1
26 Oct Middlesbrough A D 0-0
2 Nov Sheffield U H W 5-1
9 Nov Chelsea A L 1-2
16 Nov Nottingham F H W 3-1
23 Nov Manchester U A L 2-4
30 Nov Blackburn Rov A W 2-0
7 Dec Bolton W H L 1-3
14 Dec Birmingham H D 1-1
21 Dec Everton A D 1-1
25 Dec Newcastle U H D 2-2
28 Dec Sunderland H W 4-0
31 Dec Sheffield Wed A L 0-6
1 Jan Sunderland A L 2-5
2 Jan Bristol C A W 2-1
18 Jan Manchester C A L 0-4
25 Jan Preston NE H D 1-1
8 Feb Aston Villa H L 0-1
15 Feb Liverpool H W 1-0
22 Feb Middlesbrough H W 4-1
7 Mar Chelsea H D 0-0
14 Mar Nottingham F A L 0-1
21 Mar Manchester U H W 1-0
28 Mar Blackburn Rov A D 1-1
4 Apr Bolton W H D 1-1

11 Apr Birmingham A W 2-1
17 Apr Newcastle U A L 1-2
18 Apr Everton A L 1-2
20 Apr Sheffield Wed H D 1-1

FA Cup
11 Jan Hull C (1) H D 0-0
16 Jan Hull C (1R) A L 1-4

Southern Charity Cup
23 Sep Reading H L 0-1

Friendlies
16 Sep Barnsley H W 1-0
14 Oct Rest of Kent A W 3-1
26 Dec Liverpool H D 2-2
1 Feb Tottenham H A W 1-0

On Tour
21 Apr Hearts L 1-3
22 Apr Raith Rovers L 0-1
23 Apr Aberdeen L 1-4
25 Apr Dundee L 1-2
27 Apr Motherwell D 1-1
28 Apr Glasgow Rangers D 1-1
29 Apr Greenock Morton L 0-1
30 Apr Kilmarnock W 2-1

Position in Football League Table

	P	W	L	D	F:A	Pts	
Manchester C	38	23	9	6	81:48	52	1st
Arsenal	38	12	14	12	51:63	36	15th

SEASON 1908-1909
FOOTBALL LEAGUE (DIVISION 1)

2 Sep Everton H L 0-4
5 Sep Notts Co A L 1-2
7 Sep Everton A L 1-2
12 Sep Newcastle U H L 1-2
19 Sep Bristol C A L 1-2
26 Sep Preston NE H W 1-0
3 Oct Middlesbrough A D 1-1
10 Oct Manchester C H W 3-0
17 Oct Liverpool A D 2-2
24 Oct Bury H W 4-0
28 Oct Chelsea A W 2-1
31 Oct Sheffield U H D 1-1
7 Nov Aston Villa H L 0-1
14 Nov Nottingham F A L 0-1
21 Nov Sunderland H L 0-4
5 Dec Blackburn Rov H L 0-1
12 Dec Bradford C A L 1-4
19 Dec Manchester U H L 0-1
25 Dec Leicester A D 1-1
26 Dec Leicester H W 2-1
28 Dec Sheffield Wed A L 2-6
2 Jan Notts Co H W 1-0
9 Jan Newcastle U A L 1-3
23 Jan Bristol C H D 1-1
30 Jan Preston NE A D 0-0
13 Feb Manchester C H D 2-2
20 Feb Liverpool H W 5-0
27 Feb Bury A D 1-1
13 Mar Aston Villa H L 1-2
17 Mar Middlesbrough H D 1-1
20 Mar Nottingham F H L 1-2
27 Mar Sunderland A L 0-1
1 Apr Sheffield U A L 0-1
3 Apr Chelsea H D 0-0
10 Apr Blackburn Rov A W 3-1
12 Apr Sheffield Wed H W 2-0
17 Apr Bradford C H W 1-0
27 Apr Manchester U A W 4-1

FA Cup
16 Jan Croydon Common (1)* D 1-1
20 Jan Croydon Common (1R) H W 2-0
6 Feb Millwall (2) H W 1-0
10 Feb Millwall (2R) A L 0-1
*at Crystal Palace

London FA Challenge Cup
28 Sep Fulham A W 1-0
9 Nov Crystal Palace H W 2-1
22 Feb Clapton Orient (Semi-final) A L 1-2

London Professional Charity Fund
7 Dec Chelsea H W 1-0

Friendlies
7 Oct Rest of Kent A W 3-0
22 Oct Ryde A W 3-0
10 Mar Hastings A W 3-0
9 Apr Exeter A L 2-3

Position in Football League Table

	P	W	L	D	F:A	Pts	
Newcastle U	38	24	9	5	65:41	53	1st
Arsenal	38	14	14	10	52:49	38	6th

SEASON 1909-1910
FOOTBALL LEAGUE (DIVISION 1)

1 Sep Aston Villa A L 1-5
4 Sep Sheffield U H D 0-0
11 Sep Middlesbrough A L 2-5
18 Sep Bolton W A L 0-3
25 Sep Chelsea H W 3-2
2 Oct Blackburn Rov A L 0-7
7 Oct Notts Co A L 1-5
9 Oct Nottingham F H L 0-1
16 Oct Sunderland A L 2-6
23 Oct Everton H W 1-0
30 Oct Manchester U A L 0-1
6 Nov Bradford C H L 0-1
13 Nov Sheffield Wed H D 1-1
20 Nov Bristol C H D 2-2
27 Nov Bury A W 2-1
4 Dec Tottenham H H W 1-0
11 Dec Preston NE A W 4-3
18 Dec Notts Co A L 1-2

25 Dec Newcastle U H L 0-3
27 Dec Liverpool H D 1-1
1 Jan Liverpool A L 1-5
8 Jan Sheffield U A L 0-2
22 Jan Middlesbrough H W 3-0
29 Jan Bolton W H W 2-0
12 Feb Blackburn Rov H L 0-1
26 Feb Sunderland A D 1-1
2 Mar Nottingham F A L 0-1
7 Mar Everton A D 0-0
12 Mar Manchester U H D 0-0
19 Mar Bradford C A W 1-0
25 Mar Newcastle U A D 1-1
26 Mar Sheffield Wed H L 0-1
28 Mar Chelsea A W 1-0
2 Apr Bristol C H D 0-0
9 Apr Bury H W 1-0
11 Apr Aston Villa H W 1-0
16 Apr Tottenham H A D 1-1
23 Apr Preston NE H L 1-3

FA Cup
15 Jan Watford (1) H W 3-0
5 Feb Everton (2) A L 0-5

London FA Challenge Cup
20 Sep Bromley H W 4-0
11 Oct West Ham U H L 0-1

London Professional Charity Fund
1 Nov Tottenham H A L 0-3

Foord Flood Relief Fund
25 Nov Shorncliffe Garrison and W 5-2
District XI (at Folkestone)

Friendlies
22 Sep Rest of Kent A W 3-2
19 Feb Fulham H D 2-2
5 Mar Millwall A D 3-3
28 Apr Colchester W 3-2
30 Apr Ilford L 2-3

Position in Football League Table

	P	W	L	D	F:A	Pts	
Aston Villa	38	23	8	7	84:42	53	1st
Arsenal	38	11	18	9	37:67	31	18th

SEASON 1910-1911
FOOTBALL LEAGUE (DIVISION 1)

1 Sep Manchester U H L 1-2
3 Sep Bury A D 1-1
10 Sep Sheffield U H D 0-0
17 Sep Aston Villa A L 0-3
24 Sep Sunderland H D 0-0
1 Oct Oldham Ath H D 0-0
8 Oct Bradford C A L 0-3
15 Oct Blackburn H W 4-1
22 Oct Nottingham F A W 3-2
29 Oct Manchester C H L 0-1
5 Nov Everton A L 0-1
12 Nov Sheffield W H W 1-0
19 Nov Bristol C H L 1-2
26 Nov Newcastle U A L 1-2
3 Dec Tottenham H H W 3-1
10 Dec Middlesbrough H L 0-2
17 Dec Preston NE A L 1-4
24 Dec Notts Co H W 1-0
26 Dec Manchester U A L 0-5
31 Dec Bury H W 3-1
7 Jan Sheffield U A L 2-3
28 Jan Sunderland A D 2-2
11 Feb Bradford C H D 0-0
18 Feb Blackburn Rov A L 1-2
25 Feb Nottingham F H W 3-2
4 Mar Manchester C A D 1-1
6 Mar Oldham Ath A L 0-3
11 Mar Everton H W 1-0
15 Mar Aston Villa H D 1-1
18 Mar Sheffield Wed A D 0-0
25 Mar Bristol C H W 3-0
1 Apr Newcastle U A W 1-0
8 Apr Tottenham H H W 2-0
14 Apr Liverpool H D 0-0
15 Apr Middlesbrough A D 1-1
17 Apr Liverpool A D 1-1
22 Apr Preston NE H W 2-0
29 Apr Notts Co A W 2-0

FA Cup
14 Jan Clapton Orient (1)*
16 Jan Clapton Orient (1) A W 2-1
4 Feb Swindon T (2) A L 0-1
*match abandoned, fog

London FA Challenge Cup
19 Sep Q P R H W 3-0
10 Oct Millwall A L 0-1

London Professional Charity Fund
26 Sep Fulham A W 3-2

Position in Football League Table

	P	W	L	D	F:A	Pts	
Manchester U	38	22	8	8	72:40	52	1st
Arsenal	38	13	13	12	41:49	38	10th

SEASON 1911-1912
FOOTBALL LEAGUE (DIVISION 1)

2 Sep Liverpool H D 2-2
9 Sep Aston Villa A L 1-4
16 Sep Newcastle U H W 2-0
23 Sep Sheffield U A L 1-2
30 Sep Oldham Ath H D 1-1
7 Oct Bolton W A D 2-2
14 Oct Bradford C H W 2-0
21 Oct Preston NE H W 1-0
28 Oct Manchester C A D 3-3
4 Nov Everton H L 0-1
11 Nov W B A A D 1-1

18 Nov Sunderland H W 3-0
25 Nov Blackburn Rov A L 0-4
2 Dec Sheffield Wed A L 0-2
9 Dec Bury A L 1-3
16 Dec Middlesbrough H W 3-1
23 Dec Notts Co A L 1-3
25 Dec Tottenham H A L 0-5
26 Dec Tottenham H H W 3-1
30 Dec Liverpool A L 1-4
1 Jan Manchester U H D 2-2
6 Jan Aston Villa H D 2-2
20 Jan Newcastle U A W 3-1
27 Jan Sheffield U H W 3-1
10 Feb Bolton W H L 0-1
17 Feb Bradford C A D 1-1
24 Feb Middlesbrough H W 7-0
2 Mar Manchester C H W 2-0
9 Apr Oldham Ath A W 1-0
16 Mar W B A H L 0-2
23 Mar Sunderland A L 0-1
27 Mar Everton A L 0-1
5 Apr Manchester U H W 2-1
5 Apr Sheffield Wed A L 0-3
6 Apr Preston NE H W 4-1
8 Apr Bury H W 1-0
22 Apr Blackburn Rov H W 5-1
27 Apr Notts Co H L 0-1

FA Cup
13 Jan Bolton W (1) A L 0-1

London FA Challenge Cup
18 Sep Q P R A W 2-0
16 Oct Chelsea H W 1-0

London Professional Charity Fund
4 Sep Chelsea A D 2-2
30 Oct Chelsea H W 1-0

Charity Match Titanic Disaster
29 Apr Tottenham H W 3-0

Friendlies
25 Mar West Ham U H W 2-1
20 Apr Glasgow Rangers A D 0-0

On Tour
17 May Hertha Berlin W 5-0
12 May Viktoria Berliner D 2-2
16 May Prague Deutscher W 4-1
19 May Furth W 6-0
22 May Toma Graz W 6-0
24 May Tottenham Vienna W 4-0
26 May Vienna Rapide W 8-2
27 May Wiener Athletic W 5-0
29 May Budapest W 2-1

Position in Football League Table

	P	W	L	D	F:A	Pts	
Blackburn Rov	38	20	9	9	60:43	49	1st
Arsenal	38	15	15	8	55:59	38	10th

SEASON 1912-1913
FOOTBALL LEAGUE (DIVISION 1)

2 Sep Manchester U H D 0-0
7 Sep Liverpool A L 0-3
14 Sep Bolton W H L 1-2
16 Sep Aston Villa H L 0-3
21 Sep Sheffield U A W 3-1
28 Sep Newcastle U H D 1-1
5 Oct Oldham Ath A D 0-0
12 Oct Chelsea H L 0-1
19 Oct Sunderland A L 1-3
26 Oct Bradford PA A L 1-3
2 Nov Manchester C H L 0-4
9 Nov W B A A L 1-2
16 Nov Everton H D 0-0
23 Nov Sheffield Wed A L 0-2
30 Nov Blackburn Rov H L 0-1
7 Dec Derby Co A L 1-4
14 Dec Middlesbrough H L 0-3
25 Dec Notts Co H D 0-0
26 Dec Notts Co A L 1-2
28 Dec Liverpool H D 1-1
1 Jan Sunderland A L 1-4
4 Jan Bolton W A L 1-5
18 Jan Sheffield U H L 1-3
25 Jan Newcastle U A L 1-3
8 Feb Oldham Ath H D 0-0
15 Feb Chelsea A D 1-1
1 Mar Bradford PA H D 1-1
8 Mar Manchester C A W 1-0
15 Mar W B A H W 1-0
21 Mar Manchester U A L 0-2
22 Mar Everton A L 0-3
24 Mar Aston Villa A L 1-4
29 Mar Sheffield Wed H L 2-5
5 Apr Blackburn A D 1-1
9 Apr Derby Co H L 1-2
19 Apr Tottenham H A D 1-1
26 Apr Middlesbrough H D 1-1

FA Cup
11 Jan Croydon Common (I) A D 0-0
15 Jan Croydon Common (1R) H W 2-1
1 Feb Liverpool (2) H L 1-4

London FA Challenge Cup
23 Sep Clapton Orient A L 2-4

London Professional Charity Fund
30 Sep Chelsea A W 3-1

Kent Senior Shield
16 Oct Crystal Palace A L 0-1

Position in Football League Table

	P	W	L	D	F:A	Pts	
Sunderland	38	25	9	4	86:43	54	1st
Arsenal	38	3	23	12	26:74	18	20th

SEASON 1913-1914
FOOTBALL LEAGUE (DIVISION 2)

6 Sep Leicester C H W 2-1
13 Sep Wolverhampton W A W 2-1
15 Sep Notts Co H W 3-0
27 Sep Barnsley A L 0-1
4 Oct Bury H L 0-1
11 Oct Huddersfield A W 2-1
18 Oct Lincoln C H W 3-0
25 Oct Blackpool A D 1-1
1 Nov Nottingham F H W 3-2
8 Nov Fulham A L 1-6
15 Nov Grimsby T A D 1-1
22 Nov Birmingham H W 1-0
29 Nov Bristol C A D 1-1
6 Dec Leeds C H W 1-0
13 Dec Clapton Orient A L 0-1
20 Dec Glossop H W 2-0
25 Dec Bradford PA A W 3-2
26 Dec Bradford PA H W 2-0
27 Dec Leicester A W 2-1
1 Jan Notts Co A L 0-1
3 Jan Wolverhampton W H W 3-1
17 Jan Hull C A W 1-0
24 Jan Barnsley H W 1-0
7 Feb Bury A D 1-1
14 Feb Huddersfield H L 0-1
21 Feb Lincoln C A L 2-5
28 Feb Blackpool H W 2-1
7 Mar Nottingham F A D 0-0
14 Mar Fulham H W 2-0
28 Mar Birmingham A L 0-2
4 Apr Bristol C A D 1-1
10 Apr Stockport Co H W 4-0
11 Apr Leeds C A D 0-0
13 Apr Stockport Co A W 4-0
18 Apr Clapton Orient H D 2-2
23 Apr Grimsby T H W 2-0
25 Apr Glossop A W 2-0

FA Cup
10 Jan Bradford PA (1) A L 0-2

London FA Challenge Cup
22 Sep QPR H D 1-1
29 Sep QPR A W 3-2
20 Oct Chelsea A W 1-0
10 Nov Tottenham H A L 1-2

London Professional Charity Fund
27 Oct West Ham U A L 2-3

Friendly
31 Jan Everton H L 1-2

Position in Football League Table

	P	W	L	D	F:A	Pts	
Notts Co	38	23	8	7	77:36	53	1st
Arsenal	38	20	9	9	54:38	49	3rd

SEASON 1914-1915
FOOTBALL LEAGUE (DIVISION 2)

1 Sep Glossop H W 3-0
5 Sep Wolverhampton W A L 0-1
8 Sep Glossop A W 4-0
12 Sep Fulham H W 3-0
19 Sep Stockport Co A D 1-1
26 Sep Hull C H W 2-1
3 Oct Leeds C A D 2-2
10 Oct Clapton Orient H W 2-1
17 Oct Blackpool H W 2-0
24 Oct Derby Co A L 0-4
31 Oct Lincoln C H D 1-1
7 Nov Birmingham A L 0-3
14 Nov Grimsby T H W 6-0
18 Nov Nottingham F A D 1-1
21 Nov Huddersfield T A L 0-3
28 Nov Bristol C H W 3-0
5 Dec Bury A L 1-3
12 Dec Preston NE H L 1-2
25 Dec Leicester A W 4-1
26 Dec Leicester H W 6-0
1 Jan Barnsley A L 0-1
2 Jan Wolverhampton W H W 5-1
16 Jan Fulham A W 1-0
23 Jan Stockport Co H W 3-1
6 Feb Leeds C H W 2-0
13 Feb Clapton Orient A L 0-1
20 Feb Blackpool A W 2-0
27 Feb Derby Co H L 1-2
6 Mar Lincoln C A L 0-1
13 Mar Birmingham H W 1-0
20 Mar Grimsby T A L 0-1
27 Mar Huddersfield T A L 0-3
2 Apr Hull C A L 0-1
3 Apr Bristol C A D 1-1
5 Apr Barnsley H W 1-0
10 Apr Bury H W 3-1
17 Apr Preston NE A L 0-3
24 Apr Nottingham F H W 7-0

FA Cup
9 Jan Merthyr T (1) H* W 3-0
30 Jan Chelsea (2) A L 0-1
*by arrangement

London FA Challenge Cup
21 Sep Tufnell Park H W 6-0
19 Oct QPR H W 2-1
9 Nov Crystal Palace H W 2-1
7 Dec Millwall (Final) A L 1-2

London Professional Charity Fund
2 Nov West Ham U H W 1-0

Friendly
19 Dec Swindon T I 1-2

Position in Football League Table

	P	W	L	D	F:A	Pts	
Derby Co	38	23	8	7	71:33	53	1st
Arsenal	38	19	14	5	69:41	48	5th

No League football was played throughout the First World War. Competitive football was played, by Arsenal, during the seasons 1915-16 through 1919-1920, in the form of the London Football Combination and other London based friendlies. Arsenal's highest placing in the London Football combination was 3rd for seasons 1915-16 and 1918-19. Arsenal was a Second Division club at the outbreak of the First World War, finishing fifth in the last pre-war season. After the war, the First Division was increased from 20 to 22 clubs, and Arsenal illogically and possibly corruptly, were elected to one of the new places. Since then they have remained a First Division club, and from now on the records are given in more detail.

SEASON 1919-1920
FOOTBALL LEAGUE (DIVISION 1)

30 Aug Newcastle U H L 0-1
1 Sep Liverpool A W 3-2
6 Sep Newcastle U A L 1-3
8 Sep Liverpool H W 1-0
13 Sep Sunderland A D 1-1
20 Sep Sunderland H W 3-2
27 Sep Blackburn Rov A D 2-2
4 Oct Blackburn Rov H L 0-1
11 Oct Everton A W 3-2
18 Oct Everton H D 1-1
25 Oct Bradford C H L 1-2
1 Nov Bradford C A D 1-1
8 Nov Bolton W H D 2-2
15 Nov Bolton W A D 2-2
22 Nov Notts Co H W 3-1
29 Nov Notts Co A D 2-2
6 Dec Chelsea H W 1-0
13 Dec Chelsea A L 1-3
20 Dec Sheffield Wed H W 3-1
25 Dec Derby Co A L 1-2
26 Dec Derby Co H W 1-0
27 Dec Sheffield Wed A W 2-1
3 Jan Manchester C H D 2-2
17 Jan Manchester C A L 1-4
24 Jan Aston Villa H L 0-1
7 Feb Oldham Ath H W 3-2
11 Feb Aston Villa A L 1-2
14 Feb Oldham Ath A L 0-3
21 Feb Manchester U H L 0-3
28 Feb Manchester U A W 1-0
6 Mar Sheffield U A L 0-2
13 Mar Sheffield U H W 3-0
20 Mar Middlesbrough A L 0-1
27 Mar Middlesbrough H W 2-1
3 Apr Burnley A L 1-2
5 Apr W B A H W 2-0
6 Apr W B A A L 0-1
10 Apr Burnley H W 2-0
17 Apr Preston NE A D 1-1
24 Apr Preston NE H D 0-0
28 Apr Bradford PA A D 0-0
1 May Bradford PA H W 3-0

FA Cup
10 Jan Rochdale (1) H W 4-2
31 Jan Bristol C (2) A L 0-1

Appearances (Goals)
Baker A 17 · Blyth W 29 (4) · Bradshaw F 33 (2) · Buckley C 23 (1) · Burgess D 7 (1) · Butler J 21 (1) · Coopland W 1 · Cownley F 4 · Dunn S 16 · Graham J 22 (5) · Greenaway D 3 · Groves F 29 (5) · Hardinge H 13 (3) · Hutchins A 18 · Lewis C 5 (1) · McKinnon A 41 · North F 4 (1) · Pagnam F 25 (13) · Pattison G 1 · Peart J 5 · Rutherford J 36 (3) · Shaw J 33 · Toner J 15 (1) · Voysey C 5 · White H 29 (15) · Whittaker T 1 · Williamson E 26 · Total: 27 players (56)

Position in League Table

	P	W	L	D	F:A	Pts	
W B A	42	28	10	4	104:47	60	1st
Arsenal	42	15	15	12	56:58	42	10th

SEASON 1920-1921
FOOTBALL LEAGUE (DIVISION 1)

28 Aug Aston Villa A L 0-5
30 Aug Manchester U H W 2-0
4 Sep Aston Villa H L 0-1
6 Sep Manchester U A D 1-1
11 Sep Manchester C A W 2-1
18 Sep Manchester C H W 2-1
25 Sep Middlesbrough H D 2-2
2 Oct Middlesbrough A L 1-2
9 Oct Bolton W H D 0-0
16 Oct Bolton W A D 1-1
23 Oct Derby County H W 2-0
30 Oct Derby County H W 2-0
6 Nov Blackburn R A D 2-2
13 Nov Blackburn R H W 2-0
20 Nov Huddersfield T A W 4-0
27 Nov Huddersfield T H W 1-0
4 Dec Chelsea A W 2-1
11 Dec Chelsea H D 1-1
18 Dec Bradford C A L 1-3
25 Dec Everton A W 4-2
27 Dec Everton H L 1-2
1 Jan Bradford C H L 1-2
15 Jan Tottenham H H W 3-2
22 Jan Tottenham H A L 1-2
29 Jan Sunderland H L 1-2
5 Feb Sunderland A L 1-5
12 Feb Oldham Ath A L 1-2
19 Feb Oldham Ath H D 2-2
26 Feb Preston N E A L 0-2
12 Mar Burnley A L 0-1
19 Mar Burnley H D 1-1
26 Mar Sheffield U H L 2-6
28 Mar W B A H W 2-1
29 Mar W B A A W 4-3
2 Apr Sheffield U A D 1-1
9 Apr Bradford PA H W 2-1
16 Apr Bradford PA A W 1-0
23 Apr Newcastle U H D 1-1
25 Apr Preston NE H W 2-1
30 Apr Newcastle U A L 0-1
2 May Liverpool H D 0-0
7 May Liverpool A L 0-3

FA Cup
8 Jan QPR (1) A L 0-2

Appearances (Goals)
Baker A 37 (2) · Blyth W 39 (7) · Bradshaw F 21 · Buckley C 4 (1) · Burgess D 4 · Butler J 36 · Cownley F 1 · Dunn S 9 · Graham A 30 (5) · Groves G 13 (1) · Hopkins J 8 (2) · Hutchins A 39 · McKenzie A 5 (1) · McKinnon A 37 (2) · North E 8 2 · Pagnam F 25 (14) · Paterson Dr J 20 · Pattison G 6 · Peart J 1 · Rutherford J 32 (7) · Shaw J 28 · Smith J 10 (1) · Toner J 11 (3) · Walden H 2 (1) · White H 26 (10) · Whittaker T 5 · Williamson E 33 · Total: 27 players (59)

Position in League Table

	P	W	L	D	F:A	Pts	
Burnley	42	23	6	13	79:36	59	1st
Arsenal	42	15	13	14	59:63	44	9th

SEASON 1921-1922
FOOTBALL LEAGUE (DIVISION 1)

27 Aug Sheffield U H L 1-2
29 Aug Preston NE A L 2-3
3 Sep Sheffield U A L 1-3
5 Sep Preston NE H W 1-0
10 Sep Manchester C A L 0-2
17 Sep Manchester C H L 0-1
24 Sep Everton A D 1-1
1 Oct Everton H W 1-0
8 Oct Sunderland A L 0-1
15 Oct Sunderland H L 0-1
22 Oct Huddersfield T A L 1-3
29 Oct Huddersfield T H L 1-3
5 Nov Birmingham A W 1-0
12 Nov Birmingham H W 5-2
19 Nov Bolton W A L 0-1
3 Dec Blackburn Rov A W 1-0
10 Dec Blackburn Rov H D 1-1
12 Dec Bolton W H D 1-1
17 Dec Oldham Ath A L 1-4
24 Dec Oldham Ath H L 0-1
26 Dec Cardiff C H D 0-0
27 Dec Cardiff C A L 3-4
31 Dec Chelsea A W 2-0
14 Jan Chelsea H W 1-0
21 Jan Burnley H D 0-0
4 Feb Newcastle U H W 2-1
11 Feb Newcastle U A L 0-1
18 Feb Aston Villa A L 0-2
22 Feb Manchester U H W 1-0
25 Feb Liverpool A L 0-4
11 Mar Manchester U A L 0-1
18 Mar Aston Villa A L 0-2
22 Mar Liverpool H W 1-0
25 Mar Aston Villa H W 2-0
1 Apr Middlesbrough H D 2-2
5 Apr Manchester U H W 3-1
8 Apr Middlesbrough A L 2-4
15 Apr Tottenham H A L 0-2
17 Apr W B A A W 3-0
18 Apr W B A H D 2-2
22 Apr Tottenham H H W 1-0
29 Apr Bradford C A W 2-0
6 May Bradford C H W 1-0

FA Cup
7 Jan QPR (1) H D 0-0
11 Jan QPR (1R) A W 2-1
28 Jan Bradford C (2) A W 3-2
18 Feb Leicester C (3) H W 3-0
4 Mar Preston NE (4) H L 1-2
8 Mar Preston NE (4R) A L 1-2

Appearances (Goals)
Baker A 32 (4) · Blyth W 25 (1) · Boreham R 22 (10) · Bradshaw F 32 (2) · Burgess D 2 · Butler J 25 (2) · Cownley F 10 · Creegan W 5 · Dunn S 1 · Earle S 1 · Graham A 21 (3) · Henderson W 5 · Hutchins A 37 · Hopkins J 11 (3) · Maxwell T 1 · Milne W 4 · McKenzie A 3 · McKinnon A 41 · North F 11 (3) · Paterson Dr J 2 · Pattison G 2 · Rutherford J 36 · Shaw J 6 · Toner J 24 (1) · Turnbull R 5 · Voysey C 1 · Whittaker T 36 (1) · White H 35 (14) · Williamson E 41 · Young A 9 (2) · Total: 30 players (47)

Position in League Table

	P	W	L	D	F:A	Pts	
Liverpool	42	22	7	13	63:36	57	1st
Arsenal	42	15	20	7	47:56	37	17th

SEASON 1922-1923
FOOTBALL LEAGUE (DIVISION 1)

26 Aug Liverpool A L 2-5
28 Aug Burnley H D 1-1
2 Sep Liverpool H W 1-0
4 Sep Burnley A L 1-4
9 Sep Cardiff C A L 1-4
16 Sep Cardiff C H W 2-1
23 Sep Tottenham H A W 2-1
30 Sep Tottenham H H L 0-2
2 Oct Sheffield U H L 1-2
7 Oct W B A H W 3-1
14 Oct W B A A L 0-7
21 Oct Newcastle U A D 1-1
28 Oct Newcastle U H L 1-2
4 Nov Everton A L 0-1
11 Nov Everton H L 1-2
18 Nov Sunderland A D 3-3
25 Nov Sunderland H L 2-3
2 Dec Birmingham A L 2-3
9 Dec Birmingham H W 1-0
16 Dec Huddersfield T H D 1-1
23 Dec Huddersfield T A L 0-4
25 Dec Bolton W A L 1-4
26 Dec Bolton W H W 5-0
30 Dec Stoke C H W 3-0
1 Jan Blackburn Rov A W 5-0
6 Jan Stoke C A L 0-1
20 Jan Manchester C H W 1-0
27 Jan Nottingham F A D 0-0
3 Feb Nottingham F H W 2-0
10 Feb Chelsea A D 0-0
17 Feb Chelsea H W 3-1
24 Feb Chelsea H W 3-1
3 Mar Middlesbrough A L 0-2
10 Mar Middlesbrough H W 3-0
17 Mar Oldham Ath H W 2-0
24 Mar Oldham Ath A D 0-0
31 Mar Aston Villa H W 2-0
2 Apr Blackburn H D 2-2
7 Apr Aston Villa A D 1-1
14 Apr Preston NE H W 2-0
21 Apr Preston NE A W 2-1
28 Apr Sheffield U H W 2-0

FA Cup
13 Jan Liverpool (1) A D 0-0
17 Jan Liverpool (1R) H L 1-4

Appearances (Goals)
Baker A 29 (6) · Blyth W 31 (9) · Boreham R 27 (8) · Bradshaw F 17 · Butler J 18 · Clarke J 2 · Dunn S 17 · Earle S 1 (1) · Elvey J 1 · Graham A 17 (1) · Henderson W 2 · Hopkins J 2 (2) · Hutchins A 10 (1) · John R 24 · Kennedy A 24 · McKenzie A 7 (1) · Milne W 31 · Mackie J 23 · Paterson Dr J 27 · Robson J 20 · Roe A 4 (1) · Rutherford J 26 (1) · Toner J 7 · Townrow J 1 · Turnbull R 35 (20) · Voysey C 18 (4) · White H 11 (1) · Whittaker T 13 (1) · Williamson E 5 · Young A 13 (3) · Own goals 1 · Total: 30 players (61)

Position in League Table

	P	W	L	D	F:A	Pts	
Liverpool	42	26	8	8	70:31	60	1st
Arsenal	42	16	16	10	61:62	42	11th

SEASON 1923-1924
FOOTBALL LEAGUE (DIVISION 1)

25 Aug Newcastle H L 1-4
27 Aug West Ham U A L 0-1
1 Sep Newcastle U A L 0-1
8 Sep W B A A L 0-4
10 Sep West Ham U H W 4-1
15 Sep W B A H W 1-0
22 Sep Birmingham A W 2-0
29 Sep Birmingham H D 0-0
6 Oct Manchester C A L 0-1
13 Oct Manchester C H L 1-2
20 Oct Bolton W A W 2-1
27 Oct Bolton W H D 0-0
3 Nov Liverpool H W 2-1
10 Nov Liverpool A D 0-0
17 Nov Tottenham H H D 1-1
24 Nov Tottenham H A L 0-3
1 Dec Blackburn Rov H W 2-0
8 Dec Blackburn Rov A L 0-2
15 Dec Huddersfield T H L 1-3
22 Dec Huddersfield T A L 1-6
26 Dec Notts Co A W 2-1
27 Dec Notts Co H D 0-0
29 Dec Chelsea H W 1-0
5 Jan Chelsea A D 0-0
19 Jan Cardiff C H L 1-2
26 Jan Cardiff C A L 0-4
9 Feb Sheffield U H L 1-3
16 Feb Aston Villa A L 1-3
25 Feb Sheffield U H L 1-3
1 Mar Liverpool H W 3-1
12 Mar Aston Villa A L 1-2
15 Mar Nottingham F A L 1-2
22 Mar Nottingham F H W 1-0
2 Apr Liverpool A D 0-0
5 Apr Burnley H W 2-0
12 Apr Sunderland A W 2-0
18 Apr Everton A L 1-3
19 Apr Sunderland A D 1-1
21 Apr Everton H L 0-1
26 Apr Preston NE A W 2-0
28 Apr Burnley A L 1-4
3 May Preston NE H L 1-2

FA Cup
12 Jan Luton (1) H W 4-1
2 Feb Cardiff (2) A L 0-1

Appearances (Goals)
Baker A 21 (1) · Blyth W 27 (3) · Boreham R 2 · Butler J 24 · Clarke E 2 (2) · Graham A 25 (2) · Haden S 31 (3) · John R 15 · Jones F 2 · Kennedy A 29 · Mackie J 31 · Milne W 36 (1) · Neil A 11 (2) · Paterson Dr J 21 · Ramsay J 11 (4) · Robson J 42 · Rutherford J 22 (3) · Toner J 3 · Townrow 7 (2) · Turnbull R 18 (6) · Voysey C 10 (2) · Wallington E 1 · Whittaker T 8 · Woods H 36 (8) · Young A 25 (2) · Own goals 1 · Total: 26 players (40)

Position in League Table

	P	W	L	D	F:A	Pts	
H.field T	42	23	8	11	60:33	57	1st
Arsenal	42	12	21	9	40:63	33	19th

SEASON 1924-1925
FOOTBALL LEAGUE (DIVISION 1)

30 Aug Nottingham F A W 2-0
1 Sep Manchester C H W 1-0
6 Sep Liverpool H W 2-0
13 Sep Newcastle U A D 2-2
17 Sep Manchester C A L 0-2
20 Sep Sheffield U H W 2-0
27 Sep West Ham U A L 0-1
4 Oct Blackburn Rov A L 0-1
11 Oct Huddersfield T A L 0-4
13 Oct Bury H D 1-1
18 Oct Aston Villa H D 1-1
25 Oct Tottenham H H W 1-0
1 Nov Bolton W A L 1-4
8 Nov Notts Co H L 0-1
15 Nov Everton A W 3-2
22 Nov Sunderland H D 0-0
29 Nov Cardiff C A D 1-1
6 Dec Preston NE H W 4-0
13 Dec Burnley H W 6-1
20 Dec Leeds U A L 0-1
25 Dec Birmingham H L 0-1
26 Dec Birmingham A L 0-3
27 Dec Nottingham F H W 2-1
3 Jan Liverpool A L 1-2
17 Jan Newcastle U A L 1-2
24 Jan Sheffield U A L 1-2
7 Feb Blackburn Rov H L 0-5
14 Feb Huddersfield T H L 0-1
28 Feb Tottenham H A L 0-2

Huddersfield Town's keeper clears the ball at the expense of a corner at Highbury in February 1914.

1886-1939

7 Mar Bolton W H W 1-0
14 Mar Notts Co A L 1-2
21 Mar Everton H W 3-1
23 Mar West Ham U H L 1-2
28 Mar Sunderland A L 0-2
1 Apr Aston Villa A L 0-4
4 Apr Cardiff C H D 1-1
11 Apr Preston NE A L 0-2
13 Apr W B A A L 0-2
14 Apr W B A H W 2-0
18 Apr Burnley H W 5-0
25 Apr Leeds U A L 0-1
2 May Bury A L 0-2

FA Cup
14 Jan West Ham U (1) A D 0-0
21 Jan West Ham U (1R) H D 2-2
26 Jan West Ham U (1R) A L 0-1

Appearances (Goals)
Baker A 32 (2) · Blyth W 17 (1) · Brain J 28 (12) · Butler J 39 (3) · Clarke J 2 · Cock D 2 · Haden S 15 (1) · Hoar S 19 · Hughes J 1 · John R 39 (2) · Kennedy A 40 · Lewis D 16 · Mackie J 19 · Milne W 32 · Neil A 16 (2) · Ramsey J 30 4 · Robson J 26 · Roe A 1 · Rutherford J 20 2 · Toner J 26 (2) · Turnbull R 1 · Whittaker T 1 · Woods H 32 (13) · Young A 8 (2) · Total: 24 players (46)

Position in League Table

	P	W	L	D	F:A	Pts	
H.field T	42	21	5	16	69:28	58	1st
Arsenal	42	14	23	5	46:58	33	20th

SEASON 1925-1926
FOOTBALL LEAGUE (DIVISION 1)

29 Aug Tottenham H H L 0-1
31 Aug Leicester H D 2-2
5 Sep Manchester U A W 1-0
7 Sep Leicester C A W 1-0
12 Sep Liverpool H D 1-1
19 Sep Burnley A D 2-2
21 Sep West Ham U H W 3-2
26 Sep Leeds U H W 4-1
3 Oct Newcastle U A L 0-7
5 Oct West Ham U A W 4-0
10 Oct Bolton W H L 2-3
17 Oct Cardiff C H W 5-0
24 Oct Sheffield U A L 0-4
31 Oct Everton A W 4-1
7 Nov Manchester C H W 2-2
14 Nov Bury H W 6-1
21 Nov Blackburn Rov A W 3-2
28 Nov Sunderland H W 2-0
5 Dec Huddersfield T A D 2-2
12 Dec W B A H W 1-0
19 Dec Birmingham A L 0-1
25 Dec Notts Co H W 3-0
26 Dec Notts Co A L 1-4
1 Jan Tottenham H A D 1-1
16 Jan Manchester U H W 3-2
23 Jan Liverpool A L 0-3
3 Feb Burnley H L 1-2
6 Feb Leeds U A L 2-4
13 Feb Newcastle U H W 3-0
23 Feb Cardiff C A D 0-0
13 Mar Everton A W 3-2
17 Mar Sheffield U H W 4-0
20 Mar Manchester C H W 1-0
27 Mar Bury A D 2-2
2 Apr Aston Villa A L 0-3
3 Apr Blackburn Rov H W 4-2
5 Apr Aston Villa H W 2-0
10 Apr Sunderland A L 1-2
17 Apr Huddersfield T H W 3-1
24 Apr W B A A L 1-2
28 Apr Bolton W A D 1-1
1 May Birmingham H W 3-0

FA Cup
9 Jan Wolves (3) A D 1-1
13 Jan Wolves (3R) H W 1-0
30 Jan Blackburn R (4) H W 3-1
20 Feb Aston Villa (5) A D 1-1
24 Feb Aston Villa (5R) H W 2-0
6 Mar Swansea (6) A L 1-2

Appearances (Goals)
Baker A 31 (6) · Blyth W 40 (7) · Brain J 41 (33) · Buchan C 39 (19) · Butler J 41 · Cock D 1 · Haden S 25 (2) · Harper W 19 · Hoar S 21 (3) · Hulme J 15 (2) · John R 29 · Kennedy A 16 · Lawson H 13 (2) · Lewis D 14 · Mackie J 35 · Milne W 5 · Neil A 27 (6) · Parker T 7 (3) · Paterson Dr J 1 (1) · Ramsey J 16 · Robson J 9 · Rutherford J 3 · Rutherford J J 1 · Seddon W 1 · Toner J 2 · Voysey C 1 · Woods H 2 · Young A 7 · Own goals 3 · Total: 28 players (87)

Position in League Table

	P	W	L	D	F:A	Pts	
H.field T	42	23	8	11	92:60	57	1st
Arsenal	42	22	12	8	87:63	52	2nd

SEASON 1926-1927
FOOTBALL LEAGUE (DIVISION 1)

28 Aug Derby Co H W 2-1
1 Sep Bolton W H W 2-1
4 Sep Sheffield A L 0-4
6 Sep Bolton W A D 2-2
11 Sep Leicester C H D 2-2
15 Sep Manchester U A D 2-2
18 Sep Liverpool H W 2-0
25 Sep Leeds U A L 1-4
2 Oct Newcastle U H D 2-2
9 Oct Burnley A L 0-2
16 Oct West Ham U H D 2-2

23 Oct Sheffield Wed H W 6-2
30 Oct Everton A L 1-3
6 Nov Blackburn Rov H D 2-2
13 Nov Huddersfield T A D 3-3
20 Nov Sunderland H L 2-3
27 Nov W B A A W 3-1
4 Dec Bury H W 1-0
11 Dec Birmingham A D 0-0
18 Dec Tottenham H H L 2-4
27 Dec Cardiff C A D 0-0
28 Dec Manchester U H W 1-0
1 Jan Cardiff C H W 3-2
15 Jan Derby Co A W 2-0
22 Jan Sheffield U H D 1-1
5 Feb Liverpool A L 0-3
10 Feb Leicester C A L 1-2
12 Feb Leeds U H W 1-0
26 Feb Burnley H W 6-2
7 Mar West Ham U A L 0-7
12 Mar Sheffield Wed A L 2-4
19 Mar Everton H L 1-2
2 Apr Huddersfield T H L 0-2
6 Apr Newcastle U A L 1-6
9 Apr Sunderland A L 1-5
15 Apr Aston Villa H W 2-1
16 Apr W B A H W 4-1
23 Apr Aston Villa A W 3-2
28 Apr Blackburn Rov A W 2-1
30 Apr Birmingham H W 3-0
4 May Bury A L 2-3
7 May Tottenham H A W 4-0

FA Cup
8 Jan Sheffield U (3) A W 3-2
29 Jan Port Vale (4) A D 2-2
2 Feb Port Vale (4R) H W 1-0
19 Feb Liverpool (5) H W 2-0
5 Mar Wolves (6) H W 2-1
26 Mar Southampton (SF) W 2-1
(at Chelsea)
23 Apr Cardiff (F) L 0-1
(at Wembley)

Appearances (Goals)
Baker A 23 · Barley J 3 1 · Blyth W 33 3 · Bowen E 1 · Brain J 37 31 · Buchan C 33 14 · Butler J 31 · Cope H 11 · Haden S 17 4 · Harper W 23 · Hoar S 16 2 · Hulme J 37 8 · John R 41 3 · Kennedy A 11 · Lambert J 16 1 · Lee J 7 · Lewis D 17 · Milne W 6 · Moody J 2 · Parker T 42 4 · Peel H 9 · Ramsey J 12 2 · Roberts H 2 · Seddon C 17 · Shaw J 5 1 · Tricker R 4 3 · Young A 6 · Total: 27 players 77

Position in League Table

	P	W	L	D	F:A	Pts	
Newcastle U	42	25	11	6	96:58	56	1st
Arsenal	42	17	16	9	77:86	43	11th

SEASON 1927-1928
FOOTBALL LEAGUE (DIVISION 1)

27 Aug Bury A L 1-5
31 Aug Burnley H W 4-1
3 Sep Sheffield U H W 6-1
5 Sep Burnley A W 2-1
10 Sep Aston Villa A D 2-2
17 Sep Sunderland H W 2-1
24 Sep Derby Co A L 0-4
1 Oct West Ham U H D 2-2
8 Oct Portsmouth A W 3-2
15 Oct Leicester C H D 2-2
22 Oct Sheffield Wed A D 1-1
29 Oct Bolton W H L 1-2
5 Nov Blackburn Rov A L 1-4
12 Nov Middlesbrough H W 3-1
19 Nov Birmingham A D 1-1
3 Dec Huddersfield A L 1-2
10 Dec Newcastle U H W 4-1
17 Dec Manchester U A L 1-4
24 Dec Everton H W 3-2
27 Dec Liverpool A W 2-0
31 Dec Bury H D 1-1
2 Jan Tottenham H H D 1-1
7 Jan Sheffield U A L 4-6
21 Jan Aston Villa H L 0-3
4 Feb Derby Co H L 3-4
11 Feb West Ham U A D 2-2
25 Feb Leicester C A L 2-3
7 Mar Liverpool H W 6-3
10 Mar Bolton W A D 1-1
14 Mar Sunderland A L 1-5
17 Mar Blackburn Rov H W 3-2
28 Mar Portsmouth H L 0-2
31 Mar Birmingham H D 2-2
6 Apr Cardiff C H W 3-0
7 Apr Tottenham H A L 0-2
9 Apr Cardiff C A D 2-2
14 Apr Huddersfield H D 0-0
18 Apr Middlesbrough A D 2-2
21 Apr Newcastle U A D 1-1
28 Apr Manchester U H L 0-1
2 May Sheffield Wed H D 1-1
5 May Everton A D 3-3

FA Cup
14 Jan W B A (3) H W 2-0
28 Jan Everton (4) H W 4-3
18 Feb Aston Villa (5) H W 4-1
3 Mar Stoke C (6) H W 4-1
24 Mar Blackburn R (SF) L 0-1
(at Leicester)

Appearances (Goals)
Baker A 36 (3) · Barley J 2 · Blyth W 39 (7) · Brain J 39 (25) · Buchan C 30 (16) · Butler J 39 · Clark A 1 · Cope H 24 · Hapgood E 3 · Hoar S 38 (9) · Hulme J 36 (8) · John R 39 (1) · Kennedy A 2 · Lambert J 16 (3) · Lewis D 33 · Moody J 4 · Parker T 42 (4) · Paterson W 5 · Peel H 13 · H 3 · Seddon C 4 · Shaw J 6 (3) · Thompson L 1 · Tricker R 7 (2) · Own goals 1 Total: 24 players (82)

Position in League Table

	P	W	L	D	F:A	Pts	
Everton	42	20	9	13	102:66	53	1st
Arsenal	42	13	14	15	82:86	41	10th

SEASON 1928-1929
FOOTBALL LEAGUE (DIVISION 1)

25 Aug Sheffield Wed A L 2-3
29 Aug Derby Co H L 1-3
1 Sep Bolton W H W 2-0
8 Sep Portsmouth H W 2-0
15 Sep Birmingham H D 0-0
22 Sep Manchester C A L 1-4
26 Sep Derby Co A D 0-0
29 Sep Huddersfield H W 2-0
6 Oct Everton A L 2-4
13 Oct West Ham U H L 2-3
20 Oct Newcastle U A W 3-0
27 Oct Liverpool H D 4-4
3 Nov Cardiff C A D 1-1
10 Nov Sheffield U H W 3-1
17 Nov Bury A L 0-1
24 Nov Aston Villa H L 2-5
1 Dec Leicester C H D 2-2
8 Dec Manchester U H W 3-1
15 Dec Leeds A D 1-1
22 Dec Burnley H W 3-1
25 Dec Blackburn Rov A L 2-5
26 Dec Sunderland H D 1-1
29 Dec Sheffield Wed H D 2-2
1 Jan Sunderland A L 1-5
5 Jan Bolton W A W 2-1
19 Jan Portsmouth H W 4-0
2 Feb Manchester C H D 0-0
9 Feb Huddersfield A L 1-0
23 Feb West Ham U A W 4-3
9 Mar Liverpool A W 4-2
13 Mar Birmingham A D 1-1
16 Mar Cardiff C H W 2-1
23 Mar Sheffield U A D 2-2
29 Mar Blackburn Rov H W 1-0
30 Mar Bury H W 1-0
2 Apr Newcastle U H L 1-2
6 Apr Aston Villa A L 2-4
13 Apr Leicester C A D 1-1
20 Apr Manchester U A L 1-4
22 Apr Everton H W 2-0
27 Apr Leeds U H W 1-0
4 May Burnley A D 3-3

FA Cup
12 Jan Stoke (3) H W 2-1
26 Jan Mansfield T (4) H W 2-0
16 Feb Swindon T (5) A D 0-0
20 Feb Swindon T (5R) H W 1-0
2 Mar Aston Villa (6) A L 0-1

Appearances (Goals)
Baker A 32 · Barley J 3 · Blyth W 20 (1) · Brain J37 19 · Butler J 22 · Cope H 23 · Hapgood E 17 · Hoar S 6 (1) · Hulme J 41 (6) · Jack D 31 25 · John R 34 (1) · Jones C 39 (6) · Lambert J 6 (1) · Lewis D 32 · Parker T 42 (3) · Parkin R 5 3 · Paterson W 10 · Peel H 24 (5) · Roberts H 20 · Thompson L 17 (5) · Tricker R 1 · Own goals 1 · Total: 21 players (77)

Position in League Table

	P	W	L	D	F:A	Pts	
Sheffield Wed	42	21	11	10	86:62	52	1st
Arsenal	42	16	13	13	77:72	45	9th

SEASON 1929-1930
FOOTBALL LEAGUE (DIVISION 1)

31 Aug Leeds U H W 4-0
4 Sep Manchester U A L 1-3
7 Sep Sheffield Wed A W 2-0
11 Sep Manchester C H W 3-2
14 Sep Burnley H W 6-1
21 Sep Sunderland A L 2-5
29 Sep Aston Villa A L 2-5
28 Sep Bolton W H L 1-2
5 Oct Everton A D 1-1
12 Oct Derby Co H D 1-1
19 Oct Grimsby T H W 4-1
26 Oct Manchester U H L 0-1
2 Nov West Ham U H W 3-2
9 Nov Birmingham A D 1-1
23 Nov Blackburn Rov A D 1-1
27 Nov Middlesbrough H L 1-2
30 Nov Newcastle U H L 0-1
14 Dec Huddersfield T H W 2-0
16 Dec Sheffield U A L 1-4
21 Dec Liverpool A L 0-1
25 Dec Portsmouth H L 1-2
26 Dec Portsmouth A W 1-0
28 Dec Leeds U A L 0-2
4 Jan Sheffield W H L 2-3
18 Jan Burnley A D 2-2
1 Feb Bolton W A D 0-0
8 Feb Everton H W 4-0
19 Feb Derby Co A L 1-4
22 Feb Grimsby T A D 1-1
8 Mar West Ham U A L 2-3
15 Mar Birmingham H W 1-0
29 Mar Blackburn Rov H W 4-0
2 Apr Liverpool H L 0-1
5 Apr Newcastle U A W 1-0
9 Apr Middlesbrough A D 1-1
12 Apr Sheffield U H W 8-1
18 Apr Leicester H D 1-1
19 Apr Huddersfield A D 2-2
21 Apr Leicester A W 6-6
28 Apr Sunderland H L 0-1
3 May Aston Villa H L 2-4

11 Jan FA Cup (3) H W 2-0
25 Jan Birmingham (4) H D 2-2
29 Jan Birmingham (4R) A W 3-0
15 Feb Middlesbrough (5) A W 2-0
1 Mar Hull C (6) A W 3-0
22 Mar Hull C (SF) D 2-2
(at Leeds)
26 Mar Hull C (SFR) W 1-0
(at Aston Villa)
26 Apr Huddersfield T (F) W 2-0
(at Wembley)

Appearances (Goals)
Baker A 19 · Bastin C 21 (7) · Brain J 6 · Butler J 2 · Cope H 1 · Halliday D 15 (9) · Hapgood E 38 · Haynes A 13 · Hulme J 37 (14) · Humpish E 3 · Jack D 33 (12) · James A 31 (5) · John R 34 · Johnstone W 7 (3) · Jones C 31 (2) · Lambert J 20 (19) · Lewis D 30 · Parker T 41 (3) · Peel H 1 · Preedy C 12 · Roberts H 26 · Seddon C 24 · Thompson L 5 (1) · Williams J 12 (3) · Total: 24 players (78)

Position in League Table

	P	W	L	D	F:A	Pts	
Sheffield Wed	42	26	8	8	105:57	60	1st
Arsenal	42	14	17	11	78:66	39	14th

SEASON 1930-1931
FOOTBALL LEAGUE (DIVISION 1)

30 Aug Blackpool A W 4-1
1 Sep Bolton W A W 4-1
6 Sep Leeds U H W 3-1
10 Sep Blackburn Rov H W 3-2
13 Sep Sunderland A W 4-1
15 Sep Blackburn Rov A D 2-2
20 Sep Leicester C H W 4-2
27 Sep Birmingham A W 4-2
4 Oct Sheffield U H D 1-1
11 Oct Derby Co A L 2-4
18 Oct Manchester U H W 2-1
25 Oct West Ham U A W 2-1
1 Nov Huddersfield T A D 1-1
8 Nov Aston Villa H W 5-2
15 Nov Sheffield Wed A W 2-1
22 Nov Middlesbrough H W 5-3
29 Nov Chelsea A W 5-1
13 Dec Liverpool A D 1-1
20 Dec Newcastle U H L 1-2
25 Dec Manchester C A W 4-1
26 Dec Manchester C H W 7-1
27 Dec Blackpool H W 7-1
17 Jan Sunderland H L 1-3
28 Jan Grimsby T H W 9-1
31 Jan Birmingham H D 1-1
5 Feb Leicester A W 7-2
7 Feb Sheffield U A D 1-1
14 Feb Derby Co H W 6-3
21 Feb Manchester U A W 4-1
28 Feb West Ham U A W 4-2
7 Mar Huddersfield T A D 0-0
11 Mar Leeds U A W 3-0
14 Mar Aston Villa A L 1-5
21 Mar Sheffield W H W 2-0
28 Mar Middlesbrough H W 5-2
3 Apr Portsmouth A D 1-1
4 Apr Chelsea H W 2-1
6 Apr Portsmouth H D 1-1
11 Apr Grimsby T A W 1-0
18 Apr Liverpool H W 3-1
25 Apr Newcastle U H W 3-1
2 May Bolton W H W 5-0

FA Cup
10 Jan Aston Villa (3) H D 2-2
14 Jan Aston Villa (3R) A W 3-1
24 Jan Chelsea (4) A L 1-2

FA Charity Shield
8 Oct Sheffield Wed W 2-1
(at Chelsea)

Appearances (Goals)
Baker A 1 · Bastin C 42 (28) · Brain J 16 (4) · Cope H 1 · Hapgood E 38 · Harper W 19 · Haynes A 2 · Hulme J 32 (14) · Jack D 35 (31) · James A 40 (5) · John R 40 (2) · Johnstone W 2 (1) · Jones C 24 (1) · Keyser G 12 · Lambert J 34 (38) · Male G 3 · Parker T 41 · Preedy C 11 · Roberts H 40 (1) · Seddon C 18 · Thompson L 2 · Williams J 9 (2) · Total: 22 players (127)

Position in League Table

	P	W	L	D	F:A	Pts	
Arsenal	42	28	4	10	127:59	66	1st

SEASON 1931-1932
FOOTBALL LEAGUE (DIVISION 1)

29 Aug W B A H L 0-1
31 Aug Blackburn Rov A D 1-1
5 Sep Birmingham A D 2-2
9 Sep Portsmouth H D 3-3
12 Sep Sunderland A W 2-1
16 Sep Portsmouth A W 3-0
19 Sep Manchester C A W 3-1
26 Sep Everton H W 3-2
3 Oct Grimsby T A L 1-3
10 Oct Blackpool A W 5-1
17 Oct Bolton W H W 2-1
24 Oct Leicester C A W 2-1
31 Oct Aston Villa H W 2-1
7 Nov Newcastle U A L 2-3
14 Nov West Ham U H W 4-1
21 Nov Chelsea A L 1-2
28 Nov Liverpool H W 6-0
5 Dec Sheffield Wed A D 3-1
12 Dec Huddersfield H D 1-1

19 Dec Middlesbrough A W 5-2
25 Dec Sheffield U H L 1-4
26 Dec Sheffield U H L 0-2
2 Jan W B A A W 3-0
16 Jan Birmingham H W 3-0
30 Jan Manchester C A W 3-1
6 Feb Everton A W 3-1
17 Feb Grimsby T H W 2-0
20 Feb Blackpool H W 2-0
2 Mar Bolton W A L 0-1
5 Mar Leicester C H W 1-0
19 Mar Newcastle U H W 1-0
25 Mar Derby Co A D 1-1
26 Mar West Ham U A D 1-1
28 Mar Derby C H D 1-1
3 Apr Chelsea H D 1-1
6 Apr Sunderland A D 1-1
9 Apr Liverpool A L 1-2
16 Apr Sheffield Wed A D 1-1
25 Apr Aston Villa A D 1-1
27 Apr Huddersfield H L 0-1
30 Apr Middlesbrough H W 5-0
7 May Blackburn Rov H W 4-0

FA Cup
9 Jan Darwen (3) H W 11-1
23 Jan Plymouth (4) A W 4-2
13 Feb Portsmouth (5) H W 2-0
27 Feb Huddersfield (6) A W 1-0
12 Mar Manchester C (SF) W 1-0
(at Aston Villa)
23 Apr Newcastle U (F) L 1-2
(at Wembley)

FA Charity Shield
7 Oct W B A W 1-0
(at Aston Villa)

Appearances (Goals)
Bastin C 40 (15) · Beasley A 3 · Coleman E 6 (1) · Compton L 4 · Cope H 1 · Hapgood E 41 · Harper W 2 · Haynes A 7 · Hulme J 40 (14) · Jack D 34 (20) · James A 32 (2) · John R 38 (3) · Jones C 37 · Lambert J 36 (22) · Male G 9 · Moss F 27 · Parker T 38 · Parkin R 9 (7) · Preedy C 13 · Roberts H 35 · Seddon C 5 · Stockill R 3 (1) · Thompson L 1 · Williams J 1 · Own goals 5 · Total: 24 players (90)

Position in League Table

	P	W	L	D	F:A	Pts	
Everton	42	26	12	4	116:64	56	1st
Arsenal	42	22	10	10	90:48	54	2nd

SEASON 1932-1933
FOOTBALL LEAGUE (DIVISION 1)

27 Aug Birmingham A W 1-0
31 Aug W B A H L 1-2
3 Sep Sunderland H W 6-1
10 Sep Manchester C A W 3-2
14 Sep W B A A D 1-1
17 Sep Bolton W H W 3-2
24 Sep Everton H W 2-1
1 Oct Blackpool A W 2-1
8 Oct Derby Co H D 3-3
15 Oct Blackburn Rov A W 3-2
22 Oct Liverpool A W 3-2
24 Oct Leicester C H W 8-2
5 Nov Wolverhampton W A W 7-1
12 Nov Newcastle U A W 3-1
19 Nov Aston Villa A L 3-5
26 Nov Middlesbrough H W 4-2
3 Dec Portsmouth A W 3-1
10 Dec Chelsea A W 4-1
17 Dec Huddersfield H W 1-0
24 Dec Sheffield U H W 9-2
26 Dec Leeds U H L 1-2
27 Dec Leeds U A D 0-0
31 Dec Birmingham H W 3-0
2 Jan Sheffield W A L 2-3
7 Jan Sunderland A L 2-3
21 Jan Manchester C H W 2-1
4 Feb Bolton W A W 4-0
11 Feb Everton A D 1-1
18 Feb Blackpool H D 1-1
22 Feb Derby Co A D 2-2
25 Feb Blackburn Rov H W 8-0
4 Mar Liverpool H L 0-1
11 Mar Leicester C A D 1-1
18 Mar Wolverhampton W H L 1-2
25 Mar Newcastle U H W 1-0
1 Apr Aston Villa H W 5-0
8 Apr Middlesbrough A W 4-3
14 Apr Sheffield Wed H W 4-2
15 Apr Portsmouth H W 2-0
22 Apr Chelsea A W 3-1
29 Apr Huddersfield H D 2-2
6 May Sheffield U A L 1-3

FA Cup
14 Jan Walsall (3) A L 0-2

Appearances (Goals)
Bastin C 42 33 · Bowden R 7 2 · Coleman E 27 24 · Compton L 4 · Cope H 4 · Hapgood E 38 · Haynes A 6 · Hill F 26 1 · Hulme J 40 20 · Jack D 34 18 · James A 40 3 · John R 37 · Jones C 16 · Lambert J 12 14 · Male G · Moss F 41 · Parker T 5 · Parkin R 5 · Preedy C 1 · Roberts H 36 · Sidey N 2 · Stockill R 4 3 · Total: 22 players 118

Position in League Table

	P	W	L	D	F:A	Pts	
Arsenal	42	25	9	8	118:61	58	1st

SEASON 1933-1934
FOOTBALL LEAGUE (DIVISION 1)

26 Aug Birmingham H D 1-1
2 Sep Sheffield W A W 2-1

6 Sep W B A H W 3-1
9 Sep Manchester C H D 1-1
13 Sep W B A A L 0-1
16 Sep Tottenham H A D 1-1
23 Sep Everton A L 1-3
30 Sep Middlesbrough H W 6-0
7 Oct Blackburn Rov H D 2-2
14 Oct Newcastle U H W 3-0
21 Oct Leicester C H W 2-0
28 Oct Aston Villa A W 3-2
4 Nov Portsmouth H D 1-1
11 Nov Wolverhampton W A W 1-0
18 Nov Stoke C H W 3-0
25 Nov Huddersfield T A W 1-0
2 Dec Liverpool H W 2-1
9 Dec Sunderland A L 0-3
16 Dec Chelsea H W 2-1
23 Dec Sheffield U A W 3-1
25 Dec Leeds U A W 1-0
26 Dec Leeds U H W 1-0
30 Dec Birmingham A D 0-0
6 Jan Sheffield W H D 1-1
20 Jan Manchester C A L 1-2
31 Jan Tottenham H H L 1-3
3 Feb Everton H L 1-2
10 Feb Middlesbrough A W 2-0
21 Feb Blackburn H W 2-1
24 Feb Newcastle U A W 1-0
8 Mar Leicester C A L 1-4
10 Mar Aston Villa H W 3-2
24 Mar Wolverhampton W H W 3-2
30 Mar Derby Co H W 1-0
31 Mar Stoke C A D 1-1
2 Apr Derby Co A W 4-2
7 Apr Huddersfield H W 3-1
14 Apr Liverpool A W 3-2
18 Apr Portsmouth A L 0-1
21 Apr Sunderland H W 2-1
28 Apr Chelsea A D 2-2
5 May Sheffield U H W 2-0

FA Cup
13 Jan Luton (3) A W 1-0
27 Jan Crystal Palace (4) H W 7-0
17 Feb Derby Co (5) H W 1-0
3 Mar Aston Villa (6) H L 1-2

FA Charity Shield
18 Oct Everton A W 3-0

Appearances (Goals)
Bastin C 38 (13) · Beasley A 23 (10) · Birkett B 15 (5) · Bowden R 32 (13) · Coleman E 12 (1) · Cox G 2 · Dougall P 5 · Drake E 10 (7) · Dunne J 21 (9) · Hapgood E 40 · Haynes A 1 · Hill F 25 · Hulme J 8 (5) · Jack D 14 (5) · James J 22 (3) John R 31 (1) · Jones C 29 · Lambert J 3 (1) · Male G 42 · Moss F 37 · Parkin R 5 · Roberts H 30 (1) · Sidey N 12 · Wilson A 5 · Own goals 1 · Total: 24 players (75)

Position in League Table

	P	W	L	D	F:A	Pts	
Arsenal	42	25	8	9	75:47	59	1st

SEASON 1934-1935
FOOTBALL LEAGUE (DIVISION 1)

25 Aug Portsmouth A D 3-3
1 Sep Liverpool H W 8-1
5 Sep Blackburn Rov H W 4-0
8 Sep Leeds U A D 1-1
15 Sep W B A H W 4-3
17 Sep Blackburn Rov A L 0-2
22 Sep Sheffield Wed A D 0-0
29 Sep Birmingham H W 5-1
6 Oct Stoke C A D 2-2
13 Oct Manchester C H W 3-0
20 Oct Tottenham H H W 5-1
27 Oct Sunderland A L 1-2
3 Nov Everton H W 2-0
10 Nov Grimsby T A D 2-2
17 Nov Wolverhampton W H L 1-2
24 Nov Chelsea A W 5-2
1 Dec Wolverhampton W H W 7-0
8 Dec Huddersfield T A D 1-1
15 Dec Leicester C H W 8-0
22 Dec Derby Co A L 1-3
25 Dec Preston NE H W 5-3
26 Dec Preston NE A L 1-2
29 Dec Portsmouth H D 1-1
5 Jan Liverpool A W 2-0
19 Jan Leeds U H W 3-0
30 Jan W B A A W 3-0
2 Feb Sheffield W H W 4-1
9 Feb Manchester C A L 0-3
20 Feb Stoke C H W 2-0
23 Feb Manchester C A D 1-1
6 Mar Tottenham H A W 6-0
9 Mar Sunderland H D 0-0
16 Mar Everton A W 2-0
23 Mar Birmingham H D 1-1
30 Mar Aston Villa A W 3-1
6 Apr Chelsea H D 2-2
13 Apr Wolverhampton W A D 1-1
19 Apr Middlesbrough H W 8-0
20 Apr Huddersfield T H W 1-0
22 Apr Middlesbrough A W 1-0
27 Apr Leicester C A W 5-3
4 May Derby Co H L 0-1

FA Cup
12 Jan Brighton & HA (2) A W 2-0
26 Jan Leicester C (3) A W 1-0
16 Feb Reading (4) A W 1-0
2 Mar Sheffield W (5) A L 1-2

FA Charity Shield
28 Nov Man City H W 4-0

Appearances (Goals)
Bastin C 36 (20) · Beasley A 20 (6) · Birkett R 4 (2) · Bowden R 24 (14) · Compton L 5 (1) · Copping W 31 · Crayston J 37 (3) · Davidson R 11 (2) · Dougall P 8 (1) · Drake E 41 (42) · Dunne J 1 · Hapgood E 34 (1) · Hill F 15 (3) · Hulme J 16 (8) · James A 30 · Marshall Drj 4 · Moss F 33 (1) · Roberts L 36 · Rogers L 5 (2) · Sidey N 6 · Trim R 1 · Wilson A 9 · Own goals 3 Total: 25 players (115)

Position in League Table

	P	W	L	D	F:A	Pts	
Arsenal	42	23	7	12	115:46	58	1st

SEASON 1935-1936
FOOTBALL LEAGUE (DIVISION 1)

31 Aug Sunderland H W 3-1
3 Sep Grimsby T A L 0-1
7 Sep Birmingham A D 1-1
11 Sep Grimsby T H W 6-0
14 Sep Sheffield Wed H D 2-2
18 Sep Leeds U A D 1-1
21 Sep Manchester C H L 2-3
28 Sep Stoke C A W 3-0
5 Oct Blackburn Rov H W 5-1
12 Oct Chelsea A D 1-1
19 Oct Portsmouth A L 1-2
26 Oct Preston NE H W 2-1
2 Nov Brentford A L 1-2
9 Nov Derby Co H D 1-1
16 Nov Everton A W 2-0
23 Nov Wolverhampton W H W 4-0
30 Nov Huddersfield T A D 0-0
9 Dec Middlesbrough A W 7-1
14 Dec Aston Villa A W 7-1
25 Dec Liverpool H L 1-2
26 Dec Liverpool A W 1-0
28 Dec Sunderland A L 4-5
4 Jan Birmingham H D 1-1
18 Jan Sheffield Wed A L 2-3
1 Feb Stoke C H W 1-0
8 Feb Blackburn Rov H W 1-0
22 Feb Portsmouth H L 2-3
4 Mar Derby Co A W 4-0
7 Mar Huddersfield T H D 1-1
11 Mar Manchester City A L 0-1
14 Mar Preston NE A L 0-1
25 Mar Everton H D 1-1
28 Mar Wolverhampton W A D 2-2
1 Apr Bolton W H D 1-1
4 Apr Brentford A D 1-1
10 Apr W B A H W 4-0
11 Apr Middlesbrough A D 2-2
13 Apr W B A A L 0-1
18 Apr Aston Villa H W 1-0
27 Apr Chelsea H D 1-1
29 Apr Bolton W A L 1-2
2 May Leeds U H D 2-2

FA Cup
11 Jan Bristol Rov (3) A W 5-1
25 Jan Liverpool (4) A W 2-0
15 Feb Newcastle (5) A D 3-3
19 Feb Newcastle (5R) H W 3-0
29 Feb Barnsley (6) H W 4-1
21 Mar Grimsby T (SF) W 1-0 (at Huddersfield)
25 Apr Sheffield U (F) W 1-0 (at Wembley)

Appearances (Goals)
Bastin C 31 (11) · Beasley A 26 (2) · Bowden R 22 (6) · Cartwright S 5 · Compton L 12 (1) · Copping W 33 · Cox G 5 (1) · Crayston J 36 (5) · Davidson R 13 · Dougall R 8 (3) · Drake E 26 (24) · Dunne J 6 (1) · Hapgood E 33 · Hill F 10 · Hulme J 21 (6) · James A 17 (2) · John R 26 · Joy B 2 · Kirchen A 6 (3) · Male G 35 · Milne J 14 (6) · Moss F 5 · Parkin R 1 · Roberts H 26 (1) · Rogers E 11 (3) · Sidey N 11 · Tuckett E 2 · Westcott R 2 (1) · Wilson A 37 · Own goals 1 · Total: 29 players (78)

Position in League Table

	P	W	L	D	F:A	Pts	
Sunderland	42	25	11	6	109:74	56	1st
Arsenal	42	15	12	15	78:48	45	6th

SEASON 1936-1937
FOOTBALL LEAGUE (DIVISION 1)

29 Aug Everton H W 3-2
3 Sep Brentford A D 0-0
5 Sep Huddersfield T A D 0-0
9 Sep Brentford H D 1-1
12 Sep Sunderland H W 4-1
19 Sep Wolverhampton W A L 0-2
26 Sep Derby Co H D 2-2
3 Oct Manchester U A L 0-2
10 Oct Sheffield Wed H D 1-1
17 Oct Charlton Ath A W 2-0
24 Oct Grimsby T H D 0-0
31 Oct Liverpool A L 1-2
7 Nov Leeds U H W 4-1
14 Nov Birmingham A W 3-1
21 Nov Middlesbrough H W 5-3
28 Nov W B A A W 4-2
5 Dec Manchester City H L 1-3
12 Dec Portsmouth A W 5-1
19 Dec Chelsea H W 4-1
25 Dec Preston NE H W 4-1
26 Dec Everton A D 1-1
28 Dec Preston NE A W 3-1
1 Jan Bolton W H W 5-0
2 Jan Huddersfield T H D 1-1
9 Jan Sunderland A D 1-1

23 Jan Wolverhampton W H W 2-1
3 Feb Derby Co A L 4-5
6 Feb Manchester U H D 1-1
13 Feb Sheffield Wed A D 0-0
24 Feb Charlton Ath H D 1-1
27 Feb Grimsby T A W 3-1
10 Mar Liverpool H W 1-0
13 Mar Leeds U A W 4-3
20 Mar Birmingham H D 1-1
26 Mar Stoke C H D 0-0
27 Mar Middlesbrough A D 1-1
29 Mar Stoke C A D 0-0
3 Apr W B A H W 2-0
10 Apr Manchester City A L 0-2
17 Apr Portsmouth H W 4-0
24 Apr Chelsea A L 0-2
1 May Bolton W H D 0-0

FA Cup
16 Jan Chesterfield (3) A W 5-1
30 Jan Manchester U (4) H W 5-0
20 Feb Burnley (5) A W 7-1
6 Mar W B A (6) A L 1-3

FA Charity Shield
28 Oct Sunderland A L 1-2

Appearances (Goals)
Bastin C 33 (5) · Beasley A 7 (1) · Biggs A 1 · Boulton F 21 · Bowden R 28 (6) · Cartwright S 2 · Compton D 14 (4) · Compton L 15 · Copping W 38 · Crayston J 30 (1) · Davidson R 28 (9) · Drake E 26 (20) · Hapgood E 32 (1) · Hulme J 3 · James A 19 (1) · John R 5 · Joy B 6 · Kirchen A 33 (18) · Male G 37 · Milne J 19 (9) · Nelson D 8 (3) · Roberts H 30 (1) · Sidey N 6 · Swindin G 19 · Wilson A 2 · Own goals 1 · Total: 25 players (80)

Position in League Table

	P	W	L	D	F:A	Pts	
Manchester C	42	22	7	13	107:61	57	1st
Arsenal	42	18	8	16	80:49	52	3rd

SEASON 1937-1938
FOOTBALL LEAGUE (DIVISION 1)

28 Aug Everton A W 4-1
1 Sep Huddersfield T H W 3-1
4 Sep Wolverhampton W H W 5-0
8 Sep Huddersfield T A L 1-2
11 Sep Leicester C A D 1-1
15 Sep Bolton W A L 0-1
18 Sep Sunderland H W 4-1
25 Sep Derby Co A L 0-2
2 Oct Manchester C H W 2-1
9 Oct Chelsea A D 2-2
16 Oct Portsmouth H D 1-1
23 Oct Stoke C A D 1-1
30 Oct Middlesbrough H L 1-2
6 Nov Grimsby T A L 1-2
13 Nov W B A H W 3-0
20 Nov Charlton Ath A W 3-0
27 Nov Leeds U H W 4-1
4 Dec Birmingham A W 3-1
11 Dec Preston NE H W 2-0
18 Dec Liverpool A L 0-2
25 Dec Blackpool A L 1-2

27 Dec Blackpool H W 2-1
1 Jan Everton H W 2-1
15 Jan Wolverhampton W A L 1-3
29 Jan Sunderland A D 1-1
2 Feb Leicester C H W 3-1
5 Feb Derby Co H W 3-0
16 Feb Manchester C A W 2-1
19 Feb Chelsea H W 2-0
26 Feb Preston NE A D 0-0
5 Mar Stoke C H W 4-0
12 Mar Middlesbrough A L 1-2
19 Mar Grimsby H W 5-1
26 Mar W B A A D 0-0
2 Apr Charlton Ath H D 2-2
9 Apr Leeds U A W 1-0
11 Apr Leeds U H W 2-0
15 Apr Manchester U H W 1-0
18 Apr Liverpool H W 2-0
21 Apr Charlton Ath H L 1-2
25 Apr Preston NE A L 1-2
4 Mar Bolton W H L 1-2

11 Mar Leeds U A L 2-4
18 Mar Liverpool H W 2-0
25 Mar Leicester C A W 2-0
1 Apr Middlesbrough H L 1-2
7 Apr Blackpool A L 0-1
8 Apr Birmingham A W 2-1
10 Apr Blackpool H W 2-1
15 Apr Manchester U H W 2-1
22 Apr Stoke C A W 2-1
29 Apr Derby Co A W 2-1
6 May Brentford H W 2-0

FA Cup
8 Jan Bolton W (3) H W 3-1
22 Jan Wolves (4) A W 2-1
12 Feb Preston NE (5) H L 0-1

Appearances (Goals)
Bastin C 38 (15) · Biggs A 2 · Boulton F 15 · Bowden R 10 (1) · Bremner G 2 (1) · Carr E 11 7 · Cartwright S 6 (2) · Collett E 5 · Compton D 7 1 · Compton L 9 (1) · Copping W 38 · Crayston J 31 (6) · Davidson R 5 (2) · Drake E 27 (17) · Drury R 12 (2) · Griffiths W 9 (5) · Hapgood E 41 · Hulme J 7 (2) · Hunt G 18 (3) · Jones L 28 (3) · Joy B 26 · Kirchen A 19 (6) · Lewis R 4 (2) · Male G 34 · Milne J 16 (4) · Roberts H 13 · Sidey N 1 · Swindin G 17 · Wilson A 10 · Own goals 1 · Total: 29 players (77)

Position in League Table

	P	W	L	D	F:A	Pts	
Arsenal	42	21	11	10	77:44	52	1st

SEASON 1938-1939
FOOTBALL LEAGUE (DIVISION 1)

27 Aug Portsmouth H W 2-0
3 Sep Huddersfield T A D 1-1
8 Sep Brentford A L 0-1
10 Sep Everton H D 1-1
14 Sep Derby Co H L 1-2
17 Sep Wolverhampton W A L 0-1
24 Sep Aston Villa H D 0-0
1 Oct Sunderland A L 0-1
8 Oct Grimsby T H W 2-0
15 Oct Chelsea A L 2-4
22 Oct Preston NE H W 1-0
29 Oct Bolton W H D 1-1
5 Nov Leeds U H L 2-3
12 Nov Liverpool A D 2-2
19 Nov Leicester C H D 0-0
26 Nov Middlesbrough A D 1-1
3 Dec Birmingham H W 3-1
10 Dec Manchester U A L 0-1
17 Dec Stoke C H W 4-1
24 Dec Portsmouth A D 0-0
25 Dec Blackpool A L 1-2

27 Dec Charlton Ath A L 0-1
31 Dec Huddersfield T H W 1-0
14 Jan Everton A L 0-2
21 Jan Charlton Ath H W 2-0
28 Jan Aston Villa A W 3-2
1 Feb Wolverhampton W H D 0-0
4 Feb Sunderland H W 2-0
18 Feb Chelsea H W 1-0
21 Feb Grimsby T A L 1-2
25 Feb Preston NE A L 1-2
4 Mar Bolton W A L 2-4
11 Mar Leeds U A W 2-0
18 Mar Liverpool H W 2-0
25 Mar Leicester C A W 2-0
1 Apr Middlesbrough H L 1-2
7 Apr Blackpool A L 0-1
8 Apr Birmingham A W 2-1
10 Apr Blackpool H W 2-1
15 Apr Manchester U H W 2-1
22 Apr Stoke C A W 2-1
29 Apr Derby Co A W 2-1
6 May Brentford H W 2-0

FA Cup
7 Jan Chelsea (3) A L 1-2

FA Charity Shield
26 Sep Preston H W 2-1

Appearances (Goals)
Bastin C 23 (3) · Bremner G 13 (3) · Carr E 1 · Cartwright S 3 · Collett R 9 · Compton D 1 · Compton L 18 (2) · Copping W 26 · Crayston J 34 (3) · Cumner R 12 (2) · Curtis G 2 · Drake E 38 (14) · Drury G 23 (3) · Farr A 2 (1) · Fields J 28 (3) · Hapgood E 38 · Jones B 30 (4) · Jones B 30 4 · Jones L 18 · Joy B 39 · Kirchen A 27 (9) · Lewis R 15 (7) · Male G 28 · Marks G 2 · Nelson D 9 (1) · Pryde D 4 · Pugh S 1 · Swindin G 21 · Walsh W 3 · Wilson A 19 · Own goals 3 · Total: 29 players (55)

Position in League Table

	P	W	L	D	F:A	Pts	
Everton	42	27	10	5	88:52	59	1st
Arsenal	42	19	14	9	55:41	47	5th

SEASON 1939-1940
FOOTBALL LEAGUE (DIVISION 1)

(Prior to outbreak of War)
26 Aug Wolverhampton W 2 Arsenal 2
30 Aug Arsenal 1 Blackburn Rov 0
2 Sep Arsenal 5 Sunderland 2
21 Aug Jubilee Match
Arsenal 1 Tottenham H 1 (Drury)

Goal Scorers (Football League)

Drake	4
Bastin	1
Drury	1
Lewis	1
Kirchen	1

Arsenal FC 1938-39. Back Row (l to r): C. Bastin, E. Drake, J. Crayston, A. Wilson, B. Joy, C. Male, T. Whittaker (Trainer)
Front Row: R. Lewis, G. Drury, E. Hapgood (Captain), G. Allison (Sec-Manager), W. Copping, B. Jones, A. Kirchen.

1886-1939

CHAPTER 7
WHITTAKER'S ARSENAL

Altogether, 42 of Arsenal's 44 professionals in September 1939 had gone into the services. The administrators at Highbury followed, and the ground itself played a part in the war effort – Arsenal Stadium was transformed into a stronghold for ARP (Air Raid Precautions). The club was temporarily based at White Hart Lane, although for a time George Allison converted the referees' room at Highbury into a small flat. Amid the confusion of wartime competitions and the difficulties of finding who was able to play when and where, Arsenal's success nonetheless continued.

Wartime honours

In 1939–40 the South 'A' League was won, and in the following season the club reached another Wembley final in the Football League War Cup. With young Laurie Scott partnering Hapgood at full-back and Bernard Joy at centre-half, the attack was led by Les Compton, who at Wembley against Preston North End missed a penalty. Brother Denis' goal earned a replay, but with Drake now replacing the elder Compton Arsenal lost at Blackburn 2–1.

The football honours, such as they were in austere circumstances, continued: Champions of the London League in 1941–42 and the Football League South the following season, when there was also a successful return to Wembley, this time in the Football League South Cup final. Reg Lewis, who was to make his mark at the Empire Stadium in more illustrious peacetime circumstances, contributed four goals in a 7–1 thrashing of Charlton Athletic. The gifted forward whose casual approach and happy knack of scoring was to make him such a popular figure at Highbury in the early post-war years finished the 1942–43 season with a remarkable tally of 53 goals.

Two seasons later Lewis was not available and Arsenal's scoring honours were shared by Drake and Stan Mortensen from Blackpool, one of many guest players. Stanley Matthews was another in one wartime league game – he scored. For Ted Drake, though, a slipped disc proved to be one injury that even that gallant forward could not overcome, and his dramatic career finally ended.

The effort of continuing football in the war years proved extremely costly. Pre-war debts of some £150,000 were a millstone when the 1945–46 season began with regional leagues retained and the return of the FA Cup the major concession to normality. White Hart Lane was still the home venue for the most remarkable match of that confused season.

Right: Les Compton joined Arsenal in the 1931–32 season and was finally to retire from the game at the end of the disappointing 1951–52 season. When he was finally capped at the age of 36, he became the oldest ever England debutant.

Left: Tom Whittaker formally became manager in 1947 and remained in the job until his death in 1956. The parallels with Chapman's management are, to say the least, interesting. Both men were in full charge for nine years, both won two Championships, both reached two FA Cup finals, and both won the first and lost the second two years later.

Dynamo shine in Highbury fog

Late in 1945 Moscow Dynamo arrived on an unprecedented tour. With regular European football still more than a decade away, the visit was greeted with a sense of mystery mingled with anticipation.

George Allison's own account of the events surrounding the match, played in a peasouper fog, tell of the scurrying around to find a team worthy of the illustrious pre-war standards that Moscow Dynamo would expect and the opposition's misunderstanding of these efforts.

The Russians scored twice in the second half, and the match ran its allotted span; the suggestion of subterfuge could not disguise the flair and discipline glimpsed through the fog.

League fare resumed

First Division football returned to Arsenal Stadium on 4 September 1946 against Blackburn Rovers and 'Marksman' summed up the mood, without forgetting: 'You who talked Arsenal with me over a campfire in Assam and the chap with the Italy Star on the train in India who informed me of Herbert Roberts passing on, the fellow in the Skymaster on the long hop from Ceylon to the Cocos Islands who told me about our Cup final win and all those who played with or against Tom Whittaker's Arsenal Arps in the very early days of ARP. And the older ones who stuck to the job in London through a bomb and fire and rocket yet still made the long trek up to White Hart Lane to give the boys a cheer. We're home again now!'

On the field the resumption was inauspicious. It began with a defeat at Wolves where six goals and one of Bernard Joy's eyeteeth were lost. Reg Lewis, after scoring, ended up in goal, but his 11 goals in the first ten matches papered over some of the cracks. But others ran deep with little young talent immediately available; the move to White Hart Lane had deferred the production line at Highbury. Icelander Albert Gudmundsson, an amateur, was one of 31 players used in the League. The charismatic Dr Kevin O'Flanagan, an international at football and rugby, on one occasion on successive weekends, was another. Walley Barnes made his debut early in November, but it was two signings in the subsequent weeks which lifted Arsenal from the bottom of the First Division.

Joe Mercer, who had been in the England team as an attacking wing half at the outbreak of war, was in dispute with Everton. At 32 he had virtually decided to retire to concentrate on a grocery business in Wallasey. Surprise interest from Arsenal reawakened his ambition. He signed on condition that he could live and train in Liverpool. Allison and Whittaker were not worried about his ageing, bandy legs. They had purchased a football brain, and by converting Mercer to a defensive half-back they got full return for an investment of £7,000.

Two weeks after Mercer, Arsenal added another bargain. At 35 Ronnie Rooke looked an even more unlikely buy, but the short-term need for goals was critical. Rooke struck 21 in 24 League games and the details of his transfer – a fee of £1,000 plus two players moving from Highbury to Fulham – emphasised again the shrewdness of the Arsenal management. Rooke did not finish top scorer. That honour fell to Lewis with a splendid 29 in 28 First Division matches. From the foot of the table the two lifted Arsenal to the respectability of mid-table; in 13th place they still finished top of the London pecking order,

Above: In addition to the complete destruction of the North Stand, the terracing at the southern end of the ground suffered bomb damage during the Second World War, and this had to be repaired before Arsenal could return from their wartime home – White Hart Lane.

The manager's dealings finally produced six 'guests': goalkeeper Bill Griffiths from Cardiff, left-back Joe Bacuzzi from Fulham, left-half Reg Halton from Bury and three illustrious forwards – Matthews, Mortensen and Ronnie Rooke, whom Allison would sign from Fulham the following season. George Drury, now 31, and Horace Cumner, both survivors from the Arsenal pre-war scene, were the other two forwards, while Joy was at centre-half, 33-year-old Cliff Bastin at right-half and Scott at right-back.

The 54,620 spectators had only sporadic views of the proceedings when the fog occasionally lifted, as did the referee, a Russian, and his two linesmen. Moscow Dynamo scored in their first attack, through Bobrov, but Rooke equalised and then the ebullient Mortensen struck twice. At half time it was 3–2 but sinister whisperings reached the ears of George Allison that the Russian referee would abandon the match if Dynamo fell further behind. On the other hand, if they were to recapture the lead the match would be played to a finish, however thick the fog.

1945-1966

although in the third match of a five-hour FA Cup third round saga Chelsea finally triumphed on 'neutral' soil at White Hart Lane with two goals from Tommy Lawton.

Whittaker takes charge

For two tremendous servants, however, the road had come to an end. Cliff Bastin had been restricted to just six League matches, and he needed an operation on his middle ear in April 1947. The dreadful winter led to an extension of the season into June. It was too much for a wearied George Allison who, after an association with the club of four decades, announced his resignation: 'Now I feel the need for a less strenuous life and I leave the future of Arsenal in other hands.'

Those hands had already cared for so many Arsenal players and other sportsmen of great renown. Tom Whittaker, the master trainer, had modestly stayed in the background, vastly influential on the football side of the club while Allison had shown his considerable talents in the business and publicity departments. Now, for all his personal reluctance to step into the limelight, the time was right for him to accept the demanding post of secretary-manager.

Bob Wall always recalled Whittaker at work in shirtsleeves with a pot of tea never far away. A gentle, kindly man, he had spent the war in the RAF. As a qualified engineer he had repaired aircraft, sending them out to battle again with the

Ian McPherson was an RAF pilot of some distinction during the Second World War. The Scottish player was a regular for post-war Arsenal and his wing wizardry was instrumental in bringing the title to Highbury in 1948.

painstaking detail which had aided the recovery of so many Arsenal footballers. Having fought in the First World War, he was awarded the MBE for secret work in connection with the D-Day landings in the Second.

Joe Shaw returned from Chelsea, where he had been assistant manager, to become Tom Whittaker's right-hand man. The 1947–48 season began with a temporary captain. Les Compton still had cricket responsibilities for Middlesex, so Joe Mercer led out Arsenal for the opening League game at home to Sunderland. The pitch had been reseeded, the running track around it resurfaced. There was optimism in the air and it was to be well founded.

The playing strength was augmented by two more signings. Archie Macaulay from Brentford had starred for Scotland at Wembley the previous April and also represented Great Britain against the Rest of Europe.

After much persuading – Whittaker made 11 trips to see him before the deal was done – forward Don Roper arrived from Southampton and a football family. His grandfather played for Chesterfield, his father for Huddersfield Town and Royal Marines, with whom he won an Amateur Cup medal. Rejection by Hampshire County Cricket Club after trials during the summer of 1947 had sharpened Roper's appetite to make a career in football.

Gunners' record start

What was to become a historic season began on 23 August with a 3.30 kick-off at Highbury against Sunderland. Three goals, from Ian McPherson, Jimmy Logie and Rooke, all in the opening 15 minutes of the second half, produced a 3–1 victory. Four days later Charlton were swept aside 4–2 at The Valley, with McPherson running riot against the FA Cup holders, scoring one and laying on the other three for Roper, Lewis and Logie. The Scottish winger had returned to football with impressive war-time credentials as an RAF pilot, his bravery winning him the DFC and bar. Though naturally an outside right, his early contributions to Whittaker's bright start to the season were on the opposite flank.

A third successive victory came at Bramall Lane, Rooke levelling the score before Roper's 35-yarder was fumbled by the home goalkeeper Smith with only three minutes remaining. Reg Lewis then took centre stage with four goals – Rooke claimed the other two – in a 6–0 demolition of Charlton in the return match at Highbury; the visitors were handicapped by an eighth-minute injury to defender Peter Croker who went off with knee ligaments damaged trying to curb McPherson.

Manchester United were Highbury's next visitors, and the 10,000 fans locked outside when the gates were closed at 3 pm missed a memorable 2–1 victory, courtesy of goals from Rooke and Lewis. The expectation at the club was highlighted even more by the decision of Bryn Jones to turn down a move to Newport County. 'I'll stay until they chase me away, first team or not,' was the retort of the skilful Welsh international.

For the first time Arsenal extended a sequence of wins at the start of a season to six – Bolton Wanderers, the next victims, were defeated 2–0 at Highbury. McPherson and a Rooke penalty contributed the goals in a match which Arsenal finished with only seven fit men. Lewis, recently watched by England selectors, pulled a thigh muscle after ten minutes. Before half time Alf Fields strained tendons leaping over his own goalkeeper, George Swindin. Rooke and McPherson were also limping at the end of the match. Tom Whittaker sensed the need for the return of Les Compton, who had been given permission to continue his cricket with Middlesex.

Mercer still skipper

The tall wicketkeeper was back in the Arsenal dressing room at Deepdale for match number seven and, as club captain, was given a ball by Whittaker to lead out the team. Modestly Compton passed it to Mercer saying: 'If you don't mind Tom, I think Joe should have this. He's not done too badly with the job so far.' Thus Mercer retained the captaincy which was to bring more than a touch of romance to the twilight days of his career. Without Lewis at the sharp end of the attack the first point was dropped at Preston in a goalless draw, but the following week Stoke City were on the receiving end of a three-goal first-half performance, with Bryn Jones enjoying a rare first-team appearance.

Lewis was back but Mercer missing with food poisoning for a tough trip to Burnley, which brought a hard-fought success, with Barnes making one desperate clearance off the line. The winning goal from Lewis came against the balance of play. With two reserves, Paddy Sloan and the loyal George Male, as wing halves, Arsenal could only draw the next match at home to Portsmouth, but victory had been there for the taking when Rooke's 39th-minute penalty was brilliantly saved by Butler.

Goals remained hard to come by throughout October, a time when the flair of Denis Compton might have added an extra spice to Whittaker's recipe for success. But Britain's most glamorous sports star was confined to a hospital bed for the removal of some floating body from a troublesome knee. Aston Villa's visit to Highbury drew a 61,000 capacity crowd and a 1–0 win, but the goal was disputed with Rooke getting away with a push on centre-half, and ex-Gunner, Frank Moss before racing clear to score. A thumping penalty from Rooke brought a share of the points at Molineux, and it was a penalty against Arsenal, conceded by Leslie Compton and converted by Eddie Wainwright, that cost a point in the next match

against Everton at Highbury. The brilliance of visiting goal-keeper Ted Sagar had restricted Arsenal to a solitary score from Lewis in the 65th minute.

Arsenal prove the big draw

With football such an attraction after the sacrifices of war, Arsenal, as First Division leaders, had already become the major draw. Stamford Bridge played host to a crowd of 67,277 for Chelsea's clash with the Gunners on 1 November. Astonishingly some 27,000 also watched the reserve game between the two clubs at Highbury on the same afternoon; the appearance of Tommy Lawton in the Chelsea second string heightened the appeal of the fixture.

In the senior match Arsenal came away with a goalless draw, the unbeaten record still intact. It remained so seven days later when Blackpool, with Mortensen and Matthews, were beaten 2–1 at Highbury through another Rooke penalty and a Don Roper goal. Before the Blackpool match Whittaker addressed the Highbury crowd with a request to 'Keep up your reputation for sportsmanship. Don't barrack the referee.'

With more than a third of the season gone Arsenal stood proudly six points clear of Burnley at the top of the tree, with a record of: Played 17, Won 12, Drawn 5, Lost 0, goals for 31, against 8. Yet the tag of 'lucky' was still being pinned on the team. Public opinion held the view that progress had come from efficient organisation and defensive discipline rather than football of a higher level than the opposition.

Thus the inevitable first defeat, on 29 November at Derby County, was not shattering news. The Baseball Ground was packed to the rafters to see the pursuit of a record (22 games unbeaten from the start of a season) held by Preston and Sheffield United collapse to a goal in the 32nd minute.

A goal in the same minute a week later, by Black of Manchester City at Highbury, threatened another defeat, but five minutes from time Les McDowall was penalised for handball. Rooke sent his penalty past Frank Swift, and there was no disputing that, on this occasion, Arsenal were fortunate.

In such circumstances a visit to bottom club, Grimsby Town, could only be viewed as a welcome opportunity to return to the groove of earlier in the season. The Blundell Park club had conceded three goals per match on average over the first half of the season; Arsenal managed four through the reliable Rooke (2), Logie and Roper.

Gunners maintain momentum

The Saturday before Christmas has now been accepted an an attendance low spot with the demands of shopping for the festivities ahead. It was not so in 1947 when more than 58,000

1945-1966

flocked to Roker Park to watch Arsenal in the flesh. The vast majority of them almost had an early holiday treat when Davis sent Sunderland into the lead with only ten minutes remaining, but five minutes later the limping Barnes, a passenger at centre-forward, helped create an equaliser. Bryn Jones was to play only seven times in the Championship season but his Roker Park equaliser, his solitary goal of the campaign, held great significance; a second defeat with the congested holiday fixture list ahead might have badly disturbed the Arsenal momentum.

Instead the two Christmas matches produced typically contrary results. The Football League, with scant regard for the family life of footballers, paired Arsenal home and away with Liverpool! Only Mercer with his Merseyside base could have relished the Christmas morning start at Anfield, but the team responded to the challenge with two goals from Rooke and another from Roper which ended Liverpool's unbeaten home record. Two days later though, revenge was claimed. Albert Stubbins and Billy Liddell struck to stop Arsenal's invincible run at Highbury; Lewis replied too late to salvage a draw from a match for which touts did a roaring trade, with reports of tickets valued at *7s. 6d.* (37p) changing hands at more than four times that price!

On New Year's Day, Arsenal, 4–0 winners at Bolton, stood five points clear at the top. The 37-year-old George Male was pressed into service at Burnden Park and gave a sound performance. Bolton claimed that they had equalised a 32nd-minute goal from Lewis in a late scramble when the ball appeared to have crossed the line before Swindin pulled it clear. The crowd was allowed in only half-an-hour before an early start on a pitch flooded by melted snow and the referee dispensed with the half-time interval.

Arsenal's quest for football honour continued with a 3–2 victory over Sheffield United in the last game of the holiday programme. United were down to ten men when Rooke grabbed an important second goal; the player off the field was Alex Forbes, the flame-haired wing half shortly to return to Highbury as part of Whittaker's team strengthening. Forbes had been concussed and remembered nothing of his return to the pitch, during which time United scored twice in the last five minutes to give the scoreline a rather flattering look.

Shock Cup exit

With the FA Cup providing a new challenge and a break to the slog for the Championship, Tom Whittaker was not the sort of man to underestimate a kindly draw, a home tie with Second Division Bradford Park Avenue. Consequently, he took his players to Brighton (shades of pre-war delights) for a few days' preparation in the bracing sea air. It did not have the desired

Above: Denis Compton returned to the injury-hit Arsenal first team on 14 February 1948 and was vital to their run-in to the League Championship that year. Here, however, he is seen in the 0-2 defeat by Chelsea on 20 March.

effect. In Billy Elliott, the Yorkshire club possessed a locally born left-winger who would later play for England after a transfer to Burnley; the 22-year-old Elliott knocked in a first-half goal. Bradford also included centre-half Ron Greenwood as the cornerstone of their rearguard action in that third round tie at Highbury, and Arsenal's FA Cup ambitions perished.

There was little time for despondency. The next two First Division opponents also had their eyes on the League title, Manchester United and Preston. United still played their home matches at Maine Road, because of war damage at Old Trafford, and interest in the visit of the leaders was massive. More than 80,000 spectators crammed into the ground for a game that finished level after Lewis had drawn first blood and Jack Rowley equalised.

Lewis was now operating at inside right and he retained the position for the tussle with Preston, striking two more valuable goals. Rooke was also on target, while Don Roper enjoyed an inspired afternoon. With those three important points in the bag since the Cup disappointment, Arsenal continued to set a blistering pace at the top of the League. In February Stoke City took the unusual step of making their home match all-ticket against the leaders, but the 41,000 ticket-holders did not witness a goal, largely due to a succession of saves from Swindin.

For the Valentine's Day fixture against Burnley, the Arsenal team appropriately contained a touch of romance. Denis Compton, who had turned out in only one post-war League match, was called into the senior side in place of the injured

McPherson. For such a charismatic performer it was a perfect opportunity against a side which came to Highbury needing a win to close the gap at the top. Compton's return captured the imagination of the paying public; 20,000 arrived too late to get into the packed ground

It took Compton only 14 minutes to play his part. His lob was punched by goalkeeper Strong straight to Roper who drove the ball into the Burnley net. Rooke added two more, with Compton also involved in the move that led to Arsenal's third goal. With 13 matches still to play, the Gunners now held an eight-point advantage over their closest challengers.

A veteran line-up

Meanwhile, Tom Whittaker had not grown complacent about the depth of talent at the club. Because of the immediate post-war circumstances Arsenal were fielding one of the oldest sides ever to win the Championship, with Rooke, now 36, Les Compton 35 and Mercer 33 holding three of the key roles. Quietly, Whittaker was adding to his staff. Cliff Holton, an amateur from Oxford City, was signed in November 1947. Peter Goring, eternally to be dubbed as the butcher's boy, gave up his part-time football with Cheltenham Town to join the Arsenal staff the following January, and the next month a senior player arrived in the shape of Alex Forbes, whose swashbuckling performances for Sheffield United had often caught the eye of the Highbury crowd.

Alex Forbes' Arsenal debut was delayed until after the third defeat of the League campaign, at Aston Villa on 28 February, which should really not have happened at all. An own goal by Frank Moss and another from Rooke gave Arsenal a 2–1 lead when Denis Compton was tripped in the Villa penalty area. Rooke put his penalty wide, and Villa revelled in the second chance they had been given. Leslie Compton had been injured in training and played with one leg strapped from ankle to knee. In Trevor Ford, the fiery Welsh international, the home side had the perfect forward to capitalise on a weak link. Ford roasted his marker completely, and scored twice as Villa raced home to a 4–2 win.

Alex Forbes was chosen at inside left for his debut, with Wolves the opposition on a foggy Highbury afternoon. Many of the crowd were still settling down when Hancocks caught Arsenal cold with a goal after 80 seconds, but Forbes immediately began to justify his £12,000 transfer fee. His equaliser in the eighth minute delighted his new supporters and his dance back to the centre won him a place in their hearts. It was a tremendous start for a player who had once turned his back on football in favour of ice hockey. Whittaker had sent Macaulay to persuade him to come to Highbury when Forbes was in hospital recovering from appendicitis.

Above: George Male retired as a player in 1948. His very last first-class game was a perfect ending to a great career; it was on 1 May 1948 at home to Grimsby and Arsenal won 8-0, confirming their status as League Champions. Although Male played two more games on tour that summer, the Grimsby match was the last formal appearance of any of the players from the Chapman era. Like many of his colleagues, Male then went onto the coaching staff and became a tough task-master.

Wolves led again but with Denis Compton in irrepressible form in the second half Arsenal bounced back to win 5–2. A week later at Goodison Park the cricketing footballer did even better, scoring his first two post-war League goals in a 2-0 triumph over Everton.

Unpredictable Gunners

After only three defeats in 32 games, it came as a surprise that two more followed in the next three matches. The first came at Highbury where Chelsea chalked up a 2–0 victory. John Harris did a magnificent job containing Rooke and Chelsea carried enough venom in their attack to strike through Bobby Campbell and Roy Bentley. The other loss was sustained at Blackpool, where two goals from Stan Mortensen took him to the top of the First Division scorers list, with one more than the 27 of Rooke.

A week earlier fate had not been kind to Bob Anderson, whose misfortune it was to make his League debut in the Middlesbrough goal against Arsenal at Highbury. Smarting from the home defeat by Chelsea, Arsenal confronted the untried keeper in a mean mood. Among the seven goals that flashed past Anderson were two more from Denis Compton, and a hat-trick from Rooke, which was completed when he headed a tentative clearance from the goalkeeper straight back past him. So one-sided was the match that newspaper reports of the time make reference to several thousand supporters leaving at half time. Poor Bob Anderson never played again in the First Division.

Whittaker's Champs

With fewer and fewer fixtures left available for the chasing pack to close on their prey, Arsenal moved another step nearer to safety by completing a double over Blackburn Rovers at Highbury, Logie's sixth goal of the season and Rooke's 29th providing a margin of sufficient comfort; on 10 April Arsenal took the field at Huddersfield nine points clear with just five matches left. A win at Leeds Road would see Whittaker's men breasting the tape. The conclusion to the season, however, was not so decisive.

A goal from Don Roper brought only one point, and the players had to bath and change so quickly to catch the London train that they could not discover the day's other results. It was Denis Compton who broke the glad tidings. At Doncaster he ran for a paper which reported defeats for Manchester United, Burnley and Derby County. Arsenal were Champions, and had led from start to finish. George Male, the last of the great pre-war side, played at Huddersfield, and as ever turned in a highly polished performance.

1945-1966

Inevitably anticlimax followed, with Derby winning at Highbury the following Saturday, and two successive goalless draws at Portsmouth and Manchester City. There was, however, a celebration on 1 May though only 35,000, the smallest home gate of the season, were there to see it. Yorkshire-born Lionel Smith was given his League baptism at centre-half, but it was the attack which made the headlines. Arsenal ripped into Grimsby to the tune of 8–0, and four goals for Rooke confirmed him, with 33, as the Football League's leading scorer – and this at the age of 36!

George Swindin had conceded only 32 goals in the full League programme and added a second Championship medal to that gained in 1938. Rooke was the only other ever-present player, though Macaulay, Mercer and Roper missed just two matches and Logie and Laurie Scott three. Les Compton collected a League winners' medal to go with his memento of cricket Championship success the previous September (a rare double). So too did brother Denis, though he had to wait until October to receive his because of doubts as to whether his 14 appearances were sufficient qualification.

The retreating defence

Undoubtedly the consistency of the big-hearted Rooke proved to be a marvellous attribute throughout the season, but much of Arsenal's success came from the reliability of their defensive method. Joe Mercer labelled it as the 'retreating' defence. The prevailing style of the day was to try to win the ball in midfield with an attempted tackle on the opponent in possession. If that tackle was lost then there was little sophisticated covering. Mercer, with Macaulay as a shrewd ally, preferred Arsenal to leave the ball with the opposition and back off, packing the centre of the defence. Arsenal's captain had noted the success of such manoeuvres in basketball during the war, when he'd played service games with Americans. The crowd did not always like the tactic, newspaper comment denounced it as negative, but the rest of the First Division, with the exception of Derby County, who beat Arsenal twice, could not fathom out a solution. The seven-point margin at the end of the season was ample testimony to Arsenal's worth as Champions.

The players presented Tom Whittaker with a silver cigarette box inscribed 'To Tom/In Appreciation/From The Boys'. The manager, however, was already aware that the side had not been built to last. Before the end of May 1948 he had acquired the potential of Doug Lishman, a regular scorer for Walsall in the Third Division South. Nevertheless, the 1948–49 season began with the air still full of anticlimax. It took a run of wins in the autumn to lift the club from the bottom half of the table to fifth place, where Arsenal stayed. Derby County again proved to be a bogey team for the Gunners, taking three of the four

League points and knocking Whittaker's side out of the FA Cup at the Baseball Ground in the fourth round.

One match did stand out, an extravagant 4–3 victory in the Charity Shield against the Cup holders Manchester United at Highbury. Incredibly Arsenal led 3–0 after just five minutes – Jones, Lewis and Rooke – but United's resolve stood the test. Lewis scored again for Arsenal, a splendid solo goal, but the destiny of the Charity Shield was not finally settled until the last blast of the referee's whistle.

Rooke joins Palace

Rooke's magnificent contribution to the history of Arsenal Football Club ended in June 1949. His 68 goals in 88 First Division games were ample evidence of his contribution. At 37 he refused to contemplate retirement, and moved as player-manager to Crystal Palace, his pre-war club, where he paid his way in goals for two more seasons. A man of iron who never flinched from the physical contact of those who tried to stop him, he left Highbury with the satisfaction of having more than answered the call of George Allison: 'Ronnie, we're in trouble. We've got to get goals, by hook or by Rooke.'

The other half of the duo who turned the tide at Highbury in 1946 remained at the club. Joe Mercer passed his 35th birthday during pre-season training prior to the 1949–50 season, and if one target drove him to continue playing it was a search for the honour which had eluded him, an FA Cup winners' medal. Mercer had been a young reserve at Everton when they had won the most romantic of the game's trophies in 1933. The following day a kindly Albert Geldard, who had played in that final, was cleaning his boots beside Mercer at Goodison Park and offered the youthful Mercer a piece of Wembley turf. 'No thanks, I'll get some myself one day,' was the confident reply. It seemed that those words would haunt him.

Four defeats in the opening five matches of the season may well have concentrated the players' minds on the FA Cup; the only win during that dismal start had come at Chelsea where Peter Goring scored on his debut and Swindin captained the side in the absence of Mercer and Les Compton. Brother Denis had ended speculation that he had played his last for Arsenal by signing for the new season on the eve of the third Test against New Zealand, thus becoming one of 54 professionals on the staff.

The Wembley trail

League performances improved sufficiently to achieve a respectable sixth place at the end of the season but it was the Cup which cheered all at Highbury. The run began against Sheffield Wednesday on 7 January 1950.

Below: The cover of the official Arsenal yearbook for the 1948–49 season.

The Yorkshiremen were in-form opponents, unbeaten for three months. Their teamwork almost came to their rescue despite losing right-back Vince Kenny, injured in the tie. Reg Lewis finally made the breakthrough with 13 seconds on the referee's watch. The crowd was 10,000 under capacity because publicity suggesting a huge attendance had deterred many from what they believed would be a wasted journey.

The signs remained good in the draw for the fourth round, another home game against Swansea Town, who were labouring in the lower half of the Second Division. On a frosty pitch the underdogs performed gallantly while Arsenal again looked anything but potential winners of the competition. The decisive goal in a fortunate 2–1 win came ironically from a Welshman. Keane handled and Walley Barnes slotted the penalty past the left hand of goalkeeper Jack Parry.

George Swindin, the dry Yorkshireman who had been signed from Bradford City in 1936, had added the role of prophet to his more usual occupation of goalkeeper. Before each round so far he had foretold that Arsenal would be given a home tie. Again his words rang true when Burnley came out of the hat to visit Highbury in round five. In a small way the visitors had contributed to the Cup aspirations of the team they now faced, because on the opening day of the season it had been Burnley who had beaten Arsenal in the capital and thus set the Highbury League campaign off on a flat note.

The lure of the Cup, not for the first or last time, produced an indulgence in preparation. There was no seaside training in the traditional manner; instead the Arsenal squad were treated to sessions under sunray equipment to tone them up. Goals from Lewis and Denis Compton did the trick, though Mercer remembers getting away with handball in his own goalmouth.

Swindin forecast another home draw with the added prediction that Leeds United would be the opposition. Incredibly it came true, and it looked as though, in football parlance, Arsenal's 'name was on the FA Cup'. Leeds also languished in the Second Division, but their reaction to a first Cup tie at Highbury produced a creditable display. Lewis, who was to finish behind Goring in the League scoring charts, added to his catalogue of significant Cup goals by darting between two defenders to score. Arsenal were into the semi-finals and they had not been forced to leave Highbury to get there.

Semi-final fightback

A semi-final with Chelsea meant that they still did not have to leave north London, and the saga of the tie remains as memorable as the final itself. At White Hart Lane Chelsea brought back the former England international Len Goulden; at 37 he had been out of favour for six months. When Chelsea sprinted into a 2–0 lead after 25 minutes, both goals from Bentley,

Above: 1950 FA Cup Final souvenir edition of the *Sporting Mirror*, published the day before the match.

Goulden must have been dreaming of a fairy tale visit to Wembley. Arsenal had other ideas, although it needed an outright stroke of good fortune to help put those ideas into effect.

Outside right Freddie Cox knew White Hart Lane well; he had been signed from Spurs in September 1949 in an attempt to halt the slide at the start of the season. The best years of his footballing life had been sacrificed in wartime when he had flown Dakotas in Transport Command.

In the dying seconds of the first half Cox struck a corner with the outside of his foot. The ball veered in towards the Chelsea goal and was over the line before Harry Medhurst, the goalkeeper, made a vain attempt to keep it out. Cox, who died in 1973 after a career in League management, never claimed any deliberate intent, but Arsenal gratefully accepted the touch of luck, and came out for the second half in determined vein.

A family affair

Yet with a quarter-of-an-hour remaining they were still trailing. Another corner, this time from the left wing, came to the rescue. Again the goal had a story behind it. As Denis Compton prepared to take the flag kick he waved forward brother Leslie. Joe Mercer countered by telling the centre-half to stay back, but blood being thicker than water and the need for an equaliser pressing, Compton the elder ignored his captain's instructions. The fraternal pair emphatically won the argument when Denis' corner found the forehead of Les and the ball sped into the Chelsea net. On balance of play Arsenal had been fortunate to earn a replay, but this had been Chelsea's chance and it had gone.

Arsenal's form was much improved in the replay, which also took place at Tottenham, the following Wednesday. George Swindin's ability to predict the future passed, it seemed, to Eileen, the wife of Freddie Cox. On the Tuesday night she dreamed that her husband would score the goal that took Arsenal to Wembley. And so he did, but not until the 14th minute of extra time, with his weaker left foot.

Liverpool in the final

The journey to the Empire Stadium, therefore, became the longest Arsenal had had to make in the entire Cup run. By an odd coincidence Liverpool had reached the final without having to leave the north-west, beating rivals Everton at Maine Road, Manchester in the semi-final. Bob Paisley, later to become the most successful of all Liverpool managers, had scored the vital goal against Everton, but he was left out of the team for the final.

Most of the country's neutrals hoped that Joe Mercer, one of the game's best-loved characters, would at last complete his

1945-1966

collection of medals. Yet unwittingly Arsenal's captain found himself in the midst of what could have been an embarrassing situation. He had continued to train in the north-west of England – with Liverpool! Understandably he was asked not to join the Liverpool first team at Anfield for fear that he would find out too much about their Wembley battle-plan. He was not banned from the ground, but his access was restricted to afternoon sessions.

Liverpool were managed by George Kay, West Ham's captain in the first Wembley final in 1923. Kay had nurtured a team of whom the majority had come through the ranks, notably the Scottish international forward Billy Liddell. Liddell, reckoned the Arsenal players, was the most likely barrier to their winning the Cup. Moreover, Liverpool held an important psychological advantage. They had won both of that season's League meetings with Arsenal, 2–1 at Highbury in September, 2–0 at Anfield on New Year's Eve.

On the eve of the final itself Mercer was hailed Footballer of the Year by the Football Writers' Association. Tom Whittaker had already decided upon his team. Lishman, McPherson, Macaulay and Roper had their merits considered but were passed over; Goring kept his place, the Wembley setting being a perfect ending to his first season at senior level.

Rain fell heavily on 29 April 1950. Wembley was bursting at the seams, although the ticket allocation for each of the two clubs ran to only 11,500 (4,500 seats, 7,000 standing) of the 100,000 capacity stadium.

Above: The first of Reg Lewis' two goals for Arsenal in the 1950 FA Cup final. Both were sharp breaks which left Liverpool keeper Cyril Sidlow with little chance. It had been a good Cup year for Arsenal; they were drawn at home throughout and played both semis against Chelsea at White Hart Lane, and thus never left London.

Clashing Reds

Both teams had to change from their usual red shirts; Liverpool opted for white with black shorts, Arsenal took the field in shirts of old gold with white shorts. Two pre-match decisions helped turn the tide of the battle towards the north London club. Forbes had been given the task of subduing the threat of Liddell, and after some early alarms the forceful wing half, who had been recalled by Scotland two weeks before the final, coped splendidly.

An even more significant decision had been to keep faith with the 30-year-old Reg Lewis. It had not been taken lightly. Lewis undoubtedly scored goals, but at times he could look lazy and lethargic. His skill had not been in question from the moment he had begun his League career with a debut goal against Everton on New Year's Day 1938. Yet Whittaker often dropped him, and Mercer's voice, among others, was heard in defence of Lewis before his place was finally confirmed.

At Wembley he became the match-winner, collecting both goals, coincidentally, at identical times in each half. The first, after 17 minutes, came when Goring moved away, distracting the attention of Liverpool defenders. Jimmy Logie had the ball at his feet; the tiny inside right, who weighed little more than nine stones but was a giant in this match, immediately slotted a pass through a square defence for Lewis to chase.

It was a knife in Liverpool's heart. Lewis beat their Welsh international goalkeeper Cyril Sidlow. Then, 17 minutes into the second half it was Lewis again, this time with assistance

Compton gave a brilliant performance; Goring scored twice in a 2–0 victory, though Pompey eventually took the title.

While Denis Compton, after knee surgery, turned his thoughts towards representing England's cricketers in Australia, in 1950–51 football's international selectors sought the services of Les Compton. On 15 November 1950 at the age of 38 Arsenal's veteran centre-half represented his country for the first time, England's oldest international debutant. England beat Wales 4–2 at Sunderland with Lionel Smith also winning his first cap and Ray Daniel, Compton's club deputy, called up for Wales. Compton won his second, and final, cap a week later when Yugoslavia forced a 2–2 draw at Highbury.

Arsenal led the First Division at the half-way mark of the 1950–51 season, but two injuries on Christmas Day against Stoke City turned a Championship sprint into a stumble. Lishman broke a leg, thus robbing the team of its leading scorer; four of his 16 goals had come in one match against Sunderland in November. Swindin was also hurt, allowing Ted Platt an extended run in goal. Although Whittaker turned again to Lewis – who typically responded with a sequence of four games in each of which he scored twice – and for the first time to the raw Holton, the team unit did not function as smoothly in the second half of the season. Arsenal finished fifth in the League, which was won for the first time by Spurs, and lost their grip on the FA Cup to a Stan Pearson goal for Manchester United in the fifth round.

from Cox, and from then on there was little doubt that Joe Mercer would at last lay his hands on the FA Cup.

The medal to go with it almost escaped Arsenal's captain. His Majesty King George VI presented the trophy, and the personal memento came from the Queen. Joe was just about to go down the Royal Box steps with a loser's medal when the error was spotted.

Above: The victorious 1950 FA Cup squad. From left to right: Reg Lewis, Peter Goring, Freddie Cox, Denis Compton (partly hidden), Walley Barnes, George Swindin, Joe Mercer (with the Cup), Laurie Scott, Alex Forbes, Leslie Compton and Jimmy Logie.

Compton Jnr retires

One Arsenal player did retire a few days later but it was not, in fact, Joe Mercer. Approaching his 32nd birthday Denis Compton realised that the combination of international cricket, top-flight football and a knee that was protesting more and more about wear and tear was no longer viable for him. He had already decided before the Cup final to abdicate from football, a fact used to Arsenal's advantage by Tom Whittaker at half time at Wembley.

Compton's first-half contribution had been unmemorable. 'Now,' said the manager, weighing each word carefully, 'you've got 45 minutes left of your soccer career. I want you to go out there and give it every ounce you possibly can.' Compton rarely lacked confidence, but this time he needed fortification. A glass of whisky was produced, and Arsenal's outside left played a full part in a strong second-half performance. Nor was it quite his football finale. The following week Portsmouth came to Highbury needing points to win the Championship.

Gunners in Double chance

Arsenal's Double of 1970–71 is of course well documented in this history and elsewhere. Less easily recalled are the events of the 1951–52 season when the Gunners stood three games away from what would have been the first Double of modern times. Had those three games been won instead of lost the season would have been legendary. Instead it was a bold attempt which foundered in the final analysis on injuries.

Swindin had shrugged aside his injury from the previous year and played a full season in goal, Barnes was absent for just one League game though the fallibility of his knee became a major factor in the last chapter of the story. Mercer, Forbes, Logie and Roper added further threads of continuity. By now Daniel had superseded Les Compton at centre-half, and the goalscoring department lay at the feet and heads of Lishman and Holton. The cricket connection had not entirely disappeared with the Comptons; Arthur Milton, the Gloucestershire batsman, operated on the right wing on a semi-regular basis.

Progress in the First Division was steady, always in the challenging bunch of clubs, occasionally on top. Lishman enjoyed a golden spell of hat-tricks in three consecutive home games; Fulham, West Bromwich Albion and Bolton were his

1945-1966

victims. The League matches were punctuated by occasional prestige friendlies, with floodlights installed at the ground, treating the Highbury faithful to the new experience of watching evening matches. The ground also enclosed the biggest post-war attendance at the club; the visit of Spurs luring 72,164 to see whether the Champions could be toppled.

Above: The crowd rather than the players is the focus of this unusual shot taken on 16 September 1950. Peter Goring completes his hat-trick in a 6–2 thrashing of traditional rivals Huddersfield. Jimmy Logie and Doug Lishman got the others.

Lewis and Cox ensure Cup progress

The FA Cup run began at Carrow Road, where Norwich City could not rise up above their Third Division South status. Barnsley in round four provided no more testing opposition; Lewis, now a weapon to be used only occasionally, added to his personal store of Cup-tie memories with a first-half hat-trick. Lishman claimed the other in another confident triumph.

On paper the fifth round draw brought a more testing problem. Leyton Orient, who were now in the lower reaches of the Third Division South, were on the giant-killing trail. The homely East London club had already beaten two high-flying Second Division outfits, Birmingham City and Everton, both of whom were slain on their own territory. Now the 'O's' were at home and the prospect of a meeting with Arsenal attracted massive interest.

Whittaker's side, however, did not capitulate, although Lewis was injured scoring the first goal; averaging a goal a game in the League at the time plus his four in the FA Cup, he might have forced his way into another Cup final team until this misfortune. Arsenal, however, coped easily with the handicap at Brisbane Road, and Lishman hit two more goals to kill off the giant-killers.

with his second 20 minutes from time. Roper, operating at outside left, took his only corner in either game and the diminutive Cox found space to head home. Lishman made sure of Arsenal's return to Wembley with another header.

The final itself offered a showdown between the competition's two most recent superpowers, the holders Newcastle United against the winners from the previous year. It was a match which had statisticians trotting out comparisons with 20 years earlier when Arsenal had been beaten in the 'over-the-line' match.

Injuries mount

In 1932 Arsenal had also sought the Double, only to fall between the two stools of cliché. They also had to meet Newcastle at home in the League between the semi-final and final just as they had to do in the fixture-congested April of 1952 (drawing 1–1, with Milton – who did not play at Wembley – Arsenal's goalscorer). By then injuries were beginning to damage hopes of bringing the League title to Highbury.

On Good Friday, 11 April, Ray Daniel broke his arm in a goalless draw at Blackpool. The next day Lionel Smith wrenched a knee at Bolton; Arsenal lost 2–1. Leslie Compton stepped out of the shadows to help out in the crisis.

Three home games brought a fine return of five points, but at the cost of wearying key players. Mercer felt the strain so keenly that Whittaker persuaded his captain to stand down from the crucial visit to West Bromwich Albion, the clubs eighth game in 17 days. Understandably the flesh was weak, even if the spirit was strong and Albion won 3–1.

That defeat effectively ended the League challenge; only a seven-goal victory at Old Trafford on the Saturday before the Cup final would take the title from Manchester United. Reg Lewis turned out for his last senior appearance and Lionel Smith proved his recovery from injury, but United celebrated their title with a runaway 6–1 victory. Nor did Arsenal escape unscathed physically. Arthur Shaw, who might have pipped Daniel for the centre-half spot in the Wembley line-up, suffered a fractured wrist, a similar injury to his rival. Nevertheless, had the Gunners won those two last games, against West Bromwich and United, they would have been Champions.

An agonising defeat

Newcastle United's passage over the run-in to the final had been as smooth as Arsenal's had been choppy. Moreover, the holders were able to relax at the seaside while Tom Whittaker and his medical team were checking the casualty list at Highbury. Daniel had not played for more than three weeks,

Above: Leslie, the older of the Compton brothers, carried on playing football for longer than Denis as he did not have the same cricketing demands. He finally gave up professional football a few months before his 40th birthday.

Arsenal had to play away again in the sixth round, though did not have to travel very far to meet Second Division Luton Town. This draw meant that the top clubs were again avoided. After only nine minutes Luton became the first side to put the ball past Swindin in the 1952 FA Cup. Moore headed in a corner taken by Mitchell. Without Jimmy Logie to orchestrate their midfield play, Arsenal were still trailing at the interval, during which Whittaker reshuffled his forward line.

Freddie Cox was switched to the left wing and lived up to his billing as a Cup-tie specialist. Arthur Milton came back to his sparkling best. Cox equalised from a very acute angle and with Luton handicapped by injuries to Davies and Owen the match tilted away from them. Three goals inside five minutes completed the scoring, with Cox cutting in again to find the back of the net from an oblique position and then crossing for Milton to collect Arsenal's third. A penalty from Mitchell was Luton's last reply in a riveting match.

What Mrs Cox dreamed before the semi-final has not been recorded but the match certainly produced a case of *déjà vu* for her husband. Again Chelsea provided the opposition. Again White Hart Lane was the venue. And again the first match finished in a draw. In truth it rarely held the imagination of the crowd; no corners in the first hour during which Arsenal scored in the 35th minute. Almost inevitably Cox was the marksman. Chelsea equalised 27 minutes from the final whistle through Billy Gray.

Two days later the teams reassembled at Tottenham, and, as two years earlier, Arsenal won through, this time 3–0. The Cox-Logie combination eased the tensions by conjuring an early goal, and Cox broke the back of the Chelsea resistance

1945-1966

Mercer made sure his team left the pitch together to tremendous appreciation from the crowd. Later that night he addressed the guests at the traditional banquet, speaking with great emotion: 'I thought football's greatest honour was to captain England. I was wrong. It was to captain Arsenal today.'

A record seventh title

Perhaps some of the resolution forged over those 90 minutes at Wembley brought the players even closer. Certainly those who represented the club in the following 1952–53 First Division campaign proved to be too good for their rivals. The title came to Highbury for the seventh time, setting a new record, but it was to be mighty close.

Walley Barnes was missing for the entire season, though Joe Wade and John Chenhall made light of his absence. Others made meaningful contributions, like Don Oakes, who marked his League debut on the first day of the season at Aston Villa by scoring the winning goal. A tall inside forward from Rhyl, Oakes had waited almost seven years for his chance in the first team. He kept his place for the following match but suffered injury helping in another winning cause at home to Manchester United. He did not reappear at first-team level until the last nine matches of the 1954–55 season. With a regular place beckoning, he contracted a serious illness on tour in the summer of 1955. After protracted treatment, he had to accept medical advice to retire.

With two victories in those first two matches, Arsenal failed to build on such an optimistic start, winning only once in their

but with a plaster supervised by the manager so that it would pass the scrutiny of the referee the Welsh international was chosen for the fray. So too was Logie, who had been hospitalised earlier in the week leading up to the final.

Lishman, the ex-commando, who had just missed selection two years earlier, tried quickly to make up for lost time with a hooked shot that passed just wide of Newcastle's goal. Arsenal settled quickly and were looking good when fate took a hand. Barnes twisted a knee so painfully that Arsenal faced the prospect of surviving for the last 55 minutes with ten men.

Roper, strong and robust, was immediately switched from outside left to right-back; his heroic display typified Arsenal's tenacity. Smith had to clear a Milburn effort off the line, but the depleted team did not just settle for survival. Cox forayed infield and Forbes added to his usual labour with many attempts to support the undermanned attack. Then 11 minutes from the end Lishman rose to meet a corner from Cox but the ball skimmed the bar.

Five minutes later the gallant stand ended. Of the ten Arsenal players remaining Holton and Roper both went down, in urgent need of the trainer's attention. Daniel's arm was aching; Logie's damaged thigh could no longer be concealed. Mercer yelled at referee Arthur Ellis to stop the game to allow treatment for Holton and Roper. The ball was still in play and Mitchell was allowed to cross into the middle where George Robledo climbed above Smith to send in a header which dropped in off the post. Roper, still on the ground, could only sit and watch it happen. There was still time for Forbes to hit the bar, but Newcastle became the first club in the 20th century to win the FA Cup in consecutive seasons.

The 1952 Cup Final was not to see a repeat of the success of two years earlier. (Above) Swindin and Smith combine to rob Jackie Milburn of a chance, but (below) Chilean George Robledo beats Lionel Smith to a Mitchell centre and squeezes the ball in off the post to give Newcastle a 1–0 victory.

next six outings. Sunderland and Charlton both plundered two points on visits to Highbury. Only the return of Milton from cricket with Gloucestershire inspired a victory in this dismal spell; the cricketer-winger struck the bigger ball cleanly with one of the goals in a 3–1 home success against Portsmouth.

In November the spotlight turned on Jimmy Logie. His impish genius was recognised at last by Scotland's selectors. The Alex James of his generation, Logie won his first and only cap against Austria at Hampden Park. In the same month as his 33rd birthday, the honour came too late for him to make an impact for his country.

Ten days after Logie's Scotland international, Arsenal put on a display of their own from the very top drawer, demolishing Liverpool 5–1 away at Anfield. Ben Marden struck twice in his first senior match of the season and Cliff Holton weighed in with a hat-trick.

Festive goal feast

The last match of 1952 deserves special mention, not just because it brought the bonus of an away victory. On Christmas morning the Arsenal players were again a long way from their families, at Burnden Park, Bolton. The first half was above average but not exceptional. Willie Moir sent the home side into the lead but by the interval Milton had equalised and Holton, whose power of shot was formidable, had edged the visitors ahead.

In the second half those who might have had their minds on their Christmas dinners were first able to gorge themselves on a glut of goals. Within the opening five minutes of the half Logie and Roper had increased the Arsenal advantage to 4–1. Then it was Moir making it 4–2 before a Daniel penalty restored the lead to three goals. The action of the final eight minutes was even more frantic. Bolton's defensive generosities extended to the conceding of another goal to Holton, before Nat Lofthouse struck twice for Bolton. Believe it or not there was still time for Bolton to earn a penalty, which could have made it 6–5, but Kelsey, facing a spot kick for the first time in League football, saved Langton's attempt.

Title race goes to the wire

1952–53 was not to be one of the great Championship seasons – it is rightly more remembered for the FA Cup final. Arsenal eventually finished with 54 points, one of the lowest ever for a title-winning team. The excitement was in the finish with Arsenal and Preston neck-and-neck and the fixture-list taking the Gunners to Deepdale on the last Saturday of the season.

The points situation meant the Gunners' title ambitions could survive a defeat but not a heavy beating. Preston won 2–0

with goals from their two most revered forwards, Tom Finney and Charlie Wayman. Both clubs now had one match left but not on the same day.

Preston were first into action on the Wednesday before the Cup final. Away to bottom club Derby County, they won 1–0 and left for an end of season tour not knowing their fate. Arsenal's finale was staged before a packed Highbury two days later on Cup final eve; only a win would be enough. Burnley, the opposition, were in the top six of the table. It took only three minutes for the drama to take its first twist.

Roy Stephenson, Burnley's outside right, drove in a crisp, low, centre. Mercer tried to cut out the danger. He succeeded only in diverting the ball into his own net. At that moment the title looked bound for Deepdale.

It was no time for patience. Arsenal threw caution to the winds in a display of forceful attacking football which brought goals for Forbes, in one of his most passionate performances for the club, Lishman and Logie. Burnley then cut the deficit in the second half, and the all-out policy gave way to the tactics of entrenchment, and what they had Arsenal held. When the sums were done Tom Whittaker's team had won the League on goal average – by less than one-tenth of a goal.

Nightmare on Wearside

The summer of 1953 was to bring the shock of the sad and premature death, at 51, of Alex James from cancer. It was perhaps a portent – Arsenal's attempt to defend their title began dreadfully. Six of the first eight matches were lost, the other two drawn. The club's predicament reached a crisis point at Sunderland in what turned out to be Swindin's last League match. Lishman had given Arsenal the boost of a goal before the veteran goalkeeper was hurt in a collision with Trevor Ford, with Sunderland by then leading 2–1. Swindin was, in all, beaten seven times.

Dodgin had accepted the tactics more readily, and Barnes, who had not played since his Wembley injury, battled back to sufficient fitness to earn a recall though his problems were to persist. To strengthen his hand in attack Tom Whittaker sought a short-term solution. Tommy Lawton, the nation's pin-up centre-forward throughout the 1940s, was struggling as player-manager of Brentford. At 34 his best years were behind him, but Ronnie Rooke had more than risen to the challenge of a late call to Highbury. Could Lawton do the same?

The deal was done in secret and Lawton was unveiled to the Highbury public on 19 September 1953, against Manchester City. However, in his two-and-a-half seasons with Arsenal he could not sustain a regular place; it was almost seven months before his first League goal, which came against Aston Villa. Yet Lawton loved the glamour attached to being an Arsenal

1945-1966

player and recalled that his biggest mistake in football had been in not signing for the club when George Allison wanted him from Burnley in 1936 (he chose Everton instead).

The wilderness years

The years that followed were a bleak period for the club that had, by 1953, become the most celebrated in the world. They were to win nothing again until the Fairs Cup all of 17 years later. And between 1954 and 1969 they finished only once above fifth. Between 1930 and 1953 they had finished worse than fifth on only three occasions. Cup performances were, if anything, even worse – including terrible defeats by such lowly sides as Northampton (3–1) in 1958, Rotherham (2–0 after two draws) in 1960, and Peterborough (2–1) in 1965. Tom Whittaker was not there to witness the decline.

Highbury mourns death of Whittaker

Tom Whittaker died on Wednesday 24 October 1956 in University College Hospital, London, where he had undergone an operation the previous Easter. Like his great mentor Herbert Chapman he passed away in harness, which is just as he would have wished.

Both had died tragically young (neither reached 60); both in differing ways had been the very heartbeat of Highbury. Tom Whittaker perhaps had a premonition that he would not outlive his job, once admitting:

'Someone has to drive himself too hard for Arsenal. Herbert Chapman worked himself to death for the club, and if it is to be my fate I am happy to accept it.'

Joe Mercer had been lured back into football as manager of Sheffield United; his moving tribute to the guardian angel who had extended his career at Highbury to such glorious heights appeared in the *Daily Express:*

'Meeting Tom Whittaker was the best thing that ever happened to me; he was the greatest man I ever met.

As the news of his death goes around the world thousands, perhaps millions, of people will say the same thing. And how so very deeply they will mean it. Arsenal was his kingdom but in every soccer-playing country in the world he was acknowledged as a prince of the game. There never has been a greater man in football. It is a game full of hard knocks. But Tom never hit anybody. He never shirked making a hard decision, like sacking or dropping a player, or any of the other things that can hurt deeply. But the way Tom did it, it never did.

Tom made bad sportsmen into good sportsmen. He made good footballers into great footballers.

Tom was responsible for none of the bad things in football. Cynics may smile and say "I wonder". But I know.

Above: *Gunflash*, **the magazine of the Official Arsenal Football Supporters' Club – a far cry from the glossy magazines and independent fanzines of the 1990s.**

I know that he never did a bad thing. All problems had only one solution; the one done with kindness.

After Newcastle beat us in the 1952 final, Tom came into the dressing-room, looking as happy as we had ever seen him. He said: "I am really proud of you chaps. You played great football. I am as proud of Arsenal today as ever I have been." Damn it, he made us feel we had won the Cup.

The last time I saw Tom was a couple of months ago. He looked very ill, but he had already started a new phase in Arsenal history. He realised the days of big buying were over. His plans only included youngsters. And every youngster who ever went to Highbury quickly learned one thing. The only thing that mattered was the club.

Tom Whittaker never thought of the chairman, a player or anyone individually when he made a decision. If it was good for the club then it was right.'

Tom Whittaker's reputation had spread way beyond the confines of English football. When Arsenal took on the role of ambassadors on expeditions around the globe, the secretary-manager was the perfect head of the delegation. In 1949, for example, the summer tour took the club to Brazil where in Sao Paulo many supporters of the local team were of Italian extraction; Italy and the rest of the football world had just been stunned by the Superga aircrash which wiped out the brilliant Torino team. Whittaker's sensitivity recognised that there was a need for a tribute to the dead and before the match, at his suggestion, the two teams and the crowd stood, heads bowed, to the music of Ave Maria.

Yet kindness never became weakness. Bill Dodgin returned from the 7–1 humiliation at Sunderland in the dreadful opening to the 1953–54 season feeling that he had let down the side and wanted to be left out of the team. He went to see Whittaker: 'I left his office quicker than I entered it. He told me very firmly that if there was any dropping to be done, he would do it.'

In February 1956, Arsenal tried to lighten the load on Tom Whittaker by appointing Leyton Orient manager Alec Stock as his assistant. Unfortunately, Stock lasted less than two months before returning to Orient and there was no sign of Whittaker taking any fewer of the responsibilities.

Double appointment

The obvious stress of the dual role of secretary-manager persuaded the Arsenal board to split the two jobs. Bob Wall was promoted to secretary. Jack Crayston, a member of two League Championship teams and the 1936 FA Cup winning side, took over as manager. Crayston had been an assistant to Tom Whittaker, his man 'downstairs at Highbury' helping particularly with the scouting and at times, because he had received some training as an accountant, with book-keeping.

Crayston had also won eight England caps before the war. Famed for his long throws he was a strapping wing half, over six feet tall, weighing 13 stones and needing specially constructed boots for his size 12 feet.

An even longer servant, Joe Shaw, retired. He had been signed as a player in 1907 from Accrington Stanley, hanging up his boots in 1923. Following a short spell with Chelsea he had resumed his Arsenal connection under the title of Head Coach and Chief Representative, in effect Whittaker's number two.

On 13 March 1957, George Allison passed away; he had lived with indifferent health over the ten years since he had

Below: George Eastham signed for Arsenal during the 1960-61 season for £47,500 from Newcastle United. This transfer was ground-breaking as it led to the abolition of the 'retain and tranfer' system. George was a play-maker who also contributed 41 goals in his five seasons at Highbury.

resigned from his football career at Highbury. 'George Arsenal', as he had been widely known, had risen from his humble start in the club ranks as the writer of the match programme to secretary-manager. His knowledge of the game might never have been deep, but he was clever enough to realise his limitations, not frightened to consult the opinions of others. Yet as a front person for the prestigious Arsenal organisation he had been perfect. His rapport with the media would have been a strength in any era.

The next day another death was recorded, that of J. W. Julian, club captain in 1890 and the first to lead a professional side at Woolwich. He had been an enthusiastic and regular spectator at matches at Highbury up to the time of his demise.

Board and manager clash

Jack Crayston's appointment was confirmed in December 1956. The new manager on was not blind to the shortcomings of his team. He regularly asked the board for money to strengthen his hand, but it was not forthcoming. Cliff Jones was just one of a number of players he pursued, but Swansea realised the value of their winger, who was to play 59 times for Wales, and were determined not to sell him cheaply. When he finally became available it was Spurs who struck the deal.

The match programme outlined the Arsenal philosophy at the time: '... a policy not to bid for a player's transfer. We always ask the fee required, and having been told make up our mind whether the player is worth that fee.' Yet with increasing pressure for success in a market which was naturally declining after the post-war boom, the ethics of football business were to change for ever.

Crayston believed that the club did indeed have the money to invest in the transfer market. At a board meeting at the end of the season clearly the frustrations became too much. 'Gentleman Jack' Crayston resigned, severing a tie with the club that had lasted almost 25 years. He moved back to Yorkshire for a spell as secretary-manager to Doncaster Rovers, before using his accountancy skills in a business career. In 1985 he looked back on the changes in football with a twinkle in his eye: 'In my time players had short hair, wore long shorts and played in hob-nailed boots. Now they have long hair, short shorts and play in slippers.'

Although Joe Mercer was clearly the favourite to succeed, it was an Arsenal team-mate, George Swindin, who was actually offered the job. He had brought Peterborough to national prominence with their giant-killing acts and had therefore won his spurs. He was in charge for four seasons but while Arsenal were never relegation candidates, the history of the past 30 years meant that it was trophies or nothing. When Danny Clapton was chosen for England in 1959 he was the first

1945-1966

Arsenal player for five years to be capped – an excellent cameo of the decline on the field since the last Championship. Swindin also had to cope with the horrors of Nicholson, Blanchflower and the Tottenham Double of 1960–61.

Eastham wins test case

More significant in the long run was the Eastham case. George Eastham was England's most skilful creative player. He wanted to leave Newcastle United to join Arsenal, but the Geordies would not let him go. Under the rules of the League at that time (called the 'retain and transfer' system) a player's current club could stop him moving anywhere, and no club could pay any player, from the best to the worst, more than £20 per week. Eastham challenged the system in court and, after a legal battle that began in 1960 and ended in July 1963, he won. By then he had moved to Arsenal for £47,500. Of that fee he got just £20.

George Swindin remained until March 1962 and upon his departure Arsenal broke with tradition by appointing an outsider – the first since Chapman himself had arrived nearly 40 years earlier – Billy Wright.

The club's choice had won more caps than any player in the world (105) and held the then record for the most consecutive international appearances (70). He had captained Wolves to three League Championships and one FA Cup. But great players do not necessarily make great football managers. Despite the goalscoring heroics of Geoff Strong and Joe Baker (each scored 31 League and Cup goals in 1963–64) the defence was, surprisingly given Wright's pedigree, the weakness. The same year they conceded 82 goals, worse than one relegated club.

Geoff Strong was to move to Liverpool and, despite the arrival of a then rather raw Frank McLintock from Leicester, the terrible 2–1 defeat to Third Division Peterborough in 1965 was to be the symbol of the period.

Wright proves 'too nice'

Season 1965–66 was the last in first-class football for the genial, kindly Billy Wright, whose playing days had been almost devoid of failure, but whose management days were as short on success. Maybe the writing was on the wall the previous summer with the decision to change the club colours to all-red shirts, with the only white being on the collar and the cuffs; white shorts with red seams and red stockings completed the design, which was seen as a return to the style of Nottingham Forest. The change was soon reversed.

As most of football awaited the 1966 World Cup with an increasing sense of anticipation, Arsenal's and Wright's fortunes reached unprecedented depths. A home fixture against Leeds United was misguidedly rearranged for Thursday 5 May

Above: Billy Wright, then the world's most capped player, took over the manager's chair from George Swindin (who had held it for four years) in 1962. He, in his turn, was to last another four, by which time directors and fans were becoming restless as the club had not finished higher than seventh since the turn of the 1960s.

1966, the same evening Liverpool contested the European Cup Winners Cup final against Borussia Dortmund at Hampden Park, shown live on television. That attraction, combined with Arsenal's dismal form, resulted in the Gunners attracting what was the lowest First Division crowd since the First World War – 4,544 against the second placed club in the League! And they lost 3–0. Only a win over Leicester two days later elevated the club to 14th, their lowest place since 1930.

At the end of the season Billy Wright took a holiday; apart from his responsibilities at Highbury he had also been contracted by BBC Television to take part in their coverage of the World Cup finals. While he was away the board decided that recent results 'justified a change in management'. Denis Hill-Wood broke the news to him on his return. Outwardly it was accepted with the gentlemanly nature with which Wright, the player, had wooed the hearts of the football world. Inwardly it hurt bitterly: 'It was heartbreaking for me. Maybe I was too nice, but that is the way I am. But I wanted so much to make Arsenal great again, and I did feel that with the young players we were moving along the right lines.'

Many decisions were involved in the construction of the Double-winning side, which took Arsenal Football Club to the highest of all domestic achievements. Yet surely the most inspired was taken by the board of directors in the summer of 1966. While the media indulged in fruitless speculation about which of the game's big names would be appointed to succeed Billy Wright, the Highbury decision-makers were recognising a quality of leadership within the fold.

Bertie Mee was offered the manager's job at a private meeting with Denis Hill-Wood. The choice of the physiotherapist caught Fleet Street off their guard. It had the majority of the playing staff believing that it could only be a stop-gap appointment, and even surprised the recipient of the offer: 'It was a surprise, but a very pleasant one. I had not planned to become a football club manager. I was very happy in the career of my special interest, and I was enjoying a great deal of job satisfaction from it. But I was used to positions of responsibility. I had run organisations of various types. So my response was that if that's what the board would like, then I would give it a go.'

Mee appointed manager

With two successful careers already behind him – in the military and medical spheres – Bertie Mee was the right man at the right time for a club which needed an urgent injection of authority. Yet though Bertie Mee was by no means a household name, he was very well known inside the game. He had been running the treatment of injuries courses for the Football Association for almost 20 years. At establishments such as Lilleshall he had lectured to all of football's leading managers and coaches, and he had their respect. Such experiences had given the new Arsenal manager a sound working knowledge of the highways and byways of the Football League.

Mee also brought to the job an insight into what was wrong inside the dressing room. After all, it had been his area of operation for six years. The players knew that he stood for no nonsense in the discipline of recovering fitness. Most significant of all, he was not overawed at what he had been chosen to do, but with a characteristic and sensible touch of caution he did make sure that an exit was available if required: 'I asked the chairman if I could initially take the job for 12 months, and that if it didn't work out, I could revert to my previous position. He was most agreeable. So I began by approaching the task in terms of management, from purely a management point of view. It was my belief that there was nothing radically wrong, but the club had to be more professional from all angles. We needed a general tightening-up. The players were a good crowd, but I felt that they could be more dedicated to the job,

Above: The great years of 1968–72 were to see no fewer than five major Cup finals, one in each season. The memories are firmly of 1971, but three of the five were lost by tight margins. The 1968 Football League Cup final was decided by a single goal from Leeds United full-back Terry Cooper.

Left: Bertie Mee in August 1971, when he had been voted Manager of the Year for his achievement in managing Arsenal to the Double.

and certainly could care more about Arsenal. The danger was that mediocrity was being perpetuated.'

With Les Shannon also leaving the club following the change of management, Mee required a new coach, and successfully sought the services of an old friend, Dave Sexton, then with Fulham. Frank McLintock, in his 1969 autobiography *That's The Way The Ball Bounces,* summed up the players' response to Sexton: 'I haven't come across many people in the game who has his ability to get through to players without shouting the odds and screaming at them. I don't know what it is that Dave has, maybe it's a gift of leadership. That is perhaps simplifying his effect, all I know is that he could have persuaded us to do anything. He thinks deeply about football and pointed out things I wouldn't have dreamed of – and before he came I thought I knew most of it.'

League Cup disappointment

At first, relatively little seemed to have changed. Mee's first two seasons saw the side finish 7th and 9th. Arsenal had not entered the League Cup until 1966–67 but 1968 was to see them reach their first final for 16 years. Coventry, Reading, Blackburn and Burnley were the victims on the way, with Huddersfield going down 6–3 on aggregate in the two-legged semi-final. The opponents were Leeds, then still a club without a single trophy in their history. The game was not a classic, rather a forerunner of the titanic games that we were to see between the clubs in the next five years and Terry Cooper scored the only goal.

Frank McLintock was disappointed at yet another losers' medal, but the team was gaining recognition with both Bob McNab and John Radford capped by Alf Ramsey.

The solidity that was binding Arsenal together did not always please the neutrals, but Mee had already established his first priority; his team was never likely to capitulate. Bob Wilson was making great strides as a goalkeeper, his strength of character growing in the face of regular teasing from his team-mates about his background as a schoolteacher. He was ever-present in the 1968–69 League campaign. So too was the cold-eyed Peter Storey and the resident chatterbox, McNab. Court, who was to be sold to Luton on the eve of the Double, missed only two matches in midfield. Simpson was emerging as a more complete central defender than either John Ure or Terry Neill. The options in midfield were increased by experimenting with George Graham, who was blessed with a sure touch and sharp football brain, but whose lack of explosive pace was making life up front increasingly difficult for him.

The interest in the FA Cup ended in the fifth round, but hardly in disgrace, a 1–0 defeat away to West Bromwich Albion, First Division rivals. Against a background of such consistency it is unfortunate that the 1968–69 season will be recalled for another Wembley defeat in the League Cup final. Unlike the Leeds experience the players could not walk off with heads held high. This time it was a shaming experience.

The two-leg semi-final with Spurs had produced more evidence of the competitive nature of Mee's team. In front of a full house of 55,000 at Highbury, Spurs were only seconds away from a goalless draw when Radford popped up with a crucial goal. Tottenham pinned their hopes of turning the tables at White Hart Lane on the mercurial Jimmy Greaves, who scored in a tough, and at times brutal, encounter, but so did Radford and Arsenal won 2–1 on aggregate.

Humiliated by Swindon

The final was still three months away, and Mee and his players had to wait a fortnight to learn whom their opponents would be. When the news came, any thoughts that the hard part had been done by eliminating Tottenham could have been forgiven. Third Division Swindon Town had battled their way to Wembley by beating Burnley over three games.

As expected Arsenal carried the fight to Swindon from the outset, a series of attacks that in treacherous conditions took more energy to mount than to defend against. With eight of the side still touched by the after-effects of a flu virus which had caused the postponement of a League match the week before, such energy was not easily recouped. At this point in their League season Arsenal had let in just 18 goals in 30 matches. But 34 minutes into the League Cup final they allowed Swindon to take the lead with a mix-up between Ure and Wilson which presented Smart with an open goal.

Swindon kept the lead until four minutes from time. Then keeper Downsbrough, a superman on the day, ventured out of his area in an attempt to kick the ball to safety, away from the on-rushing Gould. Instead, the ball rebounded off the Arsenal forward, who reacted quickly and headed it into the unguarded

In 1969 Arsenal were back at Wembley for another League Cup final (above) and this time hot favourites to defeat Third Division Swindon Town. The result was a shock 3-1 win by the underdogs, Don Rogers, with two, and Roger Smart scoring their goals. The only Arsenal response was from Bobby Gould, who left the field in tears (below) comforted by John Radford.

net. With extra time beckoning, relieved Arsenal fans believed that their team now had a psychological advantage.

At pitch level Don Howe was not so sure. He wanted extra time to be abandoned by Bill Handley to spare the players the slog in the cloying mud. He recognised the weariness in his own players, aggravated by their recent illness. McLintock had cramp in both legs. McNab was also in distress. Graham had already replaced the weary Simpson.

For a team of Swindon's status it would have been forgivable if they had not seized their opportunity. It was a measure of their quality that they did. After 15 minutes of extra time, Don Rogers poked the ball home from a corner and in the second period the Swindon winger etched his trademark onto a Wembley final, running half the length of the pitch for a memorable solo goal. It was like sticking a knife into a dying body.

Stan Harland went up the Wembley steps to collect the League Cup from Princess Margaret. McLintock – now a four-time loser – was stunned. He had not contemplated defeat this time. A good-luck telegram from Don Revie wishing that he could 'be first up the steps this time' was ironic. The Leeds United manager had forgotten that the League Cup final's formalities have the losers collecting their mementoes first.

Stirred by defeat

Mee and Howe began the arduous task of reviving morale that had once been so high. Only the strong would swim and not sink after such a distressing experience. Among them was Bob Wilson, whose pride was aroused by the humiliation. Some 16 years later he put the desolation of defeat into perspective: 'I

1966-1972

truly believe that the rise of the Double side stemmed from that afternoon at Wembley. We came home to headlines about the "Shame of Arsenal", and a lot of us were determined that it would never happen again. We craved success with even more intensity because of it.'

The one consolation was that fourth place in the League brought them a place in the European Fairs Cup, albeit because Swindon were denied theirs by virtue of being a Third Division side. Arsenal's progress was convincing against Glentoran, Sporting Portugal, Rouen, Dinamo Bacau and Ajax in the semi-final. In retrospect Arsenal's 3–0 win over Ajax at Highbury looks a lot better now. Within a couple of years their opponents won a hat-trick of European Cups. One week later Arsenal were back in the Low Countries facing Anderlecht. The Belgians chose to play in their away strip in Brussels so that their fans could see the famous red and white shirts. It did not damage Anderlecht's performance – they were ahead 3–0 in the first leg with Jan Mulder scoring twice. It looked as though Frank McLintock would collect his fifth losers' medal. Late in the game Ray Kennedy, still a raw youngster, headed one back and the Gunners returned to Highbury 1–3 in arrears.

Wilson recalled: 'Even with the late goal we were downcast. It looked as though we could be foiled yet again in our efforts to bring the club a trophy. Initially Frank McLintock felt it the most keenly, and he was cursing about being in another losing final. But Frank was always impulsive. If he saw you in a suit he liked he had to get one like it straight away. If you'd been to a great restaurant he'd have to go there the next night. But just as suddenly the mood would change. In Brussels his initial despair turned straight into optimism. He came out of the bath yelling that we were going to win. He lifted everybody, and by the time we left the ground, nobody had their heads down. You could say that the second leg was won at that point.'

European Glory

McLintock, by his own admission, finds specific matches hard to remember, but his attitude that night remained in his memory: 'Anderlecht were good. Mulder and van Himst were special players. But defensively they had looked vulnerable when we had been able to attack. Their centre-half looked poor in the air. I believed we could do it, and I wanted to make sure the rest of the lads did.'

The second leg of the Fairs Cup final took place at Highbury on Tuesday 28 April 1970. In the match programme Bertie Mee paid tribute to McLintock's new role at centre-half, which earlier in the month had earned him a recall by Scotland after three years out of the international limelight. The manager also wrote of the crop that was being harvested from the youth policy which had been tended by Billy Wright and himself after

George Swindin had sown the seeds. Charlie George, Kennedy and Eddie Kelly were singled out for special mention.

Kelly repaid the compliment. A stunning early shot brought Anderlecht within reach. Arsenal tore into their opponents with such frantic commitment that McLintock was asked afterward by one of the Belgians if Mee's players had taken drugs. But the stimulus was not artificial; it was the desire for achievement. In the dressing room the talk about Arsenal's past glories had become more than wearisome.

The weakness in the air spotted by McLintock was exploited in the second half, and the muscular Radford found space to head Arsenal's second. Thanks to Kennedy's 'away' goal, Arsenal now led, but were in no position to relax as Mulder hit a post. Jon Sammels, who was to lose his regular place during the Double year, ensured a deserved place on the roll of honour by adding a third. Had Anderlecht managed just one in reply they would have been level on aggregate. Even Bertie Mee's considerable ability to detach himself from the emotion of match action was tested to the limit.

When the final whistle eventually sounded, the floodgates opened. Delirious supporters surged on to the pitch. George for one had his shirt pulled from his back by souvenir hunters. Sir Stanley Rous, then FIFA's President, presented the Fairs Cup, which stayed in England for the third successive year following the victories of Leeds United and Newcastle United. For Arsenal it was the end of 17 barren years. McLintock had his hands on a trophy at last and there they stayed as he was carried shoulder-high around the pitch. Oddly, despite its significance, it was not a much-heralded victory at the time and it is not particularly well remembered now.

Below: The 1970 Fairs Cup final against Anderlecht was a happier occasion. Arsenal lost the first leg 3–1 in Brussels and were left with a lot to do in the return. No team had ever come back from a two-goal deficit to win a two-legged European final, nor from a three-goal deficit at any point in a final. The goals in the second leg at Highbury were scored by Kelly, Radford and Sammels, and John Radford is seen celebrating his with the help of Charlie George.

The Arsenal Board had never made any secret of the fact that the League was the main priority. It had been nearly 20 years since Highbury had held the prize that once seemed theirs by right. But no one ever mentioned the Double – which, in 1970, achieved just once in the 20th century.

Double tip

If you were looking for a team on which to stake a few pounds to accomplish such a feat, Arsenal would not have been among the favourites. Finishing 12th in 1969–70, averaging just one point per game with 51 goals scored and 49 conceded, was hardly the foundation to suggest such glories. A much better bet would have been Leeds United, runners-up in both competitions in the previous season, or perhaps Chelsea, FA Cup winners and third in the League, or even Everton, the 1970 League Champions.

With a touch of irony, the Double year began at the home of the defending Champions. On paper it could hardly have been a tougher start, but Bertie Mee's policies of stabilising Arsenal into a side that did not readily concede defeat had already paid dividends. From the outset of his management every goal let in had been put under an analytical microscope.

With the benefit of hindsight the events at Goodison Park on Saturday 15 August 1970 said much about the qualities which were to provide the basis for such an historic campaign and the resilience which was to shine through so many battles in the months ahead.

The manager's selection had already been affected by pre-season injuries. Peter Simpson required a knee operation. Jon Sammels had a leg in plaster. John Roberts, the strong-man from Wales known as Garth, came into the defence alongside McLintock. The strength of Everton's midfield trio of Howard Kendall, Colin Harvey and Alan Ball was recognised in the role given to Peter Storey, who marked Ball throughout; Storey's job at right-back went to Pat Rice, who had played just 13 League games in the previous three seasons.

Joe Royle and Ball were to score for Everton, with Charlie George cracking two bones to provide one equaliser and Graham the second with a floater. It was only a draw, but it was away at the home of the Champions and, as Frank McLintock said afterward: 'This is the best Arsenal side in my six years with the club.'

On 1 September 1970 Arsenal had the honour of ending Leeds' perfect record so far that season. Geoffrey Green in *The Times* encapsulated the tone of the night in the pithy introduction to his match report: 'There were no goals and no broken legs at Highbury last night, and there might well have been one or two of both. Most of the plaudits of heroism went to the home side. Referee Iowerth Jones from Treharris, Glamorgan,

quite properly sent off Kelly for kicking Billy Bremner; that senseless episode after 28 minutes seemed to have condemned Arsenal to defeat. The ten men, however, resisted manfully with the raw Rice, in particular, responding to the challenge. Leeds were not allowed to make use of their advantage. Bertie Mee was never given to exaggeration, so his after-match comment deserves recording: "This was the best performance I have ever seen by an Arsenal team against a side of the calibre of Leeds. I am tremendously proud of all of them, and if we can live through an occasion like this we can live through anything."'

Brawl in Rome

It was never going to be an easy season for Arsenal, but the toughest evening proved to be in far away Rome, where the Gunners were defending their Fairs Cup. The game was a 2–2 draw but there were no feuds simmering when the two sides attended an after match dinner together. At some point in the evening Ray Kennedy was set upon by a Lazio player and the meal turned into a full scale brawl. UEFA sided with Arsenal and fined the Italians, Arsenal winning the second leg 2–0. Europe rather proved a distraction during the season – victories against Sturm Graz and Beveren Waas leading only to departure on the away goals rule to FC Köln of Germany.

A few days after their Lazio game Arsenal went to Stoke and were hammered 5–0. Bob Wilson was criticised for talking about the goals on television (Bertie Mee felt he was betraying inside information) and the nature of the defeat remains a mystery. It could have had a dramatic effect – but it didn't and the defence only let its shield down once more during the remainder of the season – and that was for another 45 minutes against Stoke. The defeat preceded the run which really laid the foundations for the Championship. After Stoke, Arsenal went 14 games without defeat, drawing just three, until a sticky patch in January when they lost against Huddersfield and Liverpool. Nonetheless, they were still not taken seriously as contenders – the League was clearly there for Leeds to lose rather than anyone else to win, and Leeds were eventually to oblige in dramatic fashion against West Bromwich.

Arsenal progress unnoticed

In the Cup, wins against Yeovil and Portsmouth were to take Arsenal to the fifth round at Maine Road against a team which was then one of England's best.

At the same time the 'high-morale' battle between Leeds United and Liverpool at Elland Road was going in Liverpool's favour – and Arsenal's. The gap was reduced to three points. Charlie George caught the eye of Brian Glanville, *The Sunday*

1966-1972

Times correspondent at the match: 'He must surely resemble the late Charlie Buchan; his height, his powerful physique, the delicacy of touch so astonishing in one so large. To see him receive a ball amidst a ruck of defenders and escape them with the skill of a Houdini is delightful.'

They were prophetic words. George was to settle the fifth round FA Cup tie against Manchester City ten days later. The match was put back from the Saturday to the following Wednesday because the Maine Road pitch was flooded, and it remained very heavy. Two goals from George, now operating as a raider from midfield in place of Graham, confirmed Arsenal's superiority in a deserved victory.

The exact date is not important, but it was around this time, in February 1971, that Bertie Mee addressed his players. To a nation which believed that the 20th-century Double could only be achieved by a team with the swagger of the Spurs 1961 side, Arsenal were not contenders. There was speculation about whether they could win the League. The pursuit of Leeds United was becoming one of the season's most fascinating features. But there were no public suggestions that Arsenal could emulate Tottenham and clear all the hurdles.

Inside Highbury it was a different matter. Mee saw the possibilities and had for some time: 'I told the players we could expect two matches a week for the rest of the season: "As this is the case now is the time for you to be really ambitious and to aim for the success which may never be possible for you as players again in your lifetimes." The point was forcibly expressed that all three trophies should be aimed for. They owed it to themselves and their colleagues to accept the challenge of the next three months.' They also owed it to the fans and to the tradition that was Highbury.

Although Leeds were clear favourites; Arsenal just kept winning. Between 6 February and 20 April they played 12 League games and won 11 of them, losing only at Derby (0–2). At the end of that run they had just four League games left to play, and had worked their way through to their first FA Cup final since 1952.

Knock-out success

Leicester City in the quarter final replay had proved to be a tough nut to crack. The match attracted Highbury's biggest crowd of the season, more than 57,000, and they witnessed a match that became the tale of two headers.

The first by Fern after 13 minutes was disallowed by referee Jim Finney on the evidence of his linesman. The Leicester forward was adjudged to have pushed Rice as he moved in to connect with Farrington's centre; it was a very close call. Then, with Mr Finney counting the seconds toward half time, George rose perfectly to meet Armstrong's corner.

Above: Charlie George scores the all-important first goal of the fifth round FA Cup tie against Manchester City at Maine Road on 17 February 1971. A free-kick had been given after Joe Corrigan handled the ball outside his area in the 18th minute. George simply shot past the City wall.

Such a blow on the interval did not diminish Leicester's efforts. An absorbing contest continued to the very last kick, and only then were Arsenal sure of their place in the last four.

Shaken by Stoke

The semi-final draw had paired together Everton and Liverpool for a special derby, while Arsenal were drawn against Stoke City, on League form the weakest of the four survivors.

The matching of the underdogs and the Arsenal machine produced a riveting contest at Hillsborough. Some 41 years earlier an FA Cup semi-final triumph in Yorkshire in dramatic circumstances provided the impetus to a decade of success. Now, in the frantic pace of a semi-final in the 1970s, the club wrote the most relevant page in the story of the Double season.

Quite simply Arsenal looked as though they had stumbled at the penultimate hurdle. Stoke might have been nervously caught up in a desire to reach their first major final, but Arsenal were at times tentative to the point of distraction in the first half and the London team's players left the field after 45 minutes trailing 2–0.

Semi-finals by nature are cautious, inhibited affairs; the price of defeat is so high that few risks are taken; winning is all-important, the means scarcely matter. Arsenal began the match in that vein, with a greater share of possession in the first 20 minutes but no end product to show for it.

The cautious approach, though, had to be thrown out of the window after a most unusual goal which lifted this semi-final tie out of the rut. Bob Wilson very properly conceded a corner by pushing behind a teasing cross from Jimmy Greenhoff, Arsenal failed to deal conclusively with the corner-kick, and as Peter Storey booted the ball away, it struck Denis Smith and flew into the Arsenal net.

In the very next attack the flame-haired Conroy played a very effective one-two with Mahoney only to put his shot inches wide. Banks twice put his stamp on the game with sharp saves, foiling Kennedy on both occasions, before Stoke, fortified by their goalkeeper, were boosted further in the 29th minute. It was a gift from George. With time to spare the 20-year-old, stricken perhaps with butterflies in this most draining of matches, sent a dreadfully underhit back pass in the direction of Wilson. Ritchie pounced and reached the ball just before the Arsenal goalkeeper, took it past him and planted it in the yawning goal. It would have been a disaster for any Sunday morning team, let alone one which was pursuing the elusive dream of a League and Cup Double. Stoke should have gone 3–0 ahead when Greenhoff broke clear a few minutes later. But, at a vital moment for both himself and his club, he lost his nerve and shot high, wide and anything but handsome. Just like Elland Road in 1930, the tide had turned.

Early in the second half Mahoney charged clear yet again through the constantly square defence. Wilson this time was able to reach the ball. It was a good piece of goalkeeping from a splendid technician, but it carried greater import as Arsenal

Above: After the scare of the 2–2 draw at Hillsborough, Arsenal made sure of the 1971 semi-final replay against Stoke. George Graham headed the first goal, then Ray Kennedy (out of shot) sent this shot past the stretching Gordon Banks.

swept upfield. What might have been 3–0 suddenly became 2–1. George Armstrong fed Kennedy, whose chip into the middle caused confusion in the Stoke ranks. Storey unleashed an instinctive drive from 20 yards and even Banks could do nothing.

Yet it was Stoke who reacted more positively to the goal. Arsenal were not allowed to dictate the play in their quest for an equaliser, largely because the impressive Greenhoff kept two and even three defenders constantly occupied. Arsenal's momentum was also interrupted by an injury to George, which brought Sammels on for the last 15 minutes. The resultant injury time proved a blessing in disguise.

Storey steps forward

It was in the two minutes that Pat Partridge, the referee, added on, that the salvation came to keep alive Arsenal's appointment with history. Banks was pressed into conceding a corner, angrily protesting after the match that he had been fouled and that the decision should have been a Stoke free-kick. Armstrong took the corner from the Arsenal right, and this time Banks was nowhere. McLintock, a rescuing figure yet again, steered his header toward the left-hand post, where only the hands of John Mahoney prevented a goal. Referee Partridge was perfectly placed to award the penalty.

The thousands of supporters who had made the journey to Sheffield roared but one Gunner was less than thrilled. Peter Storey had made the penalty job his own with a succession of nervelessly executed kicks. Even in the heat of battle he now realised the enormity of his task: 'The rest of the lads were all hugging each other as though we'd scored. But I was the one who had to stick it in. And past Gordon Banks too!'

At the other end of the ground Wilson dropped to his knees in prayer. It was one of those moments when the world stops. Had Storey missed, his name, like Waddle's or perhaps Southgate's, would have been engraved forever on the hearts of thousands. But Peter Storey was the man for Arsenal's hour of need. He repaid the faith of colleagues whose celebrations had looked so premature to the penalty taker. As Storey ran up, England's goalkeeper switched his weight on to his right foot and started to move in that direction. Storey sent his shot low, placed with the inside of his right foot, to Banks' left. Stoke City 2 Arsenal 2, the rescue was complete.

If, from the whole season, we are to choose just one moment in which the Double was won but might have been lost, then it was Jimmy Greenhoff's miss in the first half. In a remarkable display of touch football, Greenhoff had been a giant that day, but, at the vital moment, he had failed and Arsenal were saved. At 3–0 they must have been out.

There can be no doubt that the semi-final was the moment of truth. A League match can be lost (even 1–0 at Elland Road,

1966-1972

as we shall see) and the Double still won. But every Cup tie has to end positively. All Cup-winning teams have one match where luck plays its part, when they come through a game they could or even should have lost. This was Arsenal's.

Gunners claim Final berth

Psychologically, after Hillsborough Arsenal were now in the ascendant. Deep down, for all their boasts that they would finish the job at Villa Park, the Stoke squad knew that they had missed their chance. Bertie Mee's players realised that their escape came almost from the pages of schoolboy fiction. There was another omen too. Liverpool had beaten Everton in the other semi-final, and would be waiting at Wembley just as they had been waiting 21 years earlier, the last time Arsenal had won the FA Cup.

Both managers announced unchanged teams, George having recovered from his bruised ankle and spirits, but the match had a very different flavour. Arsenal assumed control from the start and maintained it.

Arsenal's skill at set pieces had kept their tally of goals ticking along for most of the season. In Armstrong the team possessed a master craftsman at corners. Radford, Kennedy, Graham, McLintock and George all relished attacking his accurate crosses. So, in the 13th minute of the FA Cup semi-final replay, Armstrong's service was again a work of precision and Graham's header was so powerful that it completely beat Banks from fully 15 yards.

After the interval Arsenal quickly reaffirmed their grip on the match with a second goal, which held special significance for the provider and the scorer. In terms of scoring the partnership of Radford and Kennedy was undergoing its most fruitless spell of the season. Neither had scored in the previous seven matches. But two minutes into the second half Radford darted down the left and as his cross slithered across

the goalmouth Kennedy was in exactly the right place to turn the ball into goal. The two danced a jig of relief and triumph. It was the end of the scoring.

McLintock emerged from the dressing room, his own positive nature sharpened by the experience: 'We are going for the Double! There is real character in this Arsenal side, and now we are going to show we can win League and Cup. This will be my fifth time at Wembley and after being on the losing side in four finals the law of averages says I must have a great chance of a winners' medal this year. The way we are playing we can certainly do it.' Bertie Mee sat for the photographers in the dressing room posed between the two goalscorers, a bottle of champagne in hand. It was a night to enjoy, but the manager soon had to restore the concentration. There were ten League games to be fitted in before the Cup final. What happened in those would determine whether Arsenal were going to Wembley simply for the Cup or for the Double.

Arsenal close on Leeds

While the dramas were unfolding at Hillsborough, Leeds United had been losing at Chelsea. Now they had 54 points from 35 games; Arsenal were on 48 points from three fewer matches. If they won them all, they would be level. Any projected forecasts about the outcome of the race had to take into account that Arsenal had to visit Elland Road.

It brought the set of matches for the clubs on 17 April into even sharper focus. By twenty-to-five that afternoon the lead had changed. Arsenal, seemingly always the more likely losers in the title race, suddenly found themselves topping the table.

The circumstances were in keeping with the story of the season for each contender. Leeds lost at home to West Bromwich Albion in a blaze of controversy. Arsenal beat Newcastle at Highbury with a display which did not easily bring poetic description to mind, but did bring them two points.

To deal with the events in north London first the two precious points were gathered courtesy of a superb goal from George 19 minutes from the end of a mediocre match. A packed penalty area ahead was not a daunting proposition when the ball dropped to George. He made sufficient inroads to disrupt the massed defence before turning sharply to drive a scorching left-footed shot past McFaul. For the rest of the action George Armstrong provided the perfect postscript: 'I don't suppose anybody will remember the game, but they'll all remember the result.'

Conversely, at Elland Road everybody will remember one particular incident. The turning point of the match concerned a decision by referee Ray Tinkler. He allowed Albion's Tony Brown to burst forward with the ball from just inside the Leeds half on the West Bromwich right. In a more central position his

Left: Bertie Mee celebrating Arsenal's passage through to the 1971 FA Cup final with the goalscorers, George Graham and Ray Kennedy.

team-mate Colin Suggett was clearly in an offside position, but not, ruled the referee, interfering with play. Brown ran on with the Leeds defence expecting the whistle, drew goalkeeper Gary Sprake out to meet him, and passed across the goal for Jeff Astle (also in an offside position) to score at will. The crowd invaded the pitch. Chaos ensued.

The Leeds protests carried such venom that the Football Association subsequently fined the club £750 and ordered them to play their opening four home games the following season away from Elland Road. Albion, who had not won away for 16 months, and were to finish the season sixth from bottom, eventually triumphed 2–1. It was a devastating blow for the Leeds' morale, made worse by repeated television showings of the crucial episode which increased their sense of grievance. Leeds were to win their last three League matches and the Fairs Cup, but will always feel that the title was taken from them on a piece of refereeing interpretation.

Nine in a row

If it was a piece of good fortune then Arsenal readily accepted it. Three days later another one-goal victory at Highbury condemned Burnley to the Second Division. With Storey and McNab on international duty for England against Greece in the European Championship, Kelly returned to midfield, and Roberts was given his only League outing over the second half of the season in defence. The absence of Storey in one other respect was covered by George because it was he, in the 26th minute, who accepted the responsibility of taking and scoring the match-winning penalty. The victory was less in doubt than some of Arsenal's one-goal successes during the season, and Wilson's only moment of real anxiety resulted from a careless back pass by Kelly. Paul Fletcher became the latest victim of the bravado of Arsenal's goalkeeper as he sped off his line to take the ball from the toes of the Burnley number nine. From 2 March to 20 April Arsenal had won all their nine League matches; the 18 points were captured with only 16 goals, but in those 13½ hours of First Division hurly-burly the defence was penetrated only once, at Southampton.

It was at The Dell where Leeds returned to winning ways on Saturday 24 April, the day that the Gunners' run of victories was halted, ironically by West Bromwich Albion, at the Hawthorns. In some ways it was an unusual match, not least because Asa Hartford scored for both sides. His goal at the right end was the first of the four. For once Wilson's charge off his line could not rescue a square defence.

Albion held their lead for only four minutes. Yet again an Armstrong corner unsettled those defending against it, particularly goalkeeper Jim Cumbes. The ball dropped for George, who was denied a goal by a block on the line. McLintock, how-

ever, was first to the rebound to notch his third goal in five games, this one at the right time to celebrate the announcement that he had been chosen as the Footballer of the Year.

Arsenal lost Rice at half time, the legacy of a twisted ankle. Storey moved to right-back but was still prepared to charge forward in the 55th minute in pursuit of a chipped pass from George. Hartford eagerly ran back, aware of the danger, only to increase it with a back pass. Cumbes was caught coming off his line and the ball rolled into goal with a simplicity which would have driven wild any Leeds United fans present. Five minutes from the end, however, Tony Brown, the scourge of the Elland Road supporters a week earlier, earned their gratitude with a thumping equaliser. Arsenal now had 61 points from 39 matches, Leeds were on 60 from 40 games.

Before leaving the Hawthorns, McLintock reflected on the impending clash of the Titans the following Monday: 'It's obviously going to be tough at Leeds, but the odds are still in our favour. I'm sure Leeds would be happy to swap positions with us. Our run of nine League wins had to end sometime.'

Summit meeting at Elland Road

Leeds had just reached the Fairs Cup final and a match with Juventus; against Arsenal they needed nothing less than victory for their Championship dreams to survive. A draw would be very much to Arsenal's liking, and for most of the game it looked the most likely outcome. The Gunners' sense of discipline and tactical organisation, a cornerstone of the season, served them well. Leeds, with Mick Bates deputising for Peter Lorimer, were kept at arm's length throughout a first half in which both teams were kept under excellent control by referee Norman Burtenshaw.

Wilson's main task in the opening 45 minutes was to gather in a succession of crosses, but the pattern altered in the second half. The home side redoubled their efforts; Arsenal partly by design, partly because of Leeds' extra determination, opted to see out the siege rather than attack. And for all the creativity of Bremner and Johnny Giles, Leeds were continually frustrated by a massed defence. It remained a stern, unrelenting battle, and though the prize was so great the conduct of the players was more orderly than in other meetings of the period between these two rivals.

It all changed in the dying moments of the game. The ubiquitous Paul Madeley triggered off another Leeds foray. Bremner, who had never ceased in his quest for an opening, played his part, and suddenly the ball broke for Jack Charlton all alone in front of Wilson's goal. England's World Cup centre-half of 1966 directed the ball past the Arsenal goalkeeper as other defenders stood frozen, arms raised in a uniform appeal for offside. Even then the gods, for once,

Opposite: Debating time at Leeds on 26 April 1971. Bob Wilson is injured, Charlie George seems cheerful enough, but Frank McLintock is engaged in a heated discussion with his Leeds counterpart, Billy Bremner (partly hidden behind Bob McNab). Leeds won the game (Arsenal's 40th – only two more to go) 1–0 with a Jack Charlton disputed goal, the Arsenal defence claiming offside. Even at this stage, Arsenal did not really seem likely Double winners. Leeds continued to do well in the League. Arsenal had to win their last two games to be sure.

favoured Leeds because the ball struck a post and rebounded out, only for a long Charlton leg to reach it before McNab. Instantly Norman Burtenshaw confirmed the goal.

Arsenal's protests were long on time and short in temper. George booted the ball into the stand and was rightly booked. Wilson and McLintock led the pursuit of the referee, and it was fully five minutes before he could restart the game. The linesman whose flag had stayed down was also turned upon by aggrieved visiting players.

There was still enough time for George Graham to send a back header flying inches over Gary Sprake's crossbar, before even more furious words were directed at the referee when he blew the final whistle.

Many off the pitch queried the goal at the time, though Bertie Mee confined himself to commenting that 'never was a defeat less deserved. Arsenal were fantastic, tremendous.' However, subsequent television re-runs convinced a number of the most bitter Arsenal players at the time that referee and linesman had been absolutely right. McNab, it seemed, had

been too slow moving out. Mr Burtenshaw was able to look forward to his next Arsenal match with confidence; he had been appointed the FA Cup final referee.

Leeds lead but Arsenal remain favourites

Whatever the actual merits of the offside decision (or not) it meant that Leeds were back on top of the First Division, but William Hill, the bookmakers, still made Arsenal, who had a game in hand, favourites for the Championship at 4–5; Leeds were quoted as even-money.

May Day brought victories for both candidates in the race to be named Champions. Leeds struck twice in the first half at Elland Road, through Bremner and Lorimer, to make sure that their League season ended with a win over Nottingham Forest. Arsenal had to wait longer before gaining a win against their semi-final victims Stoke.

The Gunnners began as though their boots were weighted down with tension. No opportunity was created until three minutes before half time. George's forward pass caught the Stoke defence in a line, and Radford bore down on the Stoke goal and its guardian, Gordon Banks. He dallied so long that Smith was able to rush back and prevent the shot. It looked a significant miss and Radford later explained: 'Initially I stopped because I thought I was offside. Then I realised I wasn't and tried to lob the ball over Banks. But he started back-pedalling so I had to hold the ball. One of their blokes came in and I've the gash to prove it.'

Early in the second half Arsenal suffered again; Peter Storey limped off with a groin strain and Eddie Kelly entered the congested midfield area. It was the start of a memorable week for the 20-year-old Scot. He had been on the field 12 minutes when he spotted the potential of a long ball into the goalmouth from Armstrong. Graham flicked it on to Radford who skilfully manipulated it into Kelly's path. The substitute blasted in the decisive goal.

Left: While both halves of the Double were won in London, neither was secured at Highbury. On 3 May 1971 Arsenal went to White Hart Lane needing a win or a goalless draw to pip Leeds for the title. A scoring draw would have given the title to Leeds. Their fate rested on their near neighbours and rivals. Those lucky enough to get inside saw just one goal, a Ray Kennedy (out of the picture) header minutes from time.

Deciders at the Lane

Arsenal knew exactly what they had to do to win the League for the first time for 18 years. Leeds had finished their League programme: Played 42, Won 27, Drawn 10, Lost 5, Goals For 72, Goals Against 30, Points 64. Arsenal's record read: Played 41, Won 28, Drawn 7, Lost 6, For 70, Against 29, Points 63.

With a wonderful sense of occasion the last fixture was against Tottenham Hotspur at White Hart Lane. The game had been originally scheduled for the day of the FA Cup semi-finals and was now rearranged for the Monday night of Cup final week. Spurs needed three points from the meeting with Arsenal and a trip to Stoke to be sure of qualifying for the next European campaign. Bonuses of £400 per man could depend on beating Arsenal.

The mathematical permutations were even more remarkable. A win would give the title to Arsenal, a defeat would send the trophy to Elland Road. But a goalless draw would mean success for Arsenal while (because of the peculiarities of the goal average system then in force) any scoring draw (even 1–1) would conclude matters in Leeds' favour.

Arsenal's players had only reached this situation through a deep yearning for success. The prospect of crossing another minefield did not alarm them. Frank McLintock rarely lost his sense of optimism: 'I'm sure we can make it. We always give good performances at White Hart Lane.' George Armstrong was equally confident: 'We're playing better away from home because we are not under the same tension, and it's in our favour that Spurs are not a defensive side.'

Alan Mullery, Tottenham's captain, reinforced the belief that it was going to be a mighty clash: 'Arsenal have got as much chance of being handed the title by Spurs as I have of being given the Crown Jewels. They are the last people we want winning the Championship. Everybody is on about the great season Arsenal are having. Well, we're not doing too badly. We have won the League Cup and reached the sixth round of the FA Cup. Now we mean to round off our season by beating Arsenal – and that will put us third in the table. That can't be bad.'

Manager Bill Nicholson recognised that the League title could be the prelude to the Double to which he had guided Spurs ten years earlier: 'We are tremendously proud of our Double achievement. I suppose some other club has got to do it again sometime but we will be doing our best to see that it isn't Arsenal. My instructions to the Tottenham players will be to go out to try to win.'

The Arsenal players rested on the Sunday as usual, but for Storey there was not enough time for recovery. When the players reported for light training on the morning of the match it was clear that Kelly would be in the team from the start. Sammels was chosen as substitute.

Kennedy the hero

The players lunched at their own homes before reconvening at the South Herts Golf Club, the regular pre-match meeting place, at 4.30 pm. Already the football fans of north London were on the march toward White Hart Lane. The gates were locked more than an hour before kick-off with 51,192 spectators inside. Twice that number were on the outside.

The volume of traffic even surprised the police. The Arsenal team coach crawled along. Bertie Mee recalled: 'We gave ourselves an hour for a drive which normally takes 20 minutes. But even then it was a very difficult journey. I have never seen scenes like it. But there was never the pressure that we

1966-1972

At the final whistle the fans celebrated Arsenal's eighth Championship on the pitch at White Hart Lane, and Frank McLintock was carried aloft, wrapped in a Leeds scarf.

At the other end George brought an athletic save from Pat Jennings in the opening minute. McLintock saw his goalbound shot bounce clear off the body of Collins. Graham's header curved on to the top of the Spurs goal. Radford and Kennedy hassled at Peter Collins and Phil Beal. Armstrong was everywhere on the pitch.

For all the energy imparted into the match by both teams, whose conduct had been first class, a goalless draw beckoned. But three minutes from time, Kinnear tried to dribble clear of trouble inside his own penalty area. George recaptured the ball from the Spurs right-back, and twisted instantly to conjure a cross from an angle which would have defeated most players. Even then it seemed as though Arsenal had been denied. Jennings made the save of the night as Radford met the ball provided so cleverly by George.

Tottenham stopped to a man, perhaps in admiration of their goalkeeper, but also because they expected the ball to run behind for a corner. Armstrong had barely stood still all season, and was not going to break the habit now. Rescuing it from near the line his chip back across goal was met by Kennedy's header. The ball sped high to Jennings' left, above the leap of Cyril Knowles behind him. It clipped the underside of the bar and was over the line.

The goal was greeted by instant exhilaration from every Arsenal player. But almost as quickly misgivings followed, particularly from the scorer. In one respect, the goal was irrelevant. A Tottenham goal would still give the Championship to Leeds and there was still time for it. 'That was the longest three minutes I have ever known,' recalled Kennedy. 'I remember thinking to myself as Tottenham came back at us that perhaps it might have been better had my header not gone into the net.' Spurs hurled themselves forward as the seconds ticked away. One last corner could still have deprived the Gunners, but Wilson's last act in an almost faultless series of performances throughout the 42-game First Division programme was to grasp the ball as though the lives of he and his team-mates depended upon it.

Champions once more

Moments later Kevin Howley blew a whistle in League football for the last time. The title belonged to Arsenal for a record eighth time. It had been won by a clear point at the last gasp of a marathon that had never been less than compelling. Leeds deserved sympathy for coming so close, but none could deny the magnificence of Arsenal's victory. Like a dog with a bone they had refused to let go right to the end.

Bedlam reigned on the pitch. George, close to the touchline, leapt into the arms of Don Howe. As thousands of fans raced to congratulate their heroes Bob Wilson found himself

were going to be late, and seeing those thronging crowds increased the sense of occasion for us. There was no way we were going to be beaten.'

The referee, Kevin Howley, had to abandon his car a mile away to fight his way on foot through the crowds. It was the last League match in a distinguished career, a great occasion on which to bow out. Making his whistle heard in the din which echoed around the ground from start to finish became a problem. The vociferous McLintock bellowed orders to his team-mates which passed largely unheard.

McLintock had his hands full coping with the powerful Martin Chivers. The wise Alan Gilzean continually sought to steal a yard on Simpson. Jimmy Neighbour probed ceaselessly down Tottenham's left and stretched Rice to the full, and all the while Martin Peters hovered menacingly in the Spurs midfield, always likely to time a late run into a scoring position. For all the attacking intent clear-cut chances were few. Peters flicked the top of the Arsenal bar with a swerving shot, and almost scored with a header. Joe Kinnear forced a courageous and painful dive from Wilson at his feet. Gilzean all but connected as the ball flashed across the Arsenal goalmouth.

marooned. Unable to contain his joy he hugged the only partic-
ipant he could reach – referee Howley! McLintock found a
Leeds United scarf wrapped around his neck as he was chaired
off shoulder high.

The celebrations became so protracted that Don Howe
found his own joy giving way to anxiety: 'My thoughts turned
straight to the Cup final and I was worried that the crowd might
injure our players. They were ripping at their shirts. Some
wanted their boots, which of course they had to wear on
Saturday. I was frightened that they would tread on some-
body's foot and keep him out of the final.'

Bertie Mee lost his club tie as he returned to the directors'
box to acknowledge the crowd's appreciation. Tottenham for
their part were most magnanimous in defeat, which the
Arsenal manager remembers with great affection: 'We were
given champagne in the dressing room by Bill Nicholson. The
club could not have done more to help us celebrate our great
night. There had been a lot of petty rivalries between the two
clubs in past years but in my time we did a lot of work to
improve relationships. They must have been very disappointed
that they had lost but they didn't let that spoil our evening.'

Final preparations for Gunners

The party spirit continued long into the night. The team moved
on to the White Hart in Southgate. There were no curfews
posted or restrictions made. Tuesday, which had already
begun by the time everyone reached home, would be a day for
recharging batteries. Wednesday was the time really to begin
the concentration on the FA Cup final.

Much of that day was given over to the needs of the media,
but not for long. Bertie Mee's medical background gave him
strong views about Wembley finals: 'Over the years so much
had been said about the problems of playing there, particularly
the victims of cramp. Now cramp is really an emotional problem. It does of course have physical symptoms, but they can
often be a result of pressure. I wanted to protect the team from
emotional stress, so there was no involvement with the press
or television after Thursday.'

Don Howe concentrated on the physical preparation.
Amidst the lush acres of the London Colney training ground,
the players did their training on a pitch marked to the exact
specifications of Wembley. The grass had been allowed to
grow to cultivate the feel of the Empire Stadium turf. Two
recent League Cup final defeats had raised doubts about the
team's ability to win at Wembley. No stone was left unturned in
an attempt to create the right atmosphere this time.

For George Wright, the physiotherapist, it was becoming a
race against the clock. Peter Storey's presence in midfield was
vital to the construction of the side; his injury was responding

Above: Bertie Mee and Bill
Shankly lead their teams out
onto the hallowed turf of
Wembley for the 1971 FA
Cup final.

to intensive treatment, but only slowly. Bertie Mee had one
major decision to make, and Storey was chosen to start the
game. It was a risk but one that was calculated; the converted
full-back had become a fearsome opponent in midfield.
Liverpool would not relish the bite in his tackles even if he was
less than one hundred per cent fit.

Mind games commence

There were psychological battles to be won. No one knew that
better than Bill Shankly, Liverpool's manager, to whom the old
cliché 'a legend in his own life-time' applied. Shankly had
rather surprisingly appeared by the side of the pitch the day
before the final when Arsenal were taking a preparatory stroll
to acclimatise to the Wembley environment. There was rain
about, and Bob Wilson was greeted by one of the masters of
gamesmanship and kidology with the comment: 'Bob, it'll be a
nightmare for goalkeepers out here tomorrow.' Directed at a
character with less perception than Wilson, it might have
induced a sleepless night.

In fact 8 May 1971 was a stiflingly hot day. The Arsenal ritual
did not include the usual lie-in of most Cup final teams. By ten

1966-1972

Below: Armstrong almost beats Ray Clemence to get a goal in what was Arsenal's fourth major final in five years.

o'clock the players were on the road to familiar surroundings. At the South Herts Golf Club they took their pre-match lunch with words of encouragement from Dai Rees, the resident golf professional.

The opportunity to gain a spot of revenge on Shankly came 15 minutes before the kick-off. Arsenal had recent memories of the formalities of Wembley finals. FA officials are keen to have the teams standing in the tunnel ready to walk out at the appropriate minute. Often the wait is so protracted that the nervous begin to suffer.

So at 2.45pm Bertie Mee politely told the FA representative that he was finishing his team-talk and his players would be out in a moment. A few minutes later the call came again. This time he replied: 'A couple of the players are just tying their boots, we won't be a minute.'

It was only at the third time of asking that Arsenal appeared. Liverpool had come out at the first request and been kept waiting. Shankly scowled, realising that for once he had been outfoxed. There was no delay for Arsenal; immediately they were led out into the sunlight and the wall of sound that was waiting beyond the end of the tunnel.

It had been six weeks since Liverpool had qualified for Wembley. While Arsenal's attentions had been very much elsewhere, at Anfield there had been no escape from the publicity machine. It had been one long round of interviews and discussions about the match in the weeks leading up to the great day itself. On the other hand, Arsenal's worries were whether the rigours of the League campaign would now begin to take their toll, and those unhappy memories of League Cup defeats. They were playing their fourth major final in five years under Mee.

Gunners grow in confidence

Liverpool's early promise brought no reward, only the bruises of battle as Storey came in high and late on Heighway. Toshack was then misused by Rice and McLintock. It took a telling pass from George to switch the balance of the opening minutes toward Arsenal. Kennedy's running was never speedy, and recovering defenders forced him away from the goal and the danger evaporated.

Indeed it was not to be Kennedy's day, and six minutes into the second half he failed with another opportunity much closer to goal. In contrast Radford recaptured the form which had been elusive toward the end of the League season. No one contributed more to Arsenal's eventual victory than the muscular Yorkshireman in the number nine shirt. Though he did not score himself he was the provider of both opportunities which were taken; throughout the match he used the Gunners' possession to excellent effect.

Armstrong was another who could not quite capture his normal excellence, though once, arriving at the far post, he almost beat Clemence for a goal which would surely have spared the players extra time. George Graham, however, strutted his way through the match with an arrogance that set him apart and he was awarded the Man of the Match prize. Just 12 minutes from time he climbed characteristically to direct Radford's long throw beyond Clemence, but it came off the bar. Smith hooked the rebound for a corner which Armstrong planted once more on Graham's head. This time left back Alec Lindsay cleared off the line.

Heighway nets opener

Both sides used their substitutes. Storey, as expected, gave way to Kelly midway through the second half. Four minutes later Peter Thompson, who was a survivor from the 1965 Cup-winning team, was brought on in an attempt to inject more thrust into Liverpool's performance; the ineffective Alun Evans was replaced. Nevertheless, neither team could break the mould of the match in normal time. It had been a highly technical 90 minutes, with both sides cautious in their attempts to seek an advantage. The uncommitted neutrals, however, were seeking a more cavalier approach in the extra 30 minutes.

They had to wait only two minutes. Steve Heighway had rarely freed himself from the shackles imposed on the Arsenal right, but suddenly he slipped past Rice and Armstrong and

Above: After Heighways' opener for Liverpool and the Kelly/Graham equaliser, it was, almost inevitably, Charlie George who scored the winner for Arsenal nine minutes from the end of extra time.

from a tight angle cut in from the left. Wilson automatically took up position covering his near post. With his usually accurate sense of anticipation already predicting that Heighway should cut the ball back for Toshack arriving in the middle, the goalkeeper slightly overcompensated for the cross. Heighway was nothing if not unorthodox and his shot fizzed into the gap that Wilson had left to his right. Only the beaten goalkeeper heard the nick as the ball glanced the post on its way in; it was no fluke, Heighway had scored from a similar angle in a Merseyside derby earlier that season.

Wilson had little time for self-recrimination. Within moments he had saved Arsenal from certain defeat, plunging to keep out a close-range shot from Brian Hall. On the bench Don Howe was sending George Wright to the touchline with a vital message: 'My first reaction was here we go again, losing at Wembley, but anyway we'd had a tremendous season. But my next thought was that we'd got to change something to pull that goal back. I told George to get to the touchline and tell George Graham to go forward. Charlie George was nearly out on his feet because of the heat and was struggling to make any runs forward, so he was told to drop back into midfield.'

Tactical switch brings equaliser

There were four minutes left in the first period of extra time when the move paid dividends. Radford hooked the ball over his shoulder into a crowded Liverpool penalty area, where the

1966-1972

congestion was perhaps too great for Clemence to risk an intervention. Larry Lloyd, Emlyn Hughes, Tommy Smith and Chris Lawler were all between the Liverpool goalkeeper and the ball, which fell for Kelly simply to touch it forward. It certainly could never be called a serious shot.

Yet on it rolled between a tangle of legs as Graham swept in to view. He swung a leg at the ball and Clemence, now very much the last line of defence, could do nothing to prevent its progress into the net. Graham wheeled away in celebration of the goal that everyone in the ground believed to be his. But football had entered a television age. The BBC and ITV were competing on the sporting front and the Cup final was the showpiece for each channel to show off its technical and editorial skills. New camera angles were one area of that competition, and the day after the final the London Weekend Television look-back at the match included a 'revelation', from a camera behind the goal, that Graham had not touched the ball. The last certain touch came from Kelly, declared Brian Moore and Jimmy Hill.

Thus the club credited the scoring of the equalising goal to Eddie Kelly. Years after the event George Graham still believes he made contact with the ball, and is understandably embarrassed at being recalled from time to time as the man who claimed a vital goal which apparently was not his. BBC Television's Barry Davies was stationed that afternoon among the photographers close to Ray Clemence's net. Watching with the eyes of a trained observer, he still believes that the goal should be Graham's. A recent study of the television pictures supports the Kelly theory, but camera angles can be deceptive. It is certainly true that the ball did not change direction whether Graham touched it or not, so Graham's swing might at least have worked like a good dummy on Clemence.

Arsenal, yet again in this astonishing season, had refused to accept second place. But back on the bench the search for victory was not quite so immediate for Don Howe: 'Once we had equalised I settled for the draw. It hadn't really been our day overall, and I felt it would be better to steady ourselves and start out afresh for the replay. I decided to get George Graham back into midfield just to make sure he got behind the ball. Charlie still looked exhausted so I wanted him back up front. Out of the way really. He found his way forward because we were trying to protect our position for the draw.'

Charlie nets famous winner

No one had explained the finer points of this theory to George himself. With the replay nine minutes away he interpassed with the magnificent Radford before letting fly from 20 yards with a right-footed shot which belied his weary appearance. The force in the drive would surely have beaten Clemence even if it

Right: Bertie Mee with an exhausted George Armstrong.

Below: George Graham and Eddie Kelly at this stage not caring which of them scored the equaliser.

Left: Charlie George, the Gunners' darling, with appropriate headgear.

had not taken a slight upward deflection off the lunging Lloyd. George marked the moment with a novel salute; his arms were outraised as in more conventional celebration, but he was lying flat on his back at the time! It remains the outstanding image of this unusual character.

How appropriate that Arsenal's Double was sealed by one of north London's own. Charlie George, born in Islington, a product of Holloway School, used to stand on Highbury's North Bank. With his flowing hair and his obvious mocking of convention he acted out the dreams of so many young Arsenal followers. At 20 years old he had earned himself and his team-mates an extra £12,000 a man with that winning goal. The money mattered, but the glory was priceless.

Frank McLintock became a Wembley victor at long last, at the fifth time of asking. Bill Shankly, generous in defeat, was quick to shake his hand. George did handsprings of jubilation. Kennedy embraced Lloyd in consolation. Bob Wilson assured Ray Clemence, a loser on his first Wembley visit, that he would certainly be back.

Wilson later admitted that on a baking afternoon he had gone cold all over at the instant George had struck his momentous goal; such was the feeling of salvation after his earlier slip. His recollections at the final whistle are also sharp: 'Frank was in so much of a hurry to go up and grab the Cup that I pulled him back. He'd waited so long. I shouted at him that it might never happen again and that he should savour every moment. Not to rush it.' Wilson was right, of course – it never did happen again for McLintock.

Wilson followed McLintock up to the Royal Box, where the second leg of the Double was presented to Arsenal's captain by the Duke of Kent. For some it was too much to take. McLintock relished the ending of his Wembley hoodoo, but years later he confessed that he had no emotion left: 'It may seem strange but I've never been able to feel that supreme thrill of winning the Double. Our Fairs Cup win the year before meant so much. And winning the League was terrific. Maybe I was just too drained at the end of it all.'

About a quarter of a million people still had enough energy to line the route from Highbury to Islington Town Hall the following day. Both trophies were displayed by the team from an open-top bus, along with the FA Youth Cup, the product of more success for the club's prospective stars. Bertie Mee had guided the club to a year of unprecedented achievement. It had taken 51 matches to win the Double, a longer road than that trodden by any of the three previous holders of that accolade. 'I wanted the boys to win the Cup for Frank McLintock. The League Championship was for my chairman Denis Hill-Wood. For myself? I wouldn't mind the European Cup next season. I know we have done the Double, but at the moment it is too much to take in.'

Don Howe departs

In any walk of life achieving success is only half the battle. Living with the difficulties it can create is another matter altogether. A month after the Double was won, north London was alive with rumours of the first split in the camp.

No member of the Highbury staff was fuelled with more ambition than Don Howe. It was understandable that other clubs looking to fill managerial positions should be attracted by his credentials. None of them knew him better than his old club, West Bromwich Albion, and on 8 July Bertie Mee had to respond to the news that Albion had attracted Howe to the Hawthorns: 'There is little need for me to repeat how highly I value Don as a coach – and how sorry I am to see him leaving.'

The popular view at the time was that Don Howe had left because he wanted to step into Mee's shoes. Ten years later he strongly refuted those rumours: 'I did want to manage in my own right. That was only natural. But I wasn't in a hurry. Being manager of Arsenal was still my ambition but I would have been prepared to wait four, five, ten years if necessary. All it would have taken to keep me at Highbury would have been a promise that when Bertie decided to finish I would have been given a go as manager for a year or two. But nobody said that.'

He was speaking then as a Highbury employee, the right-hand man to Terry Neill. Later, when Neill was dismissed, Don Howe finally fulfilled his ambition. After an initial spell as caretaker-manager he was appointed almost 13 years after his

1966-1972

departure for West Bromwich Albion. Back in 1971, what would have been a simple sense of loss became more acrimonious when Albion went further and also signed George Wright and the successful youth coach Brian Whitehouse. Denis Hill-Wood was angry enough to go into print. 'Loyalty is a dirty word, these days,' said the Chairman. 'There is nothing I can do about what West Bromwich have done in raiding our staff except just to ignore them.'

A hard act to follow

There is always the issue of what comes next. It is a truism that great football sides usually last three years. It seems to have been true of the Arsenal of 1970 to 1972. Somehow the magic

Above: Only the second team to achieve the FA Cup and League Double in the 20th century, the Arsenal players enjoy a triumphal open-top bus ride.

goes, other sides watch and learn and the unexpected is now expected. The 1971–72 season, started as Double winners, was eventually to be a disappointment. The first priority was obviously the European Cup. Of English clubs only Manchester United had ever succeeded, and the competition was still redolent of Real Madrid, of Benfica, and of impossibly long journeys across the steppes of Eastern Europe. The first two rounds brought easy draws – against Stroemsgodset of Norway and Grasshoppers of Zurich. But the real thing came next in the quarter finals. Ajax of Amsterdam were European Champions, and formed the heart of the Dutch side that should have won the World Cup two years later. In Amsterdam Gerrit Muhren scored twice although Kennedy got one back with a header. At Highbury one goal would have been enough, and Arsenal scored it. Unfortunately it was at the wrong end and Graham's own-goal ended Arsenal's chances of winning the world's premier club trophy.

The League was not to prove much kinder, despite the arrival of Alan Ball for a record £220,000. Three losses in a week in August were both a shock and too much to recover from. In the end Arsenal finished fifth, in a season which did not produce an outstanding team and one which went to the wire between Derby, Leeds and Liverpool. None of their totals came near Arsenal's of the season before.

Ball proves Cup talisman

Alan Ball's influence was most sharply felt in an FA Cup run, which with a suitable touch of irony started at Swindon. Eight of the Swindon side which had inflicted so much agony on their First Division opponents at Wembley almost three years earlier took part in the match, as did a revered opponent, Dave Mackay, who in his last season as a player at 37 was also managing the Wiltshire club.

Ball was not ravaged by memories of the gloomy day at Wembley, and while the pundits waited for Arsenal to be toppled, the recent signing started to repay some of his transfer fee. He set up the game's first goal for Armstrong before opening his own account.

There was a scare in the fourth round, at Reading of the Fourth Division. Arsenal muddled through 2–1, courtesy of an own goal and Pat Rice bursting forward to strike Arsenal's winner, which was deflected.

The fifth round brought three skirmishes with Derby County. At the Baseball Ground Charlie George netted twice, as he had in the fifth round a year earlier, but Derby matched his two efforts with an Alan Hinton penalty and a goal from Alan Durban. Neither side could break through in the replay, which went to extra time in front of a packed Highbury crowd of 63,077. Because of Arsenal's European commitments the third match was two weeks later, only five days before the quarter final. On neutral soil at Leicester, Ray Kennedy produced the crucial goal.

Away again in the sixth round, for the 18th time in the last 21 draws, Arsenal only had to travel a few miles. Leyton Orient were struggling to avoid relegation to the Third Division, but they had knocked out high-flying Chelsea at Brisbane Road in the last round.

East London was out in force to see whether Arsenal would go the way of Chelsea. With the League title now looking less likely, the Gunners had their hearts set on retaining the Cup. Orient thus met sterner opposition and shortly after half time Ball, resplendent in the white boots which were briefly in fashion, ended Orient's dreams.

Above: The final chapter of the Arsenal-Stoke semi-final story was played out at Goodison on Wednesday 19 April 1972. Arsenal won 2–1 after a seemingly offside Charlie George put John Radford through for one goal and George scored the other. The key incident was, however, at the other end when a Denis Smith (third left) header was cleared by Bob McNab. Stoke claimed the ball had crossed the line and the photographic eidence seems to support them. Geoff Barnett was in goal after Wilson's injury in the first game at Villa Park. After four semi-final matches against the Gunners and not a single victory, this was to be Stoke's last hurrah. They have yet to progress so far or have such a successful (if disappointing) spell again.

Radford earns Wembley return

By a strange coincidence Arsenal's semi-final opponents were once again Stoke City. Again the venue was Villa Park, where the thrilling saga had ended a year earlier. Arsenal's side showed only one change from the previous semi-final. Ball's inclusion meant Kennedy dropping down to substitute. George wore the number nine shirt, and Radford, recently freed from suspension, partnered him. Storey had briefly been the player to stand down to accommodate Ball, but since March had reclaimed his place in midfield.

Unlike at Hillsborough a year earlier it was Arsenal who received the boost of scoring first. Armstrong received a clearance just outside the penalty area, took the pace off the ball and drove it past Banks.

That might have been the end of the matter but for an injury to Bob Wilson, which left the goalkeeper hobbling in agony. He tore a cartilage, but the decision was made to keep him on the pitch. It made reasonable sense. Wilson's courage was unquestioned. Arsenal would be better with him on one leg than with any fit outfield player.

That judgement, however, was faulty. Defenders suddenly tried to take too much care of the wounded Wilson. In the end Peter Simpson aimed to cut out a cross he would normally have left for the goalkeeper, who moved out to try to gather it but not at sufficient speed. The end product was that Simpson nudged the ball into his own goal. With more than 15 minutes remaining it was time for a re-think. Wilson was pulled off and Kennedy brought into the action. The call for an emergency keeper was answered by Radford, a stern enough character to cope with the task of helping his team stay in the Cup in such an unfamiliar role. He was sufficiently aware of Arsenal's tradition to begin by joking about the famous jersey which was

1966-1972

blamed for the slip by Dan Lewis in the 1927 final. Radford coped admirably with the shots that Stoke managed; the stand-in gave every impression of hugely enjoying the experience. Stoke once again seemed unable to believe their good luck.

The replay was at Goodison Park – the perfect setting for Geoff Barnett's return to first team action after more than two years' patience in reserve. Arsenal's other ex-Evertonian, Alan Ball, was invited to lead out the team on his return to the pitch he had graced so often.

The first two goals were penalties: Greenhoff for Stoke, George for Arsenal, with Storey not required this time. It was fitting that Arsenal's winner fell to Radford; he had earned it with his goalkeeping stint at Villa Park. The goal was controversial, however, George breaking away from a seemingly offside position.

Leeds in Double bid

Leeds had already confirmed their place at Wembley with a one-sided 3–0 triumph over Birmingham City at Hillsborough. Arsenal's quest in the final had a double edge, not just to retain the FA Cup but to end Leeds' strong challenge for the Double, which could take some of the glitter from Arsenal's own glories of 1970–71.

The League insisted that each club should fulfil an outstanding League fixture on the Monday before the Cup final. It was not an unreasonable request although neither manager looked kindly upon it. Arsenal would still be left with two games after the final, Leeds with one.

At Coventry on Monday, 1 May, Arsenal fielded the side which had booked their Wembley places by winning 1–0, McLintock being the scorer with his first goal since August. Barnett would keep goal at Wembley, with the unfortunate Bob Wilson needing surgery. His involvement was restricted to organising the players pool for the perks of the occasion, for which he was the unanimous choice of his team-mates. Kennedy could not force his way back into the attack and was named as substitute.

The bookmakers made Don Revie's team 4–7 to lift the Cup. Arsenal were the underdogs at 6–4. The news that Eddie Gray, who had given a virtuoso Wembley performance in the 1970 Cup final, was fit to play did nothing to shorten the odds against the Gunners.

This year both clubs were able to wear their traditional colours. Both Arsenal's post-war triumphs in the FA Cup had been won in a change strip. Neither team was new to Wembley, but sadly this did little to raise the tone of the contest.

Referee David Smith from Stonehouse had barely started the game when he was reaching for his notebook. McNab, who had made a splendid return to the senior side for the semi-final

after a long absence, cut down Lorimer. From this undistinguished beginning the contest rarely improved. The kindest interpretation of the drab 90 minutes would be to point to the respect that each team clearly felt for the other. Had it been a boxing match the referee would have called for more action.

Cup goes north

The only abiding memory is of a winning goal of high quality which mercifully spared the frustrated crowd an extra 30 minutes. It did not come from Arsenal, whose attack rarely got out of second gear, even when Kennedy replaced Radford. Eight minutes into the second half the two Leeds central strikers pieced together a move which deserved to win the match. The foraging Mick Jones tricked McNab on the Leeds right. Allan Clarke met the driven cross with a diving header, stooping to conquer. Barnett and Wilson together would have had difficulty in keeping it out.

For Clarke it was a third time lucky affair. He had been voted Man of the Match as a loser for Leicester in 1969; the following year he had been beaten playing for Leeds against Chelsea. Now he had the decisive goal and another Man of the Match trophy. Jones deserved better than to collect his winners' medal in pain after dislocating an elbow in the dying minutes.

It was a costly injury. With the first leg of the Double in their pockets, Leeds needed only a point from their trip to Wolves two days after Wembley. But they badly needed Jones to respond to a very competitive performance from a team with nothing to play for. Leeds were beaten 2–1, lamenting that they should have had two penalties. It was a surprising result, and meant that for the second consecutive season Leeds missed the title by a point.

So Arsenal had lost the Cup and the League but happily not to the same club. The Gunners also had their say in the destiny of the Championship because, had Liverpool won at Highbury the night Leeds were losing at Molineux, Bill Shankly's men would have been Champions. The game, however, finished goalless, and – to their astonishment – Derby County, on a plane bound for an end-of-season holiday, heard that the League Championship was theirs. Derby finished with 58 points, one more than Leeds, Liverpool and Manchester City. Arsenal had to be content with fifth place with 52 points.

In many ways it had been a satisfactory season, though the placing in the League was not high enough to qualify for a spot in the UEFA Cup. But the standards had been set a year earlier and deep down the players who had discovered capacities for success beyond their wildest dreams knew that they had missed a great opportunity. It would not have taken too much more for the players to have really challenged for a second successive League and Cup combination.

It seemed inconceivable that greater footballing glory could await any of Arsenal's Double-winning side after they left Highbury but, although he never repeated that particular feat of lifting the League title and FA Cup in the same season, Ray Kennedy didn't exactly struggle through the remainder of his career!

His honours haul after joining Liverpool for £180,000 in the summer of 1974 – the signing was Bill Shankly's final act as Anfield boss – encompassed three European Cup triumphs, five League titles, a UEFA Cup winners' medal, a League Cup gong and 17 England caps.

Not bad for a player who left north London as a 23-year-old striker who had lost his impetus but gained a tad too much weight. In truth, he was adequate but far from outstanding in his early months as a Red, but then Bob Paisley, that incomparable judge of a player, converted the big north-easterner to a deep-lying role and he emerged as a magnificent left-sided midfielder.

In January 1982 Ray joined Swansea, later serving Hartlepool before coaching at Sunderland and then, sadly, being diagnosed with Parkinson's disease.

Kennedy's striking partner during Arsenal's finest hour, John Radford, remained at Highbury until December 1976 when he was transferred to West Ham for £80,000. The tall, oft-underrated Yorkshireman failed to score a League goal during 14 months at Upton Park, then managed ten in 36 outings for Second Division Blackburn before bossing non-League Bishop's Stortford, a friendly club he went on to serve in a variety of capacities for many years.

Frank McLintock will be revered forever as a Gunner, but they have warm memories of the inspirational Scot at Loftus Road, too, following his bargain £25,000 move to Queen's Park Rangers in April 1973. Such was the continued excellence of the Gorbals-raised defender that he fuelled the arguments of those who claimed Arsenal had released him prematurely, excelling for three campaigns and even coming close to a title triumph in 1975–76. At the end of the following term he laid aside his boots, going on to manage Leicester and Brentford before becoming a players' business representative. More recently he has sparkled as a TV pundit.

Gooners disappointed by the sale of McLintock could at least console themselves that their hero was in his thirties and therefore presumably past his best, but there was no such rationale concerning the £90,000 deal which took 24-year-old Charlie George to Derby in 1975. They were reduced to sorry

Top, right: Bill Shankly took Ray Kennedy to Liverpool for £150,000 in July 1974. At Anfield he was transformed from a striker to a creative midfielder.

Top: A mere £25,000 took the 1971 Footballer of the Year to Loftus Road. Arsenal's Double-winning captain Frank McLintock is currently enjoying a career as a TV pundit.

Above: Charlie George playing for Derby in 1978. £90,000 took him to the Baseball Ground where he enjoyed four years of top-flight football.

Right: Bob Wilson is associated more with his work as ITV's football anchorman than he is with his 1970–71 performances between the sticks.

bewilderment as their former hero spent three-and-a-half productive seasons at the Baseball Ground, the highlight of his first term being a European Cup hat-trick against Real Madrid. He went on to earn his sole England cap in 1976, later assisting Southampton, Nottingham Forest (on loan), Bulova of Hong Kong, Bournemouth and Derby again before retiring in 1982.

A less glamorous but arguably even more influential contributor to the greatness of Bertie Mee's team was George Armstrong, one of the best uncapped players of all time, who enjoyed a fascinating footballing odyssey after joining Leicester in September 1977. He didn't tarry long at Filbert Street before rounding off his playing days with Stockport in 1978–79, then travelled the world as a highly sought-after coach. 'Geordie' took his enthusiasm and expertise to Aston Villa, Narvik in Norway, Fulham, Enderby Town, Middlesbrough, Queen's Park Rangers and Worcester City before experiencing enormous success with the Kuwait national side. Then, in 1990, he returned to his spiritual footballing home of Highbury, where he has been providing an impeccable role model to the reserves ever since.

What of the rest? Bob McNab was freed to enlist with Wolves in July 1975, but he made little impact at Molineux before moving to the United States. In 1977 he assisted Barnet, then a non-League club, before coaching in Canada.

Peter Simpson was released in 1978, finishing his career with New England Teamen in the USA before a few games with Hendon heralded his departure from the game. Peter Storey was sold to west Londoners Fulham for a mere £10,000 in March 1977, but didn't linger long at Craven Cottage and subsequently faced personal problems, falling foul of the law as, perhaps, he struggled to come to terms with life outside professional football.

Eddie Kelly was transferred to Queen's Park Rangers for £60,000 in 1976, thereafter embarking on travels which took in Leicester (twice), Notts County, Bournemouth and Torquay before his retirement in 1986.

That leaves Bob Wilson, Pat Rice and George Graham, whose career paths will need little charting for Gunners' supporters. For the record, Bob played on until 1974, after which he found a happy niche on TV, while finding the time to rejoin Arsenal as goalkeeping coach in 1994. Pat moved to Watford for £8,000 in 1980, spending four years as a Hornet before re-enlisting at Highbury as youth coach. Thereafter, of course, he rose in the pecking order to serve as caretaker manager in the interregnum between fellow stop-gap Stewart Houston and Arsene Wenger, before being appointed as the Frenchman's No 2.

And so to George Graham, who joined Manchester United in December 1972, then played for Portsmouth and Crystal Palace before managing Millwall, Arsenal (for whom he did quite well) and Leeds, taking over the reins of another North London club in 1998.

BEYOND 1971

The Football League was again suspended during the Second World War, the 1939-1940 competition having been cut short after just four matches. During the seven seasons that followed the outbreak of the War, Arsenal played in a variety of competitions: the Regional League South, the London War Cup, the London League, the League Cup (South) and the Football League (South).

Arsenal won the Regional League South (A Division) in the season 1939-1940, won the London League in 1942 and retained the title the following year. They won the League Cup (South) in the season 1942-1943 and again in the season 1944-1945. Arsenal finished 11th in the League Table (South), in season 1944-1945 the full Football League was reinstated the following season.

SEASON 1946-1947
FOOTBALL LEAGUE (DIVISION 1)

```
31 Aug  Wolverhampton W   A L 1-6
4 Sep   Blackburn Rov     H L 1-3
7 Sep   Sunderland        A D 2-2
11 Sep  Everton           A L 2-3
14 Sep  Aston Villa       A W 2-0
17 Sep  Blackburn Rov     A W 2-1
21 Sep  Derby Co          H L 0-1
28 Sep  Manchester U      A L 2-5
5 Oct   Blackpool         A L 1-2
12 Oct  Brentford         H D 2-2
19 Oct  Stoke C           H W 1-0
26 Oct  Chelsea           A L 1-2
2 Nov   Sheffield U       H L 2-3
9 Nov   Preston NE        A L 0-2
16 Nov  Leeds U           H W 4-2
23 Nov  Liverpool         A L 2-4
30 Nov  Bolton W          H D 2-2
7 Dec   Middlesbrough     A L 0-2
14 Dec  Charlton Ath      H W 1-0
21 Dec  Grimsby T         A D 0-0
25 Dec  Portsmouth        H W 2-1
26 Dec  Portsmouth        A W 2-0
28 Dec  Wolverhampton W   H D 1-1
4 Jan   Sunderland        H W 4-1
18 Jan  Aston Villa       H L 0-2
1 Feb   Manchester U      H W 6-2
8 Feb   Blackpool         H D 1-1
22 Feb  Stoke C           A L 1-3
1 Mar   Chelsea           H L 1-2
15 Mar  Preston NE        H W 4-1
22 Mar  Leeds U           A D 1-1
4 Apr   Huddersfield T    H L 1-2
5 Apr   Bolton W          A W 3-1
7 Apr   Huddersfield T    A D 0-0
12 Apr  Middlesbrough     H W 4-0
19 Apr  Charlton Ath      A D 2-2
26 Apr  Grimsby T         H W 5-3
10 May  Derby Co          A W 1-0
24 May  Liverpool         H L 1-2
26 May  Brentford         A W 1-0
31 May  Everton           H W 2-1
7 June  Sheffield U       A L 1-2
```

FA Cup
```
11 Jan  Chelsea (3)       A D 1-1
15 Jan  Chelsea (3R)      H D 1-1
20 Jan  Chelsea (3R)        L 0-2
        (at Tottenham)
```

Appearances (Goals)
Barnes W 26 · Bastin C 6 · Calverley A 11 · Collett E 6 · Compton D 1 1 · Compton L 36 · Curtis G 11 · Drury G 4 · Fields A 8 · Grant C 2 · Gudmundsson A 2 · Hodges C 2 · Jones B 26 1 · Joy B 13 · Lewis R 28 (29) · Logie J 35 (8) · Male G 15 · McPherson J 37 (6) · Mercer J 25 · Morgan S 2 · Nelson D 10 · Dr O'Flanagan K 14 (3) · Platt T 4 · Rooke R 24 (21) · Rudkin T 5 2 · Scott L 28 · Sloan P 30 (1) · Smith A 3 · Swindin G 38 · Wade J 2 · Waller H 8 · Total: 31 players (72)

Position in League Table

	P	W	L	D	F:A	Pts	
Liverpool	42	25	10	7	84:52	57	1st
Arsenal	42	16	17	9	72:70	41	13th

SEASON 1947-1948
FOOTBALL LEAGUE (DIVISION 1)

```
23 Aug  Sunderland        H W 3-1
27 Aug  Charlton Ath      A W 4-2
30 Aug  Sheffield U       A W 2-1
3 Sep   Charlton Ath      H W 6-0
6 Sep   Manchester U      H W 2-1
10 Sep  Bolton W          H W 2-0
13 Sep  Preston NE        A D 0-0
20 Sep  Stoke C           H W 1-0
27 Sep  Burnley           H W 1-0
4 Oct   Portsmouth        H D 0-0
11 Oct  Aston Villa       H W 1-0
18 Oct  Wolverhampton W   A D 1-1
25 Oct  Everton           H D 1-1
1 Nov   Chelsea           A D 0-0
8 Nov   Blackpool         H W 2-1
15 Nov  Blackburn Rov     A W 1-0
22 Nov  Huddersfield T    A W 2-0
29 Nov  Derby Co          A L 0-1
6 Dec   Middlesbrough     H W 4-0
13 Dec  Grimsby T         A W 4-0
20 Dec  Sunderland        A D 1-1
25 Dec  Liverpool         A W 3-1
27 Dec  Liverpool         H L 1-2
1 Jan   Bolton W          A W 1-0
3 Jan   Sheffield U       H W 3-2
17 Jan  Manchester U      A D 1-1
31 Jan  Preston NE        H W 3-0
7 Feb   Stoke C           A D 0-0
14 Feb  Burnley           H W 3-0
28 Feb  Aston Villa       A L 2-4
6 Mar   Wolverhampton W   H W 5-2
13 Mar  Everton           A W 2-0
20 Mar  Chelsea           H L 0-2
26 Mar  Middlesbrough     H W 7-0
27 Mar  Blackpool         A L 0-3
29 Mar  Middlesbrough     A D 1-1
3 Apr   Blackburn Rov     H W 2-0
10 Apr  Huddersfield T    H L 1-2
17 Apr  Derby Co          H L 1-2
21 Apr  Portsmouth        A D 0-0
24 Apr  Manchester C      A D 0-0
1 May   Grimsby T         H W 8-0
```

FA Cup
```
10 Jan  Bradford C (3)    H L 0-1
```

Appearances (Goals)
Barnes W 35 · Compton D 14 (6) · Compton L 35 · Fields A 6 · Forbes A 11 (2) · Jones B 7 (1) · Lewis R 28 (14) · Logie J 39 (8) · Macaulay A 40 · Male G 8 · McPherson L 29 (5) · Mercer J 40 · Rooke R 42 (33) · Roper D 40 (10) · Scott L 39 · Sloan W 3 · Smith L 1 · Swindin G 42 · Wade J 3 · Own goals 2 · Total: 19 players (81)

Position in League Table

	P	W	L	D	F:A	Pts	
Arsenal	42	23	6	13	81:32	59	1st

SEASON 1948-1949
FOOTBALL LEAGUE (DIVISION 1)

```
21 Aug  Huddersfield T    A D 1-1
25 Aug  Stoke C           H W 3-0
28 Aug  Manchester U      H L 0-1
30 Aug  Stoke C           A L 0-1
4 Sep   Sheffield U       A D 1-1
8 Sep   Liverpool         H D 1-1
11 Sep  Aston Villa       H W 3-1
15 Sep  Liverpool         A W 1-0
18 Sep  Sunderland        A D 1-1
25 Sep  Wolverhampton W   H W 3-1
2 Oct   Bolton W          A L 0-1
9 Oct   Burnley           H W 3-1
16 Oct  Preston NE        A D 1-1
23 Oct  Everton           H W 5-0
30 Oct  Chelsea           A W 1-0
6 Nov   Birmingham C      H W 2-0
13 Nov  Middlesbrough     A W 1-0
20 Nov  Newcastle U       A L 0-1
27 Nov  Portsmouth        A L 1-4
4 Dec   Manchester C      H D 1-1
11 Dec  Charlton Ath      A L 3-4
18 Dec  Huddersfield T    H W 2-0
25 Dec  Derby Co          H D 3-3
27 Dec  Derby Co          A L 1-2
1 Jan   Manchester U      A L 0-2
15 Jan  Sheffield U       H W 5-3
22 Jan  Aston Villa       A L 0-1
5 Feb   Sunderland        H W 5-0
19 Feb  Wolverhampton W   A W 3-1
26 Feb  Bolton W          H W 5-0
5 Mar   Burnley           A D 1-1
12 Mar  Preston NE        H D 0-0
19 Mar  Newcastle U       H L 2-3
2 Apr   Birmingham C      A D 1-1
9 Apr   Middlesbrough     H D 1-1
15 Apr  Blackpool         A D 1-1
16 Apr  Everton           A W 2-0
18 Apr  Blackpool         H W 2-0
23 Apr  Chelsea           H L 1-2
27 Apr  Manchester C      A W 3-0
4 May   Portsmouth        H W 3-2
7 May   Chariton Ath      H W 2-0
```

FA Cup
```
8 Jan   Tottenham H (3)   H W 3-0
29 Jan  Derby Co (4)      A L 0-1
```

FA Charity Shield
```
6 Oct   Manchester U      H W 4-3
```

Appearances (Goals)
Barnes W 40 · Compton D 6 (2) · Compton L 40 · Daniel R 1 · Fields A 1 · Forbes A 25 (4) · Jones B 8 1 · Lewis R 25 (16) · Lishman D 23 12 · Logie J 35 (11) · Macaulay A 39 (1) · McPherson L 33 (5) · Mercer J 33 · Platt E 10 · Rooke R 22 (14) · Roper D 31 (5) · Scott L 12 · Smith L 32 · Swindin G 32 · Vallance T 14 (2) · Own goals 1 · Total: players 20 (74)

Position in League Table

	P	W	L	D	F:A	Pts	
Portsmouth	42	25	9	8	84:42	58	1st
Arsenal	42	18	11	13	74:44	49	5th

SEASON 1949-1950
FOOTBALL LEAGUE (DIVISION 1)

```
20 Aug  Burnley           H L 0-1
24 Aug  Chelsea           A W 2-1
27 Aug  Sunderland        A L 2-4
31 Aug  Chelsea           H L 2-3
3 Sep   Liverpool         H L 1-2
7 Sep   W B A             A W 2-1
10 Sep  Huddersfield T    A D 2-2
14 Sep  W B A             H W 4-1
17 Sep  Bolton W          A D 2-2
24 Sep  Birmingham C      H W 4-2
1 Oct   Derby Co          A W 2-1
8 Oct   Everton           H W 5-2
15 Oct  Middlesbrough     A D 1-1
22 Oct  Blackpool         H W 3-0
29 Oct  Newcastle U       A W 3-0
5 Nov   Fulham            A D 2-2
12 Nov  Manchester C      A W 2-0
19 Nov  Charlton Ath      H L 2-3
26 Nov  Aston Villa       A D 1-1
3 Dec   Wolverhampton W   A D 1-1
10 Dec  Portsmouth        A L 1-2
17 Dec  Burnley           A D 0-0
24 Dec  Sunderland        H W 5-0
26 Dec  Manchester U      A L 0-2
27 Dec  Manchester U      H D 0-0
31 Dec  Liverpool         A L 0-2
14 Jan  Huddersfield T    H W 1-0
21 Jan  Bolton W          H D 1-1
4 Feb   Birmingham C      A L 1-2
18 Feb  Derby Co          A W 1-0
25 Feb  Everton           H W 1-0
8 Mar   Middlesbrough     H D 1-1
11 Mar  Charlton Ath      A D 1-1
25 Mar  Fulham            A D 2-2
29 Mar  Aston Villa       H L 1-3
1 Apr   Manchester C      H W 4-1
8 Apr   Blackpool         A L 1-2
10 Apr  Stoke C           H W 6-0
15 Apr  Newcastle U       H W 4-2
22 Apr  Wolverhampton W   A L 0-3
3 May   Portsmouth        H W 2-0
6 May   Stoke C           A W 5-2
```

FA Cup
```
7 Jan   Sheffield W (3)   H W 1-0
28 Jan  Swansea T (4)     H W 2-1
11 Feb  Burnley (5)       H W 2-0
4 Mar   Leeds U (6)       H W 1-0
18 Mar  Chelsea (SF)        D 2-2
        (at White Hart Lane)
22 Mar  Chelsea (SFR)       W 1-0
        (at White Hart Lane)
29 Apr  Liverpool (F)       W 2-0
        (at Wembley)
```

Appearances (Goals)
Barnes W 38 (5) · Compton D 11 (1) · Compton L 35 · Cox F 32 (3) · Daniel R 6 · Forbes A 23 (2) · Kelly N 1 · Lewis R 31 (19) · Lishman D 14 (9) · Logie J 34 (7) · Macaulay A 24 · McPherson J 35 · Mercer J 35 · Platt E 19 · Roper D 27 (7) · Scott L 15 · Shaw A 5 · Smith L 31 · Swindin G 23 · Vallance T 1 · Wade J 1 · Own goals 2 · Total: 22 players (79)

Position in League Table

	P	W	L	D	F:A	Pts	
Portsmouth	42	22	11	9	74:38	53	1st
Arsenal	42	19	12	11	79:55	49	6th

SEASON 1950-1951
FOOTBALL LEAGUE (DIVISION 1)

```
19 Aug  Burnley           A W 1-0
23 Aug  Chelsea           H D 0-0
26 Aug  Tottenham H       H D 2-2
30 Aug  Chelsea           A W 1-0
2 Sep   Sheffield W       H W 3-0
6 Sep   Everton           H W 2-1
9 Sep   Middlesbrough     A L 1-1
13 Sep  Everton           A D 1-1
16 Sep  Huddersfield T    H W 6-2
23 Sep  Newcastle U       A L 1-2
30 Sep  W B A             H W 3-0
7 Oct   Charlton Ath      A W 3-1
14 Oct  Manchester U      H W 3-0
21 Oct  Aston Villa       A D 1-1
28 Oct  Stoke C           H W 3-1
4 Nov   Wolverhampton W   A W 1-0
11 Nov  Sunderland        H W 5-1
18 Nov  Liverpool         A W 3-1
25 Nov  Fulham            H W 5-1
2 Dec   Bolton W          A L 0-1
9 Dec   Blackpool         H D 4-4
16 Dec  Burnley           H L 0-1
23 Dec  Tottenham H       A L 0-1
25 Dec  Stoke C           H L 0-3
26 Dec  Stoke C           A L 0-1
30 Dec  Sheffield W       A W 2-0
13 Jan  Middlesbrough     H W 3-1
20 Jan  Huddersfield T    A D 2-2
3 Feb   Newcastle U       H D 0-0
17 Feb  W B A             A L 0-2
24 Feb  Charlton Ath      H L 2-5
3 Mar   Manchester U      A L 1-1
10 Mar  Aston Villa       H W 2-1
17 Mar  Derby Co          A L 2-4
23 Mar  Portsmouth        H L 1-1
24 Mar  Wolverhampton W   H W 2-1
26 Mar  Portsmouth        A D 1-1
31 Mar  Sunderland        A W 2-0
7 Apr   Liverpool         H L 1-2
14 Apr  Fulham            A L 2-3
21 Apr  Bolton W          H W 2-1
2 May   Blackpool         A W 1-0
```

FA Cup
```
6 Jan   Carlisle U (3)    H D 0-0
11 Jan  Carlisle U (3R)   A W 4-1
27 Jan  Northampton (4)   H W 3-2
10 Feb  Manchester U (5)  A L 0-1
```

Appearances (Goals)
Barnes W 35 (3) · Bowen D 7 · Compton L 36 · Cox F 13 (2) · Daniel R 5 · Fields A 1 · Forbes A 32 (4) · Goring P 34 (15) · Holton C 10 (5) · Kelsey J 4 · Lewis R 14 (8) · Lishman D 20 (17) · Logie J 39 (9) · McPherson J 26 · Marden B 11 (2) · Mercer J 31 · Milton A 1 · Platt E 17 Roper D 34 (7) · Scott L 17 · Shaw A 16 · Smith L 32 · Swindin G 21 · Own goals1 · Total: 23 players (73)

Position in League Table

	P	W	L	D	F:A	Pts	
Tottenham H	42	25	7	10	82:44	60	1st
Arsenal	42	19	14	9	73:56	47	5th

SEASON 1951-1952
FOOTBALL LEAGUE (DIVISION 1)

```
18 Aug  Huddersfield T    H D 2-2
22 Aug  Chelsea           A W 3-1
25 Aug  Wolverhampton W   A L 1-2
29 Aug  Chelsea           H W 2-1
1 Sep   Sunderland        A W 3-0
5 Sep   Liverpool         H D 0-0
8 Sep   Aston Villa       A L 0-1
12 Sep  Liverpool         A D 0-0
15 Sep  Derby Co          A W 3-1
22 Sep  Manchester C      A W 2-0
29 Sep  Tottenham H       H D 1-1
6 Oct   Preston NE        A L 0-2
13 Oct  Burnley           H W 1-0
20 Oct  Charlton Ath      A W 3-1
27 Oct  Fulham            H W 4-3
3 Nov   Middlesbrough     A W 3-0
10 Nov  W B A             H W 6-3
17 Nov  Newcastle U       A L 0-2
24 Nov  Bolton W          H W 4-2
1 Dec   Stoke C           A L 1-2
8 Dec   Huddersfield T    A W 3-2
15 Dec  Charlton Ath      H L 1-2
25 Dec  Fulham            A W 2-1
26 Dec  Portsmouth        H W 4-1? 
3 Jan   Chelsea           A D 1-1
14 Jan  Carlisle U        W 4-1
21 Jan  Bolton W          A L 1-1
2 May   Blackpool         A W 1-0
```

FA Cup
```
8 Jan   Tottenham H (3)   H W 3-0
29 Jan  Derby Co (4)      A L 0-1
```

FA Charity Shield
```
6 Oct   Manchester U      H W 4-3
```

Appearances (Goals)
Barnes W 40 · Compton D 6 (2) · Compton L 40 · Daniel R 1 · Fields A 1 · Forbes A 25 (4) · Jones B 8 1 · Lewis R 25 (16) · Lishman D 23 12 · Logie J 35 (11) · Macaulay A 39 (1) · McPherson L 33 (5) · Mercer J 33 · Platt E 17 Roper D 34 (7) · Scott L 17 · Shaw A 16 · Smith L 32 · Swindin G 32 · Vallance T 14 (2) · Own goals 1 · Total: players 20 (74)

Position in League Table

	P	W	L	D	F:A	Pts	
Manchester U	42	23	8	11	95:52	57	1st
Arsenal	42	21	10	11	80:61	53	3rd

SEASON 1952-1953
FOOTBALL LEAGUE (DIVISION 1)

```
23 Aug  Aston Villa       A W 2-1
27 Aug  Manchester U      H W 2-1
30 Aug  Sunderland        H L 1-2
3 Sep   Manchester U      A D 0-0
6 Sep   Wolverhampton W   A D 1-1
10 Sep  Portsmouth        H W 3-1
13 Sep  Charlton Ath      H L 3-4
17 Sep  Portsmouth        A D 2-2
20 Sep  Tottenham H       A W 1-1
27 Sep  Derby Co          A L 0-2
4 Oct   Blackpool         H W 3-1
11 Oct  Sheffield W       H D 2-2
25 Oct  Newcastle U       A W 3-0
1 Nov   W B A             A L 0-2
8 Nov   Middlesbrough     H W 5-1
15 Nov  Liverpool         A W 5-1
22 Nov  Manchester C      H W 3-0
29 Nov  Stoke C           A D 1-1
6 Dec   Burnley           H D 1-1
13 Dec  Aston Villa       H W 3-1
20 Dec  Sunderland        A L 0-2
25 Dec  Bolton W          A W 6-4
3 Jan   Sunderland        A L 1-3
17 Jan  Wolverhampton W   H W 5-3
24 Jan  Charlton Ath      H D 2-2
7 Feb   Tottenham H       H W 4-0
18 Feb  Derby Co          H W 6-2
21 Feb  Blackpool         A L 2-3
2 Mar   Sheffield W       A W 4-1
7 Mar   Cardiff           H L 0-1
14 Mar  Newcastle U       H D 1-1
19 Mar  Preston NE        H D 1-1
21 Mar  W B A             H D 2-2
28 Mar  Middlesbrough     A W 8-1? 
3 Apr   Chelsea           A D 1-1
4 Apr   Liverpool         H W 5-3
6 Apr   Chelsea           H W 2-0
15 Apr  Manchester C      A W 4-1
18 Apr  Bolton W          H W 4-1
22 Apr  Cardiff           A L 0-2
25 Apr  Preston NE        A L 0-2
1 May   Burnley           H W 3-2
```

FA Cup
```
10 Jan  Doncaster Rov (3) H W 4-0
31 Jan  Bury (4)          H W 6-2
14 Feb  Burnley (5)       A W 2-0
28 Feb  Blackpool (6)     H L 1-2
```

Appearances (Goals)
Bowen D 2 · Chenhall J 13 · Cox F 9 (1) · Daniel R 41 (5) · Dodgin W 1 · Forbes A 33 (1) · Goring P 29 (10) · Holton C 21 (19) · Kelsey J 25 · Lishman D 39 (22) · Logie J 32 (10) · Marden R 8 (4) · Mercer J 28 (2) · Milton A 25 7 · Oakes D 2 (1) · Platt E 3 · Roper D 41 (14) · Shaw A 25 · Smith L 31 · Swindin G 14 · Wade J 40 · Own goals1 · Total: 21 players (97)

Position in League Table

	P	W	L	D	F:A	Pts	
Arsenal	42	21	9	12	97:64	54	1st

SEASON 1953-1954
FOOTBALL LEAGUE (DIVISION 1)

```
19 Aug  W B A             A L 0-2
22 Aug  Huddersfield T    H D 0-0
24 Aug  Sheffield U       A L 0-1
29 Aug  Aston Villa       A L 1-2
1 Sep   Sheffield U       H D 1-1
5 Sep   Wolverhampton W   H L 2-3
8 Sep   Chelsea           A L 1-2
12 Sep  Sunderland        A L 1-7
15 Sep  Chelsea           H W 2-0
19 Sep  Manchester C      H D 2-2
26 Sep  Cardiff           A W 3-2
3 Oct   Preston NE        H W 3-2
10 Oct  Tottenham H       A W 4-1
17 Oct  Burnley           H L 2-5
24 Oct  Charlton Ath      H W 5-1
31 Oct  Sheffield W       A W 4-1
7 Nov   Manchester U      A D 2-2
14 Nov  Bolton W          H W 4-3
21 Nov  Liverpool         A W 2-1
28 Nov  Newcastle U       H W 2-1
5 Dec   Middlesbrough     A W 2-1
12 Dec  W B A             H D 2-2
19 Dec  Huddersfield T    A D 2-2
26 Dec  Blackpool         H D 1-1
28 Dec  Blackpool         A W 2-0? 
16 Jan  Wolverhampton W   A W 2-0
23 Jan  Sunderland        H L 1-4
6 Feb   Manchester C      A D 0-0
13 Feb  Cardiff           H D 1-1
24 Feb  Preston NE        A W 2-0
27 Feb  Tottenham H       H L 0-3
6 Mar   Burnley           A L 1-2
13 Mar  Charlton Ath      H D 3-3
20 Mar  Sheffield W       H W 1-0
27 Mar  Manchester U      H W 3-1
3 Apr   Bolton W          A L 1-3
6 Apr   Aston Villa       H W 1-1
10 Apr  Liverpool         H W 3-0
16 Apr  Portsmouth        H W 3-0
17 Apr  Newcastle U       A L 2-5
19 Apr  Portsmouth        A D 1-1
24 Apr  Middlesbrough     H W 3-1
```

FA Cup
```
9 Jan   Aston Villa (3)   H W 5-1
30 Jan  Norwich (4)       H L 1-2
```

FA Charity Shield
```
12 Oct  Blackpool         H W 3-1
```

Appearances (Goals)
Barnes W 19 (1) · Bowen D 10 · Dickson W 24 1 · Dodgin W 39 · Evans D 10 · Forbes A 30 (4) · Goring P 9 · Holton C 32 (17) · Kelsey J 39 · Lawton T 9 (1) · Lishman D 39 (18) · Logie J 35 (8) · Marden R 9 (3) · Mercer J 19 · Milton A 21 (3) · Roper D 39 (12) · Shaw A 2 · Smith L 7 · Sullivan C 1 · Swindin G 2 · Tapscott D 5 (5) · Tilley R 1 · Wade J 18 · Walsh B 10 · Ward G 3 · Wills L 30 · Own goals 2 · Total: 26 players (75)

Position in League Table

	P	W	L	D	F:A	Pts	
Wolverhampton W	42	25	10	7	96:56	57	1st
Arsenal	42	15	14	13	75:73	43	12th

SEASON 1954-1955
FOOTBALL LEAGUE (DIVISION 1)

```
21 Aug  Newcastle U       H L 1-3
25 Aug  Everton           A L 0-1
28 Aug  W B A             A L 1-3
31 Aug  Everton           H W 2-0
4 Sep   Tottenham H       H W 2-0
8 Sep   Manchester C      A L 1-2
11 Sep  Sheffield U       H W 4-0
14 Sep  Manchester C      H L 2-3
18 Sep  Preston NE        A L 1-3
25 Sep  Burnley           H W 2-0
2 Oct   Leicester C       A D 3-3
9 Oct   Sheffield W       A W 2-1
16 Oct  Portsmouth        H L 0-1
23 Oct  Aston Villa       A L 1-2
30 Oct  Sunderland        H L 1-3
6 Nov   Bolton W          A D 2-2
13 Nov  Huddersfield T    H L 3-5
20 Nov  Wolverhampton W   H D 1-1
27 Nov  Manchester U      A D 1-1
4 Dec   Blackpool         A W 3-1
11 Dec  Charlton Ath      H W 3-1
18 Dec  Newcastle U       A L 1-5
25 Dec  Chelsea           H W 1-0
27 Dec  Chelsea           A D 1-1
1 Jan   W B A             H D 2-2
15 Jan  Tottenham H       A W 1-0
5 Feb   Preston NE        H W 1-0
12 Feb  Burnley           A L 0-3
19 Feb  Leicester C       H D 1-1
26 Feb  Sheffield W       H W 3-2
```

Abbreviations:

Appearances (goals) refer to League games only

Figures shown as '2' etc. refer to goals scored by individual players

* own-goal

5 Mar	Charlton Ath	A	D	1-1
12 Mar	Aston Villa	H	W	2-0
19 Mar	Sunderland	A	W	1-0
26 Mar	Bolton W	H	W	3-0
2 Apr	Huddersfield T	A	W	1-0
8 Apr	Cardiff	H	W	2-0
9 Apr	Blackpool	H	W	3-0
11 Apr	Cardiff	A	W	2-1
16 Apr	Wolverhampton W	A	L	1-3
18 Apr	Sheffield U	A	D	1-1
23 Apr	Manchester U	H	L	2-3
30 Apr	Portsmouth	A	L	1-2

FA Cup

| 8 Jan | Cardiff (3) | H | W | 1-0 |
| 29 Jan | Wolves (4) | A | L | 0-1 |

Appearances (Goals)

Barnes W 25 · Bloomfield J 19 4 · Bowen D 21 Clapton Danny 16 · Dickson W 4 · Dodgin W 3 · Evans D 21 · Forbes A 20 1 Fotheringham J 27 Goring P 41 1 · Guthrie R 2 · Haverty J 6 · Herd D 31 · Holton C 8 Kelsey J 38 Lawton T 18 6 · Lishman D 32 19 · Logie J 13 3 · Marden R 7 · Milton A 8 3 · Oakes D 9 · Roper D 35 17 · Shaw A 1 · Sullivan C 2 · Swallow R 1 · Tapscott D 37 13 · Wade J 14 · Walsh J 6 · Wilkinson J 1 · Wills L 24 1 · Total: players 30 (69)

Position in League Table

	P	W	L	D	F:A	Pts
Chelsea	42	20	10	12	81:57	52	1st
Arsenal	42	17	16	9	69:63	43	9th

SEASON 1955-1956
FOOTBALL LEAGUE (DIVISION 1)

20 Aug	Blackpool	A	L	1-3
23 Aug	Cardiff C	H	W	3-1
27 Aug	Chelsea	H	D	1-1
31 Aug	Manchester C	A	D	2-2
3 Sep	Bolton W	A	L	1-4
6 Sep	Manchester C	H	D	0-0
10 Sep	Tottenham H	A	L	1-3
17 Sep	Portsmouth	H	L	1-3
24 Sep	Sunderland	A	L	1-3
1 Oct	Aston Villa	H	W	1-0
8 Oct	Everton	A	D	1-1
15 Oct	Newcastle U	H	W	1-0
22 Oct	Luton T	A	D	0-0
29 Oct	Charlton Ath	H	L	2-4
5 Nov	Manchester U	A	D	1-1
12 Nov	Sheffield U	H	W	2-1
19 Nov	Preston NE	A	W	1-0
26 Nov	Burnley	H	L	0-1
3 Dec	Birmingham C	A	L	0-4
10 Dec	W B A	H	W	2-0
17 Dec	Blackpool	H	W	4-1
24 Dec	Chelsea	A	L	0-2
26 Dec	Wolverhampton W	A	D	3-3
27 Dec	Wolverhampton W	H	D	2-2
31 Dec	Bolton W	H	W	1-0
14 Jan	Tottenham H	H	L	0-1
21 Jan	Portsmouth	A	L	2-5
4 Feb	Sunderland	H	W	3-1
11 Feb	Aston Villa	A	D	1-1
21 Feb	Everton	H	W	3-2
25 Feb	Newcastle U	A	L	0-1
6 Mar	Preston NE	H	W	3-2
10 Mar	Charlton Ath	A	L	0-2
17 Mar	Manchester U	H	D	1-1
24 Mar	Sheffield U	A	W	2-0
31 Mar	Luton T	H	W	3-0
2 Apr	W B A	H	W	2-0
3 Apr	Huddersfield T	A	W	1-0
7 Apr	Burnley	A	W	1-0
14 Apr	Birmingham C	H	W	1-0
21 Apr	W B A	A	L	1-2
28 Apr	Cardiff C	A	W	2-1

FA Cup

7 Jan	Bedford Town (3)	H	D	2-2
12 Jan	Bedford Town (3R)	A	W	2-1
28 Jan	Aston Villa (4)	H	W	4-1
18 Feb	Charlton Ath (5)	A	W	2-0
3 Mar	Birmingham C (6)	H	L	1-3

Appearances (Goals)

Barnes W 8 · Bloomfield J 32 (3) · Bowen D 22 · Charlton S 19 · Clapton Danny 39 (2) · Dickson W 1 · Dodgin W 15 · Evans D 42 · Forbes A 5 · Fotheringham J 25 · Goring P 37 · Groves V 15 (8) · Haverty J 8 (2) · Herd D 5 (2) · Holton C 31 (8) · Kelsey J 32 · Lawton T 8 (6) · Lishman D 15 (5) · Nutt G 8 (1) · Roper D 16 (4) Sullivan C 10 · Swallow R 1 (1) · Tapscott D 31 (17) · Tiddy M 21 · Walsh B 1 · Wills 15 · Own goals 1 · Total: 26 players (60)

Position in League Table

	P	W	L	D	F:A	Pts
Manchester U	42	25	7	10	83:51	60	1st
Arsenal	42	18	14	10	60:61	46	5th

SEASON 1956-1957
FOOTBALL LEAGUE (DIVISION 1)

18 Aug	Cardiff C	H	D	0-0
21 Aug	Burnley	H	W	2-0
25 Aug	Birmingham C	A	L	2-4
28 Aug	Burnley	A	L	1-3
1 Sep	W B A	H	W	4-1
4 Sep	Preston NE	H	L	1-2
8 Sep	Portsmouth	A	W	3-2
10 Sep	Preston NE	A	L	0-3
15 Sep	Newcastle U	H	L	0-1
22 Sep	Sheffield W	A	W	4-2
29 Sep	Manchester U	H	L	1-2

6 Oct	Manchester C	H	W	7-3
13 Oct	Charlton Ath	A	W	3-1
20 Oct	Tottenham H	H	W	3-1
27 Oct	Everton	A	L	0-4
3 Nov	Aston Villa	H	W	2-1
10 Nov	Wolverhampton W	A	L	2-5
17 Nov	Bolton W	H	W	3-0
24 Nov	Leeds U	A	D	3-3
1 Dec	Sunderland	H	D	1-1
8 Dec	Luton T	A	W	2-1
15 Dec	Cardiff C	A	W	3-2
22 Dec	Birmingham C	H	W	4-0
25 Dec	Chelsea	A	D	1-1
26 Dec	Chelsea	H	W	2-0
29 Dec	W B A	H	D	2-2
12 Jan	Portsmouth	H	D	1-1
19 Jan	Newcastle U	A	L	1-3
1 Feb	Sheffield W	H	W	6-3
9 Feb	Manchester U	A	L	2-6
23 Feb	Everton	H	W	2-0
9 Mar	Luton T	H	L	1-3
13 Mar	Tottenham H	A	W	3-1
16 Mar	Aston Villa	A	D	0-0
20 Mar	Wolverhampton W	H	D	0-0
30 Mar	Bolton W	A	L	1-2
6 Apr	Leeds U	H	W	1-0
13 Apr	Sunderland	A	L	0-1
19 Apr	Blackpool	H	D	1-1
20 Apr	Charlton Ath	H	W	3-1
22 Apr	Blackpool	A	W	4-2

FA Cup

5 Jan	Stoke C (3)	H	W	4-2
26 Jan	Newport Co (4)	A	W	2-0
16 Feb	Preston NE (5)	A	D	3-3
19 Feb	Preston NE (5R)	H	W	2-1
2 Mar	W B A (6)	A	D	2-2
5 Mar	W B A (6R)	H	L	1-2

Appearances (Goals)

Barnwell J 1 · Bloomfield J 42 (10) · Bowen D 30 (2) · Charlton S 40 · Clapton Danny 39 (2) · Dodgin W · 41 · Evans D 40 (4) · Goring P 13 · Groves V 5 (2) · Haverty J 28 (8) · Herd D 22 (2) Holton C 39 (10) · Kelsey J 30 · Nutt G 1 · Roper D 4 (3) · Sullivan C 12 · Swallow A 7 · Tapscott D 38 (25) · Tiddy M 15 (6) · Wills L 18 Own goals 1 · Total: 20 players 85

Position in League Table

	P	W	L	D	F:A	Pts
Manchester U	42	28	6	8	103:54	64	1st
Arsenal	42	21	13	8	85:69	50	5th

SEASON 1957-1958
FOOTBALL LEAGUE (DIVISION 1)

24 Aug	Sunderland	A	W	1-0
27 Aug	W B A	H	D	2-2
31 Aug	Luton T	H	W	2-0
4 Sep	W B A	A	W	2-1
7 Sep	Blackpool	A	L	0-1
10 Sep	Everton	H	L	2-3
14 Sep	Leicester C	H	W	3-1
21 Sep	Manchester U	H	W	2-1
28 Sep	Leeds U	H	W	2-1
2 Oct	Aston Villa	H	W	4-0
5 Oct	Bolton W	A	W	1-0
12 Oct	Tottenham H	H	L	1-3
16 Oct	Everton	A	D	2-2
19 Oct	Birmingham C	H	L	1-3
26 Oct	Chelsea	A	D	0-0
2 Nov	Manchester C	H	W	2-1
9 Nov	Nottingham F	A	L	0-4
16 Nov	Portsmouth	H	W	3-2
23 Nov	Sheffield W	A	L	0-2
30 Nov	Newcastle U	H	L	2-3
7 Dec	Burnley	A	L	1-2
14 Dec	Preston NE	H	W	4-2
21 Dec	Sunderland	H	W	3-0
26 Dec	Aston Villa	A	L	0-3
28 Dec	Luton T	A	L	0-4
11 Jan	Blackpool	H	L	2-3
18 Jan	Leicester C	A	W	1-0
1 Feb	Manchester U	H	L	4-5
8 Feb	Bolton W	A	L	1-2
22 Feb	Tottenham H	H	D	4-4
1 Mar	Birmingham C	A	L	1-4
8 Mar	Chelsea	H	W	5-4
15 Mar	Manchester C	A	W	4-2
19 Mar	Leeds U	A	L	0-2
22 Mar	Sheffield W	H	W	1-0
29 Mar	Portsmouth	A	L	4-5
7 Apr	Wolverhampton W	H	L	0-2
8 Apr	Wolverhampton W	A	W	2-1
12 Apr	Newcastle U	A	D	3-3
19 Apr	Burnley	H	D	0-0
21 Apr	Nottingham F	H	D	1-1
26 Apr	Preston NE	A	L	0-3

FA Cup

| 4 Jan | Northampton (3) | A | L | 1-3 |

Appearances (Goals)

Biggs A 2 · Bloomfield J 40 (16) · Bowen D 30 · Charlton S 36 · Clapton Danny 28 (5) · Dodgin W 23 · Evans D 32 · Fotheringham J 19 · Goring P 10 · Groves V 30 (10) · Haverty J 15 · Herd D 39 (24) · Holton C 26 (4) · Kelsey J 38 · U Roux D 5 · Nutt G 21 (3) · Petts J 9 · Standen J 1 · Sullivan C 3 · Swallow R 7 (3) · Tapscott D 8 (2) · Tiddy M 12 (2) · Ward G 10 · Wills L 18 (1) Own goals 3 · Total: 24 players (73)

Position in League Table

	P	W	L	D	F:A	Pts
Wolverhampton W	42	28	6	8	103:47	64	1st
Arsenal	42	16	19	7	73:85	39	12th

SEASON 1958-1959
FOOTBALL LEAGUE (DIVISION 1)

23 Aug	Preston NE	A	L	1-2
26 Aug	Burnley	H	W	3-0
30 Aug	Leicester C	H	W	5-1
2 Sep	Burnley	A	L	1-3
6 Sep	Everton	A	W	6-1
9 Sep	Bolton W	A	W	6-1
13 Sep	Tottenham H	A	W	3-1
17 Sep	Bolton W	H	L	1-2
20 Sep	Manchester C	H	W	4-1
27 Sep	Leeds U	A	L	1-2
4 Oct	W B A	H	W	4-3
11 Oct	Manchester U	A	D	1-1
18 Oct	Wolverhampton W	H	D	1-1
22 Oct	Aston Villa	A	W	2-1
25 Oct	Blackburn Rov	A	L	2-4
1 Nov	Newcastle U	H	W	3-2
8 Nov	West Ham U	A	D	0-0
15 Nov	Nottingham F	H	W	3-1
22 Nov	Chelsea	A	W	3-0
29 Nov	Blackpool	H	L	1-4
6 Dec	Portsmouth	H	L	1-2
13 Dec	Aston Villa	H	L	1-2
20 Dec	Preston NE	H	L	1-2
26 Dec	Luton T	A	L	3-6
27 Dec	Luton T	H	W	1-0
3 Jan	Leicester C	A	W	3-1
17 Jan	Everton	H	W	3-1
31 Jan	Tottenham H	A	W	4-1
7 Feb	Manchester C	A	D	0-0
21 Feb	W B A	A	D	1-1
24 Feb	Leeds U	H	W	1-0
28 Feb	Manchester U	H	W	3-2
7 Mar	Wolverhampton W	A	L	1-6
14 Mar	Blackburn Rov	H	D	1-1
21 Mar	Newcastle U	A	L	0-1
28 Mar	West Ham U	H	L	1-2
4 Apr	Nottingham F	A	D	1-1
11 Apr	Chelsea	H	D	1-1
14 Apr	Birmingham C	A	L	1-4
18 Apr	Blackpool	A	W	2-1
25 Apr	Portsmouth	H	W	5-2
4 May	Birmingham C	H	W	2-1

FA Cup

10 Jan	Bury (3)	A	W	1-0
24 Jan	Colchester U (4)	A	W	2-2
28 Jan	Colchester U (4R)	H	W	4-0
14 Feb	Sheffield U (5)	H	D	2-2
18 Feb	Sheffield U (5R)	A	L	0-3

Appearances (Goals)

Barnwell J 16 · Biggs A 2 (1) · Bloomfield J 29 (10) · Bowen D 16 · Charlton S 4 · Clapton Danny 39 (6) · Docherty T 38 (1) · Dodgin W 39 Evans D 37 (5) · Fotheringham J 1 · Goring P 2 · Goulden R · 1 · Goy P 2 · Groves V 33 (10) · Haverty J 10 (3) · Henderson J 21 (12) · Herd D 26 (15) · Holton C 3 (3) · Julians L 10 (5) · Kelsey J 27 · McCullough W 10 · Nutt G 16 (6) Petts J 3 · Standen J 3 · Ward G 31 (4) · Wills L 33 (1) · Own goals 3 · Total:26 players (88)

Position in League Table

	P	W	L	D	F:A	Pts
Wolverhampton W	42	28	9	5	110:49	61	1st
Arsenal	42	21	13	8	88:68	50	3rd

SEASON 1959-1960
FOOTBALL LEAGUE (DIVISION 1)

22 Aug	Sheffield W	H	L	0-1
26 Aug	Nottingham F	A	W	3-0
29 Aug	Wolverhampton W	A	D	3-3
1 Sep	Nottingham F	H	D	1-1
5 Sep	Tottenham H	H	D	1-1
9 Sep	Bolton W	A	W	1-0
12 Sep	Manchester C	H	W	3-1
15 Sep	Bolton W	H	W	2-1
19 Sep	Blackburn Rov	A	D	1-1
26 Sep	Blackpool	H	W	2-1
3 Oct	Everton	A	L	1-3
10 Oct	Manchester U	A	L	2-4
17 Oct	Preston NE	H	L	0-3
24 Oct	Leicester C	A	D	2-2
31 Oct	Birmingham C	H	W	3-0
7 Nov	Leeds U	A	L	2-3
14 Nov	West Ham U	H	L	1-3
21 Nov	Chelsea	A	W	3-1
28 Nov	W B A	H	L	2-4
5 Dec	Newcastle U	A	L	1-4
12 Dec	Burnley	H	L	2-4
19 Dec	Sheffield W	H	L	1-5
26 Dec	Luton T	H	L	0-3
28 Dec	Luton T	A	W	1-0
2 Jan	Wolverhampton W	H	D	4-4
16 Jan	Tottenham H	A	L	0-3
23 Jan	Manchester C	A	W	2-1
6 Feb	Blackburn Rov	H	W	5-2
13 Feb	Blackpool	A	L	1-2
20 Feb	Everton	H	W	2-1
27 Feb	Newcastle U	H	W	3-0
5 Mar	Preston NE	A	W	3-0
15 Mar	Leicester C	H	D	1-1
19 Mar	Burnley	A	L	2-3
26 Mar	Leeds U	H	D	1-1
2 Apr	West Ham U	H	L	1-4
9 Apr	Chelsea	H	L	1-4
15 Apr	Fulham	H	W	2-0
16 Apr	Birmingham C	A	L	0-3
18 Apr	Fulham	A	L	0-3
23 Apr	Manchester U	H	W	5-2
30 Apr	Blackpool	A	L	0-1

FA Cup

9 Jan	Rotherham U (3)	A	D	2-2
13 Jan	Rotherham U (3R)	H	D	1-1
18 Jan	Rotherham U (3R)		L	0-2
	(at Sheffield Wed)			

Joe Mercer receives the 1950 FA Cup from King George VI.

Appearances (Goals)

Barnwell J 28 (7) · Bloomfield J 36 (10) · Charles M 20 (8) · Clapton D P (Denis) 3 · Clapton D R (Danny) 23 (7) · Docherty T 24 · Dodgin W 30 · Evans D 7 (1) · Everitt M 5 · Groves V 30 (1) · Haverty J 35 (8) · Henderson J 31 (7) · Herd D 31 (14) · Julians L 8 (2) · Kelsey J 22 · Magill E 17 · McCullough W 33 · Nutt G 3 · Petts J 7 · Snedden J 1 · Standen J 20 · Ward G 15 1 · Wills L 33 (1) · Own goals 1 Total: 23 players (68)

Position in League Table

	P	W	L	D	F:A	Pts
Burnley	42	24	11	7	85:61	55	1st
Arsenal	42	15	18	9	68:80	39	13th

SEASON 1960-1961
FOOTBALL LEAGUE (DIVISION 1)

20 Aug	Burnley	A	L	2-3
23 Aug	Preston NE	H	W	1-0
27 Aug	Nottingham F	H	W	3-0
30 Aug	Preston NE	A	L	0-2
3 Sep	Manchester C	A	D	0-0
6 Sep	Birmingham C	H	W	2-0
10 Sep	Tottenham H	H	L	2-3
14 Sep	Birmingham C	A	L	0-2
17 Sep	Newcastle U	H	W	5-0
24 Sep	Cardiff C	A	L	0-1
1 Oct	W B A	H	W	1-0
8 Oct	Leicester C	A	L	1-2
15 Oct	Aston Villa	H	W	2-1
22 Oct	Blackburn Rov	A	W	4-2
29 Oct	Manchester U	A	L	1-6
5 Nov	West Ham U	A	L	0-6
12 Nov	Chelsea	H	L	1-4
19 Nov	Blackpool	A	D	1-1
26 Nov	Everton	H	W	3-2
3 Dec	Wolverhampton W	A	L	3-5
10 Dec	Bolton W	H	W	5-1
17 Dec	Bumley	H	L	2-5
23 Dec	Sheffield W	A	D	1-1
26 Dec	Sheffield W	H	D	1-1
31 Dec	Nottingham F	A	W	5-3
14 Jan	Manchester C	H	W	5-4
21 Jan	Tottenham H	A	L	2-4
4 Feb	Newcastle U	A	D	3-3
11 Feb	Cardiff C	H	L	2-3
18 Feb	W B A	A	W	3-2
25 Feb	Leicester C	H	L	1-3
4 Mar	Aston Villa	A	D	2-2
11 Mar	Blackburn Rov	H	D	0-0
18 Mar	Manchester U	A	D	1-1
25 Mar	West Ham U	H	D	0-0
31 Mar	Fulham	A	D	2-2
1 Apr	Bolton W	A	D	1-1
3 Apr	Fulham	H	W	4-2
8 Apr	Blackpool	H	W	1-0
15 Apr	Chelsea	A	L	1-3
22 Apr	Wolverhampton W	H	L	1-5
29 Apr	Everton	A	L	1-4

FA Cup

| 7 Jan | Sunderland (3) | A | L | 1-2 |

Appearances (Goals)

Bacuzzi D 13 · Barnwell J 26 (6) · Bloomfield J 12 (1) Charles M 19 3 · Clapton D R (Danny) 18 2 · Clapton D P (Denis) 1 · Docherty T 21 · Eastham G 19 5 · Everitt M 4 (1) · Griffiths A 1 · Groves V 32 · Haverty J 12 (4) · Henderson J 39 10 · Herd D 40 (29) · Kane P 4 (1) · Kelsey J 37 · Magill E 6 · McClelland J 4 · McCullough W 41 · Neill T 14 (1) · O'Neill F 2 · Petts J 1 · Skirton A 16 (3) · Snedden J 23 · Standen J 1 · Strong G 19 (10) · Ward G 9 (1) · Wills L 24 · Young D 4 · Total: 29 players (77)

Position in League Table

	P	W	L	D	F:A	Pts
Tottenham H	42	31	7	4	115:55	66	1st
Arsenal	42	15	16	11	77:85	41	11th

SEASON 1961-1962
FOOTBALL LEAGUE (DIVISION 1)

19 Aug	Burnley	H	D	2-2
23 Aug	Leicester C	A	W	1-0
26 Aug	Tottenham H	A	L	3-4
2 Sep	Leicester C	H	D	4-4
2 Sep	Bolton W	A	L	1-2
9 Sep	Manchester C	H	W	3-0
16 Sep	W B A	A	L	0-4
23 Sep	Birmingham C	H	D	1-1
30 Sep	Everton	A	L	1-4
7 Oct	Blackpool	H	W	3-0
14 Oct	Blackburn Rov	A	D	0-0
21 Oct	Manchester U	H	W	5-1
28 Oct	Cardiff C	A	D	1-1
4 Nov	Chelsea	H	L	0-3
11 Nov	Aston Villa	A	L	1-3
18 Nov	Nottingham F	H	W	2-1
25 Nov	Wolverhampton W	A	W	3-1
2 Dec	West Ham U	H	D	2-2
9 Dec	Sheffield U	A	L	1-2
16 Dec	Burnley	A	W	2-0
23 Dec	Tottenham H	H	W	2-1
26 Dec	Fulham	H	W	1-0
13 Jan	Bolton W	H	L	1-2
20 Jan	Manchester C	A	L	2-3
3 Feb	W B A	H	L	0-1
10 Feb	Birmingham C	A	D	0-0
24 Feb	Blackpool	H	D	0-0
3 Mar	Blackburn	A	D	1-1
17 Mar	Cardiff C	H	D	1-1
24 Mar	Chelsea	A	W	3-2
31 Mar	Aston Villa	H	L	4-5
7 Apr	Nottingham F	A	L	2-5
11 Apr	Fulham	A	L	2-5
14 Apr	Wolverhampton W	H	W	3-1
16 Apr	Manchester U	A	D	3-2
20 Apr	Ipswich T	A	D	2-2
21 Apr	West Ham U	A	D	3-3
23 Apr	Ipswich T	H	L	0-3
28 Apr	Sheffield U	H	W	2-0
1 May	Everton	H	L	2-3

FA Cup

| 6 Jan | Bradford C (3) | H | W | 3-0 |
| 31 Jan | Manchester U (4) | A | L | 0-1 |

Appearances (Goals)

Armstrong G 4 (1) · Bacuzzi D 22 · Barnwell J 14 (3) · Brown L 41 · Charles M 21 (15) · Clamp L 18 · Clapton Danny 5 (1) · Clarke F 1 · Eastham G 38 (6) · Griffiths A 14 (2) · Groves V 16 · Henderson J 12 · Kelsey J 35 · McLeod J 37 (6) · Magill E 21 · McClelland J 4 · McCullough J 40 · McKechnie 13 · Neill T 20 · Petts 12 ·

1940-1973

Skirton 38 (19) · Snedden 15 · Strong 20 (12) · Ward 11 · Own goals 2 · Total: 24 players (71)

Position in League Table

	P	W	L	D	F:A	Pts	
Ipswich T	42	24	10	8	93:67	56	1st
Arsenal	42	16	15	11	71:72	43	10th

SEASON 1962-1963
FOOTBALL LEAGUE (DIVISION 1)

18 Aug Leyton Orient A W 2-1
21 Aug Birmingham C H W 2-0
25 Aug Manchester U H L 1-3
29 Aug Birmingham C A D 2-2
1 Sep Burnley A L 1-2
4 Sep Aston Villa H L 1-2
8 Sep Sheffield W H L 1-2
10 Sep Aston Villa A L 1-3
15 Sep Fulham A W 3-1
22 Sep Leicester C H D 1-1
29 Sep Bolton W A L 0-3
6 Oct Tottenham H A D 4-4
13 Oct West Ham U H D 1-1
27 Oct Wolverhampton W H W 5-4
3 Nov Blackburn Rov A D 5-5
10 Nov Sheffield U H W 1-0
14 Nov Liverpool A L 1-2
17 Nov Nottingham F A L 0-3
24 Nov Ipswich T H W 3-1
1 Dec Manchester C A W 4-2
8 Dec Blackpool H W 2-0
15 Dec Leyton Orient H W 2-0
9 Feb Leicester C A L 0-2
16 Feb Bolton W H W 3-2
23 Feb Tottenham H H L 2-3
2 Mar West Ham U A W 4-0
9 Mar Liverpool H D 2-2
23 Mar Blackburn Rov H W 3-1
26 Mar Everton H W 4-3
30 Mar Ipswich T A D 1-1
6 Apr Nottingham F H D 0-0
8 Apr Wolverhampton W A L 0-1
12 Apr W B A H W 3-2
13 Apr Sheffield U A D 3-3
15 Apr W B A A W 2-1
20 Apr Manchester C H L 2-3
24 Apr Everton A D 1-1
27 Apr Blackpool A L 2-3
6 May Manchester U A W 3-2
11 May Burnley H L 2-3
14 May Fulham H W 3-0
18 May Sheffield W A W 3-2

FA Cup
30 Jan Oxford U (3) H W 5-1
12 Feb Sheffield W (4) H W 2-0
19 Mar Liverpool (5) H L 1-2

Appearances (Goals)
Anderson T 5 (1) · Armstrong G 16 (2) · Bacuzzi D (6) · Baker J 39 (29) · Barnwell J 34 (2) · Brown L 38 (1) · Clamp E 4 (1) · Clarke F 5 · Court D 6 (3) · Eastham G 33 (4) · Groves V 9 · MacLeod J 33 (9) · Magill E 36 · McClelland J 33 · McCullough W42 3 · McKechnie I (9) · Neill T 17 · Sammels J 2 (1) · Skirton A 28 (10) · Smithson R 2 · Snedden J 27 · Strong G 36 (18) · Ward G 2 · Own goals 2 · Total: 23 players (86)

Position in League Table

	P	W	L	D	F:A	Pts	
Everton	42	25	6	11	84:42	61	1st
Arsenal	42	18	14	10	86:77	46	7th

SEASON 1963-1964
FOOTBALL LEAGUE (DIVISION 1)

24 Aug Wolverhampton W H L 1-3
27 Aug W B A H W 3-2
31 Aug Leicester C A L 2-7
4 Sep W B A A L 0-4
7 Sep Bolton W H W 4-3
10 Sep Aston Villa H W 3-0
14 Sep Fulham A W 4-1
21 Sep Manchester U H W 2-1
28 Sep Burnley A W 3-0
2 Oct Everton A L 1-2
5 Oct Ipswich H W 6-0
9 Oct Stoke C A W 2-1
15 Oct Tottenham H H D 4-4
19 Oct Aston Villa A L 1-2
26 Oct Nottingham F H W 4-2
2 Nov Sheffield U A D 2-2
5 Nov West Ham U H D 3-3
9 Nov West Ham U A L 1-3
16 Nov Chelsea A L 1-3
23 Nov Blackpool H W 5-3
30 Nov Blackburn Rov A L 1-4
7 Dec Liverpool H D 1-1
10 Dec Everton H W 6-0
14 Dec Wolverhampton W A D 2-2
21 Dec Leicester C H L 0-1
28 Dec Birmingham C A W 4-1
11 Jan Bolton W A D 1-1
18 Jan Fulham H D 2-2
1 Feb Manchester U A L 1-3
8 Feb Burnley H W 3-2
18 Feb Ipswich A W 2-1
22 Feb Tottenham H A L 1-3
29 Feb Stoke C H D 1-1
7 Mar Nottingham F A L 0-2
14 Mar Chelsea H L 2-4
21 Mar West Ham U A D 1-1
24 Mar Sheffield U H D 1-1
28 Mar Sheffield U H L 1-3
30 Mar Sheffield W A W 4-0
4 Apr Blackpool H W 1-0
11 Apr Blackburn Rov H D 0-0
18 Apr Liverpool A L 0-5

FA Cup
4 Jan Wolves (3) H W 2-1
25 Jan W B A (4) A D 3-3
29 Jan W B A (4R) H W 2-1
15 Feb Liverpool (5) H L 0-1

Inter-Cities Fairs Cup
25 Sep Staevnet (1) A W 7-1
22 Oct Staevnet (1) H L 2-3
13 Nov FC Liege (2) H D 1-1
18 Dec FC Liege (2) A L 1-3

Appearances (Goals)
Anderson T 10 (3) · Armstrong G 28 (3) · Bacuzzi D 5 · Baker J 39 (26) · Barnwell J 19 2 Brown L 22 (1) · Clarke F 5 · Court D 8 · Eastham G 38 (10) · Furnell J 21 · Groves V 15 · MacLeod J 30 (7) · Magill E 35 · McClelland J 5 · McCullough W 40 (1) · McKechnie 11 (1) · Neill T 11 · Radford J 1 · Simpson P 6 · Skirton A 15 7 · Snedden J 14 · Strong G 38 (26) · Urel 41 (1) · Wilson R 5 · Own goals 1 · Total: 24 players (90)

Position in League Table

	P	W	L	D	F:A	Pts	
Liverpool	42	26	11	5	92:45	57	1st
Arsenal	42	17	14	11	90:82	45	8th

SEASON 1964-1965
FOOTBALL LEAGUE (DIVISION 1)

22 Aug Liverpool A L 2-3
25 Aug Sheffield W H D 1-1
29 Aug Aston Villa H W 3-1
2 Sep Sheffield W A L 1-2
5 Sep Wolverhampton W H W 1-0
8 Sep Blackburn Rov H D 1-1
12 Sep Sunderland A D 3-1
16 Sep Blackburn Rov A W 2-1
19 Sep Leicester C A W 3-2
26 Sep Chelsea H L 1-3
6 Oct Nottingham F H L 0-3
10 Oct Tottenham H A L 1-3
17 Oct Burnley H W 3-2
24 Oct Sheffield U A L 0-4
31 Oct Everton H W 3-2
7 Nov Birmingham C A W 3-2
11 Nov Leeds U A L 1-3
14 Nov West Ham U A L 0-3
21 Nov W B A A D 0-0
28 Nov Manchester U H L 2-3
5 Dec Fulham A W 4-3
12 Dec Liverpool H D 0-0
19 Dec Aston Villa A L 1-3
26 Dec Stoke C H W 3-2
28 Dec Stoke C A L 1-4
2 Jan Wolverhampton W A W 4-1
16 Jan Sunderland H W 2-0
23 Jan Leicester C H W 4-3
6 Feb Chelsea A L 1-2
13 Feb Leeds U H L 1-2
20 Feb Fulham H W 2-0
23 Feb Tottenham H H W 3-1
27 Feb Burnley A L 1-2
6 Mar Sheffield U H D 1-1
13 Mar Nottingham F A L 0-3
27 Mar West Ham U H L 1-2
3 Apr W B A H D 1-1
6 Apr Birmingham C H W 3-0
16 Apr Blackpool A D 1-1
19 Apr Blackpool H W 3-1
24 Apr Everton A L 0-1
26 Apr Manchester U A L 1-3

FA Cup
9 Jan Darlington (3) A W 2-0
30 Jan Peterborough (4) A L 1-2

Appearances (Goals)
Anderson T 10 (2) · Armstrong G 40 (4) · Baker J 42 (25) · Baldwin T 1 · Burns A 24 · Clarke F 15 · Court D 33 (3) · Eastham G 42 (10) · Ferry G 11 · Furnell J 18 · Howe D 40 · MacLeod J 1 · Magill E 1 · McCullough W 30 · McLintock F 25 (2) · Neill T 29 (1) · Radford J 13 (7) · Sammels J 17 (5) · Simpson P 6 (2) · Skirton A 22 (3) · Snedden J 3 · Strong G 12 (3) · Tawse B 5 · Urel 22 (1) · Total: 24 players (69)

Position in League Table

	P	W	L	D	F:A	Pts	
Manchester U	42	26	7	9	89:39	61	1st
Arsenal	42	17	18	7	69:75	41	13th

SEASON 1965-1966
FOOTBALL LEAGUE (DIVISION 1)

21 Aug Stoke C H W 2-1
25 Aug Northampton T A D 1-1
28 Aug Burnley A D 2-2
4 Sep Chelsea H L 1-3
7 Sep Nottingham F A W 1-0
11 Sep Tottenham H H D 2-2
14 Sep Nottingham F H W 1-0
18 Sep Everton A L 1-3
25 Sep Manchester U H W 4-2
28 Sep Northampton T H D 1-1
2 Oct Newcastle U A W 1-0
9 Oct Fulham H W 2-1
16 Oct Blackpool H L 3-5
23 Oct Blackburn Rov H D 2-2
30 Oct Leicester C A L 1-3
6 Nov Sheffield U H W 6-2
13 Nov Leeds U A L 0-3
20 Nov West Ham U H W 3-2
4 Dec Aston Villa H D 3-3
11 Dec Liverpool A L 2-4
27 Dec Sheffield W A L 0-4
28 Dec Sheffield W H W 5-2
1 Jan Fulham A L 0-1
15 Jan Blackburn Rov A L 1-2
29 Jan Stoke C A W 3-1
5 Feb Burnley H D 1-1
19 Feb Chelsea A D 0-0
5 Mar Blackpool A D 0-0
8 Mar Tottenham H H L 0-1
12 Mar Everton H L 0-1
19 Mar Manchester U A L 1-3
26 Mar Newcastle U A L 1-3
5 Apr W B A H D 1-1
9 Apr W B A A D 4-4
16 Apr West Ham U A L 1-2
20 Apr Sunderland H D 2-2
23 Apr Sunderland A D 1-1
25 Apr Sheffield U A L 0-3
30 Apr Aston Villa A L 0-3
5 May Leeds U H L 0-3
7 May Leicester C H W 1-0

FA Cup
22 Jan Blackburn (3) A L 0-3

Appearances (Goals)
Armstrong G 39 (6) · Baker J 24 (13) · Baldwin T 8 (5) · Burns A 7 · Court D 38 (1) · Eastham G 37 (6) · Furnell J 31 · Howe D 29 (1) · McCullough W 17 · McGill A 2 · McLintock F 36 (2) · Neill T 39 · Neilson G 2 · Pack R 1 · Radford J 32 (8) · Sammels J 32 (6) · Simpson P 8 · Skirton A 24 (9) · Storey P · 28 · Urel 21 · Walley J 9 (1) · Wilson R 4 · Own goals 4 · Total: 22 players (62)

Position in League Table

	P	W	L	D	F:A	Pts	
Liverpool	42	26	7	9	79:34	61	1st
Arsenal	42	12	17	13	62:75	37	14th

SEASON 1966-1967
FOOTBALL LEAGUE (DIVISION 1)

20 Aug Sunderland A W 3-1
23 Aug West Ham U H W 2-1
27 Aug Aston Villa H W 1-0
29 Aug West Ham U A D 2-2
3 Sep Tottenham H A L 1-3
6 Sep Sheffield W H D 1-1
10 Sep Manchester C H D 1-1
17 Sep Blackpool H D 1-1
24 Sep Chelsea A L 1-3
1 Oct Leicester C H L 2-4
8 Oct Newcastle U H W 2-0
15 Oct Leeds U A L 1-3
22 Oct W B A H L 2-3
29 Oct Manchester U A L 0-1
5 Nov Leeds U H L 0-1
12 Nov Everton A D 0-0
19 Nov Fulham H W 1-0
26 Nov Nottingham F A L 1-2
3 Dec Burnley H D 0-0
10 Dec Sheffield U A D 1-1
17 Dec Sunderland H W 2-0
26 Dec Southampton A W 4-1
27 Dec Southampton H L 1-2
31 Dec Aston Villa A W 1-0
7 Jan Tottenham H H L 0-2
14 Jan Manchester U H W 1-0
21 Jan Blackpool A W 3-0
4 Feb Chelsea H W 2-1
11 Feb Leicester C A L 1-2
25 Feb Newcastle U A L 1-2
3 Mar Manchester U H D 1-1
18 Mar W B A A W 1-0
25 Mar Sheffield W H W 2-0
27 Mar Liverpool A D 0-0
28 Mar Liverpool H D 1-1
1 Apr Stoke C A D 2-2
19 Apr Fulham A D 0-0
22 Apr Nottingham F H L 1-3
25 Apr Everton H W 3-1
29 Apr Burnley A W 4-1
6 May Stoke C H W 3-1
13 May Sheffield W A D 1-1

FA Cup
28 Jan Bristol Rov (3) A W 3-0
18 Feb Bolton W (4) A D 0-0
22 Feb Bolton W (4R) H W 3-0
11 Mar Birmingham C (5) A L 0-1

Football League Cup
13 Sep Gillingham (2) H D 1-1
21 Sep Gillingham (2R) A D 1-1
28 Sep Gillingham (2R) H W 5-0
5 Oct West Ham U (3) H L 1-3

Appearances (Goals)
Armstrong G 40 (7) · Addison C 17 (4) · Baldwin T 8 (5) · Boot M 4 (2) · Coakley T 9 (1) · Court D 13 · Furnell J 42 · Graham G 33 (11) · Howe D 1 · McNab R 26 · McGill J 8 · McLintock F 40 (9) · Neill T 34 · Neilson G 12 2 · Radford J 30 (4) · Sammels J 42 10 · Simpson P 36 (1) · Skirton A 2 2 · Storey P 34 (1) · Urel 37 · Walley J 4 · Woodward J 3 · Own Goals2 · Total: 22 players (58)

Position in League Table

	P	W	L	D	F:A	Pts	
Manchester U	42	24	6	12	84:45	60	1st
Arsenal	42	16	12	14	58:47	46	7th

SEASON 1967-1968
FOOTBALL LEAGUE (DIVISION 1)

19 Aug Stoke C H W 2-0
22 Aug Liverpool A L 0-2
26 Aug Nottingham F A L 0-2
28 Aug Liverpool H W 2-0
2 Sep Coventry C H D 1-1
6 Sep W B A A W 3-1
9 Sep Sheffield W A W 4-2
16 Sep Tottenham H H W 4-0
23 Sep Manchester C H W 1-0
30 Sep Newcastle U A L 1-2
7 Oct Manchester U A L 0-1
14 Oct Sunderland H W 2-3
21 Oct Wolverhampton W A L 2-3
28 Oct Fulham H W 5-3
4 Nov Leeds U A L 1-3
11 Nov Everton H D 2-2
18 Nov Leicester C A D 2-2
25 Nov West Ham U H D 0-0
2 Dec Burnley A L 0-3
16 Dec Stoke C A W 1-0
23 Dec Nottingham F H W 3-0
26 Dec Chelsea A L 1-2
30 Dec Chelsea H D 1-1
6 Jan Coventry C A D 1-1
13 Jan Sheffield U H D 1-1
20 Jan Tottenham H A L 0-1
3 Feb Manchester C A D 1-1
10 Feb Newcastle U H D 0-0
24 Feb Manchester U H L 0-2
9 Mar Wolverhampton W H L 0-2
23 Mar Fulham A W 3-1
29 Mar West Ham U A D 1-1
6 Apr Everton A L 0-2
10 Apr Southampton A L 0-2
12 Apr Leicester C H W 2-1
15 Apr Southampton H L 0-3
20 Apr Sunderland A L 0-2
27 Apr Burnley H W 2-0
30 Apr Sheffield W H W 3-2
4 May Sheffield W A W 2-1
7 May Leeds U H W 4-3
11 May W B A H W 2-1

FA Cup
27 Jan Shrewsbury T (3) A D 1-1
30 Jan Shrewsbury T (3R) H W 2-0
17 Feb Swansea T (4) A W 1-0
9 Mar Birmingham C (5) H D 1-1
12 Mar Birmingham C (5R) A L 1-2

Football League Cup
12 Sep Coventry C (2) A W 2-1
11 Oct Reading T (3) H W 1-0
1 Nov Blackburn Rov (4) A W 2-1
29 Nov Burnley (5) A D 3-3
5 Dec Burnley (5R) H W 2-1
17 Jan Huddersfield (SF) H W 3-2
6 Feb Huddersfield (SF) A W 3-1
2 Mar Leeds U (F) L 0-1
(at Wembley)

Appearances (Goals)
Addison C 11 (5) · Armstrong G 42 (5) · Court D 16 (3) · Davidson R 1 · Furnell J 29 · Gould R 16 (6) · Graham G 38 (16) · Jenkins D 3 · Johnston G 18 (3) · McLintock F 38 (4) · McNab R 30 · Neill T 38 (2) · Radford J 39 (10) · Rice P 6 · Sammels J 35 (4) · Simpson P 40 · Storey P 39 · Urel 21 · Wilson R 13 · Own goals 2 · Total: 19 players (60)

Position in League Table

	P	W	L	D	F:A	Pts	
Manchester C	42	26	10	6	86:43	58	1st
Arsenal	42	17	15	10	60:56	44	9th

SEASON 1968-1969
FOOTBALL LEAGUE (DIVISION 1)

10 Aug Tottenham H A W 2-1
13 Aug Leicester C H W 3-0
17 Aug Liverpool H D 1-1
21 Aug Wolverhampton W A D 0-0
24 Aug Ipswich T A W 2-1
27 Aug Manchester C H W 4-1
31 Aug Q P R A W 2-1
7 Sep Southampton A A W 1-0
14 Sep Stoke C H W 1-0
21 Sep Leeds U A L 0-2
28 Sep Sunderland H D 0-0
5 Oct Manchester U A D 0-0
9 Oct Manchester C A D 1-1
12 Oct Coventry C H W 2-1
19 Oct W B A A L 0-1
26 Oct West Ham U H D 0-0
9 Nov Newcastle U H D 0-0
16 Nov Nottingham F A W 2-0
23 Nov Chelsea H L 1-1
30 Nov Burnley A W 1-0
7 Dec Everton H W 3-1
14 Dec Coventry C A W 1-0
21 Dec W B A H W 2-0
26 Dec Manchester U H W 3-0
11 Jan Sheffield W H W 3-0
18 Jan Newcastle U A L 1-2
1 Feb Nottingham F H D 1-1
15 Feb Burnley H W 2-0
18 Feb Ipswich T H L 0-2
1 Mar Sheffield W A W 5-0
22 Mar Q P R A W 1-0
24 Mar Tottenham H H W 1-0
29 Mar Southampton H D 0-0
31 Mar Liverpool A D 1-1
7 Apr Wolverhampton W H W 3-1
8 Apr Leicester C A D 0-0
12 Apr Leeds U H L 1-2
14 Apr Chelsea A L 1-2
19 Apr Stoke C A W 3-1
21 Apr West Ham U H W 2-1
29 Apr Everton A L 0-1

FA Cup
4 Jan Cardiff (3) A D 0-0
7 Jan Cardiff (3R) H W 2-0
25 Jan Charlton Ath (4) H W 2-0
12 Feb W B A (5) A L 0-1

Football League Cup
4 Sep Sunderland (2) H W 1-0
25 Sep Scunthorpe U (3) A W 6-1
15 Oct Liverpool (4) H W 2-1
29 Oct Blackpool (5) H W 5-1
20 Nov Tottenham H (SF) H W 1-0
4 Dec Tottenham H (SF) A D 1-1
15 Mar Swindon T (F) L 1-3*
(at Wembley)
*aet. 1-1 at 90 mins

Appearances (Goals)
Armstrong G 29 (5) · Court D 40 (6) · Gould R 38 (10) · Graham G 25 (4) · Jenkins D 14 · (3) · Johnston G 3 · McLintock F 37 (1) · McNab R 42 · Neill T 22 (2) · Radford J 34 (15) · Robertson J 19 (3) · Sammels J 36 (4) · Simpson P 34 · Storey P 42 · Urel 23 · Wilson R 42 · Own goals 3 · Total: 16 players (56)

Position in League Table

	P	W	L	D	F:A	Pts	
Leeds	42	27	2	13	66:26	67	1st
Arsenal	42	22	8	12	56:27	56	4th

SEASON 1969-1970
FOOTBALL LEAGUE (DIVISION 1)

9 Aug Everton H L 0-1
13 Aug Leeds U A D 0-1
16 Aug W B A A W 1-0
19 Aug Leeds U H D 1-1
23 Aug Nottingham F H W 2-1
25 Aug West Ham U A D 1-1
30 Aug Newcastle U A L 1-3
6 Sep Sheffield W H D 0-0
13 Sep Burnley H W 1-0
16 Sep Tottenham H H L 2-3
20 Sep Manchester U A L 0-3
27 Sep Chelsea A L 0-3
4 Oct Coventry C H L 0-1
11 Oct Stoke C A D 0-0
18 Oct Sunderland A D 1-1
25 Oct Ipswich T A D 0-0
1 Nov Crystal Palace H W 5-1
8 Nov Derby Co A W 4-0
15 Nov Wolverhampton W A D 1-1
22 Nov Manchester U H D 2-2
29 Nov Liverpool A W 1-0
6 Dec Southampton H D 2-2
13 Dec Burnley A W 3-2
20 Dec Sheffield W A D 1-1
26 Dec Nottingham F H D 1-1
27 Dec Newcastle U H D 0-0
10 Jan Manchester C A L 1-1
17 Jan Chelsea H L 0-3
31 Jan Coventry C A L 0-0
7 Feb Stoke C H D 0-0
14 Feb Everton A D 2-2
18 Feb Manchester C H L 1-1
21 Feb Derby Co A L 2-3
28 Feb Sunderland H W 3-1
14 Mar Liverpool H W 2-1
21 Mar Southampton A W 2-0
28 Mar Wolverhampton W H D 2-2
30 Mar Crystal Palace A W 2-0
31 Mar Ipswich T A L 1-2
4 Apr West Ham U H W 2-1
2 May Tottenham H A L 0-1

FA Cup
3 Jan Blackpool (3) H D 1-1
15 Jan Blackpool (3R) A L 2-3

Football League Cup
2 Sep Southampton (2) A D 1-1
9 Sep Southampton (2R) H W 2-0
24 Sep Everton (3) H D 0-0
1 Oct Everton (3R) A L 0-1

European Fairs Cup
9 Sep Glentoran (1) H W 3-0
29 Sep Glentoran (1) A L 0-1
20 Oct Sp Cb de Port (2) A D 0-0
26 Nov Sp Cb de Port (2) H W 3-0
17 Dec Rouen (3) A D 0-0
13 Jan Rouen (3) H W 1-0
11 Mar Dinamo Bacau (4) A W 2-0
18 Mar Dinamo Bacau (4) H W 7-1
8 Apr Ajax (SF) H W 3-0
15 Apr Ajax (SF) A L 0-1
22 Apr Anderlecht (F) A L 1-3
28 Apr Anderlecht (F) H W 3-0

Appearances (Goals)
Armstrong G 17 3 · Barnett G 11 · Court D 21 · George C 28 (6) · Gould R 11 · Graham G 36 (7) · Kelly E 16 · (2) · Kennedy R 4 (1) · Marinello P 14 (1) · McLintock F 30 · McNab R 37 (2) · Neill T 17 (1) · Nelson S 4 · Radford J 39 (12) · Rice P 7 (1) · Roberts J 11 (1) · Robertson J 27 (4) · Sammels J 36 (8) · Simpson P 39 · Storey P 39 1 · Urel 3 · Webster M (3) · Wilson R 28 · Own goals 1 · Total: 23 players (51)

Position in League Table

	P	W	L	D	F:A	Pts	
Everton	42	29	5	8	72:34	66	1st
Arsenal	42	12	13	18	51:49	42	12th

From here on, statistics are presented in greater detail and include a full team listing, with details of goalscorers. They begin with Arsenal's Double winning season 1970-71.

SEASON 1970-1971 FOOTBALL LEAGUE (DIVISION 1)

Date	Opp				1	2	3	4	5	6	7	8	9	10	11	Subs
15 Aug	Everton	A	D	2-2	Wilson	Rice	McNab	Kelly	Roberts	McLintock	Armstrong	Storey	Radford	George1	Graham1	Marinello for George
17 Aug	West Ham U	A	D	0-0	..	Storey	..	..	McLintock	Roberts	..	Radford	Kennedy	Marinello	..	Marinello for Radford
22 Aug	Manchester U	H	W	4-0	..	Rice	..	..	..	..	..	Storey	Radford3	Kennedy	..1	Nelson for Radford
25 Aug	Huddersfield T	H	W	1-0	..	..	..	..	..	..	..	..	..	..1	..	
29 Aug	Chelsea	A	L	1-2	..	..	..	..1	..	..	..	..	Nelson	..	..	
1 Sep	Leeds U	H	D	0-0	..	..	..	..	..	..	..	..	Radford	..	..	
5 Sep	Tottenham	H	W	2-0	..	..	..	..	..	..	..2	..	..	..	..	Nelson for McLintock
12 Sep	Burnley	A	W	2-1	..	..	..	..	..	..	..	..	..	..1	..1	
19 Sep	W B A	H	W	6-2	..	..	..	..	opponents	..1	..	..	..	..2	..2	
26 Sep	Stoke C	A	L	0-5	..	..	..	..	..	..	..	..	..	..	..	
3 Oct	Nottingham F	H	W	4-0	..	..	..	..	..	..1	..	..	..	..3	..	
10 Oct	Newcastle U	A	D	1-1	..	..	..	..	..	..	..	..	..	..	..1	
17 Oct	Everton	H	W	4-0	..	..	..	..1	..	..	..	..1	..	..2	..1	
24 Oct	Coventry C	A	W	3-1	..	..	..	..	..	..	..	..	..1	..1	..1	
31 Oct	Derby Co	H	W	2-0	..	..	..	..1	..	..	..	..	..1	..	..	
7 Nov	Blackpool	A	W	1-0	..	..	..	..	..	..	..	..	..1	..	..	
14 Nov	Crystal Palace	H	D	1-1	..	..	..	..	..	..	..	..	..1	..	Sammels	
21 Nov	Ipswich T	A	W	1-0	..	..	..	..	..	Simpson	..1	..	..	..	..	Graham1 for Kelly
28 Nov	Liverpool	H	W	2-0	..	..	..	..	..	..	..1	..	..1	..	Graham1	
5 Dec	Manchester C	A	W	2-0	..	..	..	Graham	..	..	..	..	..1	..	Graham1	
12 Dec	Wolverhampton W	H	W	2-1	..	..	..	Storey	..	..	..	Sammels	..1	..	..1	
19 Dec	Manchester U	A	W	3-1	..	..	..	..	..	..1	..	..	..	..1	..1	
26 Dec	Southampton	H	D	0-0	..	..	..	..	..	..	..	..	..	..	..	
9 Jan	West Ham U	H	W	2-0	..	..	..	Nelson	..	..	..	..	..	..1	..1	
16 Jan	Huddersfield T	A	L	1-2	..	..	..	McNab	..	..	..	..	..	..1	..	
30 Jan	Liverpool	A	L	0-2	..	..	..	..	..	..	..	..	..	..	..	
6 Feb	Manchester C	H	W	1-0	..	..	..	..	..	..	..	..	..1	George	..	
20 Feb	Ipswich	H	W	3-2	..	..	..	..	..	..1	..	..	..1	..1	..	
27 Feb	Derby Co	A	L	0-2	..	..	..	..	..	..	..	..	..	..	..	Graham for Rice
2 Mar	Wolverhampton W	A	W	3-0	..	..	..	..	..	..1	..	..	..1	..1	..	
13 Mar	Crystal Palace	A	W	2-0	..	..	..	..	..	..	..	Graham1	..	..	..	Sammels1 for George
20 Mar	Blackpool	H	W	1-0	..	..	..	..1	..	..	..	..	..	..	..	
3 Apr	Chelsea	H	W	2-0	..	..	..	..	..	..	..	..	..	..2	..	Kelly for Armstrong
6 Apr	Coventry C	H	W	1-0	..	..	..	..	..	..	..	..	..	..1	..	
10 Apr	Southampton	A	W	2-1	..	..	..	..	..	..1	..	..	..	..1	..1	
13 Apr	Nottingham F	A	W	3-0	..	..	..	..	..	..1	..	..	..	..1	..1	
17 Apr	Newcastle U	H	W	1-0	..	..	..	..	..	..	..	..	..	..	..1	
20 Apr	Burnley	H	W	1-0	..	..	Roberts	Kelly	..	..	..	..	..	..	..1	
24 Apr	W B A	A	D	2-2	..	..	McNab	Storey	..1	opponents	..	..	..	..	..	Sammels for Rice
26 Apr	Leeds U	A	L	0-1	..	..	..	..	..	..	..	..	..	..	..	Kelly1 for Storey
1 May	Stoke C	H	W	1-0	..	..	..	..	..	..	..	..	..	..	..1	
3 May	Tottenham H	A	W	1-0	..	..	..	Kelly	..	..	..	..	..	..	..	..

FA Cup

Date	Opp															
6 Jan	Yeovil T (3)	A	W	3-0	Wilson	Rice	McNab	Storey	McLintock	Simpson	Armstrong	Sammels	Radford2	Kennedy1	Graham	Kelly for McNab
23 Jan	Portsmouth (4)	A	D	1-1	..	..	..	..1	..	..	..	..	..	..	..	George for Rice
1 Feb	Portsmouth (4R)	H	W	3-2	..	..	..	..1	..	..1	..	..	..	George1	..	
17 Feb	Manchester C (5)	A	W	2-1	..	..	..	..	..	..	..	..	..	..	..2	
6 Mar	Leicester C (6)	A	D	0-0	..	..	..	..	..	..	..	..	..	..	..	
15 Mar	Leicester C (6R)	H	W	1-0	..	..	..	..	..	..	..	Graham	..	..	..1	
27 Mar	Stoke C (SF) (at Sheffield W)	D		2-2	..	..	..	..2	..	..	..	..	..	..	..	Sammels for George
31 Mar	Stoke C (SFR) (at Birmingham)	W		2-0	..	..	..	..	..	..	..	..1	..	..1	..	
8 May	Liverpool (F) (at Wembley)	W		2-1*	..	..	..	..	..	..	..	..	..	..	..1	Kelly1 for Storey

*aet, 0-0 at 90 mins

Football League Cup

Date	Opp															
8 Sep	Ipswich T (2)	A	D	0-0	Wilson	Rice	McNab	Kelly	McLintock	Roberts	Armstrong	Storey	Nelson	Kennedy	Graham	
28 Sep	Ipswich T (2R)	H	W	4-0	..	..	..	..	..	..1	..	..	Radford1	..2	..	
6 Oct	Luton T (3)	A	W	1-0	..	..	..	..	..	..	..	..	..	..	..1	
28 Oct	Crystal Palace (4)	A	D	0-0	..	..	..	..	..	..	..	..	..	..	..	
9 Nov	Crystal Palace (4R)	H	L	0-2	..	..	..	..	..	..	..	..	..	..	..	

European Fairs Cup

Date	Opp															
16 Sep	Lazio Roma (1)	A	D	2-2	Wilson	Rice	McNab	Kelly	McLintock	Roberts	Armstrong	Storey	Radford2	Kennedy	Graham	
23 Sep	Lazio Roma (1)	H	W	2-0	..	..	..	..	..	..	..1	..	..1	..	..	Nelson for Graham
21 Oct	Sturm Graz (2)	A	L	0-1	..	..	..	..	..	..	..	..	..	..	..	
4 Nov	Sturm Graz (2)	H	W	2-0	..	..	..	..	..	..	..	Storey	..1	..1	..1	
2 Dec	Beveren Waas (3)	H	W	4-0	..	..	..	Sammels1	..	Simpson	..	..	..	..2	..1	
16 Dec	Beveren Waas (3)	A	D	0-0	..	..	..	Storey	Roberts	..	..	Sammels	..	..	..	Marinello for Armstrong, George for Radford
9 Mar	FC Koln (4)	H	W	2-1	..	..	..	..1	McLintock1	..	..	George	..	..	George	
23 Mar	FC Koln (4)	A	L	0-1	..	..	..	..	..	..	..	Graham	..	..	..	

Appearances (Goals)

Armstrong G 42 (7) · George C 17 (5) · Graham G 38 (11) · Kelly E 23 (4) · Kennedy R 41 (19) · Marinello P 3 · McLintock F 42 (5) · McNab R 40 · Nelson S 4 · Radford J 41 (15) · Rice P 41 · Roberts J 18 · Sammels J 15 (1) · Simpson P 25 · Storey P 40 (2) · Wilson R 42 · Own Goals 2 · **Total: 16 players (71)**

Position in League Table

	P	W	D	L	F:A	Pts	
Arsenal	42	29	6	7	71:29	65	1st

George Graham reels away after seemingly scoring Arsenal's first in the 1971 FA Cup Final. The goal was later credited to Eddie Kelly after television replays encouraged a debate as to whether Graham had touched the ball. He was distressed that anyone should think he would try to steal a colleague's goal, and remains convinced he touched the ball. What probably happened is that he did get a slight touch to the ball but the direction and speed were not varied at all. This was to prove vital. Ray Clemence's advance had been made with an allowance for a Graham touch to change the direction of the ball.

1940-1973

SEASON 1971-1972 FOOTBALL LEAGUE (DIVISION 1)

Date	Opponents		Res	Score	1	2	3	4	5	6	7	8	9	10	11	Notes
14 Aug	Chelsea	H	W	3-0	Wilson	Rice	McNab	Storey	McLintock1	Simpson	Armstrong	Kelly	Radford1	Kennedy1	Graham	
17 Aug	Huddersfield T	A	W	1-0	..	..	..	..	..	..	..	..	..	..1	..	
20 Aug	Manchester U (Liverpool)	A	L	1-3	..	..	..	..	..1	..	..	..	..	..	..	
24 Aug	Sheffield U	H	L	0-1	..	..	..	..	..	..	..	..	..	..	..	
28 Aug	Stoke C	H	L	0-1	..	..	..	..	..	..	..	..	..	..	..	Roberts for Rice
4 Sep	WBA	A	W	1-0	..	..	..	..	..	Roberts1	..	..	..	..	..	
11 Sep	Leeds U	H	W	2-0	..	..	..	..1	..	..	..	Simpson	..	..1	..1	
18 Sep	Everton	A	L	1-2	..	..	..	..	..	..	..	..	..	..1	..	Kelly for McLintock
25 Sep	Leicester C	H	W	3-0	..	..1	Nelson	..	..	Simpson	..	Kelly	.2	..	..	George for Storey
2 Oct	Southampton	A	W	1-0	..	..	..	McLintock	..1	..	..	..	..	..	..	
9 Oct	Newcastle U	H	W	4-2	..	..	..	..	..	George	..1	..	..1	..1	..1	Davies for Radford
16 Oct	Chelsea	A	W	2-1	..	..	..	..	..	Roberts	..	..	..	.2	..	Simpson for Kelly
23 Oct	Derby Co	A	L	1-2	..	..	..	..	..	..	..	..	..	..	..1	Simpson for Kelly
30 Oct	Ipswich T	H	W	2-1	..	..	..	Storey	..	McLintock	opponents	George1	..	..1	..	
6 Nov	Liverpool	A	L	2-3	..	..	..	..	..	..	opponents	..	..	..1	..	
13 Nov	Manchester C	H	L	1-2	..	..	..1	..	..	..	..	..	..	..	..	
20 Nov	Wolverhampton W	A	L	1-5	..	..	..	..	..	..	..	..	..	..1	..	
24 Nov	Tottenham H	A	D	1-1	..	..	McNab	..	..	..	..	Kelly	..	..1	..	
27 Nov	Crystal Palace	H	W	2-1	..	..	..	..	McLintock	Simpson	..	..	..1	..1	..	
4 Dec	West Ham U	A	D	0-0	..	..	..	..	..	..	..	..	..	..	..	
11 Dec	Coventry C	H	W	2-0	..	..	..	..	..	..	..	..	.2	..	..	Marinello for Simpson
18 Dec	WBA	H	W	2-0	..	..	..	..	..	Roberts2	..	..	..	..	..	
27 Dec	Nottingham F	A	D	1-1	..	..	..	..	Kelly	Simpson	..	Ball	..	..	..1	George for Armstrong
1 Jan	Everton	H	D	1-1	..	..	..	..	..	Roberts	..1	..	..	..	..	
8 Jan	Stoke C	A	D	0-0	..	..	..	..	..	McLintock	..	..	..	..	..	
22 Jan	Huddersfield T	H	W	1-0	..	..	..	Nelson	..	..	..1	..	..	..	..	George for Ball
29 Jan	Sheffield U	A	W	5-0	..	..	..	Roberts	..	..1	..	..	George2	..1	..1	
12 Feb	Derby Co	H	W	2-0	..	..	..	Kelly	..	..	..	..	.2	..	..	
19 Feb	Ipswich T	A	W	1-0	..	..	..	..	..	..	..	..	..1	..	..	
4 Mar	Manchester U	A	L	0-2	..	..	..	Storey	..	..	..	..	..	Radford	..	
11 Mar	Newcastle U	A	L	0-2	..	..	..	..	..	Simpson	Graham	..	..	Kennedy	Radford	Batson for George
25 Mar	Leeds U	A	L	0-3	..	..	..	..	..	McLintock	Simpson	..	..	..	Roberts	Marinello for Roberts
28 Mar	Southampton	H	W	1-0	..	..	..	..	..	..	..	..	..	..	Marinello1	
1 Apr	Nottingham F	H	W	3-0	..	..	..	..	..	Roberts	..	..	..1	..	Graham	Graham1 for Kennedy
4 Apr	Leicester C	A	D	0-0	..	..	..	..	..	McLintock	..	..	..	Graham	..	
8 Apr	Wolverhampton W	H	W	2-1	..	..	..	..	..	..	Marinello	..1	..	Kennedy	Graham2	Armstrong for Marinello
11 Apr	Crystal Palace	A	D	2-2	..	..	..	..	Roberts	..	Armstrong	..1	Radford1	George	..	
22 Apr	West Ham U	H	W	2-1	Barnett	..	McNab	..	McLintock	..	..	.2	Radford1	George	..	Baston for McLintock
25 Apr	Manchester U	H	W	3-0	..	..	..	Roberts	..	..1	..	Nelson	..1	Kennedy1	..	Marinello for Graham
1 May	Coventry C	A	W	1-0	..	..	..	Storey	..1	..	..	Ball	..	George	..	
8 May	Liverpool	H	D	0-0	..	..	Nelson	..	..	..	..	..	..	Kennedy	..	Roberts for Rice
11 May	Tottenham H	H	L	0-2	..	..	McNab	Nelson	..	Roberts	..	Simpson	..	..	..	Marinello for Simpson

FA Cup

Date	Opponents		Res	Score	1	2	3	4	5	6	7	8	9	10	11	Notes
15 Jan	Swindon T (3)	A	W	2-0	Wilson	Rice	Nelson	Kelly	McLintock	Simpson	Armstrong1	Ball1	Radford	Kennedy	Graham	
5 Feb	Reading (4)	A	W	2-1	..	..1	..	..	..	opponents	..	George	..	..	..	
26 Feb	Derby Co (5)	A	D	2-2	..	..	..	..	..	..	..	.2	..	..	..	Storey for Kelly
29 Feb	Derby Co (5R)	H	D	0-0	..	..	..	Storey	..	..	..	..	..	..	..	Radford for Kennedy
13 Mar	Derby Co (5R) (at Leicester)		W	1-0	..	..	..	..	..	..	..	..	..	..1	..	
18 Mar	Orient (6)	A	W	1-0	..	..	..	..	..	..	..	..1	..	..	..	
15 Apr	Stoke C (SF) (at Villa Park)		D	1-1	Wilson injured Radford ingoal	..	McNab	..	..	..	..	..1	Radford	George	..	Kennedy for Wilson
19 Apr	Stoke C (SFR) (at Everton)		W	2-1	Barnett	..	..	..	..	..	..	..	..1	..1	..	
6 May	Leeds U (F) (at Wembley)		L	0-1	..	..	..	..	..	..	..	..	..	..	..	Kennedy for Radford

Football League Cup

Date	Opponents		Res	Score	1	2	3	4	5	6	7	8	9	10	11	Notes
8 Sep	Barnsley (2)	H	W	1-0	Wilson	Rice	McNab	Storey	McLintock	Roberts	Marinello	Kelly	Radford	Kennedy1	Graham	
6 Oct	Newcastle U (3)	H	W	4-0	..	..	Nelson	McLintock	Simpson	..	Armstrong	..	.2	..1	..1	
26 Oct	Sheffield U (4)	H	D	0-0	Barnett	..	..	Storey	Roberts	McLintock	..	George	..	..	..	
8 Nov	Sheffield U (4R)	A	L	0-2	Wilson	..	..	Kelly	..	..	..	..	..	..	..	McNab for McLintock

European Cup

Date	Opponents		Res	Score	1	2	3	4	5	6	7	8	9	10	11	Notes
15 Sep	St't Drammen (1)	A	W	3-1	Wilson	Rice	Simpson1	McLintock	McNab	Roberts	Kelly1	Marinello1	Graham	Radford	Kennedy	Davies for Marinello
29 Sep	St't Drammen (1)	H	W	4-0	..	..	Nelson	Kelly	Simpson	..	Armstrong1	George	Radford2	Kennedy1	Graham	
20 Oct	Gr'pers Zurich (2)	A	W	2-0	..	..	..	McLintock	Roberts	George	..	Kelly	..	..1	..1	
3 Nov	Gr'pers Zurich (2)	H	W	3-0	..	..	..	Storey	..	McLintock	..	George1	..1	..1	..	Simpson for Roberts, McNab for McLintock
8 Mar	Ajax Ams'dam (3)	A	L	1-2	..	..	..	..	McLintock	Simpson	..	..	..	..1	..	Roberts for Nelson
22 Mar	Ajax Ams'dam (3)	H	L	0-1	..	..	..	..	..	..	..	..	Marinello	..	..	Roberts for Nelson

Appearances (Goals)

Armstrong G 42 (2) · Ball A 18 (3) · Batson B 2 · Barnett G 5 · Davies P 1 · George C 23 (7) · Graham G 40 (8) · Kelly E 23 (2) · Kennedy R 37 (12) · McNab R 20 · McLintock F 37 (3) · Marinello P 8 1 · Nelson S 24 (1) · Radford J 34 (8) · Rice P 42 (1) · Roberts J 23 (3) · Simpson P 34 (4) · Storey P 29 (1) · Wilson R 37 · Own goals 2 · **Total: 19 players (58)**

Position in League Table

	P	W	L	D	F:A	Pts	
Derby Co	42	24	8	10	69:33	58	1st
Arsenal	42	22	12	8	58:40	52	5th

SEASON 1972-1973 FOOTBALL LEAGUE (DIVISION 1)

Date	Opponents		Res	Score	1	2	3	4	5	6	7	8	9	10	11	Notes
12 Aug	Leicester C	A	W	1-0	Barnett	Rice	McNab	Storey	McLintock	Simpson	Armstrong	Ball1	Radford	Kennedy	Graham	
15 Aug	Wolverhampton W	H	W	5-2	..	..	..1	..	..	..1	..	..	.2	..1	..	Roberts for Simpson
19 Aug	Stoke C	H	W	2-0	..	..	..	..	..	Roberts	..	..	..	.2	..	
22 Aug	Coventry C	A	D	1-1	..	..1	..	..	..	Simpson	..	..	..	..	..	
26 Aug	Manchester U	A	D	0-0	..	..	..	..	..	..	..	George	..	..	..	
29 Aug	West Ham U	H	W	1-0	..	..	..	..	..	..	..	..1	Radford	..	..	George for Armstrong
2 Sep	Chelsea	H	D	1-1	..	..	..	..	..	opponents	..	..	..	..	..	George for Armstrong
9 Sep	Newcastle U	A	L	1-2	..	..	..	..	..	Roberts	Marinello	..	..	..1	..	
16 Sep	Liverpool	H	D	0-0	..	..	..	..	..	..	..	..	..	..	..	
23 Sep	Norwich C	A	L	2-3	..	..	..	..1	..	..	..	..	..1	..	..	
26 Sep	Birmingham C	H	W	2-0	..	..	..	..1	..	..	..	..	..	George1	..	
30 Sep	Southampton	H	W	1-0	..	..	..	..	..	..	..	..	..	..	..	Graham1 for Kennedy
7 Oct	Sheffield U	A	L	0-1	..	..	..	..	..	Blockley	..	..	..	Graham	..	
14 Oct	Ipswich T	H	W	1-0	..	..	..	..	..	..	..	..	..	..1	..	
21 Oct	Crystal Palace	A	W	3-2	..	..1	..	..	..	..	..	Kelly	..1	..1	..	Nelson for Kelly
28 Oct	Manchester C	H	D	0-0	..	..	..	..	..	..	..	..	..	George	Graham	
4 Nov	Coventry C	H	L	0-2	..	..	..	..	..	..	..	Ball	..	..	Kelly	Graham for Kelly
17 Nov	Wolverhampton W	A	W	3-1	..	..	..	..	..	..	..1	..	.2	..1	..	
18 Nov	Everton	H	W	1-0	..	..	..	..	Simpson	..	..	..	..1	..	..	
25 Nov	Derby Co	A	L	0-5	Wilson	..	..	..	McLintock	Simpson	..	..	..	..	..	Armstrong for Marinello
2 Dec	Leeds U	H	W	2-1	..	..	..	..	Blockley	..	Armstrong	..1	..1	Kennedy	..	
9 Dec	Tottenham H	A	W	2-1	..	..	..	..	..	..1	..	..	..1	..	..	McLintock for Simpson
16 Dec	WBA	H	W	2-1	Barnett	..	..	..	McLintock	opponents	..	..	..1	..	..	George for Rice
23 Dec	Birmingham C	A	D	1-1	Wilson	Nelson	..	..	Blockley	..	..	..	..	..	..1	
26 Dec	Norwich C	H	W	2-0	..	..	..	..	..	..	..	..	..1	..	..	George for Nelson
30 Dec	Stoke C	A	D	0-0	..	Rice	..	..	..	..	..	..	..	..	..	
6 Jan	Manchester U	H	W	3-1	..	..	..	..	..	..	..	..1	..1	..1	..	
20 Jan	Chelsea	A	W	1-0	..	..	..	..	..	..	..	..	..	..1	..	McLintock for Kelly
27 Jan	Newcastle U	H	D	2-2	..	..	..	..	..	..	..	..	..1	..1	..	George for Armstrong
10 Feb	Liverpool	A	W	2-0	..	..	..	..	..	..	..	..	..1	..1	..	George for Radford
17 Feb	Leicester C	H	W	1-0	..	..	..	..	McLintock	opponents	..	..	..	..	..	George for Blockley
28 Feb	WBA	A	L	0-1	..	..	..	Batson	McLintock	George	..	..	..	..	..	
3 Mar	Sheffield U	H	W	3-2	..	..	..	George2	..	Batson	..	..	..1	..	..	Nelson for Batson
10 Mar	Ipswich T	A	W	2-1	..	..	..	Storey	..	Simpson	..	..	..	..	..	
24 Mar	Manchester C	A	W	2-1	..	..	..	..	..	..	..	..	George1	..1	..	Nelson for Kelly
26 Mar	Crystal Palace	H	W	1-0	..	..	..	..	..	..	..	..	..	..	..	

Date	Opponents	V	R	Score	1	2	3	4	5	6	7	8	9	10	11	Substitutes
31 Mar	Derby Co	H	L	0-1	Wilson	Rice	McNab	Storey1	Blockley	Simpson	Armstrong	Ball	Radford	Kennedy	Kelly	Nelson for McLintock
14 Apr	Tottenham H	H	D	1-1	..	..	..	..	..	..	..	..	..	..	..	George for McLintock
21 Apr	Everton	A	D	0-0	..	..	..	..	Kelly	..	..	..	..	..	..	George for Blockley
23 Apr	Southampton	A	D	2-2	..	..	..	..	Kelly	..	..	..	..1	George1	Kennedy	
28 Apr	West Ham U	A	W	2-1	..	..	..	..	Blockley	..	..1	..	..	Kennedy1	George	
9 May	Leeds U	A	L	1-6	..	Batson	..	..	Blockley	..	..1	..	..	..	Hornsby	Price for Hornsby

FA Cup

Date	Opponents	V	R	Score	1	2	3	4	5	6	7	8	9	10	11	Substitutes
13 Jan	Leicester C (3)	H	D	2-2	Wilson	Rice	McNab	Storey	Blockley	Simpson	Armstrong1	Ball	Radford	Kennedy1	Kelly	
17 Jan	Leicester C (3R)	A	W	2-1	..	..	..	..	..	..	..	..1	..	..1	..	
3 Feb	Bradford C (4)	H	W	2-0	..	..	..	..	..	..	..	..1	George1	..	..	Marinello for George
24 Feb	Carlisle U (5)	A	W	2-1	Barnett	..	..	..	McLintock1	..	..	..1	Radford	..	..	Nelson for Storey
17 Mar	Chelsea (6)	A	D	2-2	Wilson	..	..	..	..	..	..	..1	George1	..	..	
20 Mar	Chelsea (6R)	H	W	2-1	..	..	..	..	..	..	..	..1	..	..1	..	
7 Apr	Sunderland (SF)	A	L	1-2	..	..	..	..	Blockley	..	..	..	..1	..	..	Radford for Blockley
(at Sheffield W)																

Football League Cup

Date	Opponents	V	R	Score	1	2	3	4	5	6	7	8	9	10	11	Substitutes
Sep	Everton (2)	H	W	1-0	Barnett	Rice	McNab	Storey1	McLintock	Simpson	Marinello	Ball	Radford	Kennedy	Graham	
3 Oct	Rotherham U (3)	H	W	5-0	..	..	Nelson	..1	..	Roberts	..1	..	..2	Graham	George1	
31 Oct	Sheffield U (4)	A	W	2-1	..	..	McNab	..	..	Simpson	..	Kelly	..1	..	Kelly	
21 Nov	Norwich C (5)	H	L	0-3	..	..	McNab	..	..	Simpson	..	Ball	..	George	Kelly	

Appearances (Goals)

Armstrong G 30 (2) · Ball A 40 (10) · Barnett G 20 · Batson B 3 · Blockley J 20 · George C 27 (6) · Graham G 16 (2) · Hornsby B 1 · Kelly E 27 (1) · McLintock F 29 · McNab R 42 (1) · Marinello P 13 1 · Nelson S 6 · Price D 1 · Radford J 38 (15) · Rice P 39 (2) · Roberts J 7 · Simpson P 27 (1) · Storey P 40 (4) · Wilson R 22 · Own goals 3 · **Total: 21 players (57)**

Position in League Table

	P	W	L	D	F:A	Pts	
Liverpool	42	25	7	10	72:42	60	1st
Arsenal	42	23	8	11	57:43	57	2nd

SEASON 1973-1974 FOOTBALL LEAGUE (DIVISION 1)

Date	Opponents	V	R	Score	1	2	3	4	5	6	7	8	9	10	11	Substitutes
25 Aug	Manchester U	H	W	3-0	Wilson	Rice	McNab	Price	Blockley	Simpson	Armstrong	Ball1	Radford1	Kennedy1	George	Homsby for Radford
28 Aug	Leeds U	H	L	1-2	..	..	..	Storey	..1	..	..	..	..	..	..1	Price for Simpson
1 Sep	Newcastle U	A	D	1-1	..	..	..	Price	..	Storey	..	..	Kelly	..	..1	
4 Sep	Sheffield U	A	L	0-5	..	..	..	Batson	..	..	..	..	..	..	..	
8 Sep	Leicester C	H	L	0-2	..	..	..	Storey	..	Simpson	Kelly	..	Radford	..	..	Armstrong for Kelly
11 Sep	Sheffield U	H	W	1-0	..	..	..1	..	..	..	Armstrong	..	..	..1	Kelly	
15 Sep	Norwich C	A	W	4-0	..	..	..	..	..	George1	..	..1	..	..1	George	Kelly for George
22 Sep	Stoke C	H	W	2-1	..	..	..	..	..	Simpson	..	..1	..1	..	George	Kelly for George
29 Sep	Everton	A	L	0-1	..	..	..	..	..	..	..	..	..	..	Kelly	Kelly for George
6 Oct	Birmingham C	H	W	1-0	..	..	..	..	..	..	..	Chambers	..	..1	Kelly	Brady for Blockley
13 Oct	Tottenham H	A	L	0-2	..	..	..	..	Simpson	Kelly	..	George	..	..	Brady	Batson for Radford
20 Oct	Ipswich T	H	D	1-1	..	..	..	..	..1	..	..	..	Batson	..	Price	
27 Oct	Q P R	A	L	0-2	..	..	..	..	..	..	..	..	..	..	Powling	
3 Nov	Liverpool	H	L	0-2	..	..	..	..	Powling	..	..	..	Radford	..	Kelly	Batson for Kelly
10 Nov	Manchester C	A	W	2-1	..	..	..	..	Kelly1	Ball	..	..	Homsby1	..	Armstrong	
17 Nov	Chelsea	H	D	0-0	..	..	..	..	..	..	..	..	..	..	..	
24 Nov	West Ham U	A	W	3-1	..	..	..	..	..	..	..	..2	..1	..	..	Nelson1 for Kelly
1 Dec	Coventry C	H	D	2-2	..	..	..	..	..	..	..	..	..1	..	..	Hornsby1 for George
4 Dec	Wolverhampton W	H	D	2-2	..	..	..	..	..	..	..	Blockley	Radford	..	..	
8 Dec	Derby Co	A	D	1-1	..	..	Nelson	..	opponents	..	Blockley	..	..	..	..	
15 Dec	Burnley	A	L	1-2	..	..	McNab	..	..	..	..	..	..	..	..	
22 Dec	Everton	H	W	1-0	..	..	McNab	..	Blockley	Simpson	Armstrong	Ball1	Homsby	..	Kelly	
26 Dec	Southampton	A	D	1-1	..	..	Nelson	..	..	..	..	..1	Radford	..	Hornsby	Homsby for Kelly
29 Dec	Leicester C	A	L	0-2	..	..	..	..	..	..	..	..	..	..	Hornsby	
1 Jan	Newcastle U	H	L	0-1	..	..	..	..	..	..	..	..	..	..	Kelly	
12 Jan	Norwich C	H	W	2-0	..	..	Storey	Kelly	..	..	..	..2	..	..	Brady	
19 Jan	Manchester U	A	D	1-1	..	..	McNab	Storey	..	..	..	..	..	..1	Kelly	
2 Feb	Burnley	H	D	1-1	..	..	Storey	Kelly	..	..	..	..1	..	..	Brady	
5 Feb	Leeds U	A	L	1-3	..	..	Nelson	Storey	..	..	..	..1	..	..	..	
16 Feb	Tottenham H	H	L	0-1	..	..	..	..	Simpson	Kelly	..	..	..	..	..	
23 Feb	Birmingham C	A	L	1-3	..	..	..	..	..	..	George	..1	..	..1	Armstrong	
2 Mar	Southampton	H	W	1-0	..	..	..	..	..	..	..	..1	..	..	Armstrong	
16 Mar	Ipswich T	A	D	2-2	..	McNab	..	..	..1	..	..	Brady	..	..1	..	
23 Mar	Manchester C	H	W	2-0	..	Rice	..	..	..	..	..	Ball	..2	..	George	
30 Mar	Stoke C	A	D	0-0	..	..	..	..	Blockley	..	Armstrong	..	..	..	George	Simpson for Kelly
6 Apr	West Ham U	H	D	0-0	..	..	..	..	..	..	..	..	..	..	..	
13 Apr	Chelsea	A	W	3-1	..	..	..	..	..	..	..	..	..1	..2	..	Simpson for Kelly
15 Apr	Wolverhampton W	A	L	1-3	..	..	..	..	..	Simpson	..	..	..	..1	..	Brady for Radford
20 Apr	Derby Co	H	W	2-0	..	..	..	..	..	Kelly	..	..	..1	George1	Brady	Simpson for George
24 Apr	Liverpool	A	W	1-0	Rimmer	..	..	..	..	..	..	..	Radford	..1	..	Simpson for Blockley
27 Apr	Coventry	A	D	3-3	Wilson	..1	..	..	Simpson	..	..	..	..1	..1	George	
30 Apr	Q P R	H	D	1-1	..	..	..	..	..	..	..	..	..	..	..	Brady1 for Ball

FA Cup

Date	Opponents	V	R	Score	1	2	3	4	5	6	7	8	9	10	11	Substitutes
5 Jan	Norwich C (3)	A	W	1-0	Wilson	Rice	McNab	Storey	Blockley	Simpson	Kelly1	Ball	Radford	Kennedy	Armstrong	
26 Jan	Aston Villa (4)	H	D	1-1	..	..	..	..	..	..	Armstrong	..	..	..1	Kelly	
30 Jan	Aston Villa (4R)	A	L	0-2	..	..	..	..	..	..	..	..	..	..	..	Brady for McNab

Football League Cup

Date	Opponents	V	R	Score	1	2	3	4	5	6	7	8	9	10	11	Substitutes
2 Oct	Tranmere Rov (2)	H	L	0-1	Wilson	Rice	McNab	Storey	Blockley	Simpson	Armstrong	Ball	Radford	Kennedy	Kelly	Chambers for Ball

FA Cup (1972-73) Third Place Play-off

Date	Opponents	V	R	Score	1	2	3	4	5	6	7	8	9	10	11	Substitutes
18 Aug	Wolverhampton	H	L	1-3	Wilson	Batson	McNab	Price	Blockley	Simpson	Chambers	Ball	Radford	Kennedy	Hornsby1	

Appearances (Goals)

Armstrong G 41 · Ball A 36 (13) · Batson B 5 · Blockley J 26 (1) · Brady L 13 (1) · Chambers B 1 · George C 28 (5) · Homsby B 9 (3) · Kelly E 37 (1) · Kennedy R 2 (12) · McNab R 23 (1) · Nelson S 19 (1) · Powling R 2 · Price D 4 · Radford J 32 (7) · Rice P 41 (1) · Rimmer J 1 · Simpson P 38 (2) · Storey P 41 · Wilson R 41 · Own goals 1 · **Total: 20 players (49)**

Position in League Table

	P	W	L	D	F:A	Pts	
Leeds U	42	24	4	14	66:31	62	1st
Arsenal	42	14	14	14	49:51	42	10th

A flying Charlie George was the icon of Arsenal during the early 1970s. The stylish flair of his attacking play was best epitomised with his 20-yard extra-time winner in 1971 FA Cup final.

CHAPTER
AND SO TO ANFIELD ...

At the beginning of 1973 Arsenal had reached five Cup finals in five seasons but Bertie Mee felt the sands of time running out. In what he later described as his greatest mistake, he bought Jeff Blockley from Coventry clearly to be the replacement for Frank McLintock. The mood was turning and, although Arsenal finished the League second to Liverpool, the final game of the season, a 6–1 defeat against Leeds at Elland Road, was to be symbolic. McLintock had been at the core of the Double team but Don Howe's departure had never adequately been dealt with and by the beginning of the 1973–74 season Howe's successor, Steve Burtenshaw, was to be replaced by Bobby Campbell.

Changing times

Gradually the Double side drifted away. Ray Kennedy went to greater and unexpected glories at Anfield, Charlie George became an unexpected failure at Derby County. Despite his central role in the Arsenal history, George had played just 169 games for the Gunners. McLintock and Kelly moved, with some success, to QPR while Alan Ball, though not part of the Double team, suffered two broken legs, failed to carry the team to similar glories, and eventually went to Southampton.

By 1976 Bertie Mee, influenced by the retirement of his friend Bill Nicholson two years earlier, decided that the time had come for him to bow out. It had been a poor season, with the club's 17th place the worst position since Herbert Chapman's arrival in 1925. It showed yet again how fragile success on a football field can be.

Mee's replacement was a surprise, although he followed the tradition of being an Arsenal man. Terry Neill, previously captain of Northern Ireland and manager of Hull, had managed Spurs with no great success for the past two years and became the youngest ever manager at Highbury.

What was to be Neill's most memorable step came almost instantly – the signature of Malcolm Macdonald for £333,333 from Newcastle. Whatever good it did Neill, it effectively ended Gordon Lee's time as manager at St James', so popular was Supermac in Newcastle. He arrived saying he would get 30 goals in his first season and he ended just one short. He also gave a boost to the careers of the then youngsters Liam Brady, David O'Leary and Frank Stapleton. Eventually even John Radford, driest and perhaps the sharpest of the Double team, moved on – after 379 League games and 111 goals – to West Ham. Now only Rice, Nelson and Armstrong remained. Additions came with Alan Hudson from Stoke and, most important of all, the return of the prodigal Don Howe.

Above: Tottenham's captain Steve Perryman is no match for a determined combination of Stewart Robson and Brian Talbot (left). Talbot had the distinction of being in the winning side in successive FA Cup finals for different teams — first for Ipswich *against* Arsenal and second *for* Arsenal.

Opposite: In an Arsenal career which lasted from 1973 to 1980, Liam Brady made 307 first-class appearances and scored a creditable 59 goals.

Cup specialists

The scene was now set for the highlight of the 20-year gap between the Championships of 1971 and 1989 – the hat-trick of Cup finals of 1978, 1979 and 1980. The Gunners contrived to win the one they were expected to lose and to lose the two they were expected to win, but that is a typical example of what appearing at Wembley can do.

The 1978 game was to be a 0–1 defeat by Ipswich, the 1979 game was to be the 'five-minute final' concluding in the 3–2 victory over Manchester United, and the 1980 final was to be the 0–1 defeat by Second Division West Ham. Arsenal became the first club to reach three successive Wembley FA Cup finals and only the third ever to achieve a hat-trick of finals.

The 1978 FA Cup rounds were to see an impressive progression – five successive wins (Sheffield United, Wolves, Walsall, Wrexham and Orient) with 17 goals scored, seven from Macdonald who scored in every game except the final. That being said, it was not the toughest test a finalist has faced, and the Wembley confrontation was to be an unhappy experience. Brady was not fit and had to be substituted, Macdonald was to end with a third losers' medal and was never to have another chance – three days later he went into hospital for the first of many knee operations that ended his career at the age of 29. Roger Osborne scored the only goal for Ipswich to win the contest.

The 'five-minute' final

1979 was more fulfilling for the Gunners, and rather more interesting for everyone. The third round should have been easy – against a Sheffield Wednesday then in the Third Division. It

Below: Pat Jennings in the 1979 FA Cup final. This was the game which was to become known as 'the five-minute final'. Arsenal were leading 2–0 in the 85th minute, Manchester United then scored twice, and Arsenal also got the winner, all in the next five minutes.

took five games and 540 minutes for Arsenal to triumph. Immediately afterward Neill acquired Brian Talbot for £400,000 from Ipswich, after Talbot's fine display in the 1978 Cup final. As a result, Talbot was to become only the second player to win Cup winners' medals with different clubs in successive seasons. Notts County were the next victims, then came the key game in the Cup run. Arsenal were drawn at the City Ground, where League Champions Nottingham Forest had not lost in 52 matches. Stapleton scored the only goal with a fine header and, after that, Southampton and Wolves were relatively easy meat. The final brought Manchester United back to London as favourites after their defeat of new Champions Liverpool in the semi-final.

It was to be a hot, stifling day. Talbot was the star again, running his heart out, but Brady and Stapleton looked world-class. In the first 85 minutes there were two goals. The first was unique at Wembley – Sunderland and Talbot arriving simultaneously for the scoring shot, although Talbot later

1973-1997

claimed it – and the second was a fine header from Stapleton. Then, in the last five minutes McQueen and McIlroy scored for United and extra time seemed a certainty. But Graham Rix set off down the left, swung the ball over for Alan Sunderland and he pushed it past Gary Bailey to make it 3–2 with no time left.

Brooking's header

The following year was memorable for the semi-final – a four-game marathon against Liverpool which was finally won by a goal from Brian Talbot. It was the longest ever semi-final at 420 minutes, and is the only semi-final to be played at Coventry. Unfortunately Arsenal had only nine days between the semi- and the final, against Second Division West Ham, and they still had two League matches to get through in those nine days. The final itself was unmemorable apart from Willie Young's terrible foul on Paul Allen with just three minutes of play left, and Trevor Brooking's stooping header which won the game for West Ham. It was one of only three headed goals that Brooking ever scored.

European failure

Just four days later an exhausted Arsenal had to travel to Brussels for their second ever European final – the Cup Winners Cup against Valencia, the reward for the 3–2 win against Manchester United a year before. Their progress in a quiet year had been against Fenerbahce, Magdeburg, IFK Gothenburg and Juventus. The Turin semi-final, after a 1–1 draw at Highbury, is among Arsenal's greatest performances in Europe. No British club had ever won there, and Juventus had not lost a European game there in ten years. Paul Vaessen, in his one moment of glory, scored the only goal two minutes from time and two minutes from elimination from the competition. Within two years of the final his playing career was cut short by a serious injury.

The final in Brussels was, like Wembley against West Ham, a poor game and scoreless. It went to a penalty shoot-out with the great Mario Kempas and Liam Brady missing the first two attempts. No one else missed until Graham Rix's shot was guessed right by Valencia keeper Pereira and this exhausting season ended without a trophy. Arsenal ended having played 15 games in 45 days, and 70 in all – no British club had played more games in a single season.

Just as the 1970–72 great period had lasted just three years, so had the four-Cup-final team of 1978–80. The decline from here on was as dramatic as in the early 1970s. Apart from a curiously symmetrical pair of semi-finals in both cup competitions against Manchester United in 1983 (Arsenal lost all three games), the news was rarely good. Defeats in Cup games by

Above: A dejected Liam Brady walks away after missing a penalty during the shoot-out at the end of the 1980 Cup Winners Cup final against Valencia.

Middlesbrough and York City were bad enough, but the real moment of truth was the 1–2 home defeat by legendary Walsall in the League Cup on 29 November 1983.

Walsall seal Neill's fate

Defeats by Third Division sides were not that uncommon, but Terry Neill was already under pressure and unlucky that it was Walsall of all clubs and that it was exactly 50 years since 1933. Little else was going right. Charlie Nicholas, who had cost £650,000 in the summer, had scored in just one game and had yet to score in front of his own fans. Neill was phlegmatic under pressure: 'They don't seem to know what it is to hunger for goals and glory. On (some) days I think they just want to pick up their money and go home. But I'll tell you now; we'll finish in the top six again this season. Whether or not I'll be around to see it is another matter.' They did finish sixth, and Neill was not around to see it.

Walsall was the match that ended the reign of Neill, and after 14 years as a coach Don Howe at last became the Arsenal trusting the imperfect Niall Quinn and showing faith in the young Tony Adams at centre-back with David O'Leary.

The side settled to a steady, if unspectacular, pattern. The rock was, in Arsenal tradition, the defence. By season's end three of the back four (Viv Anderson, Kenny Sansom and Adams) were England regulars and O'Leary, of course, had been Eire's mainstay for years. After 27 September 1986, when they lost 1–0 at League leaders Forest, the defence locked and defeat was not to be an issue until 24 January 1987, after another 22 games, setting a club record for Arsenal. In that period they won 17 and drew five, scoring 47 and conceding just 11. It was a great effort, not least because little credibility was given to Arsenal's chances at the start of the season.

Graham was adamant from the beginning of the run: Arsenal were not good enough to win the title, he insisted, and it was not said simply to generate good press copy. When the side did lose, the disappointment was, nonetheless, intense. The match was at Old Trafford, where United had been struggling all season.

Centenary celebrations

By the time of the defeat by United Arsenal were well ahead of the League and going strongly in both Cups. It had been a glorious winter, capped on 27 December 1986 by a wonderful celebration of the club's centenary, which had been two days earlier, on Christmas Day itself. An enormous crowd turned out for the game against Southampton (won 1–0) and so did a great array of stars. Most notable of many notables were, perhaps, Joe Mercer, Ted Drake and, above all others, George Male, the only man present to have played under Herbert Chapman. How appropriate that Arsenal were top of Division 1 that centenary day, how appropriate that Bob Wilson should be the master of ceremonies, how appropriate that the crowd was large, well behaved and appreciative; and, some might say, how appropriate that the defence did not concede a goal against Southampton. It was almost as if a fairy godmother had decided to shine on this great club's celebration.

And so it may have appeared three months later as the Gunners approached the series of games for which the centenary year will surely always be remembered. Having disposed of Huddersfield, Manchester City, Charlton and Forest in the League Cup, Arsenal were drawn to play, and defeated, a newly confident Spurs in the semi-final. Both clubs were also in the FA Cup quarter finals. Heady days in north London.

Frank McLintock, captain of the Double team, watched the match: 'Like us in the 1970s, they've got players who hate to be beaten. I don't remember us losing when we were a goal up.' Spurs arguably didn't remember winning when they were a goal up against Arsenal.

manager. It was not a happy two-and-a-half-years for Howe. Attendances fell dramatically – regularly to below 20,000 for the first time since Chapman's days. On 22 March 1986, after a 3–0 win over Coventry Don Howe resigned – hurt by media speculation that the club were keen to bring Terry Venables back from Barcelona.

Above: Terry Neill and Don Howe in happier times.

Stroller returns

And it was to the Double team that the club were to turn for Howe's successor – not just to the Double team, but to the player who was voted Man of the Match at the moment of ultimate triumph – George Graham, 'Stroller'.

Graham's managerial experience to date had been limited. He had done a good job at troubled Millwall, not letting crowd problems deflect from a competent young team. But he was hardly a proven quantity. Nonetheless, 12 months on, the choice seemed no less than inspired. He knew Highbury and the way the board ran things, he had the confidence of the players, the board, the public and even the sponsors, JVC, who had been totally loyal to the club since the first days of real football commercialism.

On the pitch the season was nothing less than a revelation. Firstly Graham did not spend, saying that he needed time to assess the staff and he wasn't going to buy anyone unless he was sure he was good enough. Indeed, it wasn't until season's end that he purchased Alan Smith from Leicester. So he relied on what he had – rehabilitating the impetuous Steve Williams,

1973-1997

McLintock sympathised with Howe's position: 'I couldn't help feeling a bit sorry for him sitting there. George rightly deserves the credit, but Don encouraged a lot of this success and it's all been forgotten so quickly. He wasn't that far away. The players were all his. George hasn't bought anyone.'

Early success for Graham

Arsenal had drawn the Littlewoods final card no one wanted – Liverpool. After this point any pretensions in the League disappeared completely. Players who might have found themselves suspended for the final were rested and, having played seven matches in 21 days, Graham's view on their League chances was realistic. Liverpool came to Highbury in the League. Rush scored and that was that. Was it a portent? Dalglish had done a job, but Graham's young lions contributed to the evening. At least, one no longer felt as one had in the early 1980s that the problem was not the fact that Arsenal did not win anything, but that they did not seem likely to win anything. The game against Liverpool clearly showed that Graham, as he had said, did not have the resources in depth that he really needed to run Liverpool and Everton close over a full season. But, Highbury hoped, that would come. A quarter final defeat (3–1) by Watford at Highbury ended the team's interest in the FA Cup and all that was left to think about was Wembley and Liverpool.

No matter how good they appeared in day-to-day terms, this was not the great Liverpool side of the early 1980s. They were eventually to win nothing in 1987; shades of 1985 when they not only suffered the Heysel tragedy but (it is easily forgotten) won none of the six trophies they contested. Arsenal were not short of ability. They had their defence, which remained outstanding. Tony Adams was to become Young Player of the Year and a major asset. 'If we had that boy,' said another First Division manager, 'we'd conquer the world.' And there was always the joker, Charlie Nicholas.

Arsenal won the toss for colours and, interestingly, chose to play in their own red shirts. Twice before they had met Liverpool at Wembley. In 1950 they had played in gold shirts, in 1971 in yellow shirts and blue shorts. They had won both times but this time they reverted to the familiar. It was the first time in five finals Arsenal had gone out on the pitch wearing red.

The game was on 5 April. The press unfailingly chose Liverpool, who had already won the trophy on four consecutive occasions in the 1980s. Liverpool had, of course, won 1–0 at Highbury a month before. It was to be Ian Rush's last appearance at Wembley before his move to Juventus. Liverpool had even set a record with a 10–0 defeat of Fulham on their way to the final. But this was, perhaps, all a little misleading. Arsenal had lacked Anderson, David Rocastle and Williams when they lost 1–0 four weeks before.

Below: The highlight of the centenary season, 1986–87, was a three-part League Cup semi-final tie against Spurs. Arsenal never went ahead in the 300-minute-long tie until two minutes from the end. The key moment was a last-gasp equaliser from Viv Anderson in the second of the three games. Spurs fans were quick to point out that Clive Allen (here in the first leg) scored in all three games against the club that had paid a record fee for him and then never given him a game.

Nicholas decides final

After 23 minutes Craig Johnston put Ian Rush through to open the scoring. Tediously the football world told itself, yet again, that Liverpool had never lost any of the games (almost 150) in which Ian Rush had scored. But even the oldest records have to go eventually and it was to be the enigmatic Charlie Nicholas who did the damage. The Gunners seemed remarkably unaffected by Rush's goal and took control for the remaining three-quarters of the match. Nicholas poked the ball home after a scramble on the stroke of half time and it was Liverpool under pressure in the second half.

Seven minutes from the end Perry Groves, on as a substitute, roared in from the left, depositing a trail of defenders behind him, and pushed the ball to Nicholas. The golden boy shot rather weakly, but the ball took a peculiarly spinning deflection and left Bruce Grobbelaar stranded as it meandered into the net.

The Times offered promise: 'Arsenal had no need to win the Littlewoods Cup at Wembley. Their season has already been lined with enough golden memories. To add a touch of silver as well is not only highly lucrative but it is an unexpected bonus that no one could realistically have foreseen when their centenary season began seven months ago.'

But after that unexpected bonus to conclude their first 100 years, Arsenal and George Graham were quickly brought back to a shuddering start to the second hundred. The very first game of Graham's second season in charge was at home to Liverpool on 15 August. A crowd of 55,000 saw the Gunners

Above: In 1988 Wembley was
not a lucky venue for Arsenal
against Luton. Already 2–1
ahead, the Gunners were
awarded a penalty in the League
Cup final. Andy Dibble made a
superb save from Nigel
Winterburn's spot kick and the
game was turned on its head,
with Luton coming through for
a 3–2 win.

lose 2–1 and suffer a goalless draw at Old Trafford four days later. These were to be the sides which finished first and second in the League and which the Gunners only occasionally looked like emulating. Charlie Nicholas played just the first three games of the 1987–88 season and then fell into the reserves. He was later sold to Aberdeen in January 1988 and disappeared into relative obscurity – a classic case of unfulfilled promise.

Graham kept looking for another forward to complement Smith, but made only one serious bid – £2 million for Tony Cottee at the end of the 1987–88 season. Cottee chose to go to Everton, which was perhaps an interesting comment on the perceptions of Arsenal at that time. If Cottee had come to Highbury, his transfer would at last have superseded the nine-year-old club record of £1,250,000 for the non-playing Clive Allen. Graham, perhaps more by necessity than choice, encouraged Paul Merson at the end of the 1987-88 season, partly because the previous year's leading scorer, Martin Hayes, had slipped into a surprising obscurity, scoring just once in 27 League appearances.

League Cup defence v Luton

Sunday 24 April 1988 was a delightfully bright, sunny day and an unexpectedly pleasing conclusion to a season that was otherwise disappointing. Back at Wembley for the Littlewoods Cup final, Arsenal were faced with a very different proposition

from 1987, when they had defeated hot favourites Liverpool to take the trophy for the first time. In 1988 the positions were reversed. Arsenal's opponents this time were First Division Luton Town, who had never won a trophy in their entire 102-year history and who arrived at Wembley with morale, injury and selection problems.

Arsenal won all their seven games on the way to the final, scoring 15 goals and conceding only one. Their opponents had been Doncaster, Bournemouth, Stoke, Sheffield Wednesday and Everton and the highlight was clearly the first leg of the semi-final at Goodison Park. Perry Groves had scored the only goal to give the Gunners a comfortable lead, which was built on with a pleasing 3–1 win in the second leg at Highbury.

Luton had experienced a considerably more traumatic season. A few weeks before the final all had seemed to be going so well. Luton had reached the final of the Simod Cup, the semi-final of the FA Cup and were in the Mercantile Classic Centenary celebration to be played among 16 clubs at Wembley on 17 April. It all went horribly wrong. They lost the FA Cup semi-final 2–1 to Wimbledon when they really should have done much better. Even worse, they somehow contrived to lose the Simod Cup final 4–1 to lowly Reading. Luton were then knocked out in their first game in the 16-team Mercantile tournament and came back to Wembley for the Littlewoods Cup shell-shocked.

As it happened, it was the Arsenal defence which was shell-shocked after a quarter of an hour at Wembley. After

1973-1997

Mick Harford had very nearly put Luton ahead with a powerful header, Steve Foster put Brian Stein through neatly to score well and make it Luton 1 Arsenal 0.

Arsenal's first half was no better than poor and Luton started the second half the way they did the first. After just two minutes a superb save by John Lukic from a Brian Stein header saved the day and was one of the moments of the season.

Smith, Rocastle and Groves were conspicuous by their near absence from proceedings and, indeed, after an hour Groves was replaced by Martin Hayes. This proved an excellent substitution. Hayes gave width and pace and, with a quarter of an hour left, scored after a scramble. Five minutes later Paul Davis put the ball wide to Alan Smith, who shot just between keeper Andy Dibble and the post. It was an excellent goal and, for Smith, only his second in ten games.

Winterburn misses crucial penalty

Only two minutes later Smith headed against the bar and Martin Hayes contrived to hit the post with the rebound from literally a yard out. Arsenal, after stuttering for an hour, were suddenly totally in charge, surging forward through a tired Luton midfield. Smith went through twice, only to see Dibble save well. Then with eight minutes left Rocastle fell in the area, the referee harshly said he was tripped and Nigel Winterburn, who had scored only once before for Arsenal, took the penalty. The shot went to Dibble's left, but the Luton reserve keeper

dived beautifully and tipped it round the post. It was only the second penalty ever missed in a major Wembley final.

Winterburn and Arsenal were made to pay within seconds. Gus Caesar stumbled and lost the ball in the penalty area. A chaos of bodies ensued, ending with Danny Wilson making it 2–2 with just five minutes left.

That wasn't the end, for with virtually the last move of the match Ashley Grimes came round the back of Arsenal's left side, hammered the ball with his left foot to Brian Stein and into the net it went: 3–2 to Luton.

Nonetheless, Graham was not short of talent. He had inherited Tony Adams, David Rocastle, Paul Davis and Michael Thomas. All were coming to their peak and all would attract England's attention. The full-back slots had been a problem with the decline of Kenny Sansom and the failure of Gus Caesar to replace Viv Anderson, who headed off to Old Trafford. Graham had already solved the problem by replacing Sansom with Nigel Winterburn (who had cost £400,000) and buying Lee Dixon from Stoke for the same price. Winterburn, still – so early in his Arsenal career – best known for his Wembley penalty miss, had been apprehensive about replacing Sansom: 'I was worried about being compared with Kenny – after all, he's won more caps than any other England left-back. Then I realised that the comparisons would be made anyway, so I just concentrated on my own game. Highbury's a bit like Wimbledon really. When I was there we were always being criticised, but we drew strength from these attacks. The mood's the same in the Arsenal dressing room. We scored more goals than any other team in 1988–89, yet as soon as we experiment with a sweeper we're called negative.'

Graham prepares for title tilt

Graham's other signings before the Championship season of 1988–89 were equally modest – Brian Marwood from Sheffield Wednesday for £600,000, third centre-back Steve Bould from Stoke for £390,000 and Kevin Richardson for £200,000 from Watford. It was to be a memorable year for Richardson, who became one of the few players to win a Champions' medal with two different clubs – he also has one from Everton in 1985.

Graham fitted his new players to the existing structure and covered up well where he had deficiencies. This led, toward the end of the season, to the three centre-back sweeper system after the offside trap had been battered at Highbury by both Forest and Charlton.

Like the Double side of 1971 the team depended on perspiration rather than inspiration and, in David Lacey's words, was: '... fast, fit and pragmatic. They play the long ball toward the head of Smith and depend on the breakdown of opposition movements as a springboard for counter attack.'

The Arsenal of 1989 were not as resilient as their predecessors of 1971 had proved themselves to be. They lost and drew games that many would say the Double team would have won. Radford, Kennedy, Storey, Simpson and McLintock would force results in games where the team played badly. The 1989 team were not as dependable, particularly at Highbury, where, on occasions, they looked frighteningly frail. Again, the Double team had two clear creative talents – Charlie George and George Graham – who had no real equivalents in 1989. David Rocastle came closest, winning the Barclays 'Young Eagle of the Year' Award.

Future Gunners boss Bruce Rioch said of Arsenal early in the 1988–89 season: 'They work extremely hard to take possession. If you can't stop service into the penalty area, you're in trouble. They have massive midfield strength. Once they get the ball in your half they keep it there. They pressure you on the ball so you make mistakes. It's not easy playing them, and not very pretty either.'

Arsenal were no strangers to the long-ball game, and it was when employing this style that their dependence on the brilliance and consistency of Alan Smith became clear. As the season progressed, he played better and better, ending it as the First Division's top scorer and gaining an international place. His performance at Liverpool in the final game was quite outstanding. 'You could have fired a cannonball at him that day and he'd have controlled it and laid it off to one of the midfielders without a second thought,' said one of the Liverpool defenders afterward.

Right: David O'Leary against Forest's Neil Webb in a League game in March 1989. Forest won 3–1.

Away form the key

The Championship season was, in truth, a patchy one. The Gunners did not reach the top of the League until Boxing Day, and then lost the lead to Liverpool with just 13 days left. They won more games away from home than at home (12 versus ten), which was very odd indeed for a Championship side. Far more peculiar was that the sides which finished second (Liverpool), third (Forest) and fourth (Norwich) did the same, all having better away than home records. All the top four lost at least three home games during the season.

To some extent Arsenal's League ambitions were helped by early exits in the Cups. Liverpool won a League (Littlewoods) Cup third round tie after two replays while West Ham caused a great surprise in winning an FA Cup third round replay 1–0 at Highbury. Arsenal had managed only to draw 2–2 at Upton Park, despite West Ham's dreadful League form, which eventually led to relegation. Arsenal had some minor consolation in the winning of the Mercantile Credit Trophy, another rather peculiar event which was part of the League's ill-fated centenary celebrations.

Smith starts with a trick

The League season had begun with a 5–1 victory away at FA Cup holders Wimbledon, with Alan Smith scoring a very welcome hat-trick to provide a perfect foretaste of what the season was to hold for him. It was, however, the only hat-trick that the club were to record during the season – unusual for a Championship side with such a good goalscoring record (73 in the League alone). Unfortunately this was immediately followed by a 3–2 home defeat by Villa and a 2–1 reverse at Sheffield Wednesday.

Nonetheless, other results were steady and, with mediocre starts by other contenders, Arsenal found themselves in second place early in November without having had to perform particularly well to get there.

On 6 November they had an outstanding televised win at the City Ground, totally outplaying Forest in a 4–1 crushing which, for the first time, made the press take Arsenal's season seriously. The goalscorers were Bould, Adams, Smith and Marwood and, although Arsenal were now second behind Norwich, the almost universal view was still that it was a matter of waiting for Liverpool to come good.

1973-1997

January and the ultimate denouement on 26 May. That was an astonishing achievement by Liverpool, but not unprecedented – at Christmas time 1986 Arsenal were seven points clear at the top of the League and by the end of March 1987 Liverpool were nine points ahead – a gain of 16 points in three months. So Liverpool's ability to catch up was not in doubt – it was just that this year it seemed so unlikely that they would, so vulnerable did they look (they had just lost 3–1 at Old Trafford).

But, above all else, it was Arsenal's performance at Goodison on 14 January which was particularly impressive. Kevin Richardson, who scored one of Arsenal's three goals for his first of the season, was exceptionally enthusiastic. 'It's like history repeating itself,' he said after the game. 'The pattern, team balance and tactics are all very similar to the way Everton played in 1984–85 and that is why I find it so easy to fit in.' Richardson, who won a Championship medal with that Everton team in 1984–85, continued: 'The manager has laid down the same kind of requirements on closing down opponents, denying space and putting quality balls into the box. The Arsenal players are far more experienced now, having had two seasons when they've led the League for a while, and now we have the insurance of a five-point lead. If we don't win it now, it will be the fault of the players and nobody else.'

At Goodison Arsenal brought their impressive away record to eight wins and 29 away goals, true Championship form. This was particularly good as they were troubled by injury at the centre of defence, where O'Leary and Caesar were both only second-choice options, even when available. It was David Rocastle, though, who proved Everton's downfall. The first goal was the result of a fierce cross from the right which Merson finished off with the relish of a forward enjoying his sixth goal in seven games. Just seven minutes later Rocastle went past Kevin Sheedy to the by-line, hammered over a cross and Alan Smith flung himself at the ball for goal number two. Richardson scored a clever third against his old club after a neat one-two with the outstanding Smith.

One of the few advantages of Liverpool's dominance of the 1980s was that no one else was expected to win anything, which took the pressure off them. It was only after the Everton game that Arsenal became Championship favourites and it is an interesting comment on what happened in the next four months that the bookmakers gradually changed their quotes from odds-on at the end of January to 7–1 against on 26 May.

Pressure starts to tell

As soon as Arsenal became favourites, the pressure was on. Instead of a steady, if not triumphal, progress toward their rightful prize, the campaign became one of slow attrition, with Liverpool gradually creeping up point by point, week by week,

The situation, however, had changed completely by the time Arsenal defeated Everton at Goodison Park on 14 January to go five points clear at the top of the table. This was surprising statistically as, between Forest and Everton, Arsenal played 13 first-class games of which they drew four, lost three and won only six. This was not exactly Championship form, but in an open season, it was enough to put them in front.

Below: On 28 October 1989 David O'Leary made a record-equalling 621st appearance for Arsenal.

Comfortable lead for Gunners

They were also, it must be said, playing very well when it mattered. After the 3–1 win at Goodison, Peter Ball said in *The Times*: 'In the best superstitious footballing tradition, George Graham is refusing to count the Championship until it is hatched. No one else at Goodison Park on Saturday harboured any doubts about its destination as Arsenal demolished Everton with a massively authoritative performance.' Obviously Mr Dalglish had not been at Goodison that Saturday and, indeed, Liverpool were now no fewer than 11 points behind. The gap at one time between Arsenal and Liverpool was as great as 19 points, which Liverpool clawed back between and most people thinking that Liverpool were bound, in the end, to win it as they had done so often. Between the start of the year and that dramatic evening of 26 May Liverpool, in fact, played 24 games undefeated. In a sense, that was irrelevant to Arsenal. All the Gunners had to do was keep winning and the title would be theirs. It was not like that, as we all know. Of the 17 games between Goodison and Anfield, Arsenal lost three (two at home) and drew five. Those 19 points dropped could have been, and indeed seemed, crucial as Liverpool closed a gap that had been precisely that size.

A 0–1 stutter at Coventry on 21 February was perhaps excusable, but the crisis really struck when Forest destroyed the leaders at Highbury on 11 March. This was the game that everyone attended knowing Arsenal had to win, but Forest scored three times in the first half and made the defence look ponderous, unintelligent and porous. Suddenly the Gunners, though still leading the League, looked anything but Champions. Ten days later lowly Charlton, perennial relegation candidates, drew 2–2 at Highbury and George Graham made a critical move with the change that probably secured the Championship for Arsenal.

Tactical switch

Deciding his rearguard was too vulnerable and with three experienced centre-backs now free from injury, he decided to change the pattern. Switching from the traditional four-across-the-back that Forest had so exposed, he changed to the very rare (in England) sweeper system with a third centre-back. By having David O'Leary sweep behind Bould and Adams, Graham reduced the likelihood of fast breaks cutting through a square back four.

In addition, and as important, Graham perceived that, as few opponents played more than two men up front against Arsenal, the sweeper would allow the full-backs Dixon and Winterburn to push upfield to support David Rocastle and Kevin Richardson. This, in turn, released Rocastle from defensive duties and allowed him to go forward. In attack it worked perfectly – the full-backs scored three critical goals in the games that followed and midfielders Thomas and Rocastle two each. As a system it was seen at its best against Liverpool at Anfield, when the full-backs were key elements in the intense system of constant pressure that Arsenal applied to the home club and which, in the end, won them the game and the title.

It was rare for a club leading the League to change its tactics so late in the season but, as Graham said: 'I've always been a good learner and I'm prepared to apply the things I've learned. It's up to me to come up with solutions to the problems that present themselves. The players were no problem at all. I only told them about it a week before we put it into effect

Above: Tony Adams towers above Forest's Steve Chettle at the City Ground in November of 1988. The Arsenal captain was the backbone of a defence that was becoming recognised as the meanest in the League. The Gunners powered to a 4–1 victory in this match with goals from Adams, Bould, Smith and Marwood.

(against Manchester United on 2 April), but they were very willing to try it.' Tony Adams agreed: 'In my six years with the club we've always played with four across the back, but when the boss asked us to try it, we just got on with it. Good players adapt. Our usual 4-4-2 was becoming a bit stereotyped. We were all pushing up and getting caught on the break – like we did against Forest.'

The Manchester United game was not the happiest for Adams, for he conceded an unlucky late own goal. This drew a peculiar response from what we must assume was an anti-Arsenal tabloid press, the *Mirror* in particular attacked Adams in the most puerile and unimaginative way. Happily for Arsenal, the effect was that it bonded the team closer than ever and led to Adams' most productive spell of the season.

1973–1997

Indeed, the time between the 2–2 draw with Charlton on 21 March and the game against Derby on 13 May was really the period when Arsenal won the Championship. It was their best spell of the season, with five wins and the unlucky draw against United. Coming directly after a run of five matches in which they picked up only four points, it restored belief and set up the most remarkable of pulsating finishes.

Gunners overtaken

On 8 April Arsenal were finally overtaken by Liverpool and lost first place, if only for four hours. Liverpool kicked off at Anfield in the morning that day (because the Grand National was in the afternoon) and so went to the top of the table. Arsenal took the lead back again after a hard-fought win over Everton, but the signs were ominous. The game was hardly a classic, but Chairman Peter Hill-Wood was not downhearted: 'My feeling is that whether we win the League or not, I see no reason why we shouldn't go on to have a great deal of success with this team. I've never been so hopeful about the future.'

A dull 1–0 win over Newcastle on 15 April was totally overshadowed by what happened 200 miles further north, at Hillsborough. Liverpool's sudden surge from 19 points behind, their dramatic unbeaten run since the New Year and the prospect of another Double had generated an astonishing amount of interest in the FA Cup semi-final against Forest. These were the two in-form clubs – having lost just two of 44 fixtures between them in 1989. The crowds at Hillsborough were massive, including thousands without tickets. The consequences are too well known to need repeating here, but the deaths of 96 fans were to cast long, long shadows over the English game for many years.

After the disaster there was considerable confusion as to what would happen next. Liverpool naturally suspended their fixtures, including the vital game against Arsenal at Anfield. Highbury refused the League's thoughtless request to continue as normal and cancelled their next game. Arsenal did not take the football field again for another 16 days.

Rivals 'outclassed and outplayed'

When they did, on May Day, it was for a fixture which had been expected, several months before, to determine the Championship. Norwich had led the League up to Christmas and had maintained their challenge until the past few weeks. Then their collapse had been far more comprehensive than Arsenal's and this was their last chance to struggle back into the race. The Gunners, however, chose this day for their best display of the season to date. As Stuart Jones said in *The Times*: 'Arsenal withdrew the hand of friendship and sympathy

which had been so generously extended to Liverpool. The First Division leaders, whose reaction to Hillsborough was so honourable and dignified, confirmed that now they will show no mercy to opponents or to Merseyside.'

Norwich were completely overrun. Their manager, Dave Stringer, said afterward: 'We were outclassed and outplayed. It was a hammering. We finished as also-rans. On that performance, Arsenal will walk away with the title.'

The display was electric, despite the fact that a key figure in winger Brian Marwood was injured and would be out for the remainder of the season. Dixon and Winterburn pushed up and filled the wide areas. Smith was supported everywhere and played superbly. Norwich were as vulnerable on the wings as in the centre. Winterburn, roaring through, scored the first, Smith volleyed a spectacular second just before the interval. In the second half Thomas got the third and then Smith and Rocastle provided a gala finish. It was Arsenal's biggest win of the season and it seemed to guarantee that the League race would go all the way to the end of the season.

There were now just four matches left for Arsenal. The next was rather more pedestrian – away at Middlesbrough, who were fighting to stay in the First Division.

There was just one goal, the result of what appeared to be an inspired substitution by George Graham. Martin Hayes, who had not scored all season, came on in place of Paul Merson in the 67th minute, was immediately fouled by Parkinson, got up and promptly scored a goal. The rest of the game is perhaps best forgotten, though it certainly bears comparison with the hard, taut game against Stoke City at the end of the Double season, when substitute Eddie Kelly had scored an absolutely essential goal.

Flagging at the last

After Middlesbrough came the stumble. All Arsenal needed to do by then was keep their heads up through the next two matches – at home to Derby and Wimbledon – and then the most they would need was a draw at Anfield in the last game of the season, even assuming Liverpool won all their remaining matches. But the team seemed to crack. On Saturday 13 May, Derby came to Highbury and went away with a 2–1 win. As George Graham said afterward: 'We didn't take our chances and Peter Shilton was in superb form. If anything we were too keen. We hit too many long balls when we needed to build from the back. It's easy to demand patience from the players but it's hard for them to keep showing it when there is so much at stake. We've got to bounce back. We've been written off so many times before that it would be silly to write us off just yet.' But in his programme notes Graham sounded less confident, as if he was going through the motions, saying the right things, that not even he could really believe Liverpool would be beaten now. He declared that he had derived great satisfaction from the developments of the past three seasons and that he wanted Arsenal to take over from Liverpool as the yardstick by which football was measured.

In the still small hours it was hard for anyone really to believe that they could now do it. It was statistically possible, but no longer very likely. Liverpool were back on top. There were two games left. The penultimate match was at home against Wimbledon on Wednesday 17 May. The Dons were never easy opponents, although Arsenal had destroyed them 5–1 at Plough Lane on the opening day of the season.

That was easily Wimbledon's worst defeat of the season and they came looking for revenge. They achieved it of sorts, with a 2–2 draw that seemed to spell the end of any lingering hope for the Gunners. It was a tragedy to the hordes pouring away from Highbury that night; their favourites seemed to have thrown it away by failing to win two home fixtures at the end of the season. Surely these games were the acid tests of Champions? Surely these were the games you won if you were to add your name to the panoply of greats? To take one point out of six when the Championship beckoned – it was as much as flesh and blood could bear.

Liverpool tidied up an emotional but rather stunted occasion by beating Everton 3–2 in yet another Merseyside Cup final. One game left and all Liverpool had to do was avoid defeat by two goals. A 0–1 or 1–2 defeat wouldn't be pretty, but the Double would be theirs.

Liverpool now the favourites

Arsenal were out of it – that was their great strength. The big bookmakers quoted them at 7–1 against, but you could have got 20–1 and better on any street corner. George Graham seemed relaxed when he was asked about the pressure a few days before: 'I hope we get this sort of pressure every year. Pressure is something the media like to talk about, but I'll tell you what real pressure is – it's being bottom of the Third Division. This is enjoyable pressure.' When asked whether Arsenal would still win the Championship he was more guarded. 'I don't know whether we will win. I know that we can win. Any team can win one game, particularly with an away record like we've got.'

In many respects Graham was right. Arsenal's two advantages were that no one expected them to win and that all the top four sides had played better away than at home. This was not just a statistical freak. It was a reflection of the times. Everyone now tried to build a side which could absorb pressure in defence and then score on the break. The counter-attacking game was the order of the day. Liverpool had been

Above: 17 May 1989 was the final home game of the season. A win would still make Arsenal favourites to take the title, but opponents Wimbledon managed to hold them to a 2–2 draw and the chance appeared to have gone forever. Paul Merson scored one of Arsenal's goals, here volleying past Scales, and Nigel Winterburn the other.

playing this way for some time – though with Rush, Aldridge, Barnes and Beardsley their front runners were not exactly understaffed. Graham had developed along these lines with great success during the season to the point where, as a counter-attacking force, Arsenal were perhaps comparable with the James-Bastin-Hulme triangle of the early 1930s.

Alan Smith's role was critical, his growing ability to act as a target man and control long balls forward, as well as score goals, being one of the cornerstones of the season. Brian Marwood was a key supplier, and it was fortunate that Arsenal survived his late injury so well. David Rocastle was the joker, the one man who could provide the trickery and the unexpected on the right, Michael Thomas and Kevin Richardson were the workers in midfield.

To put the task in perspective, consider the following. Only twice since the 1971 Double year had Arsenal won at Anfield – the last time in November 1974. On only nine occasions since Arsenal's Double nearly 20 years before had Liverpool lost at home by two goals, the last time to Everton in 1986. The portents were a very long way from being encouraging.

Did it seem likely that Arsenal could perform such an unlikely feat at such an emotional moment? The game was a historian's goldmine. It was only the third time in 101 years of the Football League that the two leading clubs had met on the last day of the season with the fate of the Championship resting on the result. On one other occasion the Championship had gone to the final match in slightly similar circumstances when the last game of the season had been the only match that day. Surprisingly, all three occasions had involved either Liverpool or Arsenal.

1973-1997

Showdown on Merseyside

And so to Anfield. The scene was set for a tumultuous end to a deeply emotional season. There were no fences – they had all been taken down after the terrible Hillsborough disaster. There would soon be no more Kop, because Liverpool were to install seating throughout the ground. The police made an announcement to appeal to the crowd before the game: 'Many millions are watching. Please do not come onto the pitch at any time. If we can achieve that you will see the presentation.' The crowd obeyed. They did see the presentation, but not the one they expected.

It is impossible to recreate the atmosphere there. Perhaps only United's first game after Munich or Liverpool's replayed semi-final against Forest, both played at Old Trafford, bear comparison. As David Miller said in *The Times*: 'The public came out of Merseyside's mean streets and bleak apartment blocks as the sun disappeared and poured into Anfield for the last game of the season: to share that beautiful illusion which exists inside the stadium, to enjoy the aura of reflected glory which lifts them out of the ordinariness of everyday life ... and the illusion was broken.'

The kick-off was delayed because so many Arsenal fans had been caught in traffic jams on the way to the ground. The tension was palpable, touchable. When Arsenal came out they presented a cheque for £30,000 to the Hillsborough disaster fund. All the players carried bouquets of flowers, which were taken to the supporters around the ground. It was an exceptionally thoughtful gesture, although the kindness ended right there. Here was the crunch, the moment of truth, a time which these players would almost certainly never experience again in their professional lives. Liverpool had gone 24 games undefeated. It did not seem too much to suppose that they would at least manage a draw.

But Arsenal fought; fought harder than perhaps any side representing this famous club has ever fought in its history. They battled, even kicked, Liverpool out of their majestic stride. It was pressure, pressure, pressure. Dixon forced Barnes back toward his own half. Bould prevented Aldridge from controlling the ball in the way he had done all season. Richardson, Thomas and Rocastle fought and harried in midfield and gradually overwhelmed their illustrious opponents. Were Liverpool tired, or did Arsenal just make them seem tired? They were leaden, they couldn't push forward, they couldn't compete with the fury of Arsenal's fight. It seemed to be sheer willpower which kept driving Arsenal forward. Their supporters seemed to be sucking the ball toward the Liverpool goal. Yet, for all this, Liverpool only had to survive. They didn't have to score themselves, they simply had to stop Arsenal scoring twice. And at half time it was still goalless. There had only been one real chance. Thomas, outpacing the aggressive McMahon,

whose spirit had personified Liverpool since Hillsborough, put over a beautiful cross from the right. Grobbelaar missed it but Bould rose beautifully. Somehow, Nicol got to the header and deflected it over the bar.

Smith goal panics Pool

In retrospect 0–0 at half time was a good thing. If Arsenal had scored in the first half it would have given Liverpool time to regroup and to come back, to score an equaliser and make the Gunners' task impossible. The ideal scenario had always been two late goals, preferably late enough to stop Liverpool replying or allowing the Arsenal players to relax for a moment.

The second half was as frenetic as the first. Said Patrick Barclay in *The Independent*: 'The tackling was ferocious. Seldom can English football have been played with such intensity.' The first goal came after 52 minutes. Nicol was punished for a foul on the edge of the Liverpool area. Winterburn went over to take the free-kick. The ball drifted across the goal to the far post, where Alan Smith suddenly appeared, unmarked, to deflect it off the side of his head into the corner of the net. The Liverpool players surrounded the referee, David Hutchinson. The linesman had briefly flagged. Why? Some Liverpool players claimed a foul, others that Smith had not touched the ball from that indirect free-kick. Hutchinson consulted the linesman. Ten million watching caught them in close-up, as their conversation happened in front of the touchline camera. The destination of the Championship rested on that minute. The officials finally agreed: no foul, no reason to disallow the goal. Television replays showed they were right.

Liverpool panicked. Rush had gone off in the first half after a distant shot (the best of the night from the home side) had caused him a leg injury. Beardsley was on in Rush's place, but Liverpool could not string their passes together. Everything foundered on the rock of the sweeper and Arsenal's determination and commitment. Never can a football team have expended so much energy in 90 minutes.

Clock ticks for Gunners

But while Liverpool were panicked, Arsenal were sitting on a depreciating asset – time. The minutes ticked by and it became harder to create a clear chance anywhere. Only one good one was to appear in normal time. After 74 minutes a pass from Richardson found Thomas with an instant to spare on the penalty spot. He shot quickly, but not hard enough and too predictably and Grobbelaar saved easily going slightly to his right. Grobbelaar had not appeared on the losing side in 28 appearances so far this season. As long as it stayed 1–0, he wouldn't mind losing this one.

The sands of time were running out. It was to be the nearest close miss in history. The Kop breathed a sigh of relief as Arsenal seemed to have beaten themselves out pounding on the rock of Liverpool, a rock that seemed to be saying: 'Forget tonight, history is ours. This is the season of Hillsborough and the Double. This is what was meant to be.' With the minutes ticking by, there came a lull. Kevin Richardson was injured. Liverpool had stopped pressing completely. They had hardly had an effective attack all night. It was easy to say afterward that they were unlucky knowing that even a one-goal defeat was enough. If they had to win, maybe they would have played differently. Perhaps. But when the referee correctly added two minutes on for Richardson's injury, Liverpool had just five minutes left to hold out.

The game completed

The Kop whistled frantically for the finish, not just to the match, but to a season and to its place in the history books. The seconds ticked by as Arsenal pressed forward again. Surely one last time. A clearance from Lukic was controlled by Dixon, who pushed a long ball through to the magnificent Alan Smith, 30 yards from goal. Michael Thomas ran into the inside-right slot inside Smith. The centre-forward lobbed the ball on, straight into Thomas' path. The clock said 91 minutes and 26 seconds, 86 seconds overtime. Would there even be time for Thomas to finish the move? Steve Nicol came across to tackle. The ball bounced off the defender, onto Thomas and forward. Thomas was clear. He surged into the penalty area. Nicol and Houghton flung themselves at him in desperation. Grobbelaar, everything at stake, came out and spread himself. Thomas waited, then flicked the ball over Grobbelaar's body into the right-hand corner of the net. 2–0. There was a stunned silence and then, from the Arsenal fans, euphoria. The Double was gone; the Championship surely snatched from the jaws of certain Arsenal failure. Thomas, scorer now of the most famous goal in Arsenal history, ran at the Gunners' fans and took off in a somersault. It was a gesture of astonishment rather than excitement. For the millions watching it was beyond belief. 'Re-run the video, it can't have happened. We've strayed into a film script. Seasons just don't end like this.' It was many minutes before anyone believed it really had happened.

North London celebrates

There were a few seconds left. Long enough for hero Thomas to intercept a Liverpool attack in his own penalty area and put the ball calmly back to Lukic. The whistle went. The most dramatic domestic season in living memory, probably ever, was at an end. Arsenal were Champions. For the first time the League

Championship trophy was presented as if it were the FA Cup. And how ironic that Arsenal received it at Anfield. The Kop applauded them; the dream for Liverpool was over.

The memories were inevitably of another late goal, of another Double. But that goal, from a yellow-and-blue-shirted Charlie George against a similarly red-shirted Liverpool had won a Double, whereas Michael Thomas' had prevented one. George lay down, a never to be forgotten gesture, Thomas took off in his somersault, another never to be forgotten moment.

George Graham was understandably euphoric: 'We have laid a foundation of belief at Highbury. If you lose hope, or lose belief, you may as well get out of football. Tonight was the fairy tale, the unpredictable that makes us all love football. There is no doubt that we had a mountain to climb. A lot of people thought we would get carried away and try to play gung-ho football but in fact we were very controlled and content to be 0–0 at half time.' Graham gave the credit to his players, particularly Tony Adams: 'He has suffered a lot of stick which has been very undignified and done little for football. But he has proved his strength and character, and we all did that tonight. At the end of the day it is the players who go on and do it on the pitch, and we're delighted for them. It was nice to see Michael Thomas get the winner. In the first half of the season he was the most effective midfield player in the country. He has had a lapse, but exceptional players don't go bad overnight and he has soldiered on, staying in the side because of Paul Davis' injury. He's had his reward.'

Below: Anfield, 26 May 1989. Michael Thomas scores the most dramatic goal in the whole history of the Football League – in the final minute of the final match of the season.

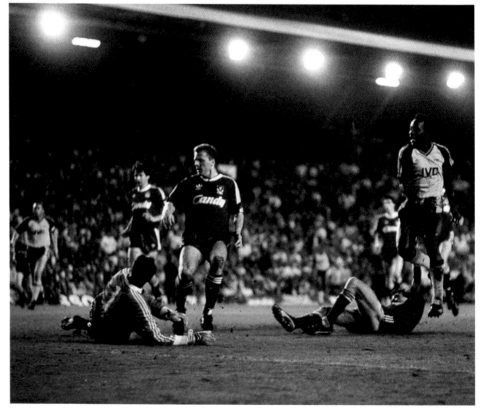

The commentators found analysis almost impossible in the shadow of such unexpected and unlikely events. Rob Hughes probably got closer than anyone else: 'Arsenal looked like nervous wrecks in surrendering home points to Derby and Wimbledon. They were lions at Anfield. The reason, I believe, is that they are better chasing a cause than protecting one. If the roles had been reversed, and if Arsenal had been three points ahead with the final game at Highbury, what then would have been the result?' What indeed, but it is difficult enough to explain what happened without speculating on what might have been. What did happen is that Arsenal won the League Championship in circumstances which no fiction writer would have dared to create. It truly was the most remarkable end to a League season ever.

Graham continues to build

But as Arsenal had seen before, winning the Championship and retaining it were different propositions. In 108 years it had happened on just 19 occasions, two of them by Arsenal in 1934 and 1935. In the season 1989–90 a final position of fourth was no disgrace, but it was 17 points behind Liverpool and there was no joy in the Cups.

Graham went out to buy, in particular paying a record for a goalkeeper to acquire David Seaman from QPR. John Lukic, a stalwart in the Championship team, went back to Leeds. Like Jimmy Rimmer a decade before, he was to be rejected by Arsenal only to win a Championship medal quickly with his new club. Anders Limpar provided variety on the wings, and Andy Linighan came from Norwich to compete in an already crowded defence.

The next season, 1990–91, was to be something of a fairy tale, with Limpar buzzing like a bluebottle, Seaman keeping 29 clean sheets in 50 matches and the season starting with 17 games undefeated. The unbeaten run came to an end in an astonishing game at Highbury when Manchester United won a League Cup tie 6–2. Young Lee Sharpe scored a hat-trick in what will probably be the game of his career. Seaman had only conceded six goals in the season's previous 17 games.

Brawl leads to two-point penalty

Four days later the Champions Liverpool were convincingly despatched 2–0 by Merson and Dixon but the Gunners had other worries. An undistinguished fight on the pitch at Old Trafford six weeks before – involving almost all 22 players – had generated an FA Commission, with Arsenal particularly concerned because they had been fined £20,000 for a similar scrap with the unlikeliest of opponents for a fight – Norwich City – the previous season.

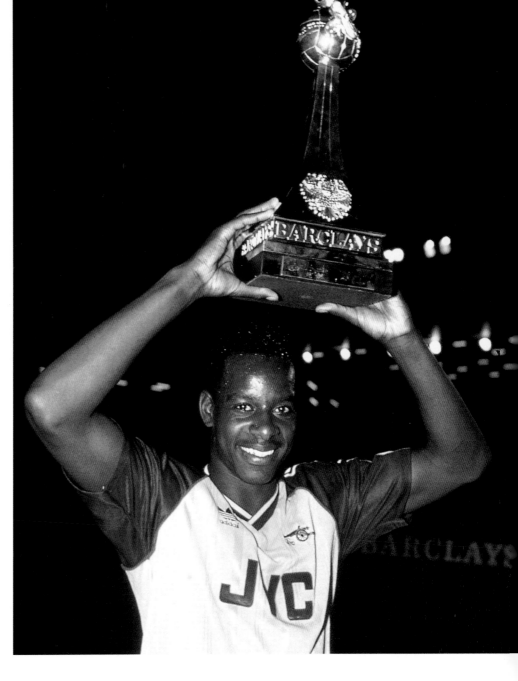

Above: Michael Thomas holds aloft the 1989 Championship trophy, which his last-minute goal had secured for Arsenal.

On November 13, a five-man FA commission deliberated for three-and-a-half hours on the Old Trafford skirmish and deducted two League points from Arsenal – precisely the punishment the directors' swift censure of their players and manager had sought to avoid. In addition, United were docked one point and both clubs were fined £50,000. To the Gunners, this was a drop in the ocean compared to the potential loss of revenue if they were pipped to the title by one or two points.

The two-point deduction left Liverpool eight points clear at the top. The Arsenal players privately conceded that the commission's verdict was tantamount to handing the Championship to Kenny Dalglish with less than a third of the season gone. But, on the pitch, they showed no signs of a side who believed they were chasing a lost cause. Four days after the FA hearing, Southampton were trounced 4–0 at Highbury and three impressive wins over the Christmas holiday period brought the Gunners back to Liverpool's shoulder. This, in itself, was triumph over adversity after another bodyblow to Graham in the week before Christmas. Tony Adams, convicted at Southend Crown Court of reckless and drunk driving, was sentenced to four months' imprisonment.

The timing of the England defender's incarceration could scarcely have been less propitious. A first-team fixture since 1986, he had just regained his international place after losing out to Des Walker and Mark Wright for Italia 90. And, for Graham, who regarded Adams as the bedrock of his back line, there was no disguising the disappointment of his captain's extended leave. 'He is my eyes and ears in the dressing room and my sergeant major on the pitch,' said the manager.

Gunners back jailed skipper

Arsenal stood four-square behind their captain who, one suspects, was something of a victim of the judiciary's modern approach: making an example of a celebrity. Managing director Ken Friar pledged: 'The player has made a mistake and has been punished for it. As far as the club are concerned, he will continue to be an Arsenal player and will receive our full support.' It is to Adams' credit that he maintained a remarkable level of physical fitness; and his unequivocal refusal to sell his story of 'life on the inside' to national newspapers who were ready to wield six-figure cheques in his direction – allowed him to resume his career with dignity.

Adams was restored to his beloved No 6 shirt in the FA Cup fifth round at Shrewsbury Town's Gay Meadow, where a team of underdogs managed by the cigar-smoking John Bond had already seen off 1988 winners Wimbledon in the previous round. In total, Tony Adams missed 13 games. Four of them comprised the fourth round FA Cup marathon with Leeds, in which Highbury witnessed two goalless draws and Elland Road most of the excitement. Limpar, with a brilliant solo goal, earned the second replay and Seaman's spectacular diversion of Gary McAllister's shot, destined for the top corner, took the sides back up the M1 for a third encore. Finally, and to the relief of both sides, Dixon and Paul Merson settled the issue. By this time, however, Arsenal had sacrificed the unbeaten League run of which they were justifiably proud.

Unbeaten run shattered by Blues

The FA Cup arm-wrestle with Leeds was clearly draining the Gunners of sharpness and stamina when, on 2 February 1991, their record perished after 23 games at Stamford Bridge. Chelsea were already 2–0 up and worthy winners by the time Smith snatched a late consolation. Dixon said: 'That defeat

Above: The fly in the ointment. Dennis Wise celebrates one of the unlikeliest goals and unexpected results of the 1990–91 season – Chelsea's 2–1 win over Arsenal on 2 February. It was Arsenal's only League defeat of the 38-game season.

hurt. A couple of years earlier, Liverpool had threatened to go unbeaten in the League all season until they came unstuck in the local derby with Everton. I suppose it was inevitable that we would lose our record in a local derby as well. We were beginning to believe that we really could go right through the season unbeaten in the League, even though we knew that was being unrealistic.'

That setback at Stamford Bridge was to be Arsenal's last of an astonishing First Division season. They had coped so well defensively in Adams' absence that it was almost a surprise when he was recalled at Shrewsbury; less startling was the hero's reception he was afforded by the travelling fans from London, and Michael Thomas made the skipper's return a happy one with the decisive goal.

The following week, the Gunners returned to Anfield for what was becoming the annual title decider. Nothing would be cut and dried with 13 games remaining, whatever the result of this proverbial six-pointer, but Merson gave Arsenal a huge psychological advantage with the winner in a thrilling match happily spared the attrition of normal top-of-the-table dogfights. Suddenly the talk around Highbury – though certainly not in George Graham's office – was of another Double.

Dreaming of the Double

The FA Cup quarter final with Third Division Cambridge, before a season's best crowd of 42,960 at Highbury, took them a step nearer the dream. It also capped Adams' rehabilitation after his prison ordeal. Kevin Campbell put the Gunners in front with a typical opportunist effort before Cambridge, whose

1973-1997

direct, primitive style had been described by one columnist as that of 'Wimbledon without the frills', hit back through Dion Dublin. The visitors had been galvanised into a stirring Cup run by manager John Beck's innovative methods of motivation, not least of which was pouring buckets of ice-cold water over his players before kick-off. Now, briefly, they threatened Arsenal's passage to the semi-finals before Adams, rising like a jump-jet at the far post, shattered the ambitions of Beck's would-be giant-killers.

Before the small matter of a north London semi-final with Tottenham at Wembley, the Gunners cemented their Championship challenge by taking 15 points from a possible 21, conceding just two goals in the process. Among those seven games was yet another meeting with Leeds; Campbell's double strike preserved the Gunners' unbeaten record against them and condemned Howard Wilkinson to his sixth match without a win in his exhausting personal test series with George Graham.

Wembley semi-final v Spurs

All eyes then focused on Wembley. Some 24 months previously 96 Liverpool supporters had died in the disaster at Hillsborough during the Liverpool-Forest semi-final. Up to this point, the FA had never allowed a tie, other than the final, to be played at Wembley, for fear of devaluing the ultimate moment. But, apart from Wembley, no football stadium in the land, and certainly no neutral venue in the south of England, could have coped with ticket demands on such a critical day for both Arsenal and Spurs.

'Common sense prevailed,' said Graham. 'After Hillsborough, staging the tie at Wembley was the only acceptable solution. I don't think it devalues the glamour or pomp of the Cup final just because we're playing the semi-final there as well.' Moreover, Wembley's lush turf was a welcome change from some of the bare, heavily-sanded surfaces to which semi-finalists had been exposed in previous seasons.

For both clubs, the match was not only an historic departure from tradition but a watershed. For Arsenal, the equation was simple: lose, and another Double was gone. But for Tottenham, whose financial plight had recently come to prominence – they were reported to be more than £10 million in the red – defeat threatened their very existence. Paul Gascoigne's express recovery from a hernia operation gave them hope of eclipsing their north London rivals, installed by bookmakers as red-hot favourites ... and although his contribution to the game lasted barely an hour, it was ultimately critical. The dramatic denouement was set to be played out with Alan Sugar and Terry Venables buying the club and it was already clear that Spurs really were in desperate straits.

Gazza proves match-winner

Less than five minutes of the semi-final had elapsed when Gascoigne's amazing 30-yard free-kick was too venomous for David Seaman's fingertips to alter its path toward the top left-hand corner. And when, 15 minutes later, Gary Lineker's predatory instincts finished a move inspired by Gascoigne's impudent back-heel, Arsenal's visions of another Double must have seemed like a cruel mirage to a desert explorer. Alan Smith briefly brought the dream back into view with a far-post header, but Lineker restored Spurs' two-goal cushion midway through the second half.

Afterward, there were tears in the Arsenal dressing room. With just five League games left, the title was still there for the taking; but the FA Cup, which had beckoned Arsenal through seven ties, was suddenly gone. It was no consolation, but Gascoigne's goal has remained one of the most startling images of a football generation. Rarely has its like been seen at such a crucial moment.

'There was nothing to choose between the sides after the first 20 minutes. That's where the match was won and lost,' reflected Graham. 'In fact, we probably shaded it from that point onward – but the damage had been done by then. You can't give a highly motivated team a two-goal start in Cup semi-finals because they're going to fight tooth and nail to protect it. It was a bitterly disappointing experience for my players, but the true test of their character is whether they can bounce back from these things.'

Liverpool sustain challenge

Arsenal had little time to lick their wounds. Three days later, Manchester City came to Highbury and exposed the frailty of their hosts' confidence. Paul Merson and Campbell hit the target, but a 2–2 draw was by no means the tonic Graham had in mind. Liverpool, despite showing their own symptoms of fallibility, were clinging to the Gunners' shirt-tails. On the same weekend as Arsenal's Wembley heartbreak, the Mersey men – now under the management of Graeme Souness – waltzed to a 4–0 half-time lead at Leeds. That they required a fifth goal after the break to sneak home 5–4 substantiated the views of those who claimed Dalglish had baled out of a club in decline. The Liverpool of old would surely have put up the shutters and sauntered past the post instead of requiring a desperate dive at the tape.

Graham, with three of the campaign's last four games at home, knew there was no margin for error. Three points separated the sides. Arsenal had held the initiative since late February, the weekend Dalglish quit Anfield, when they thrashed Crystal Palace 4–0 at Highbury and Liverpool's internal disarray was laid bare by an unexpected 3–0 defeat at lowly

Luton. Now the Gunners couldn't lose the title – they could only throw it away. Graham felt his task was to ensure that any tension he sensed went undetected among his squad.

Graham turns to flower power

Graham told pressmen that his antidote to the despair which forced Dalglish to quit was gardening. 'A bunch of pansies never won the League,' said the *Today* newspaper, 'so green-fingered George grows one in his back garden to escape the managerial pressure trap.'

Nigel Winterburn, ever-present during the season and curiously overlooked by England, recalls: 'We could easily have gone unbeaten in the League all the way to February for nothing. Nobody would have remembered us for coming second in the table and going out in the FA Cup semi-finals. Or, at least, they wouldn't have remembered us for the right reasons. If we'd blown the last few games, we'd never have lived it down. People would simply have thought we'd bottled it at Wembley and bottled it on the League run-in, and we deserved better than that for our contribution to the season.'

On 23 April, with four games to go, Arsenal's lead could still have been wiped out at a stroke as Queen's Park Rangers came to Highbury. Liverpool had, on paper at least, a comfortable home game against Crystal Palace the same evening. More than 42,000 fans came armed with smelling salts and transistor radios to Highbury for 90 minutes of ritual nail-biting. This, said Graham, was the final countdown. True to Don Howe's word, QPR were obstinate opponents and the match was hardly a classic. But as news filtered through of Liverpool's 3–0 canter against Palace, the Gunners dug deep. Merson scored for the second successive match and Dixon converted his fourth spot-kick of the season to keep the heat on Souness. Three games to go, no change in the cushion: three points.

It is not always easy to pin-point the moment when Championships are won and lost, but Liverpool will always mourn the events of the May Day Bank Holiday weekend in 1991. The demands of live television, becoming increasingly intrusive on the fixture calendar, twice fragmented the First Division programme, on each occasion leaving Arsenal to kick off knowing the result of their closest rivals. On the Saturday, the Gunners were required to commence battle with Sunderland at Roker Park at the curious hour of 5.30 pm – 45 minutes after the final whistle at Stamford Bridge, where Chelsea were entertaining Liverpool.

As the only team to get the better of Arsenal in 38 League games, it was perhaps appropriate that Chelsea should repay the debt by supplying their London neighbours with a giant helping hand toward the winning post. Liverpool's 4–2 demise

Opposite: The 1991–92 season saw the arrival at Highbury of one of football's greatest showmen, Ian Wright.

at Stamford Bridge left the Gunners safe in the knowledge that their leadership would be immune to any Roker Park revival on Wearside. As it transpired, Sunderland had neither the guile nor the firepower to breach Arsenal's dogged rearguard; Graham was far happier with a dour 0–0 draw than opposite number Denis Smith, for whom the result spelled almost certain relegation.

May Day decider

Monday 6 May was, in many ways, an average Bank Holiday: 20-mile traffic jams along coast roads caused by day trippers who wouldn't normally venture into their back gardens in such unspecial weather; the obligatory air traffic control dispute over mainland Europe; and in the pop world, Cher was No 1 with the *Shoop Shoop Song*. Arsenal's home game with Manchester United, the only team to have beaten them on home soil in 13 months, did not kick off until 8 pm, yet the players congregated at the ground from lunchtime to watch Liverpool's game with Nottingham Forest.

With Arsenal now four points to the good and only 180 minutes of the season left, the algebra was elementary: if Liverpool lost, the title returned to Highbury; a draw gave them only the tiniest mathematical hope of keeping it in the Anfield boardroom. It was the ultimate irony in their season of disruption that Liverpool's flickering hopes were finally snuffed out by a 23-year-old unknown who used to cheer them on from the Kop. Ian Woan's 64th-minute winner at the City Ground made wonderful viewing for Graham's players after Nigel Clough and Jan Molby had exchanged penalties.

Highbury celebrates in style

The result made Arsenal's fortunes against United academic. For ITV executives, who could not have foreseen Liverpool emerging pointless from their two holiday games, it was an anticlimax. But for the Highbury faithful, it turned a night of potentially unbearable nerve-jangling into a knees-up. No sooner had the Championship been clinched than the order was issued to open up the turnstiles and let 42,229 guests join the party.

Graham, returned to the boardroom from a TV interview in one of the Clock End boxes commandeered by a camera crew, found himself the recipient of a bear-hug and kiss from an East Stand season-ticket holder as he marched up the touchline, his face betraying barely a flicker of emotion. One by one the players emerged for the pre-match kick-in to thunderous acclaim. David Seaman, Lee Dixon and Michael Thomas entered the party spirit by donning a variety of headgear never previously sanctioned on matchdays by Graham. North Bank

1973-1997

fans, who filled the terrace to bursting point with more than an hour to kick-off, persuaded the players to abandon the normal practice of plying the keeper with shots and crosses; even Seaman happily bludgeoned 25-yarders into the arms of supporters going through their repertoire of victorious refrains.

Dixon conducted the singing, Anders Limpar his own personal side-show – which might have been entitled '20 Things You Never Knew You Could Do With A Football'. But such was the professionalism Graham had instilled in his side that, despite all the pre-match euphoria, there was a manifest determination not to let the party fall flat. As the sun sank reluctantly behind the North Bank, Arsenal set about United as if their medals depended on it. Champions or not, they were in no mood to show their illustrious visitors – soon to defeat mighty Barcelona and lift the European Cup Winners Cup – any clemency.

Boring, boring Arsenal

Alan Smith put the Gunners in front after 19 minutes with an accomplished finish to Dixon's right-wing cross and three minutes before the break he confirmed their swaggering superiority. Kevin Campbell's pass exposed United's back line and Smith applied another uncomplicated execution to the move from 18 yards. His night was complete when referee Bob Nixon penalised Steve Bruce for handball and regular penalty-taker Dixon stepped aside for Smith to complete his hat-trick from the spot. Perhaps the only blot on Arsenal's copybook – an eminently forgettable one – was the last-minute consolation Bruce claimed for United, which robbed Seaman of his 30th clean sheet of an outstanding term.

Graham, serenaded by the sarcastic and now ritual chants of 'Boring, boring Arsenal' from his players in the dressing room, modestly stayed in the tunnel while Tony Adams hoisted the trophy and led the team on a lap of honour. 'I didn't think it was important for me to join in ... the players are the ones who have done it. I can enjoy all the reflective glory because of their efforts, but they deserve all the credit and limelight. The fans pay their money every week to watch them play football, not to watch me sit in the dugout. I felt it was appropriate for me to stay in the background this time.' He had, after all, done it all before.

Arsenal were finally in the European Cup. In 1989 they had not entered because of the post-Heysel ban on English clubs. The competition's new format, with seeded teams kept apart in the first two rounds then thrown together in two round-robin groups of four, was thought to favour Arsenal's propensity for durability and compactness. And their chances did not seem unduly diminished by an indifferent start in the League – just three wins from their opening eight games. Graham, ostensibly satisfied with his squad depth, had surprisingly declined to increase it during the close season – a repeat of his apparent inertia after the Championship triumph of 1989.

European Cup debut

There seemed little to concern Graham about his team's quality in a European context in the first round match with Austria Vienna, though. Drawn at home in the first leg, the Gunners secured an abyss between the sides, and 24,424 fans saluted their 6–1 rout. Liverpool trounced Finland's Knusysi by the same score on the night and, like Arsenal, had their own hero. Colin Gibson of *The Daily Telegraph* wrote: 'Alan Smith emulated Liverpool's Dean Saunders with the four goals that must establish Arsenal as one of the most feared sides in this season's European Cup. Smith's goals, his first in Europe, but bringing his total to 20 in the last 20 games, demolished the Austrian challenge.'

The Gunners could even afford the luxury of Dixon's penalty miss as Andy Linighan and Limpar completed the scoring. Vienna's 1–0 victory in the return was hollow, indeed, and by then Graham had left his domestic rivals behind with the crucial record £2.5 million outlay on the Crystal Palace striker Ian Wright. Although he was ineligible for the early stages of the European Cup, Wright – capped by England seven months earlier – gave Graham an embarrassment of riches in attack.

Wright wasted little time in making an impact, scoring in the 1–1 League Cup draw at Leicester and then, spectacularly, a hat-trick in his first League game for the Gunners, at Southampton. But he had to sit out the next continental expedition, which took Arsenal to Benfica's famous Stadium of Light in Lisbon.

Benfica crush Gunners' Euro hopes

In front of 84,000 devoted Portuguese, Arsenal acquitted themselves admirably – especially Paul Davis, whose attentive marking job on Brazilian midfield player Isaias clamped the biggest single threat to the Gunners' hopes of progress. The inclusion of Isaias had raised more than a few eyebrows in the Arsenal camp in the first place, particularly when he lined up beside two Soviet internationals and two Swedish imports, an apparent contravention of UEFA's ceiling of four foreigners per team. Dissection of UEFA's small print revealed that Isaias qualified for Portuguese citizenship through marriage.

In the event, the sting was in the tail. Thanks to a disciplined rearguard action and Kevin Campbell's polished equaliser, the teams came to Highbury at 1–1, with the match well balanced. However, Isaias, so well shadowed in the

Stadium of Light, found a new sphere of influence in the second leg. Arsenal's barnstorming start yielded an early goal from Colin Pates, making only his tenth appearance in 18 months, a disallowed 'goal' from Merson and Campbell's shot against an upright. But the early optimism among expectant home supporters was to be snuffed out ruthlessly by Isaias. The Brazilian possessed that elusive ability to change the course of a match. Now, he graduated to the ability to turn the course of an entire season – Arsenal's season, that is – with one stunning swing of his boot. The 30-yard volley with which he restored parity in the tie brought all Arsenal's worst fears to the surface: they now had to chase the winner knowing that, if Benfica caught them cold at the back, the European Cup would be wrenched irrevocably from their reach. In extra time that is exactly what happened.

The Soviet, Kulkov, and then – inevitably – Isaias left the Gunners to count the cost of failing to reach the mini-league section of the competition. Conservative estimates put the loss of revenue at £1.5 million. Worse still, another potentially lucrative avenue had been sealed off to Graham between the two games with Benfica. Following the 1–0 League Cup defeat at Coventry, he had said the result 'may yet prove a blessing in disguise' because the club's fixture commitments were already 'frightening'. But elimination from two cup competitions in the space of eight days, sandwiching a home defeat against struggling West Ham, suddenly limited the scope of Arsenal's ambitions for the season.

Champions fall to lowly Wrexham

Wright's form continued to be irresistible – he scored all four goals in the 4–2 home win against Everton, for example – but Arsenal's, collectively, was erratic. Graham, sensing that his team was off the pace in the First Division, made the FA Cup 'a major priority'. A disastrous Christmas, in which the point gleaned from a 1–1 draw with Wimbledon was their only return from three games, increased the Gunners' sense of urgency in the Cup. The third round draw handed them a trip to Fourth Division Wrexham. It was one of those heads-you-win, tails-I-lose ties that top players hate.

Deprived of the suspended Wright, Graham looked to Smith – just two goals between September 21 and the New Year – for increased productivity, and after 43 minutes of embarrassing superiority the penny finally dropped. Merson burrowed his way to the byline and presented Smith with the kind of opportunity for which all strikers in a lean spell pray. Arsenal preserved their lead without undue alarm until the 82nd minute, when Mickey Thomas, a nomad with 37 years on the clock and 11 previous employers, equalised with a thunderous free-kick. Thomas had barely emerged from the

1973-1997

scrummage of delirium when Steve Watkin hooked Gordon Davies' right-wing cross past Seaman for a barely plausible winner. The media predictably feasted on the biggest Cup upset since non-League Sutton's eclipse of Coventry in 1989.

Rob Hughes wrote in *The Sunday Times* 'Oh, what lovely pandemonium, what delightful illogicality the Cup still provides! Who will believe that Arsenal, prime movers of the Premier League (and hustling) through to kill 108 years of League tradition, should fall in a theatre principally of their own making. Arsenal should have won the game by half-time ... but this was hardly the mastery of Super Leaguers.'

Graham admitted bluntly that the calamitous defeat in north Wales was 'the lowest point of my career'. Arsenal had become accustomed to adversity under his management and they were hardened against prejudice. Kicked when they were down, damned with faint praise when they won, Graham found himself yearning for the minor irritants of jealous epithets such as 'Boring, boring Arsenal'. Out of the running for the Cups, his team were also stranded in no-man's land in the Championship they had won so vibrantly seven months earlier. It seemed just like a re-run of 1990.

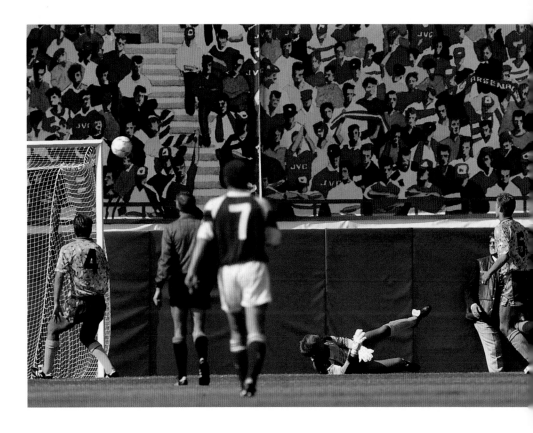

English football's brave new world

But the next season was to bring a more dramatic change – the end of the old First Division and the start of the Premier League. The Premier League's conception owed much to a handful of visionaries, including Gunners' Vice-Chairman David Dein, one of the first modern administrators to realise that aggressive marketing increased clubs' income and, in turn, provided a springboard for extra investment on facilities and players. History will judge the commercial orientation of Arsenal overseen by Dein, and the new, all-seater North Bank will perhaps come to be remembered as his personal monument to the club.

When the bulldozers moved in to replace the North Bank with a 12,500-seater edifice, brickbats flew over the methods chosen by Arsenal to finance the ground's biggest development in more than half a century. Bond schemes to pay for new facilities were pioneered successfully in the United States, and Glasgow Rangers' Ibrox Stadium was transformed without a murmur of dissent by way of a similar venture. In the face of a fierce recession, borrowing or flotation – the alternatives to a bond scheme – could have been monstrous burdens on Arsenal's finances. The board were very aware of two successive Spurs' boards being deposed as a result of the cost of new stands at White Hart Lane.

The reaction to the rebuilding programme at Highbury was perhaps a reflection of English football's parlous state in the summer of 1992. Graham Taylor's national side belly-flopped

Above: While the North Bank was being rebuilt, Arsenal broke new ground with the now famous Highbury mural. It was intended to represent a crowd and ensure that balls were returned quickly.

alarmingly in the European Championship finals in Sweden and the Premier League kicked off in funereal mood. One of the European Championship's stars, Danish midfielder John Jensen, impressed George Graham so much he spent £1 million to bring him to Highbury, while David Rocastle's love affair with Arsenal resulted in an amicable divorce. He joined the new Champions Leeds United for £2 million, but failed to impress at Elland Road and became another of the 1989 Championship stars who seemed to have faded since that glorious night at Anfield.

The North Bank mural

Jensen, a bustling, no-nonsense player, had scored Denmark's first goal against Germany in their unexpected European Championship triumph. His arrival reaffirmed Graham's determination to atone for the previous campaign's disappointments. In the 1992–93 Championship, however, they simply never got going.

Arsenal's performances at Highbury were generally as incomplete as their North Bank. In an effort to camouflage the jungle of cranes and scaffolding, the club spent large sums of money commissioning and erecting an enormous mural, 75 yards wide and 18 yards high, to hang from corner to corner behind the North Bank goal. Thousands of painted faces peered out across Highbury in a commendable initiative to retain some of the atmosphere within the stadium (not to mention its qualities as a safety net which prevented wayward shots sailing into the building site). It was fun and an unusually creative motif at a football ground.

The mural received much good-humoured criticism and became a vehicle for political point-scoring when it came to light that none of its faces was black, an oversight quickly rectified. With ground capacity temporarily reduced to 29,000, home games were virtually sold out every week. To be frank, few provided great entertainment in the Premier League; one exception was the seven-goal thriller against Southampton. But this was to be a season in which Arsenal discovered a 'home from home', a venue at which they remained unbeaten in four games ... Wembley.

Cup specialists again

Prospects of the Gunners winning the League Cup looked anything but rosy when they trailed 1–0 to Millwall at Highbury in the second round, first leg; Kevin Campbell's late introduction spared Arsenal's blushes, and he worked the miracle again at The Den a fortnight later before the Gunners scraped through on penalties with the tie deadlocked at 2–2. With Millwall moving at season's end, Arsenal were never to play again at their original 'local derby' location.

Arsenal needed two bites at the cherry to see off Derby in the next round (Campbell again scoring in both games) and two trips to the seaside before disposing of little Scarborough. The first was a wasted journey because of wintry weather, and conditions were far from ideal when Nigel Winterburn's winner

Above: An ecstatic Paul Merson celebrates Arsenal's victory over Sheffield Wednesday in the 1993 League Cup final.

earned the Gunners a quarter final tie against Nottingham Forest. Six days and two Wright goals later, Arsenal were in the semi-finals.

By now, every other game in Arsenal's tiring schedule was a Cup tie, and Graham was almost prepared to forgive his team for an 11-week barren spell without a League win. Wright scored from the spot against his old club and the resurgent Smith netted twice at Selhurst Park in the first leg as Crystal Palace's bid to throw the Gunners off their inexorable collision course with Wembley was sunk almost before it had begun. The return at Highbury smacked of going through the motions as Wright, inevitably, and the increasingly assured Andy Linighan completed a 5–1 aggregate rout of Palace.

Merson proves cup final hero

Their opponents in the League Cup final were to become frequent imposters on Graham's path to glory this season. Sheffield Wednesday, conquerors of big-spending Blackburn Rovers, arrived at Wembley with a reputation for flowing – if defensively flawed – football, and the teams treated their fans to an enthralling afternoon. Without the injured Smith, the suspended Dixon and the cup-tied Martin Keown – repatriated from Everton for £2 million, ten times the figure Arsenal received when he was sold to Aston Villa in 1986 – the Gunners were forced to shuffle their pack. Paul Davis was recalled, to unanimous amazement, after just one comeback match in the reserves following hamstring trouble. And Northern Ireland defender Stephen Morrow, so often restricted to little more than walk-on parts in previous Arsenal productions, was pressed into service beside Davis in midfield, where he was to command centre stage.

England manager Taylor, under fire from all quarters for his refusal to restore Wednesday's former Tottenham winger Chris Waddle to the international boards, will have drawn some minor, though valueless, comfort from Waddle's familiar retreat toward anonymity after a promising start. He looked worthy of all Fleet Street's platitudes about his enduring skill as the Owls snatched an early lead through American John Harkes. But Waddle was to be upstaged by Paul Merson, not least because of the 20th-minute equaliser which sparked an Arsenal revival.

Rob Hughes said in *The Times*: 'Like Wednesday's goal, Merson's goal came from a free-kick and finished, like Wednesday's, with a right-foot finish of class. When the ball was headed down to Merson just outside the penalty area, he hit across it to induce a kind of swerve that is sometimes mistakenly regarded in this country as the preserve of Brazilians. The ball obeyed his instruction and beat the diving Woods inside his left-hand post.'

1973-1997

Highs and lows for Morrow

Merson wasn't finished by any means, though. After 68 minutes, with Arsenal's vigour now firmly in the ascendancy, he fashioned the winner. Thrusting deep into Wednesday territory, his low cross from the left flank caught Carlton Palmer off balance and Morrow had the simple but joyous task of thrashing it past Chris Woods – his first senior goal for the club. For Merson, it was the perfect climax to an emotional week in which he had become a father for the second time; but for Morrow, there was to be a painful sting in the tail. On the final whistle, Tony Adams hoisted his match-winner shoulder-high by way of playful celebration, only for Morrow to come crashing to earth and break his arm, ruling him out of action for the last month of the season. Adams was so upset that assistant manager Stewart Houston had to persuade him to climb Wembley's famous steps to accept the trophy.

Poor Morrow required oxygen and was carted out of Wembley by ambulancemen instead of on the shoulders of adoring supporters. He was unable to collect his winners' medal, and Graham said: 'It was silly, really, a freak accident. But you can't tell players not to celebrate when they've just won a major Cup competition. It did, however, remove just a little of the gloss from our victory for me – you couldn't help feeling desperately sorry for the boy.' For the press the story was obvious: 'How did you break your arm?' 'I fell off a donkey', the donkey being the tabloids' less-than-friendly nickname for Tony Adams.

Campaign on two fronts

For Arsenal, the job was only half-done. They had another opportunity to test their Cup-tie expertise against Wednesday in the FA Cup final. Never has the perverse nature of Cup football been so ably demonstrated as in Arsenal's fortunes in successive seasons. After Wrexham, you wouldn't have backed them to knock out a pigeon with a tranquilliser gun, now they were the name everybody wanted to avoid when the numbered balls came out of the bag.

Not that the 1993 FA Cup started out that way. When the Gunners were required to tackle non-League Yeovil Town on their own patch at The Huish, the Press descended on the West Country ready to bury Graham again. But Ian Wright's hat-trick, and the League Cup win at Scarborough four days later, forced them to dispense with the obituaries and instead hail Arsenal's professionalism on two thankless missions. 'Sorry you've had two wasted journeys,' Graham taunted the members of media corps.

Trailing 2–0 to Leeds at Highbury in the fourth round, Arsenal demonstrated their newfound belief by bouncing back to force a replay through Ray Parlour's persistence and a 25-

yard Merson special. In the Elland Road encore, the Gunners again had to force the issue when they found themselves 2–1 down with eight minutes left. Smith's first goal for three months was already a symptom of Arsenal's resurgent morale before Wright, returning from suspension to spectacular effect, struck twice to sink Leeds in extra time.

Now Arsenal were through to the quarter finals. Already in the Coca-Cola Cup final, they were 180 minutes from another medal for the mantelpiece. Ipswich, whose defensive blanket had smothered the life out of Arsenal's Boxing Day party, were more enterprising hosts at Portman Road. Much of the build-up had focused on the gash sustained by Tony Adams in a fall

Below: Stephen Morrow, on the other hand, was in agony. He had fallen from Tony Adams' shoulders during a post-final whistle celebration and broke his arm.

during a night out with friends, which forced him out of two games. But the skipper returned to inspire those around him and Ipswich were stitched up 4–2. Adams contributed to the scoring spree, which was an overdue statement of the Gunners' attacking resources. The previous 14 League games had yielded only four goals.

North London giants clash at Wembley

The semi-final draw was, in itself, a mandate for civil strife in Sheffield and north London: Wednesday v United and Arsenal v Tottenham. Mouth-watering prospects, but powder kegs to boot. Falling at the final hurdle before the Cup final is still the most soul-destroying experience in football. Add local pride to the equation and the stakes become even greater. Adams greeted the pairing with Spurs in a cautious, circumspect manner. 'It's one for the fans to get excited about and it obviously gives us a chance to gain revenge for our semi-final defeat in 1991,' he said. 'But semis aren't about revenge or settling old scores – they're all about getting through to the final, and we mustn't lose sight of that.'

Adams' apprehension was entirely justified. Arsenal's League match at White Hart Lane four months earlier had been pock-marked by a series of niggles and unpleasantness. Spurs' 1–0 win was a travesty and their coach, Doug Livermore, was evidently carried away by euphoria when he declared it 'a great day for football'. In truth, it was nothing of the sort. Referee Alf Buksh seemed to lose his grip as early as the second minute, when Dean Austin's palpably illegal tackle on Ray Parlour warranted a penalty.

Buksh's failure to intervene became a licence for misbehaviour. Graham complained to him in the tunnel at half time that the game was almost out of control – which later earned him a £500 rebuke from he FA. Wright was not among the five names Buksh scribbled in his notebook, but TV cameras caught him aiming a rabbit-punch at Tottenham's David Howells and he was later suspended for three matches.

Above: Tony Adams scores the only goal in Arsenal's FA Cup semi-final victory over Spurs, leading to another Wembley clash with Sheffield Wednesday.

Adams goals earns passage to final

Spurs defender Justin Edinburgh admitted later that he had 'wound up' Adams by using 'the D-word' and warned of no truce in the Cup semi-final. For the Gunners, the ominous promise of more trench warfare was not necessarily as worrying as it was for Spurs. In the end the game was a great anticlimax, not remotely comparable with Gazza's game two years earlier. The only goal was a far post Tony Adams header from a Paul Merson free-kick.

By the time the big day arrived, fatigue was going to be a factor. Arsenal were playing their 48th competitive match of the campaign and their 12th in six weeks. Graham preferred Jensen to Selley in midfield, while Morrow collected his League Cup winners' medal before kick-off. He was the only man to enjoy the privilege on a desperately disappointing day.

If the rise and fall of Morrow whetted the appetite, the sequel was barely palatable viewing. Chris Waddle threatened briefly to ruffle Arsenal's feathers but, after one rasping free-kick was diverted by Seaman, he became more and more anonymous.

Wright, playing with a broken toe, struggled for 90 minutes before Graham granted him sanctuary on the bench. But he did at least make the most of his only clear-cut opportunity. After 21 minutes, Paul Davis flighted a right-wing free-kick on to Linighan's head and the big centre-half nodded it across the six-yard box. Wright, lurking with Paul Warhurst on the far post, outjumped his marker to head firmly beyond Chris Woods. Arsenal were one up, and the familiar chorus of 'Ian Wright-Wright-Wright' rang round Wembley. As Emily Bell of *The Observer*, perhaps something of a fan, said: 'Wright is the yeast in the bread, the coke in the cola, the buck in the fizz, the Pardoner in Chaucer's Tales. Without him, there is a void, an impenetrable black hole of uncertain future ...' Wednesday's renowned artistry never surfaced, but they summoned enough strength to conjure David Hirst's 68th-minute equaliser. That only hastened the onset of stalemate and neutrals agreed unanimously that parity was the only fair result.

O'Leary rewarded for 20 years' service

Two days later, Arsenal put out a full-strength side at Highbury against Manchester United in a testimonial for David O'Leary, granted a free transfer after 20 years' service. O'Leary thought the Cup final would be his last competitive appearance for the Gunners and was hoping all three major domestic trophies would be on display at his benefit game – Arsenal parading the two cups and United the Premier League trophy they had won with such panache. It turned out to be the sandwich filling between the Cup final and its replay, although 24,000 fans paid their respects to him.

O'Leary admitted: 'To be honest, I didn't want my time at Arsenal to end. But I was thrilled to be able to complete 20 full years of service with them. I would have hated to be shown the door after 19. The 20-year landmark kept me going. When I realised it was all over, that I had worn the red shirt for the last time, there was a tear or two in my eye. But I wouldn't have missed it for the world. And one day, if the club ever decide they want me back, I'd love to return to Highbury as a coach or manager. That would be the ideal happy ending to the fairy tale.' And if you're going to go out, an FA Cup final has to be the ideal setting.

1973-1997

Thursday came round and Arsenal found Wednesday waiting for them again. The FA Cup final replay attracted only 62,367 spectators, the lowest crowd ever for the fixture at Wembley and the lowest FA Cup final attendance for 71 years. But at least they saw a climax as dramatic as Anfield '89. This was in contrast with the early portents, it must be said. With the kick-off delayed by 30 minutes and Wednesday fans jamming the BBC switchboard with pleas for more time to reach Wembley after a crash caused tailbacks on the M1, the game started in heavy rain.

But if the quality of the original tie left much to be desired, it was preferable to the brutality which scarred the opening stages of its successor. Adams (on Hirst) and Jensen (on Waddle) were given the benefit of the doubt by referee Keren Barratt for challenges which looked worse than the damage they inflicted. But Mark Bright's aerial confrontation with Linighan after 19 minutes was clearly unacceptable even to the most lenient officials. Bright appeared to use his right elbow maliciously as he jumped and the yellow card scarcely seemed sufficient punishment for an offence which left Linighan with a broken nose, although he carried on playing.

Wright opens the scoring

Once football was restored to the top of the agenda, Wright deservedly put the Gunners ahead after 33 minutes. It was his 30th goal of a fragmented season, his 56th in 79 Arsenal appearances and his fourth FA Cup final goal in four Cup final appearances. Two of the goals came as a late substitute for Crystal Palace in 1990. Smith, restored to the starting line-up, provided a judicious through-ball and Wright, galloping clear, belied his excitable nature to chip Woods from 12 yards. Waddle, booed for some apparent play-acting when he hit the ground as if pole-axed by Winterburn, claimed Wednesday's equaliser after 66 minutes with a deflected volley. Now, at last, tired legs were no longer able to compress space so readily and the chances came thick and fast at either end. Mark Bright spurned the best of the lot, shaving the outside of an upright from ten yards, but perhaps this was divine retribution for his earlier offence. The excitement even stirred Mr Barratt, who chose to show yellow cards to Davis and – for the first time in his career – Smith for fouls innocuous compared to those which he allowed to disfigure the first half. Merson, struggling to live up to the high standard of his League Cup heroics, suffered from the same profligacy which afflicted Bright, and the tie was doomed to more extra-time torture when Woods recovered a Merson shot which had squirted under his body inches from the line.

Punch-drunk and dreading the prospect of a penalty shoot-out, the teams traded shots and tackles until, right on time,

Above: May 1993 and yet another trip to Wembley, Arsenal's third of the season. This time it was the FA Cup final, in which Ian Wright played with a broken toe but maintained his remarkable goalscoring record for the season, striking with his only clear-cut opportunity. After 21 minutes Wright outjumped Paul Warhurst to give Arsenal the lead after Andy Linighan had headed on a Paul Davis free-kick.

Arsenal won a left-wing corner. Paul Merson dragged his weary legs across the sodden turf as Mr Barratt checked his watch. Would there be time to take it? Adams and Linighan ventured forward for one last fling. On the bench, Graham was apoplectic. What if Wednesday hoiked the ball clear and raced upfield to score? Who would take the penalties? Had they practised them enough?

O'Leary, who had again been brought on for Ian Wright, must have let his mind wander, back to Genoa with the Republic of Ireland and to the 1980 Cup Winners Cup nightmare against Valencia, when Rix and Brady had missed. Please, God. Not penalties.

An unlikely hero

Merson's corner swung in invitingly. Woods stayed rooted to his line and Wednesday's defence followed his lead fatally. Linighan, who had spent years as a million-pound spare part in the reserves, who had heard his name greeted with groans when it was announced on the Highbury tannoy, sensed Wednesday's collective inertia. He rose like a phoenix above Bright, whose elbows this time remained firmly by his sides, and connected with a thumping header. Its power carried it through the grasp of Woods, arching back on his line, and comment on the season's end. Despite Manchester United finally winning the League, the new Premier title had seemed to create uncertainty.

As for Arsenal, it is hard to escape the conclusion that they owed it all to Wright. In the League the Gunners scored just 40 goals in 42 games, while in the two Cup competitions they managed 33 in 17 games. To score only 40 League goals and still end the season with two major trophies is an unlikely achievement. Of the season's 73 goals in all, no fewer than 30 were scored by Wright. No other player even reached double figures in all competitions, Campbell scoring just nine in all and Smith a depressing six, despite appearing in much of the Cup campaign and in no fewer than 31 League matches.

Cup Winners Cup the priority

With Manchester United running away with the League, 1993–94 was to be about the Cup Winners Cup. After Odense and Standard Liège came Torino in the quarter finals. The first leg against Arsenal was no consolation for the Italians. Arsenal were well on top, played a tight formation, and went back to Highbury with a 0–0 draw. It was not a great night for the fans and it hardly set the pulse racing, but this was Arsenal's last real chance of a trophy in 1994 and caution was the only credible watchword. A 1–0 win, with another goal scored by Tony Adams, was an appropriate reward for a very tight and conservative approach.

Interestingly, George Graham chose to play Campbell rather than Wright. Campbell had been the butt of intense jeering from Arsenal fans after a 3–1 defeat at Highbury by Bolton Wanderers. Certainly Campbell missed a number of chances, but the current Arsenal game remained directed toward Ian Wright, and Campbell had to fill the roll of foil throughout his career. As Chris Lightbown pointed out in *The Sunday Times*, Arsenal were a team that tended to run deep from defence or knock the ball over the top for Wright to run on to. They have never been a pure, instinctive passing team in the style of Liverpool or Spurs and the Highbury crowd has had a tendency to impatience with a side which doesn't show the tenacity and grit to grind out results. The passing game was probably an essential for success in Europe – here sweepers are much more capable of plucking off the long through balls that Wright thrives on. Only Merson and Anders Limpar of the contemporary players really exhibited the skills that can turn a game despite its tactical pattern and Limpar continued to be in and out of the team with Merson continuing to look uneasy on the left. Indeed, by the end of March, George Graham had sold Limpar to struggling Everton and, despite a good 1–0 defeat of Liverpool, it was clear that the only thing that counted was the Cup Winners Cup.

Nigel Worthington's attempt to hack it clear only confirmed initial impressions: it had crossed the line, Worthington's clearance hit the roof of the net and raised the roof at Arsenal's end of the stadium.

Linighan was engulfed by a tide of red-and-white delirium. Just 18 months earlier, he had asked for a transfer because he could not gain regular first-team football at Highbury. Now he will be remembered as the man who scored the latest FA Cup goal of all time.

The significance of Linighan's goal was not lost on Graham, the first man to win all three major domestic trophies as both a player and manager. He said: 'Andy's goal is strange because, like Stephen Morrow, he's scored the winner in a Cup final and has finished with broken bones. But I'm delighted that our heroes on both occasions have been players who would not normally command such attention.

'They are not really the people you think of in these situations. I never thought of taking him off just because he had a broken nose. I tried to get one throughout my career because it adds some character to your face!'

Cup Double goes unnoticed

Graham's men were, one must admit, largely ignored for their unique double. To the uncommitted, they were not Cup football experts or knockout kings. Just Arsenal. Boring Arsenal. Lucky Arsenal. But two League titles and two cups in four years can't all be down to luck. Think of Arsenal and you think of greatness. The club's very strength is in its name. But it had been an odd season. The denouement had gone on too long. Arsenal and Sheffield Wednesday had come to Wembley too often. To think that there were 18,000 empty seats at a Cup final with two such prominent teams playing is a remarkable

Above: Andy Linighan scores one of the most celebrated of all Arsenal goals – the winner in the 2–1 defeat of Wednesday in the 1993 FA Cup final replay. The goal, from a Merson corner, came in the 120th minute and is the latest ever to have won the final.

Below: Andy Linighan with the FA Cup. His last gasp header was even more remarkable for the fact that his nose had been damaged by Mark Bright's elbow earlier in the match.

Above: Eddie McGoldrick scores the final goal in the 7–0 demolition of Standard Liège in the second leg of the Gunners' tie in the Cup Winners Cup, on 3 November 1993.

On Thursday 29 March the team travelled to Paris for the semi-finals to play the French League leaders, Paris St-Germain, who were unbeaten in 35 first-class matches. For perhaps the first time realistic memories of that shoot-out with Valencia 14 years before entered the head. Graham surprised no-one by picking Ian Wright and the striker had another outstanding game, leading the line and tirelessly running off the ball to create room for Merson and Smith. Wright had just come off an excellent away hat-trick at Ipswich and was playing as well as he ever had. In the 35th minute Graham's decision paid off, with Wright beating his marker to a Paul Davis free-kick and heading just inside the far post.

After 50 minutes St-Germain equalised from a corner, but Arsenal's organisation was outstanding. At 1–1, with a precious away goal, everything was set up for the return game in London two weeks later.

Wright suspended for Euro final

This task proved not particularly difficult by Arsenal's high standards. One goal, early on in the game, from the previously abused Campbell, proved more than adequate and Arsenal held their ground in reasonable comfort. Paris St Germain were impressed. Said their manager: 'The quality of Arsenal's play surprised us. We knew they would be strong in defence but did not expect quite so much creativity upfront or in midfield.' But there were negatives, in particular a crucial second yellow card for the irreplaceable Ian Wright. George Graham was pleased to have concluded an inconsistent season with a Cup final, the first for the club in Europe for so long. In an interview with Joe Lovejoy he praised Manchester United: 'Everyone's getting out of their prams right now about United, and rightly so, but it took them 25 years to get it right. They've

got more gifted individuals than us, but they've not got a Chippy Brady or Glenn Hoddle ... The difference between them and us is that their midfield players are better than ours. I still think that Cantona will let you down at the very highest level ... If Limpar (before he was sold) or Merson would work harder, that would improve our midfield. I'm not saying it would make it right, but it would help. what I really need is a young Peter Reid to be the boss there.'

Graham believed that, if Manchester United were to be personified by Cantona, then Tony Adams was the heart of Arsenal. 'We have always been strong defensively,' says Graham, 'and what's wrong with that? What I won't have is all this talk about us being a long-ball team. Sometimes we do bypass the midfield, but not all the time. Without Alan Smith (who was having an excellent end to the season) we don't hit it as long. We play better football ... I don't know anyone who wants to be successful without playing attractive football, and I'm no different from anyone else in that respect.'

Graham refutes boring tag

On the all-too-familiar subject of boring Arsenal, Graham is direct. 'We won two Championships playing super football. We played great football with a team that had great individuals. We went to Liverpool and won it in the best Championship finale there has ever been. Then we won a second title and lost one game in the whole season. That's the first time anyone's done that in a hundred years. But I agree there was some pretty ropy stuff last season (1992–93) and in the early part of this (1993–94). We were terrible in the League last year, but we still won two Cups. I know we're not right at the moment because I know what it takes to win Championships. We've got a defence as good as any in the country, but we definitely need more quality in midfield, although we've got good forwards.'

Arsenal also proved to be the only English club for three years to have progressed to the final stages of a European competition. As they flew to Copenhagen for the 1994 Cup Winners Cup final against Parma on 4 May their worries revolved around a squad hit by injury and suspension – Wright, Jensen, Hillier and Keown would all be missing. Parma were the reigning Cup Winners Cup holders, having beaten Royal Antwerp 3–1 in the final a year before. Parma were not a grand club, but they had a rich benefactor and the Swede Tomas Brolin's outstanding skills playing just behind the front two, Tino Asprilla and Gianfranco Zola.

The absentees meant George Graham had to change the 4–3–3 formation he had introduced after the Cup defeat by Bolton. The traditional 4–4–2 had begun to go stale with too much being expected of Ian Wright, and the switch to Wright, Smith and Campbell upfront allowed Wright more freedom on given their injury problems, it had been a remarkable evening for the Gunners.

Graham was rightly effusive in his praise of Parma after the match: 'They were fitter than us, they were sharper than us. Their forwards, particularly Brolin, were outstanding and it was a marvellous defensive performance by Arsenal. We're a club with marvellous team spirit and everyone – including the guys who couldn't play – was completely involved. You have to remember that around ten of the Parma squad will be in the World Cup in a month's time and, at the end of a long, hard season, they were a very tough proposition for us.'

Parma had passed the ball around well and played the game prettily. But Arsenal, as Joe Lovejoy said, had marked and chased assiduously and kept their opponents at bay. 'Few teams do better than Arsenal when it comes to defending a lead,' said Lovejoy, 'and they slipped comfortably into the familiar "what we have, we hold" mode.' Nevio Scala, the Parma manager, also praised Arsenal: 'Tactically and technically we did not function ... because Arsenal were a better team.'

Gunners defend Euro title

The season that followed was to be all about Europe, but it was not to be until the arrival of Sampdoria in the semi-final that Arsenal faced the real test of their strength in the renewed European campaign of 1994–95. The manager of the team from Genoa was Sven Göran Eriksson, one of Europe's most successful chiefs of the past two decades. He had already won the Swedish title with Gothenburg, three Portuguese titles with Benfica and taken Roma to a European final. The last time Eriksson had been at Highbury, his Benfica team had thoroughly embarrassed Arsenal in the European Cup of 1992.

Perhaps the most surprising pre-match statistic was that Arsenal had now played 24 consecutive European Cup Winners Cup matches undefeated – easily a record for the competition. The run covered a 'who's who' of European names – Fenerbahce, Magdeburg, IFK Gothenburg, Juventus, Valencia, Odense, Standard Liège, Torino, Paris St-Germain, Parma, Omonia, Brondby and Auxerre. Of the 24 games, 13 had been won and 11 drawn. It hardly needs to be added that Arsenal didn't actually win the Cup Winners' Cup of 1980.

Sampdoria were without David Platt and Ruud Gullit at Highbury but most certainly did not come to defend. With a magnificent recent record, they were one of Europe's experienced teams. No fewer than seven of the starting 11 were over 30. The first half was full of excitement. After 28 minutes Bould flicked on a corner and Tony Adams got a touch to put it into the corner of the net. The goal was disallowed because the referee believed that Wright had jumped into goalkeeper Walter Zenga. It was a sign of things to come.

the flanks to rove around. It was a system that depended on Alan Smith's ability to hold the ball and it was to be the target-man who shocked Parma in the 21st minute of the final with a stunning left-foot volley from 20 yards. Dixon took a throw 40 yards out and Minotti, one of Italy's best sweepers, attempted a totally unnecessary overhead clearance. The ball fell to Alan Smith, who chested it down and struck it on the volley to perfection. The shot flew off the post into the net with keeper Bucci just beaten and Arsenal were 1–0 up in front of a crowded Copenhagen stadium. Just six minutes earlier, an excellent shot from Brolin had hit Seaman's right-hand post and bounced back from the inside along the line. Parma were at this stage much the better team.

Above: Celebrations at the end of the 1994 Cup Winners Cup final, which Arsenal won 1–0 thanks to an Alan Smith goal.

Alan Smith turns away after scoring a stunning volley against Parma in the Cup Winners' Cup final on 4 May 1994 in Copenhagen. It proved to be the only goal of the game as Arsenal practised their 'we hold what we have' approach, so familiar to English fans down the years.

Smith's volley proves decisive

But that, in a sense, was that. Parma had 80 per cent of the game, Brolin was outstanding, but they could not score. Adams and, in particular, Bould were excellent and both were called up to the England squad a week later. They defended superbly while Alan Smith held the ball up front and frustrated Parma. George Graham said later: 'Once we went a goal in front I knew we had a chance because our strength is keeping clean sheets. We had a team of heroes tonight and none more so than Alan Smith, who worked tirelessly up front.' In the end Brolin's shot against the post was the closest Parma came to scoring and Arsenal had won their first European title in 24 years. Steve Bould won the Man of the Match plaudits and,

Bould strikes against Samp

After 35 minutes an excellent swerving shot from Lee Dixon was brilliantly tipped away by Zenga. From the resulting corner David Hillier shot from the edge of the area, Zenga saved well but the ball fell to Steve Bould, who carefully steered the ball home with the delicacy of an Ian Wright. It was Bould's first goal of the season. It took him just two minutes to double his total. Yet another corner from Stefan Schwarz was met by Bould at the near post. The ball looped backward, Adams and Wright jumped at the near post but the only touch was a slight one by Walter Zenga and the ball was in the net. Steve Bould had scored again.

Then, 15 minutes into the second half Sampdoria pulled one back through the Yugoslav Vladimir Jugovic. But with 20 minutes left, Paul Merson drove a beautiful ball from the centre circle for Ian Wright to run onto. There were two defenders around him and Zenga came out fractionally too early, giving Wright the opportunity to flick the ball into the right-hand corner of the net. At 3–1 it all seemed set for Arsenal to reach their second consecutive final, but just eight minutes later Jugovic was again left free in the penalty area and the score was a very different 3–2. Not only that, but Sampdoria were clearly much the more creative side in the second half.

Back on the domestic front, Arsenal were in the unfamiliar throes of a relegation struggle. With four teams to go down at the end of the 1994–95 season, there was a very undignified scramble at the bottom of the Premier League. At Easter, only five points separated nine clubs in danger of ending up in the final two places. Arsenal were one of those nine teams, but two excellent wins (4–1 against Ipswich and 4–0 at Villa Park) made the flight to Genoa more comfortable than it would otherwise have been.

Schwarz hits late equaliser

Arsenal were facing a much stronger Sampdoria team than at Highbury, with Martin Keown given a marking job on Jugovic. After 13 minutes Roberto Mancini broke away with the Arsenal back four appealing for offside. He lobbed the ball over a Seaman stranded in no-man's land and it was 1–0 to Sampdoria. In many ways Arsenal were fortunate that the goal came so early. But it took until the 62nd minute for the Gunners to respond. One of numerous corners from Merson was headed on by John Hartson and the ball bounced off Wright's legs into the net; 1–1 and Arsenal were ahead again on aggregate. The game was surprisingly open, if a little aggressive, and Arsenal were openly adventurous with Wright a continual threat until he went off, battered and bruised, with ten minutes left. He had so far scored in every game. Just as Wright went off, Sampdoria won a free-kick 30 yards out. It was hit against

Ian Wright scores Arsenal's first goal in the second leg of the Cup Winners' Cup semi-final against Sampdoria on 20 April 1995. A Merson corner was headed on by Hartson and the ball virtually bounced off Wright's legs into the far corner. It meant that he had scored in every game of the tournament so far, and if he did so in the final, he would become the first player to score in every game or round of any European competition. In the end, of course, Zaragoza's Esnaider scored in the final and became the record breaker, but the Paris final could have seen two players achieve this scoring feat. Early on in the season, Wright had scored in 12 consecutive games for the club – a new record – and he finished the season with 30 goals. In truth, the team was too dependent on his scoring abilities which had perhaps, compensated for other areas of weakness.

the wall, but the return fortuitously reached substitute Claudio Bellucci, who deflected it into the net. Within a minute Attilio Lombardo broke away and, with Arsenal concentrating on attack, Bellucci was on hand to slot a third past Seaman.

With just six minutes to go Sampdoria were 3–1 up and 5–4 ahead on aggregate. It had to be all over. But on 87 minutes Stefan Schwarz took a free-kick from fully 35 yards out. He hit it low and not exceptionally hard but somehow it travelled through the wall and into the corner of Zenga's net off the keeper's left hand; 3–2 to Sampdoria, an impossibly unlikely 5-5 on aggregate at 90 minutes.

Sampdoria had much the best of extra time but could not score the all-important sixth goal. The Arsenal attack, in the unlikely shape of Chris Kiwomya, Hartson and Eddie McGoldrick made little headway against the Italian defence.

Shoot-out drama

And so to penalties. After 26 games undefeated in Cup Winners Cup matches, it was all down to David Seaman, who a year later would be England's hero at Euro 96, in the Arsenal goal. The keeper, despite conceding three goals, had had a very good night indeed.

Lee Dixon went first and scored easily. Seaman saved from Sinisa Michaelovic going to his left. Eddie McGoldrick put his shot way over the bar. Seaman then saved from Jugovic low to his right. After four shots, it was 1–0 to Arsenal. Hartson made it 2–0. Aspero scored for Sampdoria; 2–1. Tony Adams made it 3–1 to the Gunners. Then Sampdoria scored; 3–2. So it was left to Paul Merson to score and finish things. He didn't, Zenga saving. But Seaman made his third save out of five to deny

Lombardo and Arsenal were through to their third European Cup Winners Cup final.

Real Zaragoza had gone through 4–3 on aggregate against Chelsea, so the final was to be held in Paris. Had Chelsea won their semi-final, the game would have been at Wembley. Arsenal were seeking to become the first team for 35 years to retain the European Cup Winners Cup on 10 May.

A glorious end to an era rather than a new era in itself was Ian Ridley's assessment on 1994–95 for Arsenal. It was a season completely dominated by three events of significance matched only by their sheer unlikelihood. One was the dramatic departure of manager George Graham – winner of more trophies than even the incomparable Herbert Chapman – and the second was an unimaginable 5–5 draw with Sampdoria in the European Cup Winners Cup semi-final. The latter match was even more astonishing because it was the result of three goals in the last ten minutes, extra time and a truly glorious

penalty shoot-out. The third event was to come at the very end. Of the rest of the season, there is arguably little to say. The Gunners scored in only one of their first five League matches, fell immediately to mid-table mediocrity and stayed there throughout the whole season.

Graham sacked

The news that Arsenal had fired George Graham finally came on 21 February, but circumstances had been moving toward that conclusion for some time. In some regards, the whole affair was the result of a shower of sheer bad luck. In the second leg of the European Cup Winners Cup Arsenal were drawn to play Brondby of Denmark. Arsenal won the tie 4–3 on aggregate in October and November 1994. It was from Brondby that Arsenal had bought the scorer of the winning goal in the 1992 European Championship, John Jensen.

Below: Yet another penalty shoot-out. This time against Sampdoria in the 2nd leg of the 1995 Cup Winners Cup semi-final. Seaman denies Lombardo's kick to put Arsenal through on penalties 3–2 after extra time.

1973-1997

Hamburg, who had transferred Jensen to Brondby, were due 20 per cent of the fee and had recently approached Arsenal for confirmation of the amount involved. Presumably the answers they were getting from Brondby were not entirely satisfactory. Arsenal did not answer Hamburg's enquiry, but it was one reason why David Dein, Arsenal's Vice-Chairman, asked Brondby to confirm what they had received for Jensen when the two clubs met in Denmark. Both sides knew there was an agent, Rune Hauge, involved, and certainly expected him to have taken a cut. But as Peter Hill-Wood told Mihir Bose of *The Daily Telegraph*: 'The Brondby chairman said they had kept £900,000, which did surprise us.' It meant simply that some £676,000 must have gone somewhere else.

Not all the details are clear, and may never be so, but it was established that George Graham had declared to the Inland Revenue that he had received £425,000 as an unsolicited gift or gifts from Rune Hauge. Eventually Graham paid this money back to Arsenal. This happened some time before his eventual departure, and Hill-Wood later told Bose that Graham had also asked to leave Highbury with two years of his contract left. He felt he could not motivate the players and he and Hill-Wood agreed he could leave at the end of the 1994-95 season.

But on 17 February Peter Hill-Wood and Ken Friar were asked to meet the Premier League's investigation committee. Rick Parry, Robert Reid, Steve Coppell and John Quinton, the League's chairman, went through their findings of an investigation into transfers of foreign players in detail. They revealed that there had been a similar situation over the transfer of Pal Lydersen from the Norwegian club 1K Start. Although Graham had paid back everything, which he described as unsolicited gifts, and had asked for an open hearing on the whole affair, the Arsenal board felt justified in their decision to dismiss him on 21 February.

Revelations that shook football

Despite the fact that many had expected it, the mood was one of intense shock. This was after all Arsenal, the most upright of all English clubs, the bearer of the historical banner for the English game. It was inevitable that many should say that Graham was unlucky and that the allegations against him would prove to be only the tip of the iceberg, and a reflection of a season of similar behaviour elsewhere in the game. There was certainly a great deal of money sloshing about in the game since the arrival of the Premier League and the Sky television deal. Very modest players were receiving signing-on fees which made the wages of the greatest stars of George Graham's day seem like a pittance.

Stewart Houston was to be the new George Allison – taking over from the most successful manager, in terms of

Above: A, rightfully, jubilant and relieved David Seaman after his heroics in the Cup Winners Cup semi-final penalty shoot-out secured Arsenal's place in the 1995 final.

silverware won, in the club's history. But Houston inherited a team past its best and one steeped in Graham's trademarks – defensive orientation, the grinding out of results, '1–0 to Arsenal', the acquisition of numerous central defenders but only two forwards, Wright and Smith (before Hartson and Kiwomya in the 1994–95 season).

George Graham was always aware of the attitudes taken toward Arsenal, and clearly cared deeply about them. He was presumably aware of criticisms about the lack of creativity – the lack of a new Liam Brady. At the start of the 1993–94 season he had said: 'The fans keep on at me about a midfield player. They're telling me nothing I don't already know. Every paper, every radio station, every TV station is saying "George needs to buy a midfield player." In fact I actually had a T-shirt made up which said "I AM TRYING TO BUY A MIDFIELD PLAYER". I was thinking of wearing it at a press conference after a game, but eventually thought better of it ...'

End of an era

Graham's system changed in his nine years with the club. To begin with, Graham played Brian Marwood wide and his contribution to the 1989 Championship was enormous. And despite a lengthy flirtation with the massively popular Anders Limpar, Marwood was never really replaced and as a result Arsenal changed their formation to a straightforward four-man midfield, with Ian Wright up front partnered by Alan Smith, Kevin Campbell and, latterly, John Hartson. This made life much harder for the second-choice forwards. As Alan Smith said: 'We don't have a crosser anymore. If Paul Merson or Kevin Campbell play wide, they're not exactly wingers, are they? As a result, we play in straight lines. I'm flicking it on, which means I'm out of the game and someone else has to score.'

Arsenal's overdependence upon him was hardly Ian Wright's fault and it has become a truism of the modern game that without a recognised goalscorer no team achieves anything. The 1994–95 Premier League season was as good an example as any. Newcastle fell away dramatically when they lost their supply of goals in the form of Andy Cole. Blackburn won the Championship because they had two sources of goals – Alan Shearer and Chris Sutton. Nottingham Forest came from nowhere because of Stan Collymore and Liverpool lived off the efforts of Robbie Fowler.

Graham had not solved this problem by the time he left. He had created a team and a system which was very much his. As Lee Dixon said: 'The keys to the success have been the manager and the team spirit within the club. If you look at the Anfield team of 89, there is still that nucleus of players who are at the club. We've done it all. It is something George Graham can take he credit for, he's bought new players but based it around that core – built around defence. And the defence that won the League in '89 and '91 went on to Copenhagen and Paris four years later.'

Graham's legacy

George wants to be remembered as someone who has been successful,' said Brian Marwood, 'and that's definitely how people will view him. They will say he was successful but not a great character. The man (ran) a high-pressure football club and he's won two Championships, two League Cups, an FA Cup and the European Cup Winners Cup. That's good going. Practically something every year ... as time passes he will become a greater and greater figure in Arsenal's history. People's views are always kinder with history. He will be a terribly hard act to follow. I wouldn't like to think I was taking over from him.'

Dixon had insights into Graham's total coaching method. 'On the coach to away games, we'll always have the opposi-

tion's last game on the video. But you think "I only played against him a few months ago", plus there's so much football on television that you're seeing the opposition every week. The boss might get very excited watching the video and say: "Look lads, come and watch this", and we'd say: "Right, boss, and just carry on playing cards."'

The striker of strikers was, of course, Ian Wright. No successful Arsenal team had ever been so dependent on one man. Through a season beset with poor form, scandals and crises, Wright had kept scoring. By the time he ran out in the Parc des Princes on 10 May 1995, he had already scored 30 precious goals in the season. He had now scored more than one hundred for Arsenal and had already become the club's highest ever scorer in Europe. Between 15 September and 23 November 1994 he had scored at least once in each of his 12 appearances, a record for Arsenal.

Below: Stewart Houston took over when George Graham left the club so dramatically on 21 February 1995. Despite winning his first two games in charge, he always seemed to be a stop-gap. Had the team won the final in Paris, the board's position might have been more difficult, but in June they announced the arrival of Bruce Rioch from Bolton.

Nayim from the halfway line

But there were other records which needed to be achieved. No club had ever retained the Cup Winners Cup and Arsenal were to become no less than the seventh holders to be defeated in the following season's final.

There was a full house of 48,000 at the Parc des Princes, and all of them would leave with one abiding memory. The game went to extra time, Juan Esnaider scoring for Real Zaragoza to become the first man to score in every round of a European competition, and Hartson equalising for Arsenal. With just 25 seconds left of the 120 minutes, and everyone in the ground convinced it was to be penalties yet again, the truly remarkable happened – a moment which comes rarely in a lifetime of watching football. It was to be the perfect goal, not only in its execution, but also in its total unexpectedness.

Nayim, usually the Zaragoza playmaker, had been policed constantly since the game began – first by Keown, then by David Hillier. But everyone had become tired after 120 minutes of chasing back and closing down space and there was now just a little more room on the park.

Nayim picked up a loose ball out on the right. He was 15 yards from the centre line and five yards in from the touchline. Unusually, Hillier was not in attendance, and Nayim had time to look up and see if anyone was making a forward run. There was no apparent danger – no one in the penalty area. Although Nayim had played for Spurs for five years, he had been in Gascoigne's shadow, and the skills which Terry Venables recognised in Barcelona had not been much appreciated in north London. But it was to be the nightmare of the 1991 FA Cup semi-final relived as Nayim, again in white shirt and blue shorts, took aim. With no other long option available, and with time running out, Nayim lofted the ball toward the Zaragoza

1973-1997

fans. It looped off his foot in a delicate parabola, dropping finally toward Seaman's goal like a baseball pitcher's slider for a third strike. It seemed to take forever to fall, the whole ground appeared to stop breathing, and from nothing suddenly there was drama.

Seaman stranded

Seaman, who had been correctly positioned about ten yards out, started back-pedalling at speed. But the ball, by design or pure chance, was perfectly positioned. Another ten centimetres further back and it would have struck the crossbar. Another ten centimetres further forward and Seaman's hands would have pushed it over the bar. As it was the goalkeeper, hero in Genoa, could only help it into the roof of the net. There was silence, and then the sigh that accompanies news of a great disaster from the Arsenal end. Very few had any idea who had scored, or even how.

Had the shot gone over, it would have been the game's last moment. By the time Seaman had taken a goal-kick, the referee would have blown to bring on the penalty shoot-out.

The Zaragoza players and officials rolled around on the ground, completely obscuring Nayim. His shot, carefully judged, had been from all of 50 yards. Seaman later blamed himself, but he was wrong. The goal was neither a freak nor a fluke, but there are always some percentages on a football pitch that no goalkeeper can weigh the odds for. As for Nayim, he had written his epitaph. He will always be remembered for this moment. *The Sun* was astonishingly eloquent: 'In one beautiful moment, he changed the way he will be remembered in Britain for ever more. He will no longer be Nayim the playactor, Nayim the diver, Nayim the fake, the nuisance. He will be Nayim who scored probably the greatest goal ever in any European final.'

Nayim, gave his account of the goal: 'It was the last minute and the last chance. I didn't have any option but to try, really. I saw Esnaider was offside. I saw the goalkeeper was a bit forward from his line and I tried. I was quite clear in what I was trying and I was really concentrating.' Terry Venables confirmed Nayim's own account: 'I've seen him try the same thing in training and in a match. He and Gazza were always trying to outdo each other in training. If he had just lobbed it, Seaman would probably have got back, but he really whacked it and put a whip on it, and that's what beat David.'

Arsenal had now played a total of 27 games in the European Cup Winners Cup, had reached the final every time they competed, had lost only the last two of their 27 matches, and had still failed in two of their three finals. The crowd may have sung 'We'll win 'cos we're Arsenal' but it was ultimately as empty as it was unimaginative and for years Spurs fans would sing

Above: John Hartson stabs home Paul Merson's pass to equalise for Arsenal in the final of the 1995 Cup Winners Cup in Paris. Earlier, Esnaider had put Real Zaragoza ahead the the game went into extra time. With just 25 seconds left, everyone was preparing for penalties, but Nayim lobbed the ball 50 yards and the ball span under the crossbar as Seaman grabbed at air.

'Nayim from the halfway line'. A more imaginative banner read 'One life, one game, one club, one nil' and that perhaps summed up the mood of Highbury in the last two seasons. where Spurs had *The Glory Game* as their contribution to football literature, Arsenal had the very personal, anguished Nick Hornby and *Fever Pitch*. It was as good an epitaph to the Graham era as anyone was likely to produce.

Rioch takes charge

A year of transition began on 15 June. Ex-Bolton manager Bruce Rioch was named as Arsenal's new boss. Stewart Houston reverted to first team coach.

Rioch's arrival promised a positive approach after the dourness of the previous three years. The day after he was appointed, Rioch spent six hours with the coaching staff, dissecting the Gunners squad.

'They told me we probably had only one 20-goals-a-season man, Ian Wright,' remembers Rioch. He moved quickly to boost Arsenal's firepower. The Dutchman, Dennis Bergkamp, arrived from Internazionale for a club record £7.5 million, swiftly followed by England captain David Platt from Sampdoria for £4.75 million. Those signings signalled a radical change of policy for a club hitherto reluctant to spend huge sums in transfer fees or wages.

Meanwhile, Kevin Campbell left for Forest at the end of his contract – and Arsenal soon lost two more experienced players. Stefan Schwarz was one of 1994–95 successes. But the Swedish midfielder and his family never settled in London. On he moved, to Fiorentina in Italy. Then Rioch's plans took another knock when Alan Smith confirmed that a prolonged cartilage injury had ended his career.

Highbury fans saw a new-look team, in style as well as personnel. After the gloom of the months before, smiles were back in fashion. 'We go into training every morning and feel relaxed,' said Tony Adams.

By the end of the season, senior pros were admitting, they'd been through a learning process. Arsenal had gained a UEFA Cup place too, though it was a close-run thing. With eight minutes of the final Premiership Sunday left, Rioch's team were 0–1 down to relegated Bolton at Highbury. A repeat of the fixture at Burnden Park in October – when Arsenal tore Wanderers apart, but lost 0–1 – looked on the cards. Then Platt popped up with the equaliser. Two minutes later Bergkamp drilled home the winner, and another full house crowd celebrated; in relief as much as triumph.

'That's what I bought them for!' smiled Rioch.

Bergkamp shows his skills

The two new signings' fortunes contrasted sharply. After Bergkamp had scored – two corkers in the 4–2 win over Southampton – he settled down to become the fulcrum of the attack. The actor and Arsenal fanatic Tom Watt summed up his impact: 'He's made the season for me. I'd pay to watch him train, he's got that much ability.'

However, injury wrecked David Platt's season. He volleyed a brilliant goal in the fourth game, a 1–1 draw against Forest – then went into hospital for a cartilage operation that kept him out until November. More time on the sidelines followed early in the New Year.

Injuries and suspensions caused the manager all sorts of problems after an impressive start. Ligament injuries ruled out Ray Parlour for two spells. Steve Bould missed the last four months because of a groin problem. Adams was out for nearly as long after a cartilage operation. Suspensions forced Rioch to make changes too. Wright was the most high-profile victim. The manager wanted his top scorer on the pitch, not banned. In March, Wright asked for a transfer, which the club refused.

With his skipper and Bould ('the colossus') injured, Rioch switched to a 3–5–2 formation. Martin Keown, Andy Linighan and Scott Marshall formed the back line – and the Gunners conceded only seven goals in 12 matches.

Keown had an outstanding year, ending as captain in Adams' absence. It was a remarkable turn-round for the versatile defender, who'd admitted he was concerned about his future after not playing in the pre-season friendlies.

Marshall was one of several young players who came into contention. So did lively, fellow Scot Paul Dickov, left-winger Adrian Clarke and midfielder Paul Shaw. There were encouraging signs that the Arsenal youth policy was producing again. Matthew Rose, Stephen Hughes and Gavin McGowan

Above: The new order at Highbury: Manager Bruce Rioch, who took over in June 1995, flanked by his expensive signings from the Italian League, England skipper David Platt (left), who was acquired from Sampdoria, and Dutch international forward Dennis Bergkamp (right), who became Arsenal's most expensive player to date when bought from Internazionale for £7.5 million. Bergkamp's subtle brilliance, and the explosive accuracy of his finishing, brought a new dimension to Arsenal's football.

all came through from Pat Rice's 1994 Youth Cup winners to play in the first team.

David Seaman, Lee Dixon and a rejuvenated Paul Merson were ever-present. Merson finished the season with a bumper benefit match against an International Select, with the 1971 Double squad in attendance.

The low point was undoubtedly the Coca-Cola Cup semi-final against Aston Villa. Bergkamp played superbly against the competition's eventual winners, poaching two memorable goals to put Arsenal 2–0 up in the first leg. Defensive lapses enabled Dwight Yorke to strike twice in reply. The second leg at Villa Park stayed goalless despite extra time, meaning Arsenal were knocked out on the away goal rule. Aston Villa went on to beat Leeds in the final.

Rioch's reign ends abruptly

So 1995–-96 turned out to be a season of 'what might have been'. But it wasn't unsuccessful. A Cup semi-final appearance, fifth in the Premiership and a place in Europe for 1996–97 would have been something the fans would gladly have settled for during the turbulence before Bruch Rioch's arrival.

However, five days before the Premiership season started, Arsenal parted company with their manager Rioch. A statement from Peter Hill-Wood, the Arsenal chairman, announced that the board had decided that it was in the best interest of the club that Bruce Rioch should leave and that accordingly the club had released him from his position as manager. Rioch's 14-month reign was the shortest of any Arsenal manager this century. Mr Hill-Wood announced that the club had a successor in mind but that it was not possible at that stage to identify him. It did not take long for Fleet Street to name the new manager-in-waiting as a Frenchman, Arsene Wenger, who was managing Nagoya Grampus Eight in Japan, with whom he

1973-1997

had a contract which would keep him there until January 1997. Wenger had been thinking over an offer to become the FA's technical director. An intelligent man, he appeared to be a typical Arsenal type, knowledgeable and authoritative without being flamboyant.

While waiting to announce the new appointment, Stewart Houston, assisted by first-team coach Pat Rice, were responsible for team affairs. It was the second time that Houston had stepped into the shoes of the manager, as he had ably filled the gap between the departure of Graham and arrival of Rioch. Two new appointments for the season were old Arsenal men Tom Walley, the new youth team coach, and Liam Brady, head of youth development. Brady, of course, was one of Arsenal's greatest players and since then had experienced big-time management at Celtic.

French duo arrive at Highbury

On the playing side, John Jensen had returned to Brondby in Denmark and two newcomers arrived just in time for the new season. Both had French international honours. Patrick Vieira, a tall midfielder, was an Under-21 international, having been born in Senegal. He had begun his career with Cannes in France and had been made captain at just 19 years of age. He'd been snapped up by AC Milan, to whom Arsenal paid just over £3 million for him. A strong and fast player, although still only 20, he was regarded throughout France as a star of the future. The second newcomer, Remi Garde, a midfielder/sweeper, was 30, and had played for Lyon and Strasbourg, from whom Arsenal engaged him under the Bosman ruling, his contract having expired. He had made his international debut in 1990, and had won six French caps.

Below: Arsenal supporters had been demanding a stylish midfielder since Liam Brady departed in 1980. Wenger's arrival at Highbury coincided with the signing of just such a player: Patrick Vieira. The 20-year-old Frenchman proved to be not only skilful, but also strong and he could pass, shoot, head and tackle. The supporters were rightly satisfied.

So Arsenal at the last minute had signed two top players from the continent. The Bosman ruling in the European courts had denied the right of clubs to claim transfer fees on players whose contracts had expired, thus giving players a new freedom of movement. This, together with the Premiership's new wealth, arising out of Sky Television contracts, had led to the import into England of a number of top continental players.

Neither of Arsenal's imports appeared in the opening match of the season. Captain Tony Adams was also missing from the line-up although, along with Seaman, Platt and Bergkamp, he had played in the biggest football event in England for 30 years – Euro 96, the European Championships. He had played, with Bruce Rioch's blessing, despite not having fully recovered from a knee operation in January. He had another operation afterward and did not return until well into September. Ian Wright, too, was not fully fit and was to be a substitute in the first four League games of the season, during which he still scored twice.

Gunners start strongly

Arsenal got off to a good start by beating West Ham 2–0 at Highbury. Hartson and Bergkamp, with a penalty, scored the goals. It was the reverse story at Liverpool, where the Gunners lost 2–0, but an away win at Leicester, again 2–0, had them third in the table already. There was then an exciting game with Chelsea at Highbury, in which Chelsea led 2-0, but Arsenal came back to lead 3–2, only for a last-minute goal from Chelsea's Dennis Wise to restrict the Gunners to a draw. Another 2–2 draw at Villa was a good result and, with Bergkamp, Wright and Merson already on the scorer's chart with two apiece, things looked very promising for the first leg of the UEFA Cup, which was a home tie against the German Bundesliga giants Borussia Monchengladbach.

Arsenal's display was disappointing, hampered as it was by Dennis Bergkamp having to go off early in the match with a hamstring injury. Arsenal were 2–0 down soon after half time, staged a rally but finished 3–2 down. It left a big task ahead for the second leg.

Three days later (Friday the 13th) Stewart Houston resigned. He had been offered a post as assistant to George Graham who, after being banned from football management for a year, had taken over at Leeds. However Houston, who said it was clear to him he would never get the No 1 job at Highbury, stated that he was not interested in being No 2 any more. Houston's move was to facilitate him taking over the managership at First Division Queen's Park Rangers. He gave the Loftus Road side a distinctly ex-Arsenal look when he appointed his old boss at Highbury, Bruce Rioch, to be his assistant.

Wenger arrives early

With what appeared to be crisis looming at Highbury, Chairman Peter Hill-Wood revealed he had been in contact with Japan and expected Arsene Wenger to be released from his contract with Grampus Eight and to be able to take over somewhat earlier than had been expected. Meanwhile Pat Rice was the new caretaker manager at Highbury, and in his first programme notes he confessed that what he wanted for Arsenal was to get back to some 'boring' 1–0 wins again, the way to win trophies in his view.

Ian Wright emphasised Arsenal's buoyant outlook in the next game by scoring a hat-trick in a 4–1 home win over Sheffield Wednesday and he got another goal in a 2–0 win at Middlesbrough, where Adams returned as a substitute, before Arsenal went to Borussia Monchengladbach to try to win by two goals and keep themselves in Europe. Arsene Wenger flew in to join Arsenal for his first match, although for the time being Pat Rice remained in control. Wenger was encouraged by what he saw. After going one behind, Arsenal equalised just before half time through Wright and went ahead just after-ward through Merson. One more might have led to them winning on aggregate but, after Monchengladbach scored again in the 64th minute, Arsenal's pressing need was for a goal to force parity over the two legs, and in pressing they con-ceded another in injury time to lose the tie by a disappointing six goals to four.

Wenger had flown in to take over before Arsenal's next match, and saw good wins over Sunderland and Blackburn to lift Arsenal to second in the table. Two draws with Midlands

Above: Euro joy: the Arsenal bench, which included Arsene Wenger for the first time, celebrates an away goal against UEFA Cup opponents Borussia Monchengladbach. Unfortunately, it was not enough to overturn a first-leg deficit.

teams followed, at home to Coventry and away at Stoke, the second being in the third round of the Coca-Cola Cup – Arsenal, in keeping with some other top clubs, had been given a bye to this stage. Before Arsenal could beat their First Division opponents Stoke in the replay 5–2, George Graham returned to Highbury in charge of Leeds United. Former Arsenal favourite David O'Leary was with Graham as his No 2 at Leeds. The Gunners won 3–0.

Gunners go top

Arsenal's interest in the Coca-Cola Cup ended in the fourth round on 27 November when they were well beaten by Liverpool – 4–2 at Anfield, the two coming from Ian Wright penalties. However, three days later it was a different story in a remarkable match at St James' Park against the Premiership leaders, Newcastle. A minute after a 12th-minute goal by Dixon had been replied to by a 21st-minute Shearer equaliser, Tony Adams brought down Shearer when he was through on goal, and was sent off. It seemed all over for the Gunners, but they withstood the Newcastle siege and, in the 60th minute, an Ian Wright breakaway goal put Arsenal top of the table. 'There is something special about this team', said Wenger. 'They have a good camaraderie because they have been playing together for a long time'.

Arsenal's table-topping didn't last long and a surprise 2–1 defeat at relegation strugglers Nottingham Forest plus a couple of draws began a mini-slide that dropped them to third.

Right: Martin Keown enjoyed an excellent first season under Arsene Wenger. By the end of the campaign the stylish defender had impressed the new England manager, Glenn Hoddle, enough to be included in the squad for a busy summer schedule.

1973-1997

In January Arsenal negotiated the third round of the FA Cup by winning a replay 2–0 at Sunderland, this otherwise frenetic encounter was illuminated by an exquisite goal from Dennis Bergkamp. On 4 February at home to Leeds in the fourth round, they crashed 1–0 to a 12th-minute goal by Rod Wallace and inspired goalkeeping by Nigel Martyn. Apart from the UEFA Cup defeat, it was Arsenal's first defeat of the season at home, and the first time Leeds had beaten Arsenal in the Cup in ten encounters since the Cup final of 1972.

So their ejection from their third Cup competition left Arsenal with just the Premiership to fight for, or at worst a place in Europe. But the next home defeat, which quickly followed on 19 February, was a blow. Two first-half goals by leaders Manchester United, only one of which Bergkamp managed to pull back in the second half, left Arsenal trailing five points behind in third place, and with fewer games in hand than any of their rivals. After this match Wenger wrote off Arsenal's title chances.

In March Wenger completed the signing of Nicolas Anelka, a talented French striker days short of his 18th birthday, from Paris St Germain. The tall, slim youngster delighted with appearances as a sub in Arsenal's run-in.

Strangely, because Arsenal strung together some good wins and other title contenders faltered, their mathematical hopes of taking the title continued nearly to the end of the season, and their prospects of a Champions League place right to the last day. The title hopes disappeared with another home defeat – a vital one to rivals Liverpool. Arsenal's 2–1 defeat was overshadowed by a controversial penalty decision against them. Robbie Fowler stumbled over David Seaman and immediately jumped up, waving his arms to indicate that he did not think a penalty should be awarded. Referee Gerald Ashby had already pointed to the spot, and wasn't inclined to change his mind. Although the referee thought Fowler had been tripped by Seaman he did not send the keeper off. Seaman blocked Fowler's weak spot-kick, but Jason McAteer slammed in the rebound for the vital goal.

On the second-to-last day of the season Arsenal entertained close rivals Newcastle United in another vital home match. And again they lost, 1–0. Wenger noted they had lost at home to all their immediate rivals: Manchester United, Liverpool and Newcastle. Unfortunately, these late-season defeats were to cost them dear.

Champions League disappointment

With Manchester United already crowned as Champions of the 1996–97 season, any one of Liverpool, Newcastle or Arsenal could finish in second position in the Premiership and gain a Champions League place on the very last day of the season,

Above: Lee Dixon celebrates his goal against Newcastle at St James'. The long-serving full-back seemed to find a new enthusiasm for the game in 1996–97 and his energetic displays were widely acclaimed.

with Arsenal and Newcastle starting the day on identical points totals and goal differences.

Arsenal played Derby County at the last match to be played at the Baseball Ground, and things looked black after 11 minutes with Adams sent off and Arsenal one goal down, but they rallied strongly to win the game 3–1. It was all in vain however as Newcastle won 5–0. Arsenal's third place ensured a UEFA Cup place – but it could have been so much better … .

During a season in which Arsenal's charismatic ex-player Denis Compton died to worldwide tributes, Arsenal had found young players likely to uphold the reputation of the club for quality in the future. Patrick Vieira had been a great success in his first season, 20-year-old Stephen Hughes, picked for England's Under-21 side, had impressed in a late run in the team and Nicolas Anelka's promise was obvious. The 'old-stagers' were also showing no signs of slipping – Nigel Winterburn had a deserved benefit match in a 3–3 draw with Rangers on 13 May. With Arsene Wenger in charge, things looked bright for Arsenal.

It all began in August 1996, when Arsenal signed two Frenchmen – Remi Garde, and the Senegal-born Patrick Vieira. Their arrival gave a massive clue to the identity of the Gunners' new manager. Arsene Wenger had recommended both. Vice-Chairman David Dein quietly did the business. Garde came from Wenger's home town club, RC Strasbourg, on a free transfer under the Bosman ruling.

Vieira, then just 20, cost £3.5 million from AC Milan where he'd been languishing on the fringes of the first-team. Wenger, the former Monaco and Nagoya Grampus Eight coach took over, officially, as Arsenal manager at the end of September.

As he said then: 'In English football, a coach is judged by the quality of the players he recruits.' Vieira's performances quickly proved Wenger's judgement to the Highbury fans.

Vieira became the midfield link that Arsenal had lacked since the days of Paul Davis. As Ian Wright said: 'He makes dream passes for a striker.'

Garde never made the same impact due to injuries. But he played three seasons as cover in midfield or at right back – and Wenger insisted that Garde should carry on playing when he thought about retirement in the summer of 1999.

In February, 1997, the former Monaco coach added another French piece to his jigsaw: Nicolas Anelka. Anelka was an 18 year-old prodigy who couldn't get a game for Paris St-Germain. He challenged the French regulations that oblige young players to sign a contract with the club that first devel-

oped them. PS-G backed off. The Bosman judgement had sent shock waves though European clubs. PS-G feared a test case that would shatter the regulations into little pieces. So did the French federation.

So Arsenal signed Anelka for a knockdown compensation payment of around £500,000. Anelka succeeded in the English game for two reasons: his own ability – and the confidence that Wenger showed in him.

When Ian Wright was injured in the 1997–98 Double season, Wenger threw Anelka into the fray. When he did well, Wenger praised his potential. When he failed, Wenger said he was only a teenager and still learning.

Anelka ended that season in triumph, scoring the second goal in the FA Cup final against Newcastle that clinched the Double. In 1998–99, he finished Arsenal's leading scorer with 17 Premiership goals. But his veneration by the Arsenal faith-

Above, left: Emmanuel Petit arrived from Wenger's old club Monaco during the summer of 1997. After a shaky start he made himself an invaluable presence in midfield.

Above: Gilles Grimandi arrived together with Petit from Monaco. He was initially used as cover at right-back but his versatility soon saw him play in both central defence and midfield.

Above right: Nicolas Anelka blossomed into a fast striker with a clinically lethal finish whilst he was at Highbury.

Above far right: Arsene Wenger, the former coach of Monaco, arrived in 1996 and brought glory back to Highbury.

Right: Patrick Vieira is a complete midfielder who displays great touch, uncompromising tackling and visionary passing. He forged a formidable partnership with Petit that was instrumental in the success of 1997–98.

Monaco for two more players - Manu Petit and Gilles Grimandi. Petit was a versatile left-footed defender who could play in midfield. Wenger had another vision: that Petit could develop into a midfielder of the highest class. In the second half of the season, Petit more than repaid Wenger's faith. Tackler, runner and perceptive passer, he became one of Arsenal's key players.

One of France's finest too. Petit was a crucial member of Aime Jacquet's squad that won the World Cup on home ground. Somehow it was appropriate that Petit scored France's last goal in the 3–0 final win over Brazil. It was made at Highbury; created by substitute Vieira.

Grimandi came as cover, at right back or central back. Lack of first-team opportunities frustrated him. But his winning shot against Crystal Palace – on a day when injuries and suspensions reduced Arsenal to bare bones – was crucial to the Double success.

Wenger signed another ex-Monaco player too: Chris Wreh, cousin of George Weah. The Liberian international had become a French citizen. After a year on loan to Guingamp, he joined the Gunners. Wreh scored vital goals in the 'Double' season – like the winner at Bolton and the only goal in the FA Cup semi-final against Wolves.

Arsenal had set up a loose link with Cannes, Vieira's old club. In the summer of 1998, the Gunners opted for closer links with a more famous French team – St Etienne. Their youngsters had won the equivalent of the FA Youth Cup. Left-back David Grondin moved to Highbury, perhaps as a long-term replacement for Nigel Winterburn. Meanwhile, the clubs exchanged players and played regular matches against each other.

In 2001/02 Robert Pires was to prove an invaluable member of the first-team squad, making 42 appearances in all and scoring 13 goals, though injury cut short his season. With the striking power of Sylvain Wiltord, Thierry Henry and Robert Pires, the skills of Gilles Grimandi, the up-and-coming talent of Jeremie Aliadiere and the cool, calm brilliance of Arsene Wenger, it seems that Arsenal's French connection is alive and well and continues going from strength to strength. Players will come and go, but their skill and vision will always be remembered.

Wenger praised his potential, When he failed, Wenger said he was only a teenager and still learning.

Anelka ended that season in triumph, scoring the second goal in the F.A. Cup final against Newcastle that clinched the 'Double.' In 1998–99, he finished Arsenal's leading scorer with 17 Premiership goals.

Another of the French connection, Boro Primorac, arrived a few weeks after Anelka. Primorac had been Wenger's assistant at Grampus Eight. Born in Mostar, now part of Bosnia, he won 18 caps for Yugoslavia. But he had made his name as a coach in France, with Cannes and Valenciennes.

In the summer of 1997, Wenger swooped on his old club

CONNECTION

SEASON 1974-1975 FOOTBALL LEAGUE (DIVISION 1)

Date	Opp	V	R	Score	1	2	3	4	5	6	7	8	9	10	11	Notes
17 Aug	Leicester C	A	W	1-0	Rimmer	Matthews	Nelson	Storey	Simpson	Kelly	Armstrong	Brady	Radford	George	Kidd1	Price for Kelly
20 Aug	Ipswich T	H	L	0-1	..	Storey	..	Kelly	..	Matthews	..	Hornsby	..	Kidd	Brady	
24 Aug	Manchester C	H	W	4-0	..	Rice	..	..	..	Storey	Matthews	George	..2	..2	..	Armstrong for Simpson
27 Aug	Ipswich T	A	L	0-3	..	..	..	..	..	Matthews	Brady	..	..	..	Storey	
31 Aug	Everton	A	L	1-2	..	..	..	Storey	..	Kelly	Blockley	Brady	..	George	Kidd1	Powling for Kelly; Simpson for Rice
7 Sep	Burnley	H	L	0-1	..	..	..	..	Blockley	Matthews	Armstrong	..	..	..	..	
14 Sep	Chelsea	A	D	0-0	..	Kelly	Simpson	..	..	..	..	George	..	Kidd	Brady	
21 Sep	Luton T	H	D	2-2	..	Simpson	Nelson	..	..	..	..	Kelly	..	..2	..	
28 Sep	Birmingham C	A	L	1-3	..	Storey	Simpson	Kelly	..	..	George1	Ball	..	..	..	
5 Oct	Leeds U	A	L		..	..	..	..	..	..	Armstrong	..	..	..	..	
12 Oct	Q P R	H	D	2-2	..	..	..	..	..	Powling	..	..	..1	..1	..	Powling for Blockley
16 Oct	Manchester C	A	L	1-2	..	..	..	Nelson	..	Kelly	Ball	Brady	..1	..	Armstrong	
19 Oct	Tottenham H	A	L	0-2	..	..	Nelson	Kelly	..	Simpson	Armstrong	Ball	..	Brady	Kidd	
26 Oct	West Ham U	H	W	3-0	..	..	McNab	..	Mancini	..	Rice	..	..1	..1	..1	Armstrong for Rice
2 Nov	Wolverhampton W	H	D	0-0	..	Rice	..	..	..	..	Storey	..2	..	Kidd	Brady1	
9 Nov	Liverpool	A	W	3-1	..	..	..	..	..	..	Storey	..2	..	Kidd	Brady1	
16 Nov	Derby Co	H	W	3-1	..	..	..	..	..	..	..	..2	..	..	..1	
23 Nov	Coventry C	A	L	0-3	..	..	..	..	..	Simpson	Powling	Armstrong	..	..	..	George for Brady
30 Nov	Middlesbrough	H	W	2-0	..	..	..	..	..	..	George	..1	..	..	..1	
7 Dec	Carlisle U	A	L	1-2	..	..	..	..	..	Mancini	Storey	..	..	..	..1	Cropley
14 Dec	Leicester C	H	D	0-0	..	..	..	..	..	Mancini	Simpson	..	..	..	..	
21 Dec	Stoke C	A	W	2-0	..	..	..	..	..	..	..	..	..	..2	..	
26 Dec	Chelsea	H	L	1-2	..	..	..	..	..	..	..	..	..	..1	..	
28 Dec	Sheffield U	A	D	1-1	..	..	..	..	..	..	..	George1	..	..	..	Armstrong for Kelly
11 Jan	Carlisle U	H	W	2-1	..	..	..	..	..	..	Armstrong	..	Radford1	..	..1	
18 Jan	Middlesbrough	A	D	0-0	..	..	..	..	..	..	..	..	Storey	..	..	
1 Feb	Liverpool	H	L		..	..	..	Matthews	..	..	..	Brady	..	Storey		
8 Feb	Wolverhampton W	A	L	0-1	..	..	..	Ross	..	..	..2	Brady	Radford	..	Storey	Ross for Ball
22 Feb	Derby Co	A	L	1-2	..	..	..	Storey	..	..	Brady	Ball	..1	..	Brady	
1 Mar	Everton	H	L	0-2	..	..	..	..	..	..	Ball	..1	..	..	..	
15 Mar	Birmingham C	H	D	1-1	..	..	Nelson	..	..	Matthews	..	..	..1	..	..	
18 Mar	Newcastle U	H	W	3-0	..	..	..	Rostron1	..	..	..	Hornsby	..1	..	..	
22 Mar	Burnley	A	D	3-3	..	..	..	Matthews	..	..	Rostron1	..2	..	..	..	Powling for Matthews
25 Mar	Luton T	A	L	0-2	..	..	..	Storey	..	..	..	Radford	Hornsby	..	..	
29 Mar	Stoke C	H	D	1-1	..	..	McNab	..	Kelly1	Matthews	..	Stapleton	Rostron	Hornsby	..	Brady for Stapleton
31 Mar	Sheffield U	H	W	1-0	..	..	Nelson	..	Mancini	..	Kelly	Hornsby	Kidd1	Armstrong		
8 Apr	Coventry C	H	W	2-0	..	..	..	..	..	..	..	..2	..		
12 Apr	Leeds U	H	L	1-2	..	..	..	..	..	..	..	..1	..		Brady for Nelson
19 Apr	Q P R	A	D	0-0	..	..	..	..	..	Ball	..	..			
23 Apr	Newcastle U	A	L	1-3	..	..	Matthews	..	..	Brady	..	..1	Rostron		Nelson for Kelly
26 Apr	Tottenham H	H	W	1-0	Barnett	..	Nelson	..	..	Simpson	Brady	..1	Armstrong		
28 Apr	West Ham U	A	L	0-1	..	Storey	..	Kelly	..	Matthews	..	..	Rostron		

FA Cup

Date	Opp	V	R	Score												Notes
4 Jan	York C (3)	H	D	1-1	Rimmer	Rice	McNab	Kelly1	Mancini	Powling	Storey	Ball	Armstrong	Kidd	Cropley	
7 Jan	York C (3R)	A	W	3-1	..	..	..	..	Simpson	Mancini	Armstrong	..	Radford	..3		
25 Jan	Coventry (4)	A	D	1-1	..	..	..	Storey	Mancini	Simpson	..1	..	George		Matthews for George
29 Jan	Coventry (4R)	H	W	3-0	..	..	..	Matthews1	..	..2	..	Storey		Brady for Radford
15 Feb	Leicester C (5)	H	D	0-0	..	..	..	Storey	..	..	..	Brady		
19 Feb	Leicester C (5R)	A	D	1-1	..	..	..	..	..1	Matthews		Brady for Matthews
24 Feb	Leicester C (5R)	A	W	1-0	..	..	..	..	..1	Matthews		Brady for Matthews
8 Mar	West Ham (6)	H	L	0-2	..	..	..	Matthews	..	..	Brady	Armstrong for Radford

Football League Cup

Date	Opp	V	R	Score												Notes
10 Sep	Leicester C (2)	H	D	1-1	Rimmer	Kelly	Simpson	Storey	Blockley	Mathews	Armstrong	George	Radford	Kidd1	Brady	
18 Sep	Leicester C (2R)	A	L	1-2	..	Simpson	Nelson	..	..	..	..	Kelly	..	..1	

League Appearances (Goals)

Armstrong G 24 – Ball A 30 (9) – Barnett G 2 – Blockley J 6 – Brady L 32 (3) – Cropley A 7 (1) – George C 10 (2) – Hornsby B 12 (3) – Kelly E 32 (1) – Kidd B 40 (19) – Mancini T 26 – McNab R 18 – Matthews J 20 – Nelson S 20 – Powling R 8 – Price D 1 – Radford J 29 (7) – Rice P 32 – Rimmer J 40 – Ross T 2 Rostron W 6 2 – Simpson P 40 – Stapleton F 1 – Storey P 37 – **Total 24 players (47)**

Position in League Table

	P	W	L	D	F:A	Pts	
Derby	42	21	10	11	67:49	53	1st
Arsenal	42	13	18	11	47:49	37	16th

SEASON 1975-1976 FOOTBALL LEAGUE (DIVISION 1)

Date	Opp	V	R	Score	1	2	3	4	5	6	7	8	9	10	11	Notes
16 Aug	Burnley	A	D	0-0	Rimmer	Rice	Nelson	Kelly	Mancini	O'Leary	Armstrong	Cropley	Hornsby	Kidd	Brady	
19 Aug	Sheffield U	A	W	3-1	..	..1	..	..	..	..	..	..	..	..1	..1	
23 Aug	Stoke C	H	L	0-1	..	..	..	..	..	..	..	..	..	..	..	
26 Aug	Norwich C	H	W	2-1	..	..	Storey	..1	..	..	..	..	Ball1	..	..	
30 Aug	Wolverhampton W	A	D	0-0	..	..	Nelson	..	..	..	Ball	..	Radford	..	..	
6 Sep	Leicester C	H	D	1-1	..	..	..	..	..	..	..	..	Stapleton1	..	..	
13 Sep	Aston Villa	A	L	0-2	..	..	..	..	..	..	..	..	..	..	..	
20 Sep	Everton	H	D	2-2	..	..	..	..	..	..	..	..	..1	..1	..	
27 Sep	Tottenham H	A	D	0-0	..	..	..	..	..	..	..	..	..	..	Rostron	Brady for Rostron
4 Oct	Manchester C	H	L	2-3	..	..	..	..	Simpson	..	..1	..1	..	..	Brady	Rostron for Kelly
11 Oct	Coventry C	H	W	5-0	..	..	..	Powling	..	..1	..2	..	..	..2	..	Rostron for Cropley
18 Oct	Manchester U	A	L	1-3	..	..	..	Kelly1	O'Leary	Simpson	..	..	..2	..		Powling for Kelly
25 Oct	Middlesbrough	H	W	2-1	..	..	..	..	..	..	..1	..1	..	..		
1 Nov	Newcastle U	A	L	0-2	..	..	..	..	..	..	Powling	..	..	..		
8 Nov	Derby Co	H	L	0-1	..	..	Storey	..	..	Powling	Cropley	..	Hornsby	..		
15 Nov	Birmingham C	A	L	1-3	..	..	..	Nelson	..	..	..1	..	Kidd	..		Matthews for Cropley
22 Nov	Manchester U	H	W	3-1	..	..	..	Nelson	..	opponents	..1	Armstrong1	..	..		
29 Nov	West Ham U	A	L	0-1	..	..	Nelson	Storey	..	..	..1	..	..	..		
2 Dec	Liverpool	A	D	2-2	..	..	..	Storey	Nelson	..	..1	..	..1	..		
6 Dec	Leeds U	H	L	1-2	..	..	Nelson	Storey	..	Armstrong	Ball	..	..1	..		
13 Dec	Stoke C	A	L	1-2	Barnett	..	..	..	..	..	..1	..	..1	..		
20 Dec	Burnley	H	W	1-0	Rimmer	..	Simpson	Kelly	Mancini	..	..	Radford1	..	..		Simpson for Nelson
26 Dec	Ipswich	A	L	0-2	..	..	Kelly	Storey	O'Leary	..	..	..	Stapleton	..		Stapleton for Brady
27 Dec	Q P R	H	W	2-0	..	..	Nelson	..	..	..	Stapleton	..1		
10 Jan	Aston Villa	H	D	0-0	..	..	..	Powling	..	Mancini	..	..		
17 Jan	Leicester C	A	L	1-2	..	..	..	Ross1	..	..	..	..		
31 Jan	Sheffield U	H	W	1-0	..	..	..	..	Mancini	Powling	..	..1		
7 Feb	Norwich C	A	L	1-3	..	..	..	Storey	..	Simpson	..	..	..1		Rostron for Nelson
18 Feb	Derby Co	A	L	0-2	..	..	Nelson	..	..	Powling	..	Radford	..		
21 Feb	Birmingham C	H	W	1-0	..	..	..	..	..	..	..	..	..1		Simpson for Brady
24 Feb	Liverpool	H	W	1-0	..	..	..	..	..	..	..	..1		
28 Feb	Middlesbrough	A	W	1-0	..	..	..	..	..	..	..	..1		
13 Mar	Coventry C	A	D	1-1	..	..	..	..	..1	..	..	..		
16 Mar	Newcastle U	H	D	0-0	..	..	..	..	..	..	..		
20 Mar	West Ham U	H	W	6-1	..	..	..	..	..1	..2	..3		Stapleton for Rice
27 Mar	Leeds U	A	L	0-3	..	..	..	..	..	..	..		
3 Apr	Tottenham H	H	L	0-2	..	..	..	..	..	..		
10 Apr	Everton	A	D	0-0	..	..	..	..	Cropley	..		
13 Apr	Wolverhampton W	H	W	2-1	..	..	..	..	..1	Rostron	Stapleton1	..1		
17 Apr	Ipswich T	H	L	1-2	..	..	..	O'Leary	Kidd1	Radford	..		
19 Apr	Q P R	A	L	1-2	..	..	..	..	..	Stapleton	..1		Armstrong for Radford
24 Apr	Manchester C	A	L	1-3	..	..	..	..	Mancini	..	Armstrong1	Stapleton	..		

FA Cup

Date	Opp	V	R	Score												Notes
3 Jan	Wolves (3)	A	L	0-3	Rimmer	Rice	Nelson	Storey	O'Leary	Powling	Armstrong	Ball	Stapleton	Kidd	Brady	

Football League Cup

Date	Opp	V	R	Score												Notes
9 Sep	Everton (2)	A	D	2-2	Rimmer	Rice	Nelson	Kelly	Mancini	O'Leary	Ball	Cropley1	Radford	Kidd	Brady	Stapleton1 for Mancini
23 Sep	Everton (2R)	H	L	0-1	..	..	..	..	..	..	..	Stapleton	..	Rostron	

Appearances (Goals)

Armstrong G 29 (4) – Ball A 39 (9) – Barnett J 1 – Brady L 42 (5) – Cropley A 20 (4) – Hornsby B 4 – Kelly E 17 (2) – Kidd B 37 (11) – Mancini T 26 (1) – Matthews J 1 – Nelson S 36 – O'Leary D 27 – Powling R 29 (1) – Radford J 15 (3) – Rice P 42 – Rimmer J 41 – Ross T 17 (1) – Rostron W 5 – Simpson P 9 – Stapleton F 25 (4) – Storey P 11 – Own goals 1 – **Total 21 players (47)**

Position in League Table

	P	W	L	D	F:A	Pts	
Liverpool	42	23	5	14	66:31	60	1st
Arsenal	42	13	19	10	47:53	36	17th

Abbreviations:

Appearances (goals) refer to League games only

Figures shown as '2' etc. refer to goals scored by individual players

* own-goal

SEASON 1976-1977 FOOTBALL LEAGUE (DIVISION 1)

Date	Opp		Res	Rimmer	Rice	Nelson	Ross	O'Leary	Simpson	Ball	Armstrong	Macdonald	Radford	Cropley	Substitutes
21 Aug	Bristol C	H L	0-1	Rimmer	Rice	Nelson	Ross	O'Leary	Simpson	Ball	Armstrong	Macdonald	Radford	Cropley	Storey for Cropley
25 Aug	Norwich C	A W	3-1	..	..	..1	..	..	..	..	..	..1	Stapleton1	Brady	
28 Aug	Sunderland	A D	2-2	..	..	..	..	..	..	..	Brady	..	..1	Armstrong	
4 Sep	Manchester C	H D	0-0	..	..	..	..	..	..	..	..	Cropley	..	Armstrong	Cropley for Stapleton
11 Sep	West Ham U	A W	2-0	..	..	..	..1	..	Howard	..	..	Macdonald	..1	..	Storey for O'Leary
18 Sep	Everton	H W	3-1	..	..	..	..	Howard	Powling	..	..1	Macdonald1	..1	..	
25 Sep	Ipswich T	A L	1-3	..	..	..	..	O'Leary	Howard	opponents	..1	..	..	..	Storey for Nelson
2 Oct	Q P R	H W	3-2	..	..1	..	..	..	..	..	..	..1	..	..	Radford for Stapleton
16 Oct	Stoke C	H W	2-0	..	..1	Storey	..	..	..	..1	..	..	..1	..	
20 Oct	Aston Villa	A L	1-5	..	..	..	..	Matthews	..	Matthews1	..	..	..1	..	
23 Oct	Leicester C	A L	1-4	..	..	Nelson	..	Simpson	..	..	..	..1	..1	..	
30 Oct	Leeds U	A L	1-2	..	..	..	..	O'Leary	Simpson	Ball	..	..1	..1	..	Storey for O'Leary
6 Nov	Birmingham C	H W	4-0	..	..	..1	..1	..	..	..	..	..1	..1	..1	
20 Nov	Liverpool	H D	1-1	..	..	..1	..	..	..	..	..	..	..	..	
27 Nov	Coventry C	A W	2-1	..	..	..	..	..	Howard	Storey	..	..1	..3	..	Matthews for Rice
4 Dec	Newcastle U	H W	5-3	..	..	..	..1	..	Simpson	..	..1	..2	..	..	Rostron for Stapleton
15 Dec	Derby Co	A D	0-0	..	..	..	..	..	..	..	..	..2	..	Rostron	
18 Dec	Manchester U	H W	3-1	..	..	Powling	..	..	Hudson	..	..	..1	..	Armstrong	
27 Dec	Tottenham H	A D	2-2	..	..1	Nelson	..	..	..	..	..	..3	..	..	
3 Jan	Leeds U	H D	1-1	..	..	..	..	..	..	..	..	..	..	Rostron	
15 Jan	Norwich C	H W	1-0	..	..	..	Storey	..	..	..	..	..	..	Howard	Matthews for O'Leary
18 Jan	Birmingham C	A D	3-3	..	..	..	Ross	Howard	..	Matthews	Hudson	..	Rostron	Powling for Howard
22 Jan	Bristol C	A L	0-2	..	..	..	..	Powling	..	Hudson	Brady1	..1	Armstrong	
5 Feb	Sunderland	H D	0-0	..	..	..	..	Howard	Powling	Brady	Hudson	..1	..	Nelson for Matthews
12 Feb	Manchester C	A L	0-1	..	..	Young	..	..	..	..	Matthews	..1	..	
15 Feb	Middlesbrough	A L	0-3	..	..	Nelson	Price	Young	Howard	..	Powling	..1	..	Price for Hudson
19 Feb	West Ham U	H L	2-3	..	..	..	Powling	..1	..	Hudson	..	..	..	
1 Mar	Everton	A L	1-2	..	..	..	..	..	O'Leary	..	..	Price1	Stapleton	Matthews for Powling
5 Mar	Ipswich T	H L	1-4	..	..	..	..	O'Leary2	Young	Rix1	Price	..	..	
8 Mar	W B A	H L	1-2	..	..	Matthews	Price	..	..	..	Hudson	..1	..	Brady for Rix
12 Mar	Q P R	A L	1-2	..	..	..	..	..	..	Brady	..	..1	..	
23 Mar	Stoke C	A D	1-1	..	..	..	..	..	..	..	..1	..1	..	Rix for Ross
2 Apr	Leicester C	H W	3-0	..	..	..	Ross	..	..	..	..1	..1	..1	
9 Apr	W B A	A W	2-0	..	..	Nelson1	Matthews	..	..	..	..1	..	..	Howard for O'Leary / Rix for Young
11 Apr	Tottenham H	H W	1-0	..	..	..	..1	..	..	..	..	..	..	Price for Matthews
16 Apr	Liverpool	A L	0-2	..	..	..	..	..	..	Rix	..	..1	..	Rix for Young
23 Apr	Coventry C	H W	2-0	..	..	..	..	..	..1	Hudson	..1	..1	
25 Apr	Aston Villa	H W	3-0	..	..	..	..	..						
30 Apr	Newcastle U	A W	2-0	..	..	..	..	..						
3 May	Derby Co	H D	0-0	..	..	..	..	..						
7 May	Middlesbrough	H D	1-1	..	..	..	..	..						
14 May	Manchester U	A L	2-3	..	..	..	..	..						

FA Cup

Date	Opp		Res	Rimmer	Rice	Nelson	Ross	O'Leary	Simpson	Hudson	Brady	Macdonald	Stapleton	Armstrong	Substitutes
8 Jan	Notts Co (3)	A W	1-0	Rimmer	Rice	Nelson	Ross1	O'Leary	Simpson	Hudson	Brady	Macdonald..2	Stapleton	Armstrong	Storey for Macdonald
29 Jan	Coventry C (4)	H W	3-1	..	..	..	..	..	..	..	Brady	Hudson	..1	Matthews for O'Leary
26 Feb	Middlesbrough (5)	A L	1-4	..	..	..	..	..						

Football League Cup

Date	Opp		Res	Rimmer	Rice	Nelson	Ross	O'Leary	Simpson	Ball	Brady	Macdonald	Stapleton	Armstrong	Substitutes
31 Aug	Carlisle U (2)	H W	3-2	Rimmer	Rice	Nelson	Ross2	O'Leary	Simpson	Ball	Brady	Macdonald1	Stapleton	Armstrong	
21 Sep	Blackpool (3)	A D	1-1	..	..	..	..	Powling	Howard	..	..	..	..1	
28 Sep	Blackpool (3R)	H D	0-0	..	..	..	..	O'Leary	..	..	..	..1	Storey for Nelson
5 Oct	Blackpool (3R)	H W	2-0	..	..	Storey	Matthews	..1	..	..	..	..1	
26 Oct	Chelsea (4)	H W	2-1	..	..	Nelson	Ross1	Simpson	..	..	..	..1	
1 Dec	Q P R (5)	A L	1-2	..	..	..	..	O'Leary	Simpson	..	..	..1	

Appearances (Goals)

Armstrong G 37 (2) – Ball A 14 (1) – Brady L 38 (5) – Cropley A 3 – Howard P 16 – Hudson A 19 – Macdonald M 41 (25) – Matthews J 17 (2) – Nelson S 32 (3) – O'Leary D 33 (2) – Powling R 12 – Price D 8 (1) – Radford J 2 – Rice P 42 – Rimmer J 42 – Rix G 7 (1) – Ross T 29 (4) – Rostron W 5 – Simpson P 19 – Stapleton F 40 (13) – Storey P 11 – Young W 14 (1) – Own goals 1 –
Total 22 players (64)

Position in League Table

	P	W	L	D	F:A	Pts	
Liverpool	42	23	8	11	62:33	57	1st
Arsenal	42	16	15	11	64:59	43	8th

SEASON 1977-1978 FOOTBALL LEAGUE (DIVISION 1)

Date	Opp		Res	Jennings	Rice	Nelson	Ross	Young	O'Leary	Powling	Brady	Macdonald	Stapleton	Rix	Substitutes
20 Aug	Ipswich T	A L	0-1	Jennings	Rice	Nelson	Ross	Young	O'Leary	Powling	Brady	Macdonald	Stapleton	Rix	Price for Brady
23 Aug	Everton	H W	1-0	..	..	..	Powling1	O'Leary	Young	Brady	Ross	..	..	..	
27 Aug	Wolverhampton W	A D	1-1	..	..	..	..1	Young	O'Leary	Ross	Brady	..	Price	..	
3 Sep	Nottingham F	H W	3-0	..	..	..	..	O'Leary	Young	Brady1	Ross	..	Stapleton2	..	
10 Sep	Aston Villa	A L	0-1	..	..	..	Hudson	..	..	..	..	..	..	..	
17 Sep	Leicester C	H W	2-1	..	..	..	Price	..	..	..	..	..1	..1	..	
24 Sep	Norwich C	A L	0-1	..	..1	..	..	..	Simpson	Matthew	..	..	..1	..	Walford for Matthews
1 Oct	West Ham U	H W	3-0	..	..1	..	..	..	..	Brady1	..	..	..1	..	Matthews for Ross
4 Oct	Liverpool	H D	0-0	..	..	..	..	..	Young	..	Matthews	..1	..	..	Matthews for Ross
8 Oct	Manchester C	A L	1-2	..	..	..	..	..	..	..	Hudson	..1	..	..	
15 Oct	Q P R	H W	1-0	..	..	..	..	..	Young	..	..	..1	..	..1	
22 Oct	Bristol C	A W	2-0	..	..	..	..	Young	O'Leary	..	Ross	..1	..	..	Heeley for Price
29 Oct	Birmingham C	H D	1-1	..	..1	..	..	..	O'Leary	..	Sunderland	..1	..	..	
5 Nov	Manchester U	A W	2-1	..	..	..	..	..	Young	..	Sunderland	..1	..	..	
12 Nov	Coventry C	H D	1-1	..	..	..	..	..	..	opponents	..1	Hudson	..1	..	
19 Nov	Newcastle U	A W	2-1	..	..	..	..	..	..	..	..1	Macdonald	..	..	
26 Nov	Derby Co	H L	1-3	..	..	..1	..	..	..	opponents	..	..	..	
3 Dec	Middlesbrough	A W	1-0	..	..	..	..	..	..	..1	..	..	..	
10 Dec	Leeds U	H D	1-1	..	..	..	..	..	..	..1	..	..	..	
17 Dec	Coventry C	A W	2-1	..	..	..	..	..	..	..	..	..	..2	..1	
26 Dec	Chelsea	H W	3-0	..	..	..	..1	..1	..	..	..	..	..	..1	Simpson for Stapleton
27 Dec	W B A	A W	3-1	..	..	..	..	..	..	..	..1	..1	..1	..	Simpson for Macdonald
31 Dec	Everton	A L	0-2	..	..	..	..	..	..	..	..	..	..	..	Simpson for Heeley
2 Jan	Ipswich T	H W	1-0	..	..	..	..	..1	..	..	..	..	Heeley	..	
14 Jan	Wolverhampton W	H W	3-1	..	..	..	..	..	..	..	..1	..	Stapleton1	..1	
21 Jan	Nottingham F	A L	0-2	..	..	..	..	..	..	..	..	Hudson	..	
4 Feb	Aston Villa	H L	0-1	..	..	..	..	..	..	..	..	Stapleton	..	
11 Feb	Leicester C	A D	1-1	..	..	..	..	..	..	..	..1	..	..	Walford for Rix
25 Feb	West Ham U	A D	2-2	..	..	..	..	..	..	..	..	..2	Hudson	Heeley for Macdonald
28 Feb	Norwich C	H D	0-0	..	..	..	..	..	..	..	..	Heeley	Walford for Price
4 Mar	Manchester C	H W	3-0	..	..	..	..	..1	..	..1	..	..1	Hudson	Hudson	Rix for Sunderland
18 Mar	Bristol C	H W	4-1	..	..	..	..	..1	..	..	..	Macdonald	..2	Hudson	
21 Mar	Birmingham C	A D	1-1	..	..	..	..	..	..	..1	..	..	..	
25 Mar	W B A	H W	4-0	..	..	..	..	..	..	..	Rix	..3	..	Rix for Sunderland
27 Mar	Chelsea	A D	0-0	..	..	..	..	..	..	..	..	..	..	
1 Apr	Manchester U	H W	3-1	..	..	..	..	..	..	..1	Hudson	..2	..	Matthews for Young
11 Apr	Q P R	A L	1-2	..	..	..	..	..	..	..1	Rix	..	Rix	Matthews for Young
15 Apr	Newcastle U	H W	2-1	..	..	..	..	..1	Walford	..1	Rix	..	Hudson	
22 Apr	Leeds U	A W	3-1	..	Devine	..	..	..	Young	opponents	..1	..1	Matthews	Matthews for Brady
25 Apr	Liverpool	A L	0-1	..	..	..	..	..	..	..	..	Hudson	
29 Apr	Middlesbrough	H W	1-0	..	..	..	..	..	Walford	Sunderland	..1	Sunderland	..1	Matthews for Brady
9 May	Derby Co	A L	0-3	..	Price	Matthews	Harvey	..	Walford	Heeley	..	Sunderland	..	

FA Cup

Date	Opp		Res	Jennings	Rice	Nelson	Price	O'Leary	Young	Brady	Sunderland	Macdonald	Stapleton	Rix	Substitutes
7 Jan	Sheffield U (3)	A W	5-0	Jennings	Rice	Nelson	Price	O'Leary1	Young	Brady	Sunderland	Macdonald2	Stapleton2	Rix	
28 Jan	Wolves (4)	H W	2-1	..	..	..	..	..	..	..1	Hudson	Stapleton2	
18 Feb	Walsall (5)	H W	4-1	..	..	..	..	..	..	..1	Hudson	
11 Mar	Wrexham (6)	A W	3-2	..	..	..	..	..1	..	..1	..1	Hudson
8 Apr	Orient (SF) (at Chelsea)	A W	3-0	..	..	..	..	..	..	Rix1	..2	..
6 May	Ipswich (F) (at Wembley)	A L	0-1	..	..	..	..	..	..	Sunderland	..	..	Rix for Brady

Football League Cup

Date	Opp		Res	Jennings	Rice	Nelson	Powling	O'Leary	Young	Brady	Ross	Macdonald	Stapleton	Rix
30 Aug	Manchester U (2)	H W	3-2	Jennings	Rice	Nelson	Powling	O'Leary	Young	Brady1	Ross	Macdonald2	Stapleton	Rix
25 Oct	Southampton (3)	H W	2-0	..	..	..	Price	Young	Simpson	..1	Hudson	..	..1

1974-1997

Date	Opponent		Res		GK	2	3	4	5	6	7	8	9	10	11	Notes
29 Nov	Hull C (4)	H W	5-1	..	..	..	..	O'Leary	Young	..1	Matthews2	..1	..1	..	Simpson for O'Leary
18 Jan	Manchester C (5)	A D	0-0	..	..	..	..	..	..	..	..	..	..	..	
24 Jan	Manchester C (5R)	H W	1-0	..	..	..	..	..	..	..1	..	..	..	..	
7 Feb	Liverpool (SF)	A L	1-2	..	..	..	..	..	..	..	Hudson	..1	..	..	Hudson for Matthews
14 Feb	Liverpool (SF)	H D	0-0	..	..	..	..	..	..	..	..	..	..	..	

Appearances (Goals)

Brady L 39 (9) – Devine J 3 – Harvey J 1 – Heeley M 4 – Hudson A 17 – Jennings P 42 – Macdonald M 39 (15) – Matthews J 5 – Nelson S 41 (1) – O'Leary D 41 (1) – Powling R 4 (2) – Price D 39 (5) – Rice P 38 (2) – Rix G 39 (2) – Ross T 10 – Simpson P 9 – Stapleton F 39 (13) – Sunderland A 23 (4) – Walford S 5 – Young W 35 (3) – Own goals 3 – **Total: 20 players (60)**

Position in League Table

	P	W	L	D	F:A	Pts	
Nottingham F	42	25	3	14	69:24	64	1st
Arsenal	42	21	11	10	60:37	52	5th

SEASON 1978-1979 FOOTBALL LEAGUE (DIVISION 1)

Date	Opponent		Res	GK	2	3	4	5	6	7	8	9	10	11	Notes
19 Aug	Leeds U	H D	2-2	Jennings	Devine	Nelson	Price	O'Leary	Young	Brady2	Sunderland	Macdonald	Stapleton	Harvey	Kosmina for Price
22 Aug	Manchester C	A D	1-1	Barron	Rice	..	..	..	..	Devine	..	..1	..	Walford	
26 Aug	Everton	A L	0-1	..	..	..	..	..	..	Brady	..	..	..	Devine	Walford for Devine
2 Sep	Q P R	H W	5-1	Jennings	..	..	..	..	..	..1	..	Walford	..2	Rix2	
9 Sep	Nottingham F	A L	1-2	..	..	..	..	..	..	..1	..	..	..	..	Harvey for O'Leary
16 Sep	Bolton W	H W	1-0	..	..	..	..	Walford	..	..	..	Stapleton1	Heeley	..	
23 Sep	Manchester U	H D	1-1	..	..	..	..1	O'Leary	..	..	..	..	Walford	..	Heeley for Walford
30 Sep	Middlesbrough	A W	3-2	..	..	..	..1	..1	..	..	..	Devine	..	..	Walford1 for Devine
7 Oct	Aston Villa	H D	1-1	..	..	..	..	..	..	..	..1	..	Walford	..	
14 Oct	Wolverhampton W	A L	0-1	..	..	..	..	..	..	..	..	..	..	..	Stead for Sunderland
21 Oct	Southampton	H W	1-0	..	..	..	Stead	Gatting	..	..1	Heeley	..	..	..	
28 Oct	Bristol C	A W	3-1	..	..	..	Price	O'Leary	..	..2	Gatting	..1	Heeley	..	Walford for O'Leary
4 Nov	Ipswich T	H W	4-1	..	..	..	..1	..	..	..	Sunderland	..3	Gatting	..	
11 Nov	Leeds U	A W	1-0	..	..	..	..	..	..	..	..	..	..1	..	
18 Nov	Everton	H D	2-2	..	..	..	..	..	..	..2	..	..	..	..	
25 Nov	Coventry C	A D	1-1	..	..	..	..	..	..	..	..	..1	Walford	..	Heeley for Price
2 Dec	Liverpool	H W	1-0	..	..	..	..1	..	..	..	..	..	Gatting	..	
9 Dec	Norwich C	A D	0-0	..	..	..	..	..	..	..	..	..	..	..	Walford for Nelson
16 Dec	Derby Co	H W	2-0	..	..	Walford	..1	..	..	..	..	..1	..	..	
23 Dec	Tottenham H	A W	5-0	..	..	..	..	..	..	..1	..3	..1	..	..	
26 Dec	W B A	H L	1-2	..	..	..	..	..	..	..1	..	..	..	..	
30 Dec	Birmingham C	H W	3-1	..	..	..1	..	..	..	..	..1	..1	..	..	
13 Jan	Nottingham F	H W	2-1	..	Walford	Nelson	Talbot	..	..	..	..1	..1	Price1	..	
3 Feb	Manchester U	A W	2-0	..	Rice	..	..	..	..	..	..2	..	..	..	
10 Feb	Middlesbrough	H D	0-0	..	..	..	..	..	..	..	..	..	..	..	
13 Feb	Q P R	A W	2-1	..	..	..	..	..	..	..1	..	..	..1	..	Walford for Young
24 Feb	Wolverhampton W	H L	0-1	..	..	Gatting	..	..	Walford	..	..	..	..	..	
3 Mar	Southampton	A L	0-2	..	..	Nelson	..	..	..	..	Gatting	..	..	..	Heeley for Gatting
10 Mar	Bristol C	H W	2-0	..	..	..	..	..	..	..	Heeley	..1	..	..1	McDermott for Heeley
17 Mar	Ipswich T	A L	0-2	..	..	..	..	..	..	..	Sunderland	..	..	..	Gatting for Price
24 Mar	Manchester C	H D	1-1	..	..	..	..	Young	Heeley	..	..1	..	..	..	McDermott for Young
26 Mar	Bolton W	A L	2-4	..	..	..	..	Walford	Gatting	..	..	..	..1	..	Heeley1 for Talbot
3 Apr	Coventry C	H D	1-1	..	..	..1	..	Young	..	..	..	..	Heeley	..	Walford for Heeley
7 Apr	Liverpool	A L	0-3	..	..	Walford	..	..	..	..	..	..	Price	..	Brignall for Stapleton
10 Apr	Tottenham H	H W	1-0	..	..	..	..	..	Brady	..	..	..1	..	..	
14 Apr	W B A	A D	1-1	..	..	Nelson	..	..	Walford	..1	..	..	..	..	
16 Apr	Chelsea	H W	5-2	..	..	..	..	..	..	..	..1	..2	..1	..	Gatting for Rix
21 Apr	Derby Co	A L	0-2	..	..	Walford	..	Gatting	Young	..	..	..1	..	..	
25 Apr	Aston Villa	A L	1-5	..	..	..	..	..	Devine	..	..	..1	..	..	
28 Apr	Norwich C	H D	1-1	..	Devine	Nelson	..	O'Leary	Walford1	..	..	..	..	..	
5 May	Birmingham C	A D	0-0	Barron	Rice	..	..	..	Young	..	..	..	..	..	Walford for Barron – Price in goal
14 May	Chelsea	A D	1-1	Jennings	..	..	..	..	..	..	Vaessen	Macdonald1	Devine	..	

FA Cup

Date	Opponent		Res												Notes
6 Jan	Sheffield W (3)	A D	1-1	Jennings	Rice	Walford	Price	O'Leary	Young	Brady	Sunderland1	Stapleton	Gatting	Rix	
9 Jan	Sheffield W (3R)	H D	1-1	..	..	Nelson	..	..	..	..1	..	..	..	..	
15 Jan	Sheffield W (3R) (at Leicester)	D	2-2	..	..	..	..	..	..	..1	..1	..	..	..	
17 Jan	Sheffield W (3R) (at Leicester)	D	3-3	Jennings	Rice	Nelson	Price	O'Leary	Young1	Brady	Sunderland	Stapleton2	Gatting	Rix	
22 Jan	Sheffield W (3R) (at Leicester)	W	2-0	..	..	..	..	..	..	..	..	..1	..1	..	Walford for Nelson
27 Jan	Notts County (4)	H W	2-0	..	..	..	Talbot1	..	..1	..	..	..	Price	..	
26 Feb	Nottingham F (5)	A W	1-0	..	..	..	..	..	Walford	..	..	..1	..	..	
19 Mar	Southampton (6)	A D	1-1	..	..	..	..	..	Young	..	..	..1	..	..	Walford for Price
21 Mar	Southampton (6R)	H W	2-0	..	..	..	..	..	..	..	..2	..1	..	..	Walford for Brady
31 Mar	Wolves (SF) (at Aston Villa)	W	2-0	..	..	..	..	..	..	Gatting	..1	..1	..	..	
12 May	Manchester U (F) (at Wembley)	W	3-2	..	..	..	..1	..	..	Brady	..1	..1	..	..	Walford for Price

Football League Cup

Date	Opponent		Res												
29 Aug	Rotherham U (2)	A L	1-3	Jennings	Rice	Nelson	Price	O'Leary	Young	Brady	Sunderland	Macdonald	Stapleton1	Rix	

UEFA Cup

Date	Opponent		Res												Notes
13 Sep	L'motive Leipzig (1)	H W	3-0	Jennings	Rice	Nelson	Price	Walford	Young	Brady	Sunderland1	Stapleton2	Harvey	Rix	Gatting for Brady, Heeley for Harvey
27 Sep	L'motive Leipzig (1)	A W	4-1	..	..	..	..	O'Leary	..	..	..1	..1	..2	Devine	Vaessen for Price, Walford for Young
18 Oct	Hajduk Split (2)	A L	1-2	..	..	..	..	..	..	..1	Heeley	..	Kosmina	..	
1 Nov	Hajduk Split (2)	H W	1-0	..	..	..	..	..	..1	..	Gatting	..	Heeley	..	Kosmina for Heeley, Vaessen for Kosmina
22 Nov	Red Star B'grade (3)	A L	0-1	..	..	..	..	..	..	Heeley	Sunderland	..	Walford	..	
6 Dec	Red Star B'grade (3)	H D	1-1	..	..	..	..	..	..	..	..	..1	..	Gatting	Kosmina for Heeley, Macdonald for Rix

Appearances (Goals)

Barron P 3 – Brady L 37 (13) – Brignall S 1 – Devine J 7 – Gatting S 21 (1) – Harvey J 1 – Heeley M 10 (1) – Jennings P 39 – Kosmina A 1 – McDermott B 2 – Macdonald M 4 (2) – Nelson S 33 (2) – O'Leary D 37 (2) – Price D 39 (8) – Rice P 39 (1) – Rix G 39 (3) – Stapleton F 41 (17) – Stead K 2 – Sunderland A 37 (9) – Talbot B 20 – Vaessen P 1 – Walford S 33 (2) – Young W 33 – **Total: 23 players (61)**

Position in League Table

	P	W	L	D	F:A	Pts	
Liverpool	42	30	4	8	85:16	68	1st
Arsenal	42	17	11	14	61:48	48	7th

SEASON 1979-1980 FOOTBALL LEAGUE (DIVISION 1)

Date	Opponent		Res	GK	2	3	4	5	6	7	8	9	10	11	Notes
18 Aug	Brighton & HA	A W	4-0	Jennings	Rice	Nelson	Talbot	O'Leary	Young	Brady1	Sunderland2	Stapleton1	Price	Rix	Hollins for Brady
21 Aug	Ipswich T	H L	0-2	..	..	..	..	..	..	..	..	..	Hollins	..	Hollins for Price
25 Aug	Manchester U	H D	0-0	..	..	..	..	..	..	Gatting	..	..	Hollins	..	Walford for Gatting
1 Sep	Leeds U	A D	1-1	..	..	..1	..	..	..	..	..	..	..	..	
8 Sep	Derby Co	A L	2-3	..	..	..	..	..	..	Brady	..	..	..	..	
15 Sep	Middlesbrough	H W	2-0	..	..	..	..	..	..	..	..1	..1	..	..	
22 Sep	Aston Villa	A D	0-0	Barron	..	..	..	..	..	..	..	..	..	..	
29 Sep	Wolverhampton W	H L	2-3	Jennings	..	..	..	Walford	..	..	..	..	..1	..1	Price for Talbot
6 Oct	Manchester C	H D	0-0	..	..	..	..	O'Leary	..	..	..	..	..	..	
9 Oct	Ipswich T	A W	2-1	..	Walford	..	..	..	..	..	..1	..	..	..1	
13 Oct	Bolton W	A D	0-0	..	Rice	..	..	..	..	..	..	..	..	..	
20 Oct	Stoke C	H D	0-0	..	..	..	..	..	..	..	..	..	..	..	
27 Oct	Bristol C	A W	1-0	..	..	..	..	..	..	..	..1	..	..	..	
3 Nov	Brighton & HA	H W	3-0	..	..	Devine	..	..	..	..1	..1	..	..	..1	Gatting for Sunderland
10 Nov	Crystal Palace	A L	0-1	..	..	..	..	..	..	..	Gatting	..	Price	..	Walford for Devine
17 Nov	Everton	H W	2-0	..	..	..	..	..	..	..	Vaessen	..2	..	..	Gatting for Brady
24 Nov	Liverpool	H D	0-0	..	..	..	..	..	Gatting	..	Sunderland	..	..	..	
1 Dec	Nottingham F	A D	1-1	..	..	..	..	..	..	Walford	..	..	..	..	Gatting for Nelson
8 Dec	Coventry C	H W	3-1	..	..	..	..	..1	..	Brady	..1	..1	Hollins	..	
15 Dec	W B A	A D	2-2	..	..	..	..1	..	..	..	..	..1	..	..	
21 Dec	Norwich C	H D	1-1	..	..	..	..	..	..	..	..	..1	..	..	McDermott for Nelson

Date	Opponent		Res	1	2	3	4	5	6	7	8	9	10	11	Notes
26 Dec	Tottenham H	H	W 1-0	..	..	Rice	..	..	Young	..	..1	..	..	..	
29 Dec	Manchester U	A	L 0-3	..	..	..	..	..	..	..	..	..	..	..	
1 Jan	Southampton	A	W 1-0	..	..	..	..	Walford	..1	Gatting	..	..	..	..	Walford for O'Leary
12 Jan	Leeds U	H	L 0-1	..	Rice	Nelson	..	..	..	Brady	..	..	..	..	
19 Jan	Derby Co	H	W 2-0	..	..	..	..	..	..1	..1	..	..	Price	..	
9 Feb	Aston Villa	H	W 3-1	..	..	..	..	O'Leary	..	..1	..	..2	..	..1	
23 Feb	Bolton W	H	W 2-0	..	..	..	..	..	..	..1	..	..1	..	..	Vaessen for Rice
1 Mar	Stoke C	A	W 3-2	..	Devine	..	..	..	..	..1	Vaessen	..1	..1	..	
11 Mar	Bristol C	H	D 0-0	..	..	..	..	..	..	..	Vaessen	..	..	..	
15 Mar	Manchester C	A	W 3-0	..	..	..	..	..	..	..2	Sunderland	..1	..	..	Gatting for Stapleton
22 Mar	Crystal Palace	H	L 1-1	..	..	..	..	..	..	..1	Sunderland	..	..	..	
28 Mar	Everton	A	W 1-0	Barron	Rice	..	..	..	..	Gatting1	..	Vaessen	..	..	
2 Apr	Norwich C	A	D 1-2	Jennings	Devine	..	..	..	..	Brady	..	Stapleton	..	..1	Vaessen for Nelson
5 Apr	Southampton	H	D 1-1	..	..	..	Walford	..	..	..	..	..	..	..	Vaessen for Price
7 Apr	Tottenham H	A	W 2-1	Barron	Rice	..	..	..	..	Devine	Vaessen1	Hollins	Davis		Sunderland1 for Brady
19 Apr	Liverpool	A	D 1-1	Jennings	..	..	..	..1	..	Gatting	Sunderland	Stapleton	Price	Hollins	Vaessen for Stapleton
26 Apr	W B A	H	D 1-1	Barron	..	Devine	..	..	Walford	Brady	..1	Hollins	Vaessen		Gatting for Young
3 May	Coventry C	A	W 1-0	..	..	Nelson	..	..	..	Gatting	Vaessen1	Price	Hollins		Davis for Price
5 May	Nottingham F	H	D 0-0	Jennings	Devine	..	..	O'Leary	..	Brady	Vaessen	Stapleton	Rix		Hollins for Stapleton
16 May	Wolverhampton W	A	W 2-1	..	Rice	..	..	..	Walford1	Sunderland	..1	..	..		Vaessen for Price
19 May	Middlesbrough	A	L 0-5	..	..	..	..	..	..	..	..	..	..		Vaessen for Walford

FA Cup

Date	Opponent		Res	1	2	3	4	5	6	7	8	9	10	11	Notes
5 Jan	Cardiff C (3)	A	D 0-0	Jennings	Rice	Devine	Talbot	Walford	Young	Gatting	Sunderland	Stapleton	Hollins	Rix	
8 Jan	Cardiff C (3R)	H	W 2-1	..	..	Nelson	..	..	..	..	..2	..	..	..	
26 Jan	Brighton & HA (4)	H	W 2-0	..	..	..1	..1	O'Leary	..	Brady	..	..	Price	..	
5 Feb	Bolton W (5)	A	D 1-1	..	..	..	..	..	..	..	..1	..	..	..	
19 Feb	Bolton W (5R)	H	W 3-0	..	..	..	..	..	..	..2	..1	..	..	..	
8 Mar	Watford (6)	A	W 2-1	..	..	Devine	..	..	..	..	..2	..	..	..	Gatting for Sunderland
12 Apr	Liverpool (SF) (at Sheffield W)		D 0-0	..	..	Rice	..	..	..	..	..	..	..	..	Walford for Nelson
16 Apr	Liverpool (SFR) (at Aston Villa)		D 1-1	..	..	..	Walford	..	..	..	..1	..	..	..	
28 Apr	Liverpool (SFR) (at Aston Villa)		D 1-1	..	..	..	Devine	..	..	..	..1	..	..	..	
1 May	Liverpool (SFR) (at Coventry)		W 1-0	..	..	..	..1	..	..	..	..	..	..	..	
10 May	West Ham U (F) (at Wembley)		L 0-1	..	..	..	..	..	..	..	..	..	..	..	Nelson for Devine

Football League Cup

Date	Opponent		Res	1	2	3	4	5	6	7	8	9	10	11	Notes
29 Aug	Leeds (2)	A	D 1-1	Jennings	Rice	Nelson	Talbot	O'Leary	Young	Brady	Sunderland	Stapleton1	Hollins	Rix	
4 Sep	Leeds (2R)	H	W 7-0	..	..	..1	..	..	..	..2	..3	..1	..	..	
25 Sep	Southampton (3)	H	W 2-1	..	..	..	..	Walford	..	..	..1	..	..	..	
30 Oct	Brighton & HA (4)	A	D 0-0	..	..	..	..	O'Leary	..	..	..	..	..	..	Gatting for Rice
13 Nov	Brighton & HA (4R)	H	W 4-0	..	..	Devine	..	..	..	..	Vaessen2	..2	Price	..	
4 Dec	Swindon T (5)	H	D 1-1	..	..	..	..	Walford	..	Gatting	Sunderland1	..	..	..	Hollins for Price
11 Dec	Swindon T (5R)	A	L 3-4	..	..	..	Walford	..	..1	Young	Brady2	..	Hollins	..	

FA Charity Shield

Date	Opponent		Res	1	2	3	4	5	6	7	8	9	10	11	Notes
11 Aug	Liverpool (at Wembley)		L 1-3	Jennings	Rice	Nelson	Talbot	O'Leary	Walford	Brady	Sunderland1	Stapleton	Price	Rix	Young for Nelson, Hollins for Price

European Cup Winners Cup

Date	Opponent		Res	1	2	3	4	5	6	7	8	9	10	11	Notes
19 Sep	Fenerbahce (1)	H	W 2-0	Jennings	Rice	Nelson	Talbot	O'Leary	Young1	Brady	Sunderland1	Stapleton	Hollins	Rix	
3 Oct	Fenerbahce (1)	A	D 0-0	..	..	..	..	..	..	..	..	..	..	..	
24 Oct	Magdeburg (2)	H	W 2-1	..	..	..	..	..	..1	..	..1	..	..	..	
7 Nov	Magdeburg (2)	A	D 2-2	..	..	Devine	..	..	..1	Gatting	..	..	..	..	Price1 for Hollins, Walford for Nelson
5 Mar	IFK Gothenburg (3)	H	W 5-1	..	..	..	..	..	..1	..1	Sunderland2	..	Price1	..	Hollins for Brady, McDermott for Sunderland
19 Mar	IFK Gothenburg (3)	A	D 0-0	..	..	..	..	..	..	..	Vaessen	..	..	..	
9 Apr	Juventus (SF)	H	D 1-1	..	..	..	Walford	..	opponents	..	Sunderland	..	..	..	Vaessen for Devine, Rice for O'Leary
23 Apr	Juventus (SF)	A	W 1-0	..	Rice	Devine	..	..	..	..	..	..	..	..	Vaessen1 for Price, Hollins for Talbot
14 May	Valencia (F) (at Brussels)		D 0-0*	..	..	Nelson	..	..	..	..	..	..	..	..	Hollins for Price

*lost 4-5 on penalties

Appearances (Goals)

Barron P 5 – Brady L 34 (7) – Davis P 2 – Devine J 20 – Gatting S 14 (1) – Hollins J 26 (1) – Jennings P 37 – McDermott B 1 – Nelson S 35 (2) – O'Leary D 34 (1) – Price D 22 (1) – Rice P 26 – Rix G 38 (4) – Stapleton F 39 (14) – Sunderland A 37 (14) – Talbot B 42 (1) – Vaessen P 14 (2) – Walford S 19 (1) – Young W 38 (3) – **Total 19 players (52)**

Position in League Table

	P	W	L	D	F:A	Pts	
Liverpool	42	25	7	10	81:30	60	1st
Arsenal	42	18	8	16	52:36	52	4th

SEASON 1980-1981 FOOTBALL LEAGUE (DIVISION 1)

Date	Opponent		Res	1	2	3	4	5	6	7	8	9	10	11	Notes
16 Aug	W B A	A	W 1-0	Jennings	Devine	Sansom	Talbot	O'Leary	Young	Vaessen	Price	Stapleton1	Hollins	Rix	
19 Aug	Southampton	H	D 1-1	..	..	..	..	..	..	Hollins	Vaessen	Price	Stapleton1	..	McDermott for Talbot
23 Aug	Coventry C	A	L 1-3	..	..	..	..	..	..	..	Sunderland	Stapleton1	Price	..	Rice for Price
30 Aug	Tottenham H	H	W 2-0	..	..	..	..	..	..	..	..	..1	..1	..	
6 Sep	Manchester C	A	D 1-1	..	..	..	..	..	..1	..	..	..	..	..	
13 Sep	Stoke C	H	W 2-0	..	..	..	..1	..	..	..	..1	..	..	..	
20 Sep	Middlesbrough	A	L 1-2	Wood	..	..	..	..	..	..	..1	..	..	..	
27 Sep	Nottingham F	H	W 1-0	..	..	..	..	..	..	..	..	..	Gatting	..1	
4 Oct	Leicester C	H	W 1-0	..	..	..	..	..	Walford	..	..	..1	..	..	
7 Oct	Birmingham C	A	L 1-3	..	..	..	..	..	..	..	..1	..	..	..	
11 Oct	Manchester U	A	D 0-0	..	..	..	..	..	..	..	..	..	..	..	
18 Oct	Sunderland	H	D 2-2	..	..	..	..	..	..	..1	..	..	..1	..	McDermott for Talbot
21 Oct	Norwich C	H	W 3-1	..	..	..	..1	..1	..	..	..	..	..	..	McDermott1 for Hollins
25 Oct	Liverpool	A	D 1-1	..	..	..	..	..	..	..	..	..1	Price	McDermott1	Rice for Price
1 Nov	Brighton & HA	H	W 2-0	..	..	..	..	..	..	..	..	..1	..	..1	
8 Nov	Leeds U	A	W 5-0	..	..	..	..	..	..	..2	..1	Gatting1	McDermott	..1	
11 Nov	Southampton	A	L 1-3	..	..	..	..	..	..	..	..	McDermott	Gatting	..	Price for Gatting
15 Nov	W B A	H	D 2-2	Jennings	..	..	..	O'Leary	..	opponents	..1	Stapleton	..	..	Gatting for Sanson
22 Nov	Everton	H	W 2-1	..	..	..	..	..	Walford	..	..1	..	McDermott1	..	Gatting for Sanson
29 Nov	Aston Villa	A	D 1-1	..	..	..	..	..	Walford	Young	..	..	Gatting	..	Vaessen for Hollins
6 Dec	Wolverhampton W	H	D 1-1	..	..	..	..	..	..	..	McDermott	..	..1	..	Vaessen for Gatting
13 Dec	Sunderland	A	L 0-2	..	..	..	..	..	..	Price	..	..	..	Davis	Vaessen for Gatting
20 Dec	Manchester U	H	W 2-1	..	..	..	..	..	..	Vaessen1	..	..	..	Rix1	
26 Dec	Crystal Palace	A	D 2-2	..	..	..	..	..	..	Hollins	Vaessen	..1	McDermott1	Gatting	
27 Dec	Ipswich T	H	D 1-1	..	..	..	..	..	..	Sunderland1	Gatting	..	..	..	
10 Jan	Everton	A	W 2-1	..	..	..	Davis	..	..	Vaessen1	..	..1	McDermott	..	Price for Hollins
17 Jan	Tottenham H	A	L 0-2	..	..	..	McDermott	..	..	Sunderland	..	..	Rix		
31 Jan	Coventry C	H	D 2-2	..	Hollins	..	Talbot1	..	..	McDermott	..	..1	..	..	
7 Feb	Stoke C	A	D 1-1	..	..	..	..	O'Leary	..	..	..	..1	..	..	
21 Feb	Nottingham F	A	L 1-3	..	Devine	..	..	..	..	..	..	..1	..	..	Devine for Gatting
24 Feb	Manchester C	H	W 2-0	..	Devine	..	..	..1	..	Hollins	..1	..	..	..	
28 Feb	Middlesbrough	H	D 2-2	..	..	..	..	..	Walford	..	..	..1	..	..	McDermott for Sunderland / Price for Hollins
7 Mar	Leicester C	A	L 0-1	..	..	..	..	..	Young	..	..	..	..	..	
21 Mar	Norwich C	A	D 1-1	..	..	..	..	..1	..	Nicholas	..	..	McDermott	..	
28 Mar	Liverpool	H	W 1-0	..	..	..	..	..	..	Hollins	..1	..	Nicholas	..	Davis for Hollins
31 Mar	Birmingham C	H	W 2-1	..	..	..	..	..1	..	Davis	..	..	..	..	McDermott for Devine
4 Apr	Brighton & HA	A	W 1-0	..	..	..	..	..	..	..	..	Hollins1	..	..	
11 Apr	Leeds U	H	D 0-0	..	..	..	..	..	..	Hollins	..	Nicholas	Davis		McDermott for Hollins
18 Apr	Ipswich T	A	W 2-0	..	..	..1	..	..	..	..	..	..1	..	..	
20 Apr	Crystal Palace	H	W 3-2	..	..	..	..	..	..1	..	..1	..	..	..1	McDermott for Sunderland
25 Apr	Wolverhampton W	A	W 2-1	..	..	..	..	..	..	opponents	McDermott	..1	..	..	
2 May	Aston Villa	H	W 2-0	..	Hollins	..	..	..	..	..	McDermott1	Sunderland	..	..	Nelson for Talbot

FA Cup

Date	Opponent	V	R	Score											Substitute
3 Jan	Everton (3)	A	L	0-2	Jennings	Devine	Sansom	Talbot	O'Leary	Young	Hollins	Sunderland	Stapleton	Gatting	Rix	McDermott for Talbot

Football League Cup

Date	Opponent	V	R	Score											Substitute
26 Aug	Swansea (2)	A	D	1-1	Jennings	Devine	Sansom	Talbot	O'Leary	Young	Hollins	Sunderland	Stapleton1	Price	Rix	
2 Sep	Swansea (2R)	H	W	3-1	..	..	..	..	Walford1	..	..1	..1	..1	..	..	
22 Sep	Stockport Co (3)	A	W	3-1	Wood	..	..	..	O'Leary	..	..1	..1	..	..		

Appearances (Goals)

Davis P 10 (1) – Devine J 39 – Gatting S 23 (3) – Hollins J 38 (5) – Jennings P 31 – McDermott B 23 (5) – Nelson S 1 – Nicholas P 8 (1) – O'Leary D 24 (1) – Price D 12 (1) – Rice P 2 – Rix G 35 (5) – Sansom K 42 (3) – Stapleton F 40 (14) – Sunderland A 34 (7) – Talbot B 40 (7) – Vaessen P 7 (2) – Walford S 20 – Wood G 11 – Young W 40 (4) – Own goals 2 – **Total 20 players (61)**

Position in League Table

	P	W	L	D	F:A	Pts	
Aston Villa	42	26	8	8	72:40	60	1st
Arsenal	42	19	8	15	61:45	53	3rd

SEASON 1981-1982 FOOTBALL LEAGUE (DIVISION 1)

Date	Opponent	V	R	Score											Substitute
29 Aug	Stoke C	H	L	0-1	Jennings	Devine	Sansom	Talbot	O'Leary	Young	Davis	Sunderland	McDermott	Nicholas	Rix	Vaessen for Devine
2 Sep	W B A	A	W	2-0	..	..	..	..1	..	..	..	..1	..	..	..	
5 Sep	Liverpool	A	L	0-2	..	..	..	..	..	..	Hollins	..	..	..	..	Davis for Nicholas
12 Sep	Sunderland	H	D	1-1	..	Hollins	..	..	..	..	Davis	..1	..	..	..	
19 Sep	Leeds U	A	D	0-0	..	..	..	..	..	..	..	..	..	..	..	Devine for Nicholas
22 Sep	Birmingham C	H	W	1-0	..	Devine	..	..1	..	..	..	..	..	Hollins	..	
26 Sep	Manchester U	H	D	0-0	..	..	..	..	..	..	Hollins	..	Hawley	Nicholas	Davis	
3 Oct	Notts Co	A	L	1-2	..	Hollins	..	..	..	..	Davis	..	..1	..	Rix	McDermott for Hawley
10 Oct	Swansea C	A	L	0-2	..	Devine	..	..	..	..	..	..	..	..	Hollins	
17 Oct	Manchester C	H	W	1-0	..	Hollins	..	..	..	Whyte	McDermott	..	Meade1	..	Rix	
24 Oct	Ipswich T	A	L	1-2	..	..	..	..	..	Young	Davis	..	..	..	..	
31 Oct	Coventry C	H	W	1-0	..	..	..	..	opponents	Whyte	McDermott	Vaessen	Hawley	..	..	
7 Nov	Aston Villa	A	W	2-0	..	Devine	..	..1	..	..	Hollins	..	Davis	..	..1	
21 Nov	Nottingham F	A	W	2-1	..	..	..	..1	..	..	..	Sunderland1	..	..	..	
28 Nov	Everton	H	W	1-0	..	..	..	..	..	..	..	..	..	..	..	McDermott1 for Devine
5 Dec	West Ham U	A	W	2-1	..	Robson	..	..	..	..1	..1	..	..	..	..	
20 Jan	Stoke C	A	W	1-0	Wood	..	..	..	..	..	..	..1	..	..	..	
23 Jan	Southampton	A	L	1-3	..	..	..	..1	..	..	..	..	..	..	..	McDermott for O'Leary
26 Jan	Brighton & HA	H	D	0-0	..	..	..	..	Hollins	..	McDermott	..	..	..	..	Meade for Davis
30 Jan	Leeds U	H	W	1-0	..	..	Hollins	..	O'Leary	..	Vaessen1	..	..	..	..	
2 Feb	Wolverhampton W	H	W	2-1	..	..	..	..	..	..	..1	..	..	..	..1	Hawley for Sunderland
6 Feb	Sunderland	A	D	0-0	..	..	..	..	..	..	..	..	..	..	..	
13 Feb	Notts Co	H	W	1-0	..	..	..	..	..	..	..	..	..	..	..	Meade1 for Nicholas
16 Feb	Middlesbrough	H	W	1-0	..	..	..	..	..	..	..	..	..	..1	..	Meade for Nicholas
20 Feb	Manchester U	A	D	0-0	..	..	..	..	..	..	..	..	..	..	..	Meade for Vaessen
27 Feb	Swansea C	H	L	0-2	..	..	..	..	..	..	..	..	..	..	..	Meade for Vaessen
6 Mar	Manchester C	A	D	0-0	..	..	..	..	..	..	Gorman	..	..	Robson	..	
13 Mar	Ipswich T	H	W	1-0	..	..	..	..	..	..	..	..	..	..	..	
16 Mar	W B A	H	D	2-2	..	..	..	..	..	..	..	..1	..	..1	..	Meade1 for Gorman
20 Mar	Coventry C	A	L	0-1	..	..	..	..	Devine	..	..	..	..	..	..	Meade for Gorman
27 Mar	Aston Villa	H	W	4-3	..	..	..	..	O'Leary	..	Meade1	..1	..	..2	..	
29 Mar	Tottenham H	A	D	2-2	..	..	..	..	..	..	..	..2	..	..	..	Nicholas for Davis
3 Apr	Wolverhampton W	A	D	1-1	..	..	..	..	..	..	..	..	..1	..	..	Hawley for Meade
10 Apr	Brighton & HA	A	L	1-2	..	..	..	..1	..	..	..	..	..	..	..	
12 Apr	Tottenham H	H	L	1-3	..	..	..	..1	..	..	..	Hawley1	Nicholas	..	Nicholas Rix	McDermott for Robson
17 Apr	Nottingham F	H	W	2-0	..	..	..	..1	..	..	..	..	Davis	..	..1	
24 Apr	Everton	A	L	1-2	..	..	..	..	..	..	Hawley	Sunderland	..1	..	..1	Nicholas for Hollins
1 May	West Ham U	H	W	2-0	..	..	..	..	..	..	..	..1	..	..1	..	
4 May	Birmingham C	A	W	1-0	..	..	..	..	..	..1	..	..	..	..	..	
8 May	Middlesbrough	A	W	3-1	..	..	..	..1	..	..	..	..	..1	..	..1	Nicholas for Davis
11 May	Liverpool	H	D	1-1	..	..	..	..	..	..	Nicholas	..1	Hawley	..	..	Meade for Hawley
15 May	Southampton	H	W	4-1	..	..	..	..	..	..	Davis2	..	..1	..	..1	

Appearances (Goals)

Davis P 38 (4) – Devine J 11 – Gorman P 4 – Hawley J 14 (3) – Hollins J 40 (1) – Jennings P 16 – McDermott 13 (1) – Meade R 16 (4) – Nicholas P 31 – O'Leary D 40 (1) – Rix G 39 (9) – Robson S 20 (2) – Sansom K 42 – Sunderland A 38 (11) – Talbot B 42 (7) – Vaessen P 10 (2) – Whyte C 32 (2) – Wood G 26 – Young W 10 – Own goals 1 – **Total 19 players (48)**

Position in League Table

	P	W	L	D	F:A	Pts	
Liverpool	42	26	7	9	80:32	87	1st
Arsenal	42	20	11	11	48:37	71	5th

SEASON 1982-1983 FOOTBALL LEAGUE (DIVISION 1)

Date	Opponent	V	R	Score											Substitute
28 Aug	Stoke C	A	L	1-2	Wood	Hollins	Sansom	Talbot	O'Leary	Whyte	Robson	Sunderland1	Chapman	Woodcock	Rix	Davis for Sunderland
31 Aug	Norwich C	H	D	1-1	..	..	..	..	Davis	..	..	Davis	..	..1	..	Devine for Sansom
4 Sep	Liverpool	H	L	0-2	..	..	Devine	..	O'Leary	..	..	Davis	..	..	..	
7 Sep	Brighton & HA	A	L	0-1	..	..	..	..	..	..	..	..	..	..	..	Hawley for Talbot
11 Sep	Coventry C	A	W	2-0	..	..	Sansom	..	..	..	Davis	Robson	..1	..1	..	
18 Sep	Notts Co	H	W	2-0	..	..1	..	..	..	..	..	..	..	..	..1	
25 Sep	Manchester U	A	D	0-0	..	..	..	..	..	..	..	..	..	..	..	
2 Oct	West Ham U	H	L	2-3	..	..	..	..1	..	..	..1	Sunderland	..	..	..	
9 Oct	Ipswich T	A	W	1-0	..	..	..	..	..	..	..	..	Robson	..1	..	Hawley for Hollins
16 Oct	W B A	H	W	2-0	..	Devine	..	..	..	..	..	..	..1	..	..	
23 Oct	Nottingham F	A	L	0-3	..	Hollins	..	..	..	..	..	..	..	..	..	Chapman for Robson
30 Oct	Birmingham C	H	D	0-0	..	O'Shea	..	..	..	..	..	..	..	..	..	Chapman for Woodcock
6 Nov	Luton T	A	D	2-2	..	..	..	..1	..	..	..	..	..	..	..1	
13 Nov	Everton	H	D	1-1	Jennings	..	..	..	..	..	..	Chapman	..	..	..	McDermott1 for O'Leary
20 Nov	Swansea C	A	W	2-1	Wood	..	..	..	..	..	..	Sunderland	..	..1	..	Chapman1 for Woodcock
27 Nov	Watford	H	L	2-4	..	..	..	..1	..	..	..	..	..	..	..1	
4 Dec	Manchester C	A	L	1-2	..	..	..	..	..	..	..	..	Chapman	Robson	..	McDermott1 for O'Shea
7 Dec	Aston Villa	H	W	2-1	..	Hollins	..	..	..	..1	..	..	Robson	Woodcock1	..	
18 Dec	Sunderland	A	L	0-3	Jennings	..	..	..	..	..	..	..	..	..	..	Chapman for Davis
27 Dec	Tottenham H	H	W	2-0	..	..	..	..	..	Robson	..	..1	Nicholas	..1	..	
28 Dec	Southampton	A	D	2-2	..	..	..	..	..	..	..	..	..	..1	..	Chapman1 for Woodcock
1 Jan	Swansea C	H	W	2-1	..	..	..	..	..	..	..	..1	Petrovic	..1	..	Chapman for Sunderland
3 Jan	Liverpool	A	L	1-3	..	..	..	..1	..	..	Nicholas	Chapman	..1	..	..	Talbot for O'Leary
15 Jan	Stoke C	H	W	3-0	..	..1	..	Whyte	..	Nicholas	Davis	Sunderland	..1	..	..1	Talbot for Davis
22 Jan	Notts Co	A	L	0-1	..	..	..	Robson	..	..	..	..	..	..	..	
5 Feb	Brighton & HA	H	W	3-1	..	..	..	..	..	..	Talbot	Meade2	..	Davis	..1	
26 Feb	W B A	A	D	0-0	..	Key	..	..	Whyte	..	Devine	Davis	Meade	Woodcock	..	Talbot for Rix
5 Mar	Nottingham F	H	D	0-0	..	Hollins	..	..	..	..	Talbot	..	Sunderland	..	..	Meade for Sunderland
15 Mar	Birmingham C	A	L	1-2	..	..	..	..	..	..	Petrovic	..	..1	..	..	Talbot for Petrovic
19 Mar	Luton T	H	W	4-1	..	O'Leary	..	..	..	..	Talbot	..1	..	..3	..	Meade for O'Leary
22 Mar	Ipswich T	H	D	2-2	Wood	Hollins	..	Devine	..1	..	..	..	..1	..1	..	
26 Mar	Everton	A	W	3-2	..	Robson1	..	Whyte	O'Leary	..	..	..	..1	..1	..	
2 Apr	Southampton	H	D	0-0	..	Kay	..	..	..	..	..	..	..	..	..	
4 Apr	Tottenham H	A	L	0-5	..	Robson	..	..	..	..	..	..	..	..	..	Petrovic for Whyte
9 Apr	Coventry C	H	W	2-1	..	..	..	..	Kay	..	..	..	Petrovic	..1	..1	Chapman for Nicholas
20 Apr	Norwich C	A	L	1-3	..	Kay	..	Talbot	O'Leary	Whyte	McDermott	Hill	Davis1	Chapman	..	Hollins for Rix
23 Apr	Manchester C	H	W	3-0	Jennings	..	..	Whyte	..	Nicholas	Talbot3	Davis	McDermott	Woodcock	Hill	Hawley for Woodcock
30 Apr	Watford	A	L	1-2	..	..	..	..	..	..	..	..	..1	Hawley	..	Petrovic for Hawley
2 May	Manchester U	H	W	3-0	..	Devine	..	..	..1	..	..2	..	..	..	..	Petrovic for Hawley
7 May	Sunderland	H	L	0-1	..	..	..	..	..	..	..	..	Petrovic	McDermott	..	Hawley for Devine
10 May	West Ham U	A	W	3-1	..	Kay	..	..1	..	..	..	..	..1	..	..	
14 May	Aston Villa	A	L	1-2	..	Devine	..	..	..	..	..	..	..1	McDermott	Petrovic	

FA Cup

Date	Opponent	V	R	Score											Substitute
8 Jan	Bolton W (3)	H	W	2-1	Jennings	Hollins	Sansom	Talbot	O'Leary	Robson	Davis1	Sunderland	Nicholas	Woodcock	Rix1	
29 Jan	Leeds U (4)	H	D	1-1	..	..	..	Robson	..	Nicholas	Talbot	..1	Petrovic	..	..	
2 Feb	Leeds U (4R)	A	D	1-1	..	..	..	..	..	..	..	..	..	..	..1	Davis for Sunderland

Date	Opponent	V	Res	Score	1	2	3	4	5	6	7	8	9	10	11	Notes
9 Feb	Leeds U (4R)	H	W	2-1	..	..	..	..	..	..	Meade	..	..	..1		
19 Feb	Middlesbrough (5)	A	D	1-1	..	..	..	..	Whyte	..	..	Davis	..	..1		
28 Feb	Middlesbrough (5R)	H	W	3-2	..	..	..	..	..	..1	..1	Sunderland	..1			
12 Mar	Aston Villa (6)	H	W	2-0	..	..	..	..	..	Petrovic1	..	..	..1			
16 Apr	Manchester U (SF) (at Aston Villa)		L	1-2	Wood	Robson	..	Whyte	O'Leary	Hollins	Talbot	..	Petrovic	..1		Chapman for Robson

Milk Cup

Date	Opponent	V	Res	Score	1	2	3	4	5	6	7	8	9	10	11	Notes
5 Oct	Cardiff C (2)	H	W	2-1	Wood	Hollins1	Sansom	Talbot	O'Leary	Whyte	Davis1	Sunderland	Robson	Woodcock	Rix	
26 Oct	Cardiff C (2)	A	W	3-1	..	..	..	..	..	..1	..1	..1	..1			
9 Nov	Everton (3)	A	D	1-1	Jennings	O'Shea	..	..	..	..	..	..				Chapman for Sunderland
23 Nov	Everton (3R)	H	W	3-0	Wood	..	..	..	..	..	..3	..				Chapman for Sunderland
30 Nov	Huddersfield T (4)	H	W	1-0	..	..	..	..	..	..	..1					
18 Jan	Sheffield W (5)	H	W	1-0	Jennings	Hollins	..	Nicholas	..	Robson	..	Petrovic	..1			
15 Feb	Manchester U (SF)	H	L	2-4	..	..	Robson	Nicholas1	Talbot	Meade	..	..				Davis for O'Leary
23 Feb	Manchester U (SF)	A	L	1-2	..	..	..	Whyte	..	..1	..					Davis for Hollins

UEFA Cup

Date	Opponent	V	Res	Score	1	2	3	4	5	6	7	8	9	10	11	Notes
14 Sep	Spartak Moscow (1)	A	L	2-3	Wood	Hollins	Sansom	Talbot	O'Leary	Whyte	Davis	Robson1	Chapman1	Woodcock	Rix	
29 Sep	Spartak Moscow (1)	H	L	2-5	..	..	..	..	..	*opponents*	..	..1	..			Sunderland for Hollins, McDermott for Davis

Appearances (Goals)

Chapman L 19 (3) – Davis P 41 (4) – Devine J 9 – Hawley J 6 – Hill C 7 – Hollins J 23 (2) – Jennings P 19 – Kay J 7 – McDermott B 9 (4) – Meade R 4 (2) – Nicholas P 21 – O'Leary D 36 (1) – O'Shea D 6 – Petrovic V 13 (2) – Rix G 36 (6) – Robson S 31 (2) – Sansom K 40 – Sunderland A 25 (6) – Talbot B 42 (9) – Whyte C 36 3 – Wood G 23 – Woodcock A 34 (14) – **Total 22 players (58)**

Position in League Table

	P	W	L	D	F:A	Pts	
Liverpool	42	24	8	10	87:37	82	1st
Arsenal	42	16	16	10	58:56	58	10th

SEASON 1983-1984 FOOTBALL LEAGUE (DIVISION 1)

Date	Opponent	V	Res	Score	1	2	3	4	5	6	7	8	9	10	11	Notes
27 Aug	Luton T	H	W	2-1	Jennings	Robson	Sansom	Talbot	O'Leary	Hill	McDermott1	Davis	Woodcock1	Nicholas	Rix	
29 Aug	Wolverhampton W	A	W	2-1	..	..	..	..	..	..	..	..	..2	..		
3 Sep	Southampton	A	L	0-1	..	..	..	..	..	..	..	..	..			
6 Sep	Manchester U	H	L	2-3	..	..	..	..1	..	..	..	..1	..			Whyte for McDermott / Sunderland for McDermott
10 Sep	Liverpool	H	L	0-2	..	..	..	..	..	Sunderland	..	..	..			
17 Sep	Notts Co	A	W	4-0	..	..	..	Whyte	..	*opponents*	..2	..	..1			Talbot1 for Nicholas / McDermott for Nicholas
24 Sep	Norwich C	H	W	3-0	..	..	..	..	..	Chapman1	..					
1 Oct	QPR	A	L	0-2	..	..	..	..	..	..	..					
15 Oct	Coventry C	H	L	0-1	..	..	..	..	..	..	..					McDermott for Whyte
22 Oct	Nottingham F	H	W	4-1	..	..	..	..1	..1	..	Woodcock2	..				McDermott for Nicholas
29 Oct	Aston Villa	A	W	6-2	..	..	..	..	..	.5	..					McDermott for Robson
5 Nov	Sunderland	H	L	1-2	..	..	..	Adams	..	Talbot	..1					McDermott for Sunderland
12 Nov	Ipswich T	A	L	0-1	..	..	..	O'Leary	..	Davis						Gorman for Sunderland
19 Nov	Everton	H	W	2-1	..1	..	..1	Gorman	McDermott	..						Meade for Sunderland
26 Nov	Leicester C	A	L	0-3	..	..	Kay	Davis	Woodcock	..						Chapman for Rix
3 Dec	WBA	H	L	0-1	Caton	Adams	Hill	Madden	..	Allinson						Meade for Robson
10 Dec	West Ham U	A	L	1-3	Hill	Kay	Whyte1	Caton	..							Meade for Hill
17 Dec	Watford	H	W	3-1	Cork	Meade3	..									Cork for Robson
26 Dec	Tottenham H	A	W	4-2	Robson	O'Leary	..2	..2								McDermott for Caton
27 Dec	Birmingham C	H	D	1-1	Cork	Whyte	..1									
31 Dec	Southampton	H	D	2-2	..1	O'Leary	..1									
2 Jan	Norwich C	A	D	1-1	..1	..1										
14 Jan	Luton T	A	W	2-1	Kay	..1	Talbot	..1	Rix							
21 Jan	Notts Co	H	D	1-1	Adams	..1										McDermott for Adams
28 Jan	Stoke C	A	L	0-1	O'Leary	McDermott										Cork for Meade
4 Feb	QPR	H	L	0-2	Meade	Rix1										Allinson for Cork
11 Feb	Liverpool	A	L	1-2	Jennings	Hill	Sansom	Talbot	O'Leary	Caton	Cork	Davis	Woodcock	Nicolas	Rix1	
18 Feb	Aston Villa	H	D	1-1	..	..	..	..	..	..	Davis	Nicholas	Mariner	Woodcock	..1	
25 Feb	Nottingham F	A	W	1-0	..	..	..	..	..	..	..1	..1	..			
3 Mar	Sunderland	A	D	2-2	..	..	..	..	..	..	..1	..1				
10 Mar	Ipswich T	H	W	4-1	..	..	..	..1	..	..	..2	..1				Allinson for Rix
17 Mar	Manchester U	A	L	0-4	..	..	..	..	..	Robson	..					
24 Mar	Wolverhampton W	H	W	4-1	..	..	..	..	..	..1	..1	..1	..1			
31 Mar	Coventry C	A	W	4-1	..	..	Sparrow	..1	Whyte1	..1	..1					Kay for Jennings (Robson in goal) / Meade for Nicholas
7 Apr	Stoke C	H	W	3-1	Lukic	..	..	Caton	..1	..1	..1					Meade for Nicholas
9 Apr	Everton	A	D	0-0	..	Sansom	..									
21 Apr	Tottenham H	H	W	3-2	..	..	..1	..1	..1							Davis for Rix
23 Apr	Birmingham C	A	D	1-1	..	..	..1	..								Davis
28 Apr	Leicester C	H	W	2-1	Jennings	..	..1	..1	Rix							Davis1 for Talbot
5 May	WBA	A	W	3-1	..	..	..1	..1	..1							Davis for Robson
7 May	West Ham U	H	D	3-3	..	..	..1	..1	..1							Davis for Rix
12 May	Wartford	A	L	1-2	..	..	..1	Davis	Meade	..						

FA Cup

Date	Opponent	V	Res	Score	1	2	3	4	5	6	7	8	9	10	11	Notes
7 Jan	Middlesbrough (3)	A	L	2-3	Jennings	Hill	Sansom	Cork	O'Leary	Caton	Meade	Davis	Woodcock1	Nicholas1	Rix	Talbot for Cork

Milk Cup

Date	Opponent	V	Res	Score	1	2	3	4	5	6	7	8	9	10	11	Notes
4 Oct	Plymouth Arg (2)	A	D	1-1	Jennings	Robson	Sansom	Whyte	O'Leary	Hill	Sunderland	Davis	Woodcock	Nicholas	Rix1	Talbot for Woodcock
25 Oct	Plymouth Arg (2)	H	W	1-0	..	..	..	..	..	..	..1	..				
9 Nov	Tottenham H (3)	A	W	2-1	..	..	..	..	..	..	..1	..				
29 Nov	Walsall (4)	H	L	1-2	..	..1	..	..	..	..	Allinson					

Appearances (Goals)

Adams T 3 – Allinson I 9 – Caton T 26 – Chapman L 4 (1) – Cork D 7 (1) – Davis P 35 (1) – Gorman P 2 – Hill C 37 (1) – Jennings P 38 – Kay J 7 – Lukic J 4 – Madden D 2 – Mariner P 15 (7) – Meade R 13 (5) – McDermott B 13 (2) – Nicholas C 41 (11) – O'Leary D 36 – Rix G 34 (4) – Robson S 28 (6) – Sansom K 40 (1) – Sparrow B 2 – Sunderland A 12 (4) – Talbot B 27 (6) – Whyte C 15 (2) – Woodcock A 37 (21) – Own goals 1 – **Total 25 players (74)**

Position in League Table

	P	W	L	D	F:A	Pts	
Liverpool	42	22	6	14	73:32	80	1st
Arsenal	42	18	15	9	74:60	63	6th

SEASON 1984-1985 FOOTBALL LEAGUE (DIVISION 1)

Date	Opponent	V	Res	Score	1	2	3	4	5	6	7	8	9	10	11	Notes
25 Aug	Chelsea	H	D	1-1	Jennings	Anderson	Sansom	Talbot	O'Leary	Caton	Robson	Davis	Mariner1	Woodcock	Allinson	
29 Aug	Nottingham F	A	L	0-2	..	..	..	..	..	..	..	Nicholas	..	Davis	Allinson for Talbot
1 Sep	Watford	A	W	4-3	..	..	..	..1	..	..	..	Davis	..1	Nicholas2	
4 Sep	Newcastle U	H	W	2-0	..	..1	..	..1	..	..	..	..			
8 Sep	Liverpool	H	W	3-1	..	..	..	..2	..	..	..	..1			
15 Sep	Ipswich T	A	L	1-2	..	..	..	..	..	..	Rix	..	..1		
22 Sep	Stoke C	H	W	4-0	..	..	..1	..	..	..	..1	..2	..		
29 Sep	Coventry C	A	W	2-1	..	..	..	..	..	..	..1	..1			Davis for Talbot
6 Oct	Everton	H	W	1-0	..	..	..	..	..	..	..1				
13 Oct	Leicester C	A	W	4-1	..	..1	..	..2	..1	..	Allinson	..			
20 Oct	Sunderland	H	W	3-2	..	..	..	..1	..	..	..1				Davis for Woodcock
27 Oct	West Ham U	A	L	1-3	..	..	..	..	Hill	..	..1	Davis			Adams for Rix
2 Nov	Manchester U	A	L	1-4	Lukic	..	..	..	Coton	Davis	..1	Woodcock1			Allinson for Caton
10 Nov	Aston Villa	H	D	1-1	Jennings	..	..	..	..	Robson	Davis	Mariner1	..		Allinson for O'Leary
17 Nov	QPR	H	W	1-0	..	..	..	..	Adams	..	Allinson	..1			
25 Nov	Sheffield W	A	L	1-2	..	..	..	..	..	..	Mariner	..1			Allinson for O'Leary
1 Dec	Luton T	H	W	3-1	Lukic	..1	..	Adams	Caton	..	..1	Allinson1			Meade for Allinson
8 Dec	Southampton	A	L	0-1	..	..	..	O'Leary	Adams	..					
15 Dec	WBA	H	W	4-0	..	..	..1	Adams	Caton	..1	..2				
22 Dec	Watford	H	D	1-1	..	O'Leary	Hill	..	..	Nicholas	..1				
26 Dec	Norwich C	A	L	0-1	..	Anderson	Sansom	O'Leary	Adams	Caton					Nicholas for Allinson
29 Dec	Newcastle U	A	W	3-1	..	..	Caton	..1	..	Nicholas2					

Date	Opponent	Ven	Res	Score	1	2	3	4	5	6	7	8	9	10	11	Substitution
1 Jan	Tottenham H	H	L	1-2	..	..	..	..	..	Caton	..	Allinson	..	..1	Nicholas	Willams for Nicholas
19 Jan	Chelsea	A	D	1-1	..	..	Sansom	..	..	Caton	..	Willams	..1	..		
2 Feb	Coventry C	H	W	2-1	..	..	..	..	..	..	..	..	Meade1	Allinson1		Nicholas for Caton
12 Feb	Liverpool	A	L	0-3	..	..	..	..	..	Adams	..	..	..	..		Nicholas for Allinson
23 Feb	Manchester U	H	L	0-1	..	..	..	Williams	..	Caton	..	Davis	..	Woodcock	Nicholas	Talbot for Davis
2 Mar	West Ham U	H	W	2-1	..	..	..	..	..	..	..	..1	..	..1		
9 Mar	Sunderland	A	D	0-0	..	..	..	Talbot	..	..	..	..	..	..		
13 Mar	Aston Villa	A	D	0-0	..	..	..	..	..	..	..	..	..	..		Meade for Woodcock
16 Mar	Leicester C	H	W	2-0	..	..	..	Williams1	Adams	..	..	..	..	Meade1		Talbot for Nicholas
19 Mar	Ipswich T	H	D	1-1	..	..	..	..	..	..	..	..	..1			Talbot for Davis
23 Mar	Everton	A	L	0-2	..	..	..	..	O'Leary	..	Rix	..	..	..		Talbot for Robson
30 Mar	Stoke C	A	L	0-2	..	..	..	..	..	Talbot	..	..	Talbot			Allinson for Meade
6 Apr	Norwich C	H	W	2-0	..	..	..	..	..	Robson1	..	..	Talbot	..1		Allinson for Mariner
13 Apr	Nottingham F	H	D	1-1	..	..	..	..	..	..	Allinson	..	..			
17 Apr	Tottenham H	A	W	2-0	..	..	..	..	..	..	..	..	..1	..1		Mariner for O'Leary
20 Apr	QPR	A	L	0-1	..	..	..	..	Adams	..	..	..	..	..		Mariner for Adams
27 Apr	Sheffield W	H	W	1-0	..	..	..	..	O'Leary	..	..	Mariner1	..	..		Allinson for Robson
4 May	Luton T	A	L	1-3	..	..	..	Talbot	..	..	..	Allinson	..1			Davis for Caton
6 May	Southampton	H	W	1-0	..	..	..	..	Adams	Davis	..	..	..1	..		
11 May	WBA	A	D	2-2	..	..	opponents	..	O'Leary	Adams	..	..	..	Davis	..	Allinson1 for Nicholas

FA Cup

Date	Opponent	Ven	Res	Score	1	2	3	4	5	6	7	8	9	10	11	Substitution
5 Jan	Hereford (3)	A	D	1-1	Lukic	Anderson	Caton	Talbot	O'Leary	Adams	Robson	Willams	Mariner	Woodcock1	Nicholas	Allinson for Nicholas
22 Jan	Hereford (3R)	H	W	7-2	..	..1	Sansom	..2	..	Caton	..	..	..2	..1	..1	
26 Jan	York C (4)	A	L	0-1	..	..	..	..	..	..	..	..	..	..		Allinson for Nicholas

Milk Cup

Date	Opponent	Ven	Res	Score	1	2	3	4	5	6	7	8	9	10	11
25 Sep	Bristol R (2)	H	W	4-0	Jennings	Anderson1	Sansom	Talbot	O'Leary	Caton	Robson	Rix	Mariner	Woodcock1	Nicholas2
9 Oct	Bristol R (2)	A	D	1-1	..	..	..	..	..	..	..	..1	Allinson1	..	
31 Oct	Oxford U (3)	A	L	2-3	..	..	..	..	..	..	..	..	..	..	Adams for Robson

Appearances (Goals)

Adams T 16 – Allinson T 27 (10) – Caton T 35 (1) – Davis P 24 (1) – Hill C 2 – Jennings P 15 – Lukic J 27 – Mariner P 36 (7) – Meade R 8 (3) – Nicholas C 38 (9) – O'Leary D 36 – Rix G 18 (2) – Robson S 40 (2) – Sansom K 39 (1) – Talbot B 41 (10) – Williams S 15 (1) – Woodcock T 27 (10) – Own goals 1 – **Total 18 players (61)**

Position in League Table

	P	W	L	D	F:A	Pts	
Everton	42	28	8	6	88:43	90	1st
Arsenal	42	19	14	9	61:49	66	7th

SEASON 1985-1986 FOOTBALL LEAGUE (DIVISION 1)

Date	Opponent	Ven	Res	Score	1	2	3	4	5	6	7	8	9	10	11	Substitution
17 Aug	Liverpool	A	L	0-2	Lukic	Anderson	Sansom	Williams	O'Leary	Caton	Robson	Allinson	Nicholas	Woodcock	Rix	
20 Aug	Southampton	H	W	3-2	..	..	..	..	..	..1	..1	..	..	..		Davis for Williams
24 Aug	Manchester U	H	L	1-2	..	..	..	..	..	..	..	..	..	..1		Davis for Williams
27 Aug	Luton T	A	D	2-2	..	..	..	Davis	..	..	..	opponents	..	..1		Mariner for O'Leary
31 Aug	Leicester C	H	W	1-0	..	..	..	..	Mariner	..	..	..1	..	..1		
3 Sep	QPR	A	W	1-0	..	..	..	..	O'Leary	..	..	..1	..			
7 Sep	Coventry C	A	W	2-0	..	..	..	..	..	..	..	..1	..1	..		
14 Sep	Sheffield W	H	W	1-0	..	..	..	..	..	..	..	..1	..			
21 Sep	Chelsea	A	L	1-2	..	..	..	..	..	..	..	..1	..			
28 Sep	Newcastle U	H	D	0-0	..	..	..	..	..	..	Rocastle	..	..	..		Whyte for Allinson
5 Oct	Aston Villa	H	W	3-2	..	..1	..	..	..	..	Whyte1	..	..1	..		
12 Oct	West Ham U	A	D	0-0	..	..	..	..	..	..	..	..	..	..		Rocastle for O'Leary
19 Oct	Ipswich T	H	W	1-0	..	..	..	..1	..	..	..	..	..	..		Rocastle for Nicholas
26 Oct	Nottingham F	A	L	2-3	..	..	..	..1	..	..	..	..	..	..1		Rocastle for Robson
2 Nov	Manchester C	H	W	1-0	..	..	..	..1	..	..	Williams	..	..	..		Whyte for Allinson
9 Nov	Everton	A	L	1-6	..	..	..	..	..	..	..	..	..1	..		
16 Nov	Oxford U	H	W	2-1	..	..	..	..1	..	..	..	Robson	..	..1	Hayes	Allinson for Woodcock
23 Nov	WBA	A	D	0-0	..	..	..	..	Keown	..	..	..	..	..		Whyte for Hayes
30 Nov	Birmingham C	H	D	0-0	..	..	..	..	O'Leary	..	..	..	..	..		Allinson for Williams
7 Dec	Southampton	A	L	0-3	..	..	..	..	..	..	..	..	..	..		Allinson for Hayes
14 Dec	Liverpool	H	W	2-0	..	..	..	..	..	Keown	Allinson	..	..1	Quinn1	Rix	
21 Dec	Manchester U	A	W	1-0	..	Caesar	..	..	..	..	..	..	..1	..	..1	
28 Dec	QPR	H	W	3-1	..	..	..	..	..	..	..	..	..1	..	..1	Woodcock1 for Robson
1 Jan	Tottenham H	H	D	0-0	..	Anderson	..	..	..	..	..	Robson1	..	..		
18 Jan	Leicester C	A	D	2-2	..	..	..	..	..	..	Robson1	..1	Mariner	..		
1 Feb	Luton T	H	W	2-1	..	..	..	Rocastle	..	..	..1	Mariner	..	..		
1 Mar	Newcastle U	A	L	0-1	Lukic	Anderson	Sansom	Williams	O'Leary	Keown	Allinson	Rocastle	Nicholas	Woodcock	Rix	Mariner for Woodcock
8 Mar	Aston Villa	A	W	4-1	Wilmot	..	..	..	opponents	..	Hayes1	..1	..	..		
11 Mar	Ipswich T	A	W	2-1	..	..	..	..	..	..	..	..1	..1	..1		Mariner for O'Leary
15 Mar	West Ham U	H	W	1-0	Lukic	..	..	..	..	..	..	..	..1			
22 Mar	Coventry C	H	W	3-0	..	Adams	..	..	opponents	..	..1	..	..1	Quinn		Mariner for Quinn
29 Mar	Tottenham H	A	L	0-1	..	Anderson	..	..	..	..	..	..	Quinn	Mariner		Robson for Hayes
31 Mar	Watford	H	L	0-2	..	..	..	..	..	..	..	..	..	Woodcock		Allinsonfor Williams
1 Apr	Watford	A	L	0-3	..	..	..	..	Adams	..	Robson	..	..	Woodcock		
5 Apr	Manchester C	A	W	1-0	..	..	..	Allinson	..	..	..1	..	Quinn	..		Mariner for Quinn
8 Apr	Nottingham F	H	D	1-1	..	..	..	..1	..	..	..	..	..	..		Mariner for Rocastle
12 Apr	Everton	H	L	0-1	..	..	..	..	..	..	..	Davis	..	..		
16 Apr	Sheffield W	A	L	0-2	..	..	..	..	..	..	..	..	..	Woodcock		
26 Apr	WBA	H	D	2-2	..	..	..	..1	O'Leary	Adams	..1	..	Hayes	..		Quinn for Woodcock
29 Apr	Chelsea	H	W	2-0	..	..1	..	Keown	..	..	..	..	Nicholas1	..		Quinn for Rix
3 May	Birmingham C	A	W	1-0	..	..	..	..	..	..	..	..	..	..1		
5 May	Oxford U	A	L	0-3	..	..	..	..	..	..	..	..	..	..		Allinson for O'Leary

FA Cup

Date	Opponent	Ven	Res	Score	1	2	3	4	5	6	7	8	9	10	11	Substitution
4 Jan	Grimsby T (3)	A	W	4-3	Lukic	Anderson	Sansom	Davis	O'Leary	Keown	Allinson	Rocastle	Nicholas3	Quinn	Rix1	
25 Jan	Rotherham U (4)	H	W	5-1	..	..	..	Rocastle	..	..	..2	Robson1	..1	..	..1	Woodcock for Nicholas
15 Feb	Luton T (5)	A	D	2-2	..	..	..	Williams	..	..	..1	Rocastle1	..	Woodcock		Mariner for Nicholas
3 Mar	Luton T	H	D	0-0	..	..	..	..	..	..	..	..	Mariner	..		
	Extra Time (5R)															
5 Mar	Luton T (5 2nd Rep)	A	L	0-3	..	..	..	..	..	..	..	..	..	Hayes		Quinn for Hayes

Milk Cup

Date	Opponent	Ven	Res	Score	1	2	3	4	5	6	7	8	9	10	11	Substitution
25 Sep	Hereford U (2)	A	D	0-0	Lukic	Anderson	Sansom	Davis	O'Leary	Caton	Robson	Allinson	Nicholas	Woodcock	Rix	Mariner for Robson
8 Oct	Hereford U (2) (2 extra time)	H	W	2-1	..	..1	..	..	..	..	Whyte	..	..1	..		Rocastle for Davis
30 Oct	Manchester C (3)	A	W	2-1	..	..	..	..	..	..	Williams	..1	..1	..		
19 Nov	Southampton (4)	H	D	0-0	..	..	..	..	..	..	..	Robson	..	..	Hayes	Allinson for Hayes
26 Nov	Southampton (4R)	A	W	3-1	..	..	..	..	..	..	..	..1	..	..	..1	
22 Jan	Aston Villa (5)	A	D	1-1	Wilmot	..	..	Rocastle	..	..	Allinson	..1	Quinn	Rix		Woodcock for Robson
4 Feb	Aston Villa (5R)	H	L	1-2	Lukic	..	..	..	..	..	..	Mariner1	..	..		Woodcock for Allinson

Appearances (Goals)

Adams T 10 – Allinson T 33 (6) – Anderson V 39 (2) – Ceasar G 20 (1) – Caton T 20 (1) – Davis P 29 (4) – Hayes M 11 (2) – Keown M 22 – Lukic J 40 – Mariner P 9 – Nicholas C 41 (10) – O'Leary D 35 – Quinn N 12 (1) – Rix G 38 (3) – Robson S 27 (4) – Rocastle D 16 (1) – Sansom K 42 – Whyte C 7 (1) – Williams S 17 – Wilmot R 2 – Woodcock T 33 (11) – Own goals 3 – **Total 21 players (49)**

Position in League Table

	P	W	L	D	F:A	Pts	
Liverpool	42	26	6	10	89:37	88	1st
Arsenal	42	20	13	9	49:47	69	7th

SEASON 1986-1987 FOOTBALL LEAGUE (DIVISION 1)

Date	Opponent	Ven	Res	Score	1	2	3	4	5	6	7	8	9	10	11	Substitution
23 Aug	Manchester U	H	W	1-0	Lukic	Anderson	Sansom	Robson	O'Leary	Adams	Rocastle	Davis	Quinn	Nicholas1	Rix	Hayes for Rocastle
26 Aug	Coventry C	A	L	1-2	..	..1	..	..	..	..	..	..	..	..		Hayes for Rix
30 Aug	Liverpool	A	L	1-2	..	..	..	..	..	..1	..	..	..	..		Williams for Robson
2 Sep	Sheffield W	H	W	2-0	..	..	..	..	..	..1	..	..	..1	..		Hayes for Rocastle
6 Sep	Tottenham H	H	D	0-0	..	..	..	..	..	..	..	..	..	..		Hayes for Rocastle
13 Sep	Luton T	A	D	0-0	..	..	..	Williams	..	..	..	..	..	..		Groves for Rix
20 Sep	Oxford U	H	D	0-0	..	..	..	..	..	..	..	..	..	..		Groves for Rix
27 Sep	Nottingham F	A	L	0-1	..	..	..	..	..	..	..	..	..	Groves		Allinson for Rocastle
4 Oct	Everton	A	W	1-0	..	..	..	..1	..	..	..	..	..	Allinson		Caesar for Groves
11 Oct	Watford	H	W	3-1	..	..	..	..	..	..	..	..	..1	Groves1	Hayes1	Allinson for O'Leary
18 Oct	Newcastle U	A	W	2-1	..	..1	..	..1	..	..	..	..	..	..		Caesar for Quinn
25 Oct	Chelsea	H	W	3-1	..	..	..	..	..	..	..1	..	..	..2		Allinson for Quinn

Date	Opponent		Res												Substitutions
1 Nov	Charlton	A	W	2-0	..	..	..	..	..	..1	..	..	..	..	..1	Caesar for Groves
8 Nov	West Ham U	H	D	0-0	..	..	..	..	..	..	..	..	..	..	..	
15 Nov	Southampton	A	W	4-0	..	..1	..	..	..	..	..	..	..1	..1	..1	Caesar for Rocastle
22 Nov	Manchester C	H	W	3-0	..	..1	..	..	..	..1	..	..	..	Allinson	..1	Merson for Hayes
29 Nov	Aston Villa	A	W	4-0	..	..	opponents	..	..	..	..1	..	..	Groves1	..1	
6 Dec	Q P R	H	W	3-1	..	..	..	..	..	..	..	..	..1	..	..2	Nicholas for Groves
13 Dec	Norwich C	A	D	1-1	..	..	..	..	..	..	..	..	..1	..	..1	Caesar for Groves
20 Dec	Luton T	H	W	3-0	..	..	..	..	..	..1	..	..	..1	..	..1	Nicholas for Groves
26 Dec	Leicester C	A	D	1-1	..	..	..	..	..	..	..	..	..1	..	..1	Caesar for Groves
27 Dec	Southampton	H	W	1-0	..	..	..	..	..	..	..	..	..1	Nicholas	..	Allinson for Hayes
1 Jan	Wimbledon	H	W	3-1	..	..	..	..	..	..	..	..	..	..2	..1	Allinson for Rocastle
4 Jan	Tottenham H	A	W	2-1	..	..	..	..	..1	..	..1	..	..	..	..	Rix for Quinn
18 Jan	Coventry C	H	D	0-0	..	..	..	..	..	..	..	..	..	..	..	Rix for Hayes
24 Jan	Manchester U	A	L	0-2	..	..	..	..	..	..	..	..	..	..	..	Caesar for Nicholas
14 Feb	Sheffield W	A	D	1-1	..	Thomas	..	..	..	Groves	..	..	..1	Rix	..	Allinson for Williams
25 Feb	Oxford U	A	D	0-0	..	Anderson	..	Thomas	..	Rocastle	..	..	..	Groves	..	Nicholas for Groves
7 Mar	Chelsea	A	L	0-1	..	..	..	..	..	..	Caesar	..	..	Allinson	..	Merson for Hayes
10 Mar	Liverpool	H	L	0-1	..	..	..	..	..	..	Groves	..	..	..	..	Caesar for Hayes
17 Mar	Nottingham F	H	D	0-0	..	..	..	Williams	Caesar	..	..	..	Nicholas	..	Thomas	Allinson for Groves
21 Mar	Watford	A	L	0-2	..	Caesar	..	Thomas	O'Leary	..	Allinson	Davis	..	..	Hayes	Rix for Quinn
28 Mar	Everton	H	L	0-1	..	Anderson	..	Williams	..	..	Rocastle	..	..	..	..	Groves for Hayes
8 Apr	West Ham U	A	L	1-3	Wilmot	..	Thomas	..	..	..	..	..	Groves	..	..1	Rix for Hayes
11 Apr	Charlton A	H	W	2-1	Lukic	..	Sansom	..	..	..	..	..1	Quinn	..	..1	Groves for Quinn
14 Apr	Newcastle U	H	L	0-1	..	..	Thomas	..	..	..	..	..	Groves	..	..	Rix for Rocastle
18 Apr	Wimbledon	A	W	2-1	..	..	Caesar	..	..	..	..	..1	Merson1	..	Rix	Allinson for Rocastle
20 Apr	Leicester C	H	W	4-1	Wilmot	..	Sansom	..	..	..	Hayes2	..1	..	..1	..	Caesar for O'Leary
25 Apr	Manchester C	A	L	0-3	..	..	Thomas	..	Caesar	..	..	..	Quinn	..	Hayes2	Allinson for Merson
2 May	Aston Villa	H	W	2-1	..	..	..	..	O'Leary	..	Rocastle	..	..	..	Hayes2	Groves for Quinn
4 May	Q P R	A	W	4-1	..	..	..	..	Caesar	..	Rix2	..	Merson1	..	..1	
9 May	Norwich C	H	L	1-2	..	..	..	..	O'Leary	..	..	..	..	..1	..	Groves for Anderson

FA Cup

Date	Opponent		Res												
10 Jan	Reading (3)	A	W	3-1	Lukic	Anderson	Sansom	Williams	O'Leary	Adams	Rocastle	Davis	Quinn	Nicholas2	Hayes1	
31 Jan	Plymouth A (4)	H	W	6-1	..	..2	..	..	..	..	..1	..1	..1	..1	..	Groves for Hayes/Caesar for Groves
21 Feb	Barnsley (5)	H	W	2-0	..	..	..	Allinson	..	..	..	..	Groves	..1	Nicholas1 for Quinn/Thomas for Hayes
14 Mar	Watford (QF)	H	L	1-3	..	..	..	Williams	..	..	Groves	..	Allinson1	Nicholas for Allinson/Thomas for Hayes

Football League (Littlewoods) Cup

Date	Opponent		Res												
23 Sep	Huddersfield T (2)	H	W	2-0	Lukic	Anderson	Sansom	Williams	O'Leary	Adams	Rocastle	Davis1	Quinn1	Nicholas	Rix	Groves for Quinn
7 Oct	Huddersfield T (2)	A	D	1-1	..	..	..	..	..	..	..1	..1	Allinson	Groves	Hayes1 for Allinson
28 Oct	Manchester C (3)	H	W	3-1	..	..	..	..	..	..	..1	..1	Groves	Hayes1	Allinson for Quinn
18 Nov	Charlton A (4)	H	W	2-0	..	..	..	opponents	..	..	..	..1	..	..	Allinson for Groves
21 Jan	Nottingham F (QF)	H	W	2-0	..	..	..	..	..	..	..	..	Nicholas1	..1	Rix for Quinn
8 Feb	Tottenham H (SF1)	H	L	0-1	..	Caesar	..	..	..	Groves	..	..	..	Thomas for Caesar/Rix for Nicholas
1 Mar	Tottenham H (SF2)	A	W	2-1	..	Anderson1	..	Thomas	..	Rocastle	..	..1	..	Allinson for Nicholas
4 Mar	Tottenham H (SFR)	A	W	2-1	..	..	..	..	..	..1	..	..	..	Allinson1 for Thomas
5 Apr	Liverpool (F) (at Wembley)		W	2-1	..	..	..	Williams	..	..	..	..	..2	..	Groves for Quinn/Thomas for Hayes

---

Appearances (Goals)

Adams T 42 (6) – Allinson I 14 – Anderson V 40 (4) – Caesar G 15 – Davis P 39 (4) – Groves P 25 (3) – Hayes M 35 (19) – Lukic J 36 – Merson P 7 (3) – Nicholas C 28 (4) – O'Leary D 39 – Quinn N 35 (8) – Rix G 18 (2) – Robson S 5 – Rocastle D 36 (2) – Sansom K 35 – Thomas M 11 – Williams S 34 (2) – Own goals 1 – **Total 19 players (58)**

Position in League Table

	P	W	L	D	F:A	Pts	
Everton	42	26	8	8	76:31	86	1st
Arsenal	42	20	12	10	58:35	70	4th

SEASON 1987-88 FOOTBALL LEAGUE (DIVISION 1)

Date	Opponent		Res													Substitutions
15 Aug	Liverpool	H	L	1-2	Lukic	Thomas	Sansom	Williams	O'Leary	Adams	Rocastle	Davis1	Smith	Nicholas	Hayes	Groves for Rocastle
19 Aug	Manchester U	A	D	0-0	..	..	..	..	..	..	..	..	..	..	..	Groves for Nicholas
22 Aug	Q P R	A	L	0-2	..	..	..	..	..	..	..	..	..	..	..	Rix for Rocastle
29 Aug	Portsmouth	H	W	6-0	..	..	..	..	..	..1	..1	..1	..3	Groves	Rix	Merson for Groves/Richardson for Rix
31 Aug	Luton T	A	D	1-1	..	..	..	..	..	..	..	..1	..	..	..	
12 Sep	Nottingham F	A	W	1-0	..	..	..	..	..	..	..	..	..1	..	..	Hayes for Rocastle
19 Sep	Wimbledon	H	W	3-0	..	..1	..	..	..	..	..1	..	..1	..	..	Merson and Richardson for Groves and Williams
26 Sep	West Ham U	H	W	1-0	..	..	..	..1	..	..	..	..	..	..	..	Hayes for Rocastle
3 Oct	Charlton A	A	W	3-0	..	..1	..	..	..	..1	..	..	..	..1	..	Hayes for Rocastle
10 Oct	Oxford U	H	W	2-0	..	..	..	..1	..	..	..	..1	..	..	Richardson	Hayes and Caesar for Rocastle and Smith
18 Oct	Tottenham H	A	W	2-1	..	..1	..	..	..	..	..	..	..1	..	..	Hayes for Rocastle
24 Oct	Derby C	H	W	2-1	..	..	..	..	..	..	..	..	..	..	..1	Merson for Groves
31 Oct	Newcastle U	A	W	1-0	..	..	..	..	..	..	..	..1	..	..	..	Caesar and Hayes for Williams and Adams
3 Nov	Chelsea	H	W	3-1	..	..	opponents	..	..	..	..	..	..	..	..2	
14 Nov	Norwich C	A	W	4-2	..	..1	..	..	..	..	..2	..	..	..1	..	Caesar for Adams
21 Nov	Southampton	H	L	0-1	..	..	..	..	..	..	..	..	..	..	..	Quinn for Groves, Winterburn for Quinn
28 Nov	Watford	A	L	0-2	..	..	..	..	..	..	..	..	..	..	..	Hayes for Richardson
5 Dec	Sheffield W	H	W	3-1	..	..	..	..	..	..	..	..	..	..1	..1	Merson1 for Davis
13 Dec	Coventry C	A	D	0-0	..	..	..	..	..	..	..	Hayes	..	..	..	Merson for Hayes
19 Dec	Everton	H	D	1-1	..	..	..	..	..	..	..	Davis	..	..	..	Merson for Richardson
26 Dec	Nottingham F	H	L	0-2	..	..	..	..	..	..	..	Merson	Quinn	..	..	Smith and Caesar for Merson and O'Leary
28 Dec	Wimbledon	A	L	1-3	..	..	..	..	Caesar	..	..	Hayes	..1	..	..	Smith for Hayes
1 Jan	Portsmouth	A	D	1-1	..	..	Winterburn	..	..	..	..	..	..	..	..	Smith1 and Merson for Quinn and Groves
2 Jan	Q P R	H	D	0-0	..	Winterburn	Sansom	..	..	..	..	..	Smith	Merson	..	Groves for Merson
16 Jan	Liverpool	A	L	0-2	..	..	..	..	..	..	..	..	..	Quinn	..	Thomas and Groves for Caesar and Rocastle
24 Jan	Manchester U	H	L	1-2	..	Thomas	Winterburn	..	O'Leary	..	..	Rix	..	..1	..	Groves for Rix
13 Feb	Luton T	H	W	2-1	..	Dixon	..	Thomas1	..	..	..1	Hayes	..	..	..	Caesar for Adams
27 Feb	Charlton A	H	W	4-0	..	Winterburn	Sansom	..1	Caesar	..	..	..	..1	Merson2	..	Davis and Quinn for Merson and Richardson
6 Mar	Tottenham H	H	W	2-1	..	..	..	..	..	..	..	..	..1	Groves1	..	
19 Mar	Newcastle U	H	D	1-1	..	Dixon	Winterburn	..	..	..	..	Davis	..	..1	Hayes	Quinn for Smith
26 Mar	Derby Co	A	D	0-0	..	..	..	..	..	..	..	..	..	..	..	Richards and Quinn for Rocastle and Smith
30 Mar	Oxford U	A	D	0-0	..	..	Winterburn	Sansom	..	..	..	..	..	..	Marwood	Merson and Quinn for Rocastle and Marwood
2 Apr	Chelsea	A	D	1-1	..	Dixon	Winterburn	Williams	..	..	opponents	..	Quinn	..1	Hayes	
4 Apr	Norwich C	H	W	2-0	..	Winterburn	Sansom	..	..	..	..	..	Smith1	..	..	
9 Apr	Southampton	A	L	2-4	..	..	..	..	..	Thomas	..	..1	..	opponents	..	Merson for Groves
12 Apr	West Ham U	A	W	1-0	..	..	..	Thomas1	..	Adams	..	..	..	Merson	Richardson	Rix for Richardson
15 Apr	Watford	H	L	0-1	..	..	..	..	..	..	..	..	..	..	..	Hayes for Richardson
30 Apr	Sheffield W	A	D	3-3	..	..	..	..	..	..	..	..	..1	..2	Marwood	Richardson and Hayes for Davis and Winterburn

Date	Opp	V	R	Score	1	2	3	4	5	6	7	8	9	10	11	Notes
2 May	Coventry C	H	D	1-1	..	Dixon	..	..	..	..	..	..	..	..	..1	Hayes and Groves for Merson and Richardson
7 May	Everton	A	W	2-1	..	..	..	..1	..	..	..	..	..	Hayes1	..	Rix and Campbell for Caesar and Hayes

FA Cup

Date	Opp	V	R	Score	1	2	3	4	5	6	7	8	9	10	11	Notes
9 Jan	Millwall (3)	H	W	2-0	Lukic	Winterburn	Sansom	Williams	O'Leary	Adams	Rocastle1	Hayes1	Smith	Merson	Richardson	Groves for Merson
30 Jan	Brighton (4)	A	W	2-1	..	..	..	..	..	..	..	Rix	Groves1	Quinn	..1	Hayes for Rix
20 Feb	Manchester U (5)	H	W	2-1	..	..	..	Thomas	..	opponents	..	Hayes	Smith1	Groves	..	Rix for O'Leary
12 Mar	Nottingham F (6)	H	L	1-2	..	..	..	..	..	..	..1	..	..	..	..	Davis and Quinn for O'Leary and Hayes

Football League (Littlewoods) Cup

Date	Opp	V	R	Score	1	2	3	4	5	6	7	8	9	10	11	Notes
23 Sep	Doncaster (2)	A	W	3-0	Lukic	Thomas	Sansom	Williams1	O'Leary	Adams	Rocastle	Davis	Smith1	Groves1	Rix	Richardson and Quinn for Groves and Rix
6 Oct	Doncaster (2)	H	W	1-0	..	..	..	..	Caesar	..	..	..	..	..	Hayes	
27 Oct	Bournemouth (3)	H	W	3-0	..	..1	..	..	O'Leary	..	..	..	..1	..	Richardson1	Merson for Groves
17 Nov	Stoke C (4)	H	W	3-0	..	..	..	..	..	..	..1	..	..	..	..1	Hayes for Groves
20 Jan	Sheffield W (5)	A	W	1-0	..	Winterburn1	..	..	..	..	..	Rix	..	Quinn	..	Groves for Quinn
7 Feb	Everton (SF)	A	W	1-0	..	..	..	Thomas	..	..	..	Hayes	..	Groves1	..	Caesar and Quinn for Rocastle and Smith
24 Feb	Everton (SF)	H	W	3-1	..	..	..	..1	..	..	..1	..	..1	..	..	Davis for O'Leary
24 Apr	Luton (F) (at Wembley)		L	2-3	..	..	..	..	Caesar	..	..	Davis	..1	..	..	Hayes1 for Groves

Appearances (Goals)

Lukic 40 – Rocastle 40 (7) – Adams 39 (2) – Smith 39 (11) – Thomas 37 (9) – Groves 34 (6) – Sansom 34 (1) – Richardson 29 (4) – Williams 29 (1) – Davis 29 (5) Hayes 27 (1) – O'Leary 23 – Caesar 22 – Winterburn 17 – Merson 15 (5) – Quinn 11 (2) – Rix 10 – Dixon 6 – Marwood 4 (1) – Nicholas 3 – Campbell 1 – Own goals 3 – **Total 21 players (58)**

Position in League Table

	P	W	L	D	F:A	Pts	
Liverpool	40	26	2	12	87:24	90	1st
Arsenal	40	18	10	12	58:39	66	6th

SEASON 1988-89 FOOTBALL LEAGUE (DIVISION 1)

Date	Opp	V	R	Score	1	2	3	4	5	6	7	8	9	10	11	Notes
27 Aug	Wimbledon	A	W	5-1	Lukic	Dixon	Winterburn	Thomas	Bould	Adams	Rocastle	Davis	Smith3	Merson1	Marwood1	-
3 Sep	Aston Villa	H	L	2-3	..	..	..	..	..	O'Leary	..	..	..1	..	..1	Groves for Rocastle
10 Sep	Tottenham H	A	W	3-2	..	..	..1	..	..	..	..	..	..1	..	..1	Groves/Richardson for Rocastle/Marwood
17 Sep	Southampton	H	D	2-2	..	..	..	..	..	..	..	..	..	..1	..	Hayes/Richardson for Davis/Merson
24 Sep	Sheffield W	A	L	1-2	..	..	..	..	..	..	..	..	..1	..	..	Groves for Merson
1 Oct	West Ham U	A	W	4-1	..	..	..	..1	Bould	..	..1	Richardson	..2	Groves	..	Hayes for Groves
22 Oct	Q P R	H	W	2-1	..	..	..	..	..	..	..1	..	..1	Merson	..	Groves for Merson
25 Oct	Luton T	A	D	1-1	..	..	..	..	..	..	..	..	..1	..	..	
29 Oct	Coventry C	H	W	2-0	..	..	..	..1	..	..1	..	..	..	..	..	Groves/Hayes for Rocastle/Merson
6 Nov	Nottingham F	A	W	4-1	..	..	..	..	..1	..1	..	..	..1	..	..1	Hayes for Merson
12 Nov	Newcastle U	A	W	1-0	..	..	..	..	..1	..	..	..	..	Hayes	..	Merson for Rocastle
19 Nov	Middlesbrough	A	W	3-0	..	..	..	..	..	..1	..	..	..	Merson2	..	Hayes for Merson
26 Nov	Derby Co	A	L	1-2	..	..	..	..1	..	..	..	..	..	..	Hayes	Groves for Richardson
4 Dec	Liverpool	H	D	1-1	..	..	..	..	..	..	..	..	..1	..	Marwood	Hayes for Marwood
10 Dec	Norwich C	A	D	0-0	..	..	..	..	..	..	..	..	..	..	..	Hayes for Marwood
17 Dec	Manchester U	H	W	2-1	..	..	..	..1	..	..	..	..	..	..1	..	
26 Dec	Charlton A	A	W	3-2	..	O'Leary	..	..	..	..	..	..	..1	..1	..2	
31 Dec	Aston Villa	A	W	3-0	..	..	..	..	..	..1	..	..	..1	..	..	Groves1 for Merson
2 Jan	Tottenham H	H	W	2-0	..	..	..	..1	..	..	..	..	..	..1	..	Davis/Groves for Richardson/Marwood
14 Jan	Everton	A	W	3-1	..	Dixon	..	Davis	O'Leary	Caesar	..	..1	..1	..1	..	Groves/Thomas for Merson/Marwood
21 Jan	Sheffield W	H	D	1-1	..	..	..	..	..	..	..	..	..	..1	..	Groves/Thomas for Caesar/Rocastle
4 Feb	West Ham U	H	W	2-1	..	..	..	Thomas	..	Adams	..	..	..1	..	Groves1	Bould/Hayes for O'Leary/Merson
11 Feb	Millwall	A	W	2-1	..	..	..	..	..	..	..	..	..1	..	Marwood1	Bould for O'Leary
18 Feb	Q P R	A	D	0-0	..	..	..	..	..	..	..	..	..	..	..	Bould/Hayes for Dixon/Merson
21 Feb	Coventry C	A	L	0-1	..	Bould	..	..	..	..	..	..	..	..	..	Hayes for Marwood
25 Feb	Luton T	H	W	2-0	..	..	..	..	..	..	..	..	..1	Groves1	..	Merson for Rocastle
28 Feb	Millwall	H	D	0-0	..	..	..	..	..	..	..	..	..	..	..	Merson/Dixon for Rocastle/Richardson
11 Mar	Nottingham F	H	L	1-3	..	..	..	..	..	..	..	..	..1	..	..	Merson/Dixon for Bould/Groves
21 Mar	Charlton A	H	D	2-2	..	Dixon	..	Davis1	..	..	..1	..	..	Merson	..	Groves/Thomas for Richardson/Merson
25 Mar	Southampton	A	W	3-1	..	..	..	..	..	..	..1	..	..	Groves1	..	Merson1 for Groves
2 Apr	Manchester U	A	D	1-1	..	..	..	..	..	..1	..	..	..	Bould	..	Thomas/Merson for Davis/Marwood
8 Apr	Everton	H	W	2-0	..	..1	..	Thomas	..	..	..	..	Quinn1	..	..	Merson for Marwood
15 Apr	Newcastle U	H	W	1-0	..	..	..	..	..	..	..	..	..	..	..1	Merson/Groves for O'Leary/Rocastle
1 May	Norwich C	H	W	5-0	..	..	..1	..1	..	..	..1	..	Smith2	..	Merson	Quinn/Hayes for Bould/Merson
6 May	Middlesbrough	A	W	1-0	..	..	..	..	..	..	..	..	..	..	..	Hayes1 for Merson
13 May	Derby Co	A	L	1-2	..	..	..	..	..	..	..	..	..1	..	..	Hayes/Groves for Bould/Merson
17 May	Wimbledon	H	D	2-2	..	..	..1	..	..	..	..	..	..1	..	..	Groves/Hayes for Bould/Merson
26 May	Liverpool	A	W	2-0	..	..	..1	..	..	..	..	..	..1	..	..	Groves/Hayes for Bould/Merson

FA Cup

Date	Opp	V	R	Score	1	2	3	4	5	6	7	8	9	10	11	Notes
8 Jan	West Ham U (3)	A	D	2-2	Lukic	O'Leary	Winterburn	Thomas	Bould	Adams	Rocastle	Richardson	Smith	Merson2	Marwood	Davis and Groves for Bould and Marwood
11 Jan	West Ham U (3R)	H	L	0-1	..	Dixon	..	..	O'Leary	..	..	..	..	..	..	Davis and Groves for Rocastle and Marwood

Football League (Littlewoods) Cup

Date	Opp	V	R	Score	1	2	3	4	5	6	7	8	9	10	11	Notes
28 Sep	Hull C (2)	A	W	2-1	Lukic	Dixon	Winterburn1	Thomas	Bould	Adams	Rocastle	Davis	Smith	Groves	Marwood1	Hayes and Richardson for Groves and Rocastle
12 Oct	Hull C (2)	H	W	3-0	..	..	..	..	..	..	..	..	..2	Merson1	..	Hayes and Richardson for Davis and Marwood
2 Nov	Liverpool (3)	A	D	1-1	..	..	..	..	..	..	..1	Richardson	..	..	..	Groves for Merson
9 Nov	Liverpool (3R)	H	D	0-0	..	..	..	..	..	..	..	..	..	..	..	Hayes for Merson
23 Nov	Liverpool (3R2)	A	L	1-2	..	..	..	..	..	..	..	..	..	..	..1	Hayes for Marwood

Appearances (Goals)

Lukic 38 – Rocastle 38 (6) – Winterburn 38 (3) – Thomas 37 (7) – Merson 37 (9) – Adams 36 (4) – Smith 36 (24) – Richardson 34 (1) – Dixon 33 (1) – Marwood 31 (9) – Bould 30 (2) – O'Leary 26 – Groves 21 (4) – Hayes 17 (1) – Davis 12 (1) – Quinn 3 (1) – Caesar 2 – **Total 17 players (73)**

Position in League Table

	P	W	L	D	F:A	Pts	
Arsenal	38	22	6	10	73:36	76	1st

SEASON 1989-90 FOOTBALL LEAGUE (DIVISION 1)

Date	Opp	V	R	Score	1	2	3	4	5	6	7	8	9	10	11	Notes
19 Aug	Manchester U	A	L	1-4	Lukic	Dixon	Winterburn	Thomas	O'Leary	Adams	Rocastle1	Richardson	Smith	Merson	Marwood	Caesar/Groves for Adams/Merson
22 Aug	Coventry C	H	W	2-0	..	..	..	..1	..	..	..	..	..	..	..1	Groves for Rocastle
26 Aug	Wimbledon	H	D	0-0	..	..	..	..	..	..	..	..	..	..	..	Groves for Merson
09 Sep	Sheffield W	H	W	5-0	..	..	..	..1	..	..1	..	..1	..1	..1		
16 Sep	Nottingham F	A	W	2-1	..	..	..	..	..	..	..	..	..	..1	..1	Groves for Merson
23 Sep	Charlton A	H	W	1-0	..	..	..	..	..	..	..	..	..	..	..1p	Groves for Rocastle

SEASON 1989-90 FOOTBALL LEAGUE (DIVISION 1) *(continued)*

Positions 1–11: Lukic, Dixon, Winterburn, Thomas, O'Leary, Adams, Rocastle, Richardson, Smith, (10), (11)

Date	Match	V	R	Score	1	2	3	4	5	6	7	8	9	10	11	Substitutes
30 Sep	Chelsea	A	D	0-0	..	..	..	..	..	..	..	..	..	Groves	Hayes	Merson for Rocastle
14 Oct	Manchester C	H	W	4-0	..	..	..	.1	..	..	..	..	..	..2	Marwood	Jonsson/Merson1 for Richardson/Marwood
18 Oct	Tottenham H	A	L	1-2	..	..	..	.1	..	..	..	..	..	..	Hayes	Jonsson/Merson for Richardson/Smith
21 Oct	Everton	A	L	0-3	..	..	..	..	..	..	..	..	Quinn	Smith1	Merson	Smith for Hayes
28 Oct	Derby Co	H	D	1-1	..	..	..	..	..	..	..	..	Smith1	Quinn	Merson	Jonsson/Campbell for Winterburn/Quinn
4 Nov	Norwich C	H	W	4-3	..	..2.1p	..	..	..	.1	..	..	..	..1	..1	Groves for Merson
11 Nov	Millwall	A	W	2-1	..	..	..	.1	..	..	..	..	..	..1	Marwood	Groves for Quinn
18 Nov	Q P R	H	W	3-0	..	..1p	..	..	..	..	..	..	..	..1	..	Groves/Jonsson1 for Rocastle/Marwood
26 Nov	Liverpool	A	L	1-2	..	..	..	..	..	..	..	..	..	..1	Groves	Hayes/Jonsson for Quinn/O'Leary
3 Dec	Manchester U	H	W	1-0	..	..	..	..	..	..	..	..	..	Groves1	Marwood	Merson for Marwood
9 Dec	Coventry C	A	W	1-0	..	..	..	..	..	..	..	..	..	..1	..	Merson1 for Marwood
16 Dec	Luton T	H	W	3-2	..	..	..	..	..	..	..	..	..	..1	..1	Merson1/Jonsson for Smith/Groves
26 Dec	Southampton	A	L	0-1	..	..	..	..	..	..	..	..	..	Merson	..	Davis/Groves for Marwood/Merson
30 Dec	Aston Villa	A	L	1-2	..	..	..	..	..	..	.1	Groves	.1	Bould ..2	Merson	Rocastle for Bould
1 Jan	Crystal Palace	H	W	4-1	..	..1	..	..	..	.1	..	..	.1	..2	..	Rocastle/Davis for Smith/Winterburn
13 Jan	Wimbledon	A	L	0-1	..	..	..	Davis	..	..	..	..	..	..	..	Caesar/Rocastle for O'Leary/Smith
20 Jan	Tottenham H	H	W	1-0	..	..	Davis	Thomas	..	.1	Rocastle	..	..	..	Groves	Caesar/Campbell for Pates/Richardson
17 Feb	Sheffield W	A	L	0-1	..	..	Pates	Davis	..	..	..	..	..	..	Merson	Campbell for Marwood
27 Feb	Charlton A	A	D	0-0	..	..	Winterburn	Thomas	Bould	..	..	..	..	Merson	Marwood	Marwood
3 Mar	Q P R	A	L	0-2	..	..	..	..	..	..	..	..	..	..	Groves	O'Leary/Campbell for Thomas/Smith
7 Mar	Nottingham F	H	W	3-0	..	..	..	..	..	..	.1	..	..	..	..1	Campbell1/O'Leary for Merson/Groves
10 Mar	Manchester C	A	D	1-1	..	..	..	..	..	..	..	..	..	Campbell	Marwood1 Groves	Hayes for Rocastle
17 Mar	Chelsea	H	L	0-1	..	..	..	..	..	..	..	..	..	..	Groves	Hayes/O'Leary for Rocastle/Campbell
24 Mar	Derby Co	A	W	3-1	..	..	..	..	..	..	Hayes2	..	..	..1	..	O'Leary/Ampadu for Bould/Campbell
31 Mar	Everton	H	W	1-0	..	..	..	..	..	..	..	..	.1	..	..	O'Leary/Ampadu for Richardson/Campbell
11 Apr	Aston Villa	H	L	0-1	..	..	..	..	..	..	..	O'Leary	..	..	..	Merson for Hayes
14 Apr	Crystal Palace	A	D	1-1	..	..	..	..	..	..	.1	..	..	..	..	Davis/Merson for Bould/Campbell
18 Apr	Liverpool	H	D	1-1	..	..	..	..	..	..	Davis	..	..	Merson1	..	Campbell/Pates for Groves/Bould
21 Apr	Luton T	A	L	0-2	..	..	..	..	..	..	..	..	..	..	Campbell	Hayes/Rocastle for O'Leary/Merson
28 Apr	Millwall	H	W	2-0	..	..	..	..	..	..	Rocastle	Davis1	..	..1	Marwood	Campbell/Richardson for Marwood/Thomas
2 May	Southampton	H	W	2-1	..	..1p	..	..	..	..	Richardson	..	..	..	..	Rocastle1/Groves for Richardson/Marwood
5 May	Norwich C	A	D	2-2	..	..	..	Hayes	..	..	Rocastle	..	..2	Campbell	Groves	O'Leary/Thomas for Bould/Davis

FA Cup

Date	Match	V	R	Score	1	2	3	4	5	6	7	8	9	10	11	Substitutes
6 Jan	Stoke C (3)	A	W	1-0	Lukic	Dixon	Davis	Thomas	O'Leary	Adams	Quinn1	Richardson	Groves	Bould	Merson	Jonsson/Rocastle for Thomas/Quinn
27 Jan	Q P R (4)	H	D	0-0	..	..	Winterburn	Davis	..	..	Rocastle	..	Smith	..	Groves	Thomas/Merson for Davis/Bould
31 Jan	Q P R (4R)	A	L	0-2	..	..	..	Thomas	..	..	..	..	..	..	..	Merson for Groves

Football League (Littlewoods) Cup

Date	Match	V	R	Score	1	2	3	4	5	6	7	8	9	10	11	Substitutes
19 Sep	Plymouth (2)	H	W	2-0	Lukic	opponents	Winterburn	Thomas	O'Leary	Adams	Rocastle	Richardson	Smith1	Bould Groves1	Groves Hayes	Merson for Groves
3 Oct	Plymouth (2)	A	W	6-1	..	opponents	..	..3	..	..	..	..	..1	Groves1	Hayes	Caesar/Merson for Dixon/Groves
25 Oct	Liverpool (3)	H	W	1-0	..	..	..	..	..	..	..	..	Quinn	Merson	..	Smith1 for Hayes
22 Nov	Oldham A (4)	A	L	1-3	..	..	..	..	..	..	..	..	Smith	Quinn1	Jonsson	Groves for Jonsson

FA Charity Shield

Date	Match	V	R	Score	1	2	3	4	5	6	7	8	9	10	11	Substitutes
12 Aug	Liverpool (at Wembley)		L	0-1	Lukic	Dixon	Winterburn	Thomas	O'Leary	Adams	Rocastle	Richardson	Smith	Caesar	Merson	Marwood/Quinn for Caesar/Smith

Appearances (Goals)

Lukic 38 – Dixon 38 (5) – Adams 38 (5) – Smith 38 (10) – Winterburn 36 – Thomas 36 (5) – O'Leary 34 (1) – Richardson 33 – Rocastle 33 (2) – Groves 30 (4) – Merson 29 (7) – Bould 19 – Marwood 17 (6) – Campbell 15 (2) – Hayes 12 (3) – Davis 11 (1) – Quinn 6 (2) – Jonsson 6 (1) – Caesar 3 – Pates 2 (2) – **Total 19 players (54)**

Position in League Table

	P	W	D	L	F:A	Pts	
Liverpool	38	23	10	5	78:37	79	1st
Arsenal	38	18	8	12	54:38	62	4th

SEASON 1990-91 FOOTBALL LEAGUE (DIVISION 1)

Positions 1–11: Seaman, Dixon, Winterburn, Thomas, Bould, Adams, Rocastle, Davis, Smith, Merson, Limpar

Date	Match	V	R	Score	1	2	3	4	5	6	7	8	9	10	11	Substitutes
25 Aug	Wimbledon	A	W	3-0	Seaman	Dixon	Winterburn	Thomas	Bould	Adams	Rocastle	Davis	Smith1	Merson1	Limpar	Groves1 for Limpar
29 Aug	Luton T	H	W	2-1	..	..	..	.1	..	..	..	..	..	..	..	Groves for Limpar
1 Sep	Tottenham H	H	D	0-0	..	..	..	..	..	..	..	..	..	..	..	Groves for Merson
8 Sep	Everton	A	D	1-1	..	..	..	..	..	..	..	..	..	..	..	Groves1 for Smith
15 Sep	Chelsea	H	W	4-1	..	..1p	..	..	..	..1	..	..	Groves	..1	..1	Campbell/Linighan for Groves/Bould
22 Sep	Nottingham F	A	W	2-0	..	..	..	..	..	.1	..	..	Smith	..	..1	Smith for Rocastle
29 Sep	Leeds U	A	D	2-2	..	..	..	Jonsson	..	..	..	..	Smith	..	..2	Hillier/Groves for Winterburn/Merson
6 Oct	Norwich C	H	W	2-0	..	..	..	..	..	..	..	..2	..	..	..	Hillier/Groves for Limpar/Merson
20 Oct	Manchester U	A	W	1-0	..	..	..	Thomas	..	..	..	..	..	..	..1	Groves for Rocastle
27 Oct	Sunderland	H	W	1-0	..	..1p	..	..	..	..	..	..	..	..	..2	Groves for Rocastle
3 Nov	Coventry C	A	W	2-0	..	..	..	..	..	..	Groves	..	..	..	..2	Campbell/O'Leary for Smith/Groves
10 Nov	Crystal Palace	A	D	0-0	..	..	..	..	..	..	O'Leary	..	Campbell	..	..	Groves/Smith for Merson/Limpar
17 Nov	Southampton	H	W	4-0	..	..	..	..	..	..	Groves	..	Smith2	..1	..1	O'Leary/Campbell for Dixon/Groves
24 Nov	Q P R	A	W	3-1	..	..	..	..	..	..	..	..	..1	..1	..	Campbell1/O'Leary for Groves/Adams
2 Dec	Liverpool	H	W	3-0	..	..1p	..	..	..	..	O'Leary	..	..1	..1	..	
8 Dec	Luton T	A	D	1-1	..	..	..	..	..	..	Groves	..	..1	..	..	Groves for Limpar
15 Dec	Wimbledon	H	D	2-2	..	..	..	..	..	.1	Groves	..	..	..1	..	O'Leary for Winterburn
23 Dec	Aston Villa	A	D	0-0	..	..	..	..	..	Linighan	Rocastle	..	..	..	..	Rocastle for Limpar
26 Dec	Derby Co	H	W	3-0	..	..	..	..	..	..	Rocastle	..	..2	..1	..	Campbell/O'Leary for Rocastle/Limpar
29 Dec	Sheffield U	H	W	4-1	..	..1p	..	..1	..	..	Groves	..	..2	..	..	Cole/O'Leary for Groves/Winterburn
1 Jan	Manchester C	A	W	1-0	..	..	..	..	..	..	O'Leary	..	..1	..	..	Hillier/Groves for O'Leary/Limpar
12 Jan	Tottenham H	A	D	0-0	..	..	..	..	..	..	..	..	..	..	..	Hillier/Groves for Davis/Merson
19 Jan	Everton	H	W	1-0	..	..	..	..	..	Groves	..	..	..	..1	..	Campbell/Hillier for Limpar/Bould
2 Feb	Chelsea	A	L	1-2	..	..	..	..	..	Linighan	Groves	..	..1	..	..	Hillier/Campbell for Bould/Limpar
23 Feb	Crystal Palace	H	W	4-0	..	..	..	..	..	..	O'Leary1	..	..1	..1	Campbell1	Pates/Rocastle for Linighan/Merson
3 Mar	Liverpool	A	W	1-0	..	..	..	..	..	Adams	..	Hillier	..	..1	..	Rocastle/Davis for Campbell/Adams
17 Mar	Leeds U	H	W	2-0	..	..	..	..	..	..	..	..	..	..	..2	

1974–1997

Date	Opponent		Res	1	2	3	4	5	6	7	8	9	10	11	Substitutes
20 Mar	Nottingham F	H D	1-1	..	..	..	..	..	..	..	Davis	..	..	..1	Groves/Limpar for Davis/Merson
23 Mar	Norwich C	A D	0-0	..	..	..	Rocastle	..	..	..	..	..	Campbell	Limpar	Groves/Linighan for Limpar/Rocastle
30 Mar	Derby Co	A W	2-0	..	..	..	Campbell	..	..	Rocastle	..	..2	Merson	..	Groves/Hillier for Limpar/Rocastle
3 Apr	Aston Villa	H W	5-0	..	..	..	Hillier	..	..	Campbell2	..1	..2	..	..	Thomas/Groves for Hillier/Merson
6 Apr	Sheffield U	A W	2-0	..	..	..	..	..	..	..	..1	..1	..	..	Groves/Thomas for Merson/Limpar
9 Apr	Southampton	A D	1-1	..	opponents	..	..	..	..	..	..	..	Groves	..	Thomas/Merson for Hillier/Limpar
17 Apr	Manchester C	H D	2-2	..	..	..	Thomas	..	..	..	..1	..	..	Merson1	Groves Limpar/O'Leary for Merson/Dixon
23 Apr	Q P R	H W	2-0	..	..1p	..	Hillier	..	..	..	..	..	..	..1	Limpar O'Leary/Groves for Merson/Limpar
4 May	Sunderland	A D	0-0	..	..	..	..	..	..	..	..	..	..	Groves	O'Leary for Groves
6 May	Manchester U	H W	3-1	..	..	..	..	..	..	..	..	..3.1p	..	Limpar	Thomas/Groves for Hillier/Limpar
11 May	Coventry C	H W	6-1	..	opponents	..	..	..	..	..	..	..1	..	..3	Linighan/Groves1 for Merson/Campbell

FA Cup

Date	Opponent		Res	Seaman	Dixon	Winterburn	Thomas	Bould	Linighan	Groves	Davis	Smith	Merson	Limpar	Substitutes
5 Jan	Sunderland (3)	H W	2-1	Seaman	Dixon	Winterburn	Thomas	Bould	Linighan	Groves	Davis	Smith1	Merson	Limpar1	O'Leary for Limpar
27 Jan	Leeds U (4)	H D	0-0	..	..	..	..	..	Groves	O'Leary	..	..	..	..	Hillier/Campbell for O'Leary/Limpar
30 Jan	Leeds U (4R)	A D	1-1*	..	..	..	..	..	Linighan	Hillier	..	..	..	..1	
13 Feb	Leeds U (4R/2)	H D	0-0*	..	..	..	..	..	Groves	O'Leary	..	..	..	..	Campbell/Linighan for Groves/Limpar
16 Feb	Leeds U (4R/3)	A W	2-1	..	..1	..	..	..	Linighan	..	..	..	..1	Campbell	
27 Feb	Shrewsbury T (5)	A W	1-0	..	..	..	..1	..	Adams	..	Hillier	..	..	..	Rocastle for Merson
9 Mar	Cambridge U (6)	H W	2-1	..	..	..	..	..	..1	..	..	..	..	..1	Davis for Hillier
14 Apr	Tottenham H (S/F) (at Wembley)		L 1-3	..	..	..	..	..	..	Campbell	Davis	..1	..	Limpar	Groves for Limpar

*after extra time

Football League (Rumbelows) Cup

Date	Opponent		Res	Seaman	Dixon	Winterburn	Hillier	Bould	Adams	Rocastle	Davis	Smith	Merson	Groves	Substitutes
25 Sep	Chester (2)	A W	1-0	Seaman	Dixon	Winterburn	Hillier	Bould	Adams	Rocastle	Davis	Smith	Merson1	Groves	Cambell for Rocastle
9 Oct	Chester (2)	H W	5-0	..	..	..	..	..	..1	..	..	..1	..1	..2	Campbell/O'Leary for Rocastle/Bould
30 Oct	Manchester C (3)	A W	2-1	..	..	..	Thomas	..	..1	Groves1	..	..	..	Limpar	Campbell for Limpar
28 Nov	Manchester U (4)	H L	2-6	..	..	..	..	..	..	..	..	..2	..	..	Campbell for Limpar

Appearances (Goals)

Bould 38 (5) – Dixon 38 (5) – Seaman 38 – Winterburn 38 – Davis 37 (13) – Merson 37 (13) – Smith 37 (22) – Limpar 34 (11) – Groves 32 (3) – Thomas 31 (2) – Adams 30 (1) – Campbell 22 (9) – O'Leary 21 (1) – Rocastle 16 (2) – Hillier 16 – Linighan 10 – Jonsson 2 – Cole 1 – Pates 1 – Own goals 2 – **Total 19 players (86)**

Position in League Table

	P	W	D	L	F:A	Pts	
Arsenal	38	24	13	1	74:18	83**	1st

**two points deducted

SEASON 1991-92 FOOTBALL LEAGUE (DIVISION 1)

Date	Opponent		Res	Seaman	Dixon	Winterburn	Hillier	O'Leary	Adams	Campbell	Davis	Smith	Merson	Limpar	Substitutes
17 Aug	Q P R	H D	1-1	Seaman	Dixon	Winterburn	Hillier	O'Leary	Adams	Campbell	Davis	Smith	Merson1	Limpar	Rocastle/Groves for O'Leary/Campbell
20 Aug	Everton	A L	1-3	..	..	..1	..	..	..	Rocastle	..	..	..	..	Groves/Linighan for Limpar/Hillier
24 Aug	Aston Villa	A L	1-3	..	..	..	Linighan	..	..	..	..	..1	..	..	Groves/Thomas for O'Leary/Rocastle
27 Aug	Luton T	H W	2-0	..	..	..	Thomas	Linighan	..	..	..	..1	..1	..	Campbell/Pates for Rocastle/Limpar
31 Aug	Manchester C	H W	2-1	..	..	..	..	..	..	..	..	..1	..	..1	Rocastle/Limpar for Rocastle/Limpar
3 Sep	Leeds U	A D	2-2	..	..	..	..	..	..	O'Leary	..	..2	..	Campbell	O'Leary/Thomas for Limpar/Davis
7 Sep	Coventry C	H L	1-2	..	..	..	Campbell	..	..1	Rocastle	..	..	..	Limpar	Thomas1/O'Leary for Groves/Hillier
14 Sep	Crystal Palace	A W	4-1	..	..	..	Hillier	..	..	..	Groves	..1	..	Campbell2	O'Leary/Thomas for Winterburn/Groves
21 Sep	Sheffield U	H W	5-2	..	..1	..	Campbell1	..	..1	Davis	..1	..	..	Groves1	Campbell for Merson
28 Sep	Southampton	A W	4-0	..	..	..	Thomas	..	..	..1	Wright3	..	..	Limpar	Merson/O'Leary for Limpar/Wright
5 Oct	Chelsea	H W	3-2	..	..1p	..	..	Pates	..1	..	..1	..	Campbell1	..	Limpar for Campbell
19 Oct	Manchester U	A D	1-1	..	..	..	Davis	Pates	Adams	..1	..	..	Merson	Campbell	Limpar for Campbell
26 Oct	Notts Co	H W	2-0	..	..	..	..	..	..	..1	..1	..	..	..	Groves for Thomas
2 Nov	West Ham	H L	0-1	..	..	..	Thomas	..	Linighan	..	..	..	..	Limpar	Groves for Thomas
16 Nov	Oldham A	A D	1-1	..	..	..	Hillier	Bould	..	..	..	..	..	Pates	O'Leary/Groves for Bould/Pates
23 Nov	Sheffield W	A D	1-1	..	..	..	..	..	..1	..	..	..	..	..	O'Leary for Hillier
1 Dec	Tottenham H	H W	2-0	..	..	..	..	..	..	..	..1	..	..	Campbell1	Limpar/O'Leary for Wright/Rocastle
8 Dec	Nottingham F	A L	2-3	..	..	..	..	..	..	..	Campbell	..1	..1	Limpar	Carter/O'Leary for Limpar/Bould
21 Dec	Everton	H W	4-2	..	..	..	..	..	Adams	..	Wright4	..	..	..	O'Leary/Campbell for Rocastle/Merson
26 Dec	Luton T	A L	0-1	..	..	..	O'Leary	..	..	..	..	..	..	..	Campbell for Limpar
28 Dec	Manchester C	A L	0-1	..	..	..	..	..	..	..	..	..	..	Davis	Linighan/Groves for Bould/O'Leary
1 Jan	Wimbledon	H D	1-1	..	..	..	Hillier	Linighan	..	..	..	..	..1	Carter	Campbell for Wright
11 Jan	Aston Villa	H D	0-0	..	..	..	..	O'Leary	..	..	Campbell	..	..	..	Groves for Merson
18 Jan	Q P R	A D	0-0	..	..	..	Davis	..	..	..	Wright	..	..	..	Bould/Groves for O'Leary/Parlour
29 Jan	Liverpool	A L	0-2	..	..	..	Parlour	..	..	..	..	..	..	..	Pates/Limpar for Rocastle/Carter
1 Feb	Manchester U	H D	1-1	..	..	..	Hillier	Bould	..	..1	..	..	..	..	Bould/Groves for O'Leary/Parlour Pates/Limpar for Rocastle/Carter
8 Feb	Notts Co	A W	1-0	..	..	..	..	..	..	Pates	..	..1	..	Groves	Parlour/Campbell for Winterburn/Groves
11 Feb	Norwich C	H D	1-1	..	..	..	..	..	..	..	..	..	..1	Limpar	Campbell/Parlour for Limpar/Winterburn
15 Feb	Sheffield W	H W	7-1	..	..	..	..	..	..	Rocastle	..1	..1	..1	..2	Campbell2 for Smith
22 Feb	Tottenham H	A D	1-1	..	..	..	..	..	Pates	..	..1	..	..	Campbell	O'Leary/Limpar for Hillier/Rocastle
10 Mar	Oldham A	H W	2-1	..	..	..	..	..	Adams	..	..1	..	..1	Limpar	O'Leary for Limpar
14 Mar	West Ham U	A W	2-0	..	..	..	..	..	..	..	..2	..	..	Groves	Campbell/O'Leary for Smith/Groves
22 Mar	Leeds U	H D	0-0	..	..	..	..	..	..	..	..	O'Leary	..1	Campbell	Parlour/Limpar for Hillier/Rocastle
28 Mar	Wimbledon	A W	3-1	..	..	..	..	..	..	Parlour1	..1	Campbell1	..	Groves	Limpar/Lydersen for Groves/Merson
31 Mar	Nottingham F	H D	3-3	..	..1p	..	..	..	..1	Rocastle	..	..	..1	Limpar	Lydersen/Smith for Rocastle/Wright
4 Apr	Coventry C	A W	1-0	..	..	..	..	..	..	Lydersen	..	..1	..	..	Rocastle/Smith for Winterburn/Limpar
8 Apr	Norwich C	A W	3-1	..	O'Leary	Lydersen	..	..	..	Rocastle	..2.1p	..1	..	..	Morrow/Smith for O'Leary/Limpar
11 Apr	Crystal Palace	H W	4-1	..	Lydersen	Winterburn	..	..	..	..	..	..1	..3	..	Smith/Morrow for Limpar/Winterburn
18 Apr	Sheffield U	A D	1-1	..	..	..	..1	..	..	..	Campbell1	Smith	..	..	Heaney for Limpar
20 Apr	Liverpool	H W	4-0	..	..	..	..	..	..	..	Wright2	Campbell	..	..1	O'Leary for Lydersen
25 Apr	Chelsea	A D	1-1	..	Dixon1	..	..	..	..	..	..	..	..	..	Smith/Merson for Limpar/Lydersen
2 May	Southampton	H W	5-1	..	..	..	..	..	..	..	..3.1p	..1	..	..	Smith1/Parlour for Limpar/Merson

FA Cup

Date	Opponent		Res	Seaman	Dixon	Winterburn	Hillier	O'Leary	Adams	Rocastle	Campbell	Smith	Merson	Carter	Substitutes
4 Jan	Wrexham (3)	A L	1-2	Seaman	Dixon	Winterburn	Hillier	O'Leary	Adams	Rocastle	Campbell	Smith1	Merson	Carter	Groves for Campbell

Football League (Rumbelows) Cup

Date	Opponent		Res												Substitutes
25 Sep	Leicester C (2)	A D	1-1	Seaman	Dixon	Thomas	Campbell	Linighan	Adams	Rocastle	Davis	Wright1	Merson	Groves	O'Leary for Linighan
8 Oct	Leicester C (2)	H W	2-0	..	..	Winterburn	Thomas	Pates	..	..	Wright1	Smith	..1	Campbell	Groves for Writht
30 Oct	Coventry C (3)	A L	0-1	..	..	..	Davis	..	..	..	..	..	..	Limpar	Groves/Linighan for Limpar/Pates

FA Charity Shield

Date	Opponent		Res												Substitutes
18 Aug	Tottenham H (at Wembley)	D	0-0	Seaman	Dixon	Winterburn	Hillier	O'Leary	Adams	Rocastle	Davis	Smith	Merson	Campbell	Thomas/Cole for Rocastle/Campbell

European Cup

Date	Opponent		Res												Substitutes
18 Sept	FK Austria (1)	H W	6-1	Seaman	Dixon	Winterburn	Campbell	Linighan1	Adams	Rocastle	Davis	Smith4	Merson	Limpar1	Groves for Limpar
2 Oct	FK Austria (1)	A L	0-1	..	..	..	Thomas	..	..	..	Campbell	..	..	O'Leary	Groves for Merson
23 Oct	Benfica (2)	A D	1-1	..	..	..	Davis	Pates	..	..	..1	..	..	Limpar	Groves/Thomas for Campbell/Limpar
6 Nov	Benfica (2) *after extra time	H L	1-3*	..	..	..	..	..1	..	..	..	..	..	..	

Appearances (Goals)

Seaman 42 – Merson 42 (12) – Winterburn 41 (1) – Rocastle 39 (4) – Smith 39 (2) – Dixon 38 (4) – Adams 35 (2) – Campbell 31 (13) – Wright 30 (24) – Limpar 29 (4) – Hillier 27 (1) – Bould 25 (1) – O'Leary 25 – Linighan 17 – Groves 13 (1) – Davis 12 – Pates 11 – Thomas 10 (1) – Carter 6 – Parlour 6 (1) – Morrow (2) – Heaney 1 – **Total 22 players (71)**

Position in League Table

	P	W	D	L	F:A	Pts	
Leeds U	42	22	16	4	74:37	82	1st
Arsenal	42	19	15	8	81:46	72	4th

SEASON 1992-93 FA PREMIER LEAGUE

Date	Opponents		Res												Substitutes
15 Aug	Norwich C	H L	2-4	Seaman	Dixon	Winterburn	Hillier	Bould1	Adams	Jensen	Smith	Campbell1	Merson	Limpar	Wright for Merson
18 Aug	Blackburn Rov	A L	0-1	..	..	..	..	..	..	..	..	..	Carter	..	Pates/Groves for Jensen/Limpar
23 Aug	Liverpool	A W	2-0	..	..	..	..	Pates	..	..	Wright1	..	Parlour	..1	Merson for Limpar
26 Aug	Oldham	A W	2-0	..	..	..1	..	Bould	..	Parlour	..1	..	Merson	Morrow	Pates/Smith for Merson/Wright
29 Aug	Sheffield W	H W	2-1	..	..	..	..	..	..	Jensen	..	..	..1	Parlour1	Smith for Merson
2 Sep	Q P R	A D	0-0	..	..	..	..	..	..	..	..	..	..	..	Pates/Smith for Hillier/Merson
5 Sep	Wimbledon	A L	2-3	..	..	..	Pates	..	..	..	..2	..	..	..	O'Leary/Smith for Jensen/Adams
12 Sep	Blackburn Rov	H L	0-1	..	..	..	Selley	..	..	..	..	Smith	..	..	Campbell/Morrow for Parlour/Jensen
19 Sep	Sheffield U	A D	1-1	..	..	..	Parlour	..	..	..	..1	..	..	Limpar	Linighan/Flatts for Merson/Limpar
28 Sep	Manchester C	H W	1-0	..	..	..	Hillier	..	..	..	..1	..	..	Campbell	Limpar for Smith
3 Oct	Chelsea	H W	2-1	..	..	..	..	..	..	..	..1	..	..1	..	Limpar for Merson
17 Oct	Nottingham F	A W	1-0	..	..	..	..	..	..	..	..	..1	..	..	Limpar/Pates for Wright/Jensen
24 Oct	Everton	H W	2-0	..	..	..	..	..	..	..	..	..1	..	..	Pates/Limpar1 for Dixon/Wright
2 Nov	Crystal P	A W	2-1	..	..	Morrow	..	..	..	..	..1	..1	..1	..1	Limpar for Wright
7 Nov	Coventry C	H W	3-0	..	..	..	..	..	..	..	..1	Campbell	..	Limpar	Limpar for Campbell; Parlour/Miller for Hillier/Seaman
21 Nov	Leeds U	A L	0-3	..	..	..	..	..	..	..	..	..	..	..	Parlour/Flatts for Jensen/Limpar
28 Nov	Manchester U	H L	0-1	..	..	..	..	..	..	Parlour	..	..	..	Flatts	Jensen/Limpar for Dixon/Flatts
5 Dec	Southampton	A L	0-2	..	..	..	..	..	..	..	..	..	..	Parlour	Limpar for Jensen
12 Dec	Tottenham H	A L	0-1	..	Lydersen	Winterburn	..	..	..	Jensen	..	Smith	..	..	Jensen/Campbell for Merson/Parlour
19 Dec	Middlesbrough	H D	1-1	..	..	..	..	Linighan	..	Flatts	..1	..	..	..	O'Leary Limpar for Jensen/Campbell
26 Dec	Ipswich T	H D	0-0	..	..	..	..	Bould	Linighan	Jensen	..	..	Campbell	Flatts	Flatts/Limpar for Parlour/Hillier
28 Dec	Aston Villa	A L	0-1	..	..	..	..	..	..	O'Leary	..	..	..	Parlour	O'Leary for Merson
9 Jan	Sheffield U	H D	1-1	..	Dixon	..	..1	Linighan	Adams	Jensen	..	..	Merson	Limpar	
16 Jan	Manchester C	A W	1-0	..	..	..	..	Bould	..	..	Campbell	..	..1	Flatts	
31 Jan	Liverpool	H L	0-1	..	..	..	..	Linighan	..	Carter	..	..	..	Parlour	O'Leary/Heaney for Hiller/O'Leary
10 Feb	Wimbledon	H L	0-1	..	Keown	..	..	..	..	Selley	Wright	..	..	Campbell	Carter/Morrow for Merson/Smith
20 Feb	Oldham A	A W	1-0	..	..	Morrow	..	..1	..	Jensen	Selley	Campbell	..	Limpar	Carter for Limpar
24 Feb	Leeds U	H D	0-0	..	Dixon	Winterburn	..	..	..	Selley	Wright	Smith	..	Flatts	Campbell for Limpar
1 Mar	Chelsea	A L	0-1	..	..	Morrow	..	..	Keown	Jensen	Campbell	..	..	..	Lydersen/Carter for Hillier/Campbell
3 Mar	Norwich C	A D	1-1	..	..	Winterburn	Davis	..	..	..	Wright1	Parlour	Carter	Limpar	Campbell for Limpar
13 Mar	Coventry C	A W	2-0	..	..	Keown	..	..	Adams	Parlour	..1	Campbell1	Merson	Morrow	Limpar/Hillier for Wright/Merson
20 Mar	Southampton	H W	4-3	..	Keown	Winterburn	..	..1	..	Carter2	Morrow	..	..1	Limpar	Hillier/Dickov for Davis/Limpar
24 Mar	Manchester U	A D	0-0	..	Dixon	Keown	Morrow	..	..	Jensen	Wright	..	..	Carter	Parlour/Hillier for Carter/Adams
6 Apr	Middlesbrough	A L	0-1	..	O'Leary	Winterburn	Hillier	..	..	..	..	Smith	Carter	Limpar	Morrow/Keown for Hillier/O'Leary
10 Apr	Ipswich T	A W	2-1	..	..	..	Morrow	..	Keown	..	Campbell	..1	Merson1	Carter	Adams/Parlour for O'Leary/Jensen
12 Apr	Aston Villa	H L	0-1	..	Dixon	..	Selley	Keown	Adams	Morrow	Wright	..	..	Campbell	Parlour/Linighan for Wright/Campbell
21 Apr	Nottingham F	H D	1-1	..	..	..	..	Linighan	Keown	Jensen	..1	..	Parlour	Carter	Adams/Campbell for Winterburn/Parlour
1 May	Everton	A D	0-0	..	O'Leary	Lydersen	Davis	..	Bould	Keown	Selley	..	Campbell	..	Jensen/Heaney for Lydersen/Carter
4 May	Q P R	H D	0-0	Miller	Dixon	Keown	..	Adams	..	Jensen	Campbell	..	Merson	Heaney	Carter for Merson
6 May	Sheffield W	A L	0-1	..	Lydersen	..	Marshall	O'Leary	Bould	..	Selley	..	Heaney	Carter	McGowan/Flatts for Jensen/Lydersen
8 May	Crystal P	H W	3-0	Seaman	Dixon	Winterburn	Davis	Linighan	Adams	Carter	Wright1	Campbell1	Merson	Parlour	Dickov1/O'Leary for Carter/Wright
11 May	Tottenham H	H L	1-3	Miller	Lydersen	Keown	Marshall	O'Leary	Bould	Flatts	Selley	Smith	Dickov1	Heaney	McGowan/Carter for Lydersen/Flatts

FA Cup

Date	Opponent		Res												Substitutes
2 Jan	Yeovil T (3)	A W	3-1	Seaman	Dixon	Winterburn	Hillier	Bould	Adams	O'Leary	Wright3	Smith	Merson	Limpar	Carter for Jensen
25 Jan	Leeds U (4)	H D	2-2	..	..	..	..	Linighan	..	Jensen	Campbell	..1	..1	Parlour1	Campbell/O'Leary for Parlour/Winterburn
3 Feb	Leeds U (4R)	A W	3-2*	..	..	..	Selley	..	..	Morrow	Wright2	..1	..	..	Campbell/Morrow for Wright/Limpar
13 Feb	Nottingham F (5)	H W	2-0	..	..	..	Hillier	..	..	Jensen	..2	Selley	..	Limpar	Hillier/Campbell1 for Carter/Smith
6 Mar	Ipswich T (6)	A W	4-2	..	Opponents	..	Davis	..	..1	Carter	..1p	Smith	..	Morrow	Smith/Morrow for Wright/Campbell
4 Apr	Tottenham H (SF) (at Wembley)	W	1-0	..	..	..	Hillier	..	..1	Parlour	..	Campbell	..	Selley	Smith/O'Leary for Parlour/Wright
15 May	Sheffield W (F) (at Wembley)	D	1-1*	..	..	..	Davis	..	..	Jensen	..1	..	..	Parlour	Smith/O'Leary for Parlour/Wright
20 May	Sheffield W (FR) (at Wembley) *after extra time	W	2-1*	..	..	..	..	..1	..	..	..1	Smith	..	Campbell	O'Leary for Wright

Football League (Coca-Cola) Cup

Date	Opponent		Res												Substitutes
22 Sep	Millwall (2)	H D	1-1	Seaman	Dixon	Winterburn	Hillier	Bould	Adams	Parlour	Wright	Smith	Merson	Limpar	Campbell1 for Limpar
7 Oct	Millwall (2) *(won 3-1 on penalties)	A D	1-1*	..	..	..	..	..	..	Jensen	..	..	..	Campbell1	Parlour for Merson
28 Oct	Derby Co (3)	A D	1-1	..	Lydersen	Morrow	..	..	..	Parlour	Campbell1	..	..	Limpar	
1 Dec	Derby Co (3R)	H W	2-1	..	Dixon	..	..	..	..	O'Leary	Wright1	Campbell1	..	Flatts	Campbell for Merson
6 Jan	Scarborough (4)	A W	1-0	..	..	Winterburn1	..	..	..	Jensen	..	Smith	..	Limpar	Campbell for Limpar
12 Jan	Nottingham F (5)	H W	2-0	..	..	..	..	Linighan	..	Selley	..2	..2	..	..	
7 Feb	Crystal P (SF)	A W	3-1	..	..	..	..	..	..	Selley	..1p	..2	..	Campbell	Morrow for Wright

Date	Match	V	Res											Substitutes
10 Mar	Crystal P (SF)	H	W 2-0	..	..	..	Davis ..1	..	Carter ..1	..	..	Morrow		Hillier/Campbell for Winterburn/Smith
18 Apr	Sheffield W (f) (at Wembley)		W 2-1	..	O'Leary	..	Morrow1	..	..	Campbell	..	Davis ..1	Parlour	

Appearances (Goals)

Seaman 39 — Campbell 37 (4) — Adams 35 — Merson 33 (6) — Jensen 32 — Wright 31 (15) — Smith 31 (3) — Hillier 30 (1) — Dixon 29 — Winterburn 29 (1) — Bould 24 (1) — Limpar 23 (2) — Linighan 21 (2) — Parlour 21 (1) — Morrow 16 — Carter 16 (2) — Keown 16 — O'Leary 11 — Flatts 10 — Selley 9 — Lydersen 8 — Pates 7 — Davis 6 — Heaney 5 — Miller 4 — Dickov 3 (2) — Marshall 2 — McGowan 2 — Groves 1 — **Total 29 players (40)**

Position in League Table

	P	W	D	L	F:A	Pts	
Manchester U	42	24	12	6	67:31	84	1st
Arsenal	42	15	11	16	40:38	56	10th

SEASON 1993-94 FA CARLING PREMIERSHIP

Date	Match	V	Res												Substitutes
14 Aug	Coventry C	H	L 0-3	Seaman	Dixon	Winterburn	Davis	Linighan	Adams	Jensen	Wright	Campbell	Merson	Limpar	McGoldrick/Keown for Jensen/Dixon
16 Aug	Tottenham H	A	W 1-0	..	Keown	..	..	..	..	..	..1	..	McGoldrick	Parlour	Merson for Parlour
21 Aug	Sheffield W	A	W 1-0	..	..	..	..	..	..	..	..1	..	..	..	Hillier for Davis
24 Aug	Leeds U	H	W 2-1	..	opponents	..	..	..	Selley	Merson1	..	..	..	..	Merson for Hillier
28 Aug	Everton	H	W 2-0	..	..	..	Hillier	..	Adams	Jensen	..2	..	..	..	Merson for Hillier
1 Sep	Blackburn Rov	A	D 1-1	..	..	..	Merson	..	..	..	..	..1	..	..	Selley for Merson
11 Sep	Ipswich T	H	W 4-0	..	..	..	Davis	..	..	..	..1	..3	Merson	McGoldrick	Hillier/Limpar for Jensen/Merson
19 Sep	Manchester U	A	L 0-1	..	..	..	Hillier	..	..	..	..	..	..	..	Davis/Smith for Hillier/Merson
25 Sep	Southampton	H	W 1-0	..	..	..	Davis	..	..	..	..	..	..1	..	Hillier for Davis
2 Oct	Liverpool	A	D 0-0	..	Dixon	..	..	..	..	..	..	..	..	..	Campbell for Heaney
16 Oct	Manchester C	H	D 0-0	..	..	..	..	..	..	Heaney	..	Smith	Parlour	..	Campbell for Hillier
23 Oct	Oldham A	H	D 0-0	..	..	..	..	..	..	Hillier	..	..	Merson	..	Keown/Campbell for Winterburn/Smith
30 Oct	Norwich C	H	D 0-0	..	..	..	..	Bould	..	Jensen	..	..	..	Limpar	Morrow for Winterburn
6 Nov	Aston Villa	H	L 1-2	..	..	..	Selley	Keown	..	..	..1	Campbell	Merson	..	Campbell/Miller for Limpar/Wright
20 Nov	Chelsea	A	W 2-0	..	..	..	Davis	Linighan	Bould	Keown	..1p	Smith1	..	Selley	Bould/Campbell for Adams/McGoldrick
24 Nov	West Ham U	A	D 0-0	..	..	..	Keown	..	..	Morrow	..	..	..	Limpar	Campbell for Smith
27 Nov	Newcastle	A	W 2-1	..	..	..	Morrow	Keown	..	Jensen	..1	..1	..	McGoldrick	Bould/Campbell for Adams/McGoldrick
4 Dec	Coventry C	A	L 0-1	..	..	..	Davis	..	Adams	Selley	..	..	..	..	Bould/Campbell for Keown/Merson
6 Dec	Tottenham H	H	D 1-1	..	..	Keown	Selley	Bould	..	Jensen	..1	..	..	Limpar	Parlour/Morrow for Smith/Dixon
12 Dec	Sheffield W	H	W 1-0	Miller	..	Morrow	..	Keown	..	..	..1	..	..	..	Merson/Keown for Parlour/Adams
18 Dec	Leeds U	A	L 1-2	Seaman	..	Winterburn	..	Bould	..	..	..	..	Campbell1	..	Merson/Keown for Wright/Parlour
27 Dec	Swindon T	A	W 4-0	..	..	..	Parlour	..	..	..	..1	Campbell3	Hillier	McGoldrick	Keown/Merson for Dixon/Jensen
29 Dec	Sheffield U	H	W 3-0	..	..	..	..	..	..	..	..1	..2	..	..	Keown for Jensen
1 Jan	Wimbledon	A	W 3-0	..	..	..	..1	..	..	..	..1	..1	..	..	Merson/Keown for McGoldrick/Jensen
3 Jan	Q P R	H	D 0-0	..	..	..	..	..	..	..	..	..	..	..	Keown for Jensen
15 Jan	Manchester C	A	D 0-0	..	..	..	..	..	..	..	..	..	..	..	Merson/Keown for McGoldrick/Jensen
22 Jan	Oldham A	H	D 1-1	..	..	..	..	..	..	..	..1p	..	..	..	Merson/Keown for McGoldrick/Jensen
13 Feb	Norwich C	A	D 1-1	..	..	Davis	..	..	..	Campbell1	Smith	Merson	Parlour	..	Keown/Hillier for Adams/Jensen
19 Feb	Everton	A	D 1-1	..	..	..	..	..	..	..	..	..	..1	..	Keown/Hillier for Adams/Jensen
26 Feb	Blackburn Rov	H	W 1-0	..	..	..	..	..	..	..	..	..	..1	..	Merson/Keown for Limpar/Hillier
5 Mar	Ipswich T	A	W 5-1	..	opponents	..	Selley	..	..	Parlour1	Wright3.1p	..	Hillier	Limpar	Smith for Limpar
19 Mar	Southampton	A	W 4-0	..	opponents	..	Keown	Linighan	..	..	..3.1p	Campbell1	Selley	..	Campbell for Davis
22 Mar	Manchester U	H	D 2-2	..	..	..	Davis	Bould	..	Jensen	..	Smith	Merson1	Selley	Morrow/Smith for Jensen/Wright
26 Mar	Liverpool	H	W 1-0	..	..	Keown	Parlour	..	Linighan	..	..	Campbell	..1	..	Campbell/McGoldrick for Merson/Jensen
2 Apr	Swindon T	H	D 1-1	..	..	..	Davis	Linighan	Adams	..	..	Smith1	..	Parlour	Dixon/Merson for Keown/McGoldrick
4 Apr	Sheffield U	A	D 1-1	..	Keown	Winterburn	Parlour	Bould	..	Campbell1	..	..	Selley	McGoldrick	Smith for Hillier
16 Apr	Chelsea	H	W 1-0	..	Dixon	Morrow	Hillier	Keown	..	Selley	..1	Campbell	Parlour	Selley	Flatts for Davis
19 Apr	Wimbledon	H	D 1-1	..	..	Keown	Davis	Bould1	..	Campbell	Smith	..	Selley		Parlour for Davis
23 Apr	Aston Villa	A	W 2-1	..	..	..	..	..	Linighan	..	..2.1p	..	Morrow	Flatts	Selley/McGoldrick for Flatts/Keown
27 Apr	Q P R	A	D 1-1	..	..	..	Morrow	Linighan	Adams	Flatts	..	..	Merson1	Parlour	Morrow/Dickov for McGoldrick/Merson
30 Apr	West Ham U	H	L 0-2	Millier	McGoldrick	Winterburn	Davis	Bould	Linighan	Parlour	..	Campbell	..	Selley	Parlour/Linighan for Davis/Dixon
7 May	Newcastle	A	L 0-2	..	Dixon	..	..	..	Adams	McGoldrick	..	Smith	Morrow	Selley	

FA Cup

Date	Match	V	Res												Substitutes
10 Jan	Millwall (3)	A	W 1-0	Seaman	Dixon	Winterburn	Parlour	Bould	Adams1	Keown	Wright	Campbell	Hillier	McGoldrick	Merson/Jensen for Wright/Hillier
31 Jan	Bolton W (4)*	A	D 2-2	..	..	..	..	..	..1	..	..1	..	Merson		Smith for Parlour
9 Feb	Bolton W (4R) *aet	H	L 1-3*	..	..	..	Hillier	..	..	Campbell	Smith1	Merson	Parlour		Keown/McGoldrick for Hillier/Wright

Football League (Coca-Cola) Cup

Date	Match	V	Res												Substitutes
21 Sep	Huddersfield T (2)	A	W 5-0	Seaman	Keown	Winterburn	Davis	Linighan	Adams	Jensen	Wright3	Campbell1	Merson1	McGoldrick	Hillier/Smith for Jensen/Merson
5 Oct	Huddersfield (2)	H	D 1-1	..	Dixon	..	Parlour	..	Bould	..	Smith1	..	Limpar	..	Selley/Heaney for Jensen/McGoldrick
26 Oct	Norwich C (3)	H	D 1-1	..	..	..	..	..	Adams	..	Wright1	Smith	Merson	..	Campbell/Davis for Merson/McGoldrick
10 Nov	Norwich C (3R)	A	W 3-0	..	..	Keown	Selley	..	Bould	..	..2	..	..1	Limpar	
30 Nov	Aston Villa (4)	H	L 0-1	..	..	Winterburn	Morrow	Keown	..	..	..	..	..	McGoldrick	Campbell/Davis for Jensen/Dixon

FA Charity Shield

Date	Match	V	Res												Substitutes
7 Aug	Manchester U (at Wembley)		D 1-1	Seaman	Dixon	Winterburn	Davis	Linighan	Adams	Jensen	Wright1	Campbell	Merson	Limpar	Keown/McGoldrick for Dixon/Limpar

European Cup Winners Cup

Date	Match	V	Res												Substitutes
15 Sep	Odense (1)	A	W 2-1	Seaman	Selley	Winterburn	Davis	Linighan	Keown	Jensen	Wright1	Campbell	Merson1	McGoldrick	Smith for Wright
29 Sep	Odense (1)	H	D 1-1	..	Dixon	..	..	Keown	Adams	..	..	..1	..	..	Smith for Wright
20 Oct	Standard Liege (2)	H	W 3-0	..	..	..	..	..	..	..	..2	Smith	..1	..	Campbell/Linighan for Wright/Keown
3 Nov	Standard Liege (2)	A	W 7-0	..	..	..	..	..	..	..1	Selley1	..1	..1	Campbell2	McGoldrick 1/Bould for Smith/Keown
2 Mar	Torino (3)	A	D 0-0	..	..	..	..	Bould	..	..	Campbell	..	..	Hillier	Selley for Davis
15 Mar	Torino (3)	H	W 1-0	..	..	..	..	..	..1	..	Wright	..	..	..	Selley/Keown for Hillier/Jensen
29 Mar	Paris St-German (SF)	A	D 1-1	..	..	..	..	..	..	..	..1	..	..	Selley	Keown/Campbell for Davis/Smith
12 Apr	Paris St-German (SF)	H	W 1-0	..	..	..	..	..	..	..	..	..	Campbell1	Selley	Hillier/Keown for Davis/Winterburn
4 May	Parma (F) (at Copenhagen)		W 1-0	..	..	..	..	..	..	Campbell	Morrow	..1	Merson	..	McGoldrick for Merson

Appearances (Goals)

Seaman 39 — Wright 39 (23) — Campbell 37 (14) — Adams 35 — Winterburn 34 — Dixon 33 — Keown 33 — Merson 33 (7) — Jensen 27 — Parlour 27 (2) — McGoldrick 26 — Bould 25 (1) — Smith 25 (3) — Davis 22 — Linighan 21 — Selley 18 — Hillier 15 — Morrow 11 — Limpar 10 — Miller 4 — Flatts 3 — Dickov 1 — Heaney 1 — Own goals 3 — **Total 23 players (51)**

Position in League Table

	P	W	D	L	F:A	Pts	
Manchester U	42	27	11	4	80:38	92	1st
Arsenal	42	18	17	7	53:28	73	4th

SEASON 1994-95 FA CARLING PREMIERSHIP

Date	Opponent			Score	1	2	3	4	5	6	7	8	9	10	11	Substitutes
20 Aug	Manchester C	H	W	3-0*	Seaman	Dixon	Winterburn	Jensen	Bould	Adams	Campbell1	Wright1	Smith	Merson	Schwarz	Keown/Dickov for Adams/Merson
23 Aug	Leeds U	A	L	0-1	..	..	..	..	..	..	..	..	..	..	..	Keown for Bould
28 Aug	Liverpool	A	L	0-3	..	..	..	..	Keown	..	..	..	..	..	..	Linighan/Davis for Jensen/Merson
31 Aug	Blackburn Rov	H	D	0-0	..	..	..	..	..	..	..	..	..	..	..	Dickov/Linighan for Merson/Adams
10 Sep	Norwich C	A	D	0-0	..	..	..	Selley	..	..	Parlour	..	..	Campbell	McGoldrick	Smith for McGoldrick
18 Sep	Newcastle U	H	L	2-3	..	..	..	Jensen	..	..1	..	..1	Smith	Merson	..	Selley/Campbell for Jensen/Parlour
25 Sep	West Ham U	A	W	2-0	..	..	..	Davis	..	..1	Selley	..1	..	..	..	Linighan for Keown
1 Oct	Crystal P	H	L	1-2	..	..	..	..	Linighan	..	..	..1	..	..	..	Campbell for Davis
8 Oct	Wimbledon	A	W	3-1	..	..	..	Jensen	Bould	..	Parlour	..1	..1	Campbell1	..	Hillier for Schwarz
15 Oct	Chelsea	H	W	3-1	..	..	..	..	..	..	..	..2	..	..1	..	Selley/Keown for Jensen/Adams
23 Oct	Coventry C	H	W	2-1	..	..	..	Selley	..	Keown	Campbell	..2	..	Schwarz	Parlour	McGoldrick for Wright
29 Oct	Everton	A	D	1-1	..	McGoldrick	..	Jensen	Keown	Adams	Parlour	Campbell	..	Merson	Schwarz1	Selley/Linighan for Winterburn/Merson
6 Nov	Sheffield W	H	D	0-0	..	Keown	..	Selley	Bould	..	..	Dickov	..	Schwarz	Schwarz	Campbell for Smith
19 Nov	Southampton	A	L	0-1	..	Dixon	..	..	..	..	Keown	..	Campbell	McGoldrick	Schwarz	Carter for McGoldrick
23 Nov	Leicester C	A	L	1-2	..	..	..	..	..	Linighan	..	Wright1p	Dickov	Carter	..	Campbell/Morrow for Linighan/Selley
26 Nov	Manchester U	H	D	0-0	..	..	..	Jensen	..	Adams	Morrow	..	Smith	McGoldrick	Carter	Dickov/Keown for Carter/Jensen
3 Dec	Nottingham F	A	D	2-2	Bartram	..	..	Davis1	..	Keown1	Parlour	Hillier	Campbell	Flatts	Schwarz	Shaw for Flatts
12 Dec	Manchester C	A	W	2-1	..	..	..	Morrow	..	..	Jensen	Campbell	Smith1	Parlour	..1	
17 Dec	Leeds U	H	L	1-3	..	..	..	..	..	..	..	..	..	..	..	Flatts/Linighan1 for Smith/Jensen
26 Dec	Aston Villa	H	D	0-0	..	..	..	..	..	..	Hughes	Dickov	Campbell	..	..	Flatts for Hughes
28 Dec	Ipswich T	A	W	2-0	..	..	..	Jensen	..	..	Campbell1	Wright1	Smith	..	..	Linighan/Dickov for Smith/Wright
31 Dec	Q P R	H	L	1-3	..	..	..1	..	..	..	..	..	..	..	..	Clarke for Smith
2 Jan	Tottenham H	A	L	0-1	Seaman	..	..	..	..	Linighan	Selley	..	Campbell	..	..	Smith for Selley
14 Jan	Everton	H	D	1-1	..	..	..	..	Keown	..	Hillier	..1	Hartson	..	..	Kiwomya/Morrow for Parlour/Jensen
21 Jan	Coventry C	A	W	1-0	..	..	Morrow	Keown	Bould	..	Campbell	..	..1	Hillier	..	Parlour/Kiwomya for Hillier/Wright
24 Jan	Southampton	H	D	1-1	..	..	..	..	..	..	Jensen	..	..1	Parlour	..	Hillier/Kiwomya for Keown/Parlour
4 Feb	Sheffield Wed	A	L	1-3	..	..	Winterburn	Jensen	Linighan1	Adams	Selley	Campbell	..	Merson	Kiwomya	Keown/Parlour for Jensen/Selley
11 Feb	Leicester C	H	D	1-1	..	..	..	..	..	..	McGoldrick	Selley	..	..1	..	Keown/Parlour for Selley/Jensen
21 Feb	Nottingham F	H	W	1-0	..	..	..	..	Bould	Linighan	..	Merson	Kiwomya1	Schwarz	Helder	
25 Feb	Crystal P	A	W	3-0	..	..	..	..	..	..	..	..1	..2	..	..	Morrow for Winterburn, then Parlour for Morrow
5 Mar	West Ham U	H	L	0-1	Bartram	..	..	..	..	..	Parlour	Wright	Helder	Merson	Schwarz	Morrow/Kiwomya for Jensen/Helder
8 Mar	Blackburn Rov	A	L	1-3	..	..	..	Morrow1	Linighan	Adams	..	Helder	Hartson	..	..	Wright/Bould for Hartson/Linighan
19 Mar	Newcastle U	A	L	0-1	..	..	..	Jensen	Bould	..	Morrow	Wright	..	..	Helder	Parlour/McGoldrick for Helder/Hartson
22 Mar	Manchester U	A	L	0-3	..	..	..	Morrow	..	Adams	Keown	..	Kiwomya	Merson	Parlour	Helder for Parlour
1 Apr	Norwich C	H	W	5-1	..	..1	..	..	..	opponents	Hillier	..	Hartson2	..1	Helder	Keown/Kiwomya for Morrow/Hartson
8 Apr	Q P R	A	L	1-3	Seaman	..	..	Schwarz	..	Adams1	Morrow	..	..	..	..	Hillier/Kiwomya for Morrow/Hartson
12 Apr	Liverpool	H	L	0-1	..	Keown	..	..	..	..	Hillier	..	McGoldrick	..	..	Parlour/Hartson for Merson/Helder
15 Apr	Ipswich T	H	W	4-1	..	Dixon	..	..	..	..	Keown	..3	Hartson	..1	..	Parlour/Kiwomya for Winterburn/Wright
17 Apr	Aston Villa	A	W	4-0	..	..	..	..	..	..	..	..2.1p	..2	..	Parlour	Hillier/Kiwomya for Parlour/Wright
29 Apr	Tottenham H	H	D	1-1	..	..	..	..	..	..	Parlour	..1p	..	..	Helder	Parlour for Helder
4 May	Wimbledon	H	D	0-0	..	..	..	Jensen	Linighan	..	..	..	..	..	..	Kiwomya for Hartson
14 May	Chelsea	A	L	1-2	..	..	McGowan	..	Bould	..	..	..	..1	..	..	Linighan/Dickov for McGowan/Helder

*including an own goal

FA Cup

Date	Opponent			Score	1	2	3	4	5	6	7	8	9	10	11	Substitutes
7 Jan	Millwall (3)	A	D	0-0	Seaman	Dixon	Winterburn	Jensen	Bould	Linighan	Hillier	Wright	Smith	Parlour	Schwarz	Keown/Campbell for Jensen/Smith
18 Jan	Millwall (3R)	H	L	0-2	..	..	..	..	Keown	..	..	..	Campbell	..	Morrow	Adams/Flatts for Keown/Jensen

Football League (Coca-Cola) Cup

Date	Opponent			Score	1	2	3	4	5	6	7	8	9	10	11	Substitutes
21 Sep	Hartlepool U (2)	A	W	5-0	Seaman	Dixon	Keown	Davis	Linighan	Adams1	Parlour	Wright2	Smith1	Merson1	Selley	McGoldrick for Smith
5 Oct	Hartlepool U (2)	H	W	2-0	..	..	Winterburn	..	Bould	Keown	..	Dickov1	Campbell1	Hillier	McGoldrick	
26 Oct	Oldham A(3)	A	D	0-0	..	..	..	Selley	..	Adams	..	Campbell	Smith	Merson	Schwarz	Keown/McGoldrick for Dixon/Campbell
9 Nov	Oldham A (3R)	H	W	2-0	..	Keown	..	..	..	..	..	Dickov2	Campbell	McGoldrick	..	Jensen for Selley
30 Nov	Sheffield W (4)	H	W	2-0	..	Dixon	..	Morrow1	..	..	Campbell	Wright1	Smith	..	..	Bartram/Dickov/Keown for Seaman/Morrow/McGoldrick
11 Jan	Liverpool (QF)	A	L	0-1	..	..	..	Jensen	..	Linighan	Hillier	..	Campbell	Parlour	..	Morrow/Dickov for Bould/Parlour

European Cup Winners Cup

Date	Opponent			Score	1	2	3	4	5	6	7	8	9	10	11	Substitutes
15 Sep	Omonia Nicosia (1)	A	W	3-1	Seaman	Dixon	Winterburn	Schwarz	Linighan	Keown	Jensen	Wright1	Smith	Merson2	Parlour	Morrow for Schwarz
29 Sep	Omonia Nicosia (1)	H	W	3-0	..	..	..	..1	..	Adams	..	..2	..	..	..	Hillier/Campbell for Jensen/Merson
20 Oct	Brondby (2)	A	W	2-1	..	..	..	..	Bould	..	..	..1	..1	Campbell	..	
3 Nov	Brondby (2)	H	D	2-2	..	..	..	Selley1	Keown	..	..	..1p	..	Merson	..	Campbell/Bould for Wright/Dixon
2 Mar	Auxerre (3)	H	D	1-1	..	..	..	Schwarz	Bould	..	..	..1p	Kiwomya	..	McGoldrick	Hartson/Parlour for McGoldrick/Kiwomya
16 Mar	Auxerre (3)	A	W	1-0	..	..	..	..	..	..	Keown	..1	Hartson	..	Parlour	Morrow for Hartson
6 Apr	Sampdoria (SF)	H	W	3-2	..	..	..	..2	..	..	Hillier	..1	..	..	..	Kiwomya/Morrow for Wright/Merson
20 Apr	Sampdoria (SF)	A	L	2-3*	..	..	..	..1	..	..	Keown	..	..	..	Hillier	McGoldrick/Kiwomya for Hillier/Wright
10 May	Real Zaragoza (F) (at Paris)		L	1-2*	..	..	..	..	Linighan	..	..	..	..1	..	Parlour	Morrow/Hillier for Winterburn/Keown

*Arsenal won 3-2 on penalties after extra time
*after extra time

Appearances (Goals)

Winterburn 39 – Dixon 39 (1) – Schwarz 34 (2) – Bould 31 – Wright 31 (18) – Seaman 31 – Keown 31 (1) – Parlour 30 – Adams 27 (3) – Merson 24 (4) – Jensen 24 (1) – Campbell 23 (4) – Linighan 20 (2) – Smith 19 (2) – Hartson 15 (7) – Morrow 15 (1) – Kiwomya 14 (3) – Selley 13 – Helder 13 – Bartram 11 – McGoldrick 11 – Hillier 9 – Dickov 9 – Davis 4 (1) – Carter 3 – Flatts 3 – Hughes 1 – Shaw 1 – Clarke 1 – McGowan 1 – own goals 2 – **Total 30 players (50)**

Position in League Table

	P	W	D	L	F:A	Pts	
Blackburn R	42	27	8	7	80:39	89	1st
Arsenal	42	13	12	17	52:49	51	12th

SEASON 1995-96 FA CARLING PREMIERSHIP

Date	Opponent			Score	1	2	3	4	5	6	7	8	9	10	11	Substitutes
20 Aug	Middlesbrough	H	D	1-1	Seaman	Dixon	Winterburn	Keown	Bould	Adams	Platt	Wright1	Merson	Bergkamp	Parlour	Helder for Parlour
23 Aug	Everton	A	W	2-0	..	..	..	..	..	..	..1	..1	..	..	..	Jensen for Keown
26 Aug	Coventry C	A	D	0-0	..	..	..	..	..	..	..	..	..	..	..	Jensen/Helder for Dixon/Platt
29 Aug	Nottm F	H	D	1-1	..	..	..	..	..	..	..1	..	..	..	..	Helder for Parlour
10 Sept	Manchester C	A	W	1-0	..	..	..	..	..	..	Jensen	..1	..	..	..	McGoldrick for Parlour
16 Sept	West Ham U	H	W	1-0	..	Dixon	..	Jensen	..	..	Parlour	..1p	..	..	Helder	

Date				Result										
23 Sept	Southampton	H	W	4-2	..	..	..	Keown	..	..1	..	..1	..	..2
30 Sept	Chelsea	A	L	0-1	..	..	..	..	..	..	..	..	..	Jensen	Helder/Linighan for Jensen/Keown
14 Oct	Leeds U	A	W	3-0	..	..	..	..	..	..	..	..1	..1	..1	Helder
21 Oct	Aston Villa	H	W	2-0	..	..	..	..	..	..	..	..1	..1	..1	Helder
30 Oct	Bolton W	A	L	0-1	..	..	..	..	..	..	..	..	..	..	Platt for Keown
4 Nov	Manchester U	H	W	1-0	..	..	..	..	..	..	Platt	..	..	..1	Hartson for Wright
18 Nov	Tottenham H	A	L	1-2	..	..	..	..	..	..	..	Hartson	..	..1	Hillier for Helder
21 Nov	Sheffield W	H	W	4-2	..	..	..1	..	..	..	..	..1	..	..1	Dickov1 for Helder
26 Nov	Blackburn R	H	D	0-0	..	..	..	..	..	..	..	..	..	..	Hillier	Helder/Hartson for Keown/Hartson
2 Dec	Aston Villa	A	D	1-1	..	..	..	Jensen	..	..	..1	Wright	..	Hartson	Helder	Morrow/Dickov for Helder/Hartson
9 Dec	Southampton	A	D	0-0	..	..	..	Keown	..	..	..	..	..	..	Jensen	Clarke for Hartson
16 Dec	Chelsea	H	D	1-1	..	..1	..	..	..	..	..	..	..	..	..	Helder for Jensen
23 Dec	Liverpool	A	L	1-3	..	..	..	Jensen	Keown	Linighan	..	..1p	..	Parlour	..	Marshall/Hartson for Parlour/Helder
26 Dec	Q P R	H	W	3-0	..	..	..	..	..	Adams	..	..1	..2	Dickov	Clarke
30 Dec	Wimbledon	H	L	1-3	..	..	..	..	..	Linighan	..	..1	..	Bergkamp	..	Parlour/Dickov for Clarke/Jensen
2 Jan	Newcastle U	A	L	0-2	..	..	..	Keown	Bould	Adams	..	..	..	..	Parlour	Dickov/Clarke for Bould/Parlour
13 Jan	Middlesbrough	A	W	3-2	..	..	McGowan	Jensen	Keown	Adams	..1	..	..1	..	Helder1
20 Jan	Everton	H	L	1-2	..	..	Winterburn	..	Linighan	Marshall	Clarke	..1	..	..	..	Dickov for Clarke
3 Feb	Coventry	H	D	1-1	..	..	..	..	..	..	..	..	..	..1	..	Hughes for Jensen
10 Feb	Nottm F	A	W	1-0	..	..	..	..	..	Keown	Hillier	..	..	..1	..
24 Feb	West Ham U	A	W	1-0	..	..	..	Morrow	..	..	..	Hartson1	..	..	Parlour	Platt for Hillier
2 Mar	Q P R	A	D	1-1	..	..	..	..	..	..	Platt	..	..	..1	..	Rose for Morrow
5 Mar	Manchester C	H	W	3-1	..	..1	..	Rose	..	..	..	..2	..	..	..
16 Mar	Wimbledon	A	W	3-0	..	..	..1	Marshall	..	..	..1	Wright	..	..1	Hartson
20 Mar	Manchester U	A	L	1-0	..	..	..	..	..	..	..	..	..	..	..	Hillier/Helder for Bergkamp/Merson
23 Mar	Newcastle U	H	W	2-0	..	..	..	..	..	..	..	..1	..	..	..	Parlour/Helder for Wright/Winterburn
6 April	Leeds U	H	W	2-1	..	..	..	..	..	..	..	..2	..	..	..
8 April	Sheffield W	A	L	0-1	..	..	Helder	..	..	..	..	..	..	..	..	Rose/Shaw for Helder/Hartson
15 April	Tottenham H	H	D	0-0	..	..	Winterburn	..	..	..	..	..	..	..	..	Helder for Merson
27 April	Blackburn R	A	D	1-1	..	..	..	Morrow	..	..	..	..1p	..	..	..	Rose/Shaw/Hartson for Morrow/Linighan/Wright
1 May	Liverpool	H	D	0-0	..	..	..	Marshall	..	..	..	Hartson	..	..	..
5 May	Bolton	H	W	2-1	..	..	..	..	..	..	..	Wright	..	..1	..	Shaw/Hartson for Marshall/Wright

FA Cup

6 Jan	Sheffield U (3)	H	D	1-1	Seaman	Dixon	Winterburn	Jensen	Keown	Adams	Clarke	Wright1	Merson	Hartson	Helder
17 Jan	Sheffield U (3R)	A	L	0-1	..	..	McGowan	..	..	.....	Platt	..	..	Bergkamp	..	Linighan/Clarke for Dixon/Jensen

Football League (Coca-Cola) Cup

Date				Result												
19 Sept	Hartlepool (2)	A	W	3-0	Seaman	Dixon	Winterburn	Jensen	Bould	Adams2	Parlour	Wright1	Merson	Bergkamp	Helder
3 Oct	Hartlepool (2)	H	W	5-0	..	..	..	Keown	..	..	..	..3	..	..2	Jensen	Helder/Hartson for Merson/Bergkamp
24 Oct	Barnsley (3)	A	W	3-0	Seaman	..	..	..1	..	..	Jensen	..	..	..1	Helder	Hughes/Hartson for Jensen/Wright
29 Nov	Sheffield W (4)	H	W	2-1	..	..	..	Jensen	..	..	Platt	..1p	..	..	Hartson1	Helder for Bergkamp
10 Jan	Newcastle U (5)	H	W	2-0	..	..	..	Keown	..	..	..	..2	Merson	..	Helder	Jensen for Bould
14 Feb	Aston Villa (SF)	H	D	2-2	..	..	..	Jensen	Linighan	Keown	Hillier	..	..	..2	..	Parlour for Helder
21 Feb	Aston Villa (SF)	A	D	0-0	(aet)	..	..	..	Morrow	..	..	Hillier	..	..	Parlour	Platt for Winterburn

Appearances (Goals)

Seaman 38 – Dixon 38 (2) – Merson 38 (5) – Winterburn 36 (2) – Keown 34 – Bergkamp 33 (11) – Wright 31 (15) – Platt 29 (5) – Helder – 24 (1) – Parlour 22 – Adams 21 (1) – Bould 19 – Hartson 19 (4) – Linighan 18 – Jensen 15 – Marshall 11 (1) – Dickov 7 (1) – Clarke 6 – Hillier 5 – Morrow 4 – Rose 4 – Shaw 3 – McGowan 1 – McGoldrick 1 – Hughes 1 –
Total 25 players (48)

Position in League Table

	P	W	D	L	F:A	Pts	
Manchester U	38	25	7	6	73:35	82	1st
Arsenal	38	17	12	9	49:32	63	5th

SEASON 1996-97 FA CARLING PREMIERSHIP

Date				Result											
17 Aug	West Ham U	H	W	2-0	Seaman	Dixon	Winterburn	..	Bould	Linighan	Parlour	Morrow	Merson	Bergkamp1p	Hartson1	Wright/Dickov for Hartson/Bergkamp
19 Aug	Liverpool	A	L	0-2	..	..	..	..	..	..	..	..	..	..	..	Wright/Helder/Hillier for Bergkamp/Hartson/Morrow
24 Aug	Leicester C	A	W	2-0	..	..	..	..	..	..	..	..	..	..1p	..	Wright1/Hillier for Bergkamp/Hartson
4 Sept	Chelsea	H	D	3-3	Lukic	..	..	..1	..	..	..	..	..1	..	..	Platt/Wright1 for Bould/Hartson
7 Sept	Aston Villa	A	D	2-2	..	..	..	..	Morrow	..1	Platt	Wright	..1	..	Parlour	Hartson/Helder for Morrow/Bergkamp
16 Sept	Sheffield W	H	W	4-1	Seaman	..	..	..	Bould	..	..1	..3.1p	..	Parlour	Hartson	Vieira for Platt
21 Sept	Middlesbrough	A	W	2-0	..	..	..	..	..	..	..	..1	..	Vieira	..1	Adams for Dixon
28 Sept	Sunderland	H	W	2-0	..	..	..	..	..	Adams	..	..	..	..	..1	Parlour1/Shaw for ../Merson
12 Oct	Blackburn Rov	A	W	2-0	..	..	..	..	..	..	..	..2	..	..	..	Parlour for Hartson
19 Oct	Coventry C	H	D	0-0	..	..	..	..	..	..	..	..	..	..	..	Bergkamp for Hartson
26 Oct	Leeds U	H	W	3-0	..	..1	..	..	..	..	..	..1	..	Bergkamp1	Vieira	Morrow/Garde for ../Wright
2 Nov	Wimbledon	A	D	0-0	..	..	..	..	..	..	..	..1	..1	..	..
16 Nov	Manchester U	A	L	0-1	..	..	..	..	..	..	..	..	..	..	..	Garde for Bergkamp
24 Nov	Tottenham H	A	L	3-1	Lukic	..	..	..	..	..	..1	..1p	..	..1	..	Hartson/Parlour for Platt/Bergkamp
30 Nov	Newcastle U	A	W	2-1	..	..1	..	..	..	..	..	..1	..	Hartson	..	Linighan/Morrow/Parlour for Keown/Hartson/..
4 Dec	Southampton	H	W	3-1	Lukic	..	..	Linighan	..	..	..	..1p	..1	..	..	Shaw1/Parlour for Platt/Hartson
7 Dec	Derby Co	H	D	2-2	..	..	..	Linighan	..	..1	..	..	..	..	..1	Shaw for Linighan
21 Dec	Nottingham F	A	L	1-2	..	McGowan	..	Keown	..	Linighan	..	..1	..	Bergkamp	Garde	Hartson/Parlour/Morrow for McGowan/Garde/Bergkamp
26 Dec	Sheffield W	A	D	0-0	..	Parlour	..	..	..	Adams	..	..	..	..	..	Shaw/Marshall for Keown/Platt
28 Dec	Aston Villa	H	D	2-2	..	..	..	..	..	..	Garde	..1	..1	..1	Vieira	Morrow for Garde
1 Jan	Middlesbrough	H	W	2-0	..	..	..	..	..	..	..	..1	..	..1	..	Hartson/Morrow/Shaw for Garde/../Bergkamp
11 Jan	Sunderland	A	L	0-1	Seaman	..	..	..	..	..	Platt	Hartson	..	..	..	Hughes for ..
19 Jan	Everton	A	W	3-1	..	..	..	..	..	..	..	Wright	..1	..1	..1	Dixon/Hughes for Platt/Wright
29 Jan	West Ham U	A	W	2-1	..	Dixon	..	Rose	..	..	Parlour1	..1	..	Hughes	..	Hartson/Marshall/Morrow for Rose/Wright/Hughes
1 Feb	Leeds U	A	D	0-0	..	..	..	Marshall	..	..	..	Hartson	..	..	..	Wright for Hartson
15 Feb	Tottenham H	A	D	0-0	Lukic	..	..	Keown	..	..	..	Wright	..	Bergkamp	..	Hughes for ..
19 Feb	Manchester U	H	L	1-2	..	..	..	..	..	..	..	..	..	..1	..	Hughes for Adams
23 Feb	Wimbledon	H	L	0-1	..	..	..	Garde	..	Marshall	..	..	..	..	..	Hughes/Morrow/Shaw for Garde/Bould/Parlour
1 Mar	Everton	A	W	2-0	..	..	..	Keown	Garde	..	Platt	..1	Hughes	..1	..	Morrow for Garde
8 Mar	Nottingham F	H	W	2-0	..	..	..	..	Marshall	Adams	..	Hughes	Merson	..2.1p	..	Morrow for Hughes

Date	Opponent			Result													Substitutions
15 Mar	Southampton	A	W	2-0	Harper	Parlour	..	..	..	..	..	Shaw1	Hughes1	..	..		Garde for Shaw
24 Mar	Liverpool	H	L	1-2	Seaman	Dixon	..	..	..	..	..	Wright1	..	..	..		Parlour/Garde/Shaw for Dixon/Marshall/Hughes
5 Apr	Chelsea	A	W	3-0	..	..	..	..	Bould	Garde	..1	..1	..	..1			Parlour/Anelka/Selley for Wright/Hughes/Vieira
12 Apr	Leicester C	H	W	2-0	Seaman	..	..	..	..	Adams1	..1	..	..	..			Parlour for Hughes
19 Apr	Blackburn Rov	H	D	1-1	..	..	..	..	..	..	..1	..	..	..			Parlour for Hughes
21 Apr	Coventry C	A	D	1-1	..	..	..	..	..	..	..	..1p	Merson	..			Parlour/Anelka for Dixon/Merson
3 May	Newcastle U	H	L	0-1	..	..	..	..	..	..	..	..	..	..			Parlour/Anelka for Adams/Platt
11 May	Derby Co	A	W	3-1	..	..	..	..	..	..	..	..2	..	..1			Anelka/Parlour for Merson/Vieira

Football League (Coca-Cola) Cup

Date	Opponent			Result													Substitutions
23 Oct	Stoke City (3)	A	D	1-1	Seaman	Dixon	Winterburn	Keown	Bould	Adams	Platt ..1	Wright1 ..2.1p	Merson ..1	Bergkamp ..1	Vieira		Hartson for Bergkamp
13 Nov	Stoke City (3R)	H	W	5-2	..	..	..	..	..	..							Hartson/Morrow for Vieira/Bergkamp
27 Nov	Liverpool (4R)	A	L	2-4	Lukic	..	..	..	..	..		.. 2p	..	Hartson	..		Parlour/Morrow for Merson/Winterburn

FA Cup

Date	Opponent			Result													Substitutions
4 Jan	Sunderland (3)	H	D	1-1	Lukic	Parlour	Winterburn	Keown	Bould	Adams	Morrow Platt	Hartson1 Hughes1	Merson	Bergkamp ..1	Vieira		Shaw for Morrow
15 Jan	Sunderland (3R)	A	W	2-0	Seaman	..	..	..	..	..	Parlour	Wright	..	Hughes	..		Hartson for Hughes
4 Feb	Leeds U (4)	H	L	0-1	..	Dixon	Morrow	..	..	..							

UEFA Cup

Date	Opponent			Result													Substitutions
10 Sep	Moenchengladbach	H	L	2-3	Seaman	Dixon	Winterburn	Keown	Linighan	Parlour	Platt	Wright1	Merson1	Bergkamp	Hartson		Helder/Bould for Parlour/Bergkamp
25 Sep	Moenchengladbach	A	L	2-3	..	Linighan	..	..	Bould	Adams	..	..1	..1	Vieira	..		Parlour/Helder for Linighan/Adams

Appearances (Goals)

Winterburn 38 – Wright 35 (23) – Bould 33 – Keown 33 (1) – Dixon 32 (2) – Merson 32 (6) – Vieira 31 (2) – Parlour 30 (2) – Bergkamp 29 (12) – Adams 28 (3) – Platt 28 (4) – Seaman 22 – Hartson 19 (3) – Lukic 15 – Hughes 14 (1) – Linighan 11 (1) – Garde 11 – Marshall 8 – Morrow 14 – Shaw 8 (2) – Anelka 4 – Helder 2 – Hillier 2 – Dickov 1 – Harper 1 – McGowan 1 – Rose 1 – Selley 1 –
Total 28 players (62 goals)

Position in League Table

	P	W	D	L	F:A	Pts	
Manchester U	38	21	12	5	76:44	75	1st
Arsenal	38	19	11	8	62:32	68	3rd

Goalkeeper John Lukic was Bruce Rioch's last signing as Arsenal manager. It turned out to be an astute move, as the veteran keeper was called upon to make 15 League appearances during the 1996–97 season.

CHARTER
10
WENGER'S FIRST DOUBLE

As the final whistle was blown at the Baseball Ground to bring a trophyless 1996–97 campaign to a close, Arsene Wenger was already plotting how to improve his team for his first full season in charge. The summer break would be anything but rest. As Keown, Wright, Seaman and Adams travelled to Wenger's homeland to represent England in Le Tournoi, the Arsenal coach also headed to the continent as he sought to strengthen his side.

Wenger rings the changes

An abundance of European talent was available to Premiership managers – particularly those based in the capital – during the summer of 1997. The Bosman ruling and the increased profile of English football, not to mention high wages, had made the Premiership the choice of a multitude of European-based players. The Arsenal coach identified his targets and wasted no time in moving to clinch their signatures.

With Paul Merson departing for Middlesbrough, the first name on Wenger's list was the electric-paced Dutchman Marc Overmars. Some critics had expressed doubts about his fitness after a knee injury had kept him out of the game for eight months. The good news for Wenger was that these doubts had left just two clubs – Arsenal and Real Betis – willing to match the Amsterdam club's £5 million valuation. Wenger was confident that the Dutchman was fit and mentally prepared for the Premiership and later remarked: 'When I did my homework on him I discovered he was upset at the rumours he was not fit and that he could never play to his true ability again. That was a good sign for me, a hurt player. He had something to prove.' Overmars opted for Highbury, leaving Betis to look elsewhere.

Two other experienced players arrived at Arsenal over the summer, both from Wenger's former club Monaco. Gilles Grimandi and Emmanuel Petit crossed the channel in time for pre-season training and reports suggested that they were intended as ready-made replacements for members of Arsenal's veteran-filled defence. Wenger knew Petit well, having handed him his debut as an 18-year-old at Monaco. For much of his career, he had operated as a defender but Wenger had a different assignment in mind for him at Highbury. The Arsenal coach planned to pair Petit with Patrick Vieira in midfield.

Having added experience to his squad, Wenger was keen to inject youth into his first-team pool. With this in mind, two young strikers – Christopher Wreh and Luis Boa Morte – and 23-year-old midfielder, Alberto Mendez, arrived to join 18-year-old defender Matthew Upson, who had made the short trip from Luton Town in May. All would play some part in first-team affairs during a season that would see Arsenal play 54 matches in all competitions.

Opposite: One down, one to go. Wenger lifts the Championship trophy after the 4–0 win over Everton on 3 May 1998.

Below: '179, Just Done it!' Ian Wright finally breaks Cliff Bastin's 81-year-old club scoring record of 178 goals, against Bolton in September 1997. Wright confessed that the record-breaking goal was one of his easiest (tapping into an empty net from close range), but it was typical of Wright to cap the feat by completing a hat-trick as the Gunners ran out 4–1 winners.

Wright chases record

Arsenal began their Premiership campaign at Leeds. Predictably Wright grabbed the Gunners' first goal of the season to earn a share of the points. Wright was on the scoresheet two days later when Coventry visited Highbury. His double-strike gave Arsenal a comfortable victory and edged him to within a single goal of Cliff Bastin's record.

The game against a dogged Southampton side at the Dell brought the best out of Bergkamp. With an hour played and the scored at 1–1 the Dutchman made his mark. He picked up the ball in midfield and carried it into the Saints' penalty area and, with the defence fearfully backing-off, drove a precise shot past Paul Jones. Then, 20 minutes later, the Saints opted for a different approach when finding Bergkamp in possession. In an effort to restrain the Arsenal striker, Francis Benali gripped hold of Bergkamp's shirt, but his challenge was in vain. Shrugging the defender aside, the Dutchman unleashed an unstoppable shot into the Saints' goal.

Two draws followed: first there was a trip to Filbert Street to take on Martin O'Neill's Leicester City. In a match full of hard work, enterprise and far too many defensive errors, Bergkamp provided a faultless display of forward play. The Dutchman's three goals were of the highest quality and included the winner of the BBC *Match of the Day* Goal of the Season. Bergkamp used his left foot deftly to control a cross from the right, moving the ball onto his right foot before despatching it past the on-rushing Leicester keeper. A home draw against Spurs three days later left Arsenal in fifth place, four points behind Blackburn and Manchester United at the end of August.

Bergkamp's domination of Arsenal's scoring had left Ian Wright marooned on 177 goals since the second game of the season. Fortunately for Wright his partner was in generous mood as newly promoted Bolton came to Highbury in September. In the 20th minute, a Bergkamp through-ball gave Wright a sight of goal and the striker made no mistake, sliding the ball past Keith Branagan. The goal that set a new record came just five minutes later and again Bergkamp was at the hub of things. The Dutchman stabbed a shot goalward, but was foiled by Branagan and the loose ball broke to Wright two yards out in front of an unguarded net. Ray Parlour added a third goal, but nobody could gatecrash Ian Wright's party and the record-holder completed his hat-trick in the second half.

Non-flying Dutchman

Wright barely had time to bask in the glory of his goalscoring achievements before he was on a plane heading for Greece and the first leg of Arsenal's UEFA Cup tie against PAOK Salonika. One absentee was Bergkamp. His fear of flying forced Wenger to rejig his team, naming 19-year-old Nicolas Anelka alongside the experienced Overmars and Wright.

On a frustrating night for the Gunners, Wenger's attacking approach failed to reap rewards. Several good chances had been squandered by the time Greek international Fratzeskos skipped into the area to put the ball past Seaman. It was little more than the home team deserved and after the game Wenger declared: 'PAOK were more consistent overall. We dropped our level in the second half. The atmosphere was not an excuse and nor was the absence of Dennis Bergkamp. Now we have to win by two goals, which will not be easy.' Wenger's concern was well founded. Despite an early Bergkamp goal, Arsenal failed to score a second and were eliminated from the competition when the Greeks snatched an equaliser.

Between the games against Salonika, the Gunners had beaten Chelsea at Stamford Bridge – courtesy of a rare goal from Winterburn – had overcome West Ham at home and drawn away at Everton. By the end of September, Arsenal had reached the summit of the League table. Eight goals from nine games for Bergkamp had undoubtedly been the catalyst for the Gunners' storming run to pole position in the Championship.

A rare defeat

The trip to Pride Park, Derby's new ground, brought Arsenal's first defeat of the season. It was the worst possible preparation for the visit of Manchester United the following Sunday. Despite the absence of the suspended Petit and Bergkamp, Arsenal got off to a sensational start against the Champions, scoring twice in the first half hour. Bergkamp's replacement, Anelka, struck first before fellow Frenchman Vieira sent a superbly angled shot past Peter Schmeichel on 27 minutes.

United came back strongly and Teddy Sheringham grabbed two goals, but his efforts were in vain, Platt, in the team for Petit, heading a late winner. The triumph against United provided the only addition to Arsenal's points in November and by the end of the month they had slipped to fifth place in the table.

The Coca-Cola Cup was Arsenal's only early season respite from League action. However, this competition lost much of its appeal once UEFA threatened to withdraw its winners' European place. Wenger had used Arsenal's first game in the competition to field younger squad members, but for the tie against Coventry in November he selected a strong line-up that included Bergkamp. The Dutchman was eligible despite his League suspension and his extra-time goal decided the tie.

Early season form deserts Gunners

Arsenal's indifferent League form continued in December. The low point of this frustrating period coming in a 3–1 reverse at home to Blackburn. Floodlight failure in the next match, away at Wimbledon, denied Wenger's team the chance to get back on course in the title race. The match was abandoned at 0–0 after 46 minutes and rescheduled for March, by which time Wenger hoped to have Arsenal running on full power again.

Christmas brought four points but little festive cheer for Gunners fans. Arsenal were no longer playing the fluent, attacking football that had seen them waltz to the top of the table in the autumn. At New Year, Wenger's team were in sixth place, 12 points adrift of Manchester United. Most pundits considered that Arsenal's chance had gone. Fortunately, the two domestic cup competitions gave a welcome distraction and a chance to get back to form in the early weeks of 1998.

The first Saturday in January brought with it the FA Cup third round, and for Arsenal a primed and armed booby trap in the shape of a home tie against First Division Port Vale. The 37,471 crowd watched as Arsenal laboured to overcome a side that had not won for two months. A 0–0 draw gave Wenger's team a second chance at Vale Park and for the replay they would be able to call upon record goalscorer Ian Wright.

Penalties prove turning point

Cup action continued the following Tuesday as Arsenal made the short trip to take on West Ham at Upton Park. The Hammers had a formidable home record, winning 12 of their 13 home games so far in all competitions. The game turned on an incident after just ten minutes. West Ham striker Paul Kitson darted into Seaman's penalty area, only to be met by the outrushing keeper. The referee pointed to the spot and up stepped former Gunner John Hartson to take the kick. Hartson, the Premiership's top scorer v Seaman, England's top goalkeeper.

1997-2000

It was a contest which had no doubt been played out during numerous Arsenal training sessions. The outcome was strangely inevitable. Seaman comfortably collected the striker's scuffed shot. Hartson bowed his head and Arsenal were buoyed. Goals from Overmars and Wright confirmed victory and put the Gunners into a two-legged semi-final against Chelsea. The following week, Wenger's team made it to the FA Cup fourth round by overcoming Port Vale after a penalty shoot-out. In retrospect, it was perhaps the closest they came to missing the eventual Double.

In the League, a bad-tempered match against Coventry at Highfield Road saw Vieira sent off, but, more worryingly for Wenger, Seaman suffered a finger injury which would keep him out for several weeks. The experienced keeper would be replaced by 20-year-old Austrian Alex Manninger. The blow of losing Seaman was slightly diminished by the return of skipper Adams to first team duty. He had suffered a series of niggling injuries and had lost form in the first half of the season. After the defeat by Blackburn in December he sought much-needed rest and recuperation in the south of France and celebrated his recall with his first goal of the season, heading home from a corner in a 3–0 win over Southampton.

Gunners rediscover form

Arsenal were beginning to rediscover the fluency and invention that had entertained the Highbury faithful so richly during early season. In the League, Wenger was forced to employ most of his squad members as the Gunners made their way up the table despite a growing list of injuries and suspensions. Wins over Crystal Palace and Chelsea had arrived courtesy of goals from two players, Gilles Grimandi and Stephen Hughes, who had been largely confined to the bench throughout the season. Despite this upturn, the pundits' view remained that United had all but won the title and that the best Arsenal could achieve was runners-up spot and a Champions League place.

Wenger's squad continued to be stretched and the situation was not helped by increasing cup commitments. In the Coca-Cola Cup, the Gunners had taken a 2–1 lead to Stamford Bridge in the second leg of their semi-final. Arsenal's advantage was not enough. The return in west London swung in Chelsea's favour when Vieira was shown the red card just after half time. A 3–1 victory gave Chelsea a 4–3 aggregate win.

Arsenal were left to focus their attention on the Premiership and the FA Cup. Wenger's team had little time to nurse their wounds after the bruising battle at Stamford Bridge. An FA Cup fourth round replay against Palace gave the Gunners the perfect opportunity to revive their Wembley ambitions but a striker shortage was worrying Wenger before the trip to Selhurst Park. Wright was struggling to recover

Above: Stephen Hughes scores his first goal of the season against Chelsea in the first leg of the Coca-Cola Cup semi-final. Marc Overmars netted for the fifth time in five matches, but Welshman Mark Hughes came off the bench to give Chelsea a lifeline. The Gunners were guilty of spurning a hatful of chances and they would pay a heavy price for their profligacy in the return fixture at Stamford Bridge.

from a hamstring injury, Overmars had been in America with the Dutch team and was due back in the UK on the morning of the game, and Bergkamp had flu. Wenger need not have worried. First-half goals from Anelka and Bergkamp – who started the match but was replaced by Overmars in the second half – gave Arsenal a quarter final tie at home against West Ham. Afterward Wenger praised Overmars' commitment: 'It was a big surprise that we could have him playing at all. Last night he was in America playing for Holland but he was able to catch a flight to Paris and was back in London this morning.'

Fixture backlog hinders progress

Two London derbies against the Hammers followed. The first in the League was one of three games the Gunners had in hand on leaders United as they attempted to close a 12-point gap. The clash at Upton Park saw the return from injury of Petit. After playing a key role in Arsenal's upturn in form, the former Monaco man was keen to keep the momentum going, declaring: 'I think it will be difficult for us because we have to continue our good run to put pressure on Manchester United and to leave the other clubs like Chelsea, Liverpool and

Blackburn behind. We will lose some day. I just don't want it to be the next game.' A 0–0 draw was a good result given the Hammers form at Upton Park, but it was not enough. The Champions' 11-point lead seemed unassailable and several bookmakers stopped taking bets on the title race. Wenger however would not concede that Arsenal's Championship bid was over: 'It's not over yet but, of course, it will be very difficult for us now. A point was a good result when you look at the tough match we faced at West Ham but in the context of the Championship now draws are not good enough for us.'

The fixture backlog worsened six days later, when a Bergkamp penalty cancelled out a West Ham goal and forced an FA Cup quarter final replay at Upton Park. Before that game, Arsenal faced two critical League matches. First there was a return to Selhurst for the aborted clash with Wimbledon, followed three days later by a summit meeting at Old Trafford.

For both the Wimbledon and United games, Wenger rotated his young strikers. Anelka, whose form had been fitful in the early part of 1998 was replaced by Chris Wreh. The young Liberian bubbled with confidence as he lined up for his first start of the season, against the Dons. A crisp finish from Wreh on 22 minutes gave Arsenal a deserved half-time lead. The second half saw Arsenal doggedly defend their lead in the face of growing Wimbledon pressure. If the first half had belonged to Wreh, then the second went to Alex Manninger, whose faultless display secured Arsenal all three points. The efforts of Arsenal's young stars prompted a glowing testimonial from Wenger after the game. He declared: 'I am very pleased for Chris Wreh. We have not had a chance to see the best of him yet and it has been a difficult year for him. Manninger was also very good. Unfortunately, he has taken a knock on his knee and there is a slight chance he could miss the Manchester United match.'

Manninger takes his chance

Wenger needn't have worried about the fitness of his young keeper. The Austrian was in the midst of a 13-game run in the first team and was not prepared to relinquish his place. His performances would earn him many plaudits, a place in the Austrian full international squad and the Carling Player of the Month award for March. By the end of the season, he was left in no doubt about his future at Highbury, with Wenger declaring: 'I see Alex as the future Arsenal goalkeeper. He is an excellent prospect and he is willing to learn and be patient.'

The win against Wimbledon had put a new complexion on the title race. As the Gunners were collecting maximum points at Selhurst, Manchester United were settling for a single point at West Ham. The Champions' lead was still significant – nine points – but Arsenal had three games in hand. The game at

Above: Most of Highbury felt that David Seaman was irreplacable, but in Alex Manninger they had a more than adequate stand-in. The 20-year-old Austrian international was the hero of the FA Cup quarter final when ten-man Arsenal beat West Ham in a penalty shoot-out.

Old Trafford on 14 March took on a new significance; if Arsenal could leave Manchester with a win, their fate would be in their own hands. Wenger tried to play down the billing of the match: 'There is a bit more pressure on United now, but not enough,' declared the Gunners' coach. 'Even if we go there and win we will still have to win our games in hand to make it worthwhile. But I hear the bookmakers are taking bets again.'

It had seemed that United would romp to their third consecutive Premiership title, but as Arsenal closed the gap, so interest returned to the battle at the top of the table. The match kicked off at 11 am and was screened live on Sky TV. Wenger had kept faith with Wreh after his scoring start at Selhurst, but after 67 minutes he withdrew the young Liberian and sent on the inhumanly quick Anelka to unsettle the United back line. The young Frenchman had been on the field for just 11 minutes when he rose to flick a header into the path of Overmars. The Dutchman sprinted clear and despatched the ball between Schmeichel's legs. Thereafter, chances arrived for both teams but a combination of poor finishing and assured goalkeeping saw the score remain at 1–0 to Arsenal.

The leaders now looked decidedly catchable. Arsenal were in form and looked capable of converting their three games in hand into nine points and a place at the top of the table. Wenger remained circumspect: 'Manchester United have a small advantage because we have to take the points available from the games we have in hand and that won't be easy.'

Bergkamp sees red

Arsenal's punishing schedule continued with another Cup match against West Ham. Wenger, without Wright, Seaman, and Parlour, must have feared the worst when Bergkamp was

1997-2000

shown the red card by Mike Reed after 32 minutes for elbowing Steve Lomas. The Gunners had controlled the game until the Dutchman's dismissal and, though they had been thwarted by French international goalkeeper Bernard Lama, an Arsenal goal seemed inevitable. Bergkamp's dismissal visibly lifted the home side as they eagerly strove forward, relieved that their chief tormentor had departed. The Hammers' security was ill-founded and deep into first-half injury time, Anelka pinched the ball from the boot of Vieira, took aim and curled an exquisite shot into the left-hand corner of Lama's goal.

The second half brought a faultless defensive display from Wenger's team in which Manninger and Keown were outstanding. Keown's efforts in stopping Hartson were Herculean, but there was little the stopper could do as the Welshman bludgeoned his way into the penalty area to force a low drive inside Manninger's near post after 84 minutes. Extra time beckoned. With both teams flagging from an electric-paced 90 minutes, gaps began to appear at both ends, but amazingly the scores remained unaltered. Manninger was once more the Gunners' hero, saving from Eyal Berkovic and watching as Hartson and Samassi Abou placed their kicks against the frame. For the second time in 1998, Arsenal could celebrate a quarter final victory at Upton Park. Arsenal's opponents in the semi-final were to be First Division Wolverhampton Wanderers.

Arsenal close the gap

There were no Premiership fixtures for the weekend following the Gunners' Cup success in East London and for Bergkamp the break would be extended to two weeks. On the last day of March, Arsenal payed a visit to struggling Bolton, knowing that a win would take them to within three points of Manchester United with two games in hand. For Wenger, the urgent issue was his lack of striking options and the Frenchman stated: 'We will miss Dennis Bergkamp and the target for me is to find someone to replace him for Tuesday's game at Bolton.'

Once more Chris Wreh stepped into the breach, playing alongside fellow rookie Nicolas Anelka. A fourth consecutive Premiership 1–0 win duly arrived courtesy of a sharply taken 20-yarder from the young Liberian on 47 minutes. Then, 15 minutes after taking the lead, Martin Keown was dismissed for a second bookable offence and Steve Bould replaced Wreh, but Bolton rarely troubled the Gunners rearguard. United's lead was now just three points, and the confidence of the Arsenal coach was growing. 'The message for Manchester is that we go from game to game and what is important is that we have another away victory. Now, like always, it is down to the most consistent team.' Arsenal's consistency was awesome.

The FA Cup semi-final brought a routine Gunners victory. An early Wreh goal, a tightly locked defence and another win.

Above: Patrick Vieira produced a typically dominating performance at Old Trafford in March 1998. The tough-tackling Frenchman had an inspirational season that would take him back home to play in the World Cup for France.

In truth, Arsenal played well within themselves at Villa Park and though Wolves had tested them in the second half, the thought remained that if Wenger's team had conceded a rare goal – it would have been their first in five matches – they would merely have gone up the other end to restore their lead.

As spring arrived, Arsenal's run of impressive results continued. Newcastle United, who would provide the Gunners' Cup final opposition come May, arrived at Highbury when Premiership action resumed after a two-week break on 11 April. An Anelka brace and a 30-yard drive from Vieira broke a sequence of five 1–0 victories.

Blackburn chasing shadows

Arsenal were back to their fluent form of early season. The peak came on Easter Monday and the trip to Blackburn to face the last team to beat Arsenal in the League. With Dennis Bergkamp back in action the Gunners were untouchable and after 14 minutes the home side were three goals down. Wave after wave of penetrating Arsenal attacks left the Rovers defence stunned. It took Bergkamp just 75 seconds to open the scoring as he burst onto a flick from Nicolas Anelka to fire home. Two more goals from Parlour and a clinical finish from Anelka gave Arsenal an unassailable lead. It was to be their best display of the whole season Arsenal were now favourites to win the League, but Wenger would not be coaxed into offering any sound bites that might inspire Alex Ferguson and his team. 'We didn't listen to anyone when people said we didn't have a chance and we won't listen now that we are favourites. The players were happy in the dressing room, but they were not going crazy,' explained the Arsenal coach to the Ewood Park press room.

The top of the Premiership beckoned. If United failed to beat Newcastle at home and Arsenal could defeat Wimbledon at Highbury, the Gunners would top the League for the first time since October. Nothing could stop Arsenal and the Dons were hit for five without reply. A draw at Old Trafford meant the Gunners were top, their one-point lead reinforced by two games in hand. The win against the Dons saw Arsenal share the goals out among five scorers, but the loudest celebration greeted the fourth goal, from Petit. He had been an immense figure in the Arsenal midfield alongside Vieira and the Highbury faithful took immeasurable pleasure from the former Monaco star's first goal in an Arsenal shirt. The manner of Arsenal's rise to the top had the purists purring.

One win to clinch title

Another Petit strike, this time against Derby, was enough to leave Arsenal needing just one win from their final three fixtures to clinch the Championship. Between the Wimbledon and Derby games, the Gunners had condemned Barnsley to relegation with a 2–0 win at Oakwell Park courtesy of goals from Arsenal's Dutch duo. Bergkamp contributed 19 goals, and many more assists, in his 39 games but these impressive statistics fail to reveal the importance of his contribution. He had quite simply been breathtaking. He had scored goals which left his opponents open-mouthed in disbelief, his passing was intuitive and his ball skills fast and faultless. Small wonder that both the football writers and Bergkamp's fellow professionals voted him their player of the season.

Awards meant little, however, if the Gunners failed to deliver the silverware that was in their grasp at the beginning of May. Arsenal's final two League games of the season were away, so if they were to celebrate with their home fans they would need to defeat relegation-threatened Everton. In a match which the visitors could ill-afford to lose, Everton manager Howard Kendall named a defensive line-up – including Croatian defender Slaven Bilic in midfield. After just six minutes his plans were in tatters, as Bilic headed an own goal to give Arsenal the lead. On 28 minutes Arsenal had a crucial second goal, Marc Overmars accelerating past three defenders before sliding the ball underneath the advancing keeper. Overmars added a third goal, but the celebrations leapt into overdrive in the final minute when Adams latched onto a pass from Steve Bould to crash home his third goal of the season.

Highbury applauds Wenger's champs

After seven years, the title had returned to the capital. The importance was not lost on Wenger, who declared: 'This is my greatest ever achievement as a manager and I am proud for the

Above: Double jubilation. Emmanuel Petit (left) holds aloft the Premiership trophy. Tony Adams (right) raises the FA Cup aloft at Wembley to complete Arsenal's second FA Cup and League Double.

club, my staff, the players and the supporters. We have shown great spirit all season and our last goal typified that as Steve Bould sent Adams through. They have been great players for Arsenal. I am surprised but delighted that we have won the title so soon but this team can get better.'

Arsenal now had a chance to complete their second League and FA Cup Double and emulate Bertie Mee's team of 1970–71. Before the Cup clash with Newcastle United, Wenger's team faced two away matches at Liverpool and Aston Villa. Having won ten consecutive League games to clinch the title, Arsenal could be forgiven for relaxing and recording two defeats. These games were no form guide for Wembley on 16 May.

The Double is reclaimed

At Wembley, Wenger employed his tried and tested formula. A back four of Dixon, Winterburn, Adams and Keown was reinforced by the energetic presence of Petit and Vieira in midfield. The flanks were manned by Overmars and Parlour, who were to supply the bulk of service to two strikers, on this occasion, Wreh and Anelka. Wenger's game plan got off to a stunning start with Overmars and Parlour both carving out good opportunities for Anelka, but each time the teenager spurned the chance. His moment would come, but before Anelka could redeem himself, Overmars acted. The Dutchman latched onto a Petit chip to race clear of the Newcastle defence and place the ball between Shay Given's legs and into the goal.

Newcastle responded and Seaman was forced into action by a Temuri Ketsbaia effort in the first half. After the interval the Magpies had their best chance when Keown's mistake, on 63 minutes, gave Shearer a clear sight of goal. He struck a post and five minutes later Anelka collected a Parlour pass, and

1997-2000

galloped forward to drive a shot into the corner of Given's goal. It may not have provided the drama of Charlie George's late winner against Liverpool in 1971, but Anelka's goal cued celebrations of similar proportions throughout north London.

After the game even the normally restrained Wenger was in animated mood. 'The Championship was our main aim,' said the Highbury boss, 'but it would have been terrible to have lost at Wembley because we really wanted the FA Cup too.'

The 1998–99 season

The following season proved to be just as dramatic, although not as glorious. The scenes at Highbury on 16 May told their own story. Tearful fans comforted each other, as Manchester United wrested back the Championship from the Gunners. It had been another memorable season. But this time without a trophy to show for it.

The mathematics on the last day of the Premiership race were simple. Arsenal had to beat Aston Villa, and hope Spurs – now managed by George Graham – won or drew at Old Trafford.

Les Ferdinand's early goal detonated an explosion of cheers at Highbury. Never before has the old stadium rang to chants of 'Come on, you Spurs'. At least, not from Arsenal fans. But it was a forlorn hope. David Beckham levelled. Andy Cole, ironically an ex-Gunner, scored the goal that took the title back to Manchester.

So near, and yet so far. United, the new Champions of Europe, had been Arsenal's nemesis, in the Premiership, and the FA Cup. TV will replay Ryan Giggs' brilliant winner in the semi-final replay at Villa Park, for years to come. Yet Highbury fans thought the Gunners were on the brink of another trip to Wembley as Dennis Bergkamp stepped up to take that stoppage time penalty with the score at 1–1. Peter Schmeichel guessed right and flung himself to tip the ball away. The rest is history.

United were only doing what they'd promised. Giggs was one of several Old Trafford players who acknowledged the hurt they'd felt when Arsene Wenger's team won the Double. Arsenal's success galvanised United.

In the end, Giggs' strike – and Jimmy Floyd Hasselbaink's late winner in the penultimate Premiership game at Leeds – wrecked Arsenal's season. The Gunners were magnificent in the New Year. But they had left themselves too much catching up to do.

As 1998–99 approached, Alex Ferguson snapped up the towering Dutchman Jaap Stam, to remedy United's problems at centre-back. He signed the Swedish winger Jesper Blomqvist. Then, as the season began, he added a vital ingredient – Dwight Yorke from Aston Villa. At £12.6 million, Yorke

was United's record buy. He provided value for money from day one. His Champions League performances marked him as one of Europe's finest forwards.

By contrast, Arsenal signed teenage left back David Grondin, from French Youth Cup winners St Etienne, and the Argentina defender Nelson Vivas from Swiss club Lugano.

Arsenal's first choice line-up probably had a slight edge on United. But Old Trafford's back-up was formidable. United's bench regularly housed the likes of David May, Henning Berg, Wes Brown, Nicky Butt, Teddy Sheringham, Blomqvist and Ole Gunnar Solskjaer.

Wenger admitted as much at the end of the campaign. 'There are several teams in the Premiership with the same financial potential,' he said: 'Then there is Manchester United. They spent £24 million at the start of the season. I can't do that. I have money to spend and I'm looking for three players. But I have to be wise. I have to strengthen without spending too much.'

Such thoughts lead to another comparison between United and Arsenal – the capacity of their grounds. United are guaranteed a full house 55,000 for every home game. They plan to raise their capacity to 67,000. The Gunners can only accommodate 38,000. Every Highbury home match in 1998–99 was packed. Seventy-thousand-plus gates at Wembley for the Champions League games proved Arsenal's potential drawing power.

Discussions continued with Islington Council about enlarging Highbury. Studies were conducted. Meanwhile, rumours abounded, about Arsenal moving to a new site. All sorts of locations were suggested.

Whatever the rumours, United were able to generate more cash than any of their rivals, which Alex Ferguson used to good advantage.

'When you finish one point behind the winners in a 38-game season, it feels like losing a marathon by just one yard,' said Wenger. The Frenchman added: 'No one can say we had a bad season. There were three outstanding teams – United, ourselves and Chelsea. At the end, the difference was very small. But we want to be first, not second.'

Indeed, in five matches against United, the Gunners won two, drew two, and lost only the semi-final replay. That was little consolation at the end of the battle.

After the World Cup

After the Double triumph, Wenger had identified the problems the Gunners faced. Players coming back from the World Cup finals would be tired. They wouldn't be able to find their best form until later in the season. Wenger also shrewdly realised that such problems would trouble forwards – like Dennis Bergkamp and Marc Overmars – much more than defenders and midfield players.

David Seaman, Tony Adams, Martin Keown, Patrick Vieira and Manu Petit seemed to suffer little reaction. They were consistent throughout the season. But Bergkamp and Overmars did suffer. And Wenger had few alternatives.

Record goal scorer Ian Wright moved on to West Ham two months after the Gunners beat Newcastle in the FA Cup final.

On the first day of 1998 pre-season training, David Platt announced his retirement. The departure of two such experienced players left big holes. In September, Wenger signed the Swedish international midfielder Freddie Ljungberg to fill one gap. Unfortunately Ljungberg arrived a fortnight too late to play in the Champions League group games.

Wenger knew the forward he wanted too: Overmars' old Ajax colleague, Nwankwo Kanu, who had moved to Internazionale and missed more than a season because of heart-valve surgery. But Inter wouldn't sell. Not until December. By then the Gunners were out of the Champions League and fifth in the Premiership, four points behind Aston Villa and United.

'Looking back, we lost the Championship in the first half of the season,' said Wenger: 'We dropped too many points at home.' Relegated Charlton and Southampton – who narrowly escaped the drop – both nicked points at Highbury despite Arsenal's massive dominance. Spurs, Middlesbrough and Liverpool escaped with draws too.

With Bergkamp and Overmars searching for their best form in those early months, Nicolas Anelka carried a heavy burden. Anelka had not been included in France's World Cup-winning squad. His form with Arsenal made him one of the first names on new coach Roger Lemerre's team list. Despite his frequent

talk of moving on, the French striker produced some memorable performances and goals – like his stunning winner against Everton. He finished Arsenal's top scorer with 17 in the Premiership.

But Chris Wreh, striker of vital goals in the Double campaign, couldn't rediscover that form. Luis Boa Morte, so impressive for Portugal in the Toulon tournament of 1997, found it hard to fulfil his potential. The Argentinian forward Fabian Caballero came on loan from Paraguayan club Cerro Porteno but couldn't break through into Premiership football. France U-21 striker Kaba Diawara arrived from Bordeaux, but didn't score in 12 appearances.

It wasn't until February, when Kanu was fit and available, that Wenger had the options he wanted in attack.

Kanu soon became a Highbury hero. His last minute FA Cup sixth round winner against Derby won the fans over. His second goal at Middlesbrough proved his class. His strike at Tottenham was arguably Arsenal's goal of the season.

'I wish he had joined us earlier,' said Wenger, who used Kanu mainly as a tactical sub. But the Nigerian forward remained optimistic after his first season at Highbury. 'Joining Arsenal was one of the best moves of my career,' he said: 'They have allowed me to play. By the time next season starts, I'll be completely fit – for the first time in years.'

'Almost every time he came on, he changed the game,' said Wenger: 'I expect a lot of him. He will play many more games from the start next season. He can make a huge impact.'

Suspensions didn't help either. As Bruce Rioch used to say: 'You want your best players on the pitch.' Wenger, ever loyal, defended his players. But the statistics made grim reading. Petit was sent off three times; Keown twice. Lee Dixon, Vivas and Parlour took early baths too. United were at least as aggressive as Arsenal. But they channelled their fighting spirit so that they picked up far fewer cards than the Gunners.

Yet the season started so brightly. In the Charity Shield, at Wembley, Arsenal blasted United 3-0, even though Bergkamp had to retire at half time to rest his hamstring injury. Overmars, Wreh and Anelka scored. It was as if Wenger and his troops had an Indian sign on Fergie's team.

A slow start

After all the pre-match presentations, Nationwide League Champions Nottingham Forest proved surprisingly tough opponents in the Gunners opening Premiership game, a Monday night event for Sky Sports. Petit carried on where he'd left off for France, putting Arsenal ahead. Geoff Thomas levelled. The Highbury crowd were growing anxious when Overmars launched an acrobatic shot past Dave Beasant for the winner.

Marc Overmars gets Arsenal off to a flying start as his overhead lob over Dave Beasant secures a 2–1 victory on the opening fixture of the 1998–99 season at home to Forest.

1997-2000

Arsenal had the better of the play in the goalless draw against Liverpool – especially in the first half – but couldn't score. It was to be the start of a trend. Charlton survived a battering at Highbury and escaped with a point after another 0–0 draw. Petit was sent off for a second bookable offence.

Dixon walked 11 days later in a bad-tempered game at Chelsea, after flattening Graeme Le Saux. The score was 0–0, again.

Stephen Hughes, in for the suspended Petit, hit a last minute equaliser at Leicester, after Emile Heskey had put the home side in front.

The Champion's League

Then the Gunners faced their first Champions League match, away to the French Champions Lens. The Champions League campaign was another tale of 'what might have been'.

Arsenal had decided to play their home games at Wembley. Chairman Peter Hill-Wood explained: 'We'd have preferred to play at Highbury. But we couldn't play at Highbury and provide normal service for our supporters. That was the deciding factor.

'UEFA's regulations on the size of perimeter board advertising would have meant taking up several rows around the stadium with advertising boards. By the time we'd complied with that, we'd have lost many thousands of seats from our capacity, which isn't very big anyway. We'd also have lost the disabled enclosure which is very important to us.

'Then we had to consider the large number of tickets that UEFA required. That would have meant moving whole blocks of east stand season ticket holders, because UEFA would have

Denis Bergkamp fires Arsenal ahead during a a 3–0 win against Newcastle at Highbury in October. Bergkamp bagged two and Anelka made it three. The win was a welcome lift to morale as it came on the back of a defeat away to Sheffield Wednesday and was only the third of the season.

needed the areas around the Directors' Box and the press box. That would have caused huge disruption.'

The club tried to keep down the price of Wembley tickets. Season ticket holders could use their cup tie credits to get in. Many of the other tickets cost only £10. The fans – many of whom rarely managed to obtain tickets at Highbury – flocked to Wembley.

The Arsenal board had made a wise decision in all the circumstances. In football terms though, might the Gunners have done better in the tight confines of Highbury, where they could close down opponents more quickly than in Wembley's wide open spaces? At Highbury the crowd were on top of the pitch. At Wembley they were yards away. And playing at Wembley seemed to inspire the opposition, especially Dynamo Kiev and Lens.

But back to the start; at Lens' Stade Felix Bollaert. Lens had lost three key players after winning the French title – skipper Jean-Guy Wallemme, midfield playmaker Stephane Ziani, and top scorer Anto Drobnjak. Marc-Vivien Foe, the Cameroon international who later joined West Ham, was out injured. Lens hopes centred on France's Tony Vairelles and the Czech attacker Vladimir Smicer.

Arsenal took charge early on – and missed chance after chance. Overmars ran through to bury a low shot. But one goal wasn't enough. In stoppage time, Vairelles forced home a corner, off Keown. The Gunners would regret their profligacy.

Shevchenko inspires Russians

The other two teams in the group were the Greek Champions Panathinaikos, and Dynamo Kiev, famous flag bearers for Ukraine. Wenger said all along that Dynamo were favourites, even if they did lose their first game 1–2 in Athens. 'They have so much experience in this competition. They're very good at keeping the ball and Andrei Shevchenko and Sergei Rebrov are such dangerous strikers.'

First, the Gunners saw off Panathinaikos 2–1 at Wembley, thanks to headers by Adams and Keown.

Then came Kiev. After losing to Panathinaikos, they had drawn at home to Lens. At Wembley, they were inspired. Shevchenko was majestic, Rebrov a constant irritant. Oleg Luzhny charged up and down from right-back. Shevchenko had what looked a good goal disallowed. Adams produced a magnificent tackle to dispossess Shevchenko after he'd broken clear. Vieira was suspended, Petit injured. Remi Garde and Hughes in central midfield had a hard job, coping with Dynamo's fast-breaking attacks. But Bergkamp netted a rare header from Dixon's cross. Then, with time running out, came a vital moment. Overmars burst through, rounded the Kiev keeper Olexandr Shovkosky and shot. The 70,000 Arsenal fans screamed 'Goal' Somehow Luzhny raced back to hook the ball off the line. Had that gone in, Dynamo were dead. Instead they won a free-kick. As the ball flashed across the Arsenal box, Rebrov forced it home. The Gunners claimed offside. The linesman's flag stayed down.

A fortnight later, in Kiev, Arsenal crashed 1–3. Adams was out injured. So was Overmars, who'd torn a hamstring at Coventry the previous Saturday. Anelka was sidelined, after picking up a knock in that game too. Bergkamp's refusal to fly kept him out.

Two minutes before half time, Bould added to Arsenal's woe when he limped off with a hamstring injury. Rebrov struck a 27th-minute penalty – for a foul by Keown. That turned the game. Olexandr Golovko headed a second, then Shevchenko curled a free-kick past Seaman, for Kiev's third. Sub Hughes pulled one back. Wreh had a goal disallowed for offside. Suddenly Arsenal were struggling to qualify.

European Exit

The last game at Wembley, against Lens, was a disaster. Vieira was injured. So was Bergkamp. Petit was suspended. Adams had to go off at half time. Lens won 1–0 with a late goal by Mickael Debeve and Parlour was sent off for a hack at Cyril Rool. Kiev, meanwhile, beat Panathinaikos.

In the final group games, the Gunners reserves defeated Panathinaikos 3–1 in a meaningless match in Athens, while Dynamo won at Lens to reach the quarter finals. The Ukraine Champions eventually lost to Bayern in the semi-finals. But Arsenal – however fortuitously – had missed the chance to finish them off at Wembley.

The Gunners had slid out of the Worthington Cup as well. That was the least of Wenger's priorities. More a case of give the reserves a chance and see what happens. In the third round at Derby, Hughes ran the game. Arsenal led through an own goal. Vivas headed a second. 2–1 to Arsenal.

Mixed League form

Wenger fielded another mainly reserve line-up – strengthened by Bergkamp, returning after a back injury, and Ljungberg – for the fourth round tie at home to Chelsea. The Gunners stayed in the game – though a goal down – until Garde was injured. A penalty, awarded against Gilles Grimandi, gave the Blues a 2–0 lead. 'For me, Grimandi took the ball,' said Wenger. But Chelsea ran out 5–0 winners.

In the Premiership, Arsenal stuttered. They thrashed Manchester United again, 3–0 at Highbury, when Bergkamp conjured up his finest form. Adams headed Arsenal in front. Anelka converted Bergkamp's pass for the second. Ljungberg,

Andrei Shevchenko of Dynamo Kiev is halted by Tony Adams in the 1–1 draw at Wembley in October. The Russian was one of the stars of the Champions League of 1998–99 and Dynamo went on to reach the semi-finals. This result was to prove costly for the Gunners as they went on to lose in Kiev 3–2 and failed to qualify from the group stage after losing to French club Lens at Wembley.

coming on as a sub, managed to score and collect a yellow card in the space of a few minutes.

Then the Gunners went down at Sheffield Wednesday, who were rapidly becoming a bogey team. Owls striker Paolo Di Canio was sent off, after flooring the referee, Paul Alcock. Keown followed him, though the FA wiped out the defender's ban on appeal.

Kevin Pressman pulled off flying saves from Bergkamp, Anelka and Parlour, before Lee Briscoe's long shot beat Alex Manninger to send the Gunners home 0–1 losers. Said Adams: 'I was disappointed with the result because I felt we should have finished the game long before Briscoe scored. We have to kill off opponents when we're on top. Otherwise we run the risk of what happened at Hillsborough. It's a bit like killing a snake. You can chop off the tail, but unless you cut off the head, it can always bite you.'

Eight days later, Arsenal hammered Newcastle 3–0 at Highbury. Adams was outstanding. Bergkamp netted twice, one a penalty. Anelka hit the other. The happy Gunners fans taunted Geordie Alan Shearer with chants of 'There's only one England captain.'

The Gunners couldn't press home their advantage against Southampton 13 days later. Anelka made it 1–0. Then the Gunners spurned chance after chance – until ex-Spur David Howells grabbed a 67th-minute equaliser.

Petit's deflected free-kick and Anelka's finish earned a 2–1 win at Blackburn, who had Chris Sutton sent off. Overmars' run set up the winner at Coventry. Magnus Hedman palmed out his shot and Anelka tucked away the rebound.

Anelka's goal beat Everton in a game the Gunners could have won by a hatful, rather than 1–0. Enter Tottenham and George Graham. Watching Spurs that derby day was like watching so many of the Gunners' backs-to-the-wall perfor-

1997-2000

Boa Morte replied just before half time. Petit scored twice in the second. Overmars, coming back to his best, made it 4–2.

Honourable Wenger replays tie

Bergkamp from a deflection, and Overmars, scored to beat Wolves at Molineux – after Havard Flo had equalised Bergkamp's goal. But Petit said too many words to a linesman – and got himself sent off.

The fifth round tie against Sheffield United has passed into history. The score was 1–1. A Blades player had been injured and the visitors kicked the ball into touch so he could receive treatment. By the game's conventions, a Gunner should have returned it to United. Ray Parlour threw the ball to Kanu. Instead of kicking it back to United, Kanu fed Overmars who scored. The Sheffield players were incensed. So was manager Steve Bruce. At one point, he looked like calling his team off the field.

Wenger solved the problem. He was embarassed about the 'winning' goal – and immediately offered Sheffield a replay. The FA agreed. UEFA, at the last minute, tried to block the game. They were worried about future legal arguments. But they bowed to the strength of feeling in England. Overmars and Bergkamp won the tie 2–1 for Arsenal.

As the Highbury fanzines pointed out, would other clubs have been as generous to the Gunners? In 1996, for instance, Tottenham scored an equaliser when they didn't throw the ball back to Arsenal after such a stoppage. The Gunners won that game 3–1. Later in the season though, Arsenal's generosity deprived them of a Champion's League place. Blackburn should have thrown the ball back to Arsenal again. Instead, Chris Sutton went on to net an equaliser that cost the Gunners the runners-up position.

In the quarter final, sub Kanu's late strike saw off Derby's combative resistance. So Arsenal met Manchester United at Villa Park in the semi-final. Petit was suspended, the result of another dismissal, this time against Everton.

Cup exit

Vivas took his place. He was sent off for a second yellow card offence, after elbowing Nicky Butt. David Beckham clattered into Nigel Winterburn, who needed treatment for cuts and bruises. Roy Keane had a goal controversially disallowed for offside. Ljungberg and Bergkamp had chances for the ten-man Gunners in extra time. 0–0. On to a replay.

After 17 minutes, Beckham lashed a 20-yarder past Seaman. It took Arsenal 51 minutes to level, with an all-Dutch goal. Bergkamp shot, the ball hit Stam and flew past Schmeichel. The tide was running the Gunners' way. Anelka had a goal

---

mances under George. It wasn't pretty, but Tottenham departed with a goalless draw.

A 0–1 defeat against Wimbledon at Selhurst Park followed. There was, allegedly, a heated debate in the dressing room afterward. Middlesbrough left Highbury with a 1–1 draw. Arsenal, with Garde and Grimandi in midfield because of injuries, then escaped with a goalless draw at Derby.

Bergkamp, injured against Wimbledon, returned at Villa Park the following Sunday – and scored twice. Two up at half time, the Gunners seemed to be coasting to victory against the leaders. But Joachim pulled one back after 61 minutes. Dublin levelled three minutes later, then grabbed Villa's winner seven minutes from time. Villa won 3–2 and marched on, if only for another few weeks. It was the low point of Arsenal's season.

Above, left: Dennis Bergkamp turns away from Ugo Ehiogu during a 3–2 defeat at Villa Park on 13 December 1998. Aston Villa were the early-season pace setters and by Christmas they were still leading the pack.

Gunners' winning streak

By now the Gunners were trailing Villa, United and Chelsea. Wenger virtually conceded the title. Who would take it – Chelsea or Manchester United? But December 13, 1997 had been a crucial date. That home defeat by Blackburn was the last Arsenal suffered before they won the 1998 Championship. The date of the defeat at Villa was ... December 13, 1998. As if on cue, the Gunners embarked on another long unbeaten run.

They beat Leeds 3–1, with goals by Bergkamp, Vieira and Petit, then edged Wright, John Hartson and West Ham 1–0 on Boxing Day, thanks to Overmars. The Dutch winger, this time from the penalty spot, scored the only goal at Charlton two days later. Liverpool bucked the trend. Now run by Wenger's old friend Gerard Houillier, they defended in depth and left Highbury with a goalless draw.

In the FA Cup third round, five days earlier, Arsenal found themselves two down at Preston. It was a bruising contest.

Few escape the attentions of erstwhile left-back Nigel Winterburn who secures the ball from Everton striker Ibrahim Bakayoko. A 2–0 win in March was part of a sequence that saw the Gunners record eight wins out of nine and have many fans reminiscing about the 1997–98 charge to the title.

disallowed after rounding Schmeichel. Keane was sent off for a second bookable offence, à la Vivas. In stoppage time, Phil Neville tripped Parlour. Penalty. Up stepped Bergkamp. Schmeichel guessed right and saved. Giggs pounced on Vieira's misplaced pass, ran, and on, then lashed a thunderous shot past Seaman. Arsenal were out.

In the Premiership, Arsenal's famous defenders had kept them in the hunt while the forwards weren't scoring. 'The mob at the back,' Leeds manager and ex-Highbury hero David O'Leary called them, with a smile on his face and huge respect. Now they had found their goal touch again.

Keown, who makes a habit of scoring at the City Ground, headed the winner against Forest. Bergkamp struck against Chelsea, and the Gunners stayed rock solid to clinch the points. As Wenger acknowledged, not many teams could have withstood Chelsea's second-half onslaught. That afternoon summed up the calibre of Arsenal's defence. They conceded just 17 goals in 38 league games.

Parlour, Overmars, Bergkamp and Anelka scored in a 4–0 romp at West Ham. Then it was on to Old Trafford. Anelka gave Arsenal the lead, but Gunners couldn't conjure up a second. Cole levelled 20 minutes from the end. That 1–1 scoreline proved a crucial result for United at the end of the season.

O'Leary's Leeds scupper Arsenal's chances

Anelka celebrated a hat-trick as the Gunners hammered Leicester 5–0. Eight days later, they needed to win at St James'. Anelka scored again. But Didi Hamann slipped through four layers of defensive cover to hit Newcastle's equaliser. A brilliant solo goal, but a serious blow to Arsenal's hopes.

Bergkamp inspired a 3–0 win over Sheffield Wednesday and a 2–0 victory at Everton. At Goodison though, Petit was sent off again. Parlour was magnificent – on the right flank, then as a stand-in right-back – as Arsenal beat Coventry 2–0. He scored a vital goal too.

The goalless draw at Southampton was another setback. Arsenal – still without Petit – were lucky to escape with a point. Mark Hughes hit a post, then forced a blinding save from Seaman. At the other end, Francis Benali cleared off the line from Kanu.

Bergkamp again orchestrated victory over Blackburn, whose goalkeeper John Filan pulled off some marvellous saves to stop the Gunners boosting their goal difference. Then Arsenal went on the rampage. Parlour, Vieira, Kanu, Bergkamp and an own goal contributed to a 5–1 rout of Wimbledon. At Middlesbrough, Anelka and Kanu struck twice, Overmars and Vieira once each, as the Gunners defended solidly throughout the first half, then broke out to overwhelm Bryan Robson's team.

Below: A breath of fresh air. The tall Nigerian Nwankwo Kanu arrived at Highbury in December 1998 for £4 million and breathed new life into Arsenal's title challenge with some crucial goals. His exquisite touches belied his giant frame, and Gunners fans took him to their hearts immediately.

Anelka struck again, to beat Derby at Highbury. Now Tottenham – and George Graham – beckoned. Arsenal turned on the style. Bergkamp pulled off the Spurs defenders and no-one went with him. His passes set up goals for Petit and Anelka. Darren Anderton pulled one back from a free-kick. But Kanu's magificent lob over Luke Young and deadly shot past Ian Walker killed the contest.

Suddenly Arsenal were in the driving seat. Alex Ferguson, ever the pyschologist, was ready to make the Gunners title favourites. Wenger didn't accept the role. The title turned on two midweek results.

Arsenal faced a tough trip to Leeds, while United travelled to relegation-haunted Blackburn, who were managed by ex-United star Brian Kidd.

Leeds fans wanted anyone but United to win the title. Leeds manager O'Leary was a Highbury playing legend. But dedicated as ever, he did the Gunners no favours: 'It's a big game for us. We're not going to dream about our summer holidays already. I'd never let the players think that way,' said O'Leary.

Leeds piled into Arsenal from the start. Seaman saved a penalty from Jimmy Floyd Hasselbaink. Leeds' leading scorer admitted: 'When Seaman saved the spot-kick, I thought they were going to win.' Seaman was at his best. So was Nigel Martyn – three times thwarting sub Diawara.

Vivas replaced the injured Winterburn at left-back. While the Gunners regrouped, Hasselbaink bundled in Leeds' late winner. Arsenal's season was on the brink.

On that final Premiership Sunday, Arsenal duly beat Aston Villa 1–0, thanks to Kanu. But United beat Spurs and chants of 'Champions' rang round Old Trafford. At Wembley six days later, United defeated Newcastle 2–0 to win the FA Cup. In Barcelona, they pulled out an astonishing comeback to pip Bayern 2–1 and bring home the European Cup. The first English club to do the 'treble', they had ensured their place in history. The Gunners had been shaded by remarkable opponents. Yet Highbury fans could still wonder: 'What might have been?'

Anelka to go

After an exhausting 53-match season, Arsenal's players looked forward to a relaxing break, free from the interruption of major tournament football, during the summer of 1999. However, for Arsene Wenger, like all Premiership managers, the close season meant transfer dealings, and in the Frenchman's case one transfer deal in particular. Throughout the summer, Wenger would have to contend with intense media speculation over the future of star striker Nicolas Anelka, a player who had frequently made plain his discontent with life and football in England. Anelka's summer, it seemed, would not be spent on a beach but

1997-2000

in residency on the back pages of Britain's tabloid newspapers.

Wenger was fully aware of Anelka's 'situation' by the end of the 1998-99 season, but, publicly at least, the manager remained optimistic that his goalscoring prodigy would remain at the club. 'Something crazy can always happen, but I'm 95 per cent certain that he will be at Arsenal next season,' proclaimed Wenger in May 1999. Alas, the craziness soon began, with Anelka linked first with Real Madrid, then Lazio, then Juventus and, most bizarrely, with a joint deal to both Lazio and Juventus. Endless stories emerged about Anelka's suffering, about purported wages and transfer fees, about illegal approaches and about the player's brothers-cum-agents. By July, the situation seemed to have reached an impasse, although, in truth, many supporters had grown so tired of the rumours that they wanted the situation resolved one way or another.

The Anelka case would rumble throughout Arsenal's pre-season's preparations but did not prevent Arsene Wenger from making several constructive moves in the transfer market. Predictably, the Gunners' aged-defence was again targeted as an area in need of new blood. To this end, Wenger recruited the Ukraine captain and right-back, Oleg Luzhny, from Dynamo Kiev for a fee of £1.8m, and Corinthians' Brazil international left-back, Silvinho (full name Sylvio Mendes Campos Junior), for £4m. Luzhny, a versatile performer who can play at either full-back or central defence, was well known to Arsenal fans, having played against the Gunners in their Champions League encounters with Dynamo in 1998. Silvinho, however, was something of an unknown, and Wenger informed the media that his new Brazilian was: 'quick, strong, versatile and can also play in midfield'.

Silvinho's ability to play on the left of midfield was particularly significant, given the departure of Stephen Hughes to Fulham on a three-month loan deal. Another of Arsenal's home-grown players would also leave the club during the close

Above: Bergkamp's penalty is saved by Peter Schmeichel during the FA Cup semi-final. Despite the numerical disadvantage of having Roy Keane sent off, the penalty miss seemed to give United impetus and a Ryan Giggs wonder-goal meant the Gunners ended the season trophyless.

Above: Your fate in their hands. The Highbury faithful are glued to their terrace trannies in the vain hope that Spurs (of all teams!) could beat United and keep the title at Highbury.

season, Jason Crowe joining First Division Portsmouth for around £600,000. Highbury's most expensive summer departee was Kaba Diawara, whose short stay in London N5 was brought to a close with a £2.5m move to Marseille. However, the most significant exit was that of Steve Bould, the veteran defender ending an 11-year association with Arsenal by moving to newly-promoted Sunderland for £500,000.

Pre-season injury problems

With the European Championships looming at season's end, the 1999-2000 Premiership campaign was scheduled for an early start. Arsenal's first fixture was at home to Leicester City on 7 August, but before the Gunners could focus upon this match, there was the small matter of a Charity Shield meeting with Manchester United at Wembley. A game against Monaco on 26 July would be Arsene Wenger's final opportunity to assess his key players in a pre-season fixture. The match ended in a 1-1 draw but proved something of a disaster for goalkeeper David Seaman, who injured a calf when attempting a clearance in the final minute. Seaman joined a worrying injury list that already included the names of captain Tony Adams, and Dutch forwards Dennis Bergkamp and Marc Overmars. Wenger was also still wrestling to resolve the Nicolas Anelka affair in time to sign a replacement ahead of UEFA's Champions League deadline.

Neither Arsenal's injury crisis nor Anelka's transfer had been resolved by 1 August, the day of the Charity Shield, so it was a somewhat makeshift Gunners line-up that took the field at Wembley against champions Manchester United. Freddie Ljungberg and Nwankwo Kanu led the Arsenal attack, with Silvinho, Gilles Grimandi and Alex Manninger, deputising for, respectively, Overmars, Adams and Seaman. It was nothing like the team that Arsene Wenger had envisaged would start the campaign, but it was a side that produced a committed and skilful performance and, on a humid day, deservedly ran out 2-1 victors. A Kanu penalty had cancelled out David Beckham's opener, and a goal from Ray Parlour 13 minutes from time proved decisive, but nobody was reading too much into the result. After all, the Gunners had also won the previous season's Charity Shield against the same opponents, and had then watched as their rivals collected the 'treble'.

Arsene Wenger may not have allowed himself any great celebration after Arsenal's Wembley victory over Manchester United, but he undoubtedly enjoyed a well-earned sigh of relief when, the following day, Nicolas Anelka completed a £23m move to Real Madrid. There was no doubting that Highbury had lost a player of immense potential, but the size of the transfer fee, which represented a £22.5m profit on a player signed in 1997, gave Wenger every chance of finding an adequate replacement. The Arsenal manager opted to spread his risk by signing two players, both of whom had starred at the 1998 World Cup finals. First to sign was Real Madrid's Croatian international striker Davor Suker, winner of the Golden Boot at France 98 and a player of proven pedigree. Suker, whose international record read, 'played 43, scored 40', arrived for a fee of around £3m. Wenger said: 'I am delighted to get Suker, he is an Ian Wright-type of player,' but when asked whether the Croatian would be an automatic selection for his team, the manager replied: 'Nobody has that guarantee'.

Twenty-four hours after the signing of Suker, a second new striker arrived. Frenchman Thierry Henry had begun his career under Arsene Wenger at Monaco and, still only 21 years old, joined Arsenal from Juventus for a club-record fee of £11m. Henry had played mainly as a winger for Juve, but Wenger had a more central role in mind for the member of the French World Cup-winning squad and told the press: 'Thierry has the ability to do as well as Nicolas... he has all the qualities, best of all is his pace and power dribbling.' The Arsenal manager added, 'We have given ourselves the experience of a player like Suker and the promise of a young man like Henry... our ambition is there for everyone to see.'

Wenger's immediate 'ambition' was to ensure that his team got off to a better start than that of the previous season, when four draws in the first five games had proved costly in the title race. The opening day clash with Leicester City, a team who had been beaten 5-0 on their last visit to Highbury, provided the perfect opportunity for the Gunners to kick off the campaign with a win. However, the game arrived too early for the rehabilitating duo of David Seaman and Tony Adams, while Marc Overmars was considered only fit enough to merit a place on the bench. The good news was that Dennis Bergkamp, who had not managed to play 90 minutes during pre-season, was included in the starting line-up. For Arsenal supporters, however, there was the disappointing news that only two of Wenger's latest signings, Silvinho and Henry, had made the bench, while none of the newcomers were included in the starting 11.

OG secures winning start

The match against Leicester proved more difficult than many had anticipated and, with the score at 0–0, Thierry Henry was introduced for the second half. The debutant made an impressive start, getting in behind the Leicester defence on several occasions, but each time his finishing proved wayward. Then, after 57 minutes, former West Ham striker Tony Cottee opened the scoring for the visitors. The game briefly opened up, and seven minutes later Bergkamp struck an equaliser to lift the Highbury crowd. The game returned to a more frustrating pattern for the closing stages, but in the final minute Arsenal won a corner. Emmanuel Petit swung the ball over, Henry glanced it

Above: Arsenal's commitment to buying the best was underlined with the £11-million signing of Thierry Henry from Juventus in August 1999. Henry had been part of the French World Cup-winning squad and proved a revelation in his first season with the Gunners, scoring 17 League goals.

Below: Davor Suker arrived at Arsenal with an impressive pedigree. The left-footed Croatian striker, who was signed from Real Madrid in August 1999, had scored 41 goals in 49 internationals and was the Golden boot winner at France 98. However, Suker would struggle to establish himself in Wenger's line up and after eight goals and 22 appearances in the league his one-year contract was not renewed.

goalwards and Foxes defender Frank Sinclair did the rest, putting the ball into his own net and giving Arsenal an opening day victory. Wenger was relieved: 'It would have been a nightmare to lose at home on the opening day. The psychological effect would have been terrible.'

A second Premiership victory followed three days later, Arsenal defeating Jim Smith's Derby County 2–1 at Pride Park with a performance that Wenger described as 'more resilient than brilliant'. Petit and Bergkamp were the Gunners scorers, and the Dutchman had looked particularly sharp. At the start of the previous season, Bergkamp had returned still exhausted from the World Cup in France, and throughout the campaign he had struggled to contend with a series of niggling injuries and a growing sense of fatigue. This time, however, Bergkamp, appeared well-rested and focused. Alongside Bergkamp in the Gunners forward line, Thierry Henry, who began the season playing on the wing, was also showing glimpses of the form that had seen Arsenal and Juventus pay combined fees of £19m for the young Frenchman. Henry's finishing remained somewhat erratic, but the player, at least, was not unduly worried: 'I have to get fitter and find my best form. I still haven't adjusted to the Premiership and a different style of football, it takes time.'

A 0-0 draw against Sunderland at the Stadium of Light meant that Arsenal, with seven points from their first three games, had achieved the good start that Wenger had called for, and, with Adams, Overmars, Seaman and Suker recovering from injuries, the signs were that things could only get better. Unfortunately, Petit had injured his knee ligaments in the Sunderland match and would be out for more than two months. More bad news lay in the fact that Manchester United had made an equally impressive start, and it was the champions who were next on the Gunners' Premiership agenda for a Sunday meeting at Highbury. The match was to be the first screened on Sky TV's new interactive channel, which gave viewers the chance to watch the game from their chosen camera angle. Arsenal fans would, no doubt, have enjoyed Sky's new service for most of the first hour, during which the Gunners were the game's dominant force. The home team's superiority was eventually rewarded when, three minutes before the interval, Freddie Ljungberg galloped onto Bergkamp's through ball to beat United keeper Raimond Van Der Gouw. A 1–0 lead, however, proved too fragile, and when Roy Keane struck twice for the visitors in the last 30 minutes, Arsenal's 20-month League unbeaten home record reached an end.

Arsenal's gloom at the defeat against Manchester United was lifted, three days later, by the tonic supplied by a 2–0 home win against newly-promoted Bradford City. A sterner test, however, came in the shape of a trip to Liverpool the following weekend. It was Arsenal's third game in seven days, a fact that did not impress Arsene Wenger, and the Gunners, though buoyed by the returning Tony Adams and Marc Overmars, pro-

1997-2000

duced a leg-weary display to lose 2–0. The season was just three weeks old, but already Arsenal had played six Premiership matches. A tally of ten points from the season's opening exchanges was a respectable haul, but it left the Gunners six points adrift of Manchester United. Arsenal had also lost two matches, a worrying statistic given Wenger's assertion that it was unlikely that a team could lose more than four games and still win the Premiership. There was, however, clearly much more to come from Arsenal. Wenger's selections remained affected by injuries to key players, and the manager was still tinkering with his forward line to find the right blend of pace and invention. Wenger was clearly keen to combine the high velocity of Henry with the transcendental skill of Bergkamp, but the young Frenchman was still without a goal.

September began with a break from domestic football, the international game taking centre stage for a round of Euro 2000 qualifiers, but Arsenal's gruelling schedule soon resumed. This time the Gunners faced three Premiership fixtures and three Champions League matches in the space of just 18 days, and this time they coped with the workload in impressive style. In the Premiership, Wenger's team recorded three straight victories; the most memorable of which was a 3–1 home success against Aston Villa. Davor Suker, making his first appearance in the starting line-up, scored twice against Villa, while Thierry Henry at last opened his account with the only goal against Southampton at The Dell. By the end of September the Gunners were just three points behind United in the Premiership table.

Champions League kick-off

In the Champions League, Arsenal would again play their home matches at Wembley, but it was in Florence that Wenger's team began its European campaign with a 0–0 draw against Fiorentina. It could have been even better had Francesco Toldo not saved an

Above: Thierry Henry scores Arsenal's second goal in a 3–1 Champions League victory against Swedish side AIK Solna. Henry's goal came in injury time, but there was still time for Suker to add a third in a rare Wembley victory for Arsenal.

Below: Martin Keown bundles the ball over the line in the last minute of the home match against Manchester United. However, the goal was disallowed and the match ended with a 2–1 victory for United.

80th minute Kanu penalty. This was followed by a dramatic victory against Swedish champions AIK Solna, who were beaten by a late Gunners rally at Wembley. The match against AIK had looked to be heading for a 1–1 draw after Krister Nordin had cancelled out Freddie Ljungberg's opener, but as the game entered injury time Arsenal struck twice through Henry and Suker to earn the three points that took them into second place in Group B. Spanish champions Barcelona topped the group, and a trip to the Nou Camp beckoned next for the Gunners.

Arsene Wenger, still without the injured David Seaman as well as influential midfielder Emmanuel Petit, operated a rotation policy with his strikers throughout the Champions League campaign, and for the match at the Nou Camp the chosen men were Kanu and Bergkamp. Both strikers, however, saw little of the ball in the first 45 minutes. Barça, urged on by the majority of the 98,000 crowd, produced a first-half display that Wenger described as 'technically perfect', although it took a mistake from Patrick Vieira to gift the Catalans the goal their football merited.

The half-time break gave Arsenal the opportunity to regroup and, spurred on by some well chosen words from their manager and captain, the Gunners produced a much improved display in the second half. On 73 minutes Wenger, with his team now enjoying an improved share of possession, played his trump card, bringing on Henry and Suker for Parlour and Bergkamp. The introduction of Suker, a former Real Madrid player, was greeted with boos from the Barça fans, but the Croat would soon silence the home supporters. It seemed Barcelona had done enough to earn victory, particularly when Gilles Grimandi was sent off for violent conduct after 80 minutes, but within seconds Arsenal had struck an equaliser. To the annoyance of the Barça supporters Suker was the architect of the Gunners' goal, hitting a shot that Ruud Hesp could only parry into the path of Kanu. The Nigerian made no mistake and the game ended 1–1. Arsenal now had five points from their opening three Champions League matches. 'The two most difficult away matches are out of the way,' said Wenger. 'Fate is in our hands. It's at Wembley that we have to perform now.'

Alas for the second year in succession it was at Wembley that Arsenal's Champions League dreams evaporated. First came a disappointing 4–2 reverse against Barça, then a 1-0 defeat at the hands of Fiorentina. Qualification for the competition's second phase was now out of reach. 'We'll never feel at home at Wembley as we do at Highbury,' said Wenger. 'It's a psychological thing.' The only consolation for Arsenal was that, because of UEFA's radical restructuring of its two club competitions, the Gunners were now handed a place in the UEFA Cup. Home matches in Europe for the remainder of the season would, thankfully, be played in the more intimidating atmosphere of Highbury.

Vieira hammered by FA

The decline of Arsenal's Champions League campaign was accompanied by an equally dramatic series of games in the Premiership during October. The month began with the Gunners making the trip to Upton Park for the latest instalment of a London derby that had been a reliable source of high jinks over the past few seasons. The match itself ended 2–1 to West Ham, but will be remembered most for the sending-off of Patrick Vieira and the midfielder's subsequent confrontation with West Ham's Neil Ruddock. Vieira, who was dismissed after collecting a second yellow card for a foul on Paolo Di Canio, reacted angrily after a verbal exchange with Ruddock and, as he was departing the pitch, the Frenchman spat at his adversary. Vieira was quick to apologise for his moment of madness, which seemed wholly out of character, but the FA found no significant mitigation in either his apology or the provocation he had been exposed to. Three weeks later Vieira was fined £45,000 and banned for six games. Wenger was understandably disappointed and defended his player: 'I think the punishment is very severe... Patrick is not a dirty player. His attitude is right and I don't think this will affect his aggression on the field.'

The Vieira incident aside, October was also notable for two of Arsenal's best performances of the season. First came a 4–1 home victory over Everton, Davor Suker scoring twice and Lee Dixon and Kanu grabbing the other goals in a game that saw Arsenal hit 28 shots to Everton's seven. A week later, Arsenal were at Stamford Bridge to take on Gianluca Vialli's highly fancied Chelsea in, what would prove to be, a match of rare

Above: Gabriele Batistuta celebrates the goal that ended the Gunners chances of progressing to the second phase of the Champions League. Fiorentina won 1–0 at Wembley.

Below: Kanu slams home his and Arsenal's second goal in a thrilling victory against Gianluca Vialli's Chelsea at Stamford Bridge in October 1999. The Nigerian's hat-trick was rounded off in style with a goal from an improbable angle that left two World Cup winning defenders baffled.

excitement. Despite the disappointment of the Barcelona defeat just four days earlier, the Gunners started the game in positive mood, but after 52 minutes found themselves two goals down. Chelsea had not conceded a goal at home all season and, even when Kanu scored after 74 minutes, there seemed little prospect of Arsenal getting a result. The Nigerian striker, however, had failed to read the script and after 83 minutes struck an equaliser. Then, in injury time, the game took its final twist. Kanu pounced on a mistake by Albert Ferrer and took possession on the left wing, side-stepped the on-rushing Chelsea goalkeeper Ed de Goey, and with Frank Leboeuf and Marcel Desailly guarding the goal, chipped the ball into the net from the most acute angle. It was Kanu at his extravagant best. When asked whether he thought he should really have crossed the ball, he replied: 'I was never going to cross. Immediately I beat the keeper my mind was on how to score. At 2–2 there was nothing else for it.'

Victory against Chelsea pushed Arsenal into second place, just a point behind David O'Leary's Leeds at the end of October. However, during the next two months the Gunners' League form became inconsistent. The season's first North London derby provided an undoubted low point; Arsenal losing 2-1 at White Hart Lane and having both Ljungberg and Keown sent off in a bad tempered match. A better result came, two weeks later, with a 5–1 victory over Middlesbrough at Highbury. Dennis Bergkamp (2) and Marc Overmars (3) were the Gunners' goalscorers against Boro, and the same players were joined on the scoresheet by Nigel Winterburn five days later when Arsenal opened their UEFA Cup campaign with a 3-0 victory over FC Nantes. Two weeks later the Gunners drew 3–3 with the French team to book their passage into the last 16 of the competition.

In the Worthington Cup Arsenal defeated Preston 2–1 en route to a tie against Middlesbrough at the Riverside. However, the competition was low on Arsene Wenger's list of priorities, and his team for the match against Boro comprised a handful of first-teamers and a mixture of squad players and youngsters. The most notable of Arsenal's fledglings was substitute Jermaine Pennant who, at 16 years and 319 days, became the youngest first team player in the club's history. The game was eventually decided on penalties, Arsenal losing 3–1. Shoot-out defeats would become all too familiar to Gunners fans during 1999–2000.

Festive cheer for Gunners

Arsenal were unbeaten during December 1999, claiming ten Premiership points from a possible 12 and progressing to the fourth round of the FA Cup with a 3–1 victory over Second Division Blackpool. The most impressive feature of this run of good form, which included a 2–0 home victory over top-of-the-table Leeds at Highbury, was that it was achieved despite the unavailability of several key players. Most notable among

1997-2000

December's absentees were Seaman, Adams, Bergkamp, Parlour and, of course, Patrick Vieira, who was left inactive courtesy of his six-match ban. Arsene Wenger's squad was stretched to the limit, but in Gilles Grimandi, Freddie Ljungberg and Oleg Luzhny the manager found able deputies for his more established stars. Grimandi, a player who had suffered his share of brickbats from supporters and critics since arriving from Monaco in 1997, proved himself a particularly versatile performer; filling in for Vieira in midfield and producing a series of accomplished displays.

One fringe player, however, who was unable to benefit from the seasonal vacancies in Arsene Wenger's line-up was Matthew Upson. The 20-year-old central defender had spent more than a year waiting for an extended run in the first team, but, just as it seemed his chance had come, he suffered a cruciate ligament injury to his left knee in the 3–0 victory over Leicester at Filbert Street. Upson's season was over, and Wenger was left with just three first-team centre-backs.

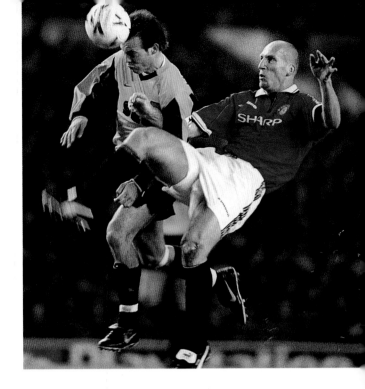

Right: Freddie Ljungberg nips in to profit from Jaap Stam's hesitation in the game at Old Trafford in January 2000. Ljungberg, playing as a makeshift striker, went on to score and put Arsenal 1–0 up, however, a Teddy Sheringham goal gave the champions a share of the points.

Rivals head for Brazil

Assistant manager Pat Rice bemoaned his club's poor luck with injuries: 'From the start of the season, I wouldn't think we've put out what people consider to be our best 11.' Nevertheless, at the turn of the year, Arsenal were well placed in third position in the Premiership. The Gunners were five points behind top club Leeds, and four points behind Manchester United, who had a game in hand. United, however, would kick off the new year in Brazil, playing in the Club World Championships. The pundits said that Arsenal and Leeds now had the opportunity to open up a lead at the top of the table; a lead which the champions, who would apparently return leg weary from their exertions in

Above: Marc Overmars slots home the first of this three goals against Middlesbrough in Arsenal's biggest league win of the season. The Gunners won the match 5–1, with Overmars' compatriot Dennis Bergkamp also scoring twice.

South America, would be unable to make up. Arsene Wenger, however, would pay little attention to such suggestions and instead focused on his own team's problems. 'We have 39 points from 20 games which is not too bad, but compared to previous seasons, we have conceded more goals [20] than before' said Wenger. 'We now have to prove to be more consistent and have to work on being much stronger defensively.'

Alas, consistency was one quality Arsenal would would find elusive during the first two months of 2000. The year began with a draw at Sheffield Wednesday but, despite a 4–1 victory over Sunderland, the Gunners remained in third place when they travelled to Old Trafford to play Manchester United on 24 January. Alex Ferguson's team had returned from Brazil level on points with Arsenal, still just a point behind Leeds and with games in hand on both. Arsenal could not afford to lose to the champions, but with Adams, Bergkamp, Kanu, Suker and Overmars all absent, avoiding defeat seemed a tall order. Wenger's chosen 11 rose to the challenge and United struggled to contend with the makeshift strike-partnership of Ljungberg and Henry. After 11 minutes Arsenal took the lead, Ljungberg scoring against the champions for the second time in one season. It was a lead that Arsenal should have added to, with good chances coming to Henry either side of the break, but the second goal did not arrive and with 17 minutes to go, Teddy Sheringham struck an equaliser. The match ended 1–1, but Wenger felt it was a point gained rather than two dropped: 'I have to give credit to the team. They showed outstanding character. Our target was to show how strong our spirit is,' said Wenger. 'One-one is a fair result.'

The draw with Manchester United was followed by a weekend of inactivity for Arsenal, who were left with no game due to their fourth round exit from the FA Cup. The Gunners had lost out 6–5 to Leicester City on penalties after a somewhat dire contest had ended goalless after 210 minutes of football. Wenger was disappointed by Leicester's defensive approach and said: 'They tried to play for a draw and in the end we were punished because we did not score a goal... It wasn't like a cup tie atmosphere. It lacked passion mainly because Leicester did not come out. They decided to defend and, to be fair, they did that well.'

Title hopes recede

Arsenal's injury list had eased little by the time the Gunners made the trip to Bradford on 5 February, but Wenger remained sanguine: 'We have shown that, even with lots of players out, we are still a good team. The problem is more of belief than in our physical abilities.' All optimism, however, would ebb away from Arsenal's Championship challenge when Dean Saunders struck the winning goal for Bradford after 57 minutes. Manchester United now had a nine-point lead at the top of the table, together with their seemingly omnipresent game in hand. Barring the most spectacular series of results, the Premiership was now out of the Gunners' reach. A top-three finish and, thereby, a Champions League place now became the priority.

Liverpool, who like Arsenal had 44 points from 24 games, appeared to be the Gunners' most likely rivals for a Champions League place, and it was the Merseysiders who were next on the Highbury guest list. Arsenal had not beaten Liverpool since August 1994 and, despite the return to the first-team line up of Dennis Bergkamp, the Gunners could not break the sequence and lost 1-0. Wenger was rightly concerned by his team's falling League position, and the manager was no less worried by the ascendancy of Liverpool, who had climbed from 12th to third in just 14 games. Patrick Vieira put it succinctly: 'We have to improve or we could end up with nothing.'

Vieira's words were heeded, and during March Arsenal produced the improved run required to maintain their position in the hunt for Champions League places. Consecutive victories against Middlesbrough, Spurs and Coventry were at the core of this good run, and it was, of course, the win against George Graham's Spurs that was most celebrated. March had also seen Arsenal return to UEFA Cup action with a tie against Spain's champions-elect, Deportivo La Coruna. The tie against Deportivo provided a keen test of Arsenal's quality, and Wenger's team passed with flying colours. The first leg was played at Highbury, and a far-post header from Lee Dixon after five minutes settled the nerves before Thierry Henry added a second on the half-hour mark. After the interval Deportivo enjoyed their best period of the game, scoring a penalty through Brazilian midfielder Djalminha, but the same player would immediately undo his good work by getting himself sent off for a clash with Grimandi. Arsenal seized the moment and added

Above: Gilles Grimandi holds his head in his hands after missing the vital penalty in the shoot-out against Leicester City in the fourth round of the FA Cup at Filbert Street.

three goals before the end of the game to give themselves an insurmountable 5–1 lead for the second leg. Henry scored twice and was named man of the match, but the pick of Arsenal's goals came from Kanu, who produced a sublime dummy to perplex the Deportivo keeper before slotting the ball home.

The second leg against Deportivo proved an intriguing affair, with Arsenal travelling to the Riazor Stadium without a recognised centre-back among their squad. Emmanuel Petit and Oleg Luzhny were deployed at the heart of the Gunners defence and performed with great composure against one of Spain's most attacking teams. It was not until the 69th minute that Arsenal's goal was breached, but by then the Gunners had already taken the lead through Henry. The match finished in a 2–1 victory for Deportivo, but it was Arsenal – 6–3 aggregate victors – who celebrated progress to a quarter-final meeting with Werder Bremen.

After the high jinks of the Deportivo match at Highbury, Arsenal's fans were treated to rather different fare against Werder Bremen. The Germans arrived at Highbury with no intention of attacking, and seemed content when they departed London N5 with a two goal deficit after conceding goals from Henry and Ljungberg. The second leg, however, proved as controversial as the first leg was frustrating. After 25 minutes, Arsenal found themselves two goals in front and, with a 4-0 aggregate lead, the tie seemed all but over. Both Gunners goals had been scored by Ray Parlour and the midfielder would complete a deserved hat-trick in the second half, however, by then his contribution had been overshadowed by the dismissal of Thierry Henry for a trip on Mike Barten. Henry's challenge was neither dangerous nor cynical and hardly seemed to warrant a yellow card, much less a red one. Wenger's disappointment at referee Kim Nielsen's decision was compounded by the fact that the manager had been attempting to substitute Henry, but had been refused permission to make two changes simultaneously. Henry, who had scored the third goal in Arsenal's 4–2 victory over Bremen, would now miss the first leg of a semi-final against Lens.

Henry the hero

Thierry Henry's suspension was a huge blow to Arsenal's plans. The young striker had enjoyed a run of breathtaking form during March, scoring seven goals and earning a recall to the blue shirt of France. Henry, who was rewarded with the *Evening Standard* Footballer of the Month award, said: 'I am feeling more confident in myself, in my play and I am developing a good understanding with the players around me.' It was a view shared by Arsene Wenger, who also believed that, good as Henry's form had been, there was still more to come from the young striker. Arsenal's number 14 did not disappoint and duly delivered his 20th goal of the season after coming on as a substitute in the 3–1 win against Wimbledon at Selhurst Park on 2 April. Victory against the Dons had been secured despite the sending off of Oleg Luzhny, and kept Arsenal in fourth place. The Gunners were now two points behind Liverpool and three behind second placed Leeds.

The chase for a Champions League place was undoubtedly Arsenal's main aim, but their only chance of silverware remained the UEFA Cup. However, to reach the final, the Gunners would have to overcome Racing Club de Lens, a team that had defeated them in the previous season's Champions League and that had already knocked out Kaiserslautern, Celta Vigo and Atletico Madrid in the UEFA Cup. The first leg of the semi-final was played at Highbury and, although Dennis Bergkamp's second-minute goal earned Arsenal a 1-0 victory, the match was overshadowed by the deaths of two Leeds United fans in Istanbul ahead of the other semi-final between Leeds and Galatasaray.

Between the two legs of the UEFA Cup semi-final, Arsenal returned to their Champions League chase with a match against Leeds United at Elland Road. The Yorkshire side were still three points ahead of Arsenal, but were in the midst of a disastrous run that had seen them lose five games in succession. The match against Leeds was preceded by a moving tribute to the supporters who had died in Istanbul, with the Arsenal players each handing a bouquet of flowers to a member of the opposition. However, Arsenal's compassion ceased once referee Steve Dunn had blown his whistle to start the game, and after 21 minutes Arsenal took the lead when Henry prodded home from Parlour's cross. The Gunners squandered a string of good chances during the remainder of the first half, but two minutes before the break their cause was aided by the dismissal of Ian Harte for an off-the-ball kick on Dennis Bergkamp. The second half saw Arsenal dominate the game, and three goals in the final 20 minutes secured a victory that took the Gunners back into the top three. Arsenal were now five points behind second-placed Liverpool but had a game in hand over the Merseysiders.

Injury problems relent

For the remainder of the season, injuries ceased to be the determining factor in Arsene Wenger's team selections, and at last the Gunners began to reveal their true calibre. For the second leg of the UEFA Cup semi-final against Lens, the manager even enjoyed the luxury of naming a line-up unchanged from that which had taken the field against Leeds. However, eight of Wenger's players were just one booking away from a UEFA suspension that would rule them out of the final, so a degree of caution would need to be employed along with the usual Arsenal competitive spirit. The red-shirted Gunners heeded their manager's instructions and produced a disciplined performance that saw them keep the game scoreless for the first 43 minutes. When the breakthrough did eventually arrive, it was via the right boot of Thierry Henry and it was Arsenal who were cel-

Above: Nwankwo Kanu sends Deportivo's Cameroon international goalkeeper, Jacques Songo'o, to ground with a sublime dummy before scoring in the 5-1 UEFA Cup victory over the Spaniards at Highbury.

Right: Kanu scores his third European goal of the season to help Arsenal beat Lens in the quarter-final of the UEFA Cup.

Below: Martin Keown celebrates scoring the second goal in Arsenal's 4–0 away win against David O'Leary's young Leeds United team at Elland Road in April 2000. Victory against Leeds put the the Gunners back in contention for a Champions League place.

ebrating. Lens did equalise midway through the second half, but it proved no more than a consolation, with Kanu scoring a second for the Londoners to ensure a 3-1 aggregate victory.

Arsenal had booked a place at their third European final in six years and would travel to Copenhagen, venue of their victory against Parma in the 1994 Cup Winners Cup, as favourites for a match against Galatasaray. However, before focusing upon the UEFA Cup final, Arsene Wenger and his team still had the small matter of Champions League qualification with which to concern themselves. According to the pundits, Arsenal's run-in was more difficult than that of their chief rivals, Liverpool and Leeds, but the experts had failed to appreciate that the Gunners had found form at the perfect time. In their final 11 matches, Arsenal dropped just five points and won nine consecutive matches. Liverpool, meanwhile, took just two points from their final five fixtures and, with a 3-3 draw in their penultimate fixture at home to relegated Sheffield Wednesday, Arsenal clinched runners-up spot and a lucrative place in the 2000-2001 Champions League.

allowed to flare. Arsenal quickly condemned the hooligans and pledged to ban them from Highbury.

The Gunners, who were 10/11 favourites to lift the Cup, had no significant injury problems, and a full strength line-up took the field in Copenhagen. Arsenal, however, struggled to live up to their star billing and, in a cagey first half that brought few clear cut chances, were well below their best. The game opened up a little after the interval, but Galatasaray remained slightly in the ascendant, although the best chance of the match fell to a Gunner. Alas, Martin Keown, who popped up in an unfamiliar position inside the opposition penalty area, crashed his close range shot over the bar. For the remainder of the second half, the better of the chances fell to the Turks, but neither side could break the deadlock and, with a certain inevitability, the game entered extra time. A goal would now be enough to win the Cup for either team and, when Galatasaray's inspirational Romanian Gheorghe Hagi was sent off four minutes into extra time, the most likely winners appeared to be Arsenal.

Penalty jinx returns

Once down to ten men, Galatasaray's ambition diminished. Fatih Terim's team now set their sights on a penalty shoot-out and, after 30 minutes of extra time, the Turks got their wish. For Arsenal fans, however, thoughts immediately returned to the shoot-out defeats against Middlesbrough and Leicester earlier on in the season and to the Cup Winners Cup defeat against Valencia in 1980. Arsenal's concerns, unlike their penalties, were well-placed. First Suker and then Vieira struck their shots against the frame of the goal, and although Parlour's effort found the net, it proved not to be enough. Former Spurs player Gheorghe Popescu was left to take the decisive spot-kick, and made no mistake. It was a bitter pill for Arsenal supporters to swallow, and Wenger was equally despondent about his team's performance: 'We did not play well in the first half, but we were much better afterwards. It is very disappointing... if we had won the shoot-out it would not have made any difference to the quality of our game and so of course I want to strengthen for next season.'

It had been a season of great drama for Arsenal. From the Anelka saga in pre-season to the defeat in Copenhagen, the Gunners had never been far from the headlines. The season's undoubted highlights had been the form of Thierry Henry and the nine-game winning sequence that had taken the club into runners-up position in the final Premiership table. In contrast, Arsenal's away form had been disappointing, and had prevented a sustained title challenge. The summer of 2000 would, no doubt, see Wenger busy himself in the transfer market once more, and, with the most accomplished youth team in England to provide further reinforcement, the disappointment of Copenhagen will soon recede to allow thoughts to drift to happier times.

Arsenal's final League fixture of 1999-2000 came against Newcastle United at St James' Park and was to be played just three days before the UEFA Cup final. Arséne Wenger, who had appealed unsuccessfully to have the game moved forward by 24 hours, fielded a weakened line-up for the clash with Newcastle and was unconcerned by his team's 4–2 defeat. One result that Wenger would have paid more attention to, however, came in the FA Youth Cup, where Don Howe's side claimed an impressive 5–1 aggregate victory over Coventry City. Arsenal would establish themselves as the pre-eminent youth team in England during 1999–2000, progressing to the finals of both the Under-17 and Under-19 Premier Youth Leagues. This unprecedented record of junior success represented a huge achievement for Liam Brady (head of the Gunners' youth section) and his coaching staff.

Above: Theirry Henry chips the ball over a prostrate Chelsea defence to score his sixth goal in seven games. The match, played in May 2000, ended in a 2–1 victory for Arsenal and secured the club's passage into the Champions League.

Below: Galatasaray's veteran forward Gheorghe Hagi clashes with Tony Adams during the UEFA Cup final. The Romanian was shown the red card for his indiscretion, however, his dismissal had little effect upon the result of a match that was decided by a penalty shoot-out.

A dark day in the 'wonderful' city

All that was left now was for Arsenal to claim the UEFA Cup and provide their supporters with the silverware that they craved. It mattered little to either players or fans that the Gunners' only chance of a trophy now rested with a competition that neither they, nor their opponents, had entered at the start of the season. 'We want to win and it's essential that the players are focused on the game and nothing else', said Wenger.

Fighting between Arsenal and Galatasaray supporters in Copenhagen's City Hall Square, however, would overshadow the build up to the UEFA Cup final. Five supporters were injured and more than 20 arrests were made. Politicians and journalists immediately began an inquest into how such trouble had been

1997-2000

THE FIRST DOUBLE

First Division appearances 1970–71				First Division Goalscorers 1970–71		FA Cup appearances 1970–71				FA Cup goalscorers 1970–71	
Armstrong	42	Graham	38	Kennedy	19	Wilson	9	Armstrong	9	George	5
Wilson	42	Simpson	25	Radford	15	Rice	9	Sammels	6	Storey	4
McLintock	42	Kelly	23	Graham	11	McNab	9	Graham	6	Kennedy	2
Kennedy	41	Roberts	18	Armstrong	7	Storey	9	Radford	9	Radford	2
Radford	41	George	17	George	5	McLintock	9	Kennedy	9	Graham	1
Rice	41	Sammels	15	McLintock	5	Simpson	9	George	8	Kelly	1
Storey	40	Nelson	4	Kelly	4			Kelly	2	Simpson	1
McNab	40	Marinello	3	Storey	2	**Total:13 players**				**Total: 16 goals**	
		Total:16 players		Sammels	1						
				Own goals	2						
				Total: 71 goals							

Ray Kennedy

THE SECOND DOUBLE

Premiership appearances 1997–98				Premiership Goalscorers 1997–98		FA Cup appearances 1997–98				FA Cup goalscorers 1997–98	
Winterburn	36	Grimandi	22	Bergkamp	16	Anelka	9	Bould	5	Anelka	3
Parlour	34	Platt	31	Overmars	12	Overmars	9	Grimandi	5	Bergkamp	3
Petit	32	Hughes	17	Wright	10	Vieira	9	Manninger	5	Overmars	2
Overmars	32	Wreh	16	Anelka	6	Winterburn	8	Bould	4	Parlour	1
Vieira	33	Manninger	7	Parlour	5	Bergkamp	7	Seaman	4	Wreh	1
Seaman	31	Garde	10	Adams	3	Keown	7	Platt	4	**Total: 10 goals**	
Bergkamp	28	Upson	5	Platt	3	Parlour	7	Boa Morte	4		
Dixon	28	Boa Morte	15	Wreh	3	Petit	7	Crowe	1		
Adams	26	Marshall	3	Hughes	2	Hughes	6	Garde	1		
I Wright	24	Mendez	3	Petit	2	Wreh	6	Upson	1		
Bould	24	Vernazza	1	Vieira	2			Wright	1		
Keown	18	Rankin	1	Grimandi	1	**Total: 21 players**					
Anelka	26	McGowan	1	Winterburn	1						
		Total: 26 players		Own goals	2						
				Total: 68 goals							

Marc Overmars

THE THIRD DOUBLE

Premiership appearances 2001–02				Premiership Goalscorers 2001–02		FA Cup appearances 2001–02				FA Cup goalscorers 2001–02	
Vieira	36	V Bronckhorst	21	Henry	24	Vieira	7	Grimandi	4	Bergkamp	3
Wiltord	33	Luzhny	18	Ljungberg	12	Wiltord	7	Keown	4	Wiltord	2
Henry	33	Seaman	17	Wiltord	10	Campbell	7	Luzhny	4	Ljungberg	2
Bergkamp	33	Edu	14	Bergkamp	9	Bergkamp	6	Parlour	4	Parlour	2
Campbell	31	Upson	14	Pires	9	Edu	5	Adams	3	Kanu	2
Cole	29	Dixon	13	Kanu	3	Henry	5	Lauren	3	Adams	1
Pires	28	R Wright (R)	12	Campbell	2	Ljungberg	5	Jeffers	2	Campbell	1
Lauren	27	Taylor	10	Cole	2	Kanu	5	V Bronckhorst	2	Edu	1
Parlour	27	Adams	10	Jeffers	2	Pires	5	Seaman	1	Henry	1
Grimandi	26	Stepanovs	6	Lauren	2	Wright	5	Stepanovs	1	Pires	1
Ljungberg	25	Jeffers	6	Vieira	2	Cole	4	Taylor	1	**Total: 16 goals**	
Kanu	23	Aliadiere	1	Edu	1	Dixon	4	Upson	1		
Keown	22	**Total: 25 players**		V Bronckhorst	1			**Total: 24 players**			
				Total: 78 goals							

Arsène Wenger and Tony Adams

SEASON 1997-98 FA CARLING PREMIERSHIP

Date	Opponents		Res	Score												Substitutes
9 Aug	Leeds United	A	D	1-1	Seaman	Garde	Bould	Grimandi	Winterburn	Parlour	Vieira	Petit	Overmars	Wright1	Bergkamp	Platt/Hughes for Vieira/Overmars
11 Aug	Coventry City	H	W	2-0	..	..	Marshall	..	..	..	..	..	..	..2	..	Platt/Hughes for Petit/Overmars
23 Aug	Southampton	A	W	3-1	..	..	Bould	..	..	..	..	..	..1	..	..2	Platt/Marshall/Boa Morte for Grimandi/Petit/Overmars
27 Aug	Leicester City	A	D	3-3	..	Dixon	..	..	..	..	..	..	..	..	..3	Anelka/Platt/Hughes for Parlour/Overmars/Wright
30 Aug	Tottenham Hotspur	H	D	0-0	..	..	..	..	..	..	..	..	..	..	..	Platt/Anelka for Parlour/Petit
13 Sep	Bolton Wanderers	H	W	4-1	..	..	..	..	..	..1	..	..	..	..3	..	Platt/Boa Morte/Anelka for Parlour/Overmars/Wright
21 Sep	Chelsea	A	W	3-2	..	..	..	Adams	..1	..	..	..	..	..	..2	Boa Morte/Grimandi for Parlour/Overmars
24 Sep	West Ham United	H	W	4-0	..	..	..	..	..	..	..	..	..2	..1p	..1	Grimandi/Platt/Anelka for Dixon/Winterburn/Wright
27 Sep	Everton	A	D	2-2	..	Grimandi	..	..	..	..	..	..	..1	..1	..	Boa Morte/Platt/Garde for Parlour/Vieira/Wright
4 Oct	Barnsley	H	W	5-0	..	Dixon	..	..	..1	..	..	..	..	..1	..2	Platt1/Anelka/Boa Morte for Parlour/Overmars/Wright
18 Oct	Crystal Palace	A	D	0-0	..	Grimandi	..	..	..	..	..	..	Boa Morte	..	..	Platt/Mendez for Parlour/Boa Morte
26 Oct	Aston Villa	H	D	0-0	..	Dixon	..	..	..	..	..	..	..	..	..	Platt/Anelka for Parlour/Boa Morte
1 Nov	Derby County	A	L	0-3	..	..	..	..	..	..	..	..	Platt	..	Anelka	Boa Morte/Wreh for Winterburn/Anelka
9 Nov	Manchester United	H	W	3-2	..	..	Grimandi	..	..	..	..1	Platt1	Overmars	..	..1	Bould/Wreh for Vieira/Anelka
22 Nov	Sheffield Wednesday	A	L	0-2	..	..	Keown	..	..	..	Platt	Grimandi	..	..	Mendez	Hughes/Marshall/Wreh for Parlour/Grimandi/Mendez
30 Nov	Liverpool	H	L	0-1	..	..	..	..	..	Hughes	..	Petit	..	..	Bergkamp	Wreh/Grimandi for Hughes/Petit
6 Dec	Newcastle United	A	W	1-0	..	..	..	..	..	Parlour	..	..	..	..	..	
13 Dec	Blackburn Rovers	H	L	1-3	..	..	..	..	..	..	..	..	..1	..	..	Vieira/Boa Morte for Parlour/Platt
26 Dec	Leicester City	H	W	2-1*	..	..	Gould	Keown	..	..	Vieira	Platt1	..	..	..	Hughes/Anelka for Platt/Wright
28 Dec	Tottenham Hotspur	A	D	1-1	..	..	..	..	..	..1	..	Petit	..	Anelka	..	Grimandi/Hughes/Rankin for Dixon/Anelka/Bergkamp
10 Jan	Leeds United	H	W	2-1	..	..	..	..	..	..	..	..	..2	Wright	..	
17 Jan	Coventry City	A	D	2-2	..	..	..	..	..	..	..	..	Upson	Anelka1	..1	Grimandi/Boa Morte for Keown/Anelka
31 Jan	Southampton	H	W	3-0	Manninger	Grimandi	..	Adams1	..	..	Hughes	..	Overmars	..1	..1	Platt/Wreh for Hughes/Anelka
8 Feb	Chelsea	H	W	2-0	..	..	..	..	..	..	..2	..	..	..	..	Dixon/Wright/Platt for Grimandi/Overmars/Anelka
21 Feb	Crystal Palace	H	W	1-0	..	Dixon	Keown	Grimandi1	Upson	Venazza	Vieira	Hughes	Boa Morte	Platt	..	McGowan for Vernazza
2 Mar	West Ham United	A	D	0-0	..	..	..	Adams	..	Hughes	..	Petit	Overmars	..	..	Winterburn/Boa Morte for Upson/Platt
11 Mar	Wimbledon	A	W	1-0	..	..	..	..	Winterburn	Parlour	..	..	..	Wreh1	..	Garde/Hughes/Boa Morte for Parlour/Overmars/Wreh
14 Mar	Manchester United	A	W	1-0	..	..	..	..	..	..	..	..	..1	..	..	Anelka/Garde for Wreh/Parlour
28 Mar	Sheffield Wednesday	H	W	1-0	..	..	..	..	..	..	..	Hughes	..	..	..1	Garde/Anelka/Grimandi for Dixon/Parlour/Wreh
31 Mar	Bolton Wanderers	A	W	1-0	..	Grimandi	..	..	..	..	..	Petit	..	..1	Anelka	Hughes/Bould/Platt for Overmars/Wreh/Anelka
11 Apr	Newcastle United	H	W	3-1	..	Garde	Gould	..	..	..	..1	..	..	Anelka2	Wreh	Platt/Hughes/Boa Morte for Overmars/Anelka/Wreh
13 Apr	Blackburn Rovers	A	W	4-1	..	..	..	..	..	..2	..	..	..	..1	Bergkamp1	Platt/Hughes for Overmars/Anelka
18 Apr	Wimbledon	H	W	5-0	..	..	Upson	..1	..	..	..	..1	..1	..	..1	Dixon/Wreh1/Platt for Garde/Vieira/Anelka
25 Apr	Barnsley	A	W	2-0	..	Dixon	Keown	..	..	Platt	..	..	..1	..	..1	Wreh for Anelka
29 Apr	Derby County	H	W	1-0	..	..	..	..	..	Parlour	..	..1	..	..	..	Wreh/Platt for Bergkamp/Anelka
3 May	Everton	H	W	4-0	..	..	..	..1	..	..	..	..	..2	..	Wreh	Wright/Bould for Anelka/Wreh - own goal
6 May	Liverpool	A	L	0-4	Manninger	..	Bould	Upson	Grimandi	..	Platt	Hughes	Boa Morte	Wright	..	Vieira/Mendez/Anelka for Parlour/Wreh/Wright
10 May	Aston Villa	A	L	0-1	Seaman	Grimandi	Keown	Adams	..	..	Vieira	Petit	Overmars	..	Anelka	Platt/Wreh for Parlour/Wright
FA Cup																
3 Jan	Port Vale (3)	H	D	0-0	Seaman	Grimandi	Keown	Bould	Winterburn	Parlour	Vieira	Petit	Overmars	Anelka	Bergkamp	Hughes/Boa Morte/Wreh for Parlour/Petit/Anelka
24 Jan	Port Vale (3R)	A	D	1-1*	..	Dixon	Bould	Keown	..	..	..	Hughes	..	Wright	..1	Grimandi/Anelka/Boa Morte for Vieira/Overmars/Wright *Won on penalties after extra time
24 Jan	Middlesbrough (4)	A	W	2-1	Manninger	..	..	Adams	..	..1	..	Petit	..1	Anelka	..	Grimandi for Dixon
15 Feb	Crystal Palace (5)	H	D	0-0	..	..	..	Grimandi	..	..	Hughes	..	..	..	..	Vieira/Platt/Wreh for Bould/Hughes/Anelka
25 Feb	Crystal Palace (5R)	A	W	2-1	..	..	Keown	Adams	Upson	Boa Morte	Vieira	Platt	Hughes	..1	..1	Overmars/Crowe for Upson/Bergkamp
8 Mar	West Ham (6)	H	D	1-1	..	..	..	..	Winterburn	Parlour	Vieira	Petit	Overmars	..	..1	Wreh for Anelka
17 Mar	West Ham (6R)	A	D	1-1*	..	..	..	..	..	Garde	..	..	..	..	..1p	Hughes/Wreh/Boa Morte for Petit/Overmars/Anelka *Arsenal won on penalties after extra time

Abbreviations:

Appearances (goals) refer to League games only

Figures shown as '2' etc. refer to goals scored by individual players

* own-goal

Tony Adams has his hands full as thousands pack the streets of Islington to hail the Double-winning heroes.

Date	Opponent			Score													Substitutes
5 Apr	Wolverhampton (SF) at Aston Villa	W	1-0	Seaman	Grimandi	..	..	..	Parlour	..	..	..	Wreh1	..	Bould/Hughes/Platt for Keown/Wreh/ Anelka
16 May	Newcastle United (F) at Wembley	W	2-0	..	Dixon	..	..	..	..	..	..1	..	..1	Platt for Wreh

Football League (Coca-Cola) Cup

Date	Opponent			Score													Substitutes
14 Oct	Birmingham City (3)	H	W	4-1 (a.e.t)	Manninger	Dixon	Marshall	Grimandi	Upson	Mendez1	Platt1	Vernazza	Hughes	Wreh	Boa Morte2	Crowe/Muntasser for Dixon/Boa Morte
18 Nov	Coventry City (4)	H	W	1-0 (a.e.t)	..	..	Bould	Keown	..	Parlour	..	Mendez	..	Anelka	Bergkamp1	Wreh/ Marshall for Mendez/Anelka
6 Jan	West Ham (QF)	A	W	2-1	Seaman	Grimandi	Keown	Bould	Winterburn	..	Vieira	Petit	Overmars1	Wright1	..	Wreh/Hughes for Overmars/Wright
28 Jan	Chelsea (SF)	H	W	2-1	Manninger	..	Bould	Adams	..	..	Hughes1	..	..1	Anelka	..	Platt for Grimandi
18 Feb	Chelsea (SF)	A	L	1-3	..	Dixon	Grimandi1	..	..	..	Vieira	..	..	..	..	Platt/Hughes for Winterburn/Parlour

UEFA Cup

Date	Opponent			Score													Substitutes
16 Sep	PAOK Salonika (1)	A	L	0-1	Seaman	Dixon	Bould	Adams	Winterburn	Parlour	Vieira	Petit	Overmars	Wright	Anelka	Platt/Boa Morte/Wreh for Parlour/Overmars/ Anelka
30 Sep	PAOK Salonika (1)	H	W	1-1	..	..	..	..	..	..	..	..	..	..	Bergkamp1	Platt/Anelka for Parlour/Overmars

---

Appearances (Goals)

Winterburn 36 (1) – Parlour 34 (5) – Petit 32 (2) – Overmars 32 (12) – Vieira 33 (2) – Seaman 31 – Bergkamp 28 (16) – Dixon 28 – Adams 26 (3) – Wright 24 (11) – Bould 24 – Keown 18 – Anelka 26 (6) – Grimandi 22 (1) – Platt 31 (3) – Hughes 17 (2) – Wreh 16 (3) – Manninger 7 – Garde 10 – Upson 5 – Boa Morte 15 – Marshall 3 – Mendez 3 – Vernazza 1 – Rankin 1 – McGowan 1 – Own goals 2 – **Total 26 players (68)**

Position in League Table

	P	W	L	D	F:A	Pts	
Arsenal	38	23	6	9	68:33	91	1st
Manchester U	38	23	7	8	73:26	73	2nd

SEASON 1998-1999 FA CARLING PREMIERSHIP

Date	Opponent			Score													Substitutes
17 Aug	Nottingham Forest	H	W	2-1	Seaman	Dixon	Keown	Adams	Winterburn	Parlour	Vieira	Petit1	Overmars1	Anelka	Bergkamp	
22 Aug	Liverpool	A	D	0-0	..	..	..	Bould	..	..	..	..	..	..	..	Vivas for Vieira
29 Aug	Charlton	H	D	0-0	..	..	..	Adams	..	..	..	..	..	..	..	Vivas, Wreh and Hughes for Dixon, Anelka and Vieira
9 Sep	Chelsea	A	D	0-0	..	..	..	..	..	..	..	..	..	..	..	Garde, Hughes and Wreh for Overmars, Anelka and Bergkamp
12 Sep	Leicester	A	D	1-1	..	..	..	Bould	..	..	..	Hughes1	..	Wreh	..	Anelka, Garde and Vivas for Wreh, Vieira and Dixon
20 Sep	Manchester United	H	W	3-0	..	..	..	Adams1	..	..	..	..	..	Anelka1	..	Ljungberg1 for Anelka
26 Sep	Sheffield Wednesday	A	L	0-1	Manninger	Vivas	..	..	..	..	..	Petit	..	..	..	Bould, Hughes and Ljungberg for Parlour, Petit and Overmars
4 Oct	Newcastle	H	W	3-0	Seaman	Dixon	..	..	..	Ljungberg	..	..	..	..1	..2(1p)	Bould, Hughes and Mendez for Keown, Petit and Ljungberg
17 Oct	Southampton	H	D	1-1	..	..	..	..	..	Parlour	..	Hughes	..	..1	..	Wreh for Parlour
25 Oct	Blackburn	A	W	2-1	..	..	..	Bould	..	Ljungberg	..	Petit1	..	..1	..	
31 Oct	Coventry	A	W	1-0	..	..	..	..	..	Parlour	..	..	..	..1	Ljungberg	Boa Morte and Hughes for Ljungberg and Overmars
8 Nov	Everton	H	W	1-0	..	..	..	Grimandi	..	..	..	..	..	..1	..	
14 Nov	Tottenham	H	D	0-0	..	..	..	Adams	..	..	..	..	..	..	..	Wreh and Boa Morte for Anelka and Ljungberg
21 Nov	Wimbledon	A	L	0-1	..	..	..	..	..	..	..	..	..	..	Bergkamp	Hughes, Wreh and Ljungberg for Overmars, Bergkamp and Vieira
29 Nov	Middlesbrough	H	D	1-1	..	..	..	Bould	..	..	Garde	Ljungberg	..	..1	Wreh	Vivas, Boa Morte and Caballero for Winterburn, Ljungberg and Wreh
5 Dec	Derby	A	D	0-0	..	..	..	..	Vivas	..	..	Grimandi	..	..	..	Ljungberg and Boa Morte for Garde and Wreh
13 Dec	Aston Villa	A	L	2-3	..	..	..	..	..	..	Vieira	Ljungberg	..	..	Bergkamp2	Grimandi and Boa Morte for Parlour and Ljungberg
20 Dec	Leeds	H	W	3-1	Manninger	..	..	..	..	Ljungberg	..1	Petit1	..	..	..	Grimandi and Wreh for Ljungberg1 and Overmars

1997-2000

Date	Opponent	V	Result	Seaman	Dixon	Keown	Adams	Winterburn	Parlour	Vieira	Petit	Overmars	Anelka	Bergkamp	Substitutions / notes
26 Dec	West Ham	H	W 1-0	..	..	..	..	..	Parlour	..	..	..	..1	..	Wreh and Grimandi for Anelka and Vivas
28 Dec	Charlton	A	W 1-0	..	..	..	..	Winterburn	..	..	..	..	..1p	Boa Morte	Vivas, Wreh and Grimandi for Winterburn, Boa Morte and Bergkamp
9 Jan	Liverpool	H	D 0-0	..	..	..	..	Grondin	..	..	..	..	Anelka	Boa Morte	Upson, Garde and Wreh for Bould, Overmars and Anelka
16 Jan	Nottingham Forest	A	W 1-0	..	..	..1	Adams	Winterburn	..	Garde	..	..	..	Bergkamp	Vivas and Upson for Overmars and Anelka
31 Jan	Chelsea	H	W 1-0	Seaman	..	..	..	..	..	..	..	..	..	..1	Upson, Vivas and Diawara for Anelka, Overmars and Bergkamp
6 Feb	West Ham	A	W 4-0	..	..	..	..	..	..1	Vieira	..	..1	..1	..1	Garde, Vivas, Diawara for Overmars, Winterburn and Kanu
17 Feb	Manchester United	A	D 1-1	..	..	Bould	..	..	..	..	..	Hughes	..1	Kanu	Diawara, Kanu and Hughes for Overmars, Anelka and Vieira
20 Feb	Leicester	H	W 5-0	..	Grimandi	..	..	Vivas	..2	Garde	..	..	..3	Bergkamp	Hughes and Upson for Garde and Overmars
28 Feb	Newcastle	A	D 1-1	..	..	Keown	..	Winterburn	..	..	..	..	..1	..	Diawara, Kanu1 and Petit for Anelka, Parlour and Ljungberg
9 Mar	Sheffield Wednesday	H	W 3-0	..	..	..	..	Vivas	..	..	Ljungberg	..	..2	..	Vivas and Upson for Overmars and Anelka
13 Mar	Everton	A	W 2-0	..	..	..	..	Winterburn	..1	..	Petit	..	..	..1(p)	Ljungberg, Diawara and Kanu for Dixon, Anelka and Overmars
20 Mar	Coventry	H	W 2-0	..	..	..	..	..	..1	..	..	..1	..	..	Boa Morte, Vivas and Bould for Ljungberg, Diawara and Keown
3 Apr	Southampton	A	D 0-0	..	..	..	..	..	..	..	Ljungberg	Diawara	..	Kanu	Kanu and Bould for Diawara and Overmars
6 Apr	Blackburn	H	W 1-0	..	..	..	..	..	Vivas	..	..	Overmars	Diawara	Bergkamp1	Kanu and Bould for Bergkamp and Keown - own goal
19 Apr	Wimbledon	H	W 5-1	..	Vivas	..	..	..	..1	..1	Petit	..	Kanu1	..1	Diawara and Bould for Kanu, Overmars and Petit
24 Apr	Middlesbrough	A	W 6-1	..	Dixon	Bould	..	..	..	..1	..	..1	Anelka2	Kanu2	Diawara, Vivas and Hughes for Kanu, Overmars and Petit
2 May	Derby	H	W 1-0	..	..	..	..	..	..	..	..	..	..1	..	Bergkamp, Hughes and Diawara for Anelka, Overmars and Kanu
5 May	Tottenham	A	W 3-1	..	..	Keown	..	..	..	..	..1	..	..1	Bergkamp	Vivas, Kanu1 and Grimandi for Parlour, Bergkamp and Overmars
11 May	Leeds	A	L 0-1	..	..	..	..	..	..	..	..	..	..	..	Kanu, Diawara and Vivas for Overmars, Parlour and Winterburn
16 May	Aston Villa	H	W 1-0	..	..	..	..	Vivas	..	..	..	..	..	..	Ljungberg, Kanu1 and Diawara for Vivas, Anelka and Overmars

Charity Shield

Date	Opponent		Result	Seaman	Dixon	Keown	Adams	Winterburn	Parlour	Vieira	Petit	Overmars	Anelka	Bergkamp	Substitutions / notes
9 Aug	Manchester United (at Wembley)		W 3-0	Seaman	Dixon	Keown	Adams	Winterburn	Parlour	Vieira	Petit	Overmars1	Anelka1	Wreh	Wreh1, Hughes, Boa Morte, Bould and Grimandi for Bergkamp, Overmars, Petit, Adams and Vieira

FA Cup

Date	Opponent	V	Result												Substitutions / notes
4 Jan	Preston (3)	A	W 4-2	Manninger	Dixon	Keown	Bould	Vivas	Parlour	Vieira	Petit2	Overmars1	Mendez	Boa Morte1	Caballero and Garde for Mendez and Overmars
24 Jan	Wolverhampton (4)	A	W 2-1	..	..	Upson	Adams	Winterburn	..	Garde	..	..1	Anelka	Bergkamp1	Vivas, Grimandi and Hughes for Garde, Anelka and Overmars
13 Feb	Sheffield United (5)	H	W 2-1	Seaman	Vivas	Grimandi	Bould	..	..	Vieira1	Garde	..1	Diawara	..	Hughes and Kanu for Garde and Diawara

(THE RESULT OF THIS MATCH WAS DECLARED VOID, BUT ARSENAL STILL INCLUDE IT IN THEIR STATISTICS)

Date	Opponent	V	Result												Substitutions / notes
23 Feb	Sheffield United (5)	H	W 2-1	..	..	Bould	Adams	..	..	..	Hughes	..	..1	Anelka ..1	Kanu, Garde, Diawara for Anelka, Bergkamp and Overmars
6 Mar	Derby	H	W 1-0	..	Dixon	Keown	..	..	..	Hughes	Ljungberg	..	..	..	Vivas, Kanu1 and Diawara for Ljungberg, Hughes and Overmars
11 Apr	Manchester United (S/F) (at Villa Park)		D 0-0	..	..	..	..	..	..	Vieira	Vivas	..	..	..	Ljungberg and Kanu for Overmars and Anelka
14 Apr	Manchester United (S/F-R) (at Villa Park)		L 1-2	..	..	..	..	..	..	..	Petit	Ljungberg	..	..1	Overmars, Kanu and Bould for Ljungberg, Parlour and Petit

League (Worthington) Cup

Date	Opponent	V	Result												Substitutions / notes
28 Oct	Derby (3)	A	W 2-1	Manninger	Vivas1	Grimandi	Upson	Grondin	Ljungberg	Garde	Mendez	Hughes	Wreh	Boa Morte	Crowe and Riza for Upson and Wreh - own goal
11 Nov	Chelsea (4)	H	L 0-5	..	..	..	..	..	..	Hughes	Boa Morte	..	Bergkamp	..	Mendez and Caballero for Garde and Bergkamp

Champions League (Group matches – all home games played at Wembley))

Date	Opponent	V	Result												Substitutions / notes
16 Sep	Lens	A	D 1-1	Seaman	Dixon	Keown	Adams	Winterburn	Parlour	Vieira	Petit	Overmars1	Anelka	Bergkamp	Hughes and Garde for Petit and Bergkamp
30 Sep	Panathinaikos	H	W 2-1	..	..	..1	..1	..	..	Garde	..	..	..	..	Vivas for Garde
21 Oct	Dynamo Kiev	H	D 1-1	..	..	..	..	..	Parlour	Garde	Hughes	..	..	..1	Vivas for Anelka
4 Nov	Dynamo Kiev	A	L 1-3	..	..	..	Bould	..	..	Vieira	Petit	Vivas	Wreh	Boa Morte	Grimandi, Hughes1 and Garde for Bould, Vivas and Boa Morte
25 Nov	Lens	H	L 0-1	..	..	..	Adams	..	..	Garde	Hughes	Overmars	Anelka	Wreh	Bould, Vivas and Boa Morte for Adams, Garde and Wreh
9 Dec	Panathinaikos	A	W 3-1	..	Vivas	Upson	Bould	Grondin	Grimandi	Vernazza	Mendez1	Boa Morte1	..1	..	M.Black for Mendez

League Appearances (Goals in brackets)

Overmars 36 (6) – Dixon 35 – Parlour 34 (6) – Anelka 34 (17) – Keown 33 (1) – Vieira 33 (3) – Seaman 31 – Winterburn 30 – Bergkamp 28 (12) – Petit 26 (4) – Adams 25 (1) – Vivas 22 – Bould 19 – Ljungberg 15 (1) – Hughes 14 (1) – Wreh 12 – Kanu 11 (5) – Diawara 11 – Garde 10 – Grimandi 8 – Boa Morte 8 – Upson 5 – Grondin 1 – Mendez 1 – Caballero 1 – Own goals 2 –
Total 25 players (59)

Position in League Table

	P	W	L	D	F:A	Pts	
Manchester U	38	22	3	13	80:37	79	1st
Arsenal	38	22	4	12	59:17	78	2nd

Date	Opp	V	R	Score	1	2	3	4	5	6	7	8	9	10	11	Subs / Scorers
7 Aug	Leicester	H	W	2-1	Manninger	Dixon	Keown	Grimandi	Winterburn	Parlour	Vieira	Petit	Ljungberg	Kanu	Bergkamp1	Henry/Overmars/Silvinho for Ljungberg/Parlour/Bergkamp [Frank Sinclair own goal]
10 Aug	Derby	A	W	2-1	..	..	..	Upson	..	..	..	..1	Henry	..	..1	Silvinho/Luzhny/Boa Morte for Parlour/Kanu/Henry
14 Aug	Sunderland	A	D	0-0	..	..	..	..	Silvinho	..	..	..	..	..	..	Ljungberg/Boa Morte for Petit/Bergkamp
22 Aug	Manchester Utd	H	L	1-2	..	..	..	..	..	..	..	Ljungberg1	..	..	..1p	Overmars/Suker for Kanu/Henry
25 Aug	Bradford City	H	W	2-0	..	Vivas	..	Grimandi	..	..	..	..1	..	..1p	..	Overmars/Suker for Upson/Henry/Bergkamp/Kanu
28 Aug	Liverpool	A	L	0-2	..	Dixon	..	Adams	Winterburn	..	..	..	Overmars	Henry	..	Suker/Silvinho for Overmars/Parlour
11 Sept	Aston Villa	H	W	3-1	..	..	..	..	..	..	..	Grimandi	..	Suker2	..	Silvinho/Kanu1/Henry for Suker/Bergkamp/Overmars
18 Sept	Southampton	A	W	1-0	..	..	..	..	..	Ljungberg	..	..	..	Kanu	..	Parlour/Henry1/Luzhny for Ljungberg/Kanu/Overmars
25 Sept	Watford	H	W	1-0	..	Luzhny	..	..	Silvinho	Parlour	..	Ljungberg	..	..1	Henry	Suker/Bergkamp/Vivas for Ljungberg/Henry/Kanu
3 Oct	West Ham	A	L	1-2	Seaman	..	..	..	..	Ljungberg	..	Grimandi	Henry	Suker1	Bergkamp	Overmars/Kanu for Luzhny/Henry
16 Oct	Everton	H	W	4-1	..	Dixon1	..	..	Winterburn	Parlour	..	..	Overmars	..2	..	Silvinho/Kanu1/Ljungberg for Overmars/Bergkamp/Parlour
23 Oct	Chelsea	H	W	3-2	..	..	..	..	Silvinho	..	Ljungberg	Petit	..	Kanu3	Suker	Henry/Vivas/Vernazza for Ljungberg/Petit/Overmars
30 Oct	Newcastle	H	D	0-0	..	Luzhny	..	..	Winterburn	Ljungberg	Vieira	Grimandi	Silvinho	Henry	..	Bergkamp/Overmars/Upson for Henry/Silvinho/Keown
7 Nov	Tottenham	A	L	1-2	..	Dixon	..	..	..	..	..1	Petit	Overmars	Kanu	Bergkamp	Suker/Grimandi for Kanu/Petit
20 Nov	Middlesbrough	H	W	5-1	..	..	Grimandi	..	..	Parlour	Ljungberg	..3	..	..2	..	Upson/Vivas/Suker for Grimandi/Dixon/Bergkamp
28 Nov	Derby	H	W	2-1	Manninger	Luzhny	Upson	..	..	Grimandi	..	..	..	Henry2	Bergkamp	Kanu/Suker/Malz for Bergkamp/Henry/Overmars
4 Dec	Leicester	A	W	3-0	..	Dixon1	..	..	Silvinho	..1	..	..1	..	Kanu	..	Vivas/Hughes/Barrett for Upson/Silvinho/Henry
18 Dec	Wimbledon	H	D	1-1	..	..	Luzhny	Grimandi	..	..	Ljungberg	..	..	..1	..	Suker for Winterburn
26 Dec	Coventry	A	L	2-3	Seaman	..	Keown	Adams	..	Ljungberg1	..	..	..	..1	..	Suker1 for Grimandi
28 Dec	Leeds	H	W	2-0	..	Luzhny	Grimandi	..	Silvinho	..1	Vieira	..	..	..1	..	Suker/Winterburn for Henry/Petit
3 Jan	Sheffield Wed	A	D	1-1	..	..	..	..	..	..	..	..	..1	..	Kanu	Winterburn/Suker for Overmars/Kanu
15 Jan	Sunderland	H	W	4-1	..	Dixon	Keown	Luzhny	..	Parlour	..	..	Ljungberg	..2	Suker2	Malz/Barrett for Ljungberg/Henry
24 Jan	Manchester Utd	A	D	1-1	..	..	..	..	Grimandi	..	..	..	..1	Hughes	Henry	Winterburn/Malz for Silvinho/Hughes
5 Feb	Bradford City	A	L	1-2	..	..	..	..	Winterburn	..	Ljungberg	Malz	Henry1	Suker	..	Bergkamp for Malz
13 Feb	Liverpool	H	L	0-1	..	..	..	..	Silvinho	..	Vieira	..	Ljungberg	..	Bergkamp	Overmars/Suker/Luzhny for Petit/Bergkamp/Ljungberg
26 Feb	Southampton	H	W	3-1	..	..	..	Adams	..	..	..	..	..2	Bergkamp1	Kanu	Overmars for Bergkamp
5 Mar	Aston Villa	A	D	1-1	..	..1	..	Grimandi	..	..	..	..	Henry	Kanu	Bergkamp	Overmars/Luzhny/Winterburn for Bergkamp/Grimandi/Petit
12 Mar	Middlesbrough	A	L	1-2	..	Luzhny	Winterburn	..	..	..	..	..	Ljungberg	Henry	Kanu	Manninger/Bergkamp1/Suker for Seaman/Ljungberg/Parlour
19 Mar	Tottenham	H	W	2-1	Manninger	Dixon	Luzhny	Adams	..	..	..	Grimandi	Overmars	..1	..	Ljungberg/Winterburn for Henry/Overmars - own goal
26 Mar	Coventry	H	W	3-0	Seaman	..	..	..1	Winterburn	..	..	Petit	..	..1	Bergkamp	Kanu1/Ljungberg/Suker for Bergkamp/Henry/Overmars
1 Apr	Wimbledon	A	W	3-1	..	..	Keown	Luzhny	Silvinho	..	..	Grimandi	..	Kanu2	..	Petit/Henry1/Winterburn for Overmars/Kanu/Bergkamp
16 Apr	Leeds	A	W	4-0	..	..	..1	Adams	..	..	..	Petit	Ljungberg	Henry1	..	Kanu1/Overmars1/Winterburn for Bergkamp/Henry/Petit
23 Apr	Watford	H	W	3-0	..	..	Luzhny	..	Grimandi	Winterburn	..1	..	Overmars	..2	..	Silvinho for Overmars
29 Apr	Everton	A	W	1-0	..	Dixon	..	Adams	Silvinho	..	..	Grimandi	..1	Kanu	..	Vieira/Winterburn/Black for Bergkamp/Overmars/Petit
2 May	West Ham	H	W	2-1	..	..	Luzhny	..	..	..	Vieira	Grimandi	..1	..	..	Petit1 for Dixon
6 May	Chelsea	H	W	2-1	..	..	Grimandi	..	..	..	..	Petit	..	Henry2	..	Winterburn/Kanu/Luzhny for Overmars/Bergkamp/Petit
9 May	Sheffield Wed	H	D	3-3	..	..1	Keown	Luzhny	Winterburn	..	Grimandi	Vieira	..	Kanu	Henry1	Bergkamp/Silvinho1 for Parlour/Winterburn
17 May	Newcastle	A	L	2-4	Manninger	Luzhny	..	Weston	Cole	..	Vernazza	Malz1	Winterburn	..1	Suker	Silvinho/McGovern/Gray for Parlour/Weston/Kanu

Charity Shield

Date	Opp	V	R	Score	1	2	3	4	5	6	7	8	9	10	11	Subs / Scorers
31 Jul	Manchester Utd (at Wembley)		W	2-1	Manninger	Dixon	Winterburn	Keown	Grimandi	Silvinho	Parlour1	Vieira	Petit	Ljungberg	Kanu1p	Boa Morte for Ljungberg/ Luzhny for Dixon

FA Cup**

Date	Opp	V	R	Score	1	2	3	4	5	6	7	8	9	10	11	Subs / Scorers
13 Dec	Blackpool (3)	H	W	3-1	Manninger	Dixon	Luzhny	Adams1	Silvinho	Ljungberg	Grimandi1	Petit	Overmars1	Suker	Henry	Kanu/Hughes for Suker/Ljungberg
9 Jan	Leicester (4)	H	D	0-0	Seaman	..	Keown	Grimandi	..	Vieira	..	Malz	..	..	..	Kanu for Malz
19 Jan	Leicester (4R)	A	D	0-0*	..	..	..	..	Parlour	..	..	..	..	..	..	Hughes for Malz

*Arsenal lost 6-5 on penalties after extra time
** Manchester United did not enter

Worthington Cup

Date	Opp	V	R	Score	1	2	3	4	5	6	7	8	9	10	11	Subs / Scorers
12 Oct	Preston (3)	H	W	2-1	Seaman	Luzhny	Grimandi	Upson	Winterburn	Parlour	Vernazza	Malz1	Silvinho	Kanu1	Henry	Overmars/Wreh for Vernazza/Kanu
30 Nov	Middlesbrough (4)	A	D	2-2*	Vivas	Luzhny	..	..	Silvinho	..	..	Black	..	Suker1	..1	Weston/Pennant/Cole for Luzhny/Black/Parlour

*Arsenal lost 3-1 on penalties after extra time

Champions League

Date	Opp	V	R	Score	1	2	3	4	5	6	7	8	9	10	11	Subs / Scorers
14 Sep	Fiorentina	A	D	0-0	Manninger	Luzhny	Keown	Adams	Winterburn	Ljungberg	Vieira	Grimandi	Overmars	Suker	Bergkamp	Kanu/Henry for Suker/Bergkamp
22 Sep	AIK Solna	H	W	3-1	..	..	..	..	..	..1	..	..	..	..1	..	Silvinho/Kanu/Henry1 for Grimandi/Overmars/Ljungberg
29 Sep	Barcelona	A	D	1-1	..	..	..	..	..	..	Parlour	..	..	Kanu1	..	Suker/Henry/Ljungberg for Bergkamp/Parlour/Overmars
19 Oct	Barcelona	H	L	2-4	Seaman	..	..	..	..	Ljungberg	..	Parlour	..1	..	..1	Upson/Suker/Henry for Keown/Kanu/Ljungberg
27 Oct	Fiorentina	H	L	0-1	..	..	..	..	..	Parlour	..	Petit	..	..	..	Ljungberg/Vivas/Suker for Parlour/Petit/Dixon
2 Nov	AIK Solna	A	W	3-2	Manninger	..	..	Luzhny	Upson	Ljungberg	..	..	..2	..	Suker1	Vivas/Malz/Hughes for Luzhny/Petit/Suker

(all home games played at Wembley)

UEFA Cup

Date	Opp	V	R	Score	1	2	3	4	5	6	7	8	9	10	11	Subs / Scorers
25 Nov	Nantes	H	W	3-0	Seaman	Vivas	Grimandi	Adams	Winterburn1	Ljungberg	Vieira	Petit	Overmars1p	Kanu	Bergkamp1	Parlour/Suker/Henry for Petit/Ljungberg/Kanu
9 Dec	Nantes	A	D	3-3	Manninger	Dixon	..1	..	..	..	..	..	..	Henry1	..	Silvinho/Vivas/Suker for Overmars/Ljungberg/Henry
2 Mar	La Coruña	H	W	5-1	Seaman	..1	Keown	Luzhny	Silvinho	..	Grimandi	..	Overmars	Henry2	Bergkamp1	Kanu1/Suker/Parlour for Overmars/Henry/Bergkamp
9 Mar	La Coruña	A	L	1-2	..	..	Luzhny	Winterburn	..	Parlour	Vieira	Petit	Ljungberg	Henry1	..	Suker/Malz/Vernazza for Henry/Kanu/Winterburn
16 Mar	Werder Bremen	H	W	2-0	..	..	..	Adams	..	..	..	Grimandi	..1	..1	Bergkamp	Kanu/Overmars/Suker for Parlour/Bergkamp/Henry
23 Mar	Werder Bremen	A	W	4-2	Manninger	..	..	..	..	..	..3	..	..	..1	Kanu	Petit/Overmars/Winterburn for Adams/Kanu/Vieira
6 Apr	Lens (SF)	H	W	1-0	Seaman	..	..	Keown	Grimandi	..	..	..	Petit	Overmars	Kanu	Bergkamp1	Ljungberg/Suker for Overmars/Bergkamp
20 Apr	Lens (SF)	A	W	2-1	..	..	..	..	..	Adams	..	..	Ljungberg	Henry1	..	Kanu1/Overmars/Grimandi for Bergkamp/Ljungberg/Henry
17 May	Galatasaray (F)	Copenhagen		0-0*	..	..	..	..	..	..	..	..	..	Overmars	..	Kanu/Suker for Bergkamp/Overmars

*lost 4-1 on penalties after extra time

League Appearances (Goals in brackets)

Henry 31 (17)–Overmars 31 (7)–Kanu 31 (12)–Silvinho 31 (1)–Vieira 31 (2)–Parlour 30 (1)–Dixon 28 (4)–Bergkamp 28 (6)–Grimandi 28 (2)–Winterburn 28–Keown 27 (1)–Petit 26 (3)–Ljungberg 26 (6)
Seaman 24–Suker 22 (8)–Adams 21–Luzhny 21–Manninger 15–Upson 8–Vivas 5–Malz 5 (1)–Hughes 2–Boa Morte 2–Barrett 2–Vernazza 2–Black 1–Cole 1–Weston 1–Gray 1–McGovern 1–own goals (2)
Total 30 players (73)

Position in League Table

	P	W	L	D	F:A	Pts	
Manchester U	38	28	7	3	97:45	91	1st
Arsenal	38	22	7	9	73:43	73	2nd

1999-2000 1997

CHAPTER

INTO THE NEW MILLENNIUM

11

The dawn of the new millennium may have coincided with football's commercial revolution and the imminent arrival of a European Super League, but for Arséne Wenger the thorny and perennial problem of team restructuring dominated the summer of 2000. Just like every manager in Arsenal's 104-year League history, Wenger would spend the close season buying and selling, however, his job had become somewhat more difficult than his predecessors' following a shift in the balance of power from clubs to players.

The sale of Nicolas Anelka in 1999 had provided ample illustration of football's new order, and a year later two more members of Wenger's Double team opted to wield their new found power. Following intense media speculation, both Marc Overmars and Emmanuel Petit made it clear that their ambitions lay away from Highbury. A £30m joint sale to Barcelona was duly agreed, leaving the Arsenal manager to fill a considerable gap in his midfield.

The departures did not end with Overmars and Petit, and in June veteran full-back Nigel Winterburn severed his ties with the Gunners after 13 years, signing for West Ham in an effort to increase his chances of first team football. However, with both Silvinho and the emergent Ashley Cole offering adequate cover at left-back, Wenger turned his attention to bolstering his midfield.

Real Mallorca's versatile Cameroon international Lauren Mayer was first to arrive, signing in a £7.2m deal in May. The remainder of Wenger's transfer business was conducted after the European Championships, a tournament at which several players with Arsenal connections would take centre stage. Patrick Vieira and Thierry Henry both starred for the victorious France team, which beat Italy in the final, while transfer targets Robert Pires and Sylvain Wiltord also made significant contributions to Les Bleus Euro 2000 success.

Marseille winger Pires, who supplied the cross for France's winning goal (scored by Wiltord), eventually signed for a bargain £6m fee in July. Pires was seen as a direct replacement for the outgoing Overmars. The final piece in Arsenal's midfield reconstruction was Brazilian Edu, a former team-mate of Silvinho's at Corinthians. However, a passport fiasco would delay Edu's arrival until January, leaving Vieira without an obvious central midfield partner. Nevertheless, Wenger decided against making a stop-gap signing and waited instead for Edu to gain the necessary international clearance. The Gunners boss would also show commendable patience over the signing of Bordeaux striker Sylvain Wiltord.

Wiltord's protracted transfer extended beyond the summer close season and was only finalised after Bordeaux agreed to accept a £13m offer for the 26-year-old toward the end of August. Arsenal's record signing would complete an impressive attacking quartet of strikers along with Henry, Dennis Bergkamp and Kanu. Wenger's team-building efforts had cost in the region of £32m, but with the departures of Overmars, Petit and several fringe players, the manager had financed his purchases entirely through sales.

Opposite: Tony Adams, the steadiest defender of the last century, celebrates his goal against Leicester with the hottest young prospect of the moment – Ashley Cole.

Below: Patrick Vieira protests his innocence but is still shown the red card for a clash with Sunderland's Darren Williams on the opening day of the 2000–01 season. The French midfielder was sent off in each of Arsenal's first two games but recovered to collect the Carling Player of the Season award in May.

Vieira dismissals mar good start

The season's opening fixture saw the Gunners travel to the Stadium of Light to take on Peter Reid's highly rated Sunderland team. Arsenal dominated the game but could not convert their superior possession into goals, spurning several good chances. Sunderland eventually made the visitors pay for their profligacy when former Gunner Niall Quinn headed into an empty net after David Seaman had misjudged a cross from Michael Gray. Worse was to follow for Wenger, with Patrick Vieira sent off late in the game for an altercation with Darren Williams. Even Reid admitted that Vieira's sending off had been harsh, commenting: 'The referee's job is very difficult but I think Vieira's a fantastic player and I thought he was unlucky to go.'

Referees and sendings-off were again the chief topic of conversation after Arsenal's next match, against Liverpool at Highbury. The Gunners hadn't beaten Liverpool for over six years, so a 2–0 victory courtesy of a home-debut goal from Lauren and a late effort from Henry, would normally have been worthy of celebration. However, the result was overshadowed by the sending-off of Vieira for the second match in succession. The France international was distraught and was left pondering his future in the Premiership. 'It's a sad night,' said Wenger, "Patrick is very upset... I don't want to repeat what he said to me. Maybe I am wrong, but after what happened against Sunderland, this may be too much.'

Fortunately, for Arsenal fans, Wenger was wrong for once and Vieira neither spoke out nor walked out on English football. The midfielder would recover from his early season setbacks to become the Premiership's most consistent performer, and he showed his professionalism with a polished display against Charlton at Highbury in Arsenal's next match. Vieira scored twice in the 5–3 win over the Addicks and had Wenger purring: 'He is committed to the club and committed to the fans... he was less aggressive today but he was playing against a team that also wanted to play football and not just antagonise him.'

After three games Arsenal sat atop the Premiership table, two points ahead of reigning champions Manchester United. Alex Ferguson's team remained 4–6 odds-on favourites to retain their title, but according to the bookmakers, Wenger's new look Gunners were their most likely challengers, at 5–1 to take United's crown. However, to stand any real chance, Arsenal would need to keep up with the leaders in the early weeks of the campaign, something they had failed to do in recent seasons.

The task was made all the more difficult by Vieira's suspen-

Above: Summer signing Lauren celebrates scoring Arsenal's first goal of the season in the 2–0 victory over Liverpool at Highbury, August 2000.

Below: Thierry Henry turns Gary Neville and volleys home a fantastic goal to earn Arsenal a well-deserved 1–0 victory over Manchester United at Highbury, October 2000.

sion, a series of niggling injuries to skipper Tony Adams, and Lauren's call up to Cameroon's Olympic team. Despite, these difficulties, Wenger's team extended their unbeaten sequence to 12 games following the defeat at Sunderland and kept United in their sights throughout the autumn.

The highlight of this impressive run, was a dogged 1–0 victory over the champions at Highbury on 1 October. The game was decided by a sublime goal from the boot of Thierry Henry, who flicked the ball up before turning to hit an unstoppable, swerving volley into the corner of the net, past his former Monaco team-mate and the world's most expensive goalkeeper, Fabien Barthez. It was Henry's first goal for seven weeks, and the Frenchman confessed, 'I was a bit down because I haven't scored recently,' and the World Cup winner added, 'This is an important result because last year there was a big gap between us and Manchester United... Now it is going to be interesting for the rest of the season.'

Leicester City moved top of the Premiership after Arsenal's victory over United, but Alex Ferguson was in no doubt as to who his main rivals were: 'Arsenal are alongside us now and as I think they will be our biggest rivals for the title,' but the Old Trafford boss added ominously, 'We are not worried, it's only October.'

Progress on the pitch was mirrored by developments behind the scenes, and in September Arsenal announced that they had signed a strategic partnership agreement with Granada Media. The deal saw Granada invest £47m into the partnership, which would be used to finance a new joint venture media company called AFC Broadband and the development of the proposed 60,000 stadium at Ashburton Grove. According to chairman, Peter Hill-Wood, the Granada deal would help the club to 'develop the Arsenal brand on a global basis by extending our fan base around the world.'

European challenge commences

Champions League football would also do much to increase Arsenal's global profile. The first group phase began with a 1–0 away victory over Sparta Prague, courtesy of Silvinho's stunning goal, but Wenger was not getting too carried away by the Gunners' winning start. A 3–2 triumph over Shakhtar Donetsk at Highbury in the next match secured another three points, but the manner of the victory was far from convincing. The Ukrainians scored twice in the first half hour and, although Wiltord pulled back a vital goal just before half time, with five minutes remaining the Gunners were still trailing. Arsenal's eventual salvation came from the unlikely figure of Martin Keown, who scored twice in the closing minutes to earn victory. Wenger was clearly grateful to his match-winning centre-half. 'We felt that Martin was a threat for them in the air...

2000–2002

He has a high motivation and his body language also shows his desire.'

Arsenal followed the victory over Donetsk with a 1–1 draw against Ipswich, earned via a late equaliser from Dennis Bergkamp. The unbeaten run continued but the results were no longer as convincing, and the Gunners forward line was beginning to display a worrying profligacy. The next Champions League fixture would offer a stern test of Arsenal's progress, with Italian double-winners Lazio providing the visiting opposition for a Group B match.

After two campaigns at Wembley, where the Gunners won just once in six 'home' fixtures, they were back at Highbury for European games. The match against Lazio vindicated the club's decision to come home, although it was the performance of Dennis Bergkamp that proved most decisive. The Dutchman was at his creative best and was the architect of both Arsenal goals; each scored by fellow midfielder Freddie Ljungberg. Lazio manager Sven Goran Eriksson was fulsome in his praise of the Gunners: 'Arsenal could win it [the Champions League]... They have been a very good team for some time. They are good technically and are physically very strong.'

The Gunners proved that their result against Lazio had been no fluke by holding the Italians to a 1–1 draw in Rome three weeks later. Robert Pires's late goal had earned Arsenal the single point they needed to guarantee qualification for the second phase of the Champions League, but it was veteran goalkeeper John Lukic who received the post-match plaudits. The 39-year-old was given a round of applause by his teammates at the end and commented, 'It might sound a bit soppy, but that really touched me.' However, it was tales of racism rather than sentimentalism that dominated the following day's papers when it was revealed that Patrick Vieira had been the target of alleged racial abuse from Lazio's Sinisa Mihajlovic. The Yugoslav would later apologise for his actions, reading out an anti-racism statement before his club's next European match a week later.

Arsenal lost one of their two remaining first phase Champions League games, but still finished top of Group B. A 4–2 home win over Sparta Prague had guaranteed the Gunners qualified as group winners for the second phase, and this time they had not lost a game at 'home'. However, Arsenal's early season momentum had begun to wane, and they won just once in seven matches during November.

The month began with a Worthington Cup defeat to Ipswich Town at Highbury, but the result of this match was overshadowed by the sad news that reserve team coach George Armstrong had died of a brain haemorrhage the previous night. Many of the players Armstrong had coached and nurtured were given the opportunity of a first team appearance

Above: A shaven-headed Freddie Ljungberg sends the ball goalwards and braces himself for the challenge of Lazio goalkeeper Luca Marchegiani in Arsenal's 2–0 victory over the Italian Champions, September 2000. The Swedish midfielder scored both Gunners goals on a memorable night of Champions League football at Highbury.

against Ipswich, and several were clearly affected on an emotional night at Highbury. Arsène Wenger summed up the occasion perfectly: 'Many of those players out there tonight worked on a daily basis with Geordie and this was a very difficult day and night for them. Losing him has been a massive blow to everybody. But they showed the same spirit that made him a true Arsenal man, a real symbol of the club who played over 600 matches and helped win the Double. If anything the boys tried too hard to live up to his example.'

Worthington Cup elimination was of no great consequence to Arsenal, but their failing Premiership form had become worrying by the start of December. Although still in second place in the table, a run of three games without scoring had seen the Gunners collect just a single point and enabled Manchester United to establish an eight-point lead. Wenger refused to admit defeat, 'Manchester United keep on winning, but we are not going to concede the Championship in November.' For Arsenal to mount a serious challenge, however, they would have to remedy their Jeckyll and Hyde home and away form. At Highbury, the Gunners seemed invincible, but on their travels they were an altogether different proposition.

Spartak and Bayern frustrate Gunners

The second phase of the Champions League began with a trip to Russia and a meeting with Spartak Moscow and, true to their away form, Arsenal lost the game 4–1. It was not a disastrous result, as there was time to recover from this early setback, and the manager remained optimistic, 'we are in a difficult period but I believe we still have the mental strength to come back and show our true form.'

It seemed that Wenger's prediction was about to come true when Henry and Kanu collaborated to give Arsenal a 2–0 lead after 55 minutes of the next Champions League match, at home to Bayern Munich. Alas, it was to be the German side who showed the greater 'mental strength' coming back to earn a 2–2 draw and leave Arsenal in a precarious position. However, with Lyon beating Spartak Moscow in the other Group C match, Bayern coach Ottmar Hitzfeld believed Arsenal were still in with a chance of qualification, 'It now looks like this will be a very tight group, which will not be decided until the very last round of matches. You cannot rule Arsenal out at this stage.'

After the Bayern game, the Champions League went into hibernation for two months, leaving Arsenal to concentrate on domestic matters. A 5–0 victory over Newcastle United at Highbury, in which Ray Parlour scored a hat-trick, hinted at a renewed title challenge and cut Manchester United's lead to six points. The differential was reduced by a further point the following week by the combined effect of Vieira's late equaliser against Spurs at White Hart Lane, and Liverpool's victory over the Champions at Old Trafford. Liverpool would provide the opposition for Arsenal's next Premiership fixture, but Wenger

had still not found a cure for his team's away day affliction and they were beaten 4–0 at Anfield. The lead was back up to eight points, and when the Gunners failed to win any of their first three league games of the New Year, they found themselves 15 points off the pace.

By the 25 February, Arsenal trailed by 13 points, and to maintain any hopes of a title challenge they required not only a victory from their away match against United but also a run of form to equal the ten successive wins of the Double season. It was not to be. A weakened Gunners team, which was without key defenders Dixon, Keown and Adams, were crushed 6–1. Latvian centre-back Igor Stepanovs was singled out for blame, but in truth the whole team defended badly. 'Everything went wrong for us today,' declared Wenger.

Even the usually enigmatic Alex Ferguson had no need for mind games and his appraisal of the situation was accurate, though painful for Gunners fans. 'If we had lost or drawn today Arsenal would have still had thoughts of catching us,' said the United boss, 'But 16 points ahead and the goal difference we have makes it impossible for them to catch us.'

Cup football the priority

Arsenal may have had to concede defeat in the title race, but the season was far from over. Premiership points were still vital to the Gunners, as a top-three finish offered the most straightforward route back into the Champions League. Wenger's team were also still in with a chance of qualifying for the quarter-finals of the current Champions League after taking four points from their two games against Lyon during February. In addition, almost unnoticed, they had made impressive progress in the FA Cup.

Victories over Carlisle, QPR and Chelsea had seen the Gunners move stealthily into the last eight of the cup, and it was only once the draw for the quarter-finals offered up a home tie against First Division Blackburn Rovers, that the fans began to anticipate a glorious cup run. Arsenal's progress owed most to the form of striker Sylvain Wiltord, who had taken an instant liking to the FA Cup, scoring five times in his first three appearances in the competition.

Wiltord's fine cup form began to carry over into the Premiership, and he struck a hat-trick against West Ham at Highbury to lift the gloom six days after the 6–1 debacle at Old Trafford. However, the Frenchman found himself back on the bench alongside Kanu for the crucial Champions League match against Spartak Moscow at Highbury. But if the night began with disappointment for Wiltord it ended in frustration for Bergkamp. The Dutchman toiled tirelessly as the Gunners struggled to find a way past Spartak's massed defensive ranks. With 18 minutes remaining, Wenger took the bold decision to

Below: White Hart Lane is silenced. Patrick Vieira wheels away after heading a late equaliser in a hard-fought North London derby.

switch to a more direct approach and substituted Bergkamp. Boos echoed around Highbury as the former Inter Milan striker trudged off the pitch. The manager, however, was proved right and with eight minutes remaining Henry struck the game's only goal to keep alive Arsenal's Champions League hopes.

The win over Spartak had left the Gunners needing to win their final Champions League group game, away to Bayern Munich, to be sure of qualification for the quarter-finals. The Champions League would dominate thoughts for the next eight days, but the Gunners did at least have the small matter of an FA Cup quarter-final against Blackburn to distract them. With Rovers chasing promotion, and Arsenal resting both Vieira and Henry ahead of the trip to Munich, it was to be no blood-and-thunder cup tie. The Gunners took an early lead through the predictable source of Wiltord, were three goals up at half-time and cruised into the last four with relative ease. A semi-final against Tottenham Hotspur would, however, offer a sterner test of Arsenal's commitment to the competition.

The match against Bayern proved a cagey affair, made no easier when the Germans took the lead after just ten minutes. It was to be the only goal of the game, however Arsenal would still qualify providing Lyon did not beat Spartak. When the final whistle blew in Munich there were still four minutes remaining in Moscow and the score was 1–1. 'It was like 90 minutes for me,' confessed Wenger. But Spartak held out for the draw and Arsenal progressed into the last eight. Valencia, beaten finalists in 2000, would provide the opposition for a two-legged quarter-final in April.

The Gunners warmed up for the first leg of the Valencia tie with a Premiership clash against North London rivals Spurs. Second half goals from Pires and Henry secured a 2–0 win, but Highbury was in no mood to celebrate victory in this dress rehearsal of the forthcoming FA Cup semi-final. On the morning of the game, former Arsenal midfielder David Rocastle had lost his battle against cancer and had passed away at the heartbreakingly young age of 33. Rocastle had played in both of George Graham's championship winning teams before moving on to Leeds United in 1992, and a minute's silence was perfectly observed by both sets of supporters prior to an unusually subdued North London derby.

Against Valencia four days later, it was one of Rocastle's former team-mates, Ray Parlour, who scored the goal that completed a dramatic comeback and gave the Gunners a narrow lead to take into the second leg. At half-time Arsenal were a goal down after a disappointing showing, but after the interval they played with greater urgency and began to create chances. Henry eventually struck a seemingly inevitable equaliser on 58 minutes and two minutes later Parlour fired home to put Wenger's team into the lead. However, Henry's subsequent failure to score when one-vs-one with the keeper, denied

Above: Arsenal and Tottenham Hotspur players observe a minute's silence for the late David Rocastle, who died of cancer at the tragically young age of 33, March 2001.

Below: Lee Dixon embraces Ryan Rocastle, son of the late David Rocastle, who was made Arsenal mascot for the 2001 FA Cup final at the Millennium Stadium.

Arsenal a two-goal cushion and left Valencia needing only a 1–0 victory in the second leg to progress to the semi-finals.

'We scored two goals but I felt the third and fourth goals were really possible,' declared Wenger, 'We missed some clear cut chances.' Arsenal's inability to convert territorial advantage into goals would dominate the remainder of the season. The FA Cup semi-final against Spurs provided further illustration of this worrying tendency. Tottenham took an early lead at Old Trafford, but despite dominating the game, Arsenal struggled to score. After 33 minutes Patrick Vieira, strode forward and showed them the route to goal. It took another 41 minutes of painfully one-sided football before Robert Pires finally put Spurs out of their misery. 'We did it the hard way because we were creating chance after chance,' said Wenger, 'Unfortunately we missed chance after chance but we scored a second goal and then it was all over.' Arsenal had made it to the FA Cup final and would meet Liverpool at the Millennium Stadium, Cardiff in May.

In the Champions League, Arsenal's dreams finally came to an end in Valencia's Mestalla stadium. On an evening of heartache and frustration for Gunners fans, Wenger's team defended their lead doggedly for 75 minutes. But with the game entering its final quarter hour, Norwegian striker John Carew rose above Tony Adams to send a header past the despairing dive of David Seaman. The Gunners, who had been just 15 minutes away from a semi-final against David O'Leary's Leeds United, were out of the competition on away goals.

Arsenal would now have to rely on their Premiership position to qualify for a place in the 2001–02 Champions League. The Gunners' cause had, however, been handicapped by a bizarre home defeat to relegation-threatened Middlesbrough the week before the Valencia game. Wenger's team had not lost at home in the league all season, but a brace of own goals from Brazilians Silvinho and Edu, had given Boro the platform for a most unlikely 3–0 victory.

Fortunately, the Middlesbrough result proved to be no more than an incomprehensible blip, and Arsenal soon recovered their form with victories over Everton and Derby. With three Premiership games to play, the Gunners took on Leeds United at Highbury knowing that victory would guarantee another season of Champions League football. The previous meeting between the two clubs, at Elland Road, had proved a bad tempered affair and this time the football was no less competitive. However, assured defending from Adams and Keown, and goals from Ljungberg and Wiltord secured a 2–1 victory along with Arsenal's continued presence among Europe's elite.

All thoughts could now turn toward the FA Cup final. The Gunners were slight favourites for the Millennium Stadium showpiece, although Liverpool were fast developing a reputation as cup specialists, having already won the Worthington Cup and progressed to the UEFA Cup final. Gerard Houllier's team were also renowned for their counter-attacking style, so it came as no surprise that they were content to defend for much of the first half of the final.

Arsenal's attacking play gradually gathered momentum, and in the 17th minute Henry rounded goalkeeper Sander Westerveld and struck a shot goalward, only to see it repelled by the arm of Reds centre-back Stephane Henchoz. Henry appealed for a penalty, but the referee had failed to notice Henchoz's handball, and the adjacent linesman considered it to be unintentional.

At half-time the game remained goalless and, although Liverpool became slightly more adventurous after the interval, the Gunners deservedly took the lead through Freddie Ljungberg 18 minutes from time. Arsenal's advantage was a narrow one, but their goal had rarely been threatened and they seemed destined to complete a hat-trick of Cup final victories over Liverpool. However, on 83 minutes the Gunners failed to deal with a Gary McAllister free-kick and Michael Owen pounced to smash the ball home and bring the scores level. Six minutes later Owen completed the most unlikely of comebacks when he outpaced Lee Dixon to reach a pass from Patrick Berger, before eluding Tony Adams and guiding a left-footed shot past the outstretched arm of David Seaman.

Just as they had against Valencia, Arsenal were left to rue missed chances and late defensive mistakes. Henry took the defeat somewhat personally and admitted, 'We should have won the game... I missed the chance to score the second goal and we missed so many chances.'

Above: Ray Parlour celebrates his goal in Arsenal's 2–1 victory over Valencia at Highbury, April 2001. Parlour's long-range strike completed a memorable comeback for the Gunners who had been 1–0 down to the Spaniards at half-time.

Arséne Wenger was clearly distressed at the way his team had lost the final and was frustrated by the injustice of the Henchoz penalty incident. Wenger complained: 'The linesman said it was not on purpose, but it's the first time I've seen anyone handle on the line and it was not deliberate.' However, despite the disappointment, Wenger retained a constructive sense of perspective and offered an accurate and succinct analysis of the match: 'It was a little bit an image of our season. We look like we should win but can't finish.'

A point still needed

In a break with tradition, the FA Cup final had not been the last domestic match of the season. Arsenal still had two Premiership games to play, and they needed a point from one of them to guarantee runners-up spot and thereby avoid having to play an early-season Champions League qualifier. The necessary point was achieved at the first attempt, via a goalless draw away to Newcastle United just three days after the Cup final. 'The players have shown a great mental strength,' enthused Wenger, 'We were in the quarter-finals of the Champions League and we were in the final of the FA Cup and we finished runners-up, and that shows the huge quality of my team.'

Wenger's positive attitude was not without foundation. For the second year running Don Howe's youth team had swept all before them in the FA Youth Cup, beating Blackburn Rovers 6–3 in the final, and with Ashley Cole already making the breakthrough from junior to senior ranks there is good reason for optimism. Cole's progress during 2000–01 was startling. He had made his Arsenal debut in the final game of the previous season, and quickly took his chance when Wenger was denied the services of first choice left-back Silvinho in the autumn of 2000. The Stepney-born defender proved himself an able deputy and his attacking instincts soon brought him to the attention of England manager Sven-Goran Eriksson, who handed him a first cap in the World Cup qualifier against Albania in March.

With the likes of Cole and Thierry Henry at Highbury, there was every reason to believe that Arsenal will make a significant impact upon European football in the years to come. However, Arséne Wenger was not ready to rest on his laurels yet, declaring: 'This team has huge potential but we need some extra quality to take us that step further. I know who I want and we have enough time to sort it all out.' Few would bet against Wenger signing the players that he needed to take Arsenal on to even greater glories.

2000–2002

Sol brightens Wenger's summer

With young stars like Cole, Ljungberg and Henry at Highbury, there was every reason to believe that Arsenal would make a significant impact in both the Premiership and Champions League in 2001–02, and for many years to come. However, Wenger was growing impatient for success. After three years as Premiership runners-up, the manager would no longer be satisfied with second place and he quickly busied himself on the transfer market.

The need for a predatory striker to complement the talents of Bergkamp and Henry had been made apparent by the frustrating Cup final defeat to Liverpool. Henry himself had even spoken about the need for a 'fox in the box' who could snaffle up the chances created by the Arsenal midfield. Everton's 20-year-old centre-forward Francis Jeffers was the player targeted to fill this role by Wenger and he became the first new arrival at Highbury in the summer of 2001.

Jeffers would be joined by the versatile Holland international Giovanni van Bronckhorst, who signed from Rangers after a successful three-year spell with the Glasgow club. However, it was the signing of a new defender on 1 July 2001 that dominated the backpages as well as conversation throughout North London.

Left: 'My decision was based on football... I felt this was the place to be.' Sol Campbell, who was to be a goliath in the Arsenal defence in 2001–02, explains his move to Highbury.

Spurs captain Sol Campbell became a free agent at the end of June and speculation had been rife about which club would sign him. Barcelona, Manchester United, Real Madrid, Roma and Liverpool had all registered their interest in the Newham-born defender, but few pundits considered Arsenal among the front runners for his signature. On 1 July a press conference was called at the club's London Colney training ground. The journalists were expecting Arsenal to announce the signing of Ipswich goalkeeper Richard Wright, and there was a fair degree of surprise when the formidable figure of Campbell was brought forward. Wenger continued his squad-strengthening with the long-anticipated signing of Richard Wright before making Japan international midfielder Junichi Inamoto his final summer addition.

Autumnal inconsistency

Arsenal kicked off the new campaign away to Middlesbrough and fielded a familiar-looking line-up. The new trio of van Bronckhorst, Jeffers and Wright were all on the bench, with Campbell the only one of the summer signings making it into the starting eleven. Wenger had tweaked his selection somewhat, deploying Parlour alongside Vieira in central midfield, switching Lauren to right-back and giving Wiltord a central striking role.

The tactical changes got the desired result at The Riverside, where Arsenal won 4–0. Henry had opened the scoring on 43 minutes against the Teessiders, but in a worrying reminder of the previous season, it took Arsenal until the final four minutes to make the game safe with a goal from Pires, which was duly followed by a brace from substitute Dennis Bergkamp.

A frustrating clash with Leeds United at Highbury ended in a 2–1 defeat for the Gunners in their first home game of the season. Arsenal would struggle for consistency throughout the early weeks of the season, and it was not until 13 October that they won back-to-back Premiership games. It was a similar story in the first group phase of the Champions League. Defeat in the opening fixture, away to Real Mallorca, had come after Ashley Cole conceded a penalty that brought the game's only goal. A home victory against Shalke 04 followed, but Arsenal lived dangerously en route to a 3–2 win over the Germans.

It seemed that Wenger's team were unable to move up a gear in the autumn of 2001, although there were occasional glimpses of the slick, incisive attacking play that would characterise their football later in the season. There were mitigating factors for this, most notably a succession of injuries to defenders that required Wenger to name six different centre-back pairings in the first eight Premiership games.

Fit defenders may have been in short supply at Highbury, but Wenger had a positive surfeit of in-form attacking players in the respectable fifth place in the Premiership, just four points behind leaders Leeds United.

Reviving the title challenge

In the Champions League, home wins in successive weeks against Panathinaikos and Real Mallorca secured progress to the second phase; although the draw, which placed Arsenal in Group D along with Juventus, Deportivo La Coruña and Bayer Leverkusen, could not have been tougher. The programme began with a tricky away fixture against Deportivo, who had already beaten Manchester United home and away in the competition's first phase. The Gunners' European curse struck again and the Spaniards won the game 2–0. This game came just four days after Arsenal had contested a typically fierce and hard-fought North London derby at White Hart Lane. The match had ended in a 1–1 draw, with Spurs equalising in injury time. While the fans were devastated at the loss against Deportivo, for Arsène Wenger the performance of his players against Tottenham had given cause for optimism. Pires had illuminated the game with a stunning 25-yard curler and had been the most creative player on show, but, it was Sol Campbell who had impressed Wenger most. The England defender gave his most commanding display yet in an Arsenal jersey.

Campbell was again at his best when Manchester United were the visitors for a clash at Highbury. After 14 minutes and against the run of play United took the lead when Paul Scholes fired past Stuart Taylor, who was making his Premiership debut in place of the injured duo of Seaman and Wright. Arsenal surged forward in formidable fashion as they attempted to restore parity, and three minutes after half-time Ljungberg struck with an exquisite chip over Fabien Barthez from the edge of the box. Arsenal pressed for the winner and in the 80th minute they gained the lead. Up until then Barthez had been a contender for man of the match, but twice in quick succession his mistakes let in Henry to score.

Wenger was delighted with his team's 3–1 victory over the reigning champions and was also pleased when Arsenal won their next two games and were up to second place in the table by mid-December.

All was going well at home, but of more immediate concern to the Arsenal manager was a Champions League match against Juventus at Highbury. It was the first time the two clubs had met since the Gunners' victory over the Italian giants in a UEFA Cup semi-final in 1980 . On the night, Henry was just one of a clutch of Arsenal players who starred in a fantastic performance that saw the Gunners win 3–1. A goal in each half from Ljungberg and a 25-yard Henry free kick clinched a victory that also owed much to an eye-catching display from Taylor in goal.

Wenger also had good reason to applaud his young charges

early weeks of 2001–02. Pires, Ljungberg, Bergkamp and Wiltord had all impressed, however, none could rival the form of the rampant Thierry Henry, who scored 14 goals in the first 15 games.

Despite Henry's goals, Arsenal's capacity to frustrate remained, as illustrated by an enthralling 3–3 draw against Blackburn Rovers at Highbury, in which the visitors clinched a point with an 89th-minute equaliser. Worse followed in the next home game in the Premiership against Charlton Athletic.

The South Londoners hadn't won at Highbury for 46 years, and when Henry opened the scoring after six minutes there seemed little hope for Charlton, who had already been spared by a post and a goal-line clearance. A procession of chances followed for the rampant Gunners but each was missed and on 35 minutes the visitors equalised when Steve Brown headed in Paul Konchesky's free kick. Richard Wright then punched another deadball delivery from Konchesky into his own net to give Charlton a barely plausible interval lead, and shortly after the resumption there were two more quick-fire goals from the Addicks. Henry's penalty reduced the deficit but it proved no more than a consolation. Arsenal had created 25 scoring attempts, 12 on target, while Charlton had fashioned just five shots on goal and had scored four times. It was a defeat that meant the Gunners had dropped more points from their first five home games of the season than throughout the whole of the previous campaign.

The good news, although of course Wenger did not know it at the time, was that Arsenal's season had reached its nadir, and despite their inconsistent form the Gunners were still in a

Above: Thierry Henry seizes on Barthez's second mistake to score Arsenal's 85th-minute winner at Highbury in November. The 3–1 victory lifted Arsenal above United to third in the table and sent Henry well on the road to the Golden Boot.

2000-2002

five days later when they overturned a 2–0 half-time deficit to beat Aston Villa 3–2. An injury-time goal from the prolific Henry – his 20th of the season – had earned the Gunners a victory that took them to within three points of leaders Liverpool. Arsenal's season had come alive and they now looked like serious contenders for the Premiership.

On 18 December Arsenal had the chance to climb to the top of the table when fellow title challengers Newcastle United visited Highbury. Just when it seemed the Gunners' Premiership assault was gathering momentum, the team were left stunned by defeat. Pires had opened the scoring after 20 minutes and Arsenal remained in control of the game. Newcastle grew in confidence after the interval but, though they equalised on the hour, Arsenal still looked like taking a point until the visitors were awarded a penalty, which Shearer duly converted. Then Robert increased Newcastle's margin of victory.

It was the third time Arsenal had lost a home game during 2001–02 and, as on both previous occasions, the result was somewhat freakish. There was all to play for, though, as Arsenal's next match saw them face title rivals Liverpool away at Anfield.

Ten Gunners triumph at Anfield

As was becoming customary, the Gunners began the match the stronger of the two teams. All could have changed, though, when Giovanni van Bronckhorst slipped and fell in the Liverpool penalty area. Although there were no theatrics nor appeals for a penalty from the Arsenal midfielder, the referee interpreted the Dutchman's fall as a dive and showed him a red card for his second bookable offence. Despite this setback Arsenal responded in impressive fashion and three minutes later Ljungberg was brought down by Liverpool goalkeeper Jerzy Dudek as he was about to score. This time the Gunners did appeal for a penalty and this time the referee pointed to the spot, from where Henry opened the scoring to put Arsenal ahead at the interval.

Wenger, showing commendable ambition, resisted the temptation to take off one of his attacking players for the second half and Pires, Ljungberg, Henry and Kanu all immediately took the fight to Liverpool. Seven minutes after the break Pires set up Ljungberg who scored what proved to be the game's decisive goal. The hosts halved the deficit three minutes later, but Arsenal held out for a deserved victory that took them ahead of Liverpool and into second place in the table.

Arsenal's resurgence had, however, coincided with a parallel improvement in the form of Manchester United and, by the time Arsenal met Liverpool in their return match at Highbury on 13 January, Sir Alex Ferguson's team had moved ahead of both their main rivals. Arsenal trailed by a point but had a game in hand. It would be nip and tuck for the remainder of the season between these two great rivals.

Reds dominate title race

After eight successive victories United finally lost a Premiership game when Liverpool's Danny Murphy struck the only goal of a tense encounter at Old Trafford on 22 January. Arsenal themselves dropped two points in a disappointing 1–1 home draw against Southampton. At the end of the first week in February just three points separated four teams (Manchester United, Newcastle United, Liverpool and Arsenal) at the top of the table.

Arsenal won their next game, away to Everton, with a somewhat fortuitous goal from Sylvain Wiltord who miscued a shot that looped over the Toffees keeper and into the corner of the net. However, fortune would rarely be required for the remainder of Arsenal's Premiership campaign. In Robert Pires the Gunners had the competition's most creative player, while in Henry they had the most potent striker, and in Ljungberg an elusive and equally predatory midfielder.

However, the most significant factor in Arsenal's progress was undeniably manager Arsène Wenger. He had long been noted for his objectivity and calm, but in the early spring of 2002 he began to speak with an assurance and an authority that bred confidence not only in the players but also the fans. There was depth in the squad, too, and when Henry was unavailable for the Premiership match against Newcastle at St James' Park, his absence gave Dennis Bergkamp the opportunity to take

Below: Freddie Ljungberg sprints away from Alessio Tacchinardi during Arsenal's magnivicent 3–1 victory over Juventus. Ljungberg scored twice against the Turin giants and underlined his value to Arsenal's attacking options.

Spaniards but it was Deportivo who were to take the honours. A 2–0 defeat left Arsenal no longer in control of their Champions League fate ahead of the final fixtures of the second group phase.

Arsenal's European woe continued as they lost their game against Juve, going down to a Marcelo Zalayeta header. Arsenal had created sufficient chances to win the game but the result mattered little as Deportivo lost 3–1 at home to Leverkusen in the other Group D game, leaving Arsenal to go no further in the competiion.

However, Wenger was in no mood for pessimism and rallied his team, and it was a refreshingly vibrant Arsenal team that swept aside Newcastle at Highbury to reach the FA Cup semifinal with goals from Pires, Campbell and Bergkamp. The Gunners' championship challenge had also been aided by an Alen Boksic goal that gave Middlesbrough a crucial and unexpected victory at Old Trafford.

Wenger's team had won five Premiership games in succession and were just two points behind Premiership leaders Liverpool with two games in hand as the Easter fixtures approached. However, on 25 March, Arsenal were hit by the news that Robert Pires's season was over due to a cruciate ligament injury sustained during the game against Newcastle.

Better news for Wenger came from Pires's compatriot Patrick Vieira who reaffirmed his commitment to Arsenal with a commanding, goalscoring display in the 3–0 victory over Sunderland at Highbury on Easter Saturday. However, for the remainder of the season another Gunners midfielder would take the limelight. Freddie Ljungberg had long been a popular figure with the Highbury faithful but his status was about to take a leap into the stratosphere with a prolific run of goalscoring that could not have been better timed.

Ljungberg's impressive scoring sequence, which would extend to seven goals in seven games, began in Arsenal's emphatic 3–0 victory over Charlton at The Valley. It was a result that took Arsenal back to the top of the table.

Rivals Liverpool and Manchester United, who were now one and two points behind Arsenal respectively, had each played a game more and were no doubt hoping that the Gunners next fixture, a North London derby at Highbury, might be the occasion on which the seemingly unstoppable league leaders dropped some points. It proved a dramatic encounter, and with the score at 1–0 to Arsenal – courtesy of a goal from the irrepressible Ljungberg – Spurs won a penalty, which was duly converted by Teddy Sheringham in the 81st minute. Just when it seemed that Tottenham might take a share of the spoils, Thierry Henry was fouled and, with the Frenchman temporarily off the pitch receiving treatment, Lauren took the penalty, coolly rolling the ball into the centre of the goal. All three points were safe and Arsenal remained top of the table.

centre stage. The Dutchman did not disappoint and he struck with a goal of sublime quality. With his back to goal Bergkamp met a pass from Pires with a delicious first touch that spun the ball round one side of his marker, while he ran round the other. With a minimum of fuss the ball was duly collected and calmly dispatched past the Newcastle keeper.

Bergkamp's goal against Newcastle helped secure a 2–0 win that cemented Arsenal's position in second place in the Premiership. It was a third successive victory for the Gunners, who were still chasing silverware on three fronts. In the Champions League they were in a strong position to qualify for the competition's knock-out stage after drawing with Bayer Leverkusen away. And they had also made good progress in the FA Cup; beating both Watford and Gillingham but most notably Liverpool – Bergkamp was the scorer of the game's only goal in the tie against the Merseysiders – en route to a sixth-round showdown with Newcastle at St James' Park. .

Above: Robert Pires was a revelation in 2001/02. His touch and vision were underlined by the fact he won the Football Writers' Player of the Year despite missing the last ten games of the season.

Cup football to the fore

March would be a month dominated by cup football for Arsenal, and the action commenced with the FA Cup tie at St James' Park. For once, however, Arsenal failed to dominate and it was they who were grateful for a goal against the run of play scored by Edu. The match ended in a 1–1 draw.

However, three days later the Gunners would lose a game on a frustrating night of Champions League misery against Deportivo at Highbury. Arsenal had their chances against the

2000-2002

Double chance

With only five Premiership games left to play and an FA Cup semi-final against Middlesbrough to contend with, whispered talk of a third Double began to be heard. The whispers grew in volume after the Gunners won their FA Cup semi-final against Middlesbrough at Old Trafford, and they soon escalated to a cacophony when further progress was made in the League.

Arsenal's seemingly ubiquitous game in hand, which was against West Ham at Highbury, was finally scheduled for 24 April. If they beat the Hammers, Wenger's team would extend their lead to four points over second-placed Liverpool with only three games to play. The tension was palpable and the atmosphere inside Highbury grew in intensity throughout a difficult first half that saw Glenn Roeder's West Ham enjoy the better chances. The Hammers even had claims for a goal waved away after Ashley Cole cleared Frederic Kanoute's shot from the goal line. Arsenal produced an improved performance in the second half but it was not until the 77th minute that they got the goal Highbury craved. Predictably it was Ljungberg who scored the decisive opener against the Hammers. Kanu added a second shortly before the final whistle to settle the nerves of the Gunners faithful.

Three days later the title race effectively became a two-way fight between Arsenal and Manchester United after Liverpool lost to Spurs at White Hart Lane. United were desperate to keep the pressure on Wenger's team in the hope that they might lose their nerve; particularly since the two rivals would meet in the penultimate fixture at Old Trafford. The Champions maintained their challenge with a 1–0 win against relegation-threatened Ipswich at Portman Road, courtesy of a penalty.

Arsenal knew that if they could win their next game, away to Bolton Wanderers, they would find themselves needing just one victory from their final two fixtures to guarantee the Premiership crown. Like most of the Gunners' recent matches the game at Bolton's Reebok Stadium proved a tense encounter and with equal predictability it was Freddie Ljungberg who opened the scoring. Sylvain Wiltord added a second. Arsenal were now two victories away from the Double.

Return to Cardiff

The victory over Bolton had also been notable for the return to fitness of Sol Campbell, who made a brief substitute appearance, after making an extraordinarily quick recovery from a hamstring injury sustained in the FA Cup semi-final.

Campbell's recovery created a defensive selection dilemma for Wenger ahead of the FA Cup final against Chelsea. The manager would have to decide which two of his three centre-halves – Adams, Keown and Campbell – would be given the task of marking the formidable strikeforce of Hasselbaink and

Above: Just days after scoring with a deft chip against Bayer Leverkusen, Dennis Bergkamp scored 'goal of the season' against Newcastle United.

Gudjohnsen. He would also have to choose between his two senior goalkeepers. David Seaman had been in exceptional form since returning from injury in February, but Richard Wright had played in five of Arsenal's six FA Cup ties and appeared to be Arsenal's FA Cup keeper. However, Wenger denied that Wright had any guarantee of playing in the final. 'There is no pact or agreement to play him in every game no matter what happens. Every individual only has one agreement with the club – to do everything to win trophies.'

Wenger was as good as his word and named the in-form Seaman in goal, with Adams and Campbell getting the nod at centre-half in preference to Keown. The Gunners were slight favourites to lift the Cup. However, Claudio Ranieri's talented team were not to be underestimated.

The first half of the final proved a rather disjointed affair and although chances came and went for both sides, it was not until the 70th minute that Arsenal took the lead. Ironically, the goal, which was scored by Ray Parlour, came at a time when Chelsea were enjoying their best spell of the game. A move involving Adams and Wiltord presented Parlour with the ball 40 yards from goal and, after assessing his options, the midfielder crashed home a 25-yard shot that Carlo Cudicini was powerless to keep out. Not to be outdone, Ljungberg then scored an even more impressive goal ten minutes later. The Swede picked up the ball on the left-hand side and surged forward, resisting a challenge from John Terry to break into the box and curl a fine shot beyond Cudicini.

Arsenal had won their first trophy for four years, but, while the fans were delighted with the FA Cup, Wenger was desperate to repeat the Double success of 1998. If the Gunners were to do so, they would need to win one of their remaining two games (away to Manchester United and at home to Everton). The supto give several of his fringe players a taste of glory and, in some cases, the chance to qualify for a Championship medal. However, even with the carnival atmosphere and some questionable defending, Arsenal retained the competitive spirit that had swept them to the Double. Winning had become a habit and an entertaining 4–3 victory extended the sequence of successive Premiership wins to a record-breaking 13 games.

A burning ambition

Despite his team's success and the adulation heaped upon him, Wenger was already mentally preparing himself for the next campaign. 'I want to maintain this success now,' declared the Arsenal manager, 'The best way to fail the season after is to celebrate and relax too much because while you are doing that everyone else tries to strengthen and catch up... The Champions League is our next challenge and I believe we have the quality in our squad to win it one day.' Few would argue after a season of incredible achievement at Highbury.

porters were desperate to see Arsenal clinch the title at Old Trafford so that they could celebrate inside the ground of their rivals, just as they had after that famous victory at Anfield in 1989.

Above: Adams, Seaman, Parlour and Vieira enjoy their second Double – long may the glory days continue for Arsenal!

And so to Old Trafford

Comparisons with 1989 were obvious and, although the 2002 showdown did not have the same finality as the game at Anfield since the title would not necessarily be decided on the night, it was unquestionably the most dramatic and significant fixture in the history of the Premiership. Arsenal, who had won 12 successive league games since drawing with Southampton at the start of February, were in confident mood.

The match itself proved a predictably dogged encounter with chances at a premium. The deadlock was eventually broken when after 57 minutes Sylvain Wiltord gave Arsenal a deserved lead after profiting from a shot by Ljungberg that Barthez could only palm into the path of his compatriot. It was the end of the scoring and the end of the title race. Not for the first time, 1–0 was enough for Arsenal and the celebrations began in earnest.

A triumphant Arsène Wenger was quick to praise the spirit of Arsenal's third Double-winning team. 'We have 84 points, completed the Double, not lost away from home and won 14 away games, and scored in every game this season,' beamed the Frenchman. 'It is absolutely tremendous. The character in this side is great.'

The official presentation of the Premiership trophy took place at Highbury three days later when Everton were the visitors for the season's final game. A much changed Gunners line-up took the field against the Toffees as Wenger attempted

A proud history

Arsenal's third Double had arrived 116 years after that Christmas Day in 1886 when 15 men met in the Royal Oak, next to Woolwich Arsenal Station, and decided that they should take their kickabouts seriously.

Memories that there ever was such a club south of the river have faded now. Few, if any, can be left alive who remember standing on the long-gone terraces of Plumstead or the original Spion Kop at the Manor Ground, and who witnessed the woe-begone Woolwich Arsenal of that disastrous season in 1913. No brick or pillar of the ground remains, no film exists of those games. That sadness is perhaps what a history must also reflect. It is not all Wembley, champagne at the Café Royal and 'We're proud to say that name.'

When Highbury is still and the underground closed on Christmas Day 2002, it still echoes to memories of the thousands of people who have walked up those dank, ill-lit Edwardian tunnels. Perhaps 15,000 every match Saturday for 90 years? That's around 30 million, equivalent to half the population of Great Britain. What dreams did they have, why did they come, what drew them to Gillespie Road, what did Arsenal mean to each and every one of them?

A quiet day is a good time to think of Bastin, of James, of Drake, of Jack, of Hapgood and Male; and, more recently, of a happier, demobbed and optimistic generation of 60,000 who would come every other week to see Reg Lewis and Ronnie Rooke, the immortal Joe Mercer and the golden 'Brylcreem Boy' Denis Compton, to live the two

2000-2002

Championships and Cup finals of Tom Whittaker's tragically brief Highbury reign.

Think of the intensity, of the hopes and fears, imagine if you can the mood on 1 May 1971, the last home game of the Double season. The tension was unbearable, nothing but a win was conceivable. It would be easy to go on, but each generation has its own memories. The next will have its own, just as glorious. It is the great-grandchildren of the men who cheered Lambert and Hulme who now pin pictures of Adams and Henry to their walls.

Arsenal are different from any other football club. Why? Because the history of English football can be told through their story, because they did dominate a crucial generation, historically a vital decade, because they are Herbert Chapman's legacy, because they did, if unexpectedly, win the Double in 1971.

So if you can, spare the time to think of Highbury, still and stolid, a repository of memories rather than cheers on the quietest of days. Think of 24 April 1915, of that same Nottingham Forest who donated the red shirts over a century ago, coming to Highbury to lose a Second Division game 7–0, the last match fifth-placed Arsenal ever played outside top company. Think of a new, shiny Wembley, almost exactly 15 years to the day later, on 26 April 1930, the moment when the pendulum swung from north to south, the day Arsenal first won the FA Cup in a game which still defines 30 years of English football, the day the Graf Zeppelin sat silently above the pitch. Think of 40 years further on, of 27 March 1971 at far away Hillsborough, of a clock which read 4.44 pm, of the dreams of a Double which paused an instant from consignment to the dustbin of football history. That was perhaps the most unforgettable moment of all, the perfect illustration that football can be, and should be, about the emotion such set-piece dramas can evoke. Think what we would say now about the game had McLintock's header hit the post rather than Mahoney's hand, or if Banks had guessed right about Storey's penalty. Think, at the end, of the glorious Double of 1997–98, when Arsenal won the Championship after being so far behind that the bookmakers had ceased betting on the result. Think about Michael Thomas and Bruce Grobbelaar. No matter how long we watch League football we will never live such a moment again.

It is one of the joys of the game that we can only wait and see. If the next hundred years can bring just moments like the last few seconds at Anfield in 1989, the joy of the second Double from such an improbable position in 1998, or the style and flair of the 2002 Double-winning team that bought the adulation of fans, critics and football purists then we will all have much to justify our enthusiasm and anticipation.

Below: Tony Adams holds aloft the Barclaycard Premiership trophy to round off a glorious season for Arsène Wenger's record-breaking team.

Memories.....

RECORDS AND AWARDS 2001–02

As Arsenal closed in on their third Double in the spring of 2002 it became virtually impossible to keep track of the achievements of Arsène Wenger's phenomenal team. A host of club and Premiership records fell to the rampant Gunners, while both Wenger and his players collected a variety of individual awards for their part in a historic season.

INDIVIDUAL AWARDS

Arsène Wenger – Voted manager of the season by both the League Managers' Association and Premiership sponsors Barclaycard
Thierry Henry – Carling-Opta Player of the Season and Golden Boot winner
Robert Pires – Football Writers' Player of the Year

RECORDS

The New Invincibles – Arsenal became the first team since Preston in 1888–89 to remain unbeaten away from home throughout an entire League season. It is also worth noting that Preston's 'Invincibles' played eight fewer away games than the Gunners.
Arsenal's winning run – Victory over Manchester United at Old Trafford on 8 May equalled United's record of 12 successive League wins. The victory over Everton three days later established a new record for the Gunners.
One–nil to the Arsenal – In 28 of their 38 Premiership games Arsenal scored first, thereby setting a new record.
Consistent entertainers – Arsenal scored in each of their 38 Premiership games.
Away-day specialists – Victory over Manchester United at Old Trafford established a new club record for successive away wins. The Gunners had won eight in a row.

Date	Opponent	V	R	Score												Substitutes
19 Aug	Sunderland	A	L	0-1	Seaman	Dixon	Keown	Adams	Silvinho	Parlour	Grimandi	Vieira	Ljungberg	Henry	Kanu	Pires/Bergkamp/Lauren for Ljungberg/Grimandi/Dixon
21 Aug	Liverpool	H	W	2-0		Luzhny	..	..	..	Lauren1	..		Pires	..1	Bergkamp	Kanu for Bergkamp
26 Aug	Charlton	H	W	5-3		Dixon			..1		..2		..2		Kanu	Bergkamp for Lauren
6 Sept	Chelsea	A	D	2-2					Luzhny	..1		Parlour	..	..1		Bergkamp/Wiltord/Ljungberg for Dixon/Parlour/Pires
9 Sept	Bradford	A	D	1-1			..		..	Cole1	Parlour		Ljungberg	..	Wiltord	Kanu for Wiltord
16 Sept	Coventry	H	W	2-1		Luzhny	..	Adams	Silvinho	..		..	..	Bergkamp	..1	Henry/Vernazza1/Kanu for Wiltord/Parlour/Bergkamp
23 Sept	Ipswich	A	D	1-1	..	Vivas	..	Luzhny	..	..	..	..	Bergkamp1	Henry	..	Kanu/Vernazza for Wiltord/Grimandi
1 Oct	Manchester Utd	H	W	1-0	..	Luzhny	..	Adams	..	..	..	..	..1		Kanu	Vivas/Wiltord for Kanu/Bergkamp
14 Oct	Aston Villa	H	W	1-0	..	Dixon	Grimandi	..		Lauren	Parlour	Vieira	Pires	Bergkamp	Henry1	Wiltord/Kanu/Luzhny for Henry/Pires/Bergkamp
21 Oct	West Ham	A	W	2-1	..	Lauren	Keown	Luzhny		Ljungberg	Grimandi	..	..1		Wiltord	Parlour/Henry/Kanu for Ljungberg/Wiltord/Bergkamp (own goal)
28 Oct	Manchester City	H	W	5-0	Lukic	Luzhny	..	Adams	Cole1	Parlour		..	..	..1	Henry2	Ljungberg/Wiltord1/Dixon for Pires/Parlour/Luzhny
4 Nov	Middlesbrough	A	W	1-0		Dixon	..		Silvinho	..			Ljungberg	..	..1	Lauren for Bergkamp
11 Nov	Derby	H	D	0-0		Luzhny	..	Grimandi	..	Ljungberg	Parlour	..	Bergkamp	Henry	Wiltord	Dixon/Kanu for Grimandi/Ljungberg
18 Nov	Everton	A	L	0-2	Manninger	Dixon	..	Luzhny	Cole	..	Pires	Parlour	..	Kanu	..	Upson for Dixon
26 Nov	Leeds	A	L	0-1	..	Luzhny	..	Adams	Silvinho	Lauren	Parlour	Vieira	Pires	Henry	..	Kanu for Lauren
2 Dec	Southampton	A	W	1-0	..	..	..			Ljungberg	Grimandi	..		Bergkamp	..	Dixon/Henry/Kanu for Silvinho/Wiltord/Pires (own goal)
9 Dec	Newcastle	H	W	5-0	..	Dixon	..	..	Vivas	..	..	Parlour3	..	Henry1	Kanu1	Lauren/Bergkamp/Luzhny for Grimandi/Kanu/Ljungberg
18 Dec	Tottenham	A	D	1-1			..		Silvinho	..	..	..	..	..	..	Vieira1/Bergkamp/Wiltord for Grimandi/Pires/Kanu
23 Dec	Liverpool	A	L	0-4			..	Luzhny	..	Parlour	..	Vieira	Ljungberg	..	Bergkamp	Pires/Wiltord/Kanu for Luzhny/Ljungberg/Bergkamp
26 Dec	Leicester	H	W	6-1			Stepanovs	Adams1	..	..	..	..1	Pires	..3	Kanu	Ljungberg1/Vivas/Cole for Kanu/Grimandi/Pires
30 Dec	Sunderland	H	D	2-2			..1	..	..	Ljungberg	..	..1	..			Parlour/Danilevicius for Kanu/Henry
1 Jan	Charlton	A	L	0-1			..	..	Grimandi	..	Parlour	Vivas	..	Ljungberg	..	Danilevicius/Cole/Malz for Pires/Silvinho/Grimandi
13 Jan	Chelsea	H	D	1-1	Seaman	..	Stepanovs	Keown	..	Ljungberg	Parlour	..	..1	Henry	Wiltord	Vivas for Ljungberg
20 Jan	Leicester	A	D	0-0	..	..	Keown	Adams	..				..	..		Edu/Bergkamp forLjungberg/Edu
30 Jan	Bradford	H	W	2-0	..	..	Stepanovs	..	Cole	Lauren1	..1	..	..		Bergkamp	Grimandi/Kanu for Lauren/Bergkamp
3 Feb	Coventry	A	W	1-0	..	..	..	..		Lauren	..	Grimandi	..	Wiltord	..1	Grimandi/Vivas for Lauren/Pires
10 Feb	Ipswich	H	W	1-0	..	..	..	..		Lauren	..	Grimandi	..			Henry1/Ljungberg for Lauren/Wiltord
25 Feb	Manchester Utd	A	L	1-6	..	Luzhny	..	Grimandi	..	Silvinho		Vieira	..	Henry1	Wiltord	Ljungberg/Vivas for Cole/Parlour
3 Mar	WestHam	H	W	3-0	..	Dixon	Grimandi	Adams	..	Ljungberg	Lauren	..	..	Wiltord3	Bergkamp	Vivas/Henry/Edu for Cole/Wiltord/Pires
18 Mar	Aston Villa	A	D	0-0	Manninger			Luzhny	Silvinho	..	..				..	Pires/Henry/Vivas for Ljungberg/Wiltord/Parlour
31 Mar	Tottenham	H	W	2-0	Seaman	..	Keown	Adams	Cole	Lauren	Parlour	..	..1	Henry1	Wiltord	Kanu/Luzhny for Lauren/Dixon
11 Apr	Manchester City	A	W	4-0	..	Luzhny	Stepanovs	Keown	..	..		Edu	Ljungberg2	Wiltord1	Kanu1	Vieira/Henry/Vivas for Edu/Wiltord/Parlour
14 Apr	Middlesbrough	H	L	0-3	..	Dixon	Keown	Adams	Silvinho	Ljungberg	Edu	Vieira	Pires	Henry	..	Wiltord/Parlour for Edu/Ljungberg
21 Apr	Everton	H	W	4-1	..	..	..		Cole	..1	Grimandi1	..	..1		Wiltord1	Vivas/Silvinho for Grimandi/Pires
28 Apr	Derby	A	W	2-1	..	..	..			Lauren	..	..	Ljungberg	Wiltord	Kanu1	Henry/Pires1/Parlour for Lauren/Ljungberg/Kanu
5 May	Leeds	H	W	2-1	..	..	..			Ljungberg1	..	..	Pires	Henry	Wiltord1	Parlour for Wiltord
15 May	Newcastle	A	D	0-0	..	Dixon	..	..		Lauren	Parlour	..		Bergkamp	Henry	Kanu for Bergkamp
19 May	Southampton	A	L	2-3	Manninger	Grimandi	..	..	..1	Parlour	Vieira	Ljungberg1	..	..	..	Kanu/Edu/Upson for Bergkamp/Ljungberg/Pires

Worthington (League) Cup

Date	Opponent	V	R	Score												Substitutes
1 Nov	Ipswich(3)	H	L	1-2	Taylor	Weston	Stepanovs1	Upson	Cole	Vivas	Pennant	Vernazza	Barrett	Wiltord	Volz	Mendez/Wreh/Canoville for Pennant/Volz/Weston

FA Cup

Date	Opponent	V	R	Score												Substitutes
6 Jan	Carlisle(3)	A	W	1-0	Manninger	Dixon	Stepanovs	Vivas	Cole	Ljungberg	Vieira	Parlour	Pires	Bergkamp	Wiltord1	Silvinho, Danilevicius, Malz for Ljungberg/Wiltord/Cole
27 Jan	QPR(4)	A	W	6-0	Seaman	..	..	Adams	..	Lauren	..	..	..1	..1	..2	Grimandi/Malz/Vivas for Lauren/Pires/Vieira (2 own goals)
18 Feb	Chelsea(5)	H	W	3-1	..	..	..	Luzhny	..		Vieira	Ljungberg	..	Henry1	Bergkamp	Wiltord2/Vivas for Pires/Bergkamp
10 Mar	Blackburn(6)	H	W	3-0	..	..	Luzhny	Adams1	..		Grimandi	..	..1	Bergkamp	Wiltord1	Silvinho/Vieira/Henry for Ljungberg/Pires/Bergkamp
8 Apr	Tottenham(SF)		W	2-1	..		Keown	..	Silvinho	..	Vieira1	Parlour	..1	Henry	..	Ljungberg/Cole for Pires/Wiltord
12 May	Liverpool(Final)		L	1-2	..	..	..	..	Cole	Ljungberg1	Grimandi	Vieira	..	..		Parlour/Kanu/Bergkamp for Wiltord/Ljungberg/Dixon

at the Millennium stadium, Cardiff

European Champions' League

Date	Opponent	V	R	Score												Substitutes
12 Sept	Sparta Prague	A	W	1-0	Seaman	Dixon	Keown	Luzhny	Silvinho1	Ljungberg	Vieira	Grimandi	Pires	Henry	Kanu	Wiltord/Vivas forHenry/Ljungberg
20 Sept	Shakhtar Donetsk	H	W	3-2	..	..2	..		..	..			..		..	Wiltord1/Bergkamp for Pires/Ljungberg
27 Sept	Lazio	H	W	2-0		Luzhny	..	Adams		..2	..	Parlour	Bergkamp	..	..	Vivas/Wiltord for Bergkamp/Henry
17 Oct	Lazio	A	D	1-1	Lukic	Dixon	..	Luzhny		Grimandi	Parlour	..	..			Pires1/Lauren/Wiltord for Parlour/Grimandi/Ljungberg
25 Oct	Sparta Prague	H	W	4-2	Seaman	..1	Vivas	..		Lauren1	..	Parlour1	Pires	..	..1	Cole/Bergkamp/Wiltord for Silvinho/Pires/Henry
7 Nov	Shakhtar Donetsk	A	L	0-3	Taylor	..	Keown	Upson	Cole	..	Vivas	..	Wiltord	..	..	Ljungberg/Vernazza for Henry/Parlour
22 Nov	Spartak Moscow	A	L	1-4	Manninger	Luzhny	..	Adams	Silvinho1	Ljungberg	..	Pires	..	..		Wiltord/Lauren for Kanu/Pires
5 Dec	Bayern Munich	H	D	2-2	..	..	..		Cole	..	Vieira	Grimandi	..	..1	..1	Wiltord/Lauren for Pires/Luzhny
13 Feb	Lyon	A	W	1-0	Seaman	Dixon	Grimandi	..		Lauren	..	Parlour	..	..1	..	Ljungberg/Vivas for Pires/Kanu
21 Feb	Lyon	H	D	1-1	..	..	..	Luzhny	..	Ljungberg	..	..	..		Bergkamp1	Wiltord/Lauren/Kanu for Bergkamp/Pires/Henry
6 Mar	Spartak Moscow	H	W	1-0	..	..	..	..	Adams	..	..	Lauren	..1	..		Wiltord/Kanu/Vivas for Pires/Bergkamp/Henry
14 Mar	Bayern Munich	A	L	0-1	..	..	..	..	..			..	..		Kanu	Wiltord/Parlour/Silvinho for Kanu/Ljungberg/Pires
4 Apr	Valencia(QF)	H	W	2-1	..	..	Keown	..	..			Parlour1	..1	..		Wiltord/Lauren for Ljungberg/Kanu
17 Apr	Valencia(QF)	A	L	0-1	..	..	..	..		Lauren	..	..	..		Wiltord	Ljungberg/Kanu for Parlour/Pires

League Appearances (Goals in brackets)

Henry 35 (17) - Pires 33 (4) - Parlour 33 (4) - Vieira 30 (5) - Ljungberg 30 (6) - Grimandi 29 (1) - Dixon 29 (1) - Keown 28 - Wiltord 27 (8) - Kanu 27 (3) - Adams 26 (1) - Bergkamp 25 (3) - Seaman 24 - Silvinho 24 (2) - Luzhny 19 - Lauren 18 (2) - Cole 17 (3) - Manninger 11 - Vivas 11 - Stepanovs 9 - Edu 5 - Lukic 3 - Vernazza 2 (1) - Upson 2 - Danilevicius 2 - Malz 1. Own goals (2)

FA Premier League

	P	W	L	D	F:A	Pts	
Manchester U	38	24	8	6	79:31	80	1st
Arsenal	38	20	10	8	68:38	70	2nd

Date	Opponent			Score	GK											Substitutions / Scorers
18 Aug	Middlesbrough	A	W	4-0	Seaman	Lauren	Campbell	Adams	Cole	Parlour	Pires1p	Vieira	Ljungberg	Henry1	Wiltord	Bergkamp2/Grimandi/Van Bronckhorst for Henry/Ljungberg/Wiltord
21 Aug	Leeds	H	L	1-2	..	..	..	..	..	..	..	..	..	..	..1	Bergkamp/Jeffers/Van Bronckhorst for Parlour/Ljungberg/Wiltord
25 Aug	Leicester	H	W	4-0	..	..	..	..	..	Ljungberg1	Vieira	Van Bronckhorst	Pires	Bergkamp	..1	Grimandi/Henry1/Kanu1 for Ljungberg/Wiltord/Bergkamp
8 Sept	Chelsea	A	D	1-1	..	..	Keown	..	..	Wiltord	Grimandi	..	..	..	Henry1	Kanu/Ljungberg/Campbell for Bergkamp/Wiltord/Adams
15 Sept	Fulham	A	W	3-1	..	..	Campbell	Keown	..	Parlour	Pires	Vieira	Ljungberg1	Henry1	Jeffers	Bergkamp1/Wiltord/Grimandi for Jeffers/Parlour/Henry
22 Sept	Bolton	H	D	1-1	..	Luzhny	Grimandi	Adams	..	..	Vieira	Van Bronckhorst	Bergkamp	..	Wiltord	Upson/Jeffers1/Pires for Grimandi/Van Bronckhorst/Parlour
29 Sept	Derby	A	W	2-0	Wright	Lauren	Upson	Keown	..	Ljungberg	..	..	Pires	..2.1p	Jeffers	Kanu/Luzhny/Grimandi for Jeffers/Ljungberg/Henry
13 Oct	Southampton	A	W	2-0	..	..	Campbell	Upson	..	..	..	..	..1	..1	Wiltord	Bergkamp/Parlour/Grimandi for Wiltord/Ljungberg/Van Bronckhorst
20 Oct	Blackburn	H	D	3-3	..	..	Keown	..	Van Bronckhorst	Parlour	..	Grimandi	..1	..1	Bergkamp1	Wiltord/Kanu for Pires/Parlour
27 Oct	Sunderland	A	D	1-1	..	..	Campbell	Keown	Upson	..	..	Van Bronckhorst	Ljungberg	Kanu1	Wiltord	Henry/Bergkamp for Wiltord/Kanu
4 Nov	Charlton	H	L	2-4	..	..	Keown	Grimandi	Cole	Ljungberg	..	..	Pires	Henry2.1p	Bergkamp	Wiltord for Cole
17 Nov	Tottenham	A	D	1-1	..	..	Campbell	Keown	..	Parlour	..	Grimandi	..1	Bergkamp	Wiltord	Kanu for Bergkamp
25 Nov	Manchester Utd	H	W	3-1	Taylor	..	..	Upson	..	..	..	Pires	Ljungberg1	Henry2	Kanu	Bergkamp/Grimandi for Kanu/Pires
1 Dec	Ipswich	A	W	2-0	..	..	..	..	..	..	..	..	..1	..1p		Bergkamp/Van Bronckhorst/Edu for Kanu/Pires/Ljungberg
9 Dec	Aston Villa	H	W	3-2	..	..	..	..	..	..	..	..	..	..2	Bergkamp	Keown/Wiltord1/Kanu for Upson/Ljungberg/Bergkamp
15 Dec	West Ham	A	D	1-1	..	..	..	Keown	..1	Grimandi	..	..	Bergkamp	..	Wiltord	Edu/Kanu for Wiltord/Pires
18 Dec	Newcastle	H	L	1-3	..	..	..	..	..	Parlour	..	..1	Kanu	..	..	Van Bronckhorst/Bergkamp for Kanu/Wiltord
23 Dec	Liverpool	A	W	2-1	..	..	..	..	..	..	Pires	Van Bronckhorst	Ljungberg1	..1p	Kanu	Upson/Luzhny/Wiltord for Pires/Kanu/Henry
26 Dec	Chelsea	H	W	2-1	..	..	..	..1	..	..	Vieira	Pires	..	..	..	Van Bronckhorst/Wiltord1/Bergkamp for Parlour/Ljungberg/Kanu
29 Dec	Middlesbrough	H	W	2-1	..	Luzhny	..	..	..	..1	Ljungberg	..	Van Bronckhorst	Pires1	..	Bergkamp/Wiltord/Grimandi for Kanu/Ljungberg/Henry
13 Jan	Liverpool	H	D	1-1	..	..	..	Upson	..1	Grimandi	..	..	..	..		Bergkamp/Wiltord/Dixon for Kanu/Pires/Luzhny
20 Jan	Leeds	A	D	1-1	Wright	..	..	..	Cole	Parlour	Pires1	Ljungberg	..	Bergkamp		Van Bronckhorst/Wiltord/Dixon for Ljungberg/Bergkamp/Luzhny
23 Jan	Leicester	A	W	3-1	..	..	..	..	..	..	Van Bronckhorst1	Pires	..1	..		Grimandi/Upson/Wiltord1 for Parlour/Van Bronckhorst/Bergkamp
30 Jan	Blackburn	A	W	3-2	..	..	..	..	..	..	Pires	Wiltord	..1	..2		Van Bronckhorst/Upson/Grimandi for Wiltord/Keown/Pires
2 Feb	Southampton	H	D	1-1	..	..	..	Upson	..	..	..	..1	..			Van Bronckhorst/Grimandi/Edu for Vieira/Cole/Bergkamp
10 Feb	Everton	A	W	1-0	..	..	Stepanovs	Upson	..	Grimandi	Van Bronckhorst	..	Wiltord1			Dixon for Upson
23 Feb	Fulham	H	W	4-1	Seaman	..	..	Van Bronckhorst	..	..1	Pires	Lauren1	..2	..		Dixon/Grimandi/Aladiere for Van Bronckhorst/Pires/Henry
2 Mar	Newcastle	A	W	2-0	..	Dixon	..1	..	Luzhny	Lauren	..	Grimandi	Pires	Bergkamp1	..	Kanu/Edu for Bergkamp/Wiltord
5 Mar	Derby	H	W	1-0	..	Lauren	..	..	..	Parlour	..	Pires1	Wiltord	Henry	Bergkamp	Dixon/Edu for Luzhny/Wiltord
17 Mar	Aston Villa	A	W	2-1	..	..	..	..	..	Ljungberg	..	Edu1	Pires1	Bergkamp	Wiltord	Dixon/Grimandi/Kanu for Stepanovs/Ljungberg/Bergkamp
30 Mar	Sunderland	H	W	3-0	..	Luzhny	..	Adams	Cole	Wiltord1	..	..	Ljungberg	..1	Henry1	Grimandi/Jeffers/Kanu for Wiltord/Ljungberg/Bergkamp
1 Apr	Charlton	A	W	3-0	..	Dixon	..	Keown	..	..	..	Grimandi	..1	..	..2	Luzhny/Edu for Cole/Bergkamp
6 Apr	Tottenham	H	W	2-1	..	Lauren1p	..	Adams	Luzhny	..	..	Edu	..1	..	..	Dixon/Parlour/Kanu/Dixon for Bergkamp/Edu/Wiltord
21 Apr	Ipswich	A	W	2-0	..	..	Keown	..	Cole	Parlour	..	..	..2	..	..	Kanu/Grimandi for Edu/Bergkamp
24 Apr	West Ham	H	W	2-0	..	..	..	..	..	..	..	..	..1	..	..	Kanu1/Grimandi/Dixon for Edu/Bergkamp/Lungberg
29 Apr	Bolton	A	W	2-0	..	..	..	..	..	..	..	..	..1	..	Wiltord1	Dixon/Kanu/Campbell for Edu/Bergkamp/Wiltord
8 May	Manchester Utd	A	W	1-0	..	..	Campbell	Keown	..	..	..	..	..	Kanu	..1	Dixon for Kanu
11 May	Everton	H	W	4-3	Wright	Dixon	Stepanovs	Luzhny	..	..	Grimandi	..	Wiltord	Bergkamp1	Henry2	Jeffers1/Vieira/Taylor for Wiltord/Parlour/Wright

League Appearances (Goals in brackets)

Vieira 36(2) – Henry 33(24) – Wiltord 33(10) – Bergkamp 33(9) - Campbell 31(2) – Cole 29 – Pires 28(9) – Lauren 27(2) – Parlour 27 – Grimandi 26 –Ljungberg 25(12) – Kanu 23(3) –Keown 22 – Van Bronckhorst 21(1) – Luzhny 18 – Seaman 17 – Edu 14(1) – Upson 14 – Dixon 13 – Wright 12 – Adams 10 – Taylor 10 – Stepanovs 6 – Jeffers 6(1) –Aladiere 1

FA Premier League

	P	W	L	D	F:A	Pts	
Arsenal	38	26	3	9	79:36	87	1st

Above: The celebrations start as the Arsenal team honour their devoted fans.

2000-2002

Above: After a hard-fought final against Chelsea, Arsenal were deserved winners after Parlour and Ljungberg scored to put the result beyound doubt.

FA Cup

Date	Opponent	V	Result													Substitutes
5 Jan	Watford(3)	A	W 4-2	Taylor	Luzhny	Campbell	Keown	Cole	Ljungberg1	Vieira	Van Bronckhorst	Pires	..	Henry1	Kanu1	Wiltord/Bergkamp1 for Henry/Kanu
27 Jan	Liverpool(4)	H	W 1-0	Wright	..	..	..	..	Wiltord	..	..	..	..	..	Bergkamp1	Parlour/Upson/Grimandi for Pires/Wiltord/Van Bronckhorst
18 Feb	Gillingham(5)	H	W 5-2	..	Dixon	..	Adams1	Juan	Parlour1	..	Edu	Wiltord2	Jeffers	Kanu	Henry/Pires/Grimandi for Jeffers/Edu/Kanu
9 Mar	Newcastle(6)	A	D 1-1	..	..	Luzhny	..	Stepanovs	Lauren	Ljungberg	..	Grimandi	Edu1	Wiltord	..	Pires/Bergkamp for Ljungberg/Edu
23 Mar	Newcastle(6R)	H	W 3-0	..	Luzhny	..	..1	Adams	Cole	..	Edu	Pires1	Bergkamp1	Wiltord	Grimandi/Jeffers/Dixon for Pires/Edu/Wiltord
14 Apr	Middlesbrough (S-F) Old Trafford		W 1-0*	..	Lauren	..	Keown	Luzhny	Wiltord	..	..	Ljungberg	..	Henry	Dixon/Parlour/Kanu for Luzhny/Campbell/Bergkamp
4 May	Chelsea(Final) Cardiff		W 2-0	Seaman	..	..	Adams	Cole	..	Parlour1	Vieira	..1	..	..	Edu/Kanu/Keown for Bergkamp/Henry/Wiltord

Worthington (League) Cup

Date	Opponent	V	Result													Substitutes
5 Nov	Manchester Utd(3)	H	W 4-0	Wright	Luzhny	Tavlaridis	Stepanovs	Van Bronckhorst	Parlour	Grimandi	Edu	Pennant	Kanu1p	Wiltord3.1p		Halls/Ricketts/Itonga for Van Bronckhorst/Pennant/Grimandi
27 Nov	Grimsby(4)	H	W 2-0	Taylor	Tavlaridis	Keown	..	Juan	Inamoto	Van Bronckhorst..1	..	Bergkamp	..1		Svart/Aliadiere/Halls for Pennant/Van Bronckhorst/Inamoto
11 Dec	Blackburn(5)	A	L 0-4	..	..	..	Upson	Van Bronckhorst ..	Grimandi	..	..	Kanu	..		Stepanovs/Aliadiere/Halls for Inamoto/Pennant/Tavlaridis

Champions League

First Group Phase

Date	Opponent	V	Result													Substitutes
11 Sept	Mallorca	A	L 0-1	Seaman	Lauren	Campbell	Keown	Cole	Ljungberg	Vieira	Van Bronckhorst	Pires	Henry	Wiltord		Kanu/Jeffers/Parlour for Ljungberg/Wiltord/Pires
19 Sept	Schalke	H	W 3-2	..	..	Grimandi	..	Van Bronckhorst	Parlour	..	Pires	Ljungberg1	..2.1p	..		Bergkamp/Inamoto/Upson for Wiltord/Pires/Henry
26 Sept	Panathinaikos	A	L 0-1	..	..	Keown	Upson	Cole	..	..	..	..	..	..		Van Bronckhorst/Jeffers/Kanu for Parlour/Wiltord/Ljungberg
16 Oct	Panathinaikos	H	W 2-1	Wright	..	Campbell	..	..	Ljungberg	..	Van Bronckhorst	Pires	..2.1p	..		Parlour/Bergkamp/Grimandi for Pires/Wiltord/Henry
24 Oct	Mallorca	H	W 3-1	..	..	..	Keown	Van Bronckhorst ..	..	Grimandi	..1	..1	Bergkamp1		Wiltord/Kanu/Parlour for Bergkamp/Ljungberg/Grimandi
30 Oct	Schalke	A	L 1-3	..	Luzhny	..	Upson	Cole	..	..	Van Bronckhorst ..	..	Kanu	Wiltord1		Stepanovs/Keown/Pennant for Upson/Campbell/Kanu

Second Group Phase

Date	Opponent	V	Result													Substitutes
21 Nov	Deportivo	A	L 0-2	Wright	Lauren	Campbell	Upson	Cole	Parlour	Vieira	Pires	Ljungberg	Henry	Wiltord		Taylor/Kanu/Edu for Wright/Wiltord/Van Bronckhorst
4 Dec	Juventus	H	W 3-1	Taylor	..	..	..	..	..	..	..	..2	..1	Kanu		Bergkamp/Grimandi/Keown for Kanu/Henry/Cole
19 Feb	Bayer Leverkusen	A	D 1-1	Seaman	..	..	Stepanovs	Van Bronckhorst ..	..	..1	Kanu	..1	Wiltord		Grimandi/Edu for Wiltord/Kanu
27 Feb	Bayer Leverkusen	H	W 4-1	..	Dixon	..	..	Lauren	Grimandi	..1	..1	Wiltord	..1	Bergkamp1		Edu/Inamoto/Pennant for Grimandi/Lauren/Wiltord
12 Mar	Deportivo	H	L 0-2	..	Lauren	..	..	Luzhny	Wiltord	..	Grimandi	Pires	Bergkamp	Henry		Kanu/Ljungberg for Wiltord/Grimandi
20 Mar	Juventus	A	L 0-1	..	Dixon	..	Luzhny	Lauren	Ljungberg	..	Edu	..	Kanu	..		Wiltord/Cole for Lauren/Kanu

Abbreviations:

Appearances (goals) refer to League games only

Figures shown as 2 etc. refer to goals scored by individual players

* own-goal

Players' names in final column, are substitutes